D0421456

SPOTTED FIREWORM
7/27/96 ~~ADULT~~
IDENTIFIED
2ND BOG

THE AMERICAN CRANBERRY

THE
AMERICAN CRANBERRY

PAUL ECK

 RUTGERS UNIVERSITY PRESS

New Brunswick and London

Library of Congress Cataloging-in-Publication Data

Eck, Paul, 1931–
    The American cranberry / Paul Eck.
      p.   cm.
    Bibliography: p.
    Includes index.
    ISBN 0–8135–1491–6
    1. Cranberries.   2. Cranberries–United States.   I. Title.
  SB383.E25 1990
  634'.76—dc20   89–10233
                                                    CIP

British Cataloging-in-Publication information available

CONTENTS

	List of Illustrations	vii
	List of Tables	xi
ONE	History	1
TWO	Industry	19
THREE	Botany	43
FOUR	Plant Improvement	56
FIVE	Environment	81
SIX	Plant Growth and Development	110
SEVEN	Plant Nutrition	136
EIGHT	Culture	165
NINE	Diseases	230
TEN	Insects	247
ELEVEN	Harvesting and Handling	283
TWELVE	Economics, Marketing, and Utilization	325
	Bibliography	359
	Index	401

LIST OF ILLUSTRATIONS

FIGURES

FIGURE 2.1   Cranberry Acreage by Decade since 1900   24

FIGURE 2.2   Distribution of Massachusetts Cranberry Acreage by County   24

FIGURE 2.3   Distribution of New Jersey Cranberry Acreage by County   25

FIGURE 2.4   Distribution of Wisconsin Cranberry Acreage by County   27

FIGURE 2.5   Distribution of Washington Cranberry Acreage by County   27

FIGURE 2.6   Distribution of Oregon Cranberry Acreage by County   28

FIGURE 2.7   Total United States Cranberry Production and Production by States for the Years 1900–1987   34

FIGURE 2.8   Cranberry Production by States as a Percentage of Total U.S. Production   34

FIGURE 2.9   Cranberry Yield per Acre for Individual States   35

FIGURE 2.10 Total Cranberry Farm Value and Price per Barrel for the Years 1900–1987   41

FIGURE 2.11 Percentage of Cranberry Production Utilized as Fresh and Processed Fruit   42

FIGURE 3.1   The Cranberry Plant Showing the Relationship between the Runners and Uprights   47

FIGURE 3.2   The Cranberry Flower   50

FIGURE 3.3   The Different Shapes of the Cranberry
                Fruit   53

FIGURE 6.1   Berry Growth Curves Based on Weight
                for the Cranberry Cultivars Early Black,
                Howes, and McFarlin   126

FIGURE 8.1   Cross Section of Dam   173

FIGURE 8.2   Incorrect Method and Correct Method
                of Installing Closed-Trunk-Type Water
                Control Gate   175

FIGURE 11.1   Schematic Representation of the Picking
                Action of the Western Picker   294

FIGURE 11.2   Schematic Representation of the Picking
                Action of the Darlington Picker   295

PLATES

PLATE 1.1   R. B. Wilcox, F. B. Chandler, and H. F.
                Bergman on Duty   15

PLATE 1.2   H. J. Franklin, Director of the
                Massachusetts Cranberry Research
                Station, 1910–1954   17

PLATE 3.1   Vaccinium macrocarpon—The American
                Cranberry   46

PLATE 3.2   Terminal Buds on Cranberry Uprights
                That Will Produce New Shoots and
                Flowers in the Spring   48

PLATE 3.3   A Typical Cranberry Flower   52

PLATE 8.1   Modern Bog Construction Showing the
                Dam, Riser on Water Supply Trunk,
                Ditch, and Bog Surface   172

PLATE 8.2   Main Supply and Drainage Channel of a
                Bog Built on the Contour   174

PLATE 8.3   A Cranberry Bog Planted by Hand at the
                Turn of the Century   179

PLATE 8.4   Different Methods of Planting Cranberry
               Vines   180

PLATE 8.5   An Aerial View of Cranberry Bogs in
               Massachusetts Showing the Relationship
               of Water Reservoir and Drainage System
               to the Bogs   182

PLATE 8.6   The Weed Mower   201

PLATE 8.7   Sanding an Established Cranberry Bog   225

PLATE 8.8   The Wisconsin Cranberry Boom,
               Applying Chemicals, and Mowing Grass   228

PLATE 10.1   Applying Pesticides by Power Sprayer
               from the Dam and by Helicopter   281

PLATE 11.1   Handpicking on Cape Cod ca. 1900   286

PLATE 11.2   The Hand Scoop   288

PLATE 11.3   The Wisconsin Scoop   289

PLATE 11.4   A Scooping Gang   289

PLATE 11.5   A Modified Wheelbarrow Used to Carry
               Quarter-Barrel Boxes from the Bog   290

PLATE 11.6   The Mathewson Picking Machine   292

PLATE 11.7   The Darlington Picking Machine   296

PLATE 11.8   A Battery of Darlington Pickers
               Harvesting Cranberries in
               Massachusetts   297

PLATE 11.9   The Getsinger Retracto Tooth Picker   300

PLATE 11.10   The Wisconsin Water Reel Harvester   301

PLATE 11.11   Narrow-gauge Track Used to Transport
               Picking Boxes during Harvesting   303

PLATE 11.12   Screening Berries at the Bog on Cape
               Cod ca. 1870   304

PLATE 11.13   Modern Cranberry Separator   306

PLATE 12.1   Packaging Cranberries in Quarter-barrel
               Boxes   340

PLATE 12.2   Hand Screening Cranberries before
                Packaging   341

PLATE 12.3   An Early Cranberry Packaging Machine
                Packing Cranberries in One-pound
                Cellophane Bags   342

PLATE 12.4   Cranberry Cheese Tarts—One of the
                Many Delicacies Made from Cranberries   357

LIST OF TABLES

TABLE 1.1   Estimates of United States Cranberry Production for the Years 1872–1899   **9**

TABLE 2.1   Total Cranberry Acreage in the United States and Individual States for the Years 1900–1987   **20**

TABLE 2.2   Total United States Production and Production by States   **30**

TABLE 2.3   Cranberry Productivity for the States and the United States   **36**

TABLE 4.1   Description of the Major Cranberry Cultivars and the New Hybrid Cultivars   **64**

TABLE 5.1   Effects of Oxygen Deficiency on Production of Three Cranberry Cultivars   **93**

TABLE 5.2   Comparison of the Climate for the Major Cranberry-Growing Regions in the United States   **105**

TABLE 6.1   Comparison of Yield Components of Different Cranberry Cultivars in Various Growing Regions   **119**

TABLE 6.2   Composition of Cranberry Fruit   **130**

TABLE 6.3   Percent Composition of Cranberries While Ripening on Vines   **131**

TABLE 7.1   Concentration of Elements in Cranberry Shoots during the Oregon Growing Season   **137**

TABLE 7.2   Proposed Nutrient Value Standards in Wisconsin for New Cranberry Shoots   **139**

TABLE 7.3   Mineral Content of Cranberry Tissue   **141**

TABLE 7.4   Effect of Nitrogen Fertilizer Rate on
               Yield and Plant Composition of Early
               Black and Ben Lear Cranberry   **149**

TABLE 8.1   Typical Swamp Vegetation Associated
               with Good Cranberry-Producing Sites   **166**

TABLE 8.2   Amounts of Sand to Apply to Attain
               Different Sanding Depths   **177**

TABLE 8.3   Fertilizer Application in Relation to Crop   **191**

TABLE 8.4   Effect of Nitrogen Fertilizer Applications
               on Cranberry Yield   **192**

TABLE 8.5   Fertilizer Recommendations for
               Producing Cranberry Bogs   **193**

TABLE 8.6   Effect of Fertilizer Source and Timing on
               Early Black Cranberry Yield Over a Six-
               Year Period   **196**

TABLE 8.7   Common Weed Problems in One or
               More of the Major Cranberry-Growing
               Areas   **202**

TABLE 9.1   A Composite Fungicide Application
               Schedule for Cranberry Diseases Found
               in the Different Growing Areas   **243**

TABLE 10.1   Percent Occurrence of Parasitic
               Nematodes in Cranberry Bogs   **275**

TABLE 10.2   A Composite Spray Schedule for
               Cranberry Insects Found in the Different
               Growing Regions   **279**

TABLE 12.1   Cash Costs of Bog Production   **329**

TABLE 12.2   Variable and Fixed Costs of Production
               from Survey of 56 Massachusetts
               Cranberry Growers, 1977   **330**

TABLE 12.3   Total Production, Utilization, Price, and
               Total Value of Cranberries for the Years
               1900–1987   **332**

TABLE 12.4   Ten-Year Average Values for Cranberry
               Acreage, Yield per Acre, Price per

	Barrel, Total Value, and Return per Acre for the Decades between 1900 and 1987	**337**
TABLE 12.5	Per Capita Consumption of Cranberries in America for the Decades between 1910 and 1987	**351**
TABLE 12.6	Chemical Composition of Fresh Cranberries and Nutritive Value of an Average Serving of Cranberry Sauce	**353**

THE AMERICAN CRANBERRY

ONE

History

Origins of the Industry

The Colonial Period

The American cranberry (*Vaccinium macrocarpon* Ait.) is indigenous to the North American continent. It is closely related to the European cranberry (*V. oxycoccus* L.) and the lingonberry, or mountain cranberry (V. *vitis-idaea* L), which can be found throughout Europe, Asia, and parts of North America. The American cranberry has the distinction of being the only cranberry that has been subjected to extensive efforts at commercial cultivation.

When the colonists arrived in North America, they found the native cranberry growing profusely in the peat bogs of Cape Cod, at Gay Head on the island of Martha's Vineyard, in the marshes along the Sudbury, Concord, Charles, and Neponset rivers in Massachusetts, and—in New Jersey—along the marshes of Barnegat Bay and in the swamps of the Great Pine Barrens (now called the Pinelands). The cranberry vine could also be found northward into the Maritime Provinces of Canada and southward along the coast into the Carolinas, as well as in isolated areas in the Allegheny Mountains from southern Pennsylvania to the peat swamps of Virginia. When the early settlers migrated westward, they found cranberries growing wild in the wetlands of Indiana, Michigan, Wisconsin, and Minnesota.

Captain John Smith was probably the first European to take note of this native berry as he explored the New England coast in 1614. The descriptions of the vegetation made by Captain Smith during his explorations included one that seems to fit the American cranberry: "The Herbes and Fruits are of many sorts and kinds: as Alkermes, currans, mulberries. . . . Of certain red berries, called Kermes, which is worth ten shillings the pound, these have been sold for thirty or forty shillings the pound, and may be yeerly gathered in a good quantity" (C. J. Hall 1948, 6).

When the Pilgrims landed at Provincetown harbor on 20 December 1620, they were undoubtedly heartened by the profusion of edible red berries that

1

grew in the marshes along the bay side of the peninsula (C. J. Hall 1941c, 17–19). Cranberries would have been the only edible fruits still available this late in the season that could be used to relieve the Pilgrims of the debilitating symptoms of scurvy, which was a common affliction among the ocean travelers. [There can be little argument about where this little red berry's place should be in American history, but that of the most American of all fruits and berries.]

The colonists soon discovered that the cranberry was already an important commodity of American Indians, not only as a source of food and medicine but also in their rituals and in their commerce. The Chippewas called the cranberry *a'ni-bimin,* meaning bitter berry, and the Narragansetts called it *sasemineash.* Roger Williams, in his 1643 "Key into the Language of America, An Help to the Language of the Natives of New England" (C. J. Hall 1949a, 12), interpreted the Narrangansett word sasemineash as follows: "Another Sharp, Cooling fruit, growing in fresh water in the Winter; Excellent to conserve against Feavors of which there are divers kinds, Sweet, like currents, Some Opening, some of a binding nature." In Wisconsin the Algonquins called the native cranberry *atoqua,* according to Le Sueur's *Fort on the Mississippi in 1700–1702* (Hintzman et al. 1953).

The Indians ate the berries raw or prepared a sweetened sauce using maple sugar. But perhaps the most common use of the cranberry by the Indians was in making *pemmican,* a mixture of dried meat (or fish) and berries pounded into a pulp, shaped into cakes, and dried in the sun. Not only did the cranberry help to preserve the meat or fish but it also insured a more balanced diet during the winter. Cranberries were used medicinally as a poultice for wounds; mixed with cornmeal it was an effective treatment for blood poisoning. The juice of the fruit was used as a dye by the Indians to brighten their rugs and blankets. Until this day a custom still exists among the American Indian descendants on Martha's Vineyard that involves setting aside one day of the year to gather cranberries along the dunes at Gay head (C. J. Hall 1941b).

Perhaps the most fascinating role of the cranberry in Indian culture was as a symbol of peace and friendship. According to John White Norwood in *The Tammany Legend,* the great Sachem of the Delawares was called *Pakimintzen,* which meant "Cranberry Eater" (Norwood 1936). His principal duty was to cement the ties of friendship and maintain peace between the Lenni-Lenape Nation, of which Pakimintzen was one of its kings, and the Iroquois Nation to the north and the Cherokee Nation to the south. This necessitated frequent state feasts at which cranberries were always eaten. In time, cranberries began to be associated with these feasts of peace.

There can be little doubt that cranberries were among the new foods that were introduced to the colonists by the American Indians. John Elliot, "Apostle to the Indians," makes mention in Thomas Shepard's 1648 *Cleare*

Sunshine of the Gospell (published in 1648) of the Indians' use of the "crane-berry" as an item of barter with the colonists (C. J. Hall, 1948). The colonists probably used that term because the stem, calyx, and petals of the flower just before expanding into a perfect flower resembled the neck, head, and bill of a crane. Another version of the name's origin is that the cranberry was a favorite food of the cranes that were abundant in the marshes along the New England and New Jersey coasts. Through usage craneberry became cranberry.

In *New England Rarities Discovered,* published in England in the early 1670s, John Josselyn was the first to describe the new species in detail (C. J. Hall 1948). Josselyn called the new berry "cran berry" or "bear berry"—the latter because it appeared to be a favorite food of bears. In addition to describing the botanical traits of the plant, Josselyn related how the berry was used by the Indians and colonists as a sauce to eat with their meat and pastry. The use of the cranberry in a poultice to control fever and its value in the prevention of scurvy are also mentioned in this early writing.

In 1686, specimens of the cranberry were sent to John Ray, a noted English botanist, who described the berry and referred to it by its American name cranberry or bear berry. This was not the first recorded transatlantic cranberry shipment, however. In 1677 the colonists sent ten barrels of cranberries plus Indian corn and 3,000 codfish to King Charles II in order to appease the royal wrath provoked when the colonists coined Pine Tree shillings.

The early settlers of New England were not the only ones to recognize the attributes of this new fruit. In Burlington, New Jersey, Thomas Budd, ancestral relative of the Budd family (one of the New Jersey cranberry industry's pioneer families), included "cramberries" among the natural resources of the region in *Good Order Established in Pennsylvania and New Jersey in America* (C. J. Hall 1948). It is interesting to note that Budd called them cramberries and not cranberries or even craneberry. Gabriel Thomas called them cramberries in his 1698 *Historical and Geographical Account of the Province and Country of Pennsylvania and of West-New-Jersey in America.* (C. J. Hall 1948). In his 1821 *Miscellanies,* William Tindov translated a 1808 memorandum from a French delegate to his superior entitled "Memoir on the consumption of Cranberry Sauce, by the Americans." In the missive, the delegate complained about the raw and simple state of the culinary preparations in the new country, in particular that "most villainous" of American sauces, cranberry sauce, "vulgarly called cramberry sauce, from the voracious manner in which they eat it" (Makepeace 1936, 5).

Mahlon Stacy, living near the Falls of the Delaware (present-day Trenton), described the use of cranberries in sauce and pastry to his brother in Yorkshire, England (Durell 1902). In a letter dated 1689, Stacy referred to the unusual keeping quality of the berry, which could be kept from one harvest to the next. He specifically mentioned the cranberry's use in sauce served with turkey, and told of how the Indians would gather and bring them to the settlers.

The cranberry is believed to have been present at the first Thanksgiving feast. Rogers Williams, in what is probably the best-known account of the event, wrote of the Pilgrims' use of the red berry—"ate plentiful of the strawberries that grew abundantly in the place" (C. J. Hall 1949a, 12). Historians generally agree that what Williams referred to was the cranberry because strawberries are a spring crop; Williams used the only word he knew to describe the yet unnamed red berry (C. J. Hall 1949a).

Birthplace of the Industry

The first attempt to cultivate the wild cranberry was made in 1810 by Henry Hall, a Revolutionary War veteran, in the town of Dennis, Massachusetts, on Cape Cod (C. J. Hall 1941a, 1949d, 1949f; Holmes 1883). Cape Cod had formed the boundary between two great tongues of ice during the last glacial epoch (Franklin 1937). One great tongue of ice was the Buzzards Bay Glacier to the south; the other was the Cape Cod Glacier, which filled Massachusetts Bay to the north. The glaciers deposited the mantle of sand that now exists over the original clay strata, creating the conditions that favored cranberry growth. Hall observed that when wind-driven sand covered wild cranberry plants growing in a marsh near his home, the plants responded with what appeared to be renewed vigor and produced abundantly. Hall proceeded to transplant portions of sod in which the wild vines were growing into a small bog behind his homestead that he prepared by draining and sanding. Hall noticed distinct differences in fruit appearance between plants, which led to such descriptive terms as "Granpaws Blues" for berries with a heavy whitish bloom on them and "Jumbos" for the exceptionally large-sized berries. The success of his sanding technique led to successful transplants on this original cultivated bog and, subsequently, to a new industry. By 1820, Hall was shipping his surplus cranberries to New York City.

Other cranberry industry pioneers in the Dennis area included Elkanah Sears and Thomas Hall, cousin of Henry Hall (C. J. Hall 1949d). Sears and his sons developed properties near Scargo Lake in East Dennis. Alexander Howes also developed so-called cranberry yards in the Dennis area during these early decades. He was the second person to be taxed on his income-producing cranberry property, the first being Henry Hall (C. J. Hall 1949f).

By 1831, cultivation began in the northern counties of Massachusetts around Boston. Augustus Leland pioneered the development of cranberry culture in Middlesex County, Massachusetts (C. J. Hall 1949c). Some of Leland's innovations were late holding of the winter flood to control the cranberry worm, the use of water reflows to protect against frost, and sanding on top of the ice. Leland was probably the first to identify the weeds present in cranberry bogs by their scientific and common names. The principal area of cultivation in Middlesex County was located at Sherborn on a peninsula between the Charles and Concord rivers. Other Middlesex County pioneers included Deacon Addison Flint of North Reading and Sylvester Reeves of Wayland. In Essex County, cranberries were abundant at Ipswich Beach. Winthrop Low was a pioneer cultivator in Essex. Low's experiments with cranberries included growing them on an upland sandy-loam soil suitable for corn. Abner Chapman of Winchester also experimented with cranberries on upland soil, as did Norman Bates of Norfolk County.

New Jersey Beginnings

Wild cranberries grew profusely in the sandy marshes and peaty bogs of southern New Jersey. The early settlers gathered the wild berries in the fall, often greedily picking them before they were fully ripe. This led the New Jersey legislature to pass a statute in 1789 that forbade the picking of cranberries before 10 October, violation of which would incur a 10-shilling fine. (C. J. Hall 1949g).

Attempts were soon made to cultivate the wild cranberry of the area. Benjamin Thomas of Pemberton has been credited with having made the first effort to culture this native berry in 1835. Other pioneers in New Jersey included William R. Braddock and John J. ("Peg Leg John") Webb of Cassville. Webb developed a bog from transplanted sods and used the Massachusetts method of sanding to improve the vigor of the vines. He has been credited with being the first individual to observe that sound berries could be separated from soft berries by bouncing them on a hard surface down a series of steps. The story has it that Peg Leg John had difficulty in moving his cranberries from his storage loft to the packing area located below because of his handicap. He resorted to bouncing the berries down the stairs rather then carrying them down. The sound berries bounced to the bottom of the stairs, whereas the rotted fruit became hung up on the treads. D. T. Stanford used this bounce principle to develop the first cranberry separator. The principle is still in use today to separate soft cranberries from sound fruit.

The industry in New Jersey developed in the rural and isolated localities of the Pinelands with such quaint names as Ongs Hat, Double Trouble, Mount Misery, Oriental, Calico, Friendship, Penny Pot, and Hog Walla. Many of these picturesque names are still in use today by the locals, who are referred to as "Pineys."

Wisconsin Beginnings

The first record of the use of cranberries in Wisconsin commerce comes from the log entries of Ebenezer Childs, a New Englander, who became a pioneer storekeeper at Green Bay (Hintzman et al. 1953). In 1828 Childs transported eight boat-loads of cranberries from Green Bay to Galena, Illinois, where he exchanged the fruit for provisions to supply a camp of Winnebago shingle makers working at the mouth of the Yellow River. Here, until the cultivation of the cranberry, the Winnebagos carried on an extensive trade in cranberries with the newcomers.

The locations of wild cranberry patches were often mentioned in the field notes of land surveyors in the area. Harvest of the wild crop was contributing tens of thousands of dollars to the local economy (Whittlesey 1937). So significant had the cranberry become in Wisconsin's commerce that a law was passed forbidding anyone from picking or having in his/her possession unripe cranberries before 20 September, upon penalty of a $50 fine.

The first attempt to cultivate the native cranberry of the region was made in 1853 by George A. Peffer in the Fox River Valley in the area that is now Berlin. By the end of the decade, so much of the native cranberry was under cultivation that all of it could not be harvested. By 1869 the Berlin area had over 1,000 acres (394 ha) under cultivation, with a crop estimated at 11,000 barrels and valued at $120,000—equivalent to the gross return from 12,000 acres (4,725 ha) of wheat or 40,000 barrels of apples (Smith 1870).

Origins on the West Coast

The last of the major cranberry-producing regions developed along the Pacific Coast of Washington and Oregon in the late 1800s. In 1883, Anthony Chabot, a Frenchman by birth, started a cranberry bog near the town of Long Beach (Washington) and another, 11 years later, at North Beach (C.J. Hall 1945, 1963). Chabot planted about 35 acres (14 ha) of the McFarlin, Native Jersey, and Cape Cod Beauty cultivars with the help of Chinese labor. He used the local Indians to help with the harvest. The young industry boomed for the first few decades, and acreage in the Long Beach area climbed to 600 (236 ha) by the end of World War II. The rapid expansion was soon to fall on hard times as absentee owners were unable to deal with the intricacies of cranberry culture. It was not until 1912 when Edward Benn started cultivating cranberries in the Grayland area that the industry in Washington again flourished.

At about the same time that Chabot was planting his cranberries at Long Beach, Charles Dexter McFarlin of south Carver, Massachusetts, planted the first vines at Empire City, Coos County, Oregon. McFarlin's original bog is still in production today (Chandler 1957).

Early Development of the Industry

The Early Decades

The second and third decades of the nineteenth century were the formative years of the cranberry industry. During this period, the fruit gathered from the wild and the cultivated fruit intermingled in the markets (C. J. Hall 1949e). During these early decades, Boston became the major market for the wild and cultivated cranberry. From Boston the fruit was shipped to Europe, where it was frequently sold for $20 a barrel. The fruit was packed in barrels in water and would arrive in England as fresh as when first gathered from the marshes. By the end of the 1830s, shipments were also sent from Boston's Faneuil Hall Market to New Orleans, Mobile, Savannah, and Charleston, selling for as high as $35 a barrel (G. T. Beaton 1959).

Eastwood (1856), however, put the real beginning of the cranberry industry at 1840. By then, all the growers in the Dennis area were practicing improved horticultural techniques such as sanding. By the 1840s cranberries began to be cultivated in Plymouth County (C. J. Hall 1949e). Saunders Walker and Thomas Pembroke were credited with being the cranberry pioneers in this new area. In 1845 Abijah Lucas was the first to cultivate the cranberry in the Plymouth County town of Carver, which is considered the center of cranberry production in Massachusetts today.

During this same period, the cranberry industry developed rapidly on Cape Cod (C. J. Hall 1949h). It was during the 1840s that Cyrus Cahoon, the developer of the Early Black cultivar, set out his first vines at Pleasant Lake (Atkins 1940). The cranberry center of Cape Cod gradually shifted from Dennis to Harwich during the century's fifth and sixth decades (C. J. Hall 1950a). In the 1855 census of Barnstable County, there were 197 acres in cranberries in the county, which produced a crop valued at $15,916 (C. J. Hall 1950e). In the entire state, there were 5,463 (2,150 ha) acres in production by this time; 15 counties were producing cranberries valued at $135,194. At this period in the history of the industry, Middlesex County was the leading county in production with 2,555 acres (1,006 ha).

Cranberry Fever

Cranberry growing as a means of livelihood took firm hold during the middle decades of the nineteenth century in both Massachusetts and New Jersey (Chandler 1956a; C. J. Hall 1949b). The expansion of the industry reached a fever pitch during the 1860s, spurred on by the high prices being paid for the fruit as a result of the increased demand of the war years. The fruit was much in demand by captains of whaling ships because its good keeping quality and its propensity to stave off scurvy (cranberries have a high vitamin C content). Despite natural disasters and financial panics, cranberry bog construction continued. Even the Civil War proved no obstacle to the growth of the industry; the higher prices being received only stimulated the planting of new acreage (C. J. Hall 1952a, 1952c).

Although the interest in and knowledge about cranberry growing was centered on Cape Cod during these middle decades of the nineteenth century, a number of Cape growers were moving westward to Plymouth County in search of the so-called red gold (C. J. Hall 1950e). The search for suitable land for cranberry production took the Crowell brothers of Sandwich to the areas around Wareham and Plymouth. Calvin Crowell became one of the most successful growers of the day, employing his expertise in water management to productive ends. Other cranberry pioneers in the Wareham area were Prince Burgess, James Williams, Samuel Beese, and Bradford Bartlett (Hamilton 1945). The cranberry fever of the period was reflected in land prices. Bogland that had not been worth even $100 per acre could not be bought for less than $10,000 once it was developed for cranberry production (C. J. Hall 1950c).

Many of the New England cranberry growers were also involved in traditional farming, fishing, salt making, and commerce. Some were seafaring men and retired sea captains, so it was not unusual for them to finance their cranberry operation by selling "64th" interests in a bog (C. D. Stevens et al., 1957). During their sailing days, they raised the capital to build new ships by selling interests in 64ths. Investors would buy one or more parts of the ship and share in the profits of its commerce. To this day, some cranberry bogs on Cape Cod are owned by as many as thirty or forty people, descendants of those early seafaring cranberry pioneers. This phase of the development of the cranberry industry on Cape Cod was poetically expressed by Captain Bill in the following old rhyme titled "Attune" (C. J. Hall 1952b, 10):

> There's nothing to me in foreign lands
>   like the stuff that grows in Cape Cod Sands;
> There's nothing in sailing of foreign seas
>   equal to getting down on your knees
>   and pulling the pizen ivy out;
> I guess I knew what I was about
>   when I put by my chart and glass
>   and took to growing cranberry sass.

Nowhere was cranberry fever more evident than in New Jersey. In 1851 Barclay White planted the first vines at Sim Place—bogs which were later operated by Isaac Harrison (C. J. Hall 1949g). A few years later, J. A. Fenwick planted the first vines at what was to become known as Whitesbog, one of the largest cranberry plantings in New Jersey (Fenwick was the father-in-law of J. J. White, Barclay's son). Although the 1850s were years of experimentation in New Jersey, the actual industry commenced, according to J. J. White (1870), with the beginning of the 1860s. By the mid-1870s, New Jersey had become a leading state in cranberry production (table 1.1), due to the organizational and horticultural ability of Barclay White, J. A. Fenwick, D. H. Shreve, and the renowned Theodore Budd, one of New Jersey's greatest cranberry growers.

TABLE 1.1. ESTIMATES OF UNITED STATES CRANBERRY
PRODUCTION FOR THE YEARS 1872–1899 (IN BARRELS)

YEAR	NEW ENGLAND*	NEW JERSEY	THE WEST†	TOTAL
1872	13,333	33,333	45,000	91,666
1873	35,000	36,666	20,000	91,666
1874	35,000	30,000	18,333	83,333
1875	25,000	36,667	14,999	76,666
1876	21,667	30,000	14,333	66,000
1877	54,743	50,700	27,166	133,609
1878	41,666	20,000	36,923	98,589
1879	65,000	30,000	26,000	111,000
1880	82,500	42,900	38,810	164,210
1881	51,942	52,338	49,395	153,675
1882	63,888	26,129	17,333	107,390
1883	47,321	39,508	45,169	131,998
1884	43,528	41,549	8,261	93,338
1885	93,626	66,042	88,144	247,812
1886	91,600	78,085	10,465	180,150
1887	102,521	54,596	46,891	204,008
1888	86,667	75,000	33,333	195,000
1889	67,167	45,000	20,583	132,750
1890	125,000	66,666	75,000	266,666
1891	160,000	83,333	10,000	253,333
1892	125,000	53,333	21,667	200,000
1893	191,667	108,333	33,333	333,333
1894	61,666	66,667	8,333	136,666
1895	140,000	66,667	3,333	210,000
1896	200,000	66,666	10,000	276,666
1897	133,333	83,333	16,667	233,333
1898	141,666	100,000	25,000	266,666
1899	208,333	83,333	36,666	328,333

SOURCE: Peterson et al. 1968.
*Includes New York.
†Includes Wisconsin, Washington, and Oregon.

Another reason for this rapid industrial expansion in New Jersey was the fact that relatively large bogs could be easily constructed in the expansive Pinelands of southern New Jersey, compared to the small individual bogs constructed on Cape Cod. By the 1880s, however, Massachusetts had become the undisputed leader in cranberry production in the nation. The coming of the railroad both on Cape Cod and in the southern counties of New Jersey was an important factor in the industry's rapid growth.

In Wisconsin there was a phenomenal growth in acreage under cranberry cultivation following the Civil War and in the early years of the 1870s (Peltier 1970). Edward Sackett from Sackett Harbor, New York, became one of the richest of the new entrepreneurs. By 1869 his crops were bringing him $70,000 in the Chicago market, which had become the principal trading site for the new commodity. Land values in the Berlin area skyrocketed as cranberry fever reached into the flatlands of Wisconsin. Establishment costs were estimated at $300 to $600 per acre, considerably less than construction costs in the East at this time, and profits were as great as two-thirds of the gross return (Smith 1870). Other pioneers in the Berlin area included the Carey brothers, Rounds and Company, and such families as Mason, Spencer, and Walters. By the end of the decade, however, the boom in the area was over. The new "marshes" (as the bogs were called in Wisconsin) had been decimated not only by drought and wildfire, but by the alkaline waters of the Fox and Willow rivers, which the growers had tapped as the water supply for their new bogs.

During the late 1870s and early 1880s, the cranberry industry shifted from the Berlin area to central Wisconsin in what is today referred to as the Cranmoor and Mather-Warrens districts. It was here that new cranberry plantings were established by such well-known Wisconsin cranberry growers as Arpin, Bennett, Fitch, Gaynor, Hamilton, Palmeter, Potter, Rezin, Searls, Smith and Whittlesey. (Many of these families are still prominent in Wisconsin cranberry growing today.) As the new lands came into production, yields slowly increased toward those heady days of the early 1870s (see table 1.1). By 1875 more than 2,500 acres (984 ha) were under cultivation in this new area.

With the rapid expansion of cranberry acreage and its establishment as a monoculture, the insect and disease infestations affecting cranberries began to emerge as serious problems of the new industry (C. J. Hall 1950b, 1950d). Holmes (1883) spoke of the appearance of the vine worm in 1856, and New Jersey growers were particularly plagued by berry rots almost from the beginnings of cultivation. The first attempt to document the existing knowledge on the culture of this crop was made in the publication of Eastwood's cranberry manual (Eastwood, 1856). Late holding floodwater and June reflows were some of the first attempts made to control serious insect infestations, as reported by Eastwood in his manual.

In 1870, the second publication concerning cranberry culture was printed, a monograph entitled *Cranberry Culture* by J. J. White of Whitesbog, New Jersey. With the publication of two books on the subject of cranberry culture within two decades, the foundation of a lasting new agricultural industry appeared to be complete. It was fortunate that the roots of the young industry were deep and sound for the new industry had to survive many economical and physical crises in the century that followed.

Grower Organizations

American Cranberry Growers' Association

The first attempt on the part of cranberry growers to come together to share their growing experiences was made by the New Jersey growers. Through the efforts of Theodore Budd, the first meeting of New Jersey growers was held at Vincentown, New Jersey, in 1869 (Rider 1909). They met once again the following year and then in 1871 established the American Cranberry Growers' Association. Its purpose, as stated in the preamble of their constitution, was the following (Rider 1909, 5): "Whereas, it is deemed practical and expedient by citizens of New Jersey, engaged in the cultivation of cranberries, to associate themselves together for the purpose of mutual benefit and protection, Therefore, we, the subscribers, to secure this and to promote the general welfare do adopt and establish the following Constitution."

Thus, the oldest cranberry growers organization in the United States was formed. At this meeting two pioneers in the New Jersey cranberry industry, J. A. Fenwick and J. J. White, were chosen as the organization's first president and secretary, respectively. The Association established committees on subjects that were of paramount concern to cranberry growers at the time, including cropping and marketing, flowing and drainage, grasses and weeds, insect enemies, scale (rot), fertilizers, and standard measure—topics that are still of concern to the cranberry grower of today. The American Cranberry Growers' Association has continued to meet semiannually since its inception, although it discontinued publishing the proceedings of its meetings in 1964. Descendants of the Budd and White families, founders of the organization, are still prominent growers of cranberries in New Jersey today.

Wisconsin State Cranberry Growers' Associations

Another early attempt by growers to organize themselves occurred in 1871, when Wisconsin cranberry growers formed the Berlin Cranberry Association (Smith 1870). This organization apparently died out with the decline of the industry in the Berlin area. It was soon superceded, however, by the

Wisconsin State Cranberry Growers' Association in 1887, developed by the growers in the Cranmoor and Mather-Warrens districts (Nash 1938). The organization meets annually to keep abreast of new developments in cranberry culture and published an annual proceedings of its meetings continuously from 1887 to 1943.

Another significant development in Wisconsin was the formation of the Wisconsin Cranberry Sales Growers' Cooperative, organized by A. U. Chaney and Judge Gaynor for the express purpose of helping Wisconsin growers market their crop. The cooperative organization introduced such innovative marketing strategies as fruit grading and price pooling, which would be later adopted by other marketing organizations. In 1907 it joined forces with eastern marketing organizations to form the National Cranberry Sales Company; this name was later changed to the American Cranberry Exchange. Other marketing organizations that were active in Wisconsin were the Midwest Cranberry Cooperative and Cranberry Growers Inc.

Cape Cod Cranberry Growers' Association

Although the cranberry industry had been in operation for some 50 years, Massachusetts growers did not develop a viable growers' organization until 1888 (an earlier effort in 1866 had failed). In that year, growers formed the Cape Cod Cranberry Growers' Association for the promotion of cranberry culture. This organization was successful in sponsoring a movement that, in 1910, established the Cranberry Experiment Station at East Wareham, with which it has cooperated ever since. The organization was instrumental in the positioning of extension personnel at the station, who disseminate cranberry information to the industry. Today the Cape Cod Cranberry Growers' Association boasts over 400 members.

State Experiment Stations

Massachusetts Cranberry Experiment Station

As briefly mentioned above, the Cape Cod Cranberry Growers' Association was persistent in efforts to get the Massachusetts State Legislature to fund a research commitment to solving the production problems of the cranberry industry. This persistence led to the establishment of the Cranberry Experiment Station at East Wareham. The State Bog, as it was to become known, was developed by Silas Besse in 1893 and purchased by the state in 1910 (Besse 1966). H. J. Franklin became its first director, a position he held until his retirement in 1952. Many of the initial objectives of the research station were still important concerns to cranberry growers today, namely, injurious and beneficial insects, diseases (their characteristic, causes, and controls), weather relations, cultivars, fertilizers, chemistry and food values of fruit, bog equipment, bog management (sanding), and water management.

During the next 75 years, many of the preeminent cranberry researchers of the country worked at one time or another at the Massachusetts Cranberry Experiment Station. In addition to being the chief administrator of the station, Franklin was a trained entomologist and was responsible for this aspect of cranberry research. In 1929 he was joined by H. F. Bergman, whose expertise was in diseases of the cranberry, an area of investigation that has been explored at the station ever since. C. E. Cross joined Franklin's staff in 1939. As a trained botanist, his responsibilities included weed investigations. Other staff added during Franklin's tenure included F. B. Chandler, who worked on cultivar evaluations, fertilizer research, and water management, and J. R. Beattie, the first extension specialist assigned to the station. Upon Franklin's retirement in 1952, Cross became director of the station, a position he held until his retirement in 1981. Currently, I. E. Demoranville heads the station with a staff of 18 technical and support personnel.

New Jersey Cranberry and Blueberry Research Laboratory

This laboratory, a substation of the New Jersey Agricultural Experiment Station of Rutgers University, was first established at Whitesbog in 1918 under the direction of C. S. Beckwith. Although it was originated to focus solely on cranberry problems, research was gradually devoted to blueberries as the new fledgling cultivated blueberry industry developed. In 1927 the station was moved to Pemberton and then, in 1966, to permanent new research facilities at Chatsworth.

In addition to the renowned Beckwith, the substation has been the laboratory for such notable cranberry scientists as C. A. Doehlert, director from 1944 until his retirement in 1960; R. B. Wilcox, U. S. Department of Agriculture plant pathologist; F. B. Chandler, horticulturist; and entomologists R. S. Filmer, P. E. Marucci, and W. E. Tomlinson, Jr. Both Chandler and Tomlinson eventually joined the staff of the Massachusetts Cranberry Experiment Station.

Today, the modern research facility located in the midst of New Jersey's cranberry and blueberry industry in the Pinelands is recognized by the federal government as the national Center for *Vaccinium* Research. In addition to providing information on the cultural needs of cranberries and blueberries, the facility supports the only cranberry breeding program in existence for the nation.

Washington Cranberry and Blueberry Station

In 1923 this substation of the Washington State Agricultural Experiment Station was opened at Long Beach under the direction of D. J. Crowley. From the beginning, the facility was utilized for research on both *Vaccinium* crops. C. C. Doughty became its director upon Crowley's retirement in 1954. In 1960 its name was changed to the Coastal Washington Experiment Station. In addition to housing modern laboratories, the facility includes six acres of cranberries that are utilized for research. It was at this station that the original cranberry crosses were made that led to the development of the Crowley cultivar. The station is presently under the direction of the noted cranberry horticulturist, A. Y. Shawa.

Wisconsin Cranberry Station 1903–1917

This cranberry research station had the distinction of being the first research facility to be devoted to cranberry research, but it was also the shortest lived of the stations. The station was established in 1903 through an act of the Wisconsin legislature, as the result of considerable pressure by the growers' organization (Peltier 1970). A five-acre bog was rented from the Wisconsin State Cranberry Growers' Association in the Cranmoor District and used for cultivar trials, insect investigations, fertilizer, and water management studies. It was used primarily for summer fieldwork by researchers from the Wisconsin Agricultural Experiment Station at Madison. Wisconsin researchers working at the rented facility included A. R. Whitson, E. P. Sandsten, R. P. Haskins, H. A. Ramsey, and O. G. Malde, who collaborated in the series of U.S. Department of Agriculture bulletins on cranberry culture in the 1920s.

Cranberry Research Pioneers

With the establishment of growers' organizations in the major cranberry-producing areas, the research needs of the industry were identified, and pressure was exerted on the state and federal agricultural research organizations to address these needs. As a result, an extraordinary amount of talent was brought to bear upon the industry's problems. It was fortunate for the industry that scientists of such caliber were available, because the problems were immense. These early cranberry research pioneers served the industry well. Cranberry growers of yesterday, today, and of tomorrow owe much to these research pioneers. It is fitting that those who have served the industry so well in the past be acknowledged.

Pathologists

Perhaps the greatest problems that the cranberry grower had to face were those of the diseases: cranberry fruit rot in the field and in storage, and later the dreaded false blossom disease. The first help from the U.S. Department of Agriculture (USDA) came when it assigned pathologists of the stature of C. L. Shear, N. E. Stevens, and H. F. Bain to investigate the disease problems of the industry. Their numerous bulletins, including their 1931 *Fungous Diseases of the Cultivated Cranberry,* remain classics to this day. To this list must be added R. B. Wilcox, USDA associate pathologist stationed in New Jersey from 1928 until his death in 1956, and senior pathologist H. F. Bergman (plate 1.1). D. M. Boone, recently retired from the University of Wisconsin, served the industry well with his productive cranberry disease investigations.

PLATE 1.1. *Left to right:* R. B. WILCOX, F. B. CHANDLER, AND H. F. BERGMAN ON DUTY (Courtesy Massachusetts Cranberry Experiment Station)

It is interesting to note that all these scientists devoted most of their professional careers to cranberry investigations, and although they were (for the most part) trained as pathologists, their interest and general knowledge of cranberries often led them far afield in their research. Steven's interest in the storage quality of cranberry fruit led to investigations on post-harvest physiology of cranberries and the interrelationship between weather and the keeping quality of cranberries. Bain's studies took him to Oregon and Wisconsin, where he not only worked on disease problems but also investigated the fruiting habit of the cranberry. He became keenly interested in the hybridization of the cranberry and, in cooperation with Wilcox and Bergman, became instrumental in carrying out the original USDA cranberry breeding project. Wilcox achieved recognition for his work on the false blossom disease, together with his New Jersey colleague, C. S. Beckwith. Bergman's greatest contributions were the studies he carried out on the role of oxygen deficiency of floodwaters on the cranberry plant and its effect on production.

Entomologists

Crop losses to insects were only second to the losses to disease. Significant contributions to our understanding of the insect problems in cranberry culture were made by H. B. Scammell (1917) and J. B. Smith (1903) in their bulletins devoted to cranberry insects. With the discovery in 1929 that the blunt-nosed leafhopper was the vector for false blossom disease, the need to control insects became crucial to the survival of the industry. The industry was fortunate to have scientists of the caliber of H. J. Franklin and C. S. Beckwith to help them combat the insect menace. R. S. Filmer and P. E. Marucci added significantly to our understanding of the pollination needs of the cranberry. W. E. Tomlinson, Jr., recently ended an illustrious career of service to New Jersey and Massachusetts cranberry growers with his retirement.

Both Beckwith and Franklin served the cranberry industry not only as trained entomologists but also as directors for their respective research stations in New Jersey and Massachusetts. Their knowledge and understanding of cranberry culture extended far beyond the realm of the insect world. In New Jersey, Beckwith researched the fertilizer, water, and cultural needs of the cranberry and published extensively on his findings. It was a tragic loss to the industry when Beckwith collapsed and died in his research plots in the prime of his career.

There probably has not been a more prolific cranberry researcher than Franklin (plate 1.2). His 50-year career (1902–1952) in cranberry research, mostly as director of the Massachusetts Cranberry Research Station, spanned a period of tremendous industrial growth. His contributions to our

PLATE 1.2. H. J. FRANKLIN, DIRECTOR OF THE MASSACHUSETTS CRANBERRY RESEARCH STATION, 1910–1952 (Courtesy Massachusetts Cranberry Experiment Station)

understanding of cranberry insects and their role in cranberry culture, of the role of the bumble bee in cranberry pollination, and the role of weather in cranberry production are classic works that remain extremely pertinent to this day.

Horticulturists

A number of scientists have served the industry well as either horticulturists or botanists. Many have also served as administrators of the various cranberry research stations. Upon Beckwith's death, C. A. Doehlert became the principal cranberry investigator in New Jersey. His research contributions included studies on the cranberry's fruiting habit and fertilizer needs and water management. His counterpart in Massachusetts was F. B. Chandler, who also conducted research on cranberry fertilizer needs, bog drainage, and cultivar trials. Also in Massachusetts, C. E. Cross carried out extensive studies on cranberry weed control in addition to his administrative duties. In Wisconsin M. N. Dana contributed extensively to our knowledge of cranberry weed control and the nutrition of the cranberry plant. On the West Coast, horticulturists D. J. Crowley and C. C. Doughty served as administrators of the research station at Long Beach and were the research principals involved in supporting the needs of the industry in Washington and Oregon. In eastern Canada, E. L. Eaton and I. V. Hall at Kentville, Nova Scotia, were the principal investigators. In western Canada, G. W. Eaton, of the University of British Columbia, studied nutrition, growth and development, and yield component analysis.

For those of us who are still actively serving the cranberry industry in some capacity, these are formidable footprints to fill. The legacy is a great one and can only be an inspiration to even greater achievement.

TWO

Industry

Acreage

United States Total

By the turn of the century, when the U.S. Department of Agriculture (USDA) began keeping statistics of the cranberry industry, a very viable industry was already in existence. In 1900 a total of 21,500 acres (8,465 ha) were harvested; this figure represented new plantings as well as improved native acres (table 2.1, fig. 2.1). Massachusetts and New Jersey contributed the bulk of this acreage, with the budding industry in Wisconsin just beginning to make an impression at the national level. In 1924 the first acreage from the West Coast were included in the USDA statistics, combining both the Washington and Oregon industries.

The industry reached its zenith with respect to acreage in production in 1930 and 1931 when 27,640 acres (10,882 ha) were harvested, reflecting the boom years following World War I. As the nation entered into the Great Depression, bogs were taken out of production, some being allowed to return to the condition of wet-lands. After a brief increase in acreage following World War II, when prices skyrocketed during the immediate postwar years, the acreage devoted to cranberry growing went into a steady decline. The poor financial returns during the 1950s and early 1960s resulted in hundreds of marginally productive acres being taken out of cranberry production. By the early 1960s, there were fewer acres being harvested than at the turn of the century. The nadir of the industry was reached in 1963 when only 20,120 acres (7,921 ha) were harvested. Only the addition of new bogs in Wisconsin and on the West Coast kept the total national losses of cranberry acreage from being worse.

Following this low point in the industry, the acreage began to increase slowly until today there are again nearly 25,000 acres in cranberry production. This increase in acreage coincided with the increasing utilization of cranberries in processing. As new consumer products were developed, the

TABLE 2.1. TOTAL CRANBERRY ACREAGE IN THE UNITED STATES AND INDIVIDUAL STATES FOR THE YEARS 1900–1987

YEAR	MASS.	N.J.	WIS.	WASH.*	OREG.*	TOTAL
1900	11,300	9,000	1,200	—	—	21,500
1901	11,700	9,100	1,300	—	—	22,100
1902	12,000	9,200	1,300	—	—	22,500
1903	12,300	9,300	1,400	—	—	23,000
1904	12,700	9,400	1,400	—	—	23,500
1905	13,000	9,500	1,500	—	—	24,000
1906	13,300	9,600	1,500	—	—	24,400
1907	13,500	9,700	1,600	—	—	24,800
1908	13,700	9,800	1,600	—	—	25,100
1909	13,900	10,000	1,700	—	—	25,600
1910	14,000	10,200	1,700	—	—	25,900
1911	14,100	10,300	1,700	—	—	26,100
1912	14,100	10,400	1,800	—	—	26,300
1913	14,200	10,500	1,800	—	—	26,500
1914	14,200	10,600	1,800	—	—	26,600
1915	14,200	10,700	1,800	—	—	26,700
1916	14,100	10,800	1,800	—	—	26,700
1917	14,100	10,900	1,800	—	—	26,800
1918	14,100	11,000	1,800	—	—	26,900
1919	14,000	*11,200*	1,800	—	—	27,000
1920	14,000	11,200	1,800	—	—	27,000
1921	14,000	11,200	1,900	—	—	27,100
1922	14,000	11,100	1,900	—	—	27,000
1923	14,000	11,000	2,000	—	—	27,000
1924	13,900	11,000	2,000	570	—	27,470
1925	13,900	10,900	2,000	570	—	27,370
1926	13,900	10,900	2,100	570	—	27,470

TABLE 2.1. (*Continued*)

YEAR	MASS.	N.J.	WIS.	WASH.*	OREG.*	TOTAL
1927	13,900	10,900	2,100	590	—	27,490
1928	13,800	10,900	2,200	670	—	25,570
1929	13,800	10,800	2,200	640	—	27,440
1930	13,800	10,800	2,300	740	—	*27,640*
1931	13,800	10,700	2,400	740	—	*27,640*
1932	13,700	10,700	2,300	620	—	27,320
1933	13,700	10,400	2,200	640	—	26,940
1934	13,700	10,100	2,100	640	—	26,540
1935	13,700	9,800	2,100	690	—	26,290
1936	13,700	9,500	2,300	700	—	26,200
1937	13,800	9,200	2,400	740	—	26,140
1938	13,800	8,800	2,400	840	—	25,840
1939	13,900	8,500	2,400	840	—	25,640
1940	13,900	8,200	2,500	840	—	25,440
1941	14,000	8,000	2,600	840	—	25,440
1942	14,100	7,800	2,700	850	—	25,450
1943	14,200	7,700	2,700	840	—	25,440
1944	14,300	7,600	2,700	800	—	25,400
1945	14,500	7,600	2,700	880	—	25,680
1946	14,700	7,700	2,700	900	—	26,000
1947	14,800	7,800	2,700	860	—	26,160
1948	*15,000*	7,800	2,800	*960*	—	26,560
1949	15,000	7,500	3,100	700	325	26,625
1950	14,800	7,000	3,500	700	390	26,390
1951	14,600	6,500	3,600	700	440	25,840

(*continued*)

TABLE 2.1. (*Continued*)

YEAR	MASS.	N.J.	WIS.	WASH.*	OREG.*	TOTAL
1952	14,300	5,800	3,700	800	450	25,050
1953	13,900	5,000	3,800	800	460	23,960
1954	13,600	4,200	3,900	800	470	22,970
1955	13,400	3,600	*4,000*	800	470	22,270
1956	13,200	3,000	3,900	950	470	21,520
1957	13,000	2,800	4,000	950	490	21,240
1958	12,900	2,500	4,100	900	520	20,920
1959	12,800	2,800	4,200	950	540	21,290
1960	12,700	2,700	4,200	1,000	540	21,140
1961	12,600	3,000	4,300	1,000	540	21,440
1962	11,800	3,000	4,300	950	520	20,570
1963	11,600	*2,600*	4,400	1,000	520	*20,120*
1964	11,500	3,100	4,500	1,000	520	20,620
1965	11,400	3,000	4,700	1,000	540	20,640
1966	11,400	3,000	4,800	1,000	560	20,760
1967	11,400	3,200	4,900	1,000	620	21,120
1968	11,000	3,300	5,200	1,000	635	21,135
1969	11,100	3,000	5,400	1,000	685	21,185
1970	10,900	3,100	5,700	1,000	745	21,445
1971	11,100	3,100	6,300	1,000	810	22,310
1972	10,900	3,000	6,500	1,000	890	22,290
1973	10,900	3,200	6,700	1,100	900	22,800
1974	10,900	3,200	7,000	1,100	900	23,100
1975	10,900	3,100	7,000	1,100	900	23,000
1976	10,900	3,100	6,800	1,100	880	22,780
1977	11,200	3,000	6,400	1,100	850	22,500
1978	11,200	3,000	7,000	1,100	820	23,120

TABLE 2.1. (*Continued*)

YEAR	MASS.	N.J.	WIS.	WASH.*	OREG.*	TOTAL
1979	11,200	3,000	7,100	1,100	800	23,200
1980	11,200	2,900	7,200	1,100	790	23,190
1981	11,200	2,900	7,100	1,000	850	23,150
1982	11,200	3,000	7,200	1,100	810	23,310
1983	11,200	3,100	7,300	1,100	850	23,550
1984	11,200	3,200	7,400	1,100	920	23,820
1985	11,300	3,300	7,500	1,200	1,100	24,400
1986	11,300	3,300	*7,900*	1,200	1,200	24,900
1987	11,300	3,300	7,900	1,200	1,200	24,900

SOURCE: USDA National Agricultural Statistics Service 1900–1987.
NOTES: Acreage may be converted to hectares by dividing by 2.54. Italicized years indicate
     years of highest acreage in production.
*Pacific Coast (Oregon and Washington) data are combined for the years 1924 through 1948
and listed under Washington.

demand for cranberries began to increase—a demand that was no longer restricted to the holiday season.

State Trends

Massachusetts. Massachusetts has always led the other states in acreage
harvested. The number of acres in production varied with the prosperity of
the industry, reaching its highest level in 1948 when 15,000 acres (5,906 ha)
were harvested. More than one-fourth (26.7%) of its acreage went out of
production during the cranberry doldrums of the next two decades. Growers
in this largest-producing state were abandoning marginal lands and concentrating their resources on the most productive acreage. Today in Massachusetts there are only as many acres in production as there were at the
beginning of the century (11,300 acres).

By the turn of the century, the center of production had moved off the Cape
(Barnstable County) into Plymouth County, concentrating around the towns
of Wareham and Carver (fig. 2.2). Bristol and Nantucket counties today grow
a fair amount of cranberries. There are a scattering of bogs still in production

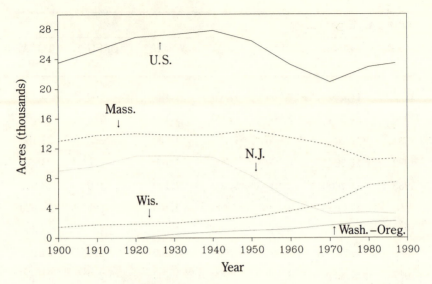

FIGURE 2.1. CRANBERRY ACREAGE BY DECADE SINCE 1900

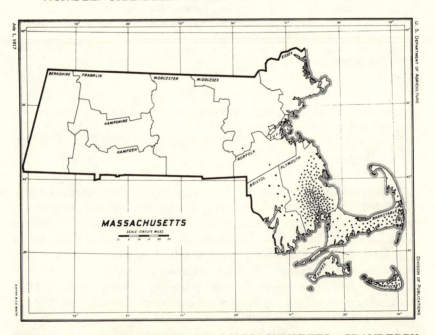

FIGURE 2.2. DISTRIBUTION OF MASSACHUSETTS CRANBERRY ACREAGE BY COUNTY (EACH DOT REPRESENTS 50 ACRES)

in Norfolk County and Middlesex County, which during the early decades of
the industry had led the state in cranberry acreage.

New Jersey. The New Jersey industry began the century with 9,000 acres
(3,543 ha) under cultivation. The industry in New Jersey differed from that in
Massachusetts in that the average holding in New Jersey was 75 acres (30 ha)
compared to 14 acres (5.5 ha) in Massachusetts. The next two decades witnessed a steady increase in the number of planted bogs in New Jersey, reaching a peak of 11,200 acres (4,409 ha) by 1919. The industry was mainly in
Burlington County, with small acreage in Ocean and Atlantic counties (fig.
2.3). A combination of factors led to a steady decline in New Jersey acreage,
beginning in the depression years of the 1930s. Poor prices, poor management, and, above all, the false blossom disease forced acreage out of production. This disease affected the industry in the latter half of the 1920s and cut
deeply into the acreage harvested throughout the 1930s. It was the losses to
this devastating disease that made the cranberry growers in New Jersey look
for some other crop to grow in their cranberry bogs.

It was Elizabeth White, a prominent cranberry grower in New Jersey and

FIGURE 2.3. DISTRIBUTION OF NEW JERSEY CRANBERRY ACREAGE
BY COUNTY (EACH DOT REPRESENTS 50 ACRES)

owner of Whitesbog, who together with F. V. Coville pioneered the development of the cultivated blueberry industry. A good part of the rapid expansion of this industry in New Jersey during the 1940s and 1950s was at the expense of cranberry acreage because both acid-loving plants thrive in the same muck soils. Cranberry growers in Massachusetts and New Jersey were also beginning to feel the pressures of urbanization during these postwar decades. Cranberry yards were becoming housing developments "marketed as "Cranberry Lakes" and "Presidential Lakes"—residential communities of the future!

Wisconsin. Only in Wisconsin and on the West Coast has the acreage story been different. With an abundance of suitable locations available for cranberry cultivation, Wisconsin made rapid strides in increasing acreage, particularly since the end of World War II. In 1955 Wisconsin replaced New Jersey as the second state in the nation in acres harvested and has kept that distinction ever since. The industry was built on the vast flatland that comprised the lake beds of Lake Wisconsin and Lake Oshkosh, which were formed after the Wisconsin Glacier retreated (Peltier 1970). This vast wetland in central Wisconsin provided a tremendous potential for development when the areas were drained. Similar areas were found to the northwest and north central part of the state, where new plantings have recently been made. Today more than 135 growers harvest nearly 8,000 acres (3,150 ha) in 18 different counties in the state (fig. 2.4; Stang and Dana 1984). In 1986 Wisconsin harvested more acres than it ever had in its history. With nearly 8,000 acres (3,150 ha) in production, it now has more than twice as many acres under production as does New Jersey.

West Coast. Although the first bogs in Washington and Oregon were established about 1885 (C. J. Hall 1963) it was not until 1924 that the USDA began to include these Western states in their annual cranberry statistical reporting service. Until 1949 the two states were combined in the USDA report from the Pacific Coast.

The industry marked time until the end of World War II, when acreage began to increase in both states. From a combined total of 960 acres (378 ha) in 1948, Pacific Coast acreage more than doubled by 1986 when 1,200 acres (472 ha) were reported in each of the two states.

The bogs in Washington and Oregon were built on peat that had accumulated between the sand dunes located along the coast. The Washington industry is concentrated in the Long Beach and Grayland districts of Pacific County with 450 acres (177 ha) and 650 acres (256 ha), respectively, and in the Copalis and North Beach sections of Grays Harbor County (fig. 2.5; Chandler 1956c). The largest holding is the Long Beach Cranguyma Farms with 150 acres (59 ha). In Oregon the bogs are located mainly in Coos County, with smaller acreages found in Clatsop and Tillamook Counties (fig. 2.6).

FIGURE 2.4. DISTRIBUTION OF WISCONSIN CRANBERRY ACREAGE BY COUNTY (EACH DOT REPRESENTS 50 ACRES)

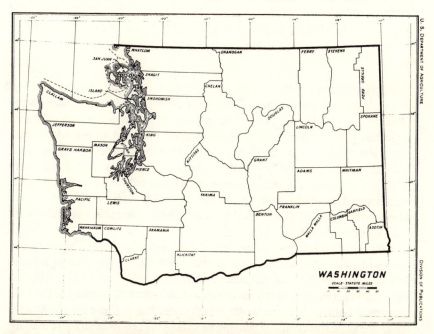

FIGURE 2.5. DISTRIBUTION OF WASHINGTON CRANBERRY ACREAGE BY COUNTY (EACH DOT REPRESENTS 50 ACRES)

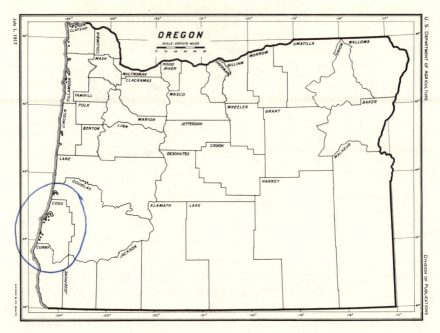

FIGURE 2.6. DISTRIBUTION OF OREGON CRANBERRY ACREAGE BY COUNTY (EACH DOT REPRESENTS 50 ACRES)

Individual plantings in Washington and Oregon are small: holdings average about 12 acres (5 ha) per farm. Most bogs will average less than three acres (1 ha) in size. A ten-acre (4-ha) planting might be considered minimal for an individual grower to make a reasonably good living. In an era when small farms are rapidly disappearing, the cranberry industry represents one of the few agricultural enterprises in the country in which the small family farm might still represent a sound economic base for an individual. Through mechanization and the use of family help, it is still possible for the cranberry grower to enjoy the good life of the small farm and realize adequate financial reward from that investment.

Canada. Cranberries are produced commercially in the Canadian provinces of British Columbia, Nova Scotia, Quebec, Ontario, Prince Edward Island, and Newfoundland (Chandler and Murray 1966). British Columbia has over 1,500 acres (590 hectares) in production, about 80 percent of the total acreage in Canada. In Nova Scotia, where according to Chandler and Murray there are large tracts of land suitable for cranberry production, there are currently over 200 acres (79 hectares) in production. The rest of the cranberry-producing acreage is located in the remaining provinces.

Although the cranberry industry has witnessed a tremendous increase in the demand for its product, it has met this need primarily through increased productivity rather than by any significant increase in acreage. It is fortunate that this has been the case since the pressures of urbanization in the East and the restrictions in the use of wetlands for agriculture are making it increasingly difficult to develop new plantings. It may well be that the industry will need to come full circle and attempt to grow the cranberry on upland soils as the early pioneers did in the area around Boston. For this to succeed, however, much more research is needed.

Production

Total Yield

At the turn of the century, 300,000-barrel yields were already being attained with regularity (table 2.2). (Early in the twentieth century, the barrel measurement was standardized at 100 pounds [45.5 kg] of fruit.) Although yields were doubled in the next four decades (fig. 2.7), it was difficult to sell more than half a million barrels on the fresh market. It seemed that whenever this threshold was reached, the price collapsed and returns suffered. It was fortunate that processing expanded the use for cranberries during the 1940s because the first million-barrel year came in 1953. In less than two decades, the two-million-barrel milestone was reached in 1970, and by 1982 the industry was producing more than three million barrels (118,110 metric tons) of cranberries per year.

Since the turn of the century, Massachusetts has been the leading state in cranberry production (fig. 2.8). By 1939 Massachusetts was producing a record 70 percent of the national cranberry crop, and Wisconsin had surpassed New Jersey in production to become the second largest cranberry-producing state in the nation. By 1950 Wisconsin was producing more than 20 percent of the total cranberry crop. As the newly planted acres came into production and other productivity gains were realized, Wisconsin cranberry production grew at a phenomenal rate until, for a brief period during the mid-1970s, Wisconsin actually produced more cranberries than did Massachusetts.

New Jersey, on the other hand, saw its share of cranberry production decrease from a third of the total production during the early decades of the century to less than 10 percent by the 1950s. Today, even though New Jersey produces more cranberries than it ever did in its history, it still accounts for less than 10 percent of the national crop. The combined total yields of Washington and Oregon have also increased significantly during the past two decades, but their combined production only amounts to less than 10 percent of

TABLE 2.2. TOTAL UNITED STATES PRODUCTION AND
PRODUCTION BY STATES (IN THOUSANDS OF
BARRELS)

YEAR	MASS.	N.J.	WIS.	WASH.*	OREG.*	TOTAL
1900	200	100	18	—	—	318
1901	264	110	40	—	—	414
1902	238	33	46	—	—	317
1903	226	175	18	—	—	419
1904	281	83	21	—	—	385
1905	165	88	18	—	—	271
1906	264	103	45	—	—	412
1907	310	121	21	—	—	452
1908	257	75	12	—	—	344
1909	402	169	30	—	—	601
1910	312	241	16	—	—	569
1911	298	145	30	—	—	473
1912	354	113	45	—	—	512
1913	367	101	30	—	—	498
1914	471	160	13	—	—	664
1915	257	184	35	—	—	476
1916	364	169	38	—	—	571
1917	137	129	27	—	—	293
1918	218	127	30	—	—	375
1919	395	155	40	—	—	590
1920	309	130	33	—	—	472
1921	208	165	24	—	—	397
1922	337	205	55	—	—	597
1923	451	200	35	—	—	686
1924	339	215	42	14	—	610
1925	447	115	25	22	—	609

TABLE 2.2. (*Continued*)

YEAR	MASS.	N.J.	WIS.	WASH.*	OREG.*	TOTAL
1926	438	215	85	24	—	762
1927	385	75	25	27	—	512
1928	348	138	45	28	—	559
1929	421	90	42	17	—	570
1930	395	146	36	7	—	584
1931	460	132	48	14	—	654
1932	415	80	75	10	—	580
1933	506	142	42	9	—	699
1934	290	72	59	24	—	445
1935	332	85	77	22	—	516
1936	346	75	62	21	—	504
1937	565	175	115	22	—	877
1938	325	62	64	23	—	474
1939	490	88	108	18	—	704
1940	322	90	121	38	—	571
1941	500	80	99	46	—	725
1942	572	95	107	38	—	812
1943	492	62	102	32	—	688
1944	159	59	115	43	—	376
1945	478	49	82	47	—	656
1946	553	101	145	57	—	856
1947	487	82	161	62	—	792
1948	605	69	238	56	—	968
1949	520	67	200	40	14	841
1950	610	103	222	33	15	983

(*continued*)

TABLE 2.2. (*Continued*)

YEAR	MASS.	N.J.	WIS.	WASH.*	OREG.*	TOTAL
1951	560	76	196	56	21	910
1952	445	104	203	30	22	804
1953	690	112	295	74	32	*1,203*
1954	590	87	250	62	30	1,019
1955	546	90	315	48	27	1,026
1956	452	73	358	65	40	988
1957	563	78	284	84	41	1,050
1958	598	89	389	57	32	1,166
1959	540	94	461	105	52	1,252
1960	805	86	379	43	28	1,341
1961	472	118	462	139	45	1,236
1962	778	103	360	54	30	1,325
1963	637	66	400	111	41	1,255
1964	660	153	430	67	35	1,345
1965	735	153	441	66	42	1,437
1966	768	135	512	135	49	1,599
1967	573	157	490	139	63	1,424
1968	660	155	438	*163*	52	1,468
1969	755	160	746	105	57	1,823
1970	957	179	702	140	61	*2,039*
1971	*1,072*	237	742	145	69	2,265
1972	819	196	805	154	104	2,078
1973	901	228	756	118	97	2,014
1974	932	250	870	92	92	2,236
1975	785	221	837	135	97	2,075
1976	935	276	*1,004*	103	89	2,407

TABLE 2.2. (*Continued*)

YEAR	MASS.	N.J.	WIS.	WASH.*	OREG.*	TOTAL
1977	875	157	854	136	80	2,012
1978	1,180	223	822	139	95	2,459
1979	1,080	253	901	147	95	2,476
1980	1,185	245	1,080	104	84	2,698
1981	1,172	228	968	129	96	2,593
1982	1,278	295	1,200	89	65	*3,039*
1983	1,421	233	1,132	125	75	2,986
1984	1,663	274	1,200	103	82	3,322
1985	1,687	321	1,255	148	96	3,485
1986	*1,813*	*325*	*1,320*	100	*122*	*3,680*
1987	1,780	325	1,312	126	132	3,675

SOURCE: USDA National Agricultural Statistics Service 1900–1987.
NOTES: Divide production values by 22 to obtain metric ton equivalent. Italicized years and
        values represent a significant milestone in the production for a specific producing area.
* Pacific Coast (Oregon and Washington) data are combined for the years 1924 through 1948
  and listed under Washington.

the national crop produced today. In 1968 Washington produced a record crop
(for that state) of 163,000 barrels (7,392 metric tons). Total Canadian production is about 253,000 barrels (11,500 metric tons) per year.

Million-barrel crops were achieved for the first time by Massachusetts in
1971 and by Wisconsin in 1976. The record crop for the entire industry, however, came in 1986 when 3,680,000 barrels (166,893 metric tons) of cranberries were produced. In this same year, record state crops were grown by
Massachusetts, New Jersey, Wisconsin, and Oregon growers.

Productivity

The most striking feature of cranberry production in the decades following
the turn of the century has been the phenomenal *yield takeoff* of the production curve (fig. 2.9). The main characteristic of the curve is the linear increase in production that occurs in an extended period during which the

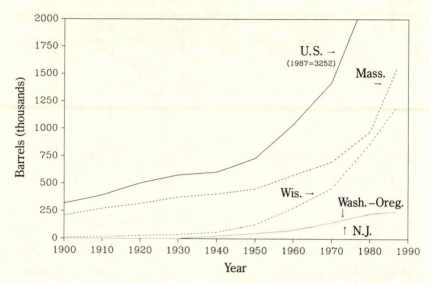

FIGURE 2.7. TOTAL UNITED STATES CRANBERRY PRODUCTION AND PRODUCTION BY STATES FOR THE YEARS 1900–1987 (IN THOUSANDS OF BARRELS)

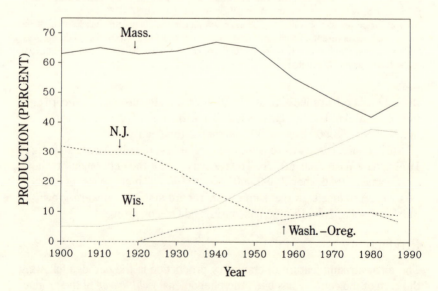

FIGURE 2.8. CRANBERRY PRODUCTION BY STATES AS A PERCENTAGE OF TOTAL U.S. PRODUCTION

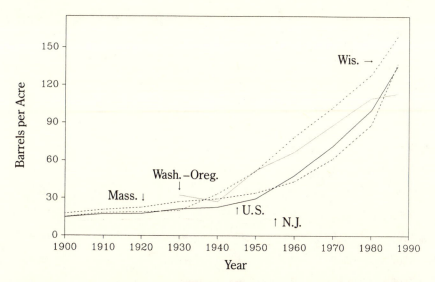

FIGURE 2.9. CRANBERRY YIELD PER ACRE FOR INDIVIDUAL STATES
(IN BARRELS PER ACRE)

acreage decreases. This type of curve is not unique to cranberries but has
been experienced by many agricultural commodities since World War II. The
phenomenon is the result of the rapid development and application of technology required to produce a given commodity. This, of course, can be directly correlated to the extensive research and extension programs that
originate from state and federal experiment stations and industry-supported
research.

A measure of productivity is the yield per acre (table 2.3). The line graph in
Figure 2.9 shows how ideally cranberries fit the yield takeoff pattern; the major takeoff points can be related to specific technological inputs. The first significant increase in productivity occurred in Wisconsin during the 1930s. Up
until 1935 Wisconsin had usually trailed Massachusetts in yield per acre. During this decade Wisconsin growers made the decision to water harvest the
majority of their crop, at first by hand raking on the flood and eventually with
mechanized water harvesters. This not only meant that most of the crop was
being harvested, but it also greatly reduced the amount of vine damage that
resulted from dry scooping the berries.

The second major boost in productivity also occurred in Wisconsin, but
this time Washington and Oregon shared in the technology. During the 1950s
Wisconsin and the West Coast were experiencing major productivity gains
because of the use of new larger-fruited cultivars such as the Searles,
McFarlin, and Ben Lear cultivars. (Fruit size is one of the yield components of

TABLE 2.3. CRANBERRY PRODUCTIVITY FOR THE STATES AND THE UNITED STATES (IN BARRELS PER ACRE)

YEAR	MASS.	N.J.	WIS.	WASH.*	OREG.*	U.S. AVE.
1900	17.7	11.1	15.0	—	—	14.8
1901	22.6	12.1	30.8	—	—	18.7
1902	19.8	3.6	35.4	—	—	14.1
1903	18.4	18.8	12.9	—	—	18.2
1904	22.1	8.8	15.0	—	—	16.4
1905	12.7	9.3	12.0	—	—	11.3
1906	19.8	10.7	30.0	—	—	16.9
1907	23.0	12.5	13.1	—	—	18.2
1908	18.8	7.7	7.5	—	—	13.7
1909	28.9	16.9	17.6	—	—	23.5
1910	22.3	23.6	9.4	—	—	22.0
1911	21.1	14.1	17.6	—	—	18.1
1912	25.1	10.9	25.0	—	—	19.5
1913	25.8	9.6	16.7	—	—	18.8
1914	33.2	15.1	18.3	—	—	25.0
1915	18.1	17.2	19.4	—	—	17.8
1916	25.8	15.6	21.1	—	—	21.4
1917	9.7	1.18	15.0	—	—	10.9
1918	15.5	11.5	16.7	—	—	13.9
1919	28.2	13.8	22.2	—	—	21.9
1920	22.1	11.6	18.3	—	—	17.5
1921	14.9	14.7	12.6	—	—	14.6
1922	24.1	18.5	28.9	—	—	22.1
1923	32.2	18.2	17.5	—	—	25.4
1924	24.4	19.5	21.0	24.6	—	22.2
1925	32.2	10.6	12.5	38.6	—	22.3
1926	31.5	19.7	40.5	41.4	—	27.7

TABLE 2.3. (*Continued*)

YEAR	MASS.	N.J.	WIS.	WASH.*	OREG.*	U.S. AVE.
1927	27.7	6.9	11.9	45.8	—	18.6
1928	25.2	12.7	20.5	41.9	—	20.3
1929	30.5	8.3	19.1	26.2	—	20.8
1930	28.6	13.5	15.7	8.8	—	21.1
1931	33.3	12.3	20.0	18.9	—	23.7
1932	30.3	7.5	32.6	15.8	—	21.2
1933	36.9	13.7	19.1	13.6	—	25.9
1934	21.2	7.1	28.1	38.0	—	16.8
1935	24.2	8.7	*36.7*	31.2	—	19.6
1936	25.3	7.9	27.0	30.4	—	19.2
1937	40.9	19.0	47.9	30.1	—	33.6
1938	23.6	7.0	26.7	27.6	—	18.4
1939	35.3	10.4	45.0	21.7	—	27.5
1940	23.2	11.0	48.4	44.6	—	22.4
1941	35.7	10.0	38.1	55.0	—	28.5
1942	40.6	12.2	39.6	44.9	—	31.9
1943	34.6	8.1	37.8	38.0	—	27.0
1944	11.1	7.8	42.6	53.4	—	14.8
1945	33.0	6.4	30.4	53.5	—	25.5
1946	37.6	13.1	53.7	63.4	—	32.9
1947	32.9	10.5	59.6	72.3	—	30.3
1948	40.3	8.8	85.0	58.0	—	36.4
1949	34.7	8.9	64.5	57.1	42.5	31.6
1950	41.2	14.7	63.4	47.1	37.7	37.2
1951	38.4	11.7	54.4	82.1	47.3	35.2

(*continued*)

TABLE 2.3. (*Continued*)

YEAR	MASS.	N.J.	WIS.	WASH.*	OREG.*	U.S. AVE.
1952	31.1	17.9	54.9	37.5	47.8	32.1
1953	49.6	22.4	77.6	92.5	70.2	*50.2*
1954	43.4	20.7	64.1	76.9	63.8	44.3
1955	40.7	25.0	78.8	59.4	58.1	46.1
1956	34.2	24.3	91.8	68.1	85.1	45.9
1957	43.3	27.9	71.0	88.4	83.7	49.4
1958	46.4	35.6	94.9	63.7	62.1	55.7
1959	42.2	33.6	*109.8*	*110.5*	95.7	58.8
1960	63.4	31.9	90.2	42.7	51.9	63.4
1961	37.5	39.3	107.4	139.0	84.1	57.7
1962	65.9	34.3	83.7	56.8	56.7	64.4
1963	54.9	25.3	90.9	111.0	78.3	62.4
1964	57.4	*49.4*	95.6	67.0	66.3	65.2
1965	64.5	51.0	93.8	66.0	77.4	69.6
1966	67.4	45.0	106.7	135.0	86.8	77.0
1967	50.3	49.1	100.0	139.0	*105.3*	67.4
1968	60.0	47.0	84.2	*163.0*	81.6	69.4
1969	68.0	53.3	138.1	105.0	83.4	86.1
1970	*87.8*	57.7	123.2	140.0	81.3	97.3
1971	97.5	76.5	117.8	145.0	84.9	*102.0*
1972	75.1	65.3	123.8	154.0	116.9	93.2
1973	82.7	71.3	112.8	107.3	108.1	92.1
1974	85.5	78.1	124.3	83.6	102.2	97.0
1975	72.0	7.13	119.6	122.7	107.9	90.2
1976	85.8	89.0	147.6	93.6	101.5	104.3
1977	78.1	52.3	133.4	123.6	95.5	93.3
1978	*105.4*	74.3	117.4	126.4	109.9	106.3

TABLE 2.3. (*Continued*)

YEAR	MASS.	N.J.	WIS.	WASH.*	OREG.*	U.S. AVE.
1979	96.4	84.3	126.9	135.6	*118.1*	106.7
1980	105.8	84.5	150.0	94.5	105.7	116.3
1981	104.6	78.6	136.3	117.3	112.9	112.0
1982	114.1	98.3	*169.0*	80.9	80.2	130.4
1983	126.9	75.2	155.1	113.6	88.2	126.8
1984	148.5	85.6	162.2	93.6	89.1	139.5
1985	149.3	97.0	168.0	123.3	90.9	142.8
1986	*159.3*	*98.5*	155.1	83.3	100.0	*147.8*
1987	157.6	98.5	166.0	105.0	110.0	147.6

SOURCE: USDA National Agricultural Statistics Service 1900–1989.
NOTES: To convert pounds per acre to metric tons per hectare multiply by 0.115. Italicized years and values indicate a productivity milestone for a specific production area.
*Pacific Coast (Oregon and Washington) data are combined for the years 1924 through 1948 and listed under Washington.

cranberry production.) At this same time, West Coast growers were pioneering the use of sprinkler irrigation for frost protection, a significant improvement in the control of this important production limitation. Wisconsin growers adopted this practice during the 1960s. The final major input of the 1950s and 1960s was the introduction of the modern pesticides. including the important organophosphates for insect control, fungicides for fruit rot control, and herbicides for weed control. In Wisconsin the single most important factor in increasing yields was weed control, beginning with the introduction of petroleum products in the 1940s and 1950s, and continuing with the introduction of casoron in the 1960s and glyphosate in the 1980s. All cranberry-growing regions benefited from the use of these modern agricultural chemicals and, as a result, saw their productivity increase. It was not surprising, however, that when the first 100-barrel-per-acre (11.5-metric-tons-per-ha) yields were achieved in 1959, it was done by Wisconsin and Washington growers.

In New Jersey, where productivity had been the lowest in the industry for decades because of the false blossom disease, the availability of the new modern insecticides was particularly beneficial. With the control of the leafhopper vector of this debilitating disease, yields doubled in a very short time.

Another factor that contributed to an increase in productivity in both New Jersey and Massachusetts during the first postwar decade was the fact that many marginally productive acres were being taken out of production; as a result, the average yield per acre increased in these states. New Jersey experienced another significant increase in productivity in 1964, when the yield per acre increased by more than 50 percent as the result of the conversion of a significant part of the state's acreage to water harvesting. By 1970 Massachusetts growers also had made significant strides in converting to water harvesting and, as a result, saw their productivity increase by more than 20 percent.

These technological advances—in addition to the increased use of bees as pollinating agents, improved weather forecasting and frost-warning services, and advances in water management and fertilization techniques—contributed to the first 100-barrel-per-acre (11.5-metric-tons-per-ha) yield achieved by the industry as a whole in 1971. This was preceded by Oregon's first 100-barrel-per-acre crop in 1967 and Washington's record 1968 crop of 163 barrels per acre (18.8 metric tons per ha). Massachusetts growers produced their first 100-barrel-per-acre crop in 1978. The record yield of 169 barrels per acre (19.5 metric tons per ha) was achieved by Wisconsin growers in 1982. Oregon's highest yield was 118 barrels per acre (13.6 metric tons per ha) in 1979, and Massachusetts' record came in 1986 when 159 barrels per acre (18.3 metric tons per ha) was the average yield for the year. New Jersey has yet to achieve the coveted century mark; its highest yield came in 1986 at 98.5 barrels per acre (11.3 metric tons per ha). For the industry as a whole, 1986 was the most productive year on record, with the national average coming to 147.8 barrels harvested for every acre (17.1 metric tons per ha) in production—an extraordinary achievement that the early cranberry pioneers could have never conceived in their wildest imaginations.

Crop Value

Concomitant with the increase in production since the turn of the century has been the increase in total value of the crop (fig. 2.10). The increase in value, however, does not show the idealistic straight-line relationship that was evident for the production curve. Value declines and plateaus are evident and reflect periods of economic depression, particularly the Great Depression of the 1930s and the recession of the 1950s. A low point was reached in 1959 when small portions of the crop were condemned by the federal government because of excessive residues of the weed killer aminotriazole. A public announcement by the secretary of health, education, and welfare, Arthur S. Fleming, of this condemnation caused a widespread buyer's boycott of cranberries because he had emphasized that the weed killer was judged to be carcinogenic to rats. For the next 10 years, the fresh market sales continued to

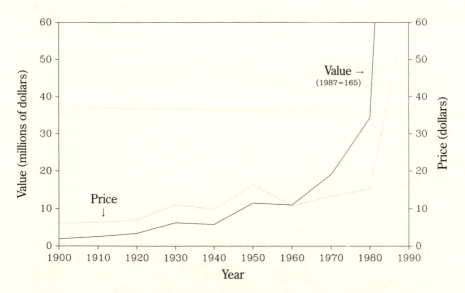

FIGURE 2.10. TOTAL CRANBERRY FARM VALUE AND PRICE PER BAR-
REL FOR THE YEARS 1900–1987

show a steady decline. The steady erosion of their market value during the
1950s and the traumatic experience of the aminotriazole cancer scare left the
industry in difficult straits as we entered what some politicians were predicting would be the "fabulous sixties."

The industry was forced to either take stock and retrench or face extinction as a viable agricultural entity. It proceeded to make every effort to regain
the public confidence. Through extensive use of advertising in all the media
and through the introduction of new products, particularly the fantastically
popular cranberry juice cocktail, the industry has recouped the losses of
these dark years and has gone on to produce a record farm value of nearly 190
million dollars in 1986.

The average price per barrel of cranberries has reflected the periods
of depression in farm value (fig. 2.10). The price per barrel during the
1960s and 1970s remained relatively stable at about $14 per barrel as the in-
dustry shifted from a predominantly fresh market to a processed market.
This price stability reflected the industry's attempts to regulate production
to meet consumer demand through a marketing quota. Those years often
saw 10 percent crop set-asides invoked in order to prevent excessive cranberry holdovers from occurring. In the last ten years, cranberry prices increased dramatically, reflecting the increased demand for processed cranberry products.

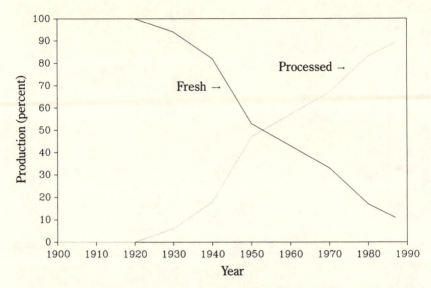

FIGURE 2.11. PERCENTAGE OF CRANBERRY PRODUCTION UTILIZED
AS FRESH AND PROCESSED FRUIT

Crop Utilization

Since 1940 the amount and percentage of fruit that was processed increased
steadily (fig. 2.11). During the war years, the processed fruit was used extensively by the military. The popularity of canned cranberry sauce continued to
increase in the postwar years, and in the 1960s the introduction of cranberry
juice cocktail added new impetus to processed sales. By 1970 about twice as
much fruit was entering processed channels as was being sold on the fresh
market. Today 90 percent of the cranberry crop is used to produce processed
cranberry products.

THREE

Botany

Taxonomy and Distribution

Genus

Within the family Ericaceae Aiton, some botanists place the American cranberry in the genus *Oxycoccus* (Porsild 1938; Scoggan 1979). Others place it in the genus *Vaccinium* together with blueberries, bilberries, and the lingonberry, relegating the cranberry to the status of a section or subgenus in the genus *Vaccinium* (Fernald 1950; Robbins 1931; Vander Kloet 1983). This lack of agreement among taxonomists has led to considerable confusion in nomenclature in the taxonomic literature on cranberry. In the following taxonomic treatment, the specific cranberry species will be listed under the *Vaccinium* genus and its equivalent binomial under the *Oxycoccus* genus will be given in parentheses.

Systematists recognize five distinct species in the subgenus *Oxycoccus,* which for the most part are easily separable by a series of well-marked morphological characters (Camp 1944). More recently, however, Vander Kloet (1983) found considerable overlap among morphological characters in *O. microcarpus, O. quadripetalus,* and *O. ovalifolius.* He placed all three of these species in *Vaccinium oxycoccus* L. (*Oxycoccus microcarpus* Turcz.) and concluded that based on the difference in size and the lack of crossability between the two groups, *Vaccinium* and *Oxycoccus* consist of two rather heterogeneous groups. One group comprises *Vaccinium macrocarpon* Ait. (*Oxycoccus macrocarpus* [Ait.] Pers.) and the other *Vaccinium oxycoccus* L. (*Oxycoccus microcarpus* Turcz.). Although some of these cranberries are harvested from the wild, only the American cranberry, *V. macrocarpon,* has been developed into a commercial industry.

Species

Vaccinium macrocarpon Ait. (*Oxycoccus macrocarpus* [Ait.] Pers.), the large or American cranberry, is the cultivated cranberry of commerce. It is native

43

to the cool, moist, boggy regions of the northern states from Maine to Minnesota and of some Canadian provinces, including Nova Scotia (Chandler and Hyland 1941; I. V. Hall and Nickerson 1986). It extends southward to West Virginia and Tennessee (Ogle 1983), where it can be found around the margins of lakes, in bogs, and along stream banks at elevations below 820 meters. It grows prolifically along the seacoast, particularly in poorly drained areas behind sand dunes. On the Pacific Coast, introduced plantings exist at the mouth of the Columbia River and behind the coastal dunes. Over 90 percent of the commercial cranberry acreage consists of selections of this species from the wild. Although indigenous to the North American continent, it was introduced in Europe prior to 1869.

The American cranberry differs from its close cousin *Vaccinium oxycoccus* (*Oxycoccus microcarpus* Turcz.), the small or European cranberry, by having larger leaves, flowers, and berries. *Vaccinium oxycoccus* has determinate solitary flowers located in the axils of bracts in the apical region of uprights. It may be more cold tolerant than the American cranberry since it has achieved a wide distribution in the alpine northern latitudes and subarctic regions of North America, Asia, and Europe. Its circumpolar distribution, however, may not be due so much to greater hardiness as to the fact that it grows close to the moss carpet of these regions, from which it gains protection from the snow cover. In North America it grows in sphagnum bogs from Labrador to Alaska and from Michigan to British Columbia. Although this berry is gathered from the wild, it is not cultivated in North America. Some of its common local names include mossberry, speckled cranberry, spiceberry, and buckberry.

A native wild cranberry found in wet mossy bogs in Europe, Asia, Greenland, and northern parts of North America is *Oxycoccus quadripetalus* Gilib. Although it is not as cold-hardy as *O. microcarpus,* this species covers the same ecological limits as the large and small cranberry. It combines characteristics of both species and is believed to be a hybrid of the two species (Camp 1944). It has small leaves, slender stems, and fruit that is intermediate in size, pink, and subacid. In the Pacific Northwest, it is found in peat bogs along the coast and in open meadows of the Cascade Mountains. It is not grown commercially.

Another wild cranberry indigenous to western North America and eastern Asia is *O. ovalifolius* Por., a vigorous plant with large leaves, black stems, and large fruit with bloom. The most vigorous of all the wild cranberry plants is *O. gigas* Hagerup. This shade- and drought-tolerant plant is found in isolated areas of Europe, Asia, and North America. The plant is sexually sterile, and appears to have originated as an autoploid of the tetraploid species. Although a small number of large berries may form, the seeds are incapable of germination.

Vaccinium vitis-idaea L., is known locally as partridge berry, foxberry, rock cranberry, mountain cranberry, and upland cranberry. *V. vitis-idaea* belongs to the genus *Vaccinium* section *Vitis-idaea,* in contrast to the cranberries already mentioned, which are members of the section or sub-genus *Oxycoccus.* It is a well-recognized cranberry species and is not considered an intermediate between cranberries and blueberries (Sleumer 1941; P. F. Stevens 1971). It is probably the most widely distributed cranberry species of all (Fernald 1902). The plant grows wild from Massachusetts northeast to Labrador and northwest to British Columbia and Alaska. It is not cultivated but is gathered in large quantities in Alaska, Nova Scotia, Newfoundland, and Scandinavia. In Europe a large-leafed form is the preisselbeere of Germany, cowberry of England, and the lingonberry of Sweden. Its distinctive, spicy, aromatic flavor makes it very popular in the Scandinavian countries.

Morphology

Shoot

The American cranberry is a low-growing, slender, vinelike, woody perennial plant with thick, narrowly elliptical leaves, whitened beneath and with rolled margins (plate 3.1). It is a long-lived plant that has been known to remain commercially productive for decades. The small (2–3 mm broad and 5–8 mm long) leaves are petiolate, leathery, and pinnately net-veined. During the growing season, the top surface of the leaves is a dark glossy green, which turns to a dull reddish brown during the dormant season. Individual leaves normally remain on the plant for at least two seasons before they abscise and new leaves take their place.

The vines (also called runners or stolons) are juvenile structures that may reach a length in excess of six feet (2 m) and spread profusely over the bog floor to form a dense mat (Porsild 1938). The leaves located along the runners are spaced relatively far apart and appear as though they alternate along the stem, but in reality they spiral around the slender stem in a $5/13$ phyllotactic pattern: 13 ranks of leaves completed in 5 spirals around the stem, which was needed to complete a phyllotactic cycle. (Bain and Dermen 1944).

Short vertical branches (referred to as uprights) can originate from runners or from older uprights at the leaf axil (fig. 3.1). The number of uprights that form may be governed by the apical dominance of the growing shoot (I. V. Hall 1970). Hall observed that as long as the vine grew upright there was continued growth of the existing shoot, but when the shoot was bent over, lateral buds (the source of the uprights) began to develop along the vine at random intervals. It is from these short uprights of two to three inches (5–8 cm) that new growth and flowers develop. The upright is terminated by a mixed bud

PLATE 3.1. *VACCINIUM MACROCARPON*—THE AMERICAN CRAN-
BERRY (USDA Photo)

which contains the differentiated tissue that will produce new shoot growth in
the spring and the flowers that are borne on this new shoot growth (plate 3.2).
Because of the closer spacing of the leaves on the short upright, they appear
as though they are whorled along the stem, but in reality they probably have
the same phyllotaxy as those on the runners. Hicks et al. (1968) observed
that cranberry plants growing in pure stands had shorter uprights than plants

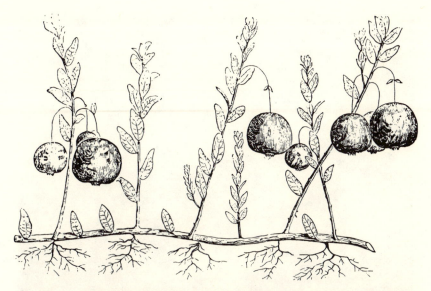

FIGURE 3.1. THE CRANBERRY PLANT SHOWING THE RELATIONSHIP
BETWEEN THE RUNNERS AND UPRIGHTS

growing in weedy areas. The shorter uprights had significantly more leaves per 10 cm of terminal growth and a smaller angle between the leaves and the stem. The lower light intensity presumably altered the auxin relation and thus affected vegetative growth (as it can in any plant). The terminal meristem of the upright always remains vegetative and continues the elongation of the upright for many years, adding as much as three inches (8 cm) of growth each year. Such decumbent uprights may be many feet long and are hard to separate in old bogs.

Root

The radicle of the germinating cranberry seed becomes a taproot that bears finely divided rootlets at the extremities. Adventitious roots develop readily from the leaf axil of the stolon when covered with soil or medium. There are no root hairs.

The fine roots of the American cranberry plant are surrounded by a loose web of fungal mycelium (Addoms and Mounce 1931). In addition, the roots have been observed to be infected with the mycelium of mycorrhizal fungi. There is considerable penetration of hyphae into the root cells where they pass from cell to cell in the cortex but do not generally enter the stele. It is believed that the mycorrhizal association is a symbiotic one in which the

PLATE 3.2. TERMINAL BUDS ON CRANBERRY UPRIGHTS THAT WILL
PRODUCE NEW SHOOTS AND FLOWERS IN THE SPRING
(Courtesy Massachusetts Cranberry Experiment Station)

fungus assists the cranberry roots in the absorption and utilization of organic
materials, especially the organic nitrogen that is contained in humus (Addoms
and Mounce 1931, 1932; Stribley and Read 1976, 1980). Addoms and Mounce
have found that the amount of mycelium in the cranberry plant is positively
correlated with the vigor of the plant and the amount of vegetative growth. It
would thus appear that the mycorrhizal association may be an important part

of the nitrogen nutrition of the cranberry plant in the low-nitrogen habitats in which they thrive.

Addoms and Mounce (1932) have discovered the mycelium not only in the roots of the American cranberry plant but also in the parenchyma tissue of the stem and in the fruit and seeds. According to Rayner and Levisohn (1940), the European cranberry (*Vaccinium oxycoccus*) exists in a mycorrhizal association with the endophytic fungus *Phoma radicis* found throughout the plant. Dana and his coworkers have disputed this because they have never been able to find mycorrhiza elsewhere than in the roots (M. N. Dana, letter to author, 1988). Bain (1937) described the colonies and mycelium that he isolated from *Vaccinium macrocarpon* as specifically distinct from those isolated by him from other *Vaccinium* species and also distinct from those of *Phoma radicis*.

Whether infection could be passed from generation to generation is doubtful. It is highly probable, however, that infection occurs from the soil, where the fungus is abundantly present.

Inflorescence

The cranberry flower originates from a bud located in the axil of the bracts borne at the base of the embryonic shoot. From one to ten axillary buds may initiate floral primordia on any upright, but the number is usually three to five (fig. 3.2a,b). As the new shoot emerges the floral axes elongate from axils below the new leaves and vegetative extension. In young plants, flowers are occasionally borne at the base of a runner, as is common in the McFarlin cultivar (Crowley 1954). Warrington and Eaton (1968) reported on a novel inflorescence in the Beaver cultivar, which consisted of a terminal raceme originating from the actively growing runners of the current season. The flowers developed on long pedicels originating from the axil of the leaves on the runners.

The cranberry flower develops in a characteristic hooked pattern, wherein just before opening, the pedicel (stem), calyx, and corolla (petals) of the flower resemble the neck, head, and bill of a crane. The flower consists of an inferior ovary, a calyx of four sepals, and a corolla of four petals that are pinkish white in color and deeply cleft (Cross 1953a). Eight stamens surround the pistil in a whorl and shed tetrad pollen grains from a terminal pore in the anther (fig. 3.3). Each flower is borne on its own stalk (pedicel) that develops from the axil of the leaf on the upright, making it a true branch of the upright. Located two-thirds of the way out on the flower stalk are two dwarfed leaves called bracteoles. Bergman (1950) was of the opinion that the relative size of

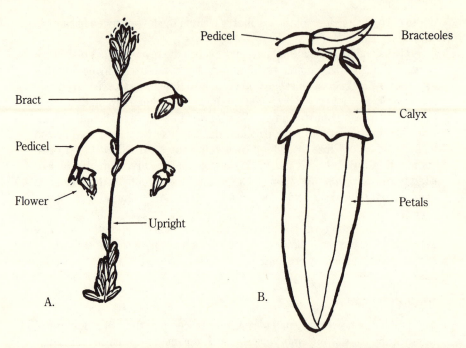

FIGURE 3.2. THE CRANBERRY FLOWER. *A,* The Relationship of the Flower to the Cranberry Upright; *B,* Closed Flower; *C,* Cross Section of Flower Exposing the Locule.

the bracteoles was an indication of the degree of oxygen deficiency injury to the flower buds: the larger the bracteoles, the greater the injury.

In the formation of the flowering shoot, a curve in the stalk develops where the flower and pedicel are joined. This curve forces the flower to nod; this appearance is characteristic of all healthy cranberry flowers (plate 3.3). Vines afflicted with false blossom disease will produce flowers that do not have this characteristic nod but are thrust upward at a sharp angle.

The ovary and calyx fuse to form a true berry that varies in shape and color. The berry consists of a relatively thin mesocarp and four rather large chambers (locules) containing a varied number of seeds (0–50). A waxy cuticle, varying in thickness from 8.7 to 13.7 microns, covers the epidermis and contributes to the ability of the cranberry to resist moisture loss after harvest. N. E. Stevens (1932), however, found no relationship between the

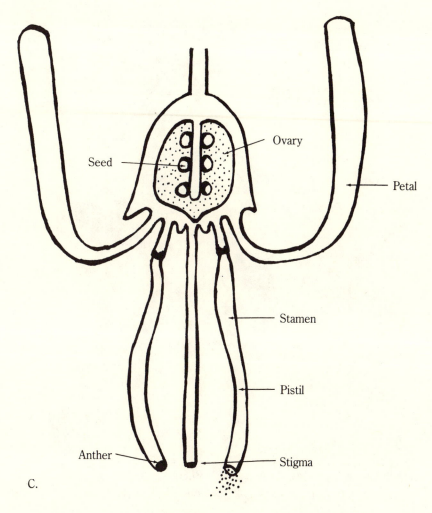

FIGURE 3.2. (*continued*)

thickness of the cranberry cuticle and fruit size, keeping quality of the fruit, or weather condition. Cuticle thickness did differ among cultivars; Early Black berries had a thin cuticle, whereas berries of the Howes cultivar had a thick cuticle. The berry may be bell, spindle, round, bugle, or olive shaped (fig. 3.3). The color can range from whitish pink to a deep purplish red.

PLATE 3.3. A TYPICAL CRANBERRY FLOWER (Courtesy Massachusetts Cranberry Experiment Station)

Anatomy and Cytology

Stomatal Apparatus

The stomatal apparatus of the cultivated cranberry was investigated by Sawyer (1931). He observed that all stomata in the cranberry leaf are located on the underside of the leaf. He measured an average of 632 stomata per sq. mm of leaf area—an extraordinarily high number for any plant. The guard cells regulating the stomatal openings appeared to function in a very erratic

FIGURE 3.3. THE DIFFERENT SHAPES OF THE CRANBERRY FRUIT.
Left to Right: Bell, Spindle, Round, Bugle, Olive.

manner. As a result, the stomatal apparatus in cranberry leaves is poorly adjusted to changing conditions of light, temperature, and moisture and responds only slowly or not at all to changing environmental conditions. Stomata also apparently exist as artifacts in the endocarp of the cranberry fruit, where they remain continuously open and appear to serve no useful purpose (Bergman 1920).

Chromosome Numbers

The basic genome for the cranberry is 12 chromosomes. The American cranberry, European cranberry, and lingonberry have been reported to be diploid ($2n=24$), although tetraploid and hexaploid species are known to exist (Ahokas 1971; Darrow et al. 1944; Vander Kloet 1983). Camp (1944) has suggested that the tetraploid ($2n=48$), *Oxycoccus* (=*Vaccinium*) *quadripetalus* Gilib., which Darrow and his associates found along the East Coast interspersed with *V. macrocarpon* and *V. oxycoccus* forms is an allotetraploid resulting from the hybridization of these two diploid species. The tetraploid form appears to occupy a distinct ecological niche located between *V. macrocarpon* to the south and *V. oxycoccus* to the north. The hexaploid cranberry species, *V. hagerupii* ($2n=64$), may have originated as an alloploid resulting from the hybridization between *Oxycoccus quadripetalus* ($2n=48$) and Vaccinium oxycoccus (*O. microcarpus*) ($2n=24$) or as an autoploid of the tetraploid population resulting from the fusion of a normally reduced gamete with a nonreduced gamete (Ahokas 1971).

By treating vegetative buds of cranberry cultivars with colchicine, Dermen (1947) was able to obtain five distinct polyploid types which he propagated. They contrasted markedly from the diploid plants, which had small stomates, small leaves, and slender stems. The five types had the following characteristics:

First polyploid type—large stomates, small leaves, and slender stems
Second polyploid type—small stomates, large leaves, and thick stems
Third polyploid type—large stomates, large leaves, and thick stems
Fourth polyploid type—small stomates, large leaves, and slender stems
Fifth polyploid type—small stomates, small leaves, and thick stems.

Each type was characterized by a cytohistologically distinct apical meristem.

Dermen traced the ontogeny of the various parts of the cranberry plant from three histogenic layers of the apical dome (apical meristem) of the bud. The epidermis of the stem, leaf, anthers, ovary, and ovule was derived from the first histogenic layer (L-I), and the second and third layers (L-II and L-III) together contributed to the formation of mesophyll and conductive tissue. Other aspects of colchicine-induced polyploidy in cranberry have been presented in a series of papers by USDA researchers Dermen and Bain (Bain and Dermen 1944; Dermen 1945; Dermen and Bain 1944).

FOUR

Plant Improvement

Origins

Native Selections

Over 80 percent of the total commercial cranberry acreage in North America is comprised of only four cultivars: Early Black, Howes, McFarlin, and Searles (often called the "Big Four"). All four represent selections from the wild by astute growers based on each fruit's superior characteristics.

The first vines of Early Black were obtained from a swamp in Harwich, Massachusetts, around 1835 (C. J. Hall 1954). Captain Cyrus Cahoon named the selection and made the first commercial Early Black planting in 1857 (C. J. Hall 1939a). The original bog is still in production but now entirely replanted in the Howes cultivar.

The Howes cultivar was selected from a wild planting in Bassett Swamp in East Dennis, Massachusetts, in 1843 by Elias Howes. Elias and his son James sold cuttings from their bog. Today the Howes cultivar is the standard late cultivar in the eastern growing regions (Chandler and Demoranville 1958).

McFarlin vines were discovered by Thomas H. McFarlin growing wild in New Meadows, a large wild cranberry bog in South Carver, Massachusetts, in 1874 (C. J. Hall 1943). This cultivar was first produced commercially in Massachusetts by Thomas's brother Charles. It was later planted in Coos County, Oregon, by Charles McFarlin, who became the first commercial cranberry grower on the Pacific Coast. This high-quality berry makes up more than 80 percent of the cranberry acreage in Washington and Oregon. Its consistent production, high-quality fruit, and vines that are not attractive to the leaf-hopper vector of the false blossom disease made it a favorite of Wisconsin growers (Barber 1938).

Searles is the only major cranberry cultivar that did not have its origin in Massachusetts. Andrew Searles of Wisconsin Rapids was the first commercial grower of this selection, which was taken from a marsh in Walker, Wisconsin, in 1893 (N. E. Stevens 1944). Originally called Searles Jumbo, through usage it has become known as the Searles cultivar. Although the berry was susceptible to bruising and the plant was not resistant to false blossom disease, it rapidly became the favored cultivar grown in Wisconsin because of its unusual productivity.

On the West Coast, Joseph Stankiewicz, a pioneer cranberry grower of Bandon, Oregon, selected what he thought were superior native vines from a marsh at New Lake (C. J. Hall 1947). The vines had actually resulted from natural hybridization of the native plants with an eastern cultivar that had been imported and allowed to grow wild in abandoned marshes. In all probability this eastern cultivar was McFarlin because that was the predominant eastern cultivar planted on the West Coast (Kranick 1937). The new selection was propagated and sold commercially as the Stankavich cultivar by Joseph and his sons.

Throughout the development of the cranberry industry, growers were continually on the lookout for vines that yielded superior fruit. In Wisconsin, New Jersey, and Nova Scotia, these wild selections were referred to as natives. One such superior selection from the wild was Beaver, selected by E. L. Eaton of the Canada Department of Agriculture and introduced for commercial production in Nova Scotia in 1956 (Brooks and Olmo 1956). Although susceptible to false blossom disease, Beaver matures about 7 to 10 days before Early Black. In New Jersey the natives were called Jerseys or Late Jerseys. These wild selections were often quite mixed and lacked uniformity of fruit characteristics. They were gradually replaced by the Big Four and, more recently, by new cultivars produced through scientific hybridization programs.

New Cultivar Production

In 1929 the USDA, in cooperation with the New Jersey and Massachusetts Agricultural Experiment stations, initiated a cranberry hybridization program with the main objective of developing new cultivars that would be resistant to the false blossom disease, a particularly debilitating disease at the time. Pioneers in the early phase of this hybridization program were C. S. Beckwith of the New Jersey Agricultural Experiment Station and H. F. Bain and H. F. Bergman of the USDA (Chandler 1944; Chandler et al. 1947). F. B. Chandler later carried out evaluations of the original selections made in the program. Other objectives of the breeding program included increased productivity, improved fruit quality, and greater storability. The fruit quality parameters that were selected for included color, glossiness, shape, size, postharvest ripening ability, season, and fruit rot tolerance. Despite its ambitious objectives, the breeding program comprised only one generation of improvement and made no attempt to build upon gains made by second-generation backcrosses.

The two cultivars that were least preferred by the blunt-nosed leafhopper were Early Black and McFarlin. In New Jersey these were used in producing crosses which led to 112 seedlings that were tested for resistance to the false blossom disease. The majority of crosses made in the program were made in Wisconsin and Massachusetts. Besides the Big Four cultivars, the parents used in these reciprocal crosses included Aviator, Bennett, Berry Berry, Centennial, Holliston (Mammoth), Paradise Meadow, Potter, Prolific, Shaw's Success (perhaps the least attractive to the blunt-nosed leafhopper), Stanley, Vose's Pride, and Whittlesey. By 1940 about 1,800 seedlings had fruited and 40 selections were made for a second test, including 6 selections from the Early Black x McFarlin cross made in New Jersey. During the next five years over 5,000 more seedlings were fruited and an additional 112 selections were chosen for further testing (I. E. Demoranville and Chandler 1957). The seedlings and selections were planted in Wisconsin, Massachusetts, and New Jersey nurseries in order to evaluate them under the growing conditions of the major cranberry-growing areas.

Since false blossom disease was particularly rampant in New Jersey, that state became the primary location for evaluating seedling resistance to the disease (R. B. Wilcox and Delap 1946). Included in the test for false blossom disease resistance was a "cafeteria" test of vines for leafhopper resistance (R. B. Wilcox and Beckwith 1933). In this test, caged blunt-nosed leafhoppers had the choice of feeding on the test seedling or two named cultivars used as a standard. The number of insects feeding on the test seedling in a day was compared to the number feeding on the standard cultivars. The standards included Shaw's Success, the least favored by the leafhopper, Early Black and McFarlin, which were moderately attractive to the insect, and Howes, which appeared to be more attractive to the blunt-nosed leafhopper.

From the original 40 selections, 18 selections were made from the second fruiting for further evaluation at the test sites (Chandler et al. 1947). Since the selections had already undergone rigorous testing for disease susceptibility and fruit quality, the evaluations for the second test were made on vine vigor, yield, berry size, seed count, berry density, berry shape, and the estimated picking date.

Only 3 of the original 40 selections were recommended for commercial trial in 1950 (USDA 1950; Brooks and Olmo 1950). By this time the original objective of false blossom resistance had become less important because of success in controlling the blunt-nosed leafhopper with modern insecticides, and increasing fruit size had become the dominant objective. The selections were named after prominent cranberry researchers who were deceased. Beckwith (McFarlin x Early Black) and Stevens (McFarlin x Potter) were berries that were much larger than either Early Black or Howes, and Wilcox (Howes x Searles) fruit was as large as Howes fruit. Both the Beckwith and

Wilcox cultivars were as resistant to false blossom disease as Early Black; Stevens proved to be more resistant than Howes to false blossom disease.

After the Beckwith, Stevens, and Wilcox cultivars were named, 32 additional seedlings out of the 152 originally selected were chosen for further observation. One reason for the additional testing was the fact that the newly named cultivars were not particularly productive in Massachusetts (Chandler and Demoranville 1961b). As the result of this additional evaluation, three more selections were named and released primarily for Massachusetts, although they have also shown promise in other parts of North America (USDA 1961). The three new cultivars—Bergman (Early Black x Searles), Franklin (Early Black x Howes), and Pilgrim (Prolific x McFarlin)—were found to be resistant to the blunt-nosed leafhopper and were recommended for locations where false blossom disease was particularly serious. The Bergman and Franklin cultivars were named in honor of H. F. Bergman and H. J. Franklin, whose careers had been devoted to the improvement of the cranberry industry (Chandler and Demoranville 1961c).

Another new introduction was the Crowley cultivar (McFarlin x Prolific), released by Washington State University in 1970 (Doughty and Garren 1970). The Crowley cultivar was named in honor of D. J. Crowley, renowned West Coast cranberry researcher and superintendent of the Coastal Washington Research and Extension Unit until his retirement in 1954. It was Crowley who originated the Washington breeding program in the early 1940s, and the Crowley cultivar, a McFarlin x Prolific cross, was one of the original 13 seedlings selected from that breeding program. This cultivar is particularly suited to the mild climate of the Pacific Northwest and produces a large, deep red berry that has a high pigment content and low astringency, making it especially suitable for processing.

Breeding Objectives and Methods

Objectives

Disease resistance has always been an important objective of cranberry-breeding programs. Even though false blossom disease can be controlled by eradicating the leafhopper vector with insecticides and fruit rots can be substantially eliminated by fungicide treatments, disease resistance in cranberry plants remains a principal objective of breeding programs. The current efforts to reduce the use of pesticides in production agriculture can be greatly augmented by the introduction of cranberry cultivars that show resistance to disease and insect injury. Resistant cultivars would be an important part of any biological or integrated pest control program.

Breeding for resistance to the blunt-nosed leafhopper, vector of the false blossom disease, warrants special mention because the disease had become so debilitating after the turn of the century that it threatened the very existence of the industry. The disease apparently originated in Wisconsin and was spread to the East and West coast growing regions by infected vine cuttings shipped there from Wisconsin (N. E. Stevens and Sawyer 1926). Whereas the disease had been found on wild vines remote from cultivated bogs in Wisconsin, it was not found on wild vines in the other major cranberry-growing regions. In 1929 Dobroscky demonstrated that false blossom was caused by a mycoplasma transmitted by the blunt-nosed leafhopper, *Ophiola striatula* Fall. (previously *Euscelis striatulus*) (Dobroscky 1929, 1931).

It was soon discovered that not all cranberry cultivars were equally affected by the disease (N. E. Stevens 1931). Stevens classified the common cultivars according to their susceptibility to the disease. Cultivars that were very susceptible to false blossom included Berlin, Centennial, Howes, Metallic Bell, Palmeter, Prolific, Searles, and Wales Henry. Bennett and Pride were considered to have moderate resistance, but not sufficient to warrant planting. Early Black was fairly resistant and McFarlin was considered to be very resistant.

Resistance to false blossom disease appeared to be related to insect preference for a particular cultivar rather than to a cultivar's actual immunity to the disease (Goldsworthy 1933; R. B. Wilcox 1951; R. B. Wilcox and Beckwith 1933). When Wilcox and Beckwith allowed the leafhoppers freedom of choice in feeding, they observed that the cultivars that were most susceptible to the disease were favored by the insects. Goldsworthy, however, showed that even McFarlin would come down with the disease if the cultivar was subjected to enforced feeding by the leafhopper. The actual mechanism for this feeding preference remains unknown (W. E. Tomlinson 1945), although Wilcox (1951) concluded from his extensive feeding trials that the ability of the insects to survive and reproduce was compromised when they were required to feed on less palatable cultivars. Wilcox and Beckwith (1933) arranged a number of cultivars in the following descending order of field susceptibility: Howes, Centennial, Champion, Early Black, McFarlin, Shaws Success. The existence of this relative susceptibility among cranberry cultivars suggested that resistance may be genetically mediated and could be accentuated by controlled hybridization. This was the approach taken when the original crosses in the USDA breeding program in 1929 were made (Bain 1940a).

Other objectives in developing new cranberry hybrids have been to increase fruit yield and quality (Sapers et al. 1983). Although productivity is associated with large fruit size, as exemplified by the large-fruited Pilgrim and Stevens cultivars, pigment production is not always the greatest in these large-fruited cultivars because the pigment is located primarily in the skin of the berry; therefore, there is less pigment per gram of fruit in large berries than in small berries (Vorsa and Welker 1985). Almost all cranberries are now mechanically harvested, so berries with firm flesh that resists bruising are highly desirable. Mechanical harvesting would be facilitated if plants could be made to bear their fruit at a uniform height above the bog. Such height uniformity would result in greater uniformity of ripening, which is another important reason for developing new cranberry hybrids. Early ripening is also much sought after in new cultivars, since this would reduce the chance of crop loss to frosts whose frequency and severity increase as the harvest season progresses.

Another important area for hybrid improvement is in bringing about changes in the fruit itself. Increased anthocyanin and vitamin C content are important objectives in the current cranberry-breeding program being conducted in New Jersey. Food scientists have developed color measurement techniques that are used by plant breeders today in making their selections for cranberry anthrocyanin (Francis 1970). (See pigment section on fruit composition in Chapter 6.) Fruit with a higher sugar and lower acid content has been another objective of hybridization research of the past few decades. Hopefully such research will result in new types of fruit that could be eaten raw and whole and out of hand. Chandler and Demoranville (1961b) reported that crosses of Black Veil, Centennial, Centerville, and Selections 8 and 28 (a total of 82 crosses) were made in 1954 for the purpose of developing new cultivars lower in acid and higher in sugar. Centennial, Centerville, and Stanley were chosen for their high sugar content and Black Veil for its low acidity. Selections 8 and 28 from the USDA breeding program and Centerville of the old cultivars had pleasing flavor. Success in attaining this objective would mean a significant breakthrough for cranberry utilization. Not only would it mean a considerable reduction in the use of sugar in processing, but an entire new market for cranberries would be possible for fresh as well as processed use.

Use of Tetraploids

In plant breeding it is sometimes helpful to artificially induce tetraploidy in a diploid plant such as *Vaccinium macrocarpon*. In the process of doubling the chromosome number, there is often a doubling in intensity of the original characteristics of the plant. This is most often expressed as an increase in the size or thickness of stems, leaves, flowers, and fruits. Reduced male and female fertility is also generally observed. One method of artificially inducing tetraploidy in the cranberry is to treat the actively growing tip with the drug colchicine (Dermen and Bain 1941, 1944; Dermen 1945). The chemical appears to interfere with normal cell division in such a way that when growth is resumed, the cells have double their former number of chromosomes, and all growth from this point will have the new ploidy level.

Although the greatest benefit of induced tetraploidy in cranberry to date has been in morphological studies, particularly in studying the phyllotaxy of the plant, scientists have been successful in producing tetraploid forms of Centennial, Early Black, Howes, McFarlin, Searles, and Vose's Pride (Bain 1943). A potential application for this technique would be to hybridize two species that were formally incompatible because of differing chromosome numbers. Thus, the tetraploid forms of the successfully treated cranberry cultivars could be crossed with the hardier northern tetraploid species, *V. quadripetalus* (Darrow 1951). So far the tetraploid hybrids that have been produced from such crosses have been found to be vigorous but less hardy and slower growing than the diploids. They set more flowers, which resulted in smaller fruit.

Interspecific Hybridization

There has been a limited effort to cross two different species of cranberries outside of the colchicine effort described above. The attempt has been made mainly by Europeans trying to combine the large fruit size of the less aromatic American cranberry with the spicy aroma of the relatively small-fruited cowberry (*V. vitis-idaea*). Some researchers were successful in crossing the two species because they were both diploid but were completely unsuccessful in getting the hybrids to bear fruit, which suggests that a certain level of incompatibility exists even though the two species have the same chromosome number (Christ 1977). When Christ attempted to cross the American cranberry with *Vaccinium quadripetalus* (*Oxycoccus quadripetalus*), a tetraploid found in Europe, he was unsuccessful in obtaining viable seeds because of sterility barriers that exist between the two species due to differing chromosome number.

Cultivar Descriptions

The Major Cultivars

In the 150 years since the commercial cultivation of the cranberry began, there have been 132 selections from the wild propagated in addition to the 7 improved cultivars obtained from controlled hybridization. Chandler and Demoranville (1958) in their bulletin "Cranberry Varieties of North America" described 56 of these selections in detail and listed 70 more, together with their common synonyms. More recently Dana (1983) compiled the most complete list of selections and cultivars ever attempted. His compilation together with the descriptions from the Chandler and Demoranville bulletin were used as the basis for table 4.1, which compares the major cultivars in use today, and for cultivar descriptions that follow.

Known Cultivars

The following list of cranberry cultivars comprises as complete a record as is known of the selections that were at one time or another grown commercially in North America. Where known, the individual making the selection and the location of the first planting are given. Unfortunately, for many of the selections there is little known other than the name given to it.

Anthony. Cuttings obtained from C. A. Cahoon of Harwich, Massachusetts, were included in the Wisconsin cultivar collection in 1894.

Applegate. No description of this cultivar is available.

Atwood. Discovered in 1889, this cultivar was propagated by Stephen Atwood of South Carver, Massachusetts. It produces a blackish red berry that is round and has a flattened calyx end. (See Fig. 3.3 for illustration of berry shapes.) The coarse vines with large, medium green leaves produce excellent early crops that keep well in storage.

Aviator. South Carver, Massachusetts, was also the site of the discovery of this wild selection made by L. S. Rogers. The fruit is light in color and medium in size, with cup counts ranging between 76 and 90 berries per cup. The spindle-shaped fruit has a protruding calyx end and is produced late in the season. It colors well in storage and has fair-to-good keeping quality. The medium coarse vines with short-to-medium uprights are moderately productive.

Bass River. This selection was made by James Smalley of South Yarmouth, Massachusetts. The berries are small, oblong to oval in shape with a squarish calyx end. They are deep red in color with a heavy waxy bloom and have good keeping quality. The coarse vines with light green, large leaves and tall uprights produce a fair crop late in the season.

Beach Berry. No description of this cultivar is available.

Beaver. This cultivar, introduced by the Canada Department of Agriculture in 1956, was selected by E. L. Eaton from seedlings of a native cranberry plant in Nova Scotia. Under the conditions of this Canadian province, the fruit consistently matures 7 to 10 days earlier than Early Black, with larger and more attractive fruit than that cultivar. The berries keep well in cold storage. The vines are susceptible to false blossom disease, but they are capable of producing fair crops.

Beckwith. This cross of McFarlin x Early Black made by H. F. Bain and H. F. Bergman of the USDA was named in 1951. The large, medium red fruit are borne high on vigorous uprights. The fruit size averages between 55 and 60

TABLE 4.1. DESCRIPTION OF THE MAJOR CRANBERRY CULTIVARS AND THE NEW HYBRID CULTIVARS

CULTIVAR	ORIGIN	HARVEST SEASON	RESISTANCE	FRUIT APPEARANCE	REMARKS
Beaver	Wild Canada 1956	Early	Susceptible to false blossom	Large bright red	Matures early; keeps well
Beckwith	McFarlin × Early Black 1950	Late	Susceptible to false blossom	Large; medium red	Good flavor
Ben Lear	Wild Wis. 1901	Early	Susceptible to storage rot	Large to medium; deep red	Good cropper
Bergman	Early Black × Searles 1961	Midseason	Resistant to false blossom	Large to medium; red	Good for processing; adapted to Mass.
Crowley	McFarlin × Prolific Wash. 1970	Midseason	Resistant to softening	Large; deep red	Good for processing; adapted to Pacific Northwest
Early Black	Wild Mass. 1857	Early	Resistant to false blossom	Medium to small; dark; firm	Broadly adapted; Good production
Franklin	Early black × Howes 1961	Early	Resistant to false blossom	Large to medium; red to dark red	Adapted to Mass.

Howes	Wild Mass. 1843	Late	Susceptible to tip worm	Medium; Good red color	Keeps well
McFarlin	Wild Mass. 1874	Late	Resistant to false blossom	Large to medium; deep red; firm	Good quality
Pilgrim	Prolific × McFarlin 1961	Late	Resistant to false blossom	Very large; dark	Adapted to Mass.
Searles	Wild Wis. 1893	Midseason	Susceptible to storage rot and false blossom	Medium; deep red	Main cultivar in Wis.
Stankavich	Wild Oreg. 1917	Late	Resistant to false blossom	Large; dark red	Low acid high sugar
Stevens	McFarlin × Potter 1950	Midseason	Resistant to softening	Very large; deep red	Adapted to Wis. and N.J.
Wilcox	Howes × Searles 1950	Early	Resistant to leafhopper	Large to medium; deep red	Adapted to N.J.; high productivity

SOURCES: Chandler and Demoranville 1958; Dana 1983.

berries per cup, and yields are generally greater than those obtained from Early Black and Howes. The berries resemble McFarlin in color (deep red) and shape (round to oblong) and ripen late, about the same time as Howes. The fruit is firm and keeps well in storage, and has excellent flavor. It has been judged unsatisfactory for Wisconsin because of poor berry appearance, but its resistance to fruit rot disease may make it a promising cultivar for New Jersey, although it is susceptible to false blossom disease (Chandler et al. 1950).

Bell and Bugle. A mixture of two native types, this was once widely cultivated in Wisconsin. The fruit was similar to that of the Bell and Cherry mixture but slightly more elongated in appearance and larger in size. The fruit was of uniform, bright red color and shipped well. Its susceptibility to false blossom disease resulted in its loss in popularity.

Bell and Cherry. These natives of Wisconsin were once the standard cranberry in Wisconsin. They were indigenous to the marshes of Central Wisconsin. The vines, although dense, are productive and do not mat to the extent that McFarlin does. The vines are quite susceptible to false blossom disease.

Bell of the Cape. This name has been used as a synonym for the Centerville cultivar, and also as a trade name.

Belvedere. This was a selection made by O. G. Malde at Belvedere, Michigan, in 1904. It produces a good yield of large, firm, round, highly colored fruit that have good flavor and keep well in cold storage.

Benjamin. No description of this cultivar is available.

Ben Lear. This cultivar was selected by D. R. Burr at Berlin, Wisconsin, before 1901. It produces a deep red berry that is pyriform shaped with a pointed stem end and is of large-to-medium size (70–90 cup count). The medium-textured vines with large, dark green leaves produce medium tall uprights that generate good crops of berries that do not store particularly well. It is currently being planted in New Jersey and British Columbia.

Bennett Jumbo. This selection was made by A. C. Bennett from a small patch of cranberries found near Grand Rapids, Wisconsin, about 1890. The fruit consist of medium (76 cup count), deep red berries that are oblong in shape with their stem end furrowed. The berries color and keep well in cold storage. The vines are vigorous and coarse, producing large, dark green leaves and tall uprights that bloom rather late in the season (which means that most of the spring frosts are escaped). The berries ripen late in the season, however, and are very susceptible to end rot fungi, which probably contributes to the poor to fair crops that are attained.

Bergman. This cross of Early Black x Searles was made in 1930 by H. F. Bain of the USDA at Whitesbog, New Jersey, and selected by F. B. Chandler and I. E. Demoranville at East Wareham, Massachusetts. The cultivar was introduced in 1961. It produces large-to-medium fruit ranging in cup count from 65 to 80 berries, which are pear-shaped and ripen at midseason. The cultivar is more productive and less susceptible to fruit rot than either Early Black or Howes. The red berry has good keeping quality and can be stored for long periods with little shrinkage. The plant produces uprights of medium length and few runners. It appears to be quite resistant to feeding by the blunt-nosed leafhopper, the vector for false blossom disease.

Berlin. This cultivar was selected at Berlin, Wisconsin. It produces fruit at midseason that is medium red in color with heavy waxy bloom. The berries are round to oblong in shape with a pointed stem end. They are of medium size, averaging 88 berries per cup. They color well in storage and their keeping quality in storage is very good. The moderately vigorous vines, however, are capable of only fair production.

Berry Berry. This selection was made in 1883 by Albert Berry on the island of Martha's Vineyard, Massachusetts. The fruit ripens about midseason into large (55–65 cup count), dark red berries with a medium waxy bloom. The nearly round berries have a calyx end that is furrowed, but they do not keep very well in storage. The vines are moderately vigorous and produce good crops on medium tall uprights.

Black Diamond. This cultivar is a synonym for the Bugle cultivar.

Black Veil. This early-ripening cultivar was selected in 1890 by Joseph McFarlin at South Carver, Massachusetts. It produces a small round berry (103–109 berries per cup) with a flat calyx end. The glossy berry is blackish red in color. Black Veil is productive and the berries color well in storage, but they are only fair in keeping quality.

Bozarthtown Pointer. No description of this cultivar is available.

Braddock Bell. This cultivar was selected at Medford, New Jersey. Produced during midseason, the fruit colors and keeps well in storage and shipping. The pyriform-shaped berry ranges in size from medium to small (85–105 cup count) and is deep red in color. The vigorous vines produce tall uprights with large leaves.

Buckalew. No description of this cultivar is available.

Budds Blues. T. H. Budd of Pemberton, New Jersey, found this cultivar in 1880. The fruit ripens late in the season and is small, averaging between 100 and 135 berries per cup, but they keep very well in storage. The berries are blackish red in color and have a heavy waxy bloom on them. They are round to oval in shape and are distinctly wrinkled around the calyx end of the berry. The very coarse vines produce tall uprights with large leaves, but production is relatively poor.

Bugle. Also known as Black Diamond, this late cultivar was selected from the wild at Sandwich, Massachusetts, in 1875 by F. Dillingham. The dark red berry has a heavy bloom and is spindle-shaped with pointed ends. The fruit is of medium size with berries ranging from 73 to 95 berries per cup. Bugle has excellent keeping quality and is considered a fancy berry for fresh use. The medium-textured vines produce tall uprights but rather poor crops.

Bumpus. No description of this cultivar is available.

Cape Cod Beauty. J. T. McFarlin of South Carver, Massachusetts, propagated this selection from the wild and sent cuttings to Wisconsin in 1894 to be included in their varietal collection. The moderately productive vines produce small, uniform fruit that are oblong in shape. The berries have fair quality, but they do not keep well in storage.

Carver Bell. This selection also was propagated by J. T. McFarlin and included in the Wisconsin cultivar collection. The large, firm, olive-shaped berries have poor flavor and do not keep well in storage.

Carver Red. No description of this cultivar is available.

Centennial. Originally selected at Holliston, Massachusetts, by George Batchelder in 1876, this cultivar was extensively planted in New Jersey during the 1920s. Centennial is as productive as Early Black but has larger berries, ranging in cup count from 47 to 75, and ripens late in the season. The round berries with furrowed stem ends are thin fleshed and uniformly red and have extrafine table quality. The plant produces coarse vines with many runners, which made hand scooping difficult. This coupled with its susceptibility to fruit rot and false blossom disease led to a loss in popularity in New Jersey.

Centerville. This productive late-ripening cultivar was selected by P. A. Fuller at Centerville, Massachusetts, in 1882. The berries are large (46–60 cup count), medium red in color, oval shaped with pointed stem end, and possess extrafine flavor, but they do not color or keep well in storage. Like Centennial it produces many coarse runners that interfere with scooping.

Champion. Selected from the wild at Carver, Massachusetts, by E. W. Shaw, this late-ripening cultivar proved to be very productive. The berries are medium red in color with a moderate amount of bloom, round to oval in shape, and average 72 berries to the cup. The fruit has excellent flavor and quality but it is susceptible to fruit rot and does not ship well. The vines are fine textured and possess short uprights. They are susceptible to false blossom disease.

Cherry Bell. No description of this cultivar is available.

Cherry Red. No description of this cultivar is available.

Chipman. G. N. Nye made this selection from the wild at East Sandwich, Massachusetts, in 1860. It produces a very small berry (110–140 cup count) that is deep red with a heavy bloom. Spindle shaped with both ends pointed, the berry colors well in storage but does not keep particularly well. The moderately vigorous vines produce tall uprights but only a poor crop late in the season.

Columbia. No description of this cultivar is available.

Crocker. No description of this cultivar is available.

Cropper. This selection from the wild was discovered by Albert Jones at Tabernacle, New Jersey, in 1930. The berry is round to oval in shape, medium red in color and rather small in size (95–105 cup count). The moderately vigorous vines produce a good crop of berries at midseason that have fair keeping quality.

Crowley. This seedling was produced from a cross of McFarlin x Prolific made by D. J. Crowley in 1940. The cultivar was introduced by Washington State University in 1970. The berry is medium large, round-oblate in shape, flattened on both ends, and has some bloom. The fruit has a high pigment content and is low in astringency, factors that make it desirable for processing. The moderately vigorous vines produce short uprights that yield consistently large crops early in the season.

Cumberland. No description of this cultivar is available.

Dill Eagle. No description of this cultivar is available.

Ear Drop. This selection from the wild was propagated by N. S. Johnson at Berlin, Wisconsin, and planted in the Wisconsin cultivar collection in 1894. The fruit is uniform, medium in size, and bell shaped, but it does not keep well. The moderately vigorous vines are productive, however.

Early Black. Although Cyrus Cahoon of Harwich, Massachusetts, commercialized this cultivar in 1857, its discovery was made by N. Robbins. The blackish red fruit ripens very early in the season; only Black Veil is known to ripen earlier. The glossy berries have no bloom, are medium to small (90–130 cup count), and pyriform in shape with a pointed stem end and a calyx end that is flat with medium-sized, flaring lobes. The firm fruit colors fairly well and keeps exceptionally well in storage. The vines of Early Black are slender and have small leaves that are light green in the summer and reddish in the winter. The plant produces many more uprights than it does runners and is considered a good producer. It is moderately resistant to frost and is resistant to false blossom disease. Its earliness, dark red color, and ability to produce on many types of cranberry soil make Early Black the standard cultivar in the eastern United States.

Early Ohio. This selection was made by L. P. Haskins from a wild bog in Walton, Michigan, in 1904. It is an early berry with a mild and pleasant flavor. The deep red berry is nearly round and is of moderate size, ranging between 80 and 95 berries per cup. The glossy fruit may color in storage, but it is a poor keeper. The vigorous vines produce only a fair crop. The cultivar most resembles Prolific—another selection made by Haskins.

Early Red. The originator of this cultivar was H. Swift of Falmouth, Massachusetts. It is a large-to-medium berry (67–84 cup count) that ripens at midseason. The medium red berry is round to oval in shape with a flat calyx end. Although it colors well in storage, it does not store very well. The medium-textured vines produce short uprights that give good production.

Early Richard. This cultivar was discovered by A. Richard of Hammonton, New Jersey, in 1870. It produces an early ripening, very dark berry that is large to medium (67–84 cup count). It is a nearly round berry with a furrowed stem end. The fruit will color in storage, but it will not keep well. The vigorous vines produce tall productive uprights with large, dark green leaves.

Excelsior. No description of this cultivar is available.

Foxboro Howes. The original planting of this selection was made by L. Handy at Wilmington, Massachusetts, in 1932. The small fruit (100–110 cup count) ripens late in the season and has good storage characteristics. The medium red, glossy berry is oblong to oval in shape but has no other distinguishing characteristics. The moderately vigorous vines, however, produce very good crops.

Franklin. This plant, a cross of Early Black x Howes made in 1930 by H. F. Bain at Whitesbog, New Jersey, and selected by F. B. Chandler and I. E. Demoranville at East Wareham, Massachusetts, was named in honor of H. J. Franklin. It was introduced by the USDA in 1961. It produces a large-to-medium fruit (57–90 cup count) that ripens early. The round berries are red to dark red and have good-to-excellent keeping quality. Producing short runners and uprights of medium length, the vines are not very vigorous, but they are resistant to attack by the blunt-nosed leafhopper.

Garwood Bell. The first planting of this selection from the wild was made by I. Garwood at Medford, New Jersey, in 1875. The medium-sized fruit ripens late in the season and has good storage qualities. The glossy, dark red berry is spindle shaped and pointed at both ends. The fairly vigorous vines produce tall uprights that give good production.

Gebhardt Beauty. This cultivar was discovered in 1893 and the original planting was made by H. H. Gebhardt at Black River Falls, Wisconsin. Ripening early in the season, the medium-sized fruit colors and keeps well in storage. The glossy, deep red berry is nearly round and has a flat calyx end. The moderately vigorous vines produce short uprights that give good production.

Gifford. No description of this cultivar is available.

Godfrey. No description of this cultivar is available.

Hall. No description of this cultivar is available.

Hardy Howes. No description of this cultivar is available.

Harlow. No description of this cultivar is available.

Harwich. No description of this cultivar is available.

Hawthorne. No description of this cultivar is available.

Henry Griffith. No description of this cultivar is available.

Hewitt Berry. Cuttings of this selection were supplied to the Wisconsin cultivar collection in 1894 by J. T. McFarlin of South Carver, Massachusetts. The plant produces small, round, and firm berries.

Hockanum. No description of this cultivar is available.

Holliston. After selecting this from the wild in 1885, George Batchelder made the first planting at Holliston, Massachusetts. The large fruit (54–75 cup count) ripens late and does not keep well in storage. The deep red berries are oblong in shape with a furrowed calyx end and are covered with a waxy bloom. The coarse vines produce tall uprights capable of giving good production.

Horseneck. No description of this cultivar is available.

Howard Bell. This is another selection made from native plantings in New Jersey. The selection was made by M. Howard of Howardville, New Jersey, in 1875. The large-sized fruit ripens late in the season and is very desirable for long shipping distances. The medium red berry is oval to spindle shaped with a pointed calyx end; it is covered with a light waxy bloom. The fine-textured vines produce tall uprights with small leaves that are quite productive.

Howes. Elias Howes discovered this cultivar in 1843 and made the first planting at East Dennis, Massachusetts. The medium-to-small fruit (80–140 cup count) ripens late but is resistant to frost; it is particularly valued for its excellent keeping quality and high pectin content (desirable for canning). The glossy, medium red berry is oblong to oval in shape (oblong when poorly seeded and round when well seeded) and has a crisp flesh. Vines are coarse with many more uprights produced than runners. Although considered a good producer, it is not as productive as Early Black nor is it as resistant to false blossom disease.

Howland. No description of this cultivar is available.

Improved Howes. Discovered by A. D. Makepeace in 1890, this cultivar was first planted at South Carver, Massachusetts. It produces a large-to-medium berry (75–82 cup count) that ripens late in the season but which does not keep very well. The glossy, medium red berry has a pyriform shape with a pointed stem end. Fine-textured vines produce short uprights that are capable of good production.

Indian Head. No description of this cultivar is available.

Jerseys. The name Jerseys (also referred to as Natives) was given to those cultivated cranberries that were taken from the wild in New Jersey without any selection and planted in bogs. The berries are variable in size, shape, and color but have been found to store and ship well.

Juneau. T. F. Hamilton discovered this cultivar in 1893 and planted the first bog at Berlin, Wisconsin. The small fruit (100 cup count) ripens early and colors well in storage, but it is only a fair keeper. The deep red berry has an oval-to-oblong shape with a pointed stem end and is covered with a moderate amount of bloom. Coarse vines produce tall uprights that give good production.

Keystone. Cuttings of this cultivar were sent to Wisconsin in 1893 by J. T. McFarlin of South Carver, Massachusetts, to be included in the Wisconsin cultivar trial. The plant produces a moderate crop of small, bell-shaped fruit that is of fair quality but does not keep well.

Klondike. No description of this cultivar is available.

Late Cape. No description of this cultivar is available.

Late Jersey. No description of this cultivar is available.

Late Reds. No description of this cultivar is available.

LeMunyon (Norman?). No description of this cultivar is available.

Leonard Robbins. No description of this cultivar is available.

Mammoth. No description of this cultivar is available. It may be the same variety as Holliston, but it is found in a different locality.

Matthews. Isaiah Matthews made the first planting of this cultivar about 1880 at South Yarmouth, Massachusetts. Although a good producer with a cup count ranging from 59 to 80, this medium red berry with its pyriform shape and pointed stem end is regarded as a poor keeper in storage. This fancy berry was rated prime for fresh table use in the 1920s for the Central and Eastern markets. The coarse vines produce short uprights that bear fruit with a heavy bloom. It is very similar to Centerville.

Maxim Randall. This cultivar, also referred to as Randall in the literature, was discovered by L. Randall at Rochester, Massachusetts. It is a good, late-season producer of large, deep red berries that keep very well. The wax-coated berries are oblong to spindle shaped with a stem end that is both point-ed and furrowed. The fine-textured vines give rise to medium tall uprights with light green, small leaves.

McFarlin. This cultivar was discovered by T. H. McFarlin in 1874 and planted by him at South Carver, Massachusetts. The fruit is large to medium (65 to 95 cup count) but the berries are not uniform in size and do not color in storage. They ripen midseason (usually in the second and third week of October) but they are frost resistant. The berries have tender flesh and fine flavor, but their keeping quality is only fair. The deep red berries are round to oblong in shape with a very prominent calyx and heavy waxy bloom. The cultivar produces a prolific amount of coarse vine growth, which makes it par-ticularly difficult to harvest by hand scoops or with mechanical dry harvesters. Where water harvesting is practiced, this drawback is not serious. The plant is very resistant to false blossom disease. McFarlin makes up about 20 per-cent of the production in Wisconsin and over 80 percent in the Pacific North-west.

Metallic Bell. Another cultivar selected by T. F. Hamilton, it was first planted by him at Shennington, Wisconsin. The large, lightly colored fruit is bell shaped and possesses a metallic gloss. The plant is susceptible to false blossom disease.

Middleboro. Discovered by J. W. Howes in 1885, this was first planted by him at Middleboro, Massachusetts. Middleboro is a large berry (54–58 cup count) that ripens late but does not keep well. It is a glossy, deep red, oval-shaped berry with a pointed calyx end. The vines are fine to medium textured, and the uprights are tall with very large, dark green leaves. The cultivar is considered a good producer.

Middlesex. George Batchelder was the discoverer of this cultivar which he planted at Holliston, Massachusetts. The fruit is medium sized (90–96 cup count), ripens late in the season, and keeps well in storage. The glossy, deep red berries are oval shaped with a pointed stem end. The medium coarse vines and tall uprights have very large, dark green leaves. Production by this cultivar is only fair.

Monmouth. No description of this cultivar is available.

Mosquito Damn. No description of this cultivar is available.

Murdock. No description of this cultivar is available.

Nancy LeMunyon. No description of this cultivar is available.

Natives (of Wisconsin). This wild cranberry of Wisconsin is a mixture of Bell and Cherry types of variable size, shape, and color intensity.

Newton. No description of this cultivar is available.

North Cape Howes. No description of this cultivar is available.

Nova Scotia Bell. No description of this cultivar is available.

Old Homestead. No description of this cultivar is available.

Oxhart. No description of this cultivar is available.

Pacific Beauty. No description of this cultivar is available.

Palmeter. D. C. Palmeter of Berlin, Wisconsin, made the first planting of this cultivar. Palmeter produces medium-sized fruit that ripens early in the season but does not keep well even though it colors up in storage. The glossy, medium-red berry is nearly round with a flat calyx end. Medium coarse vines support tall uprights with light green, small leaves. The cultivar is a poor producer.

Paradise Meadow. W. P. Turner discovered this cultivar in 1873 and made the first planting at Sharon, Massachusetts. The large berries (58–68 cup count) ripen late in the season, and although they will not color in storage, they will store well. The medium red berry is round to oval in shape and is covered with a heavy waxy bloom. The vines are coarse and the uprights tall with large, light green leaves. Paradise Meadow's production is rated as fair to good.

Paul. No description of this cultivar is available.

Perkins. No description of this cultivar is available.

Perry Red. Discovered in 1888, Perry Red was named by J. Perry and planted at Marion, Massachusetts. The medium-sized fruit (80–100 cup count) ripens early and colors well in storage. The berry is round with a flat calyx end and is covered with a heavy bloom. Coarse vines support tall uprights with large, dark green leaves that are capable of producing good crops.

Pilgrim. This late-season cultivar resulted from a cross of Prolific x McFarlin made by H. F. Bain in 1930 at Whitesbog. It was selected by F. B. Chandler and I. E. Demoranville at East Wareham, Massachusetts. The berries are long and oval shaped, very large (43–66 berries per cup), purplish red with yellow under-color, and covered with a waxy bloom. They keep well in storage. The plant is moderately vigorous, producing a medium number of runners and medium-to-long uprights, and is resistant to feeding by the false blossom disease vector. It is considered to be a very good producer.

Pittsberg. No description of this cultivar is available.

Plum. This cultivar was selected from the wild in 1872 by E. Staten and planted in his Toms River, New Jersey, bogs. The cultivar produces a medium-sized berry that ripens at midseason and stores well. The dark red berry is oblong in shape and is covered with a moderate amount of bloom. Coarse vines produce tall uprights with large, dark green leaves. The cultivar is considered only a fair producer.

Potter. Also called Potter's Favorite, this productive early cultivar was discovered in 1895 by M. O. Potter and planted by him at Wisconsin Rapids, Wisconsin. The deep red berries are oval shaped with a pointed stem end and ripen early in the season. The fruit are fairly large (68 berries per cup) and color well in storage, but unfortunately they do not keep well in storage. The coarse vines produce tall uprights with large, light green leaves.

Pride. This is a highly productive cultivar selected by B. F. Vose of Massachusetts in 1873 and planted by him at Marion, Massachusetts. It is also referred to as Vose's Pride in the literature. Pride is a midseason cultivar with a cup count of 88 to 98. The berries are glossy red to dark red and pyriform shaped with a very pointed stem end. They are firm fleshed and keep and ship well. The plant produces coarse vines with many runners that are enlarged at the juncture of branches. The fruiting uprights have a tendency to produce one or more branchlets in the season they fruit. The cultivar, however, appears to be quite susceptible to cranberry fruit worm.

Prolific. C. D. Leach of Walton, Michigan, selected this productive cultivar in 1904. The large, dark red, cherry-shaped berries have excellent flavor and are borne on vigorous vines that tend to flower early in the season.

Reckless. No description of this cultivar is available.

Reds. No description of this cultivar is available.

Rhode Island. No description of this cultivar is available.

Round Howes. H. W. Chapman discovered this cultivar in 1910 and planted it in his bogs in South Yarmouth, Massachusetts. The medium-sized fruit (80 cup count) ripens late in the season and has only fair keeping quality. The light red berries are round to oval in shape and carry a heavy waxy bloom. The moderately vigorous vines produce very good crops.

Round Red. No description of this cultivar is available.

Russell Bell. No description of this cultivar is available.

Rutherford. The originator of this cultivar is unknown, but the first planting is believed to have existed at East Falmouth, Massachusetts. Large-to-medium fruit (73–98 cup count) ripen late in the season and store well. The dark red fruit is spindle shaped with both ends pointed and is lightly covered with bloom. Short uprights on coarse vines with medium leaves produce fair-to-good crops.

St. Clair. Cuttings of this cultivar were supplied by C. D. McFarlin of Empire City, Oregon, for inclusion in the 1894 Wisconsin cultivar collection. The berries are medium in size and oblong in shape, and they have good flavor. Their keeping quality, however, is judged as only fair.

Samuel Small's Bugles. No description of this cultivar is available.

Searles. Also known as Searles Jumbo, this Wisconsin selection was made by A. Searles in 1893 and planted by him at Wisconsin Rapids. This midseason cultivar produces deep red berries that ripen by the third or fourth week in September. The fairly uniform fruit averages 80 berries per cup. Fruit flesh is firm and the berries color well in storage but they do not keep particularly well. The berries are round to oblong with a protruding calyx and are devoid of bloom. The fruit is susceptible to rot and the plants are susceptible to false blossom disease. Searles is the standard cultivar in Wisconsin, comprising about 65 percent of the cranberries grown in that state. The medium coarse vines produce tall uprights that give excellent production.

Settler. No description of this cultivar is available.

Shaw's Success. A. M. Shaw discovered this midseason cultivar in 1890 and made the original planting in South Carver, Massachusetts. The berries are very small (110–139 berries per cup) and blackish red, but the cultivar is a good producer and the fruit keeps very well. The berries are spindle shaped with both ends pointed. The vines are fine textured and produce short uprights. Shaw's Success is very resistant to the spread of false blossom disease.

Shurtleff. No description of this cultivar is available.

Silver Lake. No description of this cultivar is available.

Smalley Howes. This cultivar was discovered in 1853 by J. A. Smalley and originally planted at East Dennis, Massachusetts. The fruit is medium to small (89–125 cup count) and is harvested late in the season. It colors well in storage but has only fair keeping quality. The glossy, medium red berry is pyriform in shape and has a pointed stem end. Moderately vigorous vines generally produce good crops.

Smith. This very productive late-season cultivar was selected by R. Smith in 1880 and planted in his bogs at Chatham, Massachusetts. The deep red, round-to-oval berry with a pointed stem end has a moderate amount of bloom and colors well in storage but is only a fair keeper. The coarse vines produce tall uprights with large dark green leaves.

Smith No. 1. No description of this cultivar is available.

Smith No. 2. No description of this cultivar is available.

Snipatuit. No description of this cultivar is available.

Stankavich. This cultivar originated in Oregon as the result of a cross between an Oregon native and an Eastern cultivar believed to be McFarlin. It was selected by Joseph F. Stankavich sometime between 1914 and 1917 in Bandon, Oregon, and was introduced to the industry in 1926. Stankavich ripens early and produces well. The large fruit has a low acid content and a good sugar content, and it keeps well in storage. The glossy, deep red, nearly round berry is flat on both ends. It is a moderately vigorous plant with tall uprights that are very productive. In the milder growing regions, it does have a tendency to bloom a second time in the fall, which can adversely affect its production the following year.

Stanley. J. W. Shaw found this late-season, productive plant in 1890 and planted it in his bogs at Carver, Massachusetts. The light red berry is pyriform to spindle shaped with a pointed stem end. Although the plant produces exceptionally well, the berry does not keep well in storage. The moderately vigorous plant has fine-to-medium-textured vines with medium tall uprights.

Stevens. This cultivar resulted from a cross of McFarlin x Potter made by H. F. Bain of the USDA at Beltsville, Maryland. The cultivar was first tested at Whitesbog, New Jersey, and introduced in 1950. The berries are exceptionally large, averaging 50 to 55 berries per cup. This productive cultivar ripens midseason between Early Black and Howes. The deep red, round-to-oval berry resembles Howes and keeps exceptionally well in storage. The plants are vigorous, producing many coarse, strong vines. Its vigorous growth habit would make it suitable to cranberry soils low in organic matter.

Taylor. In 1905 G. Taylor found this cultivar growing wild and planted it in his bogs at Indian Mills, New Jersey. It produces a fair-to-good crop of dull red fruit early in the season. The round-to-oval berry has a moderate amount of waxy bloom on it, and it has good keeping quality. The vines are fine textured and the uprights are short with small, light green leaves.

Wales Henry. This midseason cultivar was considered a promising cranberry in Massachusetts during the 1920s. It was discovered by W. A. Andrews in 1887 and first planted at North Carver, Massachusetts. The berries are round to oval with a calyx end that is flat and striped. A heavy waxy bloom covers the berry. The fruit is firm fleshed, has fair-to-good keeping quality, and has excellent flavor. The plant produces coarse vines with many uprights but few runners, which makes it well adapted to hand scooping.

Wellman Cherry. No description of this cultivar is available.

Whiting Randall. This very late cultivar was discovered by George Randall in 1888 and planted in his bogs at Plympton, Massachusetts. It is a small (111–140 cup count), medium red berry with a light bloom. The fruit is spindle shaped with both its ends pointed, and it colors and keeps well in storage. The fine-textured vines give rise to short uprights that produce good crops.

Whitman Park. No description of this cultivar is available.

Whittlesey. No description of this cultivar is available. It was, however, one of the cultivars used in the U.S. Department of Agriculture breeding program.

Wilcox. This early cultivar resulted from a cross of Howes x Searles made by H. F. Bain of the USDA at Beltsville, Maryland, and tested at Whitesbog, New Jersey. The cultivar is both precocious and productive, quickly covering the bog surface when newly planted and coming into bearing at an early age. The large-to-medium fruit (73–98 cup count) resembles Howes in size but has better color, keeps well, and is of excellent quality. It also produces very vigorous growth that is characterized by long coarse vines and a dense mat of uprights. The plant is as resistant to false blossom disease as is Early Black and appears to be particularly promising in New Jersey.

Winslow. No description of this cultivar is available.

Winter Queen. No description of this cultivar is available.

Wisconsin. No description of this cultivar is available.

Woolman. A. W. Woolman discovered this cultivar in 1897 and put out the first planting at Indian Mills, New Jersey. This midseason cultivar is a very good producer but its fruit does not color in storage, nor does it keep all that well. The deep red berry, covered with a moderate amount of bloom and averaging 105 berries per cup, is spindle shaped with both its ends pointed. The moderately vigorous vines are medium in texture with uprights of medium length.

Cultivar Trials

Wisconsin

The first documented effort at carrying out a systematic evaluation of the known commercial cranberry cultivars of the time was the Wisconsin State Cranberry Growers Association's 1893 attempt to put together a collection of all the known cultivars of cranberries and to test new selections from many sources (Boone and Dana 1971). With a grant from the Wisconsin Legislature, the association put out three separate plantings. One of these survived and was incorporated into the newly created Cranberry Experiment Station at Cranmoor in 1903. More than 200 new selections were evaluated at this facility in addition to the eastern cultivars of Early Black, Howes, and McFarlin as well as the cultivars originating in Wisconsin, including Ben Lear, Bennett Jumbo, Berlin, Early Ohio, Metallic Bell, Palmeter, Potter's Favorite, Prolific, and Searles. Although an extensive effort was made to evaluate the selections for size, color, form, gloss, uniformity, keeping qualities, firmness, productiveness, season, vigor of vines, time of flowering, and flavor, no new cultivar was ever named by the time the station closed in 1917. The commercial acceptance of the cultivar Searles Jumbo (Searles), however, was probably confirmed as a result of these trials.

The next attempt to carry out systematic studies on cultivar adaptability to Wisconsin growing conditions was made in 1931 with the establishment of a nursery at the Weiss and Hamre Marsh in Wood County. It was here that H. F. Bain was able to separate the true clone of McFarlin, which by this time had become thoroughly intermeshed with Wisconsin natives. In addition 21 selections were made that were established in a test planting at the Biron Company in 1939. It was at this test planting that the USDA seedlings from the new breeding program were tested under the supervision of H. F. Bain. With the withdrawal of federal funds, this program was ended in 1960. Of the six new hybrids named from the USDA breeding program, only the cultivar Stevens appears to be particularly suited to Wisconsin growing conditions.

In 1969 a new cooperative effort between the Wisconsin cranberry industry and the State Experiment Station was initiated to reevaluate existing commercial cultivars on the basis of the modern needs of the industry and to assemble and preserve cranberry germ plasm so that it could be utilized in future breeding programs. Plantings were established at the Du Bay Cranberry Company at Dancy, at Jacob Searles Cranberry Company at Cranmoor, and at Tomahawk Cranberry Company at Tomahawk. More than 50 cultivars, selections, and seedlings were evaluated. Among the characteristics examined were yield, color, keeping quality, disease resistance, insect resistance, processing quality, and season of ripening.

Massachusetts

Although the seedlings emanating from the USDA breeding program were being tested throughout the 1940s at the Massachusetts Agricultural Experiment Station, State Bog, it was not until 1955 that a systematic evaluation of existing cultivars and new selections was begun in Massachusetts (Chandler 1956b). In addition to evaluating the new selections for adaptability to Massachusetts growing conditions, it was hoped that by growing existing cultivars under identical growing conditions, valid comparisons could be made between them. It was also anticipated that pure clones could be established that would be kept free of disease and would serve as a source of propagating material for the industry. The trial planting included 22 Massachusetts cultivars including: Aviator, Berry Berry, Black Veil, Centennial, Centerville, Champion, Early Black, Early Red, Foxboro Howes, Holliston, Howes, McFarlin, Matthews, Paradise, Meadow, Perry Red, Randall, Round Howes, Shaw's Success, Smalley Howes, Stanley, Vose's Pride, and Wales Henry; three Wisconsin cultivars: Ben Lear, Potter, and Searles; and the Stankavich cultivar from the West Coast. In addition the newly named cultivars Beckwith, Stevens, and Wilcox were included in the trial as well as other selections from the USDA breeding program. This extensive trial contributed to the naming of Bergman, Franklin, and Pilgrim—the last of the cultivars to be named from the USDA breeding program.

Washington

In 1940 D. J. Crowley, superintendent of Washington State University's Coastal Washington Research and Extension Unit at Long Beach, initiated a cranberry-breeding program together with systematic trials to test the new seedlings as well as existing cultivars under Washington conditions. Most of the Eastern cultivars were not able to thrive under the cooler growing season of the Pacific Northwest (Crowley 1954). The exception was McFarlin, which under Pacific Coast conditions produced a late-maturing berry with consistent productivity. This became the standard commercial cultivar in Washington, and by 1954 it made up 95 percent of the crop. The Wisconsin cultivar Searles also produces well on the Pacific Coast, but it ripens at the same time as does McFarlin.

One of the 13 seedlings selected from Crowley's breeding program was WSU No. 72, which in 1970 was named Crowley in honor of its originator (Doughty and Garren 1970). This very productive cultivar, although developed in Washington, appeared to be even more adapted to growing conditions in Coos County, Oregon. It has been readily accepted by the industry because it provided the early-ripening cultivar needed to augment the late-ripening McFarlin cultivar. Of the new cultivars available, Stevens appears to be particularly adapted to the growing conditions of the Pacific Coast, where it ripens a few weeks before McFarlin (Shawa et al. 1984).

New Jersey

During the early days of testing the cranberry seedlings and selections that emanated from the USDA breeding program, evaluations were conducted at Whitesbog and, later, in cooperation with other New Jersey cranberry growers. With the establishment in 1966 of the Rutgers University Cranberry-Blueberry Research Station at Chatsworth, New Jersey, however, a concerted effort was made to establish a cultivar planting of as many existing cultivars as could be acquired. Today this planting contains most of the cultivars, selections, and improved cultivars known and serves as a valuable germ plasm source for an ongoing cranberry breeding program carried out under the auspices of the New Jersey Agricultural Experiment Station.

As the industry has grown and changed with respect to the utilization of its product, so have the objectives of today's modern breeding programs. Although insect and disease resistance, including fruit and root rot, are still important objectives, they now share a priority with such things as early ripening, anthocyanin content, sugar content, and resistance to softening—factors that are significant to today's harvest methods and to the processed product.

Europe

Trials of the large-fruited American cranberry are underway in a number of European countries including Germany, Poland, and the USSR. In the Latvian SSR (Ripa 1984, 1985), American cultivars have been under trial since 1972. In this northern province, the berries ripen from August to September. Wilcox produces the largest fruit, but Franklin and Bergman are the highest yielders of the cultivars tested. In southern Germany, Fiedler and Christ (1986) have been testing 17 American cultivars since 1970 on the high moorland of this district. Of these, 5 were found to have commercial possibilities.

FIVE

Environment

Temperature

Critical Temperature

As a perennial evergreen plant indigenous to the temperate zone, the cranberry does not appreciably grow below 40°F (4.4°C). As with other ericaceous plants, it begins to accumulate sugars as temperatures begin to drop at the end of the growing season in preparation for dormancy (Sieckmann and Boe 1978). Temperatures below 10°F (−12.2°C) during the dormant period, however, can be expected to cause considerable injury to the unprotected cranberry plant; even temperatures below freezing can be particularly injurious to the cranberry, depending upon the physiological stage of development of the plant (Doughty and Shawa 1966). Once the cranberry plant has completed its physiological rest period (chilling requirement), it is capable of active growth and will do so if environmental conditions are favorable. After completion of its rest requirement, spells of warm weather during winter will greatly decrease the cranberry plant's ability to withstand sudden sharp temperature drops (loss in hardiness). For this reason bogs in Wisconsin, Massachusetts, and New Jersey are sometimes kept flooded well into the beginning of the growing season. The prolonged flood protects the developing bud from severe spring frosts. The more physiologically active the cranberry bud, the greater its susceptibility to cold injury.

Optimum growth occurs in the range of 60°F to 80°F (15.6°C to 26.7°C), but lethal high temperatures may be as low as 80°F (26.7°C) if warm drying winds follow a period of cool moist growing conditions and coincide with a particularly susceptible stage of growth, as can often occur in the Pacific Coast growing region. The use of sprinklers over the plants to produce evaporative cooling has proven effective in reducing high bog temperatures.

Winter Injury

Although the dormant cranberry plant can probably tolerate a temperature as low as 0°F (−17.8°C) from the standpoint of the plant's genetic capability to resist ice formation within individual cells, cell desiccation may occur well above this lethal temperature if low temperatures are accompanied by moderate winds (Dana and Klingbeil 1966). Winter injury is observed when the leaves of the dormant plants change from their normal reddish color to a dull brown. The environmental conditions that generally prevail when winter injury occurs are a frozen root zone in the soil, a subfreezing temperature throughout both day and night, and winds of moderate velocity (Cross 1969b). The normal procedure for protecting the cranberry plant against this type of injury is to submerge the plant under a winter flood during the critical period.

Another form of winter injury is the damage to blossom buds that sometimes occurs when exposed vines are subjected to temperatures below 10°F (−12.2°C). In dormant cranberry plants, the injury often occurs at the abscission layer between the bud and the stem (Doughty and Shawa 1966). This type of injury does not always occur to all dormant buds—suggesting that differences in the stage of development, nutrition, or plant vigor might influence the relative hardiness of a bud. Under Washington conditions cranberries are most resistant to cold injury during the middle of the dormant period, normally between November and January (Doughty and Dodge 1966). It was found that the minimum temperature at which injury occurs increases as physiological activity increases in the plant. It is the abscission zone, a layer only a few cells thick between the upright stem and the terminal bud, that is most susceptible to low temperature injury (Doughty 1961). Uprights that fail to grow and instead start a side shoot out from a leaf axil below the bud are usually injured at this point. If the abscission layer is only partially injured, the bud may develop slowly and may even start new growth but that growth generally dies before the end of the growing season.

Other parts of the dormant bud that are susceptible to injury are the young shoot and the individual flower buds. If the young shoot is killed, an umbrella upright (characterized by two or three hooks) will form from the top of the upright. In this case, a new shoot arising from an axial bud does not occur. Blossom buds that develop first or lowest on the inflorescence are generally more susceptible to injury than those which develop later.

From the latter part of the dormant season through the hook (pink) stage, the flower parts most easily injured by low temperature are the anthers, style, and nectaries. Anther tubes injured by subfreezing temperatures during development twist and curl so that pollen dehiscence is extremely difficult. Damage to the ovaries and ovules can also occur. If all of the blossom buds are killed, only the young vegetative shoot grows.

Frost Injury

With the completion of the cranberry's rest requirement and the cessation of environmental conditions that maintain dormancy, the cranberry undergoes an explosive rate of growth. This is associated with the withdrawal of the winter flood in the East and Midwest and with warming temperatures in the bogs of the Pacific Northwest. After bud break any temperature below 31°F (−0.6°C) can cause a serious crop reduction, according to Doughty and Shawa (1966). Even prolonged exposure to 32°F (0°C) may damage as much as one-fourth of the crop if the plants are at an advanced stage of bud break. Prior to the Washington work (Doughty and Shawa 1966) on low-temperature injury, it was generally accepted that the rapidly expanding cranberry bud could tolerate temperatures as low as 30°F (−1.1°C) without sustaining injury (Franklin 1920). According to Franklin, the overwintering cranberry buds can tolerate temperatures as low as 25°F (−3.9°C) in the spring without injury until the buds swell to a diameter of 2 mm.

Soon after the withdrawal of the winter flood, the buds need protection at 27°F (−2.8°C). More recently, however, Massachusetts' researchers (Cross et al. 1967) concluded that when the winter flood on bogs was withdrawn early (before mid-March), cranberry buds grew more slowly in the spring and remained resistant to frost damage throughout April. Bogs that remained flooded later into the spring were likely to have cranberry buds more advanced in development and therefore more sensitive to frost. Consequently, Massachusetts growers tend to withdraw the winter flood by mid-March, particularly if the long-term forecast is for cool temperatures.

Any part of the open flower may be injured by temperatures below 31°F (−0.6°C) including the ovary and ovules, the style and pistil, the anthers and pollen grains, and the nectaries (Doughty 1961, 1962b). Low-temperature injury at this stage may result in a deformed berry or in complete failure of fruit set. When injury to the ovary wall occurs, a deformed fruit referred to as a *catfaced* berry may develop. If anthers or pollen are killed, viable pollen would be necessary from another flower to bring about fertilization. G. W. Eaton (1966) has shown that Early Black flowers injured by frost produced fruit with fewer seeds and of smaller size than comparable uninjured flowers. Injury to the nectaries may result in the curtailment of nectar production and thereby adversely affect the attractiveness of the flower to the bee (I. V. Hall and Newberry 1972).

The injury to these susceptible flower parts will be dependent upon the duration of the low temperature as well as the temperature itself. Injury results when ice forms within the plant tissue, and this does not occur until after the tissues have supercooled. This is generally 2 to 3 F° below freezing (−1.1° to −1.7°C). When ice forms within the plant cell or in the intercellular spaces, the cell walls are ruptured and the protoplasm is disorganized, which leads to the death of the cell. Another important factor related to the severity of frost injury is the rate at which the temperature drops. Sudden and rapid lowering of the temperature results in rapid ice formation within the cell rather than in the intracellular space—a condition more likely to lead to injury.

In the late summer it is the developing flower primordia and the developing fruit that can be injured by early fall frosts. Hall and Newberry (1972) have shown that plants injured by frost not only had fewer flower primordia but those that did form developed more slowly. The developing cranberry fruit continues to be susceptible to frost damage throughout the growing season. In the colder cranberry growing regions of Wisconsin, a frost can occur in any month of the summer. Franklin (1920) maintained that cranberries in the greenish white stage of fruit development can tolerate 26°F (−3.3°C) without injury and 25°F (−3.9°C) with some injury. Most fruit will be damaged at 24°F (−4.4°C) especially if the low temperature occurs for any length of time. Ripe Early Black and Howe berries can withstand temperatures to 23°F (−5.0°C). In fact, ripe berries of the Howes variety are so resistant to frost injury that under bog conditions only 10 percent have been found to freeze at temperatures as low as 16°F (−8.9°C), and 20 percent at 14°F (−10.0°C). Losses of Early Black cranberries are much greater at these low temperatures. In an interesting observation, Zuckerman (1961b) has noted that cranberries receiving fungicide treatments were notably more tolerant of frost. Because the actual freezing point of the berries was not affected by the fungicide application, he concluded that the fungicides in some way influenced the environment of the berries so as to reduce the severity of the frost.

Most frosts that occur in cranberry-growing areas are radiation frosts, that is, the injury occurs on clear, calm nights as the result of the plants' loss of heat by radiation to the sky. Cranberry bogs are particularly susceptible to this type of frost because the thick peat layer of the bog effectively insulates the plant from the stored heat of the soil, which would be useful in maintaining plant warmth during the cooling night (Bates 1971). Cranberry bogs are usually constructed in low areas; this prevents air movement that would be useful in mixing the warm upper layers of air with the cold air surrounding the plant.

Flooding is the traditional method of protecting the cranberry plant from frost damage. Protection by flooding is based upon the fact that water has a very high specific heat (ability to absorb heat). During the night the heat that the water has absorbed all day is released and can be utilized by the plant to maintain a temperature above freezing. Reflows (repeated bog floodings) can be kept to one-inch depths when frosts are light, but if temperatures are predicted for the low 20s (between −6° and −4°C), 3 to 4 inches (7.6–10.2 cm) of water would be necessary for protection. The greatest disadvantage of the flooding method is that plants that are experiencing intense physiological activity can be adversely affected by the submergence because of the rapid depletion of oxygen in the floodwater. Floodwaters must be removed as quickly as possible after a reflow in the spring, otherwise production may be impaired. In the fall when bogs are flooded to protect fruit, the rapid removal of floodwater is not as critical although fruit quality may be adversely affected (Kenny 1949).

Another popular method of frost control is the use of low-gallonage sprinklers (Norton 1959, 1969). Protection in this case depends upon the latent heat of fusion of water, that is, as water freezes it changes from a high energy state (liquid) to a low energy state (solid) with a subsequent release of energy (heat). This heat release is substantial (144 BTU per lb. of water [317 BTU per kg of water]) and can be utilized by the plant to maintain tissues above the critical temperature. It is extremely important to continue sprinkling the vines as the ice begins to melt after ambient temperatures go above freezing because the plant may experience a heat loss as energy is utilized by the melting ice. Continued sprinkling until all the ice is gone will insure sufficient heat energy from the irrigation water to prevent plant damage.

The continuous application of approximately 0.1 inch (2.5 mm) of water per hour through low-gallonage sprinklers during the frost period will protect plants against temperatures as low as 20°F (−6.7°C). During the cranberries' most susceptible period, sprinklers should be turned on when temperatures fall to 34°F (1.1°C). This will reduce the probability of spotty frost damage occurring because of microclimate differences between locations in the bog.

Wind machines can be effective in preventing frosts when a strong temperature inversion (lowest temperatures exist at ground level and rise rapidly with increasing elevation) exists over the bogs (Kranick 1940; Wallis 1964). The wind machines are mounted on towers 20 to 30 feet (6–9 m) high and are used to mix the air mass over the bogs, thus forcing the warmer upper layers of air down to vine level. Temperatures can be raised as much as 8 F° (4.4 C°) by this method when temperature inversions are great.

Radiation frosts occur primarily during the early and latter portions of the vegetative growing season. This type of frost is most apt to occur when there is rapid clearing developing under the influence of a high-pressure air mass. The drier the air mass is, the lower the minimum temperature because a moist air mass partly absorbs the heat radiated from the bog and reradiates it to the bog surface. During late summer when maximum day temperatures occur in the 70s (21° to 26°C), it is not likely that a frost will occur the first night these atmospheric conditions occur because of the amount of heat absorbed by the soil. If conditions for frost continue, the following night might be frosty. Light, sandy soils sparsely covered with vines will absorb greater amounts of heat than thickly vined bog sections and will have more heat to radiate at night.

Because of the strong influence of microclimate on temperature, it is important that temperatures are monitored at the vine level—usually about five inches (12.7 cm) from the bog surface. Temperatures at vine level may be as much as 10 F° (5.6 C°) colder than shelter temperatures. In order to be of value to cranberry growers, predicted minimum bog temperatures must be forecast early enough for the grower to make preparations for protecting his bog. The Bliss formula was developed to provide a predicted minimum bog temperature (Bliss 1922, 1924). The formula was arrived at empirically from the statistical evaluation of thousands of observations of dew point and temperature. The following relationship was found to be highly related to minimum bog temperature when dew point and bog temperature were taken one-half hour after sunset:

$$\text{Dew Point} + \text{Bog Temperature} \times 0.31 = \text{Predicted Minimum Bog Temperature (°F)}$$

In New Jersey, where some of the frost control is still obtained by flooding bogs, it was found desirable to modify the Bliss formula so that dew-point and air temperature readings taken earlier in the day could be related to a predicted minimum temperature. The following noon formulae were developed when dew points and air temperature were taken at noon:

$$\tfrac{1}{2} \text{Dew Point} + \tfrac{1}{10} \text{Dew Point} = \text{Predicted Minimum Bog Temperature (°F)}$$

or

$$\tfrac{1}{2} \text{Dew Point} + \tfrac{1}{10} \text{Air Temperature} = \text{Predicted Minimum Bog Temperature (°F)}$$

Equations to predict minimum bog temperatures have also been developed by Hovey and Shulman (1966). In Massachusetts formulae have been developed for specific periods during the growing season (I. E. Demoranville 1978). Frost forecasting for the cranberry industry in Wisconsin is particularly difficult because of the northern latitudes in which cranberries are grown and the relatively large growing area covered, roughly equivalent to the distance between Massachusetts and New Jersey (C. F. Hall 1950f).

As valuable as frost forecasts are, they will never be as reliable as the actual measurement of the bog temperature. When bogs were flooded to protect against frost, it was necessary to have a reliable forecast because it could take hours to flood the bogs in a large holding. Today, with most bogs protected by solid set irrigation systems, which can be turned on with the flick of switch, an accurate frost forecast hours before its expected occurrence is no longer essential. Accurate temperature monitoring of the bogs, however, becomes paramount. In this case it becomes important not only to monitor the temperature at the vine level but also to locate the temperature-recording equipment in the coldest part of the bog. The entire frost alarm system lends itself to rather sophisticated automation. One such alarm system was described by Norton (1967). It consists of a thermostat located in the critical bog area, a private telephone line provided by the local telephone company in their Private-Line-Signal-Service, and a bell or similar alarm device. The thermostat is joined to the telephone line that conveys the signal to the grower's house, where a sensitive relay completes the circuit. A second circuit containing the alarm device is incorporated into the original circuit to complete the alarm system. The system can be calibrated to give an alarm at whatever temperature the grower may feel he or she needs in order to give sufficient lead time to get the sprinklers started. Today the alarms may be digital and radio-relayed in many cases.

Heat Injury

Cranberries may also be injured by high temperatures. Three types of high-temperature injury are possible. First, desiccation may occur as the result of excessive transpiration; secondly, a depletion of food reserves may occur because of excessive respiration; and finally, the death of the protoplasm may occur, the thermal death point in this case ranging from 120° to 140°F (48.8° to 60.0°C).

High temperatures combined with high humidity in late May and early June favor vigorous and tender new growth. This type of growth is particularly susceptible to desiccation injury when drying southerly winds prevail. This type of injury has been referred to as *blast*. Berries may also be adversely affected by high temperatures, a condition that has been termed *scalding*. When high temperatures coincide with low humidity, sprinkling has been found to be an effective method of reducing bog temperature (Cross 1969b; Doughty and Dodge 1966). Temperature can be lowered by as much as 10 F° (5.6 C°) by evaporation using this sprinkler technique. Under the cool growing conditions of the Pacific Coast, the tender growth that is produced may be injured by temperatures as low as 80°F (26.7°C) (Shawa 1984). White (1870) claimed that in New Jersey when berries changed from green to white, they could be damaged by summer temperatures as low as 85°F (29.4°C).

Other Temperature Aspects

Temperature may have important manifestations in cranberry growth and development beyond the effects of excessively low or high temperatures. Bain (1926) was firmly convinced that part of the poor fruit set that Wisconsin growers sometimes experienced was due to low temperatures (above freezing) that often prevailed at the critical bloom period. Although Bain offered no explanation for this viewpoint other than the empirical evidence of its occurrence, other researchers working with the closely related blueberry (Knight and Scott 1964) have shown that low temperature at time of bloom can seriously retard pollen tube growth after pollination and thus reduce the potential for successful fertilization.

Temperature also plays a critical role in anthocyanin formation in the cranberry plant, which is a significant attribute in the marketing of the cranberry fruit. I. V. Hall and Stark (1972) showed that there was a dramatic increase in the anthocyanin content of both the plant and fruit as ambient temperatures decreased, with the greatest increases in color occurring under the coolest conditions. Warm temperatures during the late stages of fruit development can be expected to be quite detrimental to color formation and, therefore, to the marketability of the fruit.

Additional aspects of temperature as it relates to weather influences on cranberry production are discussed later in this chapter in the section dealing with weather factors.

Oxygen Deficiency

Occurrence

The first suggestion that oxygen deficiency of floodwater may have a debilitating effect upon cranberry plants came from work conducted in the cranberry-producing regions of Massachusetts and Wisconsin in 1919 (Bergman 1921). Following June reflows for insect control, it was noted that many flower buds and growing tips were injured and killed. Subsequent experiments led to the verification of the occurrence of oxygen deficiency injury not only during summer reflow periods but also after the winter flood and occasionally even after spring and fall reflows for frost protection (Bergman 1921, 1925, 1931; Franklin et al. 1943).

Originally, the problem of oxygen deficiency injury was thought to be limited to the Wisconsin and Massachusetts cranberry-growing areas because of the more severe winter weather that prevailed in these areas. After a survey of New Jersey bogs, however, it was conclusively shown that the problem also existed in New Jersey (Bergman 1954; Doehlert 1955b; Marucci and Moulter 1955). The severity of the situation was often compounded by the fact that much of the floodwater used in New Jersey was highly colored, which tended to exclude light that would favor photosynthesis and subsequent oxygenation of bog water. Oxygen deficiency remains largely a nonexistent problem in the West Coast cranberry-growing region because of the milder winter conditions that prevail there.

Oxygen deficiency injury in the flooded cranberry plant occurs when the demand for oxygen by the plant exceeds the rate of supply of oxygen to the floodwater (Bergman 1953). Injury, therefore, becomes a function of the oxygen content of the water, the oxygen requirement of the plant tissues (a measure of growth activity), and the ability of the plant to withstand a lack of oxygen. The greater the difference between the oxygen demand by the plant and the oxygen supply of the water, the greater is the degree of injury. Since the cranberry plant is an evergreen plant and carries on oxygen-requiring physiological functions that are vital to its survival throughout the year, the oxygen balance in floodwater is of prime importance to the plant whenever flooding is necessitated. These periods of flooding can be grouped according to the season of year and according to their specific cultural function. Spring and summer reflows are used to combat insect infestations. Reflows for frost control are made in both the spring and fall, and a winter flood is placed on bogs for varying lengths of the winter season in the different cranberry-growing regions. The degree of oxygen deficiency injury that is experienced at these different flood periods varies considerably depending upon the stage of plant growth and upon the many environmental factors that may influence the oxygen content of the floodwater.

Late spring and summer reflow for insect control is a particularly critical flood period because of the ease at which an unfavorable oxygen balance can develop in the floodwater (Bergman 1931). This unfavorable balance occurs because during this period the vines are undergoing their most active growth and the floodwaters have a relatively low oxygen content because of the high water temperatures that prevail. Flooding for insect control is complicated because low oxygen content of the water is most suitable for insect control but unfortunately also unfavorable to the growing cranberry plant (Marucci and Moulter 1971). Flooding for longer than 48 hours during this active plant growth period can be extremely dangerous to the plant, particularly if accompanying environmental conditions are not conducive to rapid oxygenation of the water.

Oxygen deficiency injury during reflows for frost control does not occur frequently. This is generally true because the flood lasts for less than 24 hours and occurs at a time of low temperatures, which would favor relatively high oxygen levels in the water. If, however, the flood is allowed to remain for longer than a 24-hour period, particularly if water from swamp reservoirs low in oxygen is used, injury to the plants and fruit may occur. An increase in susceptibility to fruit rot has been observed to occur under these conditions (Wakabayashi 1925).

Winter flooding is practiced in the colder cranberry-growing regions in order to prevent winter killing and frost heaving of the plants and to delay growth until after most of the early spring frosts. Except for specifically local conditions, such as a prolonged period of calm and cloudy weather or the use of poor-quality floodwater, little oxygen deficiency injury is apt to occur on winter-flooded bogs unless they are covered by ice and snow (Bergman 1931). Unfortunately, this is the condition prevalent in Wisconsin, Massachusetts, and New Jersey for most winters. By mid-December, flooded Wisconsin bogs are often frozen and snow-covered and, in most years, remain so until mid-March (Bergman 1930a). This results in a comparatively long flood period during which an unfavorable oxygen balance in the floodwater is likely to occur. The situation in Massachusetts is little better, although the flooded bogs generally freeze over later in December than they do in Wisconsin, and ice-free periods are apt to occur during a midwinter thaw. Snow cover also presents a problem in Massachusetts. Although New Jersey bogs can be expected to be free of ice and snow for longer periods during the winter season than bogs in Wisconsin and Massachusetts, the winter flood problem is complicated by the fact that much of the floodwater used in New Jersey is highly colored and not favorable to the factors that contribute to a high oxygen level in the floodwater.

Forms of Injury

The death of stems and terminal buds and the loss of leaves are diagnostic symptoms readily noticed and easily identified with oxygen deficiency (Bergman 1953). The injury to flower buds, embryonic leaf tissue, and fruit, however, is not as readily associated with oxygen deficiency and is often attributed erroneously to other causes. The outright death of the terminal bud and its bearing upright represents the effects of a very severe oxygen deficiency. When the difference between the oxygen requirement of plant tissues and the oxygen supply is not great enough to produce these dramatic effects, intermediate symptoms of injury are often manifested in several ways (Franklin et al. 1943).

For example, terminal buds may be killed without injury to the stems. This results in the development of side shoots originating from buds lower down on the upright. The presence of a larger number of uprights bearing this type of shoot growth on vines that have been under a winter flood is proof of the existence of oxygen deficiency during the flood period. Although the terminal buds are more susceptible to injury than the old leaves, occasionally leaf drop occurs without any appreciable injury to terminal buds. There are times when all the flower buds within the terminal bud are killed without injury to the embryonic leaves or to the apex of the stem axis within the terminal bud. This results in a new upright that will be both retarded in growth and flowerless. Upon careful examination, vestiges of the flowers may be seen. These are characterized by the presence of pedicels, each bearing two small leaves at its summit with a very small dead structure between them (representing a flower bud killed very early in its development). When deformed leaves develop from these flowerless shoots, it is an indication that small areas of tissue in the embryonic leaves had been destroyed (Bergman 1945).

Sometimes the flower buds are not killed outright but are injured to the extent that they do not completely differentiate. Depending upon the severity of the injury, the buds may continue development for a short time and then die, or they may go on to produce flowers that are incapable of setting fruit. When ovary tissue is damaged, fertilization does not occur and the further development of the ovary into a fruit is prevented. Under these circumstances the presence of even a large number of pollinators would be of no avail. This delayed effect of oxygen deficiency injury is sometimes referred to as *flower bud absorption*. In some cases, the cells that form the nectaries are injured to the extent that the amount of nectar secreted by individual flowers is reduced, consequently affecting the attractiveness of the flowers for bees.

Finally, the fruit itself may be affected by oxygen deficiency injury (Bergman 1953). Berries may either die before they are one-fourth grown or fail to mature. Fruit that does mature may be reduced in size.

In summary, it is apparent that all the factors that influence yield—namely, the number of uprights per unit area (density of stand of uprights), percentage of flowering uprights, number of flower buds per upright, fruit set, and size of berries—can be adversely affected by oxygen deficiency injury. The importance of oxygen deficiency injury in determining the potential yield of a cranberry bog is undeniable.

Oxygen Requirement

The amount of oxygen required by specific parts of the cranberry plant and, therefore, their susceptibility to oxygen deficiency injury are directly related to their degree of growth activity (Bergman 1953). The synthesis of proteins and their assimilation into tissues that makes up growth are energy-requiring processes. This energy is obtained by the oxidation of simple sugars within the plant cells, an oxygen-requiring process referred to as *respiration*. During the winter flood period, the flower buds, young leaves, and the growing point of the stem within the terminal buds are the most active plant parts and so are the first tissues to be injured when critical oxygen levels are reached. Because stems and old leaves are the least active parts of the plant during the overwintering period, they are the most tolerant of low oxygen levels in the floodwater.

The respiration rate of cranberry plants at temperatures of 32° to 34°F (0° to 1.1°C) is very slow. With each increase in temperature of 10 C°, the respiration rate of a plant doubles. At 10°C the respiration rate is twice the rate at

0°C, and at 20°C (often the temperature of water when flooding for insect control) respiration occurs at a rate four times greater than the rate at 0°C. The very active growth that takes place during late spring and early summer is an important reason for the extreme caution that needs to be exercised when flooding for insect control. The oxygen demand by the growing cranberry plant is probably at its greatest during this period.

Bergman (1925, 1930b) has measured the respiration rate of different parts of the cranberry plant in terms of carbon dioxide (CO_2) evolution (a by-product of the respiration process). He found that flowers released between 22.0 and 76.5 cc of CO_2/hr/100 g of tissue at 0°C and 760 mm pressure. Under the same experimental conditions, cranberry growing tips released 19.3 to 46.2 cc CO_2/hr/100 g of tissue and old plants released 6.1 to 28.3 cc CO_2/hr/100 g of tissue. He noted that there were two periods of maximum respiratory activity in the development of the flower. The first peak occurred in the bud stage, during which the stamens and corolla were undergoing rapid development. During the period that the flower was opened, a lower respiration rate prevailed due to the fact that the stamens and corolla had reached their maximum growth and the pistil remained unchanged for awhile. Soon after pollination, the rate of respiration of the flower increased to a second peak of short duration due to an increase in the respiration rate of the pistil. Young fruits respired very rapidly for a period of one to three days after petal fall, the rate equalling or exceeding the respiration rate of buds. With the further development of the fruit, the respiration rate decreased very rapidly.

Both the buds and young fruits had a greater respiratory rate than young shoots. The respiration rate of young shoots was very similar to that of opened flowers but was two to three times greater than that of old shoots. Leaves are more resistant to oxygen deficiency injury than are buds and shoots, partly due to a lower respiration rate and possibly also due to the accumulation of oxygen in intercellular spaces from the water surrounding the leaves. The respiration rate of mature leaves was less than that of growing leaves of the same season. Leaves of the preceding season were least active.

The critical oxygen level of floodwater at which some oxygen deficiency injury may be expected to occur has been put at 5.7 ppm by Bergman (1953). The extent of the injury is directly related to the concentration reached below this critical level and to the length of time the oxygen content remains at that level. There is some indication that this critical oxygen level may vary for different cranberry plants depending upon the amount of carbohydrates (sugars and starches) stored by the plant in the fall (Franklin et al. 1943). Vines with large amounts of stored carbohydrates appear to be more resistant to oxygen deficiency injury than do vines with small amounts of stored carbohydrates. Apparently the cranberry plant is able to break down the carbohydrates to obtain the oxygen needed for respiration. Factors which favor the accumulation of large amounts of stored carbohydrates in vines during the late fall are a light crop, favorable fall growing conditions, and freedom from vine injury. It has been observed that oxygen deficiency injury is greatest in years following a heavy crop, a condition that would have made great demands on the carbohydrate reserves of the cranberry plant. Autumn weather conditions determine to a great extent the amount of photosynthetic activity (carbohydrate-producing capacity) of the vines after harvest, although light nitrogen fertilization may also serve to increase the plant's capacity to produce carbohydrates during this period. Excessive damage to vines by the harvest operation would most definitely be a deterrent to the carbohydrate-producing capacity of the plant.

There is some indication of cultivar differences in the cranberry plant's susceptibility to oxygen deficiency injury (Franklin et al. 1943). In a comparison of the Early Black, Howes, and McFarlin cultivars, flowers and fruits of the Early Black cultivar were found to be the most susceptible to oxygen deficiency injury (table 5.1). In this experiment the degree of injury was found

TABLE 5.1. EFFECTS OF OXYGEN DEFICIENCY ON PRODUCTION OF THREE CRANBERRY CULTIVARS

CULTIVAR AND DEGREE OF O_2 DEFICIENCY*	FLOWERS		FRUIT		
	Per Upright %	Dead Buds %	Fruit Set %	Yield bbls/a (mt/ha)†	Size cc‡
Early Black					
Severe	3.1	12.6	21.6	26 (3.0)	158
Moderate	3.5	12.9	28.0	55 (6.4)	118
Slight	4.0	5.2	28.3	75 (8.6)	110
Howes					
Severe	3.1	16.8	33.3	50 (5.8)	115
Moderate	3.5	17.6	34.9	72 (8.3)	105
Slight	3.7	4.8	49.4	110 (11.5)	100
McFarlin					
Severe	3.9	16.1	20.9	39 (4.5)	94
Moderate	4.0	12.9	23.5	—	94
Slight	4.0	10.0	30.0	81 (9.3)	84

SOURCE: Franklin et al. 1943.

*Degree of O_2 deficiency was obtained by artificially excluding light from the flooded plants. Severe deficiency resulted when O_2 content of water dropped below 2 ppm; moderate deficiency at 2–4 ppm O_2; and slight deficiency above 4 ppm O_2.

†bbls/a = Barrels per acre; mt/ha = metric tons per hectare.

‡Berries per 8-oz. cup.

to be directly related to the length of time the vines were subjected to an oxygen level in the floodwater of less than 4 ppm. Howes flowers and fruits were intermediate in their resistance to oxygen deficiency and those of McFarlin appeared to be the most resistant to oxygen deficiency.

Factors Affecting Oxygen Level in Floodwater

The physical factors that influence the solubility of oxygen in water are pressure and temperature. An increase in pressure causes more oxygen to go into solution, but since flooding depths are relatively shallow, pressure is not an important factor in the overall oxygen content of floodwater. The amount of oxygen dissolved in floodwater is, therefore, essentially a function of temperature (Bergman 1946; N. E. Stevens and Thompson 1943). It is greatest at 32°F (0°C) and decreases as the temperature rises. At 32°F (0°C) water is saturated with oxygen when the level reaches 14.6 ppm; at 40°F (4.4°C), 12.4 ppm; at 50°F (10.0°C), 11.0 ppm.

Photosynthesis, respiration, and biological oxidation are biological processes that have a significant influence on the oxygen balance in floodwater. *Photosynthesis* is an oxygen-producing cellular process in which carbon dioxide and water in the presence of light and the green pigment, chlorophyll, are combined to produce simple sugars and oxygen. All photosynthesizing plants contribute to the oxygen level of the water. In a bog this would include the chlorophyll-containing mosses and algae, in addition to the cranberry vines. The rate of photosynthesis is influenced by temperature, light, and carbon dioxide level. Between 32°F and 39°F (0° to 3.9°C, the temperature of water under ice), the rate of photosynthesis is very slow but it will increase as the temperature is increased provided no other factor is limiting photosynthesis. The temperature coefficient of photosynthesis is about two for many temperate plants, that is, for every celsius degree increase in temperature the rate of photosynthesis is increased by a factor of two within a favorable temperature range.

In flooded bogs light is the most common factor limiting photosynthesis. The amount of light reaching the vines is dependent upon the intensity of the incident light, the depth and clearness of the water, the thickness and clearness of the ice, and the presence or absence of light-obstructing substances upon the ice such as snow or sand (Bergman 1921, 1940; N. E. Stevens and Thompson 1943). The intensity of light on a clear day at high noon is least about 21 December and greatest around 21 June. Cloudiness may be sufficient to decrease the rate of photosynthesis and cause an overall reduction in the oxygen content of the water. The effects of cloudiness are most serious when the cloudiness persists for several days and if the water used for flooding was initially low in oxygen content.

Although the light rays that are most effective in photosynthetic activity (550–650 nm) readily penetrate bog water, the transmittance of the water decreases the longer the water remains on the bog. Water appreciably colored by organic matter may allow only one-third to one-fourth as much light to be transmitted as does clear water. In New Jersey, colored flood-water causes only one-half of the light received at the bog surface to penetrate to a depth of one foot, and at two feet only one-fourth of the surface light reached the vines (Bergman 1945). Conclusive proof of the significance of light on the photosynthetic activity of cranberry vines and subsequent oxygen level in floodwater was presented by Bergman in a series of experiments in which vines underwater were artificially shaded (Franklin et al. 1943).

The formation of ice over the flooded vines can be an effective deterrent to light penetration if snow becomes occluded with the ice or if snow or sand cover the ice (Bergman 1940). Clear ice up to four inches thick will allow as much as 88 percent of the incident light to penetrate the water. Some light may be lost by reflection from the ice. The penetration of light through the ice is greatest at midday and diminishes progressively with the decreasing altitude of the sun. When melted snow becomes mixed with ice, the penetration of light is reduced considerably. An even more effective exclusion of light occurs when a snow cover exists over the ice. An inch of snow will allow only one-fourth to one-third of the incident light to penetrate to the vines; four inches of snow cuts light penetration down to one-twentieth of the incident light. A layer of sand 0.25 inch thick over the ice would have the same effect on light penetration as four inches of snow.

The carbon dioxide level in floodwater rarely limits photosynthesis. The carbon dioxide level in bog water may often exceed the level in air because continuous supplies of the gas are contributed by plant and animal respiration and by the oxidation of organic matter in the water or on the bog or reservoir floor.

Respiration is the antithesis of photosynthesis in that oxygen is utilized to break down the products of photosynthesis in order to obtain the energy required for plant growth. Each living cell carries on this process continuously throughout the life of the cell. The rate at which this process proceeds depends upon the growth activity of the tissue of which the cell is a part. Since respiration involves the utilization of oxygen, this process must play an important role in determining the oxygen balance in floodwater. The rate of respiration is directly related to temperature but, unlike photosynthesis, it is not influenced by light.

Biological oxidation (such as bacterial decomposition) and direct oxidation of organic matter compete for oxygen that might otherwise be available to plants. Bacterial decomposition of organic matter generally places greater demand upon oxygen reserves than does direct oxidation. Water chemists have referred to the demand created for oxygen by organic material in the water as the *biochemical oxygen demand* (BOD) of water. The significance of the BOD of floodwater to oxygen deficiency injury in the cranberry is not known but it could be great. When used for insect control reflows, Wisconsin reservoirs having a high BOD caused considerable damage (C. H. Lewis 1946). High temperatures favor biological oxidation in floodwater. Bergman (1930b) maintained that using floodwater taken from a swamp reservoir on a cloudy day at a temperature greater than 65°F (18.3°C) provides a set of flooding conditions under which injury is almost inevitable. In peat bogs, sanding is sometimes effective in minimizing the suspension of organic matter in floodwater by providing a physical barrier between the organic matter of the bog and the floodwater.

The density of vine growth, the abundance of algae, and the amount of organic matter all influence respiration and photosynthesis and, therefore, the oxygen balance in floodwater. On clear days and in the absence of ice formation, there is little danger of oxygen deficiency injury because photosynthesis produces oxygen at a faster rate than is required by plant and bacterial respiration. Local oxygen deficiencies may arise, however, on exceptionally calm days in the vicinity of the respiring plant and oxidizing organic matter because of the failure of adequate oxygen distribution.

The oxygen content of a flooded bog will tend to remain uniform because the forces of diffusion, convection, and wind action tend to distribute the oxygen throughout the water mass (Bergman 1925, 1931). Diffusion is the molecular movement of oxygen from a region of high concentration to a region of lower concentration. The transfer of oxygen from air to water and from water to air occurs very rapidly by the process of diffusion, but the diffusion of oxygen from one layer of water to another occurs very slowly. It is the rapid diffusion of oxygen from the air to the water that enables convection currents and wind action to equilibrate the oxygen content of the bog water so effectively.

Convection currents occur in floodwater because of temperature differentials that develop. Water has its greatest density at 36°F (2.2°C) and becomes lighter as it becomes warmer or colder. Convection currents are set up if the surface water becomes heavier than the underlying water. The surface water sinks and the water below rises, thereby distributing the oxygen-rich surface water to lower zones. Convection currents are slower and less effective in distributing oxygen than is wind action. However, in the absence of wind they can become important in those situations where the surface of the water is cooled to a greater extent than the lower depths.

An oxygen deficiency may occur on calm days at a depth of only a few inches below the surface of the water, indicating that convection currents and diffusion are not entirely adequate to equalize the oxygen content throughout the water. Wind action represents the most effective means of oxygen distribution. Through wind action the surface water is set in motion, producing currents that carry small masses of surface water saturated with oxygen to lower depths. The effectiveness of wind action depends upon the velocity of the wind and upon its direction. The higher the wind velocity is, the more rapid the mixing process and the greater the depth to which the water is exchanged. The direction of the wind becomes important when bogs are sheltered from wind from certain directions. In ice-covered bogs, wind is eliminated as an agent for oxygen distribution, and it remains for the processes of diffusion and convection to distribute oxygen throughout the floodwater.

The dissolved oxygen content of exposed bog water may vary appreciably between day and night (Bergman 1921). This diurnal variation is affected by the relative rates of photosynthetic and respiratory activities of the submerged plants, the temperature of the water, and the distribution of oxygen throughout the water. Wakabayashi (1925) has shown that the oxygen content in floodwater covering plants in a growth cylinder peaks during the afternoon hours and is at its lowest level during the early morning hours. Similar variation is obtained from submerged open bogs, although the extent of the minimum oxygen levels obtained in the experimental cylinders is not realized in open bogs.

Remedial Measures

The prevention of oxygen deficiency injury depends upon the early and accurate determination of the existence of a critical oxygen level in the floodwater. Bergman (1932) has detailed the procedures for sampling bog water and analyzing the water for oxygen. When it has been determined that a critical situation exists, the alternatives are to add water of a higher oxygen content, to oxygenate the water by some mechanical or chemical means, or to remove the oxygen-depleted water completely.

The Winkler determination (American Public Health Association Inc. 1965, 405–413) is the most common method for the estimation of dissolved oxygen in water. The principle of this method involves the oxidation of manganous hydroxide in a highly alkaline solution by the dissolved oxygen present. In the presence of potassium iodide-azide reagent, molecular iodine is released when sulfuric acid is added to the sample. The liberated iodine is titrated with a standard sodium thiosulfate solution, using starch as an internal indicator. The normality of the thiosulfate solution is adjusted so that 1.0 ml of the titrating solution is equivalent to a dissolved oxygen concentration of 1 ppm.

The recent development of an oxygen sensitive sensor (E. H. Sargent and Co. 1966) has made it possible to determine directly the dissolved oxygen content in water. A portable galvanic cell consisting of a lead anode surrounded by a silver cathode in an epoxy plastic housing is battery operated and capable of measuring dissolved oxygen content in water in the range of 0 to 50 ppm. Its accuracy is ± 0.1 ppm. The chief advantages of this method of oxygen analysis are the ability to make direct determinations of oxygen in the field; the ease of monitoring the dissolved oxygen content of different depths (simply by raising or lowering the probe); and the quickness of the process (just the time it takes to read the galvanometer dial). This portable instrument has an initial cost of approximately $400 and requires another $10 per year to maintain.

In addition to keeping a check on the dissolved oxygen level in bog water, it is desirable to take certain precautions when flooding for specific purposes. The development of effective, modern insecticides has led to the nearly complete elimination of spring and summer reflows as a method of insect control. Insect reflows may still be used in the event of a severe infestation by a particular insect that threatens an entire crop. The effectiveness of this method of control depends upon timing the flood so that maximum insect destruction is attained. Some consideration should be given, however, to the quality of the water and the environmental conditions that prevail so that minimum oxygen deficiency injury is experienced. Floodwater low in organic matter content and applied during a period of clear weather would favor minimum injury. Maintaining the flood for longer than 48 hours at this time would entail considerable risk to the plants (Bergman 1931).

Frost reflows ordinarily would not be expected to cause any appreciable oxygen deficiency injury. Precautions that should be considered include using clear water and removing the floodwater immediately after the frost danger is past. When injury does occur, it is generally the result of allowing the water to remain on the bogs for longer than 24 hours because of the lack of water reserves for frequent reflows. Shallow reflows are all that is necessary for frost control. When a prolonged cold spell requires consecutive reflows, it may be possible to drain the bogs partially so as to allow the water to remain high in the ditches. Subsequent reflows would not require as great a volume of water as that required when the bog is completely drained. This technique is effective if the bogs are uniformly level.

During the winter flood, oxygen deficiency injury can be minimized by flooding shallowly, by drawing the floodwater from under the ice, and by keeping the winter flood period as short as possible. Franklin et al. (1943) recommend a shallow flood of 12 to 15 inches (30–38 cm) even for bogs considerably out of grade. This often results in a large number of vines becoming frozen into the ice. It has been observed that vines frozen in the ice produce larger crops and bear more regularly than deeply flooded vines (Bergman 1947, 1948, 1949). The temperature of the ice is, of course, never greater than 32°F (0°C) and it may often be less. The temperature at the surface of the ice is always near that of the air when air temperatures are below freezing. At temperatures below freezing, a temperature gradient is established in the ice between the upper and lower surfaces of the ice. When air temperatures are below freezing, the ice temperature may be considerably less than the water beneath the ice. When air temperatures are above freezing, the ice temperature remains about 3 to 4 Fahrenheit degrees colder than the water under the ice. At these low temperatures, the respiration rate of plant tissues is extremely slow and therefore little oxygen is required. The small amount of oxygen needed by the vines is adequately provided by the dissolved oxygen content of the ice.

After the formation of 4 to 6 inches (10–15 cm) of ice, winter floodwaters are often drawn from under the ice in Massachusetts and Wisconsin (Franklin et al. 1943). If the ice becomes snow covered before the ice reaches this thickness, the water should be drawn immediately before the oxygen content of the water is appreciably lowered. In the absence of light, the dissolved oxygen content of the water may be consumed within three or four days. By drawing the water from under the ice, the ice is allowed to drop upon the vines where it remains until it melts. The temperature of vines under a layer of ice would be much lower than the temperature of vines in water under the ice. If the ice melts during a midwinter thaw (as is often the case in Massachusetts and New Jersey), it would be necessary to reflood the bogs.

The decision to draw water from under clear ice is, therefore, influenced by the availability of water for reflows. When the ice becomes snow covered, the availability of water for reflow can no longer be considered in the decision; the bogs should be drawn. When the ice is allowed to drop on the surface of the bog, the vines freeze only to the lower surface of the ice and do not become embedded into the ice. If a bog is reflooded before the ice melts, the water is generally warm enough to melt the ice around the vines so that the vines are not torn out when the ice lifts.

Franklin et al. (1943) recommend that the winter flood be held for as short a period as possible. This may be accomplished both by delaying the flooding of the bog and by withdrawing the flood as early as possible. The date for initiating the winter flood depends upon the severity of the winter in the different growing areas. The winter flood is placed on Wisconsin bogs by mid-November, by early December in Massachusetts, and by mid-December on New Jersey bogs. Floodwaters are withdrawn by mid-April in Wisconsin and anywhere from early April to mid-May in Massachusetts and New Jersey. When water reserves are short, growers tend to retain the winter flood longer in order to reduce the need for a large number of spring reflows for frost control. Massachusetts growers often draw the winter flood in early April, allow the bogs to remain open for two to three weeks, and then reflow until about mid-May (Bergman 1949).

Attempts to oxygenate floodwater by mechanical aeration and chemical additives have been confined to experimental trials. In Wisconsin a system of splash boards placed at angles in the flooding gates has been used to agitate and thereby aerate the water (C. H. Lewis 1946). The results were neither replicated nor compared to controls, so no definite conclusions could be drawn as to the effectiveness of this method in increasing the oxygen level of the floodwater. In New Jersey Wakabayashi (1925) has successfully increased the oxygen level in bog water by chemical means. When applied during an active period of photosynthetic activity, gaseous oxygen and carbon dioxide increased the oxygen level of floodwater to the extent that oxygen deficiency injury was prevented on experimental plants. Hydrogen peroxide (H_2O_2) also was an effective source of oxygen. It was nontoxic to the plants and, when applied to floodwater in even dilute solutions, it rendered highly colored bog water entirely colorless. Sodium bicarbonate stimulated photosynthetic activity when added at the rate of 0.5 g per gallon (3.78 l) of water, although sodium carbonate and calcium carbonate did not. No recorded attempts have been made to expand upon these results. Additional experimental data are needed not only to determine rates and concentrations of these active oxygenating agents and any others that are capable of contributing to the oxygen level of bog water but also to determine whether it may be practical under certain conditions to artificially oxygenate bog water.

Soil and Water

Soil Requirements

Cranberries can be grown successfully in a wide range of soils extending from pure sand to peat provided the substrate has an acidic soil reaction (Darrow et al. 1924a; Franklin 1948a). Whereas most agronomic crops prefer a soil pH closer to neutrality (7.0), cranberries (like the related blueberries) require a soil pH between 4.0 and 5.5. (E. L. Eaton 1957). Chandler and Demoranville (1961a) found that the pH of the majority of cranberry bogs in Massachusetts ranged between 4.2 and 4.6. Bogs with the best production records were most often found to have a soil pH at the lower (more acidic) end of the range. They found that the lower the pH, the higher the available soil phosphorus level and the fewer the weeds. In Wisconsin, the pH of bogs can range from a low of 3.5, in sphagnum moss bogs, to a high of 7.0, in bogs that had been irrigated for years with alkaline water (Peltier 1964).

Cranberry vines have been known to respond to limestone applications on soils below a pH of 4.0. When the soil pH is near neutrality, it was observed that not only did the cranberries not grow well but the bog grasses and sedges were replaced by annual and perennial weeds common to upland soils. The pH in such cases must be lowered by sulfur addition. Szpunar (1985) has suc-

cessfully grown cranberries in swamp soil with a pH of 6.6 when it was treated with 10 tons of sulfur per hectare before planting and top dressed with
another 5 tons in four doses.

The preferred substrate is an acid peat soil (Shear 1915). The organic matter content in well-decomposed peat or muck has a number of beneficial characteristics that favor cranberry growth. Bear (1949) has shown that acid peat
can be a significant source of nitrogen and boron, which become available to
the plant as the organic matter decomposes. The organic matter in peat soil
also has a very high cation-exchange capacity, which gives it the potential for
storing a large amount of nutrient elements (Colby 1947). The predominance
of the hydrogen ion at these cation-exchange sites is what gives the cranberry
soil its acid pH. Cranberries appear to thrive in this relatively infertile environment. Finally, the organic matter provides a tremendous capacity to
store water, which is crucial to good cranberry growth.

Cranberry soils can vary tremendously in organic matter content, depending upon the conditions under which they developed. Underwater or poorly
drained conditions, organic matter tends to decompose very slowly. In this
environment organic matter may accumulate faster than it decomposes.
When bogland is drained, the organic matter begins to decompose very
rapidly, releasing its stored-up nutrients. Plantings made on these recently
drained soils usually make excessive vine growth at the expense of fruiting
and, therefore, require special management practices. With the rapid decomposition of the organic material in deep, highly organic bogland soils, there
also occurs an appreciable amount of subsidence that can cause planting diffi-
culties. It is often desirable to wait a number of years after draining bog land to
allow the land to settle before planting vines. These highly organic soils are
referred to as cranberry muck soils or as mud bottom soils.

A more common and perhaps preferred soil profile is that of a plow layer of
mixed mineral soil and organic muck 6 to 12 inches (15–30 cm) deep overlay-
ing 8 to 12 inches (20–30 cm) of sand on top of a hardpan (Beckwith 1922).
Such a soil environment can be found in all of the major cranberry-growing
areas of North America. In New Jersey these are the so-called savannas (gray
sands) that are favored for cranberry production. The organic matter in these
soils can vary from as little as 2 percent to as much as 20 percent (above which
they would be classified as a muck soil). These soils are classified as Berryland sands in the current soil classification scheme of the Soil Conservation
Service.

Microbial Populations in Cranberry Soils

It is generally believed that the highly acidic nature of cranberry soils and the
high degree of moisture saturation that is maintained precludes the existence
of a significant variety of soil microflora other than the molds (Waksman

1918). Both of these soil conditions are unfavorable for the soil nitrifiers needed to complete the nitrogen cycle (Colby 1947). Because cranberries are able to thrive on the reduced forms of nitrogen, it would appear that the complete nitrogen cycle is not essential to the normal functioning of the cranberry plant (Addoms and Mounce 1931, 1932). Waksman (1918), however, demonstrated that by raising the pH of cranberry soil (a savanna soil) from pH 5.2 to 6.2, *Azotobacter* and *Actinomyces* could be induced to grow in the cranberry soil. Moreover, the rise in pH, brought about by the addition of four tons of limestone per acre (9.2 metric tons per ha), resulted in a doubling in yield that Waksman (1919) attributed to both the activity of the *Actinomyces* in decomposing the organic matter and the nitrogen fixation by *Azotobacter*.

The microflora of cranberry soils can affect the degradation of the insecticide parathion. This was the conclusion that Ferris and Lichtenstein (1980) arrived at when they studied the radioactive by-products of ^{14}C parathion breakdown as influenced by different agricultural chemicals. Fungicides and herbicides tended to suppress parathion breakdown, and nitrogen fertilizers tended to alter the degradation by-products.

Pesticide Residues in Soils

Both the chlorinated hydrocarbon insecticides and herbicides appear to be rather persistent in cranberry soils. In part their effectiveness as insecticides or herbicides is dependent on the compounds' ability to remain in the root environment of the plant. In controlled experiments, Miller (1966) and Deubert (1971) showed not only that most of the applied insecticide dieldrin remained in the soil but also that 87 percent remained in the top two inches of the profile. Persistence in the soil was directly related to the organic matter content of the soil. Deubert and Zuckerman (1969) found that large amounts of dieldrin and DDT could still be found in cranberry soils 13 years after the last application of the chemicals, again pointing to the lack of vertical movement of the compounds in the soil. There was some indication, however, that the materials tended to move horizontally with the movement of floodwater.

Miller and his associates (Miller et al. 1966b) also demonstrated that the herbicide dichlobenil persisted mainly in the top four inches of the cranberry soil profile, where it was held primarily by the organic matter. Residues of Casoron and its breakdown product found two years after application points to the persistence of this herbicide in cranberry soil (Miller et al. 1966a). Most of the herbicide was restricted to the upper four inches of the profile and there was no indication of significant lateral movement in the soil.

Water Quality

A problem that appears to be indigenous to the Wisconsin cranberry-growing region is that of alkaline water and the associated hardness (mineral content) of the water. Stevens and his colleagues (N. E. Stevens et al. 1940) described some of the cranberry growth manifestations associated with alkaline water as follows: the occurrence of different, and sometimes more serious, weeds; excess vine growth; overgrowth and absorption of flower buds (failure of uprights to flower); excess leaf drop; and abnormally small crops over a period of years. The critical pH for floodwater was set at 7.0, which represents the dividing line between soft and medium-hard water.

A water quality problem associated with the East Coast cranberry-growing regions is that of saltwater intrusion resulting from hurricanes and severe coastal storms. Chandler (1954d) and Chandler and Demoranville (1959) have documented the harmful effects of saltwater intrusion and other injury caused by a series of hurricanes to hit the Massachusetts coast in 1954. Bogs that were inundated with salt water had their vines killed when chloride levels in the soil exceeded 500 ppm (20 to 200 ppm Cl^- is normal). Salt injury appeared to be most severe on bogs that had been recently disturbed, such as by scooping, and on bogs low in organic matter. Water supplies were severely contaminated by salt water, reaching levels 80 percent of seawater (8200 ppm) in some instances. Three years after the inundation, some water supplies were still registering chloride levels four times higher than prehurricane levels. Chlorides are also difficult to remove from the soil profile. Thirty years after the 1938 hurricane, chloride levels in one contaminated bog still measured nearly 200 ppm chloride. The use of road salt to maintain ice-free roads during the winter can be another potential source of salt contamination if road runoff is allowed to drain into cranberry water supplies (Deubert 1969b).

Another water-quality concern is the potential for contamination by pesticides. Contamination of runoff and groundwater is of concern because of the possible lethal effect of the chemicals on aquatic life and possible pollution of drinking water. Massachusetts researchers have studied the persistence and movement of dieldrin and parathion in bog floodwaters and the effect of pesticide residues on aquatic life in considerable detail (Miller, Tomlinson, and Norgren 1967; Miller, Zuckerman, and Charig 1966, 1967). Although most of the chemicals disappeared from the treated water in 144 hours, fish and freshwater mussels accumulated the pesticides or their metabolites often to levels far in excess of those found in the water. The level of diazinon contamination studied did not result in fish or mussel mortality, but levels of 0.07 ppm parathion in the water resulted in extensive fish kill. Movement of parathion from the irrigation waters to an associated water system can occur readily, and because the concentration at which aquatic toxicity can occur persists for as much as 96 hours, it is important that no water movement be allowed through the bogs during this critical period. In subsequent studies, however, Zuckerman and Mackiewicz (1969) found that applied parathion to stream water did not mix readily with subsurface water but instead tended to remain at the surface, where it volatilized readily. Examination of brain tissue of trout caught downstream showed no evidence of parathion or its metabolites.

Another chemical that has the potential to pollute water systems is copper sulfate, although it does not have the aquatic phytotoxicity of parathion. Copper sulfate is used to control algal growth in cranberry bogs during the winter flood period. Deubert and Demoranville (1970) found that if the floodwater was retained for at least four weeks after the application of the copper sulfate, the copper concentration of the water will have returned to its original level, the copper having been adsorbed to the soil and organic particles on the bog floor. It is generally accepted that copper so adsorbed is released only very slowly to the environment.

Runoff from cranberry bogs is apparently very low in soluble nitrogen and phosphorus, the elements that contribute most to the eutrophication of lakes (Deubert 1972). Nitrate levels in bog discharge waters were less than 0.2 ppm, well below the level considered significant for water contamination. Phosphorus levels averaged 0.038 ppm, below the level considered optimum for algae growth. These small nutrient losses are in keeping with the relatively small amount of fertilizer that is required for cranberry production, when compared to an upland agronomic crop such as corn. Similarly low values for soluble phosphorus and nitrate nitrogen were found in discharge waters from cranberry bogs in the Manitowish Waters area of Wisconsin (Konrad and Bryans 1975). The discharge water from these cranberry bogs contained less than 2 percent of the nitrogen applied in the fertilizer and 4 percent of the phosphorus.

Gray (1972) analyzed water samples from point sources that were subject to cranberry-growing activity in Massachusetts and those that were not. In every case there was no significant difference in water composition between the two sources, which suggests that cranberry culture had not changed the quality of the water in the region.

Climate and Weather

Comparison of the Major Growing Areas

Under native conditions the American cranberry needs about 150 frost-free days to successfully mature a crop of berries. Although this would not appear to be a particularly significant limitation to growth for the major cranberry growing areas, the specific microclimatic conditions of the flat, low-lying sites favor frequent late frosts in the spring and early frosts in the fall. It is for this reason that yields from wild plantings are usually small and very erratic. In Wisconsin, frosts are known to occur in any month of the year, whereas on the East and West coasts midsummer frosts are unknown (Cox 1910). In addition, the cranberry plant appears to favor a growing season with moderate temperature—one that is not too cool so as to retard fruit development nor too warm so as to cause the death of flowers and fruits or to encourage fruit rot (Darrow et al. 1924a). New Jersey, therefore, appears to be the southern limit for successful commercial production of the cranberry. The coolness of summer and the shortness of the growing season would set the northern limits for commercial production.

Of the four major cranberry producing regions, the Pacific Coast has the most moderate climate and perhaps the most favorable for cranberry growth and development (table 5.2). The cool summers in this region are due to the frequent fogs that affect the area during the growing season. Poole (1986) attributes the high anthocyanin content that West Coast cranberries are noted for to this long, cool growing season. Although the Pacific Coast receives 65 inches (1650 mm) of rain per year on average, only about 12 percent of it falls during the growing season, which makes some form of irrigation essential. Evapotranspiration averages about 1.5 inches (38 mm) per week during the long days of June and July, much more than is supplied by rainfall during this period.

Effects of Weather Extremes

The damaging effects of frost and of inundations of salt water by coastal storms have already been addressed. There is another weather extreme, however, that is the bane of all farmers, and that is hail. Hail is associated with

TABLE 5.2. COMPARISON OF THE CLIMATE FOR THE MAJOR CRANBERRY-GROWING REGIONS IN THE UNITED STATES

GROWING REGION	GROWING SEASON* DAYS	TEMPERATURE† °F (°C)	RAINFALL* IN. (mm)	SUNSHINE§ %
Pacific Coast	280	57 (13.9)	65 (1650)	50
Massachusetts	180	61 (16.1)	44 (1118)	61
New Jersey	190	68 (20.0)	47 (1194)	62
Wisconsin	170	60 (15.5)	21 (813)	64

*Number of days between the average date for the last frost in the spring and the average date for the first frost in the fall.
†Average daily mean temperature during the growing season.
‡Average annual precipitation.
§Percentage of total possible sunshine during the growing season at Bandon, Oregon; Boston, Massachusetts; Philadelphia, Pennsylvania; LaCrosse, Wisconsin.

thunderstorms that occur most often from May to September. Crop losses caused by hail can take three forms: (1) immature berries knocked off by the force of the hail are considered a total loss; (2) berries that have deep wounds are also considered a total loss; and (3) berries that are merely dented and are able to continue their maturation can still be used in processing (Peltier 1959). If the storms occur early enough in the season, the uprights are tender enough to be severely damaged by hail (Chandler 1954c). Chandler described the damage to the berry in detail. Berries hit by hail develop a little red pigment around the impact area before the remaining part of the berry colors. Below the impact area, a cork layer develops and the injured spot becomes a darker brown than a spot resulting from rot or mechanical injury. As long as the skin is not broken, there is little chance for rot to occur, but the appearance of the fruit relegates its use to strained sauce. The extent of hail damage is dependent on the vine density and the percentage of top berries. Growers that are insured for hail damage must calculate the percentage of damage incurred by the hailstorm in order to determine the insurance company's liability.

Effect on Specific Growth Parameters

The role of weather in influencing the oxygen content of the winter flood has already been discussed in detail. Bergman (1948) demonstrated that severe winter conditions of prolonged ice and snow contributed to the low oxygen levels in floodwater that were responsible for the death of cranberry flower buds and for the reduction in fruit set as the result of damaged flower parts. Weather can affect fruit set in yet another way. Peltier (1954) reported that the combination of heavy rains and muggy nights during bloom in Wisconsin resulted in poor pollination and blasted flowers.

Temperature and rainfall during the growing season may also influence the size (weight) of the berry and hence its production, although the response may be cultivar dependent (I. E. Demoranville 1960). The size of Early Black cranberries is favored by warm temperatures and heavy rainfall, whereas the late-harvested Howes cultivar produced heavier berries following dry growing seasons. Franklin (1943) observed that cranberries tended to be larger in size when March temperatures were above normal. He attributed this to the favorable conditions that would result from the early and rapid disappearance of the winter ice under these conditions. Large cranberries were also associated with more than 300 hours of sunshine during December and January, presumably because of the better quality of buds surviving the winter flood under these conditions. Franklin also observed that large cranberries were produced when there was ample rainfall during August and September, when the berries undergo their final and most rapid period of growth.

The relationship between temperature and fruit ripening was examined by Franklin (1943). He found that warmer-than-normal temperatures during March through June favored the early ripening of Early Black cranberries. Warmer-than-normal temperatures during August, on the other hand, retarded berry ripening. July temperatures had no effect on ripening whatsoever. Franklin concluded that when the sum of the mean monthly temperatures at Middleboro, Massachusetts, for the months of March through June was greater than 141, Early Black cranberries will ripen early, and if the sum was less than 133, they would ripen late.

N. E. Stevens (1927) carried out a long-term investigation in which he studied weather conditions during the growing season and related them (specifically temperature) to the keeping quality of fruit, which he ascertained by incubator tests. His conclusions on the relationship between weather and berry keeping quality were as follows: (1) low temperatures during May and June were related to good keeping quality; (2) this relationship was strengthened when the cool May–June period was followed by a warm July and August; (3) a warm May–June period was associated with poor keeping quality; (4) keeping quality was reduced even more if the warm May–June period was followed by a cool July and August. In other words, the weather combination for best fruit quality was cool weather in May and June followed by warm weather in July and August; the worst combination was a warm May and June followed by a cool July and August. Stevens had hoped that by being able to forecast the quality of the cranberry crop, marketing strategies could be developed that would maximize returns to the grower. The introduction of effective modern fungicides and the move to processing has lessened the need for this type of fruit-quality forecast.

Effect on Production

As described above, weather can have a profound effect on cranberry production through temperature extremes, frosts, and oxygen deficiency in the floodwater. The ability to forecast cranberry yields would be valuable to producers in developing management and marketing strategies for their prospective crop. Ever since Franklin (1946) made his detailed observations on the relationship between various weather parameters and cranberry yield, there has been considerable interest in fine-tuning these relationships particularly in light of the recent technological advances that have led to rapid increases in productivity (Degaetano and Shulman 1987; Morzuch et al. 1983). The weather factors that appear to consistently affect cranberry yield are temperature, sunshine, and precipitation (Cross 1983). Factors such as snow cover, evapotranspiration, and available soil moisture do not show up significantly in the correlations with yield (Degaetano and Shulman 1987).

The amount of sunshine that the cranberry plant receives was found by Franklin (1946) to be the most important weather factor in predicting cranberry yield. High crop yields were not related to the amount of sunshine the plants received in the current growing season, however, but rather to the amount of sunshine in the growing season the year before. Franklin attributed this sunshine response to the increased production of nonfruiting uprights during the year prior to crop response. More sunshine meant more favorable conditions for photosynthesis and subsequent vegetative growth. He also found that lots of sunshine in February of the current crop year also favored production, which he interpreted as a response to more favorable oxygen levels in the floodwater. Later, Franklin and Cross (1948) refined the positive sunshine relationship to specifically include the amount of sunshine that cranberry plants received during the months of May, August, September, and November of the previous year. The sunshine response in the late summer and fall was attributed by the authors to the improved condition of the over-wintering buds that would have resulted from the increased photosynthates produced by the favorable growing conditions. In their study of the relationship between weather factors and cranberry yield in New Jersey for the period from 1906 to 1984, Degaetano and Shulman (1987) added the mid-May to mid-June period of the current crop year to the list of periods during which the high incidence of sunshine favors cranberry production. Abundant sunshine during this period would favor less potential loss due to frost (more radiant heat available to plants), rapid bud development, and favorable conditions for early pollination.

Although Franklin (1946) showed only a weak correlation to exist between cold March temperatures and high cranberry yields, Degaetano and Shulman (1987) found temperature to be the most important weather variable in predicting crop yields in New Jersey. Warm but not excessive temperatures during the periods of mid-May to mid-June and mid-October to mid-November in the year prior to the crop year were particularly conducive to high cranberry yields. Warm temperatures during the spring months would favor photosynthetic activity and subsequent new upright formation. Warm temperatures in the fall would favor bud development and its ability to survive the winter flood. In contrast, temperatures much above normal during most of the growing season, particularly during May and June, were detrimental to cranberry production. Cross (1969b) was also of the opinion that high temperatures during late May and early June were particularly debilitating to the cranberry plant. The tender new shoot growth is very susceptible to blast, or desiccation by hot temperatures and drying winds. High temperatures during the final stage of berry development in late August can bring about the condition known as berry scald (Cross 1983). As the berry begins to develop color, the ability to absorb the sun's heat rays increases, resulting in berry temperatures that exceed the ambient temperature. Temperatures as high as 119°F (48.3°C) have been recorded in the cranberry when air temperatures exceeded 100°F (37.8°C). This is sufficient to scald cranberries when the high temperature is accompanied by bright sunshine and no wind. Finally, the New Jersey workers (Degaetano and Shulman 1987) also found that cold temperatures during February and March favored high cranberry yield, which tends to corroborate Franklin's early observations on temperature.

With respect to rainfall, Franklin (1946) concluded that cranberry production was favored when the monthly precipitation during the growing season was between two and four inches (51–102 mm). Both drought and excessive rainfall could result in lowered yields. Drought in August was particularly detrimental because of its adverse effect on berry size. Insufficient rainfall during the spring months could result in insufficient water for frost control. Excessive rainfall during the bloom period can interfere with pollination, and too much rain during the growing season can increase fruit losses due to field rots. Cross (1969b) maintained that adequate precipitation was particularly significant in October of the year prior to the crop. The precipitation at this time, he argued, was needed to enable the vines to recuperate from the mechanical damage caused by the harvest operation.

Morzuch and his associates (Morzuch et al. 1983) took the findings of Franklin and Cross and applied them as variables in a predictive model for cranberry yield. In developing their regression model, the Massachusetts workers factored in the influence that technological advances have on cranberry productivity. They were able to show that 91 percent of the variability in a cranberry crop was attributed to technological factors, and an additional 2 percent of the variability could be explained by the meteorological factors. The predictive model developed by Morzuch and his coworkers is presently being used by some producers to predict their cranberry yields.

SIX

Plant Growth and Development

Growth Habit

Rest Requirement

In late summer or early fall, the terminal bud of the cranberry, which contains the vegetative and floral growing points, enters into a rest period. During this phase of development, the internal conditions within the plant are unfavorable for growth of the meristematic bud, particularly for the processes of cell division and cell enlargement. In this respect the cranberry is similar to other temperate fruit crops such as peaches, apples, and blueberries, which also have a rest requirement. The significance of the rest period is in the fact that this internal control of growth would prevent the plant from initiating growth if a period of abnormally warm temperatures occurs during winter months, when subsequent environmental conditions would not be suitable for the survival of premature growth.

A certain period of chilling is necessary to fulfill the rest requirement of the terminal bud. This chilling requirement, usually expressed in terms of number of hours of plant exposure below 45°F (7.2°C), differs for different plant species and may also differ between cultivars within a plant species. Experiments in Massachusetts by Chandler and Demoranville (1964) have shown that 2500 hours of plant exposure below 45°F were sufficient to produce normal bud break in the cultivars Early Black, Franklin, Howes, and McFarlin. The authors observed that when plants received less than 1500 hours below 45°F, abnormal blossoming occurred. This abnormality in bloom was characterized by the formation of terminal flowers on the upright, that is, the vegetative portion of the bud failed to produce a normal upright above the uppermost flower. This type of bloom, sometimes referred to as *umbrella bloom,* has been attributed to frost injury and other types of damage to the terminal bud such as insect attack or mite injury (I. E. Demoranville and Chandler 1962).

Chandler and Demoranville noted that the longer the cranberry plants were exposed to temperatures below 45°F, the shorter was the period required for the plants to bloom when they were returned to a favorable growing environment. The authors went on to suggest that this might explain the prolonged blossoming that occasionally occurs in Washington and Oregon where 2500 hours below 45°F may not accumulate in some years.

More recently, Eady and Eaton (1969) have shown that the acceleration of bud break in McFarlin cranberries was inversely related to the length of exposure below 45°F when the total cold accumulation was between 650 and 2500 hours. In their experiments McFarlin buds broke after only 650 hours of chilling. This apparent contradiction in response may be explained in part by the differences in cold treatments given to the plants. The cold treatments given the McFarlin plants used by Eady and Eaton in British Columbia were interrupted daily with 4 hours at 58°F (14.4°C), whereas the plants used by the Massachusetts workers were given no interruption in their cold treatment. It appears likely that the interrupted cold period may have influenced internal biochemical changes within the bud tissues, the effect of which was to shorten the buds' rest requirement. This possibility was further supported by the Canadian experiments, in which abnormal vegetative and flower growth (umbrella bloom) was not evident when 650 hours below 45°F (7.2°C) were made available to the plant. In the Pacific Northwest, the type of chilling that cranberry plants receive would resemble the conditions of the Canadian experiment, while in the East and in Wisconsin the conditions under which the Massachusetts work was performed (winter flood) would be the most prevalent.

In subsequent studies, Eady and Eaton (1972a) again found that cranberry buds broke sooner after the completion of the rest requirement when a warm period of about 50°F (10°C) was alternated daily with inductive chilling temperatures. For normal flower development, 125 days of chilling were needed. Chilling for less than 100 days resulted in only vegetative growth. In British Columbia these conditions were met by late February. By the end of April, the flower buds were well differentiated.

Rigby and Dana (1972b) investigated the rest requirement for normal flower development in the Stevens cultivar in Wisconsin. They concluded that all that was needed for normal flowering in the cranberry was 600 to 700 hours of chilling. They further found that for normal flower development to occur after the completion of the rest period, the plant had to receive long days; no flowers were produced under short days. The authors suggested that if the Massachusetts workers had failed to give their cranberry plants long days when testing them for the completion of rest, it might explain the failure of the plants to bloom normally even when they received as much as 1600 hours of chilling. The Wisconsin workers also observed that the completion of rest did not always insure the formation of normal flowers; therefore, flower development may be a separate process to that of the rest requirement. They concluded that a certain amount of heat accumulation must occur interspersed with the cold period in order to produce normal flowers. This supports the Canadian workers' findings of normal flower development from buds that had their cold period interrupted with a four-hour period of warmer temperatures.

Rigby and Dana (1972b) were able to substitute an exogenous application of gibberellic acid (GA_3) for the rest requirement of cranberry buds. The treatment caused more than 80 percent of the buds to break even if they had no cold treatment. In addition, buds that had received their chilling requirement were found to break faster after dormancy if they were treated with gibberellic acid. Flowers that were produced as the result of the plant growth regulator treatment, however, were abnormal in that they were unable to dehisce pollen; they were essentially male-sterile flowers. They were, however, able to produce seed when pollinated with pollen from a normal flower. When Eady and Eaton (1972b) attempted to substitute a gibberellic acid treatment for cold treatment, they were successful in only producing vegetative growth from the terminal buds of the McFarlin cultivar.

Vegetative Growth

The cranberry plant has essentially three types of vegetative buds: terminal, axillary, and adventitious. The terminal bud, as its name suggests, is the bud that terminates the extension of a shoot. In cranberry the bud contains the rudiments of a vegetative shoot and perhaps flowers. As a result the bud can produce either flowers or shoots; more likely it produces both. It is most often located on the tip of the upright but can also be found at the end of a runner. In the terminal bud, the vegetative meristem occupies the apex of the bud.

Axillary buds located at a leaf node either on the runner or on an upright are the source of new shoots, which can be either vertical uprights or horizontal runners, although axillary buds have been known to form flowers on runners, particularly in the McFarlin cultivar. They appear to be controlled by apical dominance exerted by the terminal bud, since the buds will be inclined to break if the terminal bud is destroyed. In this case a shoot will develop from an axillary bud located at a leaf node subtending the terminal bud. These new shoots, however, have been known to go on to flower (Rigby and Dana 1972b). I. V. Hall (1970) demonstrated conclusively that the cranberry plant is strongly influenced by the apical dominance of the terminal bud. In controlled growth-chamber studies, he showed that when the cranberry vine grew in a vertical position, there was a continued growth of the existing shoot, whereas when the shoot was bent over, lateral buds began to develop all along the vine. The practice of sanding vines would serve to bend vines and thus contribute to a loss in apical dominance and an increase in lateral shoot growth. Increased upright density is one of the results of sanding. Pruning vines also serves to remove terminal buds and encourages the breaking of axillary buds, which contributes to an increase in upright density. More recently, Scorza et al. (1984) have been able to increase axillary shoot proliferation from cranberry nodes in tissue culture with the addition of specific growth regulators.

Bain (1940b) has demonstrated the existence of adventitious buds in the cranberry shoot. He showed that if the hypocotyl of cranberry seedlings was severed a few millimeters below the cotyledons, the nodeless stalks invariably produced adventitious buds near the cut end. The shoots originated in the epidermal cell layer of the stalk and were capable of normal growth.

Light intensity and photoperiod are important factors affecting vegetative growth. R. H. Roberts and Struckmeyer (1942) showed that the shade produced by a single layer of cheesecloth increased the length of uprights by 48 percent. The significance of this effect becomes apparent when it is realized that there is an optimum upright length associated with cranberry production. Roberts and Struckmeyer determined this optimum upright length for the Searles cultivar to be between 2.5 and 3.5 inches (6.4–8.9 cm). A heavy density of uprights can bring about shading that can lead to increased upright length, which further compounds the shading effect. The Wisconsin workers concluded that the optimum upright density for the Searles cultivar was from 200 to 300 uprights per square foot (0.09 m^2). The shading produced by weeds can have a similar effect on cranberry uprights (Hicks et al. 1968).

Vegetative growth in the cranberry plant is stimulated by long days (G. W. Eaton and Ormrod 1968; Lenhardt et al. 1976). Eaton and Ormrod found that both the length of cranberry shoots and the total dry matter production increased with increasing day length—up to 21 hours. If the plants were given 24 hours of daylight, they did not produce as much growth as with a 21-hour day. Later, Lenhardt and his associates showed that a 13-hour day was necessary to stimulate growth and accelerate bud break in the spring. In the field the most vigorous vegetative growth of both uprights and runners occurs under the long days of summer. The Canadian workers noted also that short days were not a prerequisite for the beginning of dormancy in the cranberry plant.

The role of endogenous plant growth regulators in cranberry growth was investigated by Eady and Eaton (1972b) and by Luke and Eck (1978). Both groups of researchers extracted gibberellin-like (GA) substances from the cranberry plant at various stages of plant development and attempted to relate the hormonal activity to specific growth occurrences. A novel method of extraction for GA from cranberry tissue was developed by Luke and her associates (Luke et al. 1977) and involved a simple dialysis extraction procedure.

Eady and Eaton extracted GA substances from both the terminal buds and the leaves and found that a translocation of these substances occurred from the leaves to the buds during March and early April. This coincides with the period of terminal bud elongation, but since flower buds are well formed by this time in British Columbia, the GA substances probably do not have an important role in flower bud development. Luke and Eck found that buds and young leaves of Early Black cranberry plants contained relatively high levels of GA activity. The activity in the leaves of uprights declined during July, coinciding with active elongation of the stems, and increased again in August, after terminal bud formation. The authors found high levels of GA activity in the leaves of the runners, which they suggested may represent important sources of GA production during active runner growth.

Photosynthesis and Respiration

Cranberries appear to be able to carry on more efficient photosynthesis (Pn) than its ericaceous relative, the lowbush blueberry (Bonn et al. 1969). The researchers calculated the rate of Pn by measuring the rate at which carbon dioxide (CO_2) was removed by a photosynthesizing plant from an enclosed environment. When measured at a light intensity of 1,000 ft.-c, the Pn rate for a McFarlin cranberry leaf was equivalent to the assimilation of 40.0 mg CO_2/dm^2/hr, as compared to 14.4 for the lowbush blueberry. At 2,000 ft.-c of light intensity, the rate of apparent Pn was still below the saturation level for the cranberry shoots but well above the saturation level for the blueberry plant, which suggests that the cranberry leaf is much more efficient per unit of leaf area than the lowbush blueberry in removing carbon dioxide from the ambient air. Stang and his coworkers (Stang et al. 1982), on the other hand, found much lower rates of apparent Pn in cuttings of the Ben Lear, Crowley, and Searles cultivars. They found that a maximum Pn rate of 22.5 mg CO_2/dm^2/hr occurred at a light level of 700 micro Einsteins and declined to 15.0 mg CO_2/dm^2/hr at 1,650 micro Einsteins, indicating that light saturation had occurred at some intervening light level. When Hicks and her associates (Hicks et al. 1968) measured the Pn rates of cranberry leaves in the field, they found that rates were higher in weedy areas early in the season but higher in pure cranberry stands later in the growing season, possibly because of the shading by the developing weed canopy in the weedy cranberry stand.

Forsyth and Hall (1967b) observed that the rate of apparent Pn increased linearly in the Howes cultivar as temperature increased from 3.5° to 25.0°C.

Up until 15°C the rate of Pn was greater than the rate of oxygen removal by respiration. Even at the low temperature of 3.5°C, which would be common in floodwater, Pn can more than meet the oxygen requirement for respiration.

In addition to being a function of temperature, respiration increases dramatically with the increase in growth activity of the tissue. Bergman (1925) measured the respiration rates of different tissues at different stages of development in the Early Black and Howes cultivars. He found the maximum rates of respiration to occur in the breaking bud and then again in the young fruit one to three days after petal fall. The rate decreased rapidly in the fruit as it developed. The young emerging shoots respired two to three times faster than older shoots. The respiration rates of buds or shoots did not differ substantially between the two cranberry cultivars.

Exogenous Growth Regulator Effects

Plant growth regulators are generally applied to plants either to stimulate some type of growth or reaction or to retard growth or some specific physiological activity. We have already seen how the application of GA has been used as a substitution for the chilling requirement of the cranberry. The use of GA to promote fruit set in the cranberry flower will be discussed under the section on fruit set. The role of growth promoters in the culture of cranberry explants has also been already mentioned. Another group of growth promoters are those that stimulate anthocyanin formation in the cranberry. They will be discussed in the chapter dealing with cranberry harvest. This leaves the second group of plant growth regulators, those referred to as the growth inhibitors or retardants.

Excessive vine growth has been the bane of cranberry growers since the beginning of cranberry cultivation. Not only was an inverse relationship often observed between excessive vegetative growth and production but the added runner growth contributed to a vine environment that was conducive to fruit rot and made it difficult to scoop-harvest the berries. The control of this excessive vegetative growth with a simple application of a plant growth retardant would have great practical significance. Daminozide (succinic acid-2,2-dimethylhydrazide), marketed commercially as Alar, is one such growth retardant that has been used experimentally on cranberries. When Alar was applied two weeks before full bloom, shoot growth was retarded in the current growing season, but after a cold period, shoots from the same plants were greatly stimulated in growth (Doughty and Scheer 1969). Similarly, Luke and Eck (1978) found that in the year following Alar treatment, plants receiving Alar produced more runners than did untreated plants. Although Lenhardt et al. (1976) noticed a reduction in the growth rate of greenhouse plants (McFarlin cultivar) that had been treated with Alar earlier in the growing season, they concluded that their growth control was not satisfactory. In a field study of the McFarlin cultivar, however, Lenhardt and Eaton (1976) observed an increase in the number of uprights that set flower buds. There were no apparent harmful effects. To date, Alar has only been used experimentally on cranberry plants and has not been approved for commercial use.

Maleic hydrazide was found to be a powerful suppressant of cranberry runner growth (Marucci and Moulter 1957, 1958). Not only was the length of the runners reduced by maleic hydrazide treatment but the number of runners that were produced was greatly reduced, indicating that the chemical also acted as an inhibitor. There was a significant increase in the number of uprights produced by the treatment, suggesting that the retardant had affected apical dominance in the plant in some way. Flower, fruit set, and yield were not affected by maleic hydrazide, but some phytotoxicity—characterized by shoot tip yellowing and dieback of uprights—was noted. Since maleic hydrazide is suspected to be a carcinogen, it is no longer being used experimentally on cranberry bogs. Herbicides also have been known to have growth retardant effects on the cranberry (I. E. Demoranville and Devlin 1976).

Recently it has been reported that the cranberry may have its own natural growth inhibitor (Devlin 1980b; Devlin and Deubert 1981). The Massachusetts workers found that extracts of cranberry leaves contained a substance that strongly inhibited the germination of wheat seeds and suppressed wheat seedling growth. Devlin (1980a) speculated that the beneficial effect that the removal of floaters after dry harvest had on subsequent yields was in part due to the removal of dead leaves and trash with the floaters, the implication being that this trash may have been the source of a natural growth inhibitor that suppressed cranberry growth.

Fruiting Habit

Flowering

Blossom induction in the newly forming cranberry terminal bud occurs soon after flowering in June and early July. This is the consensus of those researchers that have studied flowering in the different cranberry-growing regions (Goff 1901; I. V. Hall and Newberry 1972; Lenhardt and Eaton 1977; R. H. Roberts and Struckmeyer 1943). Blossom induction coincides with the period of maximum day length in the northern hemisphere. In fact, Lenhardt and his coworkers (1976) have demonstrated that if plants are kept under short days, they will not form flower buds.

Cranberry uprights have a tendency to biennial bearing (Lenhardt and Eaton 1976, 1977). G. W. Eaton (1978) suggested that this tendency could be altered in either year of the cycle. Defoliation of nonflowering uprights prior to 4 July resulted in a decrease in floral induction but not when the defoliation occurred after this date, suggesting that a floral stimulus existed in the leaf and that 4 July was the date of floral induction for the Bergman cultivar in British Columbia. Early removal of flowers and developing fruit of flowering uprights resulted in an increase in floral induction. The longer the defloration was delayed the greater was the depression in subsequent floral induction of the fruiting upright, which would be consistent with the existence in flowers or developing fruits of an inhibitor of floral induction.

Flower primordia become visible under the microscope by late July in British Columbia (Lenhardt and Eaton 1977), Nova Scotia (Hall and Newberry 1972), and Wisconsin (R. H. Roberts and Struckmeyer 1943), and a few weeks later in Massachusetts (Lacroix 1926). The rate at which the flower bud differentiates is apparently dependent on the vigor of the cultivar and the growing conditions that exist. Lacroix found that the flower buds of Early Black and Howes had differentiated and developed petals and sepals by the end of October. He concluded that in Massachusetts the cranberry flower bud overwinters in this state under the winter flood, and it does not undergo any further development until the water is removed. This is also the stage of bud development that Bell and Burchill (1955) found in overwintering native cranberries in Nova Scotia. In the vigorous Stevens cultivar, however, Hall and Newberry found that by 5 October in Nova Scotia the calyx, corolla, stamens, and pistil were clearly defined in the bud. In Massachusetts this stage was not reached until after the winter flood had been removed for a week or more. In areas not having severe winters and where winter flooding is not practiced, some bud development probably does occur during the winter months.

Each terminal bud may contain two to seven flowers, rarely more than five, as well as leaves and a growing point. With the removal of the winter flood in mid-May, a prolonged flowering period commences in mid-June and lasts into July. Cranberry blossoms in the Stevens cultivar were found to open in about 2 to 12 hours (Rigby and Dana 1972a). Within the next two days, the style had elongated and the stigma had emerged through the anther ring. The stigma became pollen receptive at about the time the petals separated—even before it had emerged through the anther ring. This was sooner than reported for other cultivars (Bain 1933a; Cross 1953a; R. H. Roberts and Struckmeyer 1942).

Pollination is normally performed by bees (Filmer 1955). The viable pollen is shed from the terminal pores in the anther tubes when the flower is agitated. This may occur even before the elongating stigma reaches the position of the pores. The pollen grains of the cranberry are shed as tetrads, each capable of germinating four individual pollen tubes. Rigby and Dana (1972a) found that the pollen tube had traversed the style within 48 hours after pollination, and that within 72 hours fertilization had occurred. Berry development occurs throughout the growing season and is followed by a two-month harvest period starting in September.

Types of Uprights

Uprights may originate from an older vine, as is common in the McFarlin cultivar, from new vines (runners), common to the Bergman cultivar, or from another upright (Tallman and Eaton 1976). The new uprights normally do not flower in their first year, needing first to develop a terminal bud that undergoes the prescribed rest period. The uprights may not always bear a terminal bud, but when they do the buds are one of three types, according to Lacroix (1926): (1) a round, compact, solid bud covered with tightly fitting scales; (2) a loosely set rosette of scales and small leaves; or (3) an elongate, sharply pointed, scale-covered shoot bud. The first type contains flower primordia; the second, usually developing as a result of some injury to the normal terminal bud, does not; and the third type develops only a vegetative shoot. By early October these different bud types are easily discernible in the bog.

Uprights bearing a flower bud or originating from another upright were termed old uprights by Bergman (1950) to distinguish them from the new uprights that originated from the vine and did not flower. Most of the fruit is borne on old uprights, although some cultivars under certain conditions may produce a part of their crop on runners (Crowley 1954). Not all old uprights will flower, however, as indicated by a New Jersey survey which discovered that the old uprights ranged in number from 126 to 563 per square foot whereas the number of flowering uprights ranged from 72 to 478 per square foot (Bergman 1954). The survey also found that the total number of uprights including both flowering and nonflowering types may reach as high as 1,000 per square foot. In a survey of four Wisconsin bogs, Bain (1946) found that the number of uprights per square foot was rarely less than 400 and more often was near 500.

Yield Components

Optimum production would therefore appear to be dependent upon a large population of uprights or, more precisely, upon a large concentration of flowering uprights. Doehlert (1953b) showed that high production was associated with the percentage of uprights with flower buds the previous autumn. He found that in low-yielding areas only 22 percent of the uprights had flowered, as compared to 32 percent in high-yielding areas. He also noted that uprights with 3, 4, and 5 flowers produced 80 percent of the crop. In a detailed survey of the fruiting habit of the Searles cultivar in Wisconsin, Bain (1948) found that 14 to 66 percent of the total number of uprights bloomed with an average of 27 percent. The number of flowers per square foot ranged from 55 to 1128 with an average of 300, and fruit set ranged from 9 to 85 percent with an average of 37 percent. The number of flowers per blossoming upright ranged from 1.2 to 3.5, with 2.5 as the average number of flowers per upright. Bain concluded that when the percentage of blooming uprights was low, there was no compensating increase in the set of berries, and that large yields were the result of an increase in the number of blooming uprights rather than an increase in the percentage of flowers setting fruit. A comparison of Bain's observations on the Searles cultivar with those by other researchers on different cultivars in different cranberry-growing regions is shown in table 6.1.

Perhaps the most striking comparison to be made in these data is the difference in the production of flowering uprights in Massachusetts compared to the other growing regions. Under Massachusetts growing conditions, the

TABLE 6.1. COMPARISON OF YIELD COMPONENTS OF DIFFERENT CRANBERRY CULTIVARS IN VARIOUS GROWING REGIONS

| | YIELD COMPONENT | | |
Cultivar and Region	Uprights Blooming %	Flowers/Upright N	Fruit Set %
Searles Wisconsin	27 (14–66)	2.5 (1.2–3.5)	37 (9–85)
Early Black New Jersey	30 (26–33)	3.2 (2.4–4.0)	44 (42–47)
Early Black Massachusetts	87 (77–94)	3.4 (2.2–4.1)	25 (22–46)
Howes Massachusetts	84 (72–93)	3.1 (2.2–4.2)	21 (8–55)
McFarlin Massachusetts	89 (87–90)	3.5 (2.6–4.5)	30 (12–61)
Bergman British Columbia	—	3.0*	13*

SOURCES: Searles data from Bain 1948; Early Black New Jersey data from Filmer 1955; Early Black Massachusetts data as well as Howes and McFarlin data from Bergman 1950; Bergman data from G. W. Eaton and Macpherson 1978.
NOTES: Values in parentheses represent range found in samples.
*Range not calculated.

proportion of uprights flowering is nearly three times that found in Wisconsin and New Jersey. This difference does not seem to be cultivar related since it appears to hold for all the cultivars tested in Massachusetts. The difference appears to be a result of the method used to determine the number of flowering uprights. In New Jersey and Wisconsin the upright was not considered to be a flowering upright unless it actually produced a flower. In Massachusetts, on the other hand, Bergman scrutinized every upright with a hand lens, and if he observed what he thought was a bud with flower primordia, he would classify it as a flowering upright. His tabulations would, therefore, include many uprights that never actually flowered. Bergman attributed the failure of these uprights to flower to possible oxygen deficiency and frost injury. Because his flowering upright counts included these nonflowering uprights with flower primordia, and because they were used in assessing percentage fruit set, the result was that fruit set data reported from Massachusetts were consistently lower than the data reported from the other major growing regions.

Studies of the morphological components of cranberry yield in British Columbia and Washington bogs showed that the number of flowering uprights per unit area and the fruit set percentage made the most important contributions to cranberry yield (G. W. Eaton and Kyte 1978; G. W. Eaton and MacPherson 1978; Shawa et al. 1981). The number of total uprights, the number of flowers per upright, and the size of the individual berry were less important. In later studies Baumann and Eaton (1986) confirmed that fruit set was the most important component in cranberry yield, but berry size and the number of flowers per centimeter of upright were next in importance. The Ben Lear cultivar was found to set more fruit than either the McFarlin or Bergman cultivar. Although the Searles cultivar has about 25 percent fewer flowers per upright than the Early Black, Howes, and McFarlin cultivars, its large fruit size contributes to its high productivity.

Edaphic and environmental factors which favor the initiation and development of flower buds as well as the formation of uprights would therefore be necessary for optimum yield. The influence of temperature on flower bud initiation and development serves as an example. Under commercial conditions, the largest crops seem to be harvested in years following a high mean annual temperature. It is axiomatic that those edaphic conditions which include the nutritional status of plant and soil would also influence flower bud development and subsequent yield.

Objective Yield Analysis

The ability to forecast a potential crop weeks before it is harvested has distinct advantages for management, marketing, and promotional purposes. Two approaches have been taken in developing the predictive models that can be used in such a crop forecast: (1) a model based on the actual measurement of some parameter related to crop yield (objective analysis); and (2) a model based on aggregate yield over time which reflects technological advances and certain weather parameters.

The New Jersey Crop Reporting Service uses a cranberry objective yield analysis model based on the weight of berries taken from sample squares in mid-August (Barrowman 1968; St. Pierre 1966). Using this method the authors were able to improve upon former forecasts that were based on growers' subjective yield estimates. To further improve on the forecasts, they felt that additional information was needed, such as weather factors that might influence berry development from the period of measurement to final harvest.

Morzuch and his associates (Morzuch 1982; Morzuch and Dudek 1984) used a different approach to predicting yield. They developed an econometric structural model that factored in the effects of technological advances on yield over a specified period of time as well as selected precipitation and temperature variables (based on Franklin's weather studies [Franklin 1943]). When the authors compared the yield values obtained from their mathematical model with the actual yield for the period from 1932 to 1982, they were able to come up with a very close fit that statistically was highly significant with a correlation coefficient of 0.91. The model can be altered to growers' specific situations if the necessary parameters are known.

Pollination

Requirement

The formation of the cranberry fruit is dependent upon the successful fertilization of the ova within the cranberry flower with the subsequent formation of one or more seeds. Pollination, the transfer of pollen from an anther to the stigma of a flower, is a prerequisite to fertilization and seed formation. Although seedless cranberry fruit do occur, they generally are very small and are of no commercial value (R. H. Roberts and Struckmeyer 1942). There is, in fact, a direct relationship between berry size and the number of seeds found in the berry (Filmer et al. 1958).

Method

The cranberry is self-fruitful, that is, the pollen from a given flower may fertilize the ova of that same flower. This fact, combined with a flower anatomy that is conducive to self-pollination, led some researchers to suggest that agitation of the flower was sufficient to bring about pollination. Roberts and

Struckmeyer (1942) suggested that bees did not transfer pollen directly via body contact with the flower parts but rather indirectly by jarring the flower, thus releasing the pollen in close proximity to the stigma. Rigby and Dana (1972a) have since shown, however, that cranberry pollen is mature before the stigma emerges from the anther ring, which would argue against self-pollination.

Roberts and Struckmeyer were of the opinion that wind-borne pollination was effective over short distances. Filmer (1949), however, showed that wind and the mechanical jarring of blossoms were ineffective in promoting pollination of cranberries. The heavy and sticky nature of cranberry pollen would support this conclusion (Stricker 1946), although pollen traps set above a bog surface have collected significant amounts of wind-borne pollen (Papke et al. 1980). Nevertheless, Papke and coworkers observed a pronounced dilution effect with distance from the pollen source and concluded that compared to goldenrod and ragweed, there is relatively little cranberry pollen produced per cubic meter of air, making wind pollination unlikely in cranberry bogs. Observations by Farrar and Bain (1946) that bees did indeed probe between anthers and pistil in their attempt to reach nectar at the base of the flower, and in so doing came in contact with the stigmatic surface, suggested that bees were probably very much involved in cranberry pollination. The sugar content of cranberry nectar is apparently fairly high, averaging between 46 and 55 percent in different cultivars (Shaw et al. 1956).

Subsequent research, in which caged plants were either subjected to insects or protected from insects, well documented the need for insect pollination—whether indirectly as flower agitators or directly as agents for pollen transfer (Farrar and Bain 1946; Filmer 1949, 1953; Hutson 1925, 1929). Filmer and Doehlert (1959) proved conclusively that flower agitation was not adequate to produce a commercial cranberry crop when they included in their caging experiments various agitation methods designed to dislodge pollen. Only 15 berries per square foot developed on caged plants receiving agitation as compared to 90 to 152 berries per square foot on plants that received insect pollination.

Self-Pollination versus Cross-Pollination

Although there is no doubt that the cranberry is self-fertile, it is seldom possible to increase fruit set in cranberry to more than 50 percent even with a heavy concentration of bees. In a few instances when a higher percentage of fruit set has been reported, it was usually in vines containing a mixture of cultivars (Stricker 1946). Mixtures are probably not unusual because there is little reason why seedlings cannot become established in older bogs. Pure stands of old cultivars are rare. Marucci and Filmer (1964) showed that greater fruit set, larger berries, and higher seed count occurred when cranberry flowers were cross-pollinated. In a bog where cranberry cultivars were interplanted, fruit set was measured at 68 percent compared with 30 to 40 percent for solid block plantings of a single cultivar. Similarly, Bain (1933a) showed that more seed were produced when the stigmas of the McFarlin and Early Black cultivars were pollinated with pollen from another cultivar than when self-pollination occurred. This would suggest that cross-pollination might result in larger berries.

Fruit Set

Importance

An acre of cranberries is capable of producing as many as 20 million blossoms (Marucci and Filmer 1957). If every blossom matured a fruit, that acre would produce about 450 barrels of cranberries. Yields of this magnitude, although theoretically possible, have not as yet been achieved in the cranberry industry. The principal reason for the failure to attain this theoretical yield is that only about one-third of the potential blossoms in a cranberry bog will set fruit (Bain 1946; Bergman 1950). It is also doubtful that one could ever attain the uniformity in stand necessary to obtain maximum production over a large area. Based on the harvest of a single square-foot sample of the Bergman cultivar, G. W. Eaton (letter to author, 1989) calculated a yield at the rate of 510 barrels per acre, which points to the potential of cranberry production if all factors that affected yield were optimum.

In order for fruit set to occur, a number of things must happen after pollination (Cross 1966). Only pollen which adheres to a receptive stigma will germinate. The stigma of the cranberry flower becomes receptive about 24 to 36 hours after the male parts of the flower have begun shedding pollen. Rigby and Dana (1972a), however, have observed that stigma receptivity in the Stevens cultivar occurs at the time of petal separation. Apparently the exact time of stigma receptivity varies for different cultivars.

Each pollen tetrad consists of four pollen grains which are each capable of germination and eventual union with an egg. Germination occurs when the pollen tube grows from the surface of the stigma down through the canal in the center of the style and enters one of the locules in the ovary. With the union of the nuclear material from the pollen grain with the nuclear material of the ovule, fertilization is consummated and a seed begins to form. Within 36 to 48 hours after pollination, a noticeable swelling of the ovary tissues occurs. Unfertilized flowers may hang on for more than three weeks, the petals taking on a rosy coloration during this time. For good fruit set, most of the flowers should open and fertilization take place followed by petal fall within a two-week period (Marucci and Moulter 1978).

Factors Affecting Fruit Set

The failure of the cranberry flower to set fruit—*blossom blast,* as some researchers have called it (Marucci and Filmer 1957; R. B. Wilcox 1940a)—may result for a number of reasons. Marucci (1967) was of the opinion that most blossom blast is the result of natural attrition of the blossoms due to an overproduction of blossoms and an inadequate energy reserve to produce a fruit from every flower. Such an energy theory might also explain the *physiological blast* or *natural blast* that Wilcox (1940a) described as occurring the year after a heavy crop and after a season of excessive rainfall throughout the late summer. The lack of pollination, of course, could seriously aggravate the natural blast present in the cranberry. The fact that Marucci and Filmer (1964) found that a high concentration of bees did not decrease blossom blast supports the natural blast theory.

Weather also has a strong influence on fruit set. Wilcox (1940a) observed that poor fruit set was associated with severe cold before flooding in the fall and with severe frost in the spring before flower buds expand. Excessively high temperature in the spring, especially where moisture supply was deficient, was particularly detrimental to fruit set. Cold night temperatures (short of freezing) during the bloom period did not appear to affect fruit set (Bain 1926). Adverse weather conditions, which influence insect activity, may have a significant effect on fruit set (Marucci and Filmer 1957). Cold daytime temperatures, rain, and high winds for any prolonged period during bloom would adversely affect pollination and, consequently, fruit set.

Other conditions that have been associated with poor fruit set are oxygen deficiency during the winter flood and particularly during June reflows, nutrition imbalance, tipworm injury, false blossom disease, and fungus attack (Bergman 1948; Marucci and Filmer 1957).

The application of fungicides during bloom may influence fruit set by affecting pollen germination (Shawa et al. 1966; Bristow and Shawa 1981). Pollen germination was reduced by 50 percent when flowers were sprayed with Captan, Ferbam, Maneb, or Phaltan. The reduction in pollen germination was associated with significant yield losses. Zineb was less phytotoxic to cranberry pollen than the other fungicides and did not reduce cranberry yields. Bristow and Shawa found that triforine-EC, when sprayed on flowers, reduced pollen germination and produced smaller and lighter berries. As a result, there was a 41 percent yield reduction.

Parthenocarpy

The production of seedless cranberries through the use of plant growth-regulating chemicals has been shown to be possible (Devlin and Demoranville

1967; Mainland and Eck 1968). Gibberellic acid has proven to be particularly effective in increasing fruit set and yield; however, serious growth side effects have made its use questionable. In addition to small fruit size, plants produced few flowers and abnormally long uprights in the year after gibberellic acid application. Devlin and Demoranville found that Gibrel, a commercial preparation of gibberellic acid, produced less severe growth effects than laboratory-grade gibberellin.

Auxins have also been found to increase fruit set in the cranberry (Doughty 1962a). Materials that increased yield the year after its application were CPA (p-chlorophenoxyacetic acid) and 2,4,5-T (2,4,5-trichloroacetic acid). Increased fruit set without increased yield was obtained with NAA (1-naphthaleneacetic acid), 2,4,5 TP (2,4,5-trichlorophenoxypropionic acid), and NOA (β-naphthoxyacetic acid). Doehlert (1956), on the other hand, was unable to increase fruit set in cranberries with a commercial fruit-setting hormone preparation containing auxin that has been successfully used on vegetables and other fruits.

Fruit Development

Size

With the successful consummation of fertilization, fruit growth and development are initiated. The enlargement of the ovary occurs rapidly throughout the major part of the growing season and slows perceptively as the harvest season approaches (fig. 6.1). Unlike the blueberry which has two distinct periods of rapid fruit growth (Eck and Childers 1966), the growth curve of the cranberry is characterized by a single initial growth surge that is sustained (Chandler 1952b). Chandler observed that the growth curves for the larger-fruited McFarlin and the smaller-fruited Early Black and Howes cultivars were qualitatively similar. By mid-July fruit of these three cultivars averaged 0.5 g/berry. During the next six weeks, Early Black and Howes berries increased at the rate of approximately 0.020 g/day, and McFarlin berries at an even faster rate. Fruit from Early Black and Howes bogs in which the winter flood was held until late May averaged a daily increase of 0.024 g/berry during the month of August. Growth rates during September averaged only 0.0005 g/berry/day for Early Black and Howes from early-drawn bogs and 0.005 g/berry/day for fruit from late-held bogs. Growth rates were exceedingly slow after mid-September, suggesting that there was no size advantage in delaying harvest beyond this period. Early Black and Howes cranberries from late-held bogs attained berry sizes by the end of the growing season comparable to those from early-drawn bogs.

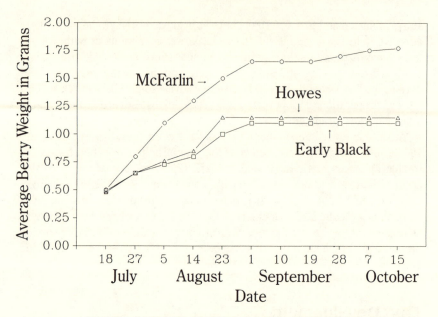

Cross (1954), however, observed that Early Black berries increased in weight by 12 percent, 86.5 to 96.5 g per 100 berries, between 26 August and 26 September. On late-held bogs, weight per berry increased 14 percent between 10 September and 29 September. Late-held Howes increased 15 percent in weight between 29 September and 1 November.

In summarizing seven years' data, I. E. Demoranville (1960) showed that the average size increase for Early Black cranberries, from both early- and late-drawn bogs, was 12 percent from date of first harvest to the date of maximum berry size, which was 13–19 September for early-drawn bogs and 23–29 September for late-drawn bogs. Howes averaged a 6 percent increase in size for early-drawn bogs and a 4 percent increase for late-drawn bogs. Optimum harvest dates were 3–9 October for early-drawn bogs and 9 October for late-drawn bogs. Demoranville observed that the heaviest Early Black berries occurred in years that coincided with the greatest amount of rainfall, whereas the heaviest Howes berries were produced in the drier years. Smaller berries were associated with those growing seasons in which temperatures were below normal.

Chandler (1953b) has analyzed various methods of measuring berry size.

He compared cup count (the number of berries contained in a standard half-pint cup) to the average volume of berries, the number of berries per pound, the average weight per berry, and the distribution of berries by size classes. Chandler published curves which show the interrelationships between these parameters for different cultivars. For example, a cup count of 80 berries for the Howes, Early Black, and McFarlin cultivars would be equivalent to an average berry volume of 1.78 cc, an average berry weight of 1.25 g, and 370 berries per pound. It would consist of berries that could pass through a 22/32-inch grader but not through a 18/32-inch space. (Small berries average > 95 berries per cup, medium berries 75–95, and large berries < 75 berries per cup.) Specific gravity was also used as a measure of berry size by Chandler. Small berries were found to have a higher specific gravity than large berries: 0.71 g/cc as compared to 0.56 g/cc. Pie berries with a cup count of 306 had a specific gravity of 0.74 g/cc. Chandler concluded that although specific gravity, average berry weight, and average berry volume represent the best methods of size measurement, cup count still affords the most practical method of size evaluation. He calculated that for a given cultivar the average weight per berry for a given cup count varies less than 0.07 g from year to year.

Herbicides and plant growth regulators have been known to decrease cranberry size in some instances. Devlin and Demoranville (1968) found that the herbicide dichlobenil reduced berry size, but the small size reduction was more than made up for by the yield increase that resulted from the weed control. When the plant growth regulator CEPA (2-chloroethyl phosphoric acid) was applied before or at full bloom, it decreased berry size (Devlin and Demoranville 1970). When applied late in the growing season, however, the CEPA application enhanced the pigment content of the fruit without causing a size reduction in the berry.

Seeds

Seed formation is apparently necessary to sustain fruit development in the cranberry since a seedless cranberry is a rare occurrence (Filmer et al. 1958). There is evidence to suggest that a strong relationship exists between the number of seeds contained in a berry and its ultimate size (Rigby and Dana 1971). I. V. Hall and Aalders (1965) found a strong correlation existed between seed number and berry size in the Howes cultivar. Large Howes berries averaged 1.31 g per berry and contained 19.9 viable seeds, whereas small Howes berries weighed only 0.46 g per berry and contained only 5.3 seeds per berry. The authors calculated that each additional seed increased the weight of the berry by 36 mg. A similar relationship was found to exist between seed number and the diameter of the berry (G. W. Eaton 1966). Each additional seed increased berry diameter by 0.09 mm, or 2.1 percent.

Filmer and his associates (1958) reported on the maximum number of seeds found in the most important New Jersey cultivars. Champion berries contained a maximum of 32 seeds per berry, Howes and Jerseys had 20 seeds per berry, and Early Black contained a maximum of 18 seeds per berry. The authors found that berries averaging less than one seed per carpel (there are four carpels per berry) were nonuniform in shape and small in size. The maximum number of seeds found in a single carpel was 12. In small berries, 24 percent of the carpels did not have seeds. Berries with seedless carpels were misshapen and probably would not produce normal-sized berries regardless of the length of the growing period.

Before the cranberry seed can germinate, it apparently must go through a period of dormancy, or *afterripening*. Bain (1933a) observed that cranberry seeds obtained in the spring from the previous season's crop germinated much better than seeds from freshly harvested berries. This dormancy factor is important to the plant breeder who is interested in reducing the time between seed formation and seedling production in order to speed up his breeding program. Normally, cranberry seeds need to be stored for six to seven months at 0°C in order for them to germinate at 25°C (Schultz 1944). Devlin and his associates (Devlin et al. 1976) suggested that this seed dormancy is brought about by high levels of abscisic acid (ABA) in the dormant seed. Not only did they find that ABA levels were much higher in dormant seeds than in nondormant seeds but they also observed that extracts of dormant seeds could inhibit germination. Extracts from nondormant seeds had no adverse effect on seed germination. For good germination of the cold-treated cranberry seed to occur, light (Devlin and Karczmarczyk 1974) and temperatures of at least 22°C (I. E. Demoranville 1974) were both necessary. Sand, peat moss, and a mixture of sand and peat moss have been used successfully to germinate cranberry seeds when misting was used (Greidanus et al. 1971; Stone 1982).

Color

During the initial part of its development, the fruit is green owing to the predominance of the chlorophyll pigment. As the fruit enlarges, the green pigment becomes less dominant and the berry appears increasingly white in color. The red anthocyanin and yellow flavonol and carotene pigments become dominant as the harvest season approaches (Puski and Francis 1967). These pigments (see Fruit Composition section), concentrated in the epidermal and subepidermal layers of the berry, impart the attractive red color that is so important to the cranberry's commercial application.

Ethylene treatment promotes the synthesis of anthocyanin in the cranberry (Craker and Wetherbee 1973). This response to ethylene forms the basis for the growth regulator treatments employed to enhance anthocyanin development in early-harvested cranberries (see chapter 11). Craker and Wetherbee demonstrated that this ethylene effect on anthocyanin promotion could be prevented or greatly reduced by the inclusion of a carbon dioxide treatment with the ethylene.

Climacteric

Respiration measurements of developing cranberry fruit suggest that the cranberry undergoes a slight respiratory climacteric sometime between 11 and 13 weeks after full bloom (Doughty et al. 1967; Forsyth and Hall 1967a). Respiration in the developing cranberry fruit was greatest during the early green stage of the fruit (approximately 4 weeks after full bloom) and decreased rapidly as the fruit matured, reaching a fairly steady state at maturity. Ethylene production in the fruit also peaked during the early green stage of fruit development and decreased sharply as the berry enlarged. With the onset of red color development, the ethylene content in the fruit increased to a secondary maximum and steady state after the fruit had become fully colored (Forsyth and Hall 1969). It is at this time of minimum respiration and steady state of ethylene production that optimum maturity is believed to occur and the fruit is ready for harvest.

Fruit Composition

Chemical Content

The chemical composition of the cranberry has been well documented. Much of the impetus for this documentation has been the widespread interest in the fruit's nutritional benefits and its potential therapeutic effects. Fellers and Esselen (1955) have compiled the composition data for the cranberry, a summary of which is given in table 6.2. The ripe cranberry consists primarily of fruit sugars, organic acids, and pectin. The sugar found in cranberries is formed during berry development on the vine inasmuch as there is very little starch present in the ripe fruit from which sugars could be converted.

Sugar

Cranberries are relatively low in sugar when compared to other small fruits. The low sugar content makes it necessary to add considerable amounts of sucrose to achieve the necessary jelling property to produce sauce. There

TABLE 6.2. COMPOSITION OF CRANBERRY FRUIT

CHEMICAL COMPOSITION	%	ENERGY VALUE	kcal per 100 g
Moisture	88.00	Fresh berries	26
Reducing sugars	4.20	Sauce	125
Acids (as citric)	2.40		
Pectin	1.20	VITAMIN CONTENT	per 100 g
Fat (ether extract)	0.40	Vitamin A	40 I.U.
Protein	0.20	Vitamin C	7.5–10.5 mg
Ash	0.25	Thiamine (B_1)	13.5 mcg
Fiber	1.60	Riboflavin (B_2)	3.0 mcg
Undetermined	1.80	Nicotinic acid	33.0 mcg
		Pantothenic acid	25.0 mcg
MINERAL CONTENT	ppm	Pyridoxine (B_6)	10.0 mcg
Potassium	530	Biotin	trace
Sodium	20		
Calcium	130	ACID CONTENT	%
Phosphorus	80	Citric	1.10
Magnesium	55	Malic	0.26
Iodine	0.05	Quinic	0.5–1.0
Sulfur	50	Benzoic	0.065
Chlorine	40		
Iron	4		
Manganese	6		
Copper	4		
ALKALINITY OF ASH	2.2 cc		

SOURCE: Fellers and Esselen 1955.

are, however, greater differences in sugar content between cultivars than was noted for total acid content (Morse 1930). The cultivars Centennial and Centerville were found to have as much as 50 percent more sugar than the Early Black or Howes cultivar when measured in the mature berry (table 6.3). If this difference is genetically related, the high-sugar cultivars may be useful in plant breeding programs to raise the natural sugar content of new hybrids. Morse found that there was a marked increase in the sugar content of the berry in the weeks just prior to harvest, nearly doubling in some cases in the last three weeks before harvest.

Organic Acids

The astringency of the cranberry owes its existence to the high levels of organic acids—mainly quinic, citric, malic, and benzoic—although the pres-

TABLE 6.3. PERCENT COMPOSITION OF CRANBERRIES WHILE RIPENING ON VINES

CULTIVAR	DRY MATTER	TOTAL ACID	TOTAL SUGAR
Early Black*	10.3–11.5	2.81–2.86	2.2–3.5
Howes*	10.5–11.9	2.71–2.61	1.8–3.7
McFarlin†	12.2	2.35	4.60
Searles†	11.6	2.23	4.00
Centennial†	12.8	2.10	5.20
Centerville†	12.5	2.20	5.20

SOURCE: Morse 1930.
*Fruit analyzed on 9/1 and 9/28; the ranges represent both data sets.
†Fruit analyzed in November only.

ence of polyphenolic compounds may also contribute to its astringency (Coppola et al. 1978; Wang et al. 1978). Cranberry juice was found to contain 1.32% quinic acid, 0.92% malic acid, and 1.08% citric acid, as determined by high-pressure liquid chromatography (Coppola et al. 1978). Nelson (1927) reported that cranberries contain on average 0.062% benzoic acid. Mason (1905) found that the benzoic acid content increased as the berries ripened and that the levels attained were high enough to preserve perishable foods. It is interesting to note in this regard that American Indians often pounded cranberries into their meat to preserve it.

Morse (1930) analyzed cranberries from the major cranberry-growing regions and found the total acid content to vary relatively little among regions and cultivars. The percent acid in the fruit at harvest averaged between 2.30 and 2.41 and decreased with storage. Despite the acidity of the fruit, there is no indication that the consumption of moderate amounts affects the alkali reserve of the blood (Fellers et al. 1933). The high organic acid content of cranberries has been associated with urinary acidification and the reduction in size of struvite-type renal stones (Fellers et al. 1933; Light et al. 1973; Zinsser et al. 1968; see also chapter 12). The benzoic acid level in cranberry juice has been found to exert a significant in vitro antifungal effect on eight representative species of dermatophyte (Swartz and Medrek 1968).

Minerals

Compared to other fruits, the ash content of cranberries is low (Morse 1929), which means that cranberries are rather low in minerals. Potassium is the predominant mineral present in the berry, whereas the sodium content is quite low (table 6.2). Compared to other fruits and vegetables, cranberries have a relatively high iodine content (Morse 1928). Despite the high acidity of the fresh cranberry, the ash of the fruit is slightly alkaline.

Vitamins

Cranberries are a very good source of vitamin C (ascorbic acid), the antiscorbutic vitamin. The amount is about equal to the vitamin C content of tomato juice. The ascorbic acid content of fresh cranberries ranges from 7.5 to 10.5 mg per 100 g of fresh fruit (table 6.2). There is a gradual loss in vitamin C during cold storage, but freezing does not destroy the vitamin (Fellers et al. 1935). Whole cranberry sauce will retain about 80 percent of the fresh berries' vitamin C content, but strained sauce and jelly have virtually no vitamin C left because of the extensive heat processing it undergoes. Cranberries are a fair source of vitamin A, which is not lost in processing. Cranberries are relatively low in the B complex vitamins.

Pigments

The red pigments of cranberry were identified as the four major anthocyanins, cyanidin-3-monogalactoside, peonidin-3-monogalactoside, cyanidin-3-monoarabinoside, and peonidin-3-monoarabinoside (Sakamura and Francis 1961; Zapsalis and Francis 1965), and two minor pigments, cyanidin-3-glucoside, and peonidin-3-glucoside (Fuleki and Francis 1967). In addition, the yellow flavonol glycosides, quercetin-3-galactoside, quercetin-3-rhamnoside, quercetin-3-arabinoside, quercetin, myricetin-3-arabinoside, and myricetin-3-digalactoside, have been isolated (Puski and Francis 1967). When Sapers and Hargrave (1987) measured the proportions of the individual anthocyanins in fruits of different cranberry cultivars at different stages of ripeness, they found no differences between the clones studied, indicating that the different anthocyanins were being produced at about the same rate during berry ripening.

In a series of papers, Fuleki and Francis (1968a, 1968b, 1968c) developed the methods of separation, purification, and identification of the anthocyanins in the cranberry. In addition they established the extinction coefficients for the cranberry anthocyanins, which enabled them to calculate the absolute quantities of the pigment in the berry. Thus, analytical procedures could be developed to monitor quality control in the processing operation. Similar procedures were developed for the flavonols in cranberry by Lees and Francis (1971). Lees and Francis (1972) went on to propose a standard method for the quantitative determination and reporting of total cranberry pigment content.

Total anthocyanin content recovered has become an important factor in the processing of cranberries because it is such an important constituent in cranberry juice cocktail, which now utilizes more than half of the cranberry crop grown in the United States. Breeding strategies are being developed for increasing the anthocyanin content of cranberries (Sapers et al., Breeding strategies . . . , 1986). Three approaches suggested by Sapers and coworkers in order to maximize the potential genetic gains in anthocyanin content were to select for (1) increased pigmentation, (2) small berries, and (3) early and concentrated color development. Although color development, even in the same cultivar, can vary substantially depending upon the environmental conditions under which the plant is being grown, there are indications of differences between cultivars in not only their ability to accumulate anthocyanin but how early and how quickly they are able to accomplish color development. This suggests some sort of genetic control. So it is that such cultivars as Early Black and Ben Lear and the new hybrids Crowley and Franklin, which appear to approach the biological limit for anthocyanin production, may be useful as parents in carrying out the first and third breeding strategies.

The second breeding strategy, that of selecting for small berries, is based on the premise that small berries will contain more anthocyanin for a given weight of fruit than large berries (Francis 1957; Vorsa and Welker 1985). Supporting this premise is the fact that the pigments of the cranberry are concentrated in the skin; therefore, the total pigment content is proportional to the surface area of the berry. Vorsa and Welker warned that the selection for larger-berried genotypes to increase yield may actually work against increasing total anthocyanin recovery. When Sapers et al. (factors affecting anthocyanin content . . . , 1986) calculated the actual anthocyanin recovered in the juicing operation, however, they came to the conclusion that both juice yield and anthocyanin recovery were independent of berry coloration and size. Only total anthocyanin content varied in proportion to the surface-to-volume ratio. It would seem, therefore, that selecting for smaller berries might lead to greater anthocyanin production if the smaller berry is attained with no change in the surface anthocyanin content.

Volatiles

The volatile components of cranberry juice have been isolated and identified by Anjou and von Sydow (1968) and by Croteau and Fagerson (1968). Analyzing the juice of the American cranberry cultivar Early Black, the Swedish workers Anjou and von Sydow isolated 43 different compounds that comprised 87 percent of the concentrate of the volatiles. The majority of the compounds consisted of aliphatic alcohols, aliphatic aldehydes and ketones, terpene derivatives, aromatic compounds, and a few other compounds. The volatile in highest concentration was a terpene compound, alpha-terpineol.

This was in agreement with the results obtained by the American workers Croteau and Fagerson.

Of the aromatic compounds that contribute to the aroma of the cranberry, Croteau (1977) found that benzaldehyde was the most important contributor to the aroma complex, which also included benzyl alcohol and benzyl benzoate. The aromatics were apparently synthesized from benzoic acid during the ripening of the berry, since they were not detected in the green fruit. Croteau and Fagerson (1971b) found that the volatiles were concentrated in the cuticle wax of the cranberry where, the authors speculated, they may serve as a defense against pathogenic attack.

Anjou and von Sydow (1968) also found the presence of 2-methylbutyric acid in the American cranberry, but at much lower concentrations than existed in the lingonberry (*Vaccinium vitis-idaea*), in which the acid is the predominant volatile. They suggested that this difference, together with the very high alpha-terpineol levels found in the American cranberry, is the major reason for the difference in aroma between the two cranberry species.

Other Compounds

Cranberries contain a considerable amount of pectin, which is responsible for the high jellying power of cranberry sauce (Fellers and Esselen 1955). The high quality of cranberry pectin enables the formation of a firm jelly with as little as 40 percent sugar, compared to the 65 percent sugar required for most other fruit pectins. The pectin content of cranberries can vary greatly between cultivars, from bog to bog, and from one growing season to the next. A comparison of different cultivars in some New Jersey bogs over a period of years found the pectin content of cranberry fruit to range from 0.40 to 1.36 percent, with an overall average content of 0.79 percent.

The pectin is removed in the processing of the cranberry. There remains in the cranberry pomace a great many compounds that may be extracted by petroleum ether or by ether (Markley and Sando 1934). According to Markley and Sando, these compounds make up the waxy cuticle of the cranberry and are primarily free liquid (unsaturated) fatty acids, principally oleic acid. The authors attributed the imperviousness of the cranberry cuticle to water and the unusual stickiness observed in berries that have been frozen to the large amount of these free liquid fatty acids (unsaturated fatty acids). In addition to these fatty acids, the authors found the skins to contain small amounts of hydrocarbons, solid (saturated) fatty acids, glycerol, and free ursolic acid. Ursolic acid is used as an emulsifying agent in pharmaceutical preparations. Arnold and Hsia (1957) have shown that it can be extracted from cranberry skins on a commercial basis (see chapter 12).

More recently the chemical composition of the cranberry cuticle was analyzed by thin-layer and gas-liquid chromatography in conjunction with mass spectrometry and infrared spectroscopy (Croteau and Fagerson 1971a, 1972). Although these authors confirmed the presence of saturated (solid) fatty acids in the cuticle, they were of the opinion that the unsaturated (liquid) fatty acids identified by Markley and Sando (1934) were derived from the seed portion of the experimental material rather than from the cuticle. In previous work (Croteau and Fagerson 1969) had found the presence of sizeable amounts of unsaturated fatty acids (oleic, linoleic, and linolenic acids) in the cranberry seed. The authors also differed with Markley and Sando on the alcohol composition of the berry cuticle in that the presence of long-chain alcohols was actually detected. In addition to the saturated fatty acids and long-chain alcohols, Croteau and Fagerson (1971b) detected several triterpenoid classes, including acids, alcohols, esters, and hydrocarbons. Although 50 percent of the wax of the cranberry cuticle is made up of these cyclic triterpenes, it is the aliphatic component, of which the aldehydes are the main compounds, that is believed to contribute significantly to the prevention of water loss from the berry. When Croteau and Fagerson (1972) removed the surface wax layer from the underlying cutin polymer and analyzed just the cutin material, they separated seven classes of cutin acids. From these seven classes of acids, they identified 41 individual compounds of which two trihydroxy monobasic acids comprised more than 60 percent of the total.

Polyphenolic polymers, such as leucoanthocyanins, are believed to contribute to the flavor and appearance of food. The unique flavor of the cranberry, characterized as an astringent taste with a little bitterness, is probably due to the presence of such polymeric polyphenols (Wang et al. 1978). Using paper and thin-layer chromatography of extracts from cranberries, the authors were able to show a complex pattern of separation that was indicative of such large polymers.

Cranberry leaves have been found to contain N-methylindolic and N-methylazatricyclo-type alkaloids (Jankowski 1973). It has been speculated that the role of the cranberry in folklore medicine (various cures attributed to cranberries based on anecdotal evidence) may be related to the presence of such alkaloids in the fruit. Using column chromatography fractionation, Jankowski isolated 19 different basic products from the cranberry, the three principal alkaloids being cannivonines 1, 2, and 3.

SEVEN

Plant Nutrition

General Aspects

Nutrient Requirement

As a member of the higher order of plants, the cranberry shares with other plants the need for the following 16 essential elements for normal growth and development: carbon (C), hydrogen (H), oxygen (O), nitrogen (N), phosphorus (P), potassium (K), calcium (Ca), magnesium (Mg), sulfur (S), iron (Fe), manganese (Mn), copper (Cu), zinc (Zn), boron (B), molybdenum (Mo), and chlorine (Cl). Carbon and oxygen are obtained from the atmosphere as gaseous components of the air and require no additional amelioration by the cranberry grower. The remaining elements must be supplied to the plant either via a soil and water resource or by supplemental application through a fertilizer.

The cranberry belongs to the Ericaceae family of plants, a group of plants that have evolved under conditions of low fertility and low pH. The plant thrives best when the substrate pH ranges between pH 4 and 5. The requirement for the essential elements supplied by the soil and water is correspondingly low, much lower than for most agronomic crops. Young cranberry plants grown in nutrient solution were found to respond only very slowly to the nutrient medium (Rupasova 1984). Colby (1945) has calculated that 100 barrels of cranberries and one ton of dried vines contains only 23 pounds of nitrogen, 3 pounds of phosphorus, 15 pounds of potassium, and 2 pounds of calcium. This low nutrient requirement of the cranberry has a profound influence on the nutrition of the cranberry plant and subsequent fertilizer practices.

Seasonal Distribution of Elements

The low nutrient-element requirement of the cranberry is reflected in the relatively low concentration of the elements in the plant tissue. Chaplin and Martin (1979) measured the seasonal changes in leaf element composition of cranberry in Oregon (table 7.1). Over the course of the growing season, they found that nitrogen, phosphorus, potassium, and zinc concentrations in the leaf decreased while concentrations of calcium, magnesium, iron, manganese, and boron increased. They found that the period during which a specific element did not vary significantly in concentration occurred between 15 June and 15 September and depended on the particular element. The authors concluded that in order to adequately diagnose the nutrient status of the cranberry it would be necessary to sample plant tissue during this period of minimum elemental flux. This would require taking two samples: one between 15 June and 15 July to analyze for magnesium, manganese, and iron; and the other from 15 August to 15 September to analyze for nitrogen, phosphorus, potassium, calcium, copper, zinc, and boron. A great deal of yearly variability was observed in the magnesium and iron content of the plant, which may make it difficult to diagnose the nutritional status of these elements by leaf tissue analysis.

Standard Elemental Values

The first attempt to systematically establish a set of standard values for cranberry plant nutrition was made by Dana (1981) in Wisconsin. He proposed

TABLE 7.1. CONCENTRATION OF ELEMENTS IN CRANBERRY SHOOTS DURING THE OREGON GROWING SEASON

ELEMENT	1 JUNE	1 JULY	1 AUGUST	1 SEPTEMBER
Nitrogen (N)	1.25%	1.00	0.97	0.95
Phosphorus (P)	0.18	0.14	0.12	0.13
Potassium (K)	0.55	0.47	0.44	0.40
Calcium (Ca)	0.51	0.58	0.64	0.77
Magnesium (Mg)	0.21	0.20	0.20	0.22
Iron (Fe)	80 ppm	75	90	100
Manganese (Mn)	75	90	130	190
Copper (Cu)	25	12	9	10
Zinc (Zn)	45	33	34	33
Boron (B)	30	35	35	40

SOURCE: Chaplin and Martin 1979.

that by sampling healthy, productive vines in several bogs in widely separated areas a range of nutrient values could be obtained from which median standard values could be derived. He concluded that these tissue values would reflect the nutrient status of a healthy cranberry plant and could be used for interpretive purposes in diagnosing the nutritional needs of the cranberry plant.

Basic to the establishment of such standard values is the need to standardize the sampling procedure, including the tissues to be analyzed and the time to take the sample. Dana opted to sample the new cranberry shoot rather than just the leaf, arguing that the mineral concentrations in the new leaves are very similar to those in the stem and are easier to harvest than just the leaves. He pointed out that new shoots give a more reliable estimate of changing elemental concentrations than do older tissues and are apt to be less contaminated by spray and winter flood residues. Dana recommended that the period of tissue sampling under Wisconsin conditions be from 20 June to 1 August , pointing out that this is when most of the essential elements in the cranberry plant are at their median level. Earlier sampling was made difficult by the lack of sufficient tissue, and later sampling ran the risk of contamination by spray residues. This sampling period, however, may not represent a period of minimum elemental flux as reported above for West Coast data (Chaplin and Martin 1979). The elemental standards for cranberry shoots proposed by Dana based on three experimental sampling programs are given in table 7.2.

Mycorrhizal Relationships

An important aspect of cranberry nutrition is the plant's association with an endophytic mycorrhizal fungus (*Phoma radicis*) that permeates the parenchymatous cells as well as the stem system, fruits, and seeds of the plant (Addoms and Mounce 1931). It is believed that the branching mycelium of this fungus, which covers the surface of the cranberry's hairless roots, greatly expedites the uptake of essential nutrients from the substrate. It may well be that the survival of the cranberry in its natural habitat prior to human intervention may have been dependent upon this mycorrhizal association. Recent research by Hunt et al. (1975), however, failed to show any difference in the cranberry's root-to-shoot ratio between the plants that possessed a mycorrhizal fungal association and those that did not. Nevertheless, the role of mycorrhizal fungi in cranberry nutrition is one of the least understood aspects of cranberry nutrition and warrants more research.

Cranberry Yield Components

One approach to ascertaining the importance of plant nutrition to cranberry growth and production is to evaluate the nutrition of the plant in the context of the yield components of the cranberry plant. These components include: (1)

TABLE 7.2. PROPOSED NUTRIENT VALUE STANDARDS IN
WISCONSIN FOR NEW CRANBERRY SHOOTS

Element	Deficiency Level	PROPOSED STANDARD VALUE		
		Low	Median	High
Nitrogen (N)	0.70%	< 0.90	0.90–1.00	> 1.00
Phosphorus (P)	0.09	< 0.14	0.14–0.18	> 0.18
Potassium (K)	0.17	< 0.50	0.50–0.90	> 0.90
Calcium (Ca)	< 0.05	< 0.31	0.31–0.60	> 0.60
Magnesium (Mg)	0.02	< 0.16	0.16–0.20	> 0.20
Iron (Fe)	26.0 ppm	< 40.0	40–80	> 80
Manganese (Mn)	< 2.0	< 10	10–200	> 200
Copper (Cu)	3.1	< 6	6–10	> 10
Zinc (Zn)	3.8	< 15	15–30	> 30
Boron (B)	< 1.0	< 10	10–20	> 20

SOURCE: Dana 1981.

the number of uprights produced, (2) the proportion of uprights that flower, (3) the number of flowers per flowering upright, (4) percentage fruit set, and (5) berry size. Bain (1946) and Doehlert (1953b) both associated high cranberry yields with a high percentage of flowering uprights. Bain concluded that when the percentage of blooming uprights was low, there was no compensating increase in fruit set. Doehlert found that 80 percent of cranberry production was produced on uprights having at least three berries per upright.

In more recent studies (G. W. Eaton and Kyte 1978; G. W. Eaton and MacPherson 1978; Shawa et al. 1981), it was consistently shown that the proportion of uprights bearing flowers and the percentage of those flowers setting fruit were the most important components contributing to cranberry yield. It is therefore important that the nutrition of the cranberry plant be so regulated as to achieve the optimum level of these two parameters. Not only must the nutrient needs of the cranberry plant be addressed but also the adverse effects of excessive nutrition must be guarded against. Most cranberry growers are painfully aware that excessive vegetative growth manifested in prolific runner growth is the antithesis to flowering upright development. The most important nutrient that is capable of influencing this vegetative-reproductive balance is the element nitrogen.

Nitrogen

Requirement

Of the elements essential to plant growth, nitrogen appears to have the greatest effect on the development, flowering, and productivity of the cranberry plant. It is a component of all proteins, including those that make up the enzymes and growth regulators responsible for the metabolic functions essential to the plant—including those that regulate flowering and vegetative growth in cranberry. Colby (1945) has calculated that 100 barrels (5 tons) of cranberries would remove 23 pounds (10.4 kg) of nitrogen from an acre of bog. Dana (1968a) has estimated that the new growth of leaves, stems, and roots would require an additional 30 pounds (13.6 kg) of nitrogen per acre. This nitrogen requirement, in addition to the nitrogen lost by leaching and denitrification, must be supplied by the natural reservoir of nitrogen in the soil, including that released by the decaying of vegetative matter, or by mineral supplement.

Plant and Fruit Content

The nitrogen content of cranberry tissue readily responds to increased levels of nitrogen nutrition. Eck (1971) found that the nitrogen content of nonfruiting uprights was more highly correlated to nitrogen nutrition levels than the nitrogen content of fruiting uprights or of leaves taken from vines. No relationship at all was found to exist between the nitrogen content of stem tissue and nitrogen fertilization. This suggests that uprights rather than runners should be used to diagnose the nitrogen status of cranberry plants and, more specifically, the leaves of uprights. Using greenhouse conditions, Torio and Eck (1969) found that the nitrogen content of leaf tissue of Early Black plants was strongly associated with nitrogen levels in the nutrient solution, and Leschyson and Eaton (1971) found a similar relationship to exist in McFarlin cranberry plants grown on bog soil.

Reported values for nitrogen content in cranberry leaves range from 0.73 to 1.59 percent nitrogen and in stem tissue from as low as 0.37 to 0.43 percent, with similarly low values for nitrogen content in the fruit (table 7.3). This represents a concentration range considerably lower than exists for most of our commercial fruit crops. Somogyi et al. (1964) and Torio and Eck (1969) have identified 0.80 percent nitrogen in the leaves of the Early Black cranberry plant as the level below which nitrogen deficiency symptoms characterized by the extensive reddening of the foliage occur. Prolific vine growth was associated with a leaf nitrogen content of 0.98 percent, suggesting that the optimum nitrogen level in the Early Black cultivar lies within this narrow range. Greidanus et al. (1972) observed nitrogen deficiency in Stevens

TABLE 7.3. MINERAL CONTENT OF CRANBERRY TISSUE

TISSUE	CULTIVAR	ELEMENT	% OF ELEMENT IN DRY MATTER	REMARKS	REFERENCE
Nonfruiting shoots	McFarlin	N	1.25–0.95	June–Sept. sampl.	Chaplin & Martin (1979)
Leaf of uprights	Ben Lear	N	0.80–1.06	N fertilizer rates, 0–34 kg/ha	G. W. Eaton & Meehan (1973)
Uprights	Stevens	N	0.72–0.91	NH_4-fed plants showing N deficy.	Greidanus et al. (1972)
Nonfruiting uprights	Early Black	N	0.89–1.10	N fertilizer rates, 16–64 lbs N/A	Eck (1971)
Fruiting uprights	Early Black	N	0.84–1.04	Same as above	,,
Runner leaf	Early Black	N	0.92–1.09	Same as above	
Runner stem	Early Black	N	0.40	Ave. of plants receiving 3 different levels of N	,,
			,,		
Leaf	McFarlin	N	1.03–1.22	N fertilizer rates of 0–120 lbs N/A	Leschyson & Eaton (1971)
Leaf	Ben Lear	N	1.48	Received N fertilizer	Townsend & Hall (1971)
Leaf	Stevens	N	1.59	Received N fertilizer	,,

(continued)

TABLE 7.3. (*Continued*)

TISSUE	CULTIVAR	ELEMENT	% OF ELEMENT IN DRY MATTER	REMARKS	REFERENCE
Leaf	Natives	N	1.25	Received no fertilizer during year analyzed	Townsend & Hall (1971)
Leaf	Howes	N	1.31	Received no fertilizer during year analyzed	"
Leaf	Ben Lear	N	0.84–1.44	Young planting	G. W. Eaton (1971b)
Leaf	McFarlin	N	0.84–1.44	0–135 lbs N/A applied to young producing bogs, ave. of 3 years	G. W. Eaton (1971b)
Leaf	McFarlin	N	0.73–0.95	Samples from mature producing bogs in 1966 & 1967, respectively.	G. W. Eaton (1971a)
Leaf	Early Black	N	0.78–0.98	Plants fertilized with nutrient solution, 20 ppm & 60 ppm N, respectively	Torio and Eck (1969)
Fruit	Early Black	N	0.44–0.49	Same as above	
Leaf	Early Black	N	0.72–0.98	Plants grown on bog soil in greenhouse	Somogyi et al. (1964)
Stem	Early Black	N	0.37–0.43	Same as above	"

Tissue	Cultivar	Element	Value	Conditions	Reference
Leaf	Early Black	N	0.90–1.13	Plants grown in sand culture in greenhouse	Kender & Childers (1959)
Nonfruiting uprights	McFarlin	P	0.180–0.140	June–Sept. sampling	Chaplin & Martin (1979)
Upright leaves	Ben Lear	P	0.110–0.210	0–29 kg/ha applied	G. W. Eaton & Meehan (1973)
Uprights	Stevens	P	0.034–0.080	Deficiency	Greidanus & Dana (1972)
			0.090–0.110	Hidden hunger	
			0.120–0.270	Sufficiency	
Leaf	Ben Lear	P	0.089–0.384	0–25 lbs P/A on a young bog	G. W. Eaton (1971b)
Leaf	Early Black	P	0.076–0.088	5–15 ppm P in nutrient solution	Torio & Eck (1969)
Fruit	Early Black	P	0.070–0.078	Same as above	"
Leaf	Ben Lear	P	0.170	Bogs fertilized with NPK	Townsend & Hall (1971)
Leaf	Stevens	P	0.170	Same as above	"
Leaf	Natives	P	0.130	Bogs not fertilized	"
Leaf	Howes	P	0.120	Same as above	"

(continued)

TABLE 7.3. (*Continued*)

TISSUE	CULTIVAR	ELEMENT	% OF ELEMENT IN DRY MATTER	REMARKS	REFERENCE
Leaf	Early Black	P	0.063–0.119	Fertilized at the rate of 0–120 lbs P_2O_5/A	Eck (1964b)
Nonfruiting uprights	McFarlin	K	0.55–0.40	June–Sept. sampling	Chaplin & Martin (1979)
Fruit	McFarlin	K	0.62–0.49	Increasing lime application	Shawa (1979b)
Leaf	Ben Lear	K	0.68	Bogs fertilized with NPK	Townsend & Hall (1971)
Leaf	Stevens	K	0.73	Same as above	"
Leaf	Natives	K	0.48	Bogs not fertilized	"
Leaf	Howes	K	0.38	Same as above	"
Leaf	McFarlin	K	0.23–0.37	Ave. of plantings receiving 0–60 lbs K_2O/A	G. W. Eaton (1971a)
Leaf	Ben Lear	K	0.24–0.90	Young planting receiving different rates of K_2O	G. W. Eaton (1971b)
Leaf	Early Black	K	0.59–0.74	Greenhouse plants grown in 20 & 60 ppm K, respectively	Torio and Eck (1969)

Tissue	Cultivar	Element	Value	Conditions	Reference
Fruit	Early Black	K	1.37–1.61	Same as above	"
Nonfruiting uprights	McFarlin	Ca	0.51–0.73	June–Sept. sampling	Chaplin & Martin (1979)
Upright leaves	Ben Lear	Ca	0.75–0.62	P rates of 0–29 kg/ha	G. W. Eaton & Meehan (1973)
Fruit	McFarlin	Ca	0.056–0.068	Increasing lime application	Shawa (1979b)
Leaf	Ben Lear	Ca	0.86	Bogs fertilized with NPK	Townsend & Hall (1971)
Leaf	Stevens	Ca	0.70	Same as above	"
Leaf	Natives	Ca	1.21	Bogs not fertilized	"
Leaf	Howes	Ca	1.03	Same as above	"
Leaf	McFarlin	Ca	0.26–0.30	Plantings on peat, 2 years of sampling	G. W. Eaton (1971a)
Leaf	Ben Lear	Ca	0.24–0.30	Young planting	G. W. Eaton (1971b)
Nonfruiting uprights	McFarlin	Mg	0.21	June–Sept. sampling	Chapling & Martin (1979)
Fruit	McFarlin	Mg	0.083–0.070	Increasing lime	Shawa (1979b)
Leaf	Ben Lear	Mg	0.22	Bogs fertilized with NPK	Townsend & Hall (1971)

(continued)

TABLE 7.3. (*Continued*)

TISSUE	CULTIVAR	ELEMENT	% OF ELEMENT IN DRY MATTER	REMARKS	REFERENCE
Leaf	Ben Lear	Mg	0.22	Bogs fertilized with NPK	Townsend & Hall (1971)
Leaf	Natives	Mg	0.22	Bogs not fertilized	"
Leaf	Howes	Mg	0.24	Same as above	"
Leaf	McFarlin	Mg	0.38–030	Plantings on 2 years sampling	G. W. Eaton (1971a)
Nonfruiting uprights	McFarlin	Fe	0.008–0.010	June–Sept. sampling	Chaplin & Martin (1979)
Leaf	Ben Lear	Fe	0.0094	Bog fertilized with NPK	Townsend & Hall (1971)
Leaf	Stevens	Fe	0.0100	Same as above	"
Leaf	Natives	Fe	0.0122	Bogs not fertilized	"
Leaf	Howes	Fe	0.0075	Bogs not fertilized	"
Leaf	McFarlin	Fe	0.0074–0.0093	Plantings on peat, 2 years sampling	G. W. Eaton (1971a)
Leaf	Ben Lear	Fe	0.003–0.012	Young planting	G. W. Eaton (1971b)
Nonfruiting uprights	McFarlin	Mn	0.008–0.019	June–Sept. sampling	Chaplin & Martin (1979)

Leaf	Ben Lear	Mn	0.0305	Bogs fertilized with NPK	Townsend & Hall (1971)
Leaf	Stevens	Mn	0.0324	Bogs fertilized with NPK	Townsend & Hall (1971)
Leaf	Natives	Mn	0.0438	Bogs not fertilized	"
Leaf	Howes	Mn	0.0908	Same as above	"
Leaf	McFarlin	Mn	0.0524–0.736	Plantings on peat, 2 years sampling	G. W. Eaton (1971a)
Leaf	Early Black	S	0.106–0.127	Greenhouse plants receiving 20 & 60 ppm S, respectively	Torio & Eck (1969)
Fruit	Early Black	S	0.085–0.082	Same as above	"
Nonfruiting uprights	McFarlin	Zn	0.0045–0.0032	June–Sept. sampling	Chaplin & Martin (1979)
Nonfruiting uprights	McFarlin	Cu	0.0025–0.0010	June–Sept. sampling	"
Nonfruiting uprights	McFarlin	B	0.0030–0.0040	June–Sept. sampling	"

cranberry manifested as pink leaves at a concentration of 0.72 to 0.91 percent nitrogen. G. W. Eaton (1971b) has suggested that 1.00 percent nitrogen in the Ben Lear cultivar probably represented a luxury level of nitrogen.

The narrow range in nitrogen content between which symptoms of deficiency and excess are manifested in the cranberry plant suggests that the vegetative-reproductive balance in the cranberry plant is extremely sensitive to nitrogen level. The optimum nitrogen level in the cranberry plant for maximum yield has yet to be determined experimentally for the major cranberry cultivars. In the meantime, however, some understanding of the optimum nitrogen level in cranberry might be obtained by analyzing for the element in consistently good and poor producing vines.

Eck (1976b) has questioned the value of nitrogen analysis of plant tissue as an effective diagnostic method of measuring nitrogen response in cranberry because of the dilution of the nitrogen content in the plant as a result of the increased vegetative growth that nitrogen treatment produces. The complexity of the problem was demonstrated by the recent results of Stieber and Peterson (1987) wherein they observed active growth of cranberry vines taking place at the same time that nitrogen deficiency symptoms were being expressed.

Numerous workers (G. W. Eaton and Meehan 1973, 1976; Eck 1971; Leschyson and Eaton 1971) have shown that the nitrogen content can be increased in the cranberry plant by nitrogen fertilization (table 7.4). Nitrogen applications have also reportedly increased the leaf potassium content and decreased the zinc content in the cranberry plant (G. W. Eaton 1971a,b).

Chaplin and Martin (1979) have shown that the maximum flux in nitrogen content in the cranberry plant occurs during the first part of the growing season (table 7.1) and again toward the end of the growing season. Cranberry shoots measured 1.25 percent nitrogen in June and 0.95 percent in September. This is important to know if plant analysis is to be used for diagnostic purposes. It is necessary to measure the nitrogen content during a period of minimum change or flux to adequately diagnose nutrient status. Chaplin and Martin found this period of minimum nitrogen flux in cranberry shoots to occur in a period between mid-August and September.

Greidanus et al. (1972) have suggested that tissue nitrogen concentration may not be a suitable indicator of plant growth response and that the analysis for a particular nitrogen fraction might better reveal the association between nitrogen content and growth. They based their conclusion upon data that showed that plants receiving nitrate nitrogen exhibited nitrogen deficiency symptoms despite a nitrogen content of 1.34 percent, whereas plants receiving ammonium nitrogen produced vigorous growth with a tissue nitrogen concentration of 0.91 percent.

TABLE 7.4. EFFECT OF NITROGEN (N) FERTILIZER RATE ON YIELD AND PLANT COMPOSITION OF EARLY BLACK (EB) AND BEN LEAR (BL) CRANBERRY

Rate of N lbs./acre (kg/ha)	% of N in leaf (d.w.)	Fruit yield tons/acre (mt/ha)
0 (0)	0.96	6.5 (15.0) (BL)
10 (11.5)	0.97	8.1 (18.7) (BL)
15 (17.3)	0.92	10.8 (24.9) (EB)
20 (23.0)	1.03	9.7 (22.4) (BL)
30 (34.5)	1.15	11.4 (26.3) (BL)
30 (34.5)	1.01	9.6 (22.1) (EB)
45 (51.8)	1.09	6.8 (15.7) (EB)

SOURCES: Early Black data from Eck 1976b; Ben Lear data from G. W. Eaton and Meehan 1973.

Form of Nitrogen

The cranberry plant has been observed to respond under field conditions to the nitrate, ammonium, and organic forms of nitrogen (Beckwith 1931; Crowley 1954; Doehlert 1954; Schlatter 1916; Somogyi et al. 1964; Voorhees 1914). Addoms and Mounce (1932) were the first investigators to study the response of the cranberry plant to the nitrate and ammonium form of nitrogen under controlled greenhouse conditions. They observed that both forms stimulated vegetative growth but the ammonium ion produced the most growth. Nitrate nitrogen stimulated growth at low concentrations but suppressed growth at higher nitrate levels. Similar results were reported by Greidanus et al. (1972). This suggests that the nitrate reduction mechanism in the cranberry is quickly overloaded in the presence of high nitrate levels, thus preventing the metabolism of the nitrogen for growth. It would also explain the high nitrogen values found by Greidanus in plants supplied with nitrate nitrogen.

The question of whether the cranberry plant is capable of utilizing nitrogen in the nitrate form is still debated. Addoms and Mounce (1932) noted that the cranberry plant grew well in the presence of nitrate nitrogen when the pH was low (pH 4.0) but at higher pH (pH 6.5) ammonium nitrogen was essential.

They could not detect the presence of nitrates in cranberry tissue, which meant that its assimilation must have been extraordinarily rapid—despite the fact that tests for reductase (the enzyme required to assimilate NO_3-N) activity within various tissues of the cranberry plant gave only the faintest indication of any activity. Further evidence of the absence of any nitrate reductase activity in the aboveground portions of the cranberry plant was presented by Greidanus et al. (1972), although some activity was noted in the roots which the authors attributed to activity associated with the mycorrhizal fungi. Again, no nitrate nitrogen was detected in the plant tissue. Greidanus and his coworkers postulated that the cranberry, having evolved in an environment that was not conducive to nitrification (highly acidic, high-moisture soils), does not possess the genes for producing nitrate reductase and therefore the favored form of nitrogen for cranberry growth is ammonium.

Dirr (1974) showed that Early Black cranberries grew equally well with either the ammonium or nitrate form of nitrogen. He was unable to detect nitrates in the cranberry leaves but did measure considerable amounts in the roots of the cranberry plant. After examining the tissues of the plant and determining them to be free of mycorrhizal fungi, Dirr concluded that the cranberry plant must be capable of reducing nitrate nitrogen and that this reduction probably occurs in the roots.

Under bog soil conditions, the evidence appears to favor the conclusion that the cranberry plant can utilize the nitrate form of nitrogen to produce satisfactory growth (Beckwith 1930; Kender and Childers 1959; Leschyson and Eaton 1971), which would suggest that nitrate reduction must occur in the cranberry plant. The strongest evidence for the occurrence of nitrate reduction in cranberry is the failure on the part of all the investigators to find any nitrates in the aerial portions of the plant. This would suggest that any nitrates that are taken up by the plant are either stored in the roots as nitrates or are being reduced in the roots and assimilated into organic fractions. The fact that the cranberry plant does respond to nitrate nitrogen fertilization with increased vegetative growth would suggest the latter course. The question that remains is whether the cranberry plant is capable of carrying out the reduction or whether this function is carried out by the associated mycorrhizal fungi. Perhaps this is one of the benefits of mycorrhizal fungi in cranberries.

Role of Fungal Mycorrhiza

If the cranberry plant is unable to reduce nitrate nitrogen, an important question arises as to how the plant under field conditions is able to respond to nitrate fertilizers. It has been observed that both the roots and aerial parts of the cranberry plant are ramified with fungal mycelium (Addoms and Mounce 1931 1932). Bain (1937) isolated the fungus and observed that the hyphal complexes found represented not one but four different fungi, none of which was *Phoma radicis,* the endophytic fungus common to many ericaceous species. Although the mycorrhizal fungus (or fungi) alone was not able to supply the cranberry's need for nitrogen, there was no doubt as to the symbiotic relationship that exists between the fungus (fungi) and the plant. Addoms and Mounce observed that the amount of mycelium present within the plant appeared to be directly related to the vigor of growth in the host plant. Recently, Read (1987) has shown that cranberry plants infected with mycorrhizal fungi were able to utilize protein nitrogen after it was assimilated by the fungi and that this assimilation led to higher nitrogen content and yield in the cranberry plant.

Greidanus et al. (1972) have postulated that the fungal mycorrhiza within the cranberry plant is capable of reducing nitrate nitrogen in the plant. When chloramphenicol was used to inhibit the activity of the microbial systems, all evidence of nitrate reduction in the cranberry plant disappeared. The implication was that the endophytic fungi perform the nitrate reduction that the cranberry plant is unable to do and thereby enables the plant to respond to nitrate fertilizers.

Stribley and Read (1974) have reported that mycorrhizal plants were heavier, contained more nitrogen, and had a greater concentration of nitrogen on a dry-weight basis than nonmycorrhizal plants. They hypothesized that mycorrhizal roots perhaps could absorb nitrogen compounds unavailable to nonmycorrhizal plants. In subsequent studies Stribley and Read (1976) observed that the beneficial effect of mycorrhizal association could be easily masked by incremental additions of ammonium nitrogen fertilizer. It thus appears that the mycorrhizal association plays an important role in the cranberry's survival under indigenous conditions and may be even essential, but the association becomes much less important under the conditions of commercial production where nitrogen fertilizers are applied.

The possibility exists that the endophytic fungus may contribute to the nutrition of the cranberry in terms of water relationships and cation uptake as well as nitrogen utilization. The mass of mycelium over the surface of cranberry roots observed by Addoms and Mounce (1931) would greatly extend the amount of absorptive surface available to the cranberry plant inasmuch as the fungal hyphae penetrate the epidermis and cortical parenchyma of the root cells.

Vegetative Responses

Nitrogen deficiency in the cranberry plant is readily diagnosed. The leaves remain small, become pale yellow, and often develop a red pigmentation or bronzing beginning at the leaf margins (Dana 1968b). Uprights remain short and have abnormally small leaves, and vine growth is retarded. The stimulation of vine and upright growth is perhaps the most consistent response to nitrogen fertilization that has been observed (Addoms and Mounce 1931; Kender and Childers 1959; Torio and Eck 1969). Some stimulation of vine growth is desirable particularly when new bogs are being established. Bogs that are rapidly covered with vines will have a lower incidence of weed infestation and will bear a commercial crop sooner than bogs covered sparsely with vines.

In the presence of an excessive level of nitrogen, vine growth is often overstimulated to the extent that yield reductions result because of an apparent imbalance in the factors that govern vegetative and reproductive responses. Torio and Eck (1969) have shown that a cranberry plant receiving 60 ppm N in a nutrient solution produced 50 vines as compared to only 19 vines by a plant receiving only 20 ppm N in solution. A similar response under bog conditions was observed by Eck (1971, 1976b). Both the number of runners and the total runner growth per square foot increased with increasing nitrogen fertilization. Cranberry plants receiving 16 pounds (7.3 kg) of nitrogen per acre produced 35 vines per square foot as compared to the 67 vines per square foot produced by plants receiving 64 pounds (29 kg) of nitrogen per acre.

Chandler (1961) has maintained that adequate supplies of nitrogen must be made available to the cranberry plant to insure optimum production of uprights per square foot of bog area. According to Dana (1968b), the optimum production for the Searles cultivar would be from 250 to 300 uprights per square foot—comprising both flowering and vegetative uprights. Chandler has observed that the increase in upright production in response to nitrogen is primarily the result of the formation of new uprights with little increase in the number of flowering uprights. In fact, Eck (1976b) reported that the number of flowering uprights decreased from 189 to 107 per square foot as the nitrogen fertilizer rate increased from 15 to 45 pounds (6.8—20.4 kg) per acre.

Upright length also responds to nitrogen application. Eck (1971) has shown this to be the case under field conditions. Vegetative uprights averaged 6.3 cm in length when plants received 16 pounds (7.3 kg) of nitrogen per acre as compared to 7.4 cm when plants were treated with 64 pounds of nitrogen per acre. Flowering uprights responded similarly to nitrogen fertilization (Eck 1976b). Chandler (1955b) based his nitrogen recommendations for the Early Black cultivar upon existing upright length. The highest rates of nitrogen application (40 lbs., or 18.2 kg, per acre) were recommended for vines with new uprights less than one inch (2.5 cm) in length. Vines with new uprights 1 to 1½ inches (2.5—4.0 cm) required a medium rate of nitrogen (20 lbs., or 9.1 kg, per acre), and vines with new uprights over 2 inches (5 cm) in length required no added nitrogen. For the Searles cultivar, the optimum growth for new uprights would be 3 inches (7.5 cm) and for McFarlin it would be 2½ inches (6.5 cm), according to Dana (1968b).

Luke and Eck (1978) looked at the endogenous gibberellin activity in the cranberry plant under low and high nitrogen fertilization. Cranberry buds and young leaves contained high levels of gibberellin activity. Gibberellin activity in the leaves of uprights declined during July, coinciding with active elongation of the upright stem, and increased in August after terminal bud formation. The authors found that runner leaves contained high levels of gibberellin activity and postulated that the leaves may be important sources of gibberellin production during active runner growth. Interestingly, they found that plants receiving the lowest level of nitrogen had the highest gibberellin activity in both runners and uprights. Luke and Eck attributed this to the increased growth associated with the high nitrogen treatments, which effectively diluted the endogenous gibberellin levels.

Production Response

Cranberry production can be increased if nitrogen is added when it is a limiting factor to growth. In a long-term experiment covering 11 years, Beckwith (1930) showed that cranberry yield from plantings on savanna soil could be nearly doubled by the application of 30 pounds (13.6 kg) of nitrogen per acre. Earlier, both Beckwith (1919) and Voorhees (1914) had found that 40 pounds (18.2 kg) of nitrogen was detrimental to fruit production. Voorhees observed that this high rate of nitrogen caused runners to grow at the expense of fruit bud formation and fruit development. On a Berryland sand, Eck (1976b) found no benefit from applying more than 15 pounds (6.8 kg) of nitrogen per acre to a producing Early Black bog (Table 7.4). G. W. Eaton and Meehan (1973) found 30 (13.6 kg) pounds of nitrogen to be the optimum rate for bearing Ben Lear vines (Table 7.4). In an earlier study on peat soil in British Columbia, Eaton (1971a) showed that 45 pounds (20.4 kg) of nitrogen did not increase yield over a 15-pound (6.8-kg) rate and 135 (61.3 kg) pounds of nitrogen per acre reduced fruit yield to nearly a third of the production obtained at the 15-pound (6.8-kg) rate.

The production response to increased nitrogen must be manifested in one or more of the following ways: (1) an increase in the number of fruiting uprights, (2) an increase in the number of flowers per bud, (3) an increase in fruit set, and/or (4) an increase in berry size. A nitrogen deficiency would probably influence all these factors. As a constituent of the chlorophyll molecule and of proteins that are the building blocks of enzymes necessary for cranberry growth, nitrogen is directly related to the production of both flowering and nonflowering uprights. Healthy flower buds are better able to withstand the winter flood, according to Doehlert (1953b), who advocates nitrogen applications to undernourished bogs after harvest and prior to applying the winter flood. Nitrogen is also a constituent of the plant hormones that contribute to fruit set. A deficiency of nitrogen can therefore contribute to reduced fruit set. Nitrogen contributes to berry growth by virtue of its role in the many metabolic functions that contribute to growth.

Chandler (1961) showed that when nitrogen was limiting, the application of 20 pounds (9.1 kg) of nitrogen per acre increased the number of uprights that bore at least one or more fruits. In a controlled greenhouse study (Torio and Eck 1969), nitrogen treatment resulted in a greater number of flowers per upright. Doehlert (1953a) was able to increase the percentage of fruiting uprights by 20 percent the following growing season when he applied nitrogen in a complete fertilizer early in November. Since the fertilizer was applied too late in the season to affect the number of flower buds, the added nutrients may have contributed to the vitality of the existing buds, enabling them to overwinter more successfully. Eck (1976b) observed a biennial bearing pattern in Early Black cranberries that appeared to be related to new upright production. Fewer new uprights were formed during heavy production years than during light producing years.

There is no direct evidence that nitrogen fertilization beyond what is necessary to prevent nitrogen deficiency increases the percentage fruit set in cranberry. However, Shawa (1982) has speculated that nitrogen sprayed on cranberries at flowering may increase fruit set because the application increased pollen germination (as measured in vitro). On the contrary, Torio and Eck (1969) have shown that under greenhouse conditions the percent fruit set decreased with increasing nitrogen level.

The size of fruit can be significantly increased with nitrogen fertilization. Doehlert (1955a) had shown this to be the case by demonstrating that larger Early Black fruit were produced when 20 pounds (9.1 kg) of nitrogen were applied early in June, as compared to no fertilizer treatment. Eck (1964a) has also shown that nitrogen fertilization (60 lbs., or 27.4 kg, of N per acre) was associated with larger cranberry fruit. However, fewer cranberries per square foot were produced which might partially account for the size response to nitrogen at this high rate.

Fruit Quality

Nitrogen appears to have an important influence upon the quality of the fruit. Thienes (1955) reported that under Oregon conditions, the application of more than 30 pounds (13.6 kg) of actual nitrogen per acre can be expected to cause soft fruit of poor keeping quality. In Washington, berries treated with ammonium nitrogen alone had a high rate of breakdown in storage compared with berries receiving a complete fertilizer containing $N-P_2O_5-K_2O$ in a 1-4-2 ratio (Washington State College 1963). Atwood and Zuckerman (1961) correlated increased fruit rot with an increased nitrogen rate. The authors postulated that the high rate of nitrogen produced an environment favorable to rot infection. Chandler (1956d) also was of the opinion that excess nitrogen fertilization impaired the keeping quality of fruit and that poor fruit quality was in some way related to the excessive vine growth associated with high nitrogen fertilization. The high incidence of fruit rot often observed in young bearing bogs may be partially the result of large quantities of nitrogen becoming available from the rapidly decomposing organic matter of the new bog. Eck (1976b) observed an increase in fruit rot associated with higher nitrogen fertilization in a bearing Early Black planting. In sand culture studies in which nitrogen nutrition and fruit rot infection were controlled, Torio et al. (1966) were able to show that high nitrogen was associated with increased fruit rot.

Anthocyanin development in cranberry fruit may also be influenced by nitrogen nutrition. Francis and Atwood (1961) found that the red pigment content of fresh cranberries decreased with the application of increasing amounts of nitrogen fertilizer. The highest pigment content was always found in fruit harvested from plants that had received no nitrogen. The low pigment content associated with the high levels of nitrogen nutrition may have resulted from the shading effect by increased vegetative production stimulated by the added nitrogen. The possibility also exists, however, that the rate of the biochemical reactions that produce anthocyanins in cranberry fruit is retarded by the presence of high nitrogen levels that would favor active plant growth and tend to delay senescence. Eaton (1971a) observed that increased nitrogen nutrition decreased the redness and increased the yellowness and lightness in McFarlin fruit. A similar response was reported in a mature Early Black planting (Eck 1976b).

Phosphorus

Plant Response

Phosphorus (P) is necessary for cranberry growth because it is an essential constituent of compounds that are involved in the plant's energy transfer reactions, of which photosynthesis is a critical example. Approximately 4½ pounds (2 kg) of phosphorus are removed in each 100 barrels of cranberries harvested from an acre (Colby 1945). As early as 1914, Voorhees showed that cranberry yields could be increased by applications of phosphorus fertilizer. More recently, Eaton (1971a) found that tissue phosphorus increased with increasing phosphorus fertilization; tissue phosphorus was positively related to fruit yield but negatively correlated with fruit redness. Eck (1985) obtained the highest yields from the Early Black cranberry at a phosphorus fertilizer rate of 40 kg P/ha. Phosphorus fertilization was associated with increased phosphorus content in the plant and increased available soil phosphorus (Eck 1964b, 1985). Torio and Eck (1969) showed that runner growth increased with increasing phosphorus content of the leaf as phosphorus fertilization was increased.

At fertilizer rates below 34 kg P/ha, phosphorus deficiency in the Stevens cranberry under Wisconsin field conditions was manifested in a general restriction of growth and in a purplish bronze coloration of the leaves (Greidanus and Dana 1972). When soil levels of phosphorus were maintained above a range of 45 to 60 pounds (20.4–27.2 kg) of available phosphorus per acre by a fertilizer rate in excess of 30 pounds (13.6 kg) of phosphorus per acre, no symptoms or limitation of growth occurred in the Stevens cranberry. However, Shawa (A. W. Shawa, letter to author, 1988) has observed that the tips of cranberry uprights yellow at these soil phosphorus levels in Washington, which he attributes to phosphorus-induced zinc deficiency. Similar conclusions regarding the optimum P fertilizer rate and soil level were drawn by Massachusetts (Chandler and Demoranville 1961a) and New Jersey researchers (Eck 1985) working with the Early Black cultivar.

Under greenhouse conditions, new shoots turn pink in the upper stem and at the leaf edges when phosphorus is deficient. At a later stage of deficiency, the terminal leaves become pink and the older leaves of the shoot develop a purplish red speckling and die. When cranberry plants were grown in nutrient solution, Medappa and Dana (1970a) were unable to show a response to phosphorus when the solution levels were increased from 2 to 120 ppm in a medium adjusted to pH 4. These available phosphorus levels far exceed the solution levels found in most soils. Cranberry plants were capable of accumulating comparable amounts of radiophosphorus even at low levels of P^{32} activity in the external solution (Medappa and Dana 1968). Shoot tissues accumulated low amounts of phosphorus at pH 3 and at pH 8. High levels of aluminum in the nutrient solution markedly depressed the uptake of phosphorus by the cranberry plant.

Plant and Fruit Content

Greidanus and Dana (1972) found that deficiency symptoms in the Stevens cranberry developed when the phosphorus content of young cranberry shoots ranged from 0.034 to 0.080 percent (table 7.3). A range from 0.09 to 0.11 percent represented an area of hidden hunger, and 0.12 to 0.27 percent represented phosphorus sufficiency in the plant. Eck (1964b) found that phosphorus levels in the Early Black cultivar ranged from 0.063 percent when no phosphorus fertilizer was added to 0.119 percent when fertilizer was added.

Maximum yield in an Early Black planting was associated with 0.088 percent phosphorus in the fruiting upright (Eck 1985).

G. W. Eaton (1971b) found that the phosphorus content in leaf tissue of a young Ben Lear planting to be as high as 0.384 percent when fertilized at the rate of 53 pounds (24 kg) of phosphorus per acre. Eaton (1971a) reported that the phosphorus content in McFarlin leaves of a mature planting increased from 0.089 to 0.105 percent as the phosphorus fertilizer rate was increased from 0 to 27 pounds (12.3 kg) per acre. The phosphorus levels found in the fruit tissue of these plants were as high (0.070—0.078 percent) as those found by Torio and Eck (1969) in fruit tissue in their greenhouse-grown Early Black plants.

According to Chaplin and Martin (1979), the phosphorus content of cranberry shoots decreases during the growing season, ranging from 0.18 percent in June to 0.14 percent in September. The greatest change in phosphorus content of the shoots occurred during June. Sidorovich et al. (1986) also studied the seasonal dynamics of phosphorus accumulation in the American cranberry and found not one but two accumulation maxima: one occurring in May and the other in the period between August and September. Torio and Eck (1969) observed that the phosphorus content of the cranberry plant decreased with the age of the plant, decreasing from 0.26 percent as a rooted cutting to 0.08 percent in its third growing season. This observation appears to support Eaton's findings of high phosphorus levels in young cranberry plants in the field.

Both nitrogen and sulfur applications were observed to influence phosphorus content in the cranberry plant (Torio and Eck 1969). Early Black plants grown in nutrient solution containing a high level of nitrogen (60 ppm N) had a lower phosphorus content than plants receiving a low level of nitrogen (20 ppm N). Plants that received a high level of sulfur nutrition (60 ppm S) had a higher phosphorus content than plants receiving a low sulfur level (20 ppm S). Under field conditions, however, G. W. Eaton (1971a) observed that the addition of nitrogen fertilizer was associated with increased phosphorus uptake.

Potassium

Plant Response

Although potassium is not a constituent of any major metabolite in cranberry, it is undoubtedly involved in regulatory processes within the plant, particularly that of stomatal regulation. Colby (1945) has calculated that a hundred barrels of cranberries removes 15 pounds of potassium from an acre of cranberries. Its essentiality to cranberries is demonstrated by the fact that cranberries are known to respond to potassium nutrition. As early as 1914, Voorhees observed that potassium applied without any other nutrient supplement increased both yield and size of Early Black fruit from vines grown on a savanna soil. Vine growth increased in a young McFarlin bog when potassium was added by G. W. Eaton (1971b). Under greenhouse conditions Torio and Eck (1969) found that Early Black cranberry plants receiving a high level of potassium (60 ppm K) in the nutrient solution had consistently more uprights per plant than did plants receiving a low supplement of potassium (20 ppm K). Fisher (1951) has reported that cranberry yields in Washington were reduced when soil test values drop below 50 pounds (22.7 kg) of available potassium per acre. Peltier (1955) has suggested a soil test value of 250 pounds (113.5 kg) of available potassium per acre for Wisconsin cranberry soils in order to balance the high phosphorus requirement for their soils. In British Columbia, however, Eaton (1971a) was not able to show any yield increase or change in fruit quality in the McFarlin cultivar as the potassium fertilizer rate was increased from 0 to 50 pounds (22.7 kg) of potassium per acre.

Despite its importance to cranberry nutrition, potassium has received very little study by cranberry researchers. As a result, we do not know what constitutes potassium sufficiency or deficiency in the cranberry plant. To date, the classical symptoms of marginal leaf scorch that signify potassium deficiency under greenhouse conditions have not been observed in the field.

Plant and Fruit Content

The addition of potassium to the growing substrate is readily reflected in increased potassium content of cranberry tissue (G. W. Eaton 1971a, 1971b; Torio and Eck 1969). Reported values for potassium in cranberry leaf tissue have ranged from a low of 0.23 percent to a high of 0.74 percent (table 7.3). In a mature McFarlin bog, Eaton (1971a) reported a range of potassium content in the leaf from 0.23 to 0.37 percent as the potassium fertilizer rate was increased from 0 to 60 pounds (27.3 kg) per acre. Potassium fertilization was found to have a marked depressant effect on the magnesium content of McFarlin leaf tissue (Eaton 1971a). Increased levels of potassium fertilization consistently lowered magnesium leaf content in all three years of Eaton's test. Chaplin and Martin (1979) observed that the potassium content in McFarlin cranberry shoots was highest in June (0.55 percent) and decreased to 0.40 percent by September. The period of minimum potassium flux in the plant occurred between mid-August and mid-September.

The cranberry fruit appears to serve as an extraordinary sink for potassium. The potassium content of Early Black cranberries was found to range from 1.37 to 1.61 percent—nearly three times as great as the leaf potassium content (Torio and Eck 1969).

Other Major Elements

Calcium

Cranberries apparently have a very low requirement for the element calcium, even though it is an essential part of cell wall structure and maintains the integrity of cell membranes. A hundred barrels of cranberries only removes about 2 pounds (0.9 kg) of calcium from the soil, according to Colby (1945). This need not be very surprising inasmuch as the cranberry thrives in an acid substrate that would normally be very low in calcium content. Nonetheless, Washington recommendations have included the annual application of 200 pounds (90.8 kg) of calcium to an acre of cranberries (Doughty 1972). The plant's response to this amount of calcium, however, lessens after three years of annual application. Medappa and Dana (1970a) increased calcium levels in a nutrient solution maintained at pH 4 but were unable to obtain a growth response. Recently, Russian workers have shown that the American cranberry will respond to lime application with increased shoot growth (Sharstsyanikina and Zaranchuk 1986). Shawa (1979b) has reported both a significant yield increase and reduced fruit breakdown during storage of McFarlin cranberries as the result of the application of 446 pounds (202 kg) per acre of agricultural lime ($CaCO_3$). This lime rate increased the soil pH from 5.8 to 6.1. Higher rates of lime application resulted in chlorotic uprights and reduced yields.

The calcium content of cranberry leaves has been found to vary appreciably between cranberry-growing areas and between cultivars (table 7.3). The difference in calcium content of the plant tissue might reflect a difference in the composition of the organic matter found in the different locales. Shawa (1979b) measured increases in calcium content of the fruit from 0.056 to 0.068 percent as lime rates were increased but observed decreased contents of potassium and magnesium. According to Chaplin and Martin (1979), the calcium content of cranberry shoots increases as the growing season progresses, from 0.51 percent in June to 0.73 percent in September. The best time to take tissue samples for calcium analysis is between mid-August and mid-September.

Magnesium

Although there have been no reports that the cranberry plant will respond to magnesium supplements, magnesium is an important essential element to the cranberry because of its role as a constituent of the chlorophyll molecule. Because of their extreme acidity, cranberry soils do not have significant magnesium reserves in them. It is entirely possible that cranberries could be existing at a marginal magnesium sufficiency level when consideration is given to the fact that its close relative, the blueberry, frequently shows magnesium deficiency when grown on these same soils.

Reported values for magnesium content in the cranberry plant appear to be fairly constant between cultivars and between different cranberry-growing regions (table 7.3). The magnesium content of the tissue, however, can be depressed by applying increasing amounts of potassium fertilizer, as reported by G. W. Eaton (1971b). Chaplin and Martin (1979) concluded that there was a great deal of variability in the magnesium content of cranberry shoots during the growing season, another indication that, at best, the cranberry may be functioning in only a marginal sufficiency range. This variability would tend to make it difficult to diagnose the magnesium status of the cranberry plant by tissue analysis.

Sulfur

Although sulfur is also a constituent of essential metabolites in the cranberry, deficiencies are unknown. The high levels of sulfur dioxide as an air pollutant may in part contribute to the sulfur needs of the cranberry plant. Wood et al. (1950), however, have reported that a low incidence of fruit rot and large berry size were associated with sulfur use in Oregon. A sulfur response in cranberries in Oregon is entirely plausible since other crops have been known to respond to sulfur in that part of the country. Since the prevailing winds are westerly, those growing regions would not be exposed to the levels of sulfur dioxide in the air that more easterly regions of the country exposed to the emissions of coal-fired generating plants are.

When sulfur was used to lower pH in the Wisconsin River area, sulfur had no effect on cranberry yields after three years of use (Peltier 1964). Nor was it very effective in lowering the pH in the bog, presumably because of the absence of sulfur bacteria capable of oxidizing sulfur. More recently, Torio and Eck (1969) have shown that sulfur application may interact with nitrogen treatment to produce significant effects on the production potential of the cranberry plant. At a low level of nitrogen nutrition, increasing the sulfur application increased both the flowering and the percentage fruit set in plants, but at a high level of nitrogen nutrition, both flowering and fruit set were depressed as the sulfur application rate increased. Both yield and resistance to fruit breakdown in storage were found to increase with the application of sulfur-coated urea to McFarlin bogs under Washington conditions (Shawa 1972b).

The sulfur content of cranberry leaves was found to range from 0.106 to

0.127 percent in plants receiving low and high rates of sulfur nutrition (table 7.3). In comparison, the fruit contained over three-fourths the sulfur content of the leaf and did not appear to be influenced by the rate of sulfur application.

Trace Elements

Iron

Iron plays a significant role in the energy transfer system of metabolic reactions in the cranberry plant. Iron availability in the soil is at its greatest at a low pH; therefore, cranberry soils might be expected to contain adequate amounts of iron. Fisher (1951) observed a direct correlation between yield and the available iron content of the soil in a survey of the nutritional status of Washington cranberry bogs. The high-yielding bogs were found to contain at least twice as much available iron as aluminum. When the content of iron was several times that of aluminum, the actual amount of iron needed to supply the plant's needs apparently could be less than if the aluminum content was high—suggesting an aluminum antagonism to iron uptake by the plant. Because aluminum availability increases as soil pH decreases and aluminum in high concentration can be toxic to plants, the significant role of iron in the soil may, in part, be that of preventing aluminum from reaching toxic levels in the soil.

Medappa and Dana (1970b) found that plants in nutrient solution culture supplied with iron in chelate form (FeEDTA) produced better growth above pH 6 than did plants receiving iron as iron sulfate. Above pH 7, plants developed chlorosis when supplied with iron sulfate but not with the iron chelate. The authors postulated that the chlorosis developed because of the inactivation of the iron in the plant tissue.

Cranberry response to iron has been reported in Washington (Washington State College 1963) but not in Massachusetts (Chandler 1955b). Doughty (1984) was able to correct what appeared to be iron chlorosis in the terminal growth of McFarlin vines and increase yield with applications of iron chelate. The applications of iron chelate also reduced the levels of aluminum in the cranberry leaves. Iron content has been found to range from 30 ppm in a young Ben Lear planting to 122 ppm in Natives found in the Annapolis Valley of Nova Scotia (Townsend and Hall 1971). In McFarlin cranberry shoots, iron was measured at 80 ppm in June and 100 ppm in September by Chaplin and Martin (1979). They found the iron content in the cranberry plant to fluctuate widely during the growing season.

Manganese

Cranberries contain very high concentrations of manganese in their leaves, ranging from 300 to 908 ppm (table 7.3). These levels far exceed the manganese levels required by most higher plants to carry out the metabolic processes that manganese regulates. Again, the low soil pH at which cranberries thrive greatly favors the availability of manganese from the soil. Chaplin and Martin (1979) reported a range of 80 to 190 ppm manganese in cranberry shoots. Levels were lowest in June and highest in September and appeared to fluctuate least in the plant during the early part of the growing season. G. W. Eaton (1971b) has observed that whenever the level of applied nitrogen was increased, the level of manganese in the leaf would decrease significantly.

When manganese was applied to Washington cranberries showing chlorotic symptoms, a response was obtained (Washington State College 1963). Doughty (1984), however, observed a negative relationship between yield and foliar manganese level. Eck (1966) has presented evidence that suggests that it may be important to maintain a balance between manganese and copper and between manganese and boron. When copper chelate was added without also adding manganese, a reduction in yield resulted. Highest yields were obtained when both manganese chelate and copper chelate were added. In a similar manner, berry size was reduced when boron was added without also adding manganese. The largest berries were produced when the plants received both boron and manganese and when the plants received no additional boron or manganese, thereby maintaining the natural balance that existed before the initiation of amendments.

Zinc

This element also functions in a regulatory capacity in the cranberry plant and thus is only required in very low amounts. Again, it is the West Coast cranberry-growing region from which reports of response to the trace element come, suggesting that the cranberry soils that developed in this part of the country were of parent material significantly different from that of the eastern growing regions. Shawa (1972a) has reported that yellow tips of cranberry uprights in Washington can be greened up by the application of zinc chelate. Three pounds of zinc chelate has been recommended for zinc deficiency correction in Washington. A foliar spray application of a liquid fertilizer containing nitrogen, phosphorus, and 2 percent zinc at the hook stage of flowering and one week after fruit set increased berry size and weight of the McFarlin cranberry and reduced fruit breakdown in storage (Shawa 1973). Zinc chelate applied to McFarlin vines corrected leaf chlorosis, improved terminal growth, and decreased foliar levels of iron but did not affect yield (Doughty 1984).

Chaplin and Martin (1979) found the zinc content in cranberry shoots to range from 45 ppm in June to 32 ppm in September with the least tissue fluctuation occurring in August tissue samples. Similarly, Russian researchers (Sidorovich et al. 1987) found the zinc content to be highest in the new growth. They observed that the zinc content in the plant increased with increasing zinc levels in the soil and that zinc tended to accumulate in the fruit.

Copper

The high acidity of cranberry soils makes copper toxicity a distinct possibility because only very small amounts of copper are required by the cranberry plant to perform the regulatory functions of this element. Reports of copper toxicity in cranberries have come from Washington (Doughty 1972) and from Massachusetts (Chandler 1955b). Symptoms of copper toxicity are similar to the chlorosis that develops as the result of iron deficiency. Feeder roots are often injured in high-copper environments. This injury will prevent the uptake of adequate amounts of water and nutrients so that eventual growth restriction occurs. If copper toxicity is known to exist, attempts must be made to raise the pH of the soil by the addition of lime to render some of the soluble copper into an unavailable form. Copper is sometimes added to cranberry bogs as copper sulfate to control moss and algae growth and in copper-based fungicides. Its level should therefore be carefully monitored in soils where copper toxicity is suspect.

Shawa (1981) observed a deformity in McFarlin cranberry fruit in Washington, which he described as a "cat-facing" on the berry, that he attributed to copper deficiency. He was able to decrease the number of the so-called cat-faced berries by sprays of copper before bloom and after fruit set. Cranberry shoots ranged in copper content from a high of 25 ppm in June to 10 ppm in September (Chaplin and Martin 1979).

Boron and Molybdenum

Both boron and molybdenum are normally found in soils in very minute quantities, particularly in highly acid soils such as those that exist in cranberry bogs. Although one might expect responses in cranberry to these elements because the plants are grown under such acid soil condition, little conclusive work has been done to show whether the cranberry responds to either of these elements. Eck (1966) has reported a significant interaction between these two elements on the yield of Early Black cranberries under New Jersey soil conditions. In two years of testing under field conditions, he observed that yields were increased by 25 percent when molybdenum was applied without added boron. When boron and molybdenum were both applied, the yield was depressed when compared to plants receiving only added boron. This suggests that in the cranberry some interrelationship exists between boron and molybdenum that affects fruit set and/or berry development. Chaplin and Martin (1979) have reported the boron content in cranberry shoots to vary in the narrow range of 30 to 40 ppm.

Recently, C. J. Demoranville and Deubert (1987) have presented evidence that suggests that two foliar spray applications of a commercial calcium-boron formulation, timed at one week before full bloom and at full bloom, will increase the percentage fruit set in both Early Black and Howes cranberry. Experimental applications increased fruit set by 45 percent in Early Black and 68 percent in Howes. Commercial applications of the compound by aerial and sprinkler application also increased the percentage fruit set in these cultivars but not to the extent of the experimental hand-spray applications.

EIGHT

Culture

Site Selection

Indicator Plants

In the major commercial growing areas, cranberries can be found growing naturally in swamps that have undergone various stages of ecological development. The type of plants found associated with the cranberry is an indication of the stage of development of the swamp. The ecological sequence of vegetation beginning with the impounded water body consists of water lilies, followed by rushes, moss, and then the bushes, which may include leatherleaf ("brown brush"), wild blueberry, and sheep laurel. Finally come the tree species that may include white cedar, red maple, or mixtures of red maple and pine, depending on the depth of the organic matter layer. The cedars are found on the deep peat swamps in the East, but in northern Wisconsin it is spruce and tamarack that will be found in the deep peat. A swamp that is at the leatherleaf stage of development is considered ideal for cranberry growing. Swamps covered in rushes and sedges are not considered good locations because these weeds spread rapidly when the ground is cleared and are difficult to eradicate.

The peat marshes or swamps upon which commercial plantings are established usually have a pH of 4.0 to 5.0; pH 5.5 is about the upper limit for successful production. The low pH appears to favor cranberry growth and probably discourages a great many weed species. Typical vegetation that is indicative of good cranberry land is given in table 8.1 taken from *Cranberry Growing in New Jersey* (Beckwith 1922).

Other plant species common to New Jersey swamp areas are sphagnum moss, pitcher plant (*Sarracenia purpurea* L.), cinnamon fern (*Osmunda cinnamomea* L.), royal fern (*Osmunda regalia* L.), wintergreen (*Gaultheria procumbens* L.), golden club (*Orontium aequaticum* L.), and white water lily (*Castalia odorata*). In Massachusetts the plant species associated with cranberry growing are the same as those found in New Jersey. In Wisconsin,

TABLE 8.1. TYPICAL SWAMP VEGETATION ASSOCIATED WITH
GOOD CRANBERRY-PRODUCING SITES

Common name	Scientific name	% of ground covered
White cedar	*Chamaecyparis thyoides* B.S.P.	85
Pitch pine	*Pinus rigida* Mill	5
Swamp magnolia	*Magnolia virginiana* L.	2
Leatherleaf	*Chamaedaphne calyculata* Moench	2

The remaining 6% would consist of the following:

Button bush	*Cephalanthus occidentales* L.	
Alder	*Alnus rugosa* Koch	
Swamp maple	*Acer rubrum* L.	
Sweet pepperbush	*Clethra alnifolia* L.	
Poison sumac	*Pihus toxicodendron* L.	
Sour gum	*Nyssa sylvatica* Marsh	

SOURCE: Beckwith 1922.

in addition to leatherleaf (*Chamaedaphne calyculata*), it is tamarack (*Larix laricina*) that is the chief indicator plant for successful cranberry growing. In Washington Crowley (1954) lists the following species that are found in swamps growing with the native cranberry: *Spirea douglasii* Hook (buckbrush), *Ledum columbianum* Piper, *Kalmia polifolia* Wang, *Alnus oregona* Nutt. (alder), *Picea sitchensis* (spruce), *Myrica gale* (sweet gale), *Vaccinium oxycoccus intermedius* (Gray) Piper (or *V. quadripetalum*) wild cranberry, and *Salix* sp. (willow).

The University of Wisconsin Cooperative Extension Service (Dana and Klingbeil 1966) recommends the use of the following criteria in selecting a site for the commercial production of cranberries: (1) a soil acidity in the range of pH 4.0 to pH 5.0; (2) a marsh area large enough to be profitable and permit mechanization (generally a minimum of 30 acres of established vines); (3) a large supply of water available for frost protection, irrigation, and harvesting (accessibility may include legal restrictions as well as quantity restrictions); (4) a virgin peat soil, although a sandy soil may be used; (5) good drainage of cold air away from the marsh and little or no elevated area from which cold air will drain onto the marsh; (6) a convenient supply of coarse sand that may be used in the development and management of the marsh; (7) and sufficient grade to provide for rapid water drainage from the marsh without constant pumping to remove seepage.

Soils

Cranberries are grown commercially on acid peat and sandy loam soils with an organic matter depth varying in thickness from a fraction of an inch to as much as 20 feet. Common to some of these soils is a high water table supported by an underlying hardpan that can be manipulated to carry out the cultural practices essential for commercial production. These soils would be classified as wetland soils. Commercial cranberry production on upland soils is possible as long as good water supplies are available and the soils are not excessively drained. An example of this upland cranberry production is the successful cranberry industry that has developed on the sandy elevated marine terraces in Oregon.

In the wetland soils, the organic matter layer, which may be of variable thickness, is underlain by a layer of leached sand overlying a layer of yellowish to coffee brown sand. Below these layers of sand, a hardpan consisting of iron oxides or clay is present. It is this hardpan that is impervious to water and contributes to the high water table that is essential for commercial cranberry production. Care must be taken not to break through this hardpan when the site is prepared for planting. The destruction of the hardpan would lead to excessive drainage and render an otherwise suitable site too dry for commercial cranberry production. When the sand layers and relatively thin layers of organic matter are incorporated, the sand takes on a black appearance. As mentioned above (chapter 5), in New Jersey this is called savanna land. On the West Coast, this type of soil is called *blacklock*. Most new cranberry plantings are being made on these loamy sand, mineral-type soils. Deubert (1969a) analyzed 136 Massachusetts bog soil samples and found that they averaged 87 percent sand and only 3 percent silt and clay. The organic matter content in the top four inches of these soils ranged from less than 1 percent to 5 percent, with 2.34 percent as a mean value. The cation exchange capacity in these same soils ranged from 5.9 to 20.4 meq.

The prerequisite of low silt and clay levels was emphasized as early as 1870, when Joseph White in his monograph *Cranberry Culture* (p. 28) noted that "clay and loam are to be avoided, under all circumstances, by those desiring a profitable and permanent investment in cranberry meadows."

Muck and mud bottom soils in New Jersey and Massachusetts consist of deeper layers of partially decomposed organic matter. Muck layers may be as thick as 25 feet but most cranberry muck soils average about 5 feet in depth. This is the type of soil most often encountered when a pond is drained and used for cranberry growing. The organic matter in a muck soil ranges between 20 and 50 percent and is more highly decomposed than the organic matter in peat.

It is not advisable to plant cranberries on undecomposed peat until sufficient time is allowed for the peat to settle after drainage. As the peat dries, the increased aeration favors the microbial decomposition of the organic matter, which ultimately leads to the formation of the muck soil. The rate and extent of decomposition and settling of the peat can be controlled by regulating the water table depth. The moisture-holding capacity of muck soils makes them particularly suitable for cranberry production. Coarse mucks, however, are not capable of holding much moisture nor are they able to absorb moisture from below. Without irrigation, plantings established on coarse muck would suffer more than plantings on sand. Planting on pure peat and muck soils also greatly increases the risk of plant heaving during the winter months. The use of peat and muck soils for cranberry growth is discouraged in Washington because of the high levels of nitrogen that are released upon decomposition, which often contributes to excessive vine growth and poor fruit production. Another drawback to the use of peat for cranberry bogs is that often the peat may be poorly drained (Chandler 1952a). Chandler described this peat as being "greasy" because it tended to be very slippery to the touch yet it would stick to shovels. The well-decomposed peat was usually very densely packed and had very small pore space and would not support good cranberry root development. Such bogs were always slow to vine over when first planted.

Water Supply

An abundant supply of good-quality water for irrigation, frost protection, and the winter flood is essential for commercial cranberry production. Water low in dissolved minerals, high in oxygen, and low in pH would be considered of good quality. The source of this water might be either a series of reservoirs located upstream from the bogs (reservoirs located adjacent to the bogs can create wet areas in the bogs because of excessive seepage), a large river or stream, or deep wells dug especially for irrigation purposes. When reservoirs are relied upon for the water supply, a general rule of thumb has been to have two acres of reservoir for each acre of cranberry bog, assuming a 48-to-72-hour recharge rate. A winter flood would require at least 300,000 gallons of water per acre (Cross 1969a), but conceivably even more water would be needed if frequent flooding is needed to protect against frost, since a four-inch flood would use as much as 100,000 gallons per acre.

The use of sprinkler irrigation for frost protection and for summer irrigation can reduce the demand for water. It has been estimated that sprinkling for frost control can reduce the water need by 80 percent of that required by conventional frost flooding. Because of the many legal restrictions that exist on water use, it is imperative that prospective cranberry producers thoroughly familiarize themselves with the state and local legal aspects involved in the acquisition of water supplies before making any investment in a cranberry property.

Drainage

The ability to drain the intended cranberry-growing site is extremely important. If the site cannot be drained at least 18 inches below the surface, it should be rejected. Early producers of cranberries found out very quickly that stagnant water is fatal to the cranberry plant and, as succinctly stated by White (1870, p. 34), "water is essential, but *it must be under control.*" Poorly drained bogs are more prone to severe weed infestations as well as disease and insect infestations. Good drainage also speeds water removal after spring frost reflows, which is important because the plants are undergoing rapid growth during this period and can suffer from the poor aeration that results from water logging. F. B. Chandler was a strong advocate for good drainage in cranberry bogs (Chandler 1953a). He observed that bogs with good drainage invariably yielded more than bogs with poor drainage. Compared to poorly drained bogs, well-drained bogs had plants with deeper root systems, which helped sustain the cranberry plant during periods of moisture stress and the stress from mechanical injury associated with harvest operations. The frequent occurrence of upright dieback and vine browning in poorly drained areas of a bog was attributed by Chandler (1955b) to the shallow roots of the cranberry plant, which succumbs quickly to moisture stress during periods of drought. His observations led him to conclude that New Jersey bogs were amongst the most poorly drained, Massachusetts bogs were intermediate in drainage, and Wisconsin bogs were the best drained. Chandler was of the opinion that when poorly drained bog conditions existed, some remedial measures were absolutely essential to obtain good yields.

To achieve the necessary drainage, ditches are usually dug at least 2 feet in depth around the periphery of the bog and 18 inches deep in the cross ditches. In addition, sufficient grade is needed to allow for the rapid removal of water by gravity flow. Through the use of water control structures, the water table can be controlled in the bog. If internal soil drainage is restricted, it is necessary to install tile drainage in those sections that drain poorly. These areas in the bogs are often characterized by the presence of rushes and sedges, which favor these wet areas. Chandler (1954b) successfully drained such areas with perforated plastic tubing that was put in place using a mole plow with very little damage to the vines.

Air drainage is also an important consideration because of the frost

implications. Cranberry bogs are by necessity located on land that is extensively flat from which air is likely to drain only slowly, increasing the potential
for frost pockets to develop. Radiation frosts are much more prevalent on
these flat, low-lying areas than on adjacent upland. If the bogs are surrounded
by forest land, air drainage is further impeded. Air drainage can be improved
in these instances by cutting down the trees at the end of the bogs at the
lower elevation, enabling the cold air to drain away from the bogs.

In special cases, such as on the Pacific Coast, windbreaks may be needed
to protect against drying winds during the growing season. Not only are these
drying northwesterlies capable of desiccating the new cranberry growth but
they are also strong enough to cause sand to encroach upon the bog. If sites
cannot be selected with natural northwest windbreaks, they must then be
constructed and maintained.

Sand Supply

A convenient source of clean, sharp sand or fine gravel is highly desirable
when locating a cranberry site. Sand is important in site preparation and bog
maintenance. During bog construction, a three-inch layer on top of muck requires 400 cubic yards of sand per acre, and a half-inch layer for resanding will
take 65 to 70 cubic yards. The cost of moving this amount of sand will depend
in part on how far the source is from the bogs and how easy it is to get at.

The quality of the sand is extremely important. Sand containing silt and
clay should be avoided because it often encourages weed growth. A convenient test of the suitability of the sand can be made by dropping a handful of the
sand into clear, still water. If the sand contains loam or clay, the water will
become muddy, but if the sand is pure it will sink without a trace of turbidity.

Bog Establishment

Clearing

The first step in establishing a new cranberry bog is to clear all the living vegetation, both tops and roots, from the site. This is imperative in order to insure
proper leveling of the bog as well as to eliminate weeds and other undesirable
agents. Roots and buried stumps that are allowed to remain will eventually rot
and cause settling in the bog after it is planted, forming pockets that could
cause management problems in the future. One approach has been to burn
the site after any valuable timber has been removed and to flood it for two
years (Beckwith 1922). In this procedure, care must be taken to keep the
water table fairly high during the burning so as not to ignite the peat because
peat fires can be difficult to extinguish. After the flood is withdrawn, the re-

mainder of the vegetation is removed. This had been the favored method of clearing new land in New Jersey, but today the long-term flooding operation is no longer used because of capital considerations.

An alternative to flooding is called *turfing* or *scalping.* After the swamp has been drained, the tops of all the vegetation are removed and the turf containing the roots of the plants is cut into squares and turned over with turf hooks (Franklin 1948a). When the turf is thoroughly dry, it can be easily broken up with a grading hoe in order to remove the roots of undesirable vegetation. In the early days of cranberry growing, turfing was an arduous hand process, but today sites are scalped with draglines and bulldozers that remove the root-containing turf completely and transport it to the dam sites, where it will be used to secure the sides of the dam. The same equipment is then used to level the fields. The leveling of the field is an important part of site preparation because level bogs make water management for frost protection and water harvesting much easier. The techniques of leveling have progressed over the years from eyeballing, to the use of land levels, to the modern day use of laser-leveling techniques. The clearing and leveling procedures are completed in the summer preceding the spring planting.

Sites that are free of trees and brush, such as the grassed marshes of Wisconsin and Massachusetts, need only be plowed and planted in cranberries (Darrow et al. 1924a). In Massachusetts growers have been known to merely cover such grasslands with a thick layer of sand and plant cranberries without disturbing the turf at all. Such easily developed sites, however, have been utilized long ago. Today, considerably more labor and capital must be invested in preparing new sites for cranberry production (plate 8.1). In addition to the heavy equipment and modern technology that are available, growers have at their disposal new herbicides that can be used in clearing brush from the site.

Dams and Ditches

After clearing the bog area, a decision must be made on the size and shape of the bogs. It is generally accepted that a bog encompassing two to four acres constitutes the best management unit (Dana and Klingbeil 1966). To provide for the efficient use of equipment for pest control, fertilization, weed control, and harvesting, the bogs should be no wider than 160 feet. The length of the bogs may vary depending on the natural contour of the area. The bogs can be either shaped to fit the natural contour or constructed into rectangular sections. At any rate, each section must be surrounded by a roadway that serves as a dam and provides the access for the management operations.

The dam essentially consists of three parts: (1) a 2-foot core extending through any peat to the mineral substrata; (2) the main body of the dam, com-

PLATE 8.1. MODERN BOG CONSTRUCTION SHOWING THE DAM, RISER ON WATER SUPPLY TRUNK, DITCH, AND BOG SURFACE—ALL OF WHICH WOULD BE ACCOMPLISHED TODAY BY HEAVY EARTH-MOVING EQUIPMENT (Courtesy Massachusetts Cranberry Experiment Station)

posed of sand; (3) and a turf veneer for stabilization (fig. 8.1). The core is constructed along the centerline of the dam and should extend through the peat so as to impede seepage across the dam. The main body of the dam consists of sand, preferably containing some silt and clay for better compaction, and is constructed to a height that will exceed the maximum water level in the bog or reservoir by 2 feet. The top of the dam should be at least 12 feet wide to facilitate the movement of equipment. The slope of the dam is generally about 60° and is covered with a layer of turf to stabilize the dam. When construction of the dam is completed, water is raised against it to the highest attainable head and then allowed to drain slowly. This serves to compact the materials and allows for the detection of leaks. Dams constructed in this way can easily contain 5-foot heads of water. Dikes that are not meant to serve as roadways or do not require so large a head of water need not be so elaborately constructed; often turfing may be unnecessary. On the other hand, larger bodies of water that may be subject to considerable wave action may need

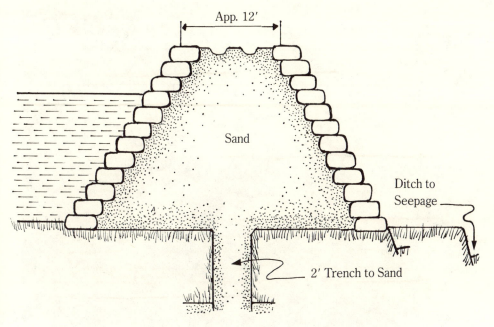

FIGURE 8.1 CROSS SECTION OF A CRANBERRY DAM

more slope protection than just turf. Large bodies of water that are impounded also require that spillways be constructed that will divert excess water during periods of heavy rainfall.

An essential part of bog construction, ditching maintains ample drainage and provides channels for the rapid movement of water onto the fields for irrigation or flooding (plate 8.2). Three sizes of ditches are usually constructed, with size depending upon function. The main supply channel, or canal, that conveys water from its source to the bog is the largest of these ditches, usually measuring 5 to 8 feet in width with a depth of 2 feet. A somewhat smaller ditch about 3 feet wide and 2 feet deep is dug along the periphery of the bog. This ditch is the main supply channel for the bog from which smaller lateral ditches extend into the main bog area. The smaller cross-ditches are 18 to 24 inches wide at the top, 10 inches wide at the bottom, and 18 inches deep to allow for water table control. The sides of the ditches are sloped at 60° to facilitate annual cleaning. The distance between these supply ditches may vary depending upon soil conditions, but generally they are dug at 100-to-150-foot intervals.

There remain but two final structures required to complete the movement of water to and from the bog: the head gate, which controls the movement of water from the supply source into the supply channels, and the drainage gate,

PLATE 8.2. MAIN SUPPLY AND DRAINAGE CHANNEL OF A BOG BUILT
ON THE CONTOUR. Note the Well House and Irrigation Pipe For
Supplying a Sprinkler System For Frost Protection (Courtesy
Massachusetts Cranberry Experiment Station).

which provides a method for the water to recess from the bog. Water that
moves by gravitational flow can be controlled either by an open-flume-type of
control gate or by a closed-trunk-type. Common to both types is the need to
provide multiple walls of matched sheet piling to prevent water from leaking
through the embankment around the structure and eventually causing the
gate to wash out. The open flume type is usually constructed in bogs being
supplied by a free-flowing stream and is designed to carry the entire flow of
the stream. The gates may be constructed of reinforced concrete or cre-
osoted wood and will have wings extending out from each side of the gate into
the dike to discourage the passage of muskrats. The water is controlled from
the top by means of flashboards made to fit into slots on each side of the head
gate.

The preferred method of water control in New Jersey and Massachusetts
is with the covered trunk gate (fig. 8.2). The gate consists of a sill and a trunk.

Again, the sides of the gate are double-sheathed so as to minimize water seepage. The trunk portion of the flume traverses the dike and is placed below the permanent water level of the bog. Since this part of the structure remains underwater, it need not be constructed of creosote-treated wood. However, the sill, which may extend above the waterline, is constructed with wood treated with creosote under pressure. The receiver is positioned away from the dike to minimize soil contact that can lead to rapid deterioration. At the outlet end, a short uptake serves to cut down on the velocity of the water coming through the trunk, thereby reducing the potential for scouring, and insures that the trunk remains full of water. Water flow is also controlled by flashboards positioned across the receiver sill. At the other end of the bog, a similar covered trunk is fitted across the dike to control the flow of water leaving the bog. This control gate is used when it is desired to raise the water table in the bog.

When gravity cannot be used to move water into the bog, some type of

A.

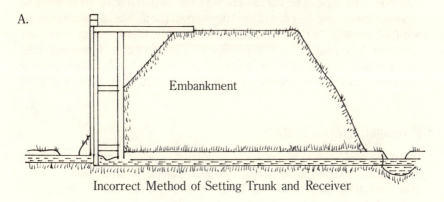

Incorrect Method of Setting Trunk and Receiver

B.

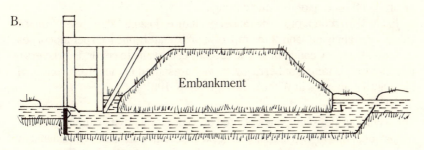

Correct Method of Setting Trunk and Receiver

FIGURE 8.2 INSTALLING CLOSED-TRUNK-TYPE WATER CONTROL GATE. *A*, incorrect method; *B*, correct method.

water pump is required. In Wisconsin highly efficient low-lift pumps can move water a height of 14 feet, although most pumps are designed to lift water only 3 to 6 feet. A 40-horsepower engine can power a lift pump with a 5-foot lift that can provide 10,000 gallons per minute—enough to apply an inch of water each half hour to 10 acres. When lifts of more than 14 feet are needed, centrifugal pumps, preferably a submerged type, are required.

With the completion of the ditching and installation of the water-control structures, the final grading can be completed. It is also at this time that the piping is installed for solid-set sprinkler irrigation. The polyethylene piping used to deliver the minimum gallonage needed for frost protection will last much longer if it is buried rather than exposed to sunlight (Norton 1957). The diameter of the laterals will vary with the length of the run from the mains. Using a 1/10-inch application rate, three sprinklers can be operated on a 145-foot run of 3/4-inch flexible polyethylene pipe (65 ft. between sprinklers), four sprinklers on a 230-foot run of 1-inch pipe, or six sprinklers on a 390-foot run of 1¼-inch pipe. The laterals are supplied by portable mains that can be located either along the edge of the bog or down the middle, depending on the width of the bog. In the submerged condition, the plastic piping is not only protected from sunlight but also protected against freezing. Typical sprinkler spacings in Oregon are 35 to 40 feet by 35 to 40 feet. Most installations are of polyvinylchloride (PVC) plastic pipe set in the bed (A. Poole letter to author, 1988).

Propagation and Planting

When the final leveling of the bog is completed, sanding may be necessary if the planting is to be made on muck or peat. Under no circumstances, however, should the sand be used to level the bog. The success of sanding over peat is dependent on the application of a level layer of sand over the peat to insure good rooting of the vine cuttings.

In his 1870 monograph on cranberry culture, Joseph White tells of the advisability of applying sand at the rate of approximately one inch per foot of peat under New Jersey conditions. The case for using sand to cover deep layers of peat before planting cranberries was well presented in the letter from S. H. Shreve that appears in White's monograph (p. 108):

> Without the sand, vines planted upon peat will grow luxuriantly, and may bear one or two crops. The surface becomes covered with a dense growth of long runners and uprights of twice the usual length. The runners become woody, and the uprights are soft and flimsy. The presence of sand is absolutely necessary in the growth of the healthful and fruitful vine. The vigorous, short uprights, full of berries, will have, when

drawn through the fingers, a rough, grating feeling, compared with the long, barren uprights, grown upon pure peat.

In spite of Shreve's experiences, the sanding of new bogs did not develop into an established prerequisite for cranberry bog construction during the early years of development of the industry in New Jersey. The early growers in New Jersey opted to set out as much acreage as possible with their initial capital investment. Therefore, the costly operation of sanding was omitted more often than not. It was not until Beckwith's research in the 1920s demonstrated the beneficial effects of sanding that sanding became a widely accepted cultural practice in New Jersey (Beckwith 1937).

Just before planting, the sand is spread evenly over the surface of the leveled bog at a depth of two to six inches, depending on the depth of peat (table 8.2). In this way, the sand is still loose enough to allow for easy striking of the plant cutting. Two inches should be the minimum sand depth, with added one-inch increments of sand for each additional foot of peat beyond two feet—up to a six-inch maximum sand depth. Crowley (1954) recommends a maximum of two inches for Washington conditions. The layer of sand prevents the peat surface from becoming hard and dry and provides a better rooting medium for the cranberry cuttings. The cuttings will generally root at the interface of the

TABLE 8.2. AMOUNTS OF SAND TO APPLY TO ATTAIN DIFFERENT SANDING DEPTHS

Depth of sand in. (cm)	Volume of Sand	
	Cubic Yards Per Acre (cu.m/ha)	Wheelbarrow Loads Per Acre
0.25 (0.64)	33.6 (64)	185
0.33 (0.85)	44.8 (85)	246
0.50 (1.27)	67.2 (127)	370
0.67 (1.70)	89.6 (170)	493
0.75 (1.92)	100.8 (192)	554
1 (2.54)	134.4 (250)	739
2 (5.08)	268.8 (500)	1478
3 (7.62)	403.2 (750)	2218
4 (10.16)	537.6 (1000)	2957

SOURCE: B. Tomlinson 1937.

peat and sand if the sand is not too deep. The layer of sand also prevents the germination of weed seeds that may be present in the peat. As an additional benefit, sanding may shorten the prefruiting period of a new bog. New bogs constructed from sands rich in organic matter and underlain by a high water table (savanna type) are generally not sanded at the time of planting.

Cranberries are propagated vegetatively from vine cuttings. With the removal of the terminal bud of the vine, apical dominance is lost—allowing the buds in the leaf axils to break. The vine cuttings root readily in two to three weeks after the cuttings are struck. Good quality vines of the variety wanted for plantings are selected, and care is taken to avoid bogs that are particularly weedy. The vines to be used as propagating material were traditionally harvested in the early spring before bud break with a scythe or pruning tool; more recently, mechanized mowing machines are used. A bog well cared for will yield as much as four tons of prunings per acre. Prunings from young bogs generally root better than those taken from older bogs. The prunings are further cut into six-to-eight-inch lengths for striking (planting for propagation). If the vines cannot be struck immediately, they must be stored in a moist environment until they can be used. The best time to plant a new field is from early April to mid-May. Cuttings made after 1 June do not make good growth.

In the early days of cranberry culture, planting was a laborious process requiring much handwork (plate 8.3). Planting grids were laid out on the leveled and sanded bog to mark the position for striking the cranberry cutting. The distance between the cuttings depended on the amount of planting material available. Planting the corners of a 16-inch (40-cm) square would require about 200 pounds (91 kg) of vines per acre, whereas 1,600 pounds (727 kg) would be needed if the cuttings were spaced 6 by 8 inches (15 × 20 cm). The closer spacing, of course, meant that the bog was vined over much quicker, and it greatly reduced the need for weeding. The vine cuttings were struck, usually two or three per location, with a blunt dibble that pressed the cutting down through the sand into the peat. Little more than an inch or two of the vine needed to be exposed; in fact, if too much vine laid exposed it had to be pruned back so the wind would not whip the cutting loose. The cuttings were firmed in place with the heal of the foot.

Today, few bogs are still planted by hand unless a very limited supply of a new cultivar is available, in which case the cuttings can be rooted in peat pots under mist. For this purpose, Welker and Vass (1983) have recommended that cuttings, five nodes in length, be taken and struck vertically rather than horizontally in the propagating media. The rooted cuttings are then hand planted, pot and all, into the prepared bog, where they can begin growth almost immediately since they are already rooted. More commonly, however, vine prunings are now broadcast over the prepared bog surface at either one

PLATE 8.3. A CRANBERRY BOG PLANTED BY HAND AT THE TURN OF THE CENTURY (Courtesy Massachusetts Cranberry Experiment Station)

or two tons of prunings per acre, depending upon the quantity of material available. The cuttings are disced into the sand with a tractor-powered set of blunt discs that have been so designed as not to cut the vines but merely pass them some three to four inches into the sand. The final process is to firm the soil around the cuttings with a roller, again powered by a tractor, and the excess vines are mowed off with a power mower (plate 8.4). In this method of planting, most of the hand labor has been replaced by machine.

During the first few weeks after the cuttings are struck, the soil is kept quite moist by raising the water in the ditches. As the cuttings root and new shoots begin to appear, the water level is gradually dropped to improve drainage and aeration in the root zone. Lowering the water table will also encourage the root system to develop at a greater soil depth, making the plant less susceptible to drought. Thereafter, it is necessary to protect the young vines from frost and insects and insure an adequate water supply. Light broadcast applications of nitrogen fertilizer at the rate of 15 to 30 pounds

A.

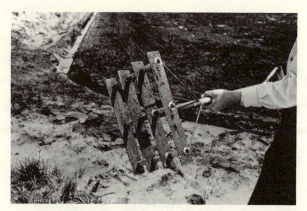

B.

C.

PLATE 8.4. DIFFERENT METHODS OF PLANTING CRANBERRY VINES; *A*, HAND-HELD DIBBLE; *B*, SELF-PROPELLED PLANTER; *C*, TRACTOR-DRIVEN DISC (Courtesy University of Wisconsin Extension Service)

(17–35 kg/ha) of nitrogen per acre every three weeks during the growing season will encourage vine growth for more rapid bog coverage (Dana and Klingbeil 1966). Washington researchers (Shawa 1984) recommend a weekly application of 2 pounds of nitrogen per acre (2.4 kg/ha) per week starting after the first of June. This is slowly increased to 5 pounds (5.75 kg/ha) of nitrogen by the end of the growing season. In Canada the use of fertilizer is also recommended during the establishment years (I. V. Hall 1969) To bring about rapid vegetative growth, Hall recommends applying 200 pounds per acre (230 kg/ha) of a 5-20-20 fertilizer about the middle of June and another 100 pounds (115 kg/ha) after 1 July. In addition, 40 pounds (46 kg/ha) of ammonium nitrate are applied in mid-July and another 60 pounds (69 kg/ha) at the end of July.

Despite the fact that the addition of fertilizer can promote weed growth as well as cranberry vine growth, the benefit of prolific vine growth appears to outweigh the weed stimulation possibility, particularly if the weeds can be controlled with selective herbicides. Weeds can be controlled also by hand and through the proper maintenance of the water table. Sanding the new vine growth will encourage additional rooting to occur and more rapid population of the bog surface. The newly planted bog must be flooded earlier in the winter than established bogs because of the danger of the young plants being heaved out of the soil by frosts. With the successful establishment of the new bog, the first commercial crop can be expected in the fourth year after planting.

Water Management

General Aspects

The cranberry plant is indigenous to wet bogland and in its evolution has developed the ability to withstand partial and even complete submergence during certain stages of growth. A dormant plant may withstand complete submergence for months as it does during the normal winter flood period, but when the plant is actively growing, even partial submergence may prove injurious if allowed to remain submerged for longer than 24 hours.

Water management is therefore a critical phase of cranberry growing (plate 8.5). The winter flood, early vs. late drawing of the winter flood, reflows for frost and insect control, and the control of water table depth for summer irrigation are all aspects of the intricate water management system required for successful cranberry production. To successfully manage their water resources, experienced growers rely not only on their knowledge of how, when, and why to use available water but also upon an intuition which develops from knowing each individual bog. The frost-danger periods in spring and fall are particularly critical periods of heavy demand on available

PLATE 8.5. AN AERIAL VIEW OF CRANBERRY BOGS IN MASSACHU-
SETTS SHOWING THE RELATIONSHIP OF WATER RESER-
VOIR AND DRAINAGE SYSTEM TO THE BOGS (USDA-SCS
photo)

water resources, and the cranberry grower is frequently required to exercise intuition and unerring judgment at these times.

Winter Flood

Cranberry bogs are generally kept flooded during the winter months of December through March. The winter flood is essential in order to prevent the heaving-out of plants by alternate freezing and thawing. It protects the plants from the desiccation that would result if they were to remain exposed to winter winds while rooted in a frozen ground from which no water was available (Beckwith 1940a). Even in regions of heavy snow, such as the Maritimes in Canada and in northern Wisconsin, bogs must be flooded in winter because the snow cover is often blown from the bog or may be inadequate to protect the plants.

The criterion usually used to determine when to apply the winter flood is the observation that the sand surface in the bog remains frozen throughout the day (Franklin 1948a). This may occur as early as 1 December in northern Wisconsin and as late as the end of December in New Jersey. The timing of the winter flood is important because it is postulated that the shorter the duration of the winter flood the greater the crop potential (Cross 1969a).

It takes 300,000 gallons of water to flood an acre bog to a depth of one foot (3,000 cubic meters to flood a hectare of bog to a depth of 30 cm). This is generally adequate to cover the vines on fairly level bogs. Deeper floods would be necessary in bogs that are uneven. The object is to just cover the vines with the water. Often the vines are frozen into the ice, where they are adequately protected. To prevent the vines from tearing as the result of movement in the ice cover, the water is often drawn from beneath the ice, particularly in locales where the ice is apt to remain for most of the winter. Drawing the flood from beneath the ice is also an effective means of insuring against oxygen deficiency that may develop in floodwater when the ice is covered with snow or when the ice has been sanded. The snow or sand effectively excludes light from the plant so that photosynthesis within the cranberry plant ceases and the respiring plants quickly use up the available oxygen dissolved in the floodwater. The removal of the water from beneath the ice enables fresh air to again envelop the plants and the ice blanket resting on the vines provides an even temperature of 32°F (0°C), which the plants can tolerate. If the ice should melt during a prolonged thawing period, the winter flood must, of course, again be applied.

Late Holding vs. Early Drawing of the Winter Flood

The conditions for which the winter flood is applied generally no longer exist in cranberry bogs after 1 April. In fact, Massachusetts records show that winter killing of vines has never occurred after 20 March in that state. If one accepts the thesis that the shorter the submergence period of the cranberry plant the greater the cropping potential of the plants, then there must be some compelling reasons for keeping a winter flood on the bogs through the months of April and May.

First, however, let us look at the advantages of early drawing of the winter flood. For New Jersey, Beckwith (1940a) advocated 10 April as the date for drawing of the winter flood. Beckwith maintained that the reason for the winter flood no longer existed in New Jersey by this date and later holding of the water would result in some loss of crop. In Massachusetts, shorter winter flooding has been associated with larger crops (Cross 1969a). Short winter floods reduce the chances of oxygen deficiency injury. Exposure of vines to cool temperatures results in short, stocky uprights, which is an advantage on heavily vined bogs, and retards the development of terminal buds, making them less susceptible to spring frosts. Bloom on early-drawn bogs tends to be prolonged because of the uneven development of buds, often lasting from mid-June to early August. This extended bloom gives added insurance against complete crop losses to frost and provides a longer pollination period.

If greater crop potential is realized from early-drawn bogs, then why is late holding of the winter flood commonly practiced in the Canadian Maritimes (growers in western Canada do not usually flood their bogs in winter) and in New Jersey? In Canada the winter flood is normally held until 24 May (E. L. Eaton 1957) and in New Jersey until 10 May (Beckwith 1940c). The principal reason for late holding appears to be to bypass the early spring frost period. In New Jersey ambient temperatures in April can already be high enough to be conducive to very rapid growth. This tender new growth would be particularly susceptible to frost damage and it would be necessary to protect it with frequent reflows. Frequent reflows would make a heavy demand on water reserves and the constant resubmergence of actively growing tissue may in itself be injurious to the plant. The late spring in the Canadian Maritimes would subject early-drawn bogs to a particularly long frost season; therefore, the late May date for flood removal will effectively shorten the frost season. The installation of solid-set sprinkle irrigation systems with frost control capabilities, however, would eliminate this requirement for late holding.

Late holding also has some marked effects on the insect populations of cranberry bogs. Many insects can be effectively controlled by this method of water management (Beckwith 1940c), which makes it a valuable tool in an integrated pest management program designed to gain maximum efficiency of pest control with the minimum use of pesticides. The yellow-headed fireworm, which overwinters as an adult and lays its eggs on the vines in late April and early May can be controlled by late holding. The black-headed fireworm winters on the leaves as an egg, which is unable to hatch if the water is held until the first of June.

Another insect controlled by late holding is the cranberry girdler, which over-winters as a larva in a cocoon in the trash under the vines.

Late holding of the winter flood may also influence the weed population in a bog. The invigorated vine growth associated with late holding will overcome small clumps of cut grass (*Carex bullata*). Saucer grass (*Calamovilfa brevepiles*) and red root (*Lachnanthes tinctoria*) are weakened but not eliminated as are also the ferns and brush. Algal scum, however, often develops in late-held bogs. This can generally be overcome by changing the flood-water in early April and allowing the bogs to be exposed to the air for about a week.

Another advantage of late holding listed by K. L. Beaton (1953) is that bet-ter-quality fruit results because the late-held bogs bloom later during a drier part of the growing season, which is less favorable for fungal infection. Beaton also stressed that when water reserves are limited, late holding will conserve the grower's water supply because the need to reflow for frost is less fre-quent.

In Massachusetts a late-water flood is equivalent in effect to late holding in New Jersey. A late-water flood is any deep flood (the depth is required to insure cool water temperature) of several weeks duration in the spring ap-plied after the removal of the winter flood, usually applied in mid-April and lasting to mid-May or the end of May (Cross 1969a). A late-water flood is generally used where water supplies are inadequate for frequent reflows for frost protection in the early spring.

After the water is withdrawn from late-held bogs, the buds grow rapidly and evenly and must be protected from temperatures below 29.5°F (−1.4°C). Vegetative growth is extremely rapid in the warm temperatures of early June. Uprights and berries are generally longer and larger than their counterparts in early-water vines (bogs from which the winter flood had been drawn earlier). There is danger of overfertilizing late-water vines, causing them to become overly vegetative. Flowering tends to be later in late-drawn vines with fewer flowers per upright and fewer flowering up-rights in general, but percent flower set is usually always greater for late-water vines than for early-water vines. Berries are often pear shaped in late-water vines, as compared to the more spherical early-water berries, and tend to develop rapidly and evenly to produce large, well-colored ber-ries that continue to develop color in storage. Quality is generally better in late-water berries than in early-water berries, although crops generally average 10 percent less than early-water crops.

Late holding as it is practiced in New Jersey and Massachusetts is not rec-ommended as an annual water management practice. In New Jersey, Beck-with (1940c) has recommended that late holding should be practiced only one year in three. In Massachusetts, late holding every other year has been advo-cated (Franklin 1948a). Further precautions against the use of late holding are advised for Massachusetts when the winter has been long and severe, especially if oxygen deficiency is suspected and if the bogs were sanded during the fall or winter (Cross 1969a).

A final type of late holding is practiced when it is desired to rejuvenate run-down bogs (Beckwith 1940c). In this procedure the winter flood is allowed to remain until 5 July or 10 July. An important prerequisite for this form of late holding is that ample supplies of fresh water are available for circulating through the bog. The effect of this extremely late hold is the production of only vegetative growth in the current growing season. Healthy vines do not appear to be injured. The growth that follows is very vigorous, characterized by uprights and leaves that are as much as 30 percent larger than their counterparts in normally held bogs. Many flower buds are formed and the next year's crop is usually very heavy. The warm water temperatures (usually greater than 60°F) that are apt to develop in this extreme late-hold treatment is particularly effective in combating insects and weeds. Fruitworm infestations are eliminated since no current crop is produced, and annual weeds are effectively controlled as are the brambles.

Reflows

Throughout the growing season, a cranberry bog is apt to be intentionally flooded any number of times for various reasons. The grower must exercise complete control over depth and duration of the flood because the actively growing cranberry plant is very susceptible to oxygen deficiency injury. Therefore, flooding is restricted to as short an interval of time as is necessary for the purpose applied and is accomplished preferably with as cool a water as possible.

The most common reason for reflows is to protect plants from frost damage in the spring and fruit from frost damage in the fall. The tender new growth on cranberry vines may be injured by temperatures only slightly below freezing (29°F, or −1.7°C) and, therefore, must be protected. In the late summer and early fall, young developing fruits must also be protected from freezing. Immature green fruits must also be protected from freezing. Immature green fruits are more susceptible than ripe red fruits, which can withstand temperatures down to 26°F (−3.3°C). Fruit that has been exposed to frost may have a shorter storage life (E. L. Eaton 1957). Often it is not necessary to completely submerge the bog to protect the vines from frost but necessary only to raise the water to the level of the bog surface. Since reflows for frost protection in the spring occur during periods when water temperatures are still quite cold, the duration of the flood is not as critical as it will be later in the growing season. However, a 24-hour limitation on the duration of the flood is a good practice to follow unless another night of frost is predicted, in which case the flood may be kept on for another 24 hours. In many cranberry operations in Massachusetts and Wisconsin, reflows for frost protection has been replaced with permanently installed overhead sprinkler systems that effectively insure against frost damage (see temperature section for a more detailed account).

Another reason for reflows is to control insects. This is accomplished by a June reflow usually in early June before bloom (Beckwith 1931). Reflows during bloom are not recommended because of the increased potential for spreading fruit rot inoculum. A June reflow consists of a flood that just covers the tips of the highest vines and is then withdrawn as soon as possible. A well-developed and adequate drainage system is imperative in order to remove the floodwater rapidly. Normally a 24-hour submergence should be all that is needed. Most insects will succumb within 10 hours of submergence (Franklin 1948a). Insects that are controlled by June reflows include the black-headed fireworm (*Rhopobata vacciniane*), the blossom worm (*Epiglaea apiata*), and the blunt-nosed leafhopper (*Euscelis striatulus*).

A reflow after harvest, lasting about a week, is beneficial to the planting because it helps to anchor disturbed roots and removes much of the debris that remains after the harvest operation. This reflow is particularly important when bogs have been dry scooped since considerably more vine damage can be anticipated than when plantings are water harvested. Although bogs in the Pacific Northwest are not usually flooded in winter, a postharvest flood for 3 to 4 weeks is effective in controlling larvae of the black vine weevil (*Otiorhynchus sulcatus* Fabr.).

Irrigation

The most common method of supplying the water requirements for cranberry growth during the growing season is by maintaining the water table depth at some optimal level. The installation of permanent irrigation systems in many cranberry plantings, however, has provided an alternative system for supplying the cranberry's water needs. When the sprinkler irrigation system is supplied by deep wells, it has the distinct advantage over the necessity of maintaining a sustained water table depth during prolonged periods of drought when reservoirs may become depleted.

Nevertheless, when water resources are adequate, the control of water table represents a convenient and efficient method of providing the water needs to the growing cranberry plant. One immediate question arises: What is the optimum depth at which the water table should be maintained for maximum production of highest quality fruit? Beckwith (1940b) sought to answer this question for a muck soil in New Jersey in a long-term study in which he controlled the water table depth in square-rod plots at various depths. When he averaged yields for Howes over a four-year period, he found that the highest yield (80 barrels/acre) was obtained when the water table was maintained at a depth of 9 to 12 inches (23–30 cm). The poorest yield (56 barrels/acre) was obtained when the water table depth was set at 0 to 3 inches (0–7.5 cm). Yields at depths of 3 to 6 inches (7.5–15 cm), 6 to 9 inches (15–23 cm), and 12 to 15 inches (30–37.5 cm) were 68, 77, and 77 barrels per acre, respectively. Other observations made by Beckwith during this experiment were that the length of uprights increased with increasing water table depth and that the maximum number of uprights per square foot were produced at a depth of 9 to 12 inches (23–30 cm). In a later report, Beckwith (1944) recommended a water table depth of 12 to 15 inches (30–37.5 cm) for muck bogs that were sanded.

The optimum water table depth for best production of Early Black cranberry from new plantings on a Berryland sand was found by Eck (1976a) to be 12 to 15 inches (30–37.5 cm). At this depth the greatest number of uprights were produced, but at lower water table depths longer vines developed. In an earlier study Driggers (1924) had concluded that a depth of 12 to 15 inches (30–37.5 cm) was best from the standpoint of fruit rot development. At higher water table depths, the incidence of fruit rot increased dramatically.

Doehlert (1940) has cautioned against rapidly changing the water table depth on unsanded bogs. Roots concentrate near the surface in moist bogs, and lowering the water table beyond the reach of the root system will damage the vines. If it is necessary to lower the water table, it should be at the rate of no more than two inches per year. When an unsanded bog is sanded, the water table can be lowered twice the thickness of the applied sand layer. Doehlert maintained that when bogs are sanded and replanted, however, the water table can be safely lowered because the roots of the new plants will only develop at depths where water is available.

Similarly, I. V. Hall (1971) has observed that cranberry plants that are grown at a high water table depth (2 in. or 5 cm) develop a dense root mat near the (unsanded) surface with no root growth developing below the water level. In his experimental setup, Hall grew Beckwith and Pilgrim plants in containers containing a prepared soil mix and maintained water table depths of 2, 7.5, and 13 inches (5, 19, and 33 cm). He then proceeded to measure total linear growth over a period of 210 days and observed that although the initial growth was most rapid at the highest water level, the growth rate at the medium water level exceeded the high-water-level rate after three months. The least growth occurred at the lowest water level. The root system of plants grown at the medium water table depth was not as thick as the root system of the plants at the high water level, but the roots extended much deeper. The root system of plants grown at the low water level was long with few root laterals until near the water level.

The lateral movement of subsurface water through a bog depends greatly upon the nature of the soil. Chandler (1951) observed that the lateral movement through peat was extremely slow, whereas movement through sand was fairly rapid. When he measured soil moisture tension as close as five feet from a supply ditch in a peat soil, he found little relationship between the water level in the ditch and the supply of available water in the root zone of the cranberry plant. However, where 10 to 12 inches (25–30 cm) of sand existed, there was a close relationship between the water level in the ditch and the water table in the bog when the water level was maintained above 12 inches (30 cm). The importance of this observation is that the level of water in the supply ditch cannot be relied upon as a sole determinant of the water level within a peat bog. Observation wells within the bog would provide a means of determining whether water levels within the bog are at the optimum level. In all probability it would be necessary to provide more lateral water supply ditches in peat bogs than in sand bogs, where there is no real impediment to lateral water movement.

With respect to the movement of water through cranberry soil, Dickey and Baumer (1985) have made some interesting observations. It has been estimated that a producing cranberry bog will require about 0.25 inch (0.6 cm) of water per day during sunny summer days; this must be provided either from the water table or by surface irrigation. If a water table is to provide the required moisture, the following physical properties must be kept in mind:

1. The capillary rise of water in coarse sand is 30 cm (about 1 foot); therefore, the water table under the plants must be maintained at 15 to 18 inches (38–46 cm) to provide a steady source of moisture to the cranberry roots.

2. Capillary action cannot take water across a soil interface (the boundary between sand and organic matter, for example) until saturation is reached from the direction the water is moving.

In a bog that has undergone periodic sanding, there will be numerous alternate layers of sand and organic debris. With each new sanding another interface is created. When subirrigation is used, the saturation at the interface cannot occur until the water table is raised to the interface. The result is that in stratified organic-layered cranberry soils, the water table must be kept higher than the normal 15 to 18 inches (38–46 cm) if adequate moisture is to be moved through these interfaces. These same interfaces serve to impede the downward movement of surface-applied water; therefore, a surface irrigation or rainfall is probably more efficient in providing water to the cranberry plant.

Alternative methods of supplying water to the cranberry bog to solid-set sprinkler irrigation and irrigation from a raised water table are ditch irrigation, buried perforated pipe, or flash flood (Chandler 1955d; Cross 1953b). Cross cautioned that if water is supplied by lateral ditches, it should be done early in the drought period because lateral water movement in most cranberry bogs is very slow. Buried perforated plastic pipe has the advantage of doubling as a drainage conduit if needed, but water supplied by this underground means is also subjected to the limitations of capillarity observed by Dickey and Baumer (1985). Flash flooding has limited application since drought stress usually occurs during the most active stage of cranberry growth, when the plant is most susceptible to oxygen deficiency injury. This irrigation method could only be used in small bogs that can be rapidly drained.

Fertilizer Practices

Requirements

The fertilizer requirements of the cranberry are relatively low compared with most other crops. Colby (1945) has calculated that a crop of 100 barrels of cranberries per acre (1 barrel = 1 cwt.) plus one ton of dried vines contains 23 pounds (10.5 kg) of N (nitrogen), 10 pounds (4.5 kg) of P_2O_5 (phosphorus), 18 pounds (8.2 kg) of K_2O (potassium), and only 9 pounds (4.1 kg) of CaO (calcium). Dana (1968a), on the other hand, estimated the level of N removal to be higher. He calculated that 100 barrels of cranberries contain 23 pounds (10.5 kg) of N but that the additional N utilized in producing new stems and roots represented another 10 pounds (4.5 kg) of N. The amount of N contained in old leaves that are lost can be an additional 20 pounds (9.1 kg) of N. An acre of cranberry vines producing 100 barrels of cranberries, therefore, may remove as much as 53 pounds (24 kg) of N.

Based on Colby's calculations, Chandler (1955a) has summarized the loss of N in terms of fertilizer applications necessary to replace crop removal (table 8.3).

Responses

As noted previously (chapter 7), cranberry yield can be increased in one or more of the following ways: (1) an increase in the number of uprights produced and the percentage of them bearing flowers, (2) an increase in the number of flowers per upright, (3) an increase in fruit set, and (4) an increase in berry size. The beneficial influence of fertilizer on cranberry yield has been recognized as early as 1921. Using Berryland sand in New Jersey, Beckwith (1921b) was able to demonstrate significant increases in yield in response to 30 pounds per acre (34.5 kg/ha) of N and 80 pounds per acre (92 kg/ha) of P_2O_5. Doehlert (1954) found that the application of 200 pounds per acre (230 kg/ha) of an 8-8-8 (N-P_2O_5-K_2O) fertilizer in August significantly increased the number of uprights that flowered in a sample of 100 uprights, and June applications of 18 to 21 pounds per acre (20.7–24.2 kg/ha) of N increased

TABLE 8.3. FERTILIZER APPLICATION IN RELATION TO CROP

Crop in barrels per acre (mt/ha)	Pounds of N removed per acre*	POUNDS OF FERTILIZER PER ACRE TO REPLACE N REMOVED BY CROP				
		5-10-5†	8-16-8	Urea	Ammonium Sulfate	7-7-7
50 (5.75)	11.5	230	144	26	55	164
75 (8.63)	17.3	345	216	39	83	246
100 (11.50)	23.0	460	288	51	110	328
150 (17.25)	34.5	690	432	77	165	493
200 (23.00)	46.0	920	575	102	220	657

SOURCE: Chandler (1955a).
*To convert lbs./a to kg/ha, multiply values by 1.15.
†N-P_2O_5-K_2O.

berry size. In a controlled nutrition study, Torio and Eck (1969) reported that adequate nitrogen nutrition can increase the percentage fruit set in cranberry. In a factorial study on New Jersey bogs, Eck (1964a) reported a significant increase in berry weight in response to phosphorus fertilizer and a highly significant increase in berry size in response to N and P. More recently, Eck (1976b) concluded that Early Black cranberries grown on Berryland sand in New Jersey did not require more than 17 kg N/ha/yr (table 8.4). Rates as high as 51 kgN/ha were found to be detrimental to cranberry production under these growing conditions mainly because of a reduction in the number of uprights that flowered. G. W. Eaton (1971a) showed that McFarlin cranberry yield could be increased in British Columbia with the addition of 22 kg N/ha (table 8.4). Ben Lear responded to somewhat higher nitrogen fertilizer rates of 34 kg N/ha (G. W. Eaton and Meehan 1973). Current recommendations in Washington (Shawa and Kresge 1976) call for an annual application of 44.8 kg N/ha.

Nitrogen fertilization markedly increases the vegetative growth of the plant. Both the amount of vine growth and the length of uprights is strongly affected. Chandler (1961) stressed that adequate nitrogen fertilizer be applied to insure optimum production of uprights, which Dana (1968b) maintained is between 250 to 300 uprights per square foot for the Searles variety. Excessive vine and upright growth results not only in fruit shading that can lead to poor berry color but also in a microclimate that can increase the incidence of fruit disease, according to Atwood and Zuckerman (1961). Chandler (1961) has suggested that the amount of nitrogen fertilizer applied should be determined by the length of the new uprights (table 8.5).

Research in Wisconsin (Peltier 1955) has pointed to the need for at least

TABLE 8.4. EFFECT OF NITROGEN (N) FERTILIZER
APPLICATIONS ON CRANBERRY YIELD

Rate of N kg/ha (lbs./a)	Fruit Yield mt/ha	Barrels Per Acre	Cultivar
17 (15)	24.1	215	Early Black
34 (30)	21.5	192	Early Black
51 (45)	15.3	136	Early Black
0 (0)	19.4	173	McFarlin
11 (10)	21.3	190	McFarlin
22 (20)	23.1	206	McFarlin
0 (0)	14.5	129	Ben Lear
11 (10)	18.2	162	Ben Lear
22 (20)	21.8	194	Ben Lear
34 (30)	25.5	227	Ben Lear

SOURCES: Early Black data from Eck 1976b; McFarlin data from G. W. Eaton 1971a; Ben Lear data from G. W. Eaton and Meehan 1973.

100 pounds per acre (115 kg/ha) of available phosphorus (P) for good production on some of Wisconsin's muck and peat soils. Early in the decade, Voorhees (1914) showed that cranberry yields in New Jersey could be increased by using phosphorus fertilizer. Eck (1985) was able to demonstrate a yield response to P on Berryland sand in New Jersey. Highest yields were obtained at the 40 kg P/ha (115 kg P_2O_5/ha) rate of phosphorus fertilization, which resulted in an available soil phosphorus level of 22 pounds per acre (25.3 kg/ha).

In New Jersey Voorhees (1914) reported a fruit size and yield response in Early Black cranberry to potassium fertilizer applied to the Berryland soil. Cranberry yields in Washington were decreased when soil test values fell below 50 pounds per acre (57.5 kg/ha) of available potassium, according to Fisher (1951). On the muck and peat soils of Wisconsin, 250 pounds per acre (287.5 kg/ha) of available potassium were needed to maintain a desirable nutritional balance in these soils (Peltier 1955), but too much potassium fertilizer could seriously depress the amount of magnesium taken up by the cranberry plant (G. W. Eaton 1971a).

The application of 1000 kg/ha (870 lbs./acre) of agricultural lime ($CaCO_3$) increased yield and reduced storage rot in McFarlin cranberries, according to Shawa (1979b). This rate of lime increased the soil pH to 6.1 without apparent phytotoxic effects on the plant. Higher rates of lime application resulted in

TABLE 8.5. FERTILIZER RECOMMENDATIONS FOR PRODUCING CRANBERRY BOGS

Length of Vines	When to Apply	Fertilizer Grade	Application Rate lbs./a (kg/ha)		Remarks & Recommendation
New uprights 1″–1.5″ (2.54–3.8 cm)	April or June or July or Oct.	5-10-5 8-16-8 6-12-12 4-12-8	400 250 333 500	(460) (288) (383) (575)	Uprights of good color; to maintain fertility only; add 20 lbs./a (23 kg/ha) of N
New uprights <1″ (2.54 cm)	Same as above	5-10-5 8-16-8 6-12-12 4-12-8	800 500 667 1000	(920) (575) (767) (1150)	Vines of poor color; low production; add 40 lbs./a (46 kg/ha) of N
New uprights >2″ (5 cm)	April	0-25-25 0-20-20 0-14-14 20% super phosphate	200 250 350 250	(230) (288) (403) (288)	Excessive vine growth; poor yield; no nitrogen needed

SOURCE: Chandler 1961.

chlorotic uprights and reduced yields. Washington fertilizer recommendations have called for annual applications of 200 pounds per acre (230 kg/ha) of lime (Doughty 1972).

Wood and his associates (1950) have reported large berry size and a low incidence of fruit rot associated with sulfur use in Oregon. Shawa (1972b) reported a similar response in McFarlin cranberries treated with sulfur-coated urea. In controlled nutrition studies, Torio and Eck (1969) found that at a low nitrogen fertility level, an increase in sulfur application resulted in greater flowering and percentage fruit set. The response to sulfur did not occur when nitrogen level was high.

In Washington Fisher (1951) observed an increase in cranberry yield to be associated with the available iron content of the soil. The best-yielding bogs were found to contain twice as much available iron as aluminum. The response to lime that has been observed in Washington may be due in part to a reduction in aluminum availability, which decreases markedly with increasing pH.

Shawa (1973) has used foliar sprays of manganese and zinc to significantly reduce storage breakdown in the McFarlin cranberry. In Washington, foliar sprays of copper applied at prebloom and again after set decreased the amount of deformed (cat-faced) berries in the McFarlin variety and increased the size, weight, and total yield of fruit (Shawa 1981). Recently, C. J. Demoranville and Deubert (1987) have increased fruit set and cranberry yield in the Early Black cultivar with a combination calcium-and-boron spray applied at bloom.

Materials

As early as 1919, sodium nitrate was found to be an effective source of nitrogen (N) for New Jersey soils (Beckwith 1919, 1921b). Although Beckwith determined that a mixture of mineral and organic sources was not superior to sodium nitrate alone, he recommended that a cranberry fertilizer contain the following materials in a mixture: 75 pounds (34 kg) sodium nitrate, 75 pounds (34 kg) dried blood, 300 pounds (136 kg) rock phosphate, and 50 pounds (23 kg) sulfate of potash (Beckwith 1921a).

The relative superiority of the ammonium and nitrate sources of N for cranberries is a controversial matter in the research literature. Addoms and Mounce (1932) found nitrate-N to be superior to ammonium-N at pH 4 but the ammonium-N source was superior at pH 6 and pH 8. Since most cranberry bogs are in the pH 4 to 5 range, it would appear from this basic work that nitrate-N would be preferable to ammonium-N. The authors go on to note, however, that ammonium-N was being used effectively in acid bog soils in New Jersey and that this possibly could be attributable to the buffering capacity of the soil.

Fisher (1951) has indicated that ammonium sulfate is the most widely used fertilizer in Washington, despite the fact that his findings indicated that soil ammonium-N levels greater than 45 pounds per acre (52 kg/ha) were detrimental to yields. Washington State recommendations call for ammonium sulfate applications only (Crowley 1954). In Massachusetts Chandler (1961) indicated that ammonium sulfate produced crops as large as those produced with sodium nitrate. More recently, Kender and Childers (1959) have shown that ammonium sulfate produced the poorest plant growth in bog soil cultures in the greenhouse when four different N sources were compared. In a Massachusetts experiment, ammonium sulfate was found to increase field rot significantly when applied even at the lowest rate of 20 pounds per acre (23 kg/ha) (Atwood and Zuckerman 1961).

Nonetheless, it appears that ammonium sulfate can be used effectively for cranberry production especially in soils which have a relatively high buffering capacity. Excessive use on the sandier soils probably would be undesirable.

The unavailability and high cost of natural organic materials such as dried blood, cottonseed meal, and fish meal have given some impetus to investigations of synthetic organic sources of N which release their N slowly over a prolonged period. As mentioned above, there is considerable evidence that the cranberry will benefit from sustained N sources throughout the growing season. Urea formaldehyde-N has proven to be an effective N source in a number of experiments (Atwood and Zuckerman 1961; Kender and Childers 1959; Somogyi et al. 1964). Urea appears to give excellent results on cranberries (Chandler 1961; Kender and Childers 1959; Washington State College 1963). Somogyi et al. (1964) reported that a mixture of urea and urea formaldehyde produced more uprights, runner growth, and total dry matter than either urea or urea formaldehyde separately. Shawa and Kresge (1976) recommend that sulfur-coated urea (SCU) be used under the high rainfall conditions of the Pacific Northwest. In their studies, a single application of slow-release SCU with dissolution rates (amount of N dissolved in water at 38°C in 7 days followed daily by 1 percent or less thereafter) of 18 to 40 percent replaced multiple applications of urea at rates ranging from 22.4 to 44.8 kg N/ha and increased the yield of McFarlin cranberries without causing excessive cranberry vegetative growth. Isobutylidene diurea (IBDU), also a slow-release nitrogen formulation, was found to be an effective nitrogen source for cranberries in western Washington (Shawa 1979c). A single application of IBDU was as effective as four lighter fertilizer applications made at monthly intervals during the growing season.

In a long-term field experiment comparing yield of Early Black cranberry from plots receiving different formulations and timings of fertilizer material, Eck (unpublished data) found that a slow-release fertilizer yielded more berries per acre than any other treatment (table 8.6). These data would suggest that small dosages of fertility during the growing season would be a more efficient method of supplying the cranberry's nutritional need than a single surge of fertility. Along this line of reasoning, Shawa (1982) presented evidence that the timing of three light doses of liquid urea fertilizer at 4.48 kg N/ha during bloom can effectively increase yield of the McFarlin cranberry.

Rates and Ratios

Fertilizer rates and ratios vary primarily on the basis of the soil type to which the materials are being applied and on the basis of vigor of the vines and uprights. Rates of N will vary from 0 to 40 pounds per acre (0–46 kg/ha) depending upon the relative vigor of the vines (Chandler 1961). On the sandier soils, a 1-1-1 ratio appears to be satisfactory (Doehlert 1954), although earlier New Jersey work indicated a 1-2-1 ratio to be desirable (Beckwith 1930). More recently, Eck (1985) has presented evidence to support Beckwith's original recommendation of a 1-2-1 fertilizer for the Berryland sand in New Jersey. On soils of higher organic matter content, as occur in Wisconsin

TABLE 8.6. EFFECT OF FERTILIZER SOURCE AND TIMING ON
EARLY BLACK CRANBERRY YIELD OVER A SIX-YEAR
PERIOD

Fertilizer Source and Timing*	Yield Barrels/a/yr (mt/ha)	Yield as % of 10-10-10 Split Treatment†	Difference in Dollar Return Per Acre/yr‡
14-14-14 Slow release	127 (14.6)	108	+ $450
10-10-10 Dry split app.	118 (13.6)	100	0
10-10-10 Dry single app.	114 (13.1)	97	− 200
20-20-20 Liq. single app.	111 (12.8)	94	− 350
20-20-20 Liq. split app.	109 (12.5)	92	− 450
No fertilizer	108 (12.4)	92	− 500

Source: Eck, P. Unpublished data.
*All fertilizers were applied at the rate of 20 lbs. N, P_2O_5, K_2O per acre (23 kg/ha).
†The 10-10-10 split application of dry fertilizer was used as the standard cranberry fertilizer practice for comparison purposes.
‡Calculations were based on a return of $50 per barrel of cranberries.

marshes, a fertilizer ratio of 1-4-4 has been found to be best (Sorensen 1955). For Wisconsin soils, an available soil phosphorus level of 60 pounds per acre (69 kg/ha) and 250 pounds of potassium per acre (288 kg/ha) were deemed desirable (Greidanus and Dana 1972; Peltier 1955). On Massachusetts bogs, a 1-2-1 ratio has given the best results (Chandler 1961). Under Massachusetts conditions, it appears that the P and K may be applied at four-to-five-year intervals, thus applying only N on a yearly basis. Fertilizer rates are usually based on the desired amounts of N to be applied.

Wisconsin researchers have proposed the following general outline on which to base the development of individual fertilizer management programs for Wisconsin marshes (Dana 1968b):

1. On thrifty vines, use 50 pounds per acre (66 kg/ha) of ammonium nitrate (33-0-0) about 1 May followed by 300 pounds per acre (397 kg/ha) of mixed fertilizer (0-10-30) about 1 June for a total annual nitrogen application of about 16 pounds per acre (18.4 kg/ha).

2. On medium-vigor vines, use 75 pounds per acre (86.3 kg/ha) of ammonium nitrate (33-0-0) about 1 May followed by 300 pounds per acre (345 kg/ha) of mixed fertilizer (3-9-27) about 1 June for a total N application of about 35 pounds per acre (40 kg/ha).

3. On vines in poor condition, use 100 pounds per acre (115 kg/ha) of am-

monium nitrate (33-0-0) about 1 May followed by 300 pounds per acre (345 kg/ha) of complete fertilizer (5-9-27) about 1 June for a total nitrogen application of about 48 pounds per acre (55 kg/ha).

Time of Application

Researchers have put considerable emphasis on the time of fertilizer application for optimum results. Applications early in May appear advantageous in Wisconsin because of the relatively short growing season (Peltier 1955). During this comparatively cool and wet period, the application of nitrate nitrogen creates a very rapid response. Applications later than mid-June tend to encourage vine growth at the expense of the fruit crop. Another advantage of early N application appears to be the fact that N is taken up before some of the weeds and grasses get started.

In New Jersey, Doehlert (1954) found fertilizer applications in June and split applications in June and August to be superior to full applications in August and October alone. Large berry size appeared to be favored by the June application, whereas the August application tended to increase the number of flower buds formed. November applications applied to weak vines were found to increase the number of flowering uprights the following spring (Doehlert 1953a). Split applications were not recommended by Chandler (1961) because of the added cost.

In the heavy-rainfall cranberry-growing areas of the Pacific Northwest, Washington researchers recommend a single application of slow-release sulfur-coated urea to replace multiple applications of soluble N (Shawa and Kresge 1976). The alternative was to divide the fertilizer in four equal portions and apply them separately in May, June, July, and August in order to minimize runner growth and enhance fruit production.

In New Jersey, 200 pounds per acre of an 8-8-8 (standard blueberry fertilizer) is recommended to be applied as soon after the frost reflow period as possible (N.J.A.E.S. 1960). A high analysis formulation such as a 5-20-20 is recommended in Wisconsin (Peltier 1955) in order to economize from the standpoint of original cost per unit of plant nutrient as well as the labor involved in its application. In addition, low-analysis fertilizers (containing low nutrient percentages) may contain limestone as a filler, which would be undesirable in many cases. To date, applications of potassium and phosphorus have given no increase in production in Washington bogs. Ammonium sulfate at the rate of 20 pounds of N per acre (23 kg/ha) is recommended for bogs not exhibiting excessive vine growth (Crowley 1954).

Method of Application

Practically all fertilizing is done in the solid form (Sorensen 1955), although solution application through sprinkler systems has found some application in

Massachusetts (Chandler 1952b, 1955c). Norton (1963) was of the opinion that liquid and readily soluble fertilizers could be effectively applied through the irrigation system. Based on an application rate of 50 gallons per minute per acre, he recommended that the actual application be extended over a 30-minute period and that sprinkling then be continued for an additional three to four hours in order to insure that the fertilizer was washed from the vines into the soil. The application of fertilizers to the floodwaters also has been tried with limited success. Since relatively small amounts of fertilizers are required and excessive traffic on the vines is undesirable, fertilizers are generally broadcast by hand or, more recently, by airplane (Doehlert 1951). The pelletizing of fertilizer has considerably improved the distribution pattern of aerial application.

Weed Control

Available Publications

There are currently available a number of excellent publications from the major cranberry-growing regions illustrating in color the important weed species that are of economic significance to growers in the area. The weeds of economic importance in one region are not necessarily the same as those in another growing area. For example, the rushes and sedges that are the bane of cranberry growers on the East Coast are not nearly as troublesome to growers in Wisconsin and on the West Coast. Conversely, some of the broadleaf weeds that plague Wisconsin and West Coast growers are of little concern to cranberry growers in the East.

I. E. Demoranville (1984, 1986) has recently prepared two excellent monographs on the *Weeds of Massachusetts Cranberry Bogs* (SP-148,149). The publications contain descriptions, current control recommendations, and excellent color plates of the major weeds that are a problem to Massachusetts cranberry growers. Many of the weeds discussed by Demoranville are also a problem to New Jersey cranberry growers. The publications are currently available from the University of Massachusetts Cooperative Extension Service at Amherst. Although no longer available, an earlier monograph by C. E. Cross (1952), of the University of Massachusetts, is also worthy of mention because of its excellent line drawings and detailed botanical descriptions of many of the weed species. Beckwith and Fiske (1925) published a similarly illustrated monograph (also out of print) on the weeds found in New Jersey cranberry bogs.

T. D. Planer (1986) has recently prepared a *Cranberry Pest Control—Weed Identification Series* of the major weed species infesting Wisconsin cranberry bogs. The series takes the form of individual one-page leaflets containing color plates of four different weeds on the front page and their description and current recommended control measures on the back side of the page. To date, there are eight such leaflets describing 32 different weeds of economic importance to Wisconsin cranberry growers, some of which are of concern to cranberry growers in other growing regions as well. The leaflets are available from the University of Wisconsin Cooperative Extension Service at Madison.

The recent Pacific Northwest Cooperative Extension Bulletin PNW 247 entitled *Cranberry Production in the Pacific Northwest* (Shawa et al. 1984) contains color photographs of the problem weeds in West Coast cranberry bogs. The bulletin is available from the Cooperative Extension Service at any of the state universities of Washington, Oregon, or Idaho.

Major Weed Problems

Recently, Dana (1987) has compiled a master list of 423 plant species that have been found as weeds in Massachusetts, New Jersey, Washington, or Wisconsin cranberry fields. Many, of course, are only a minor nuisance to cranberry growers, but those that are a significant problem in one or more of the major growing areas are listed in table 8.7. Often the same species of weed is called by a different local name in the different growing regions; therefore, both the scientific name as well as the common names given to the weed are included. Although control recommendations continually change as new herbicides come into use, current control measures for some weeds are included in the table. For a detailed description of the weeds listed, readers are encouraged to avail themselves of the publications mentioned above.

One of the problems cranberry growers have is to distinguish between the rushes, sedges, and grasses, of which there are many different species. For this reason, and because Cross's 1952 bulletin is no longer in print, the following "Key to Rushes, Sedges, and Grasses" from the University of Massachusetts Agricultural Experiment Station Bulletin 463 entitled "Weeds of the Massachusetts Cranberry Bogs" is reprinted below in its entirety (Cross 1952, 11).

Rushes
The rushes are the easiest to identify. They are distinguished by the following characteristics:

1. Stems tubular, round in cross section, often filled with a spongy pith; the nodes inconspicuous, not swollen.

2. Leaves usually tubular, resembling the stems.

3. Flowers small and starlike, associated with narrow (not leafy) bracts.

4. Fruit a small capsule containing hundreds of very minute seeds and surrounded by the persistent sepals and petals.

Sedges

If the "grassy weed" does not possess the above characteristics it is probably a sedge or a true grass. These weeds are more difficult to distinguish from one another, as indicated by the common names woolgrass, nutgrass, needlegrass, cottongrass, three-square grass, and fresh meadowgrass, all of which "grasses" are sedges. Sedges are characterized by the following:

1. Stems usually angular (often triangular) in cross section (except in *Dulichium*), unbranched; nodes inconspicuous, not swollen.

2. Leaves, when present on the stem, 3-ranked, lower edges united about the stem forming a "closed" sheath.

3. Flowering in spikelets; inflorescence with one or more leaflike bracts at the base or, if not, inflorescence small, terminal, and conelike.

4. Fruit nutlike, brown at maturity, easily separated from the scales (except in *Carex*), frequently surrounded by hairs or bristles.

Grasses

If the "grassy weed" has neither the characteristics of a rush nor a sedge, it should be a true grass with the following:

1. Stems tubular, round in cross section and hollow, usually branched; the nodes conspicuous, hard and swollen.

2. Leaves always present on the stem, 2-ranked; lower edges overlapping, not united, forming an "open" sheath (except in *Glyceria*).

3. Flowering in spikelets; inflorescence not associated with leaflike bracts, obviously branched.

4. Fruit a grain, tightly enclosed by several scales or husks.

Control Measures

Hand weeding has been the traditional method of weed control in cranberry bogs since the beginnings of the industry. Even today with the modern herbicides available to the grower, it is still practical to remove woody-stemmed weeds such as swamp maple, leatherleaf, and wild blueberry by hand. For this purpose, the grower had an assortment of weeding hooks available to help extricate the tops and roots of these woody plants. The task was greatly simplified if the plants were discovered and removed before they were more than two years old. The rotary mowing machine was another significant tool in the grower's arsenal against weeds (plate 8.6). By mowing the tops of seed-bearing weeds before the seeds matured, many of these weeds could be kept in check. Another important deterrent to the introduction of weeds into the bog was to maintain healthy and vigorous vines. Weak vines are poor weed competitors. B. Tomlinson and Franklin (1936) summarized these early methods of weed control in their Special Circular No. 29. Cross (1937) outlined the

A.

B.

PLATE 8.6. *A,* CLOSE-UP OF A WEED MOWER; *B,* MOWING THE TOPS OF WEEDS BEFORE THEY GO TO SEED (Courtesy University of Wisconsin Extension Service)

methods of weed control available at the time in a presentation to American Cranberry Growers' Association.

Good soil drainage and proper water management were also significant weed control measures at the disposal of cranberry growers. Many of the grasses and sedges prosper only under wet soil conditions. Often their presence was the sign of poor drainage conditions that could be detrimental to cranberry growth. In soils without impeded drainage, the wetland grasses and sedges can be easily controlled by keeping the water table below a foot. This is also the recommended procedure for controlling red-root, a wetland weed. Areas with impeded drainage would need to have the condition ameliorated either by ditching or by the installation of underground tiles. Late holding the winter flood until July has also been an effective means of eliminating severe weed infestations, although in so doing a crop is sacrificed.

Among the more effective of the early weed control chemicals that cranberry growers had were the petroleum derivative products, which included kerosene, Stoddard Solvent, and fuel oil (Crowley 1940; Dana 1975). Applied as oil sprays in the early spring, they acted as a contact herbicide and effectively killed the tops of many of the emerging perennial weeds. During

TABLE 8.7. COMMON WEED PROBLEMS IN ONE OR MORE OF THE MAJOR CRANBERRY-GROWING REGIONS

SCIENTIFIC NAME	COMMON NAMES	CONTROL MEASURES
Grasses (Gramineae)		
Agrostis hyemalis (Walt) BSP	Summer grass, hairgrass (Mass.)	Chloro-IPC, Dichlobenil, Evital
A. scabra Willd.	Harsh ticklegrass (Oreg., Wis.), Witch grass	Consult current Oreg. and Wis. recommendations
A. stolonifer L. var. *palustris* (Huds.) Pers.	Creeping bentgrass (Oreg.)	Consult current Oreg. recommendations
A. tenuis Sibth.	Colonial bentgrass (Oreg.)	Consult current Oreg. recommendations
Amphicarpon purshii (Pursh.) Nash	Double-seeded millet (N.J.)	Mowing and pulling
Andropogan scoparius Michx	Poverty grass (Mass.) Little blue stem, Broom beardgrass	Devrinol; keep dams closely mowed
Anthoxanthum odoratum L.	Sweet vernalgrass (Oreg.)	Consult current Oreg. recommendations
Aristida longespica Poir.	Triple-awned grass (Mass.)	Increase water and fertility
Calamagrostis canadensis	Blue joint grass (Wis.)	Consult current Wis. recommendations
Calamovilfa brevepilis Hack	Reed grass (N.J.), Saucer grass	Late holding until July; hoe dams
Danthonia californica	Danthonia (Oreg.)	Consult current Oreg. recommendations
Deschampsia cespitosas (L.) Beauv.	Tufted hairgrass (Oreg.)	Consult current Oreg. recommendations
Digitaria sanguinalis Scop.	Crabgrass (Mass.), Finger grass	Dichlobenil, Chloro-IPC, Fusilade
Distichlis spicata (L.) Greene	Seashore saltgrass (Wash.)	Consult current Wash. recommendations

TABLE 8.7. (*Continued*)

SCIENTIFIC NAME	COMMON NAMES	CONTROL MEASURES
Echinochloa crusgalli Beauv.	Barnyard grass (Mass., Oreg.)	Maintain vigorous vines; Chloro-IPC, Devrinol, Evital
E. punguns	Pungent barnyard grass (Wis.)	Consult current Wis. recommendations
Eragrostis hypnoides	Love grass (Wis.)	Consult current Wis. recommendations
Glyceria canadensis (Michx.) Trin.	Rattlesnake grass (Mass., Wis.)	Dichlobenil, Roundup
G. obtusa (Muhl.) Trin.	Blunt manna grass (Mass.), Manna gras	Mowing; improve drainage; Roundup,
Holcus lanatus L.	Velvet grass (Mass., Oreg.)	Kerosene, Dichlobenil, Chloro-IPC
Hordeum jubatum L.	Squirrel tail grass (Wis.)	Consult current Wis. recommendations
Leersia oryzoides (L.) Swartz	Rice-cutgrass (Mass., Oreg., Wash.)	Improve drainage; Chloro-IPC, Devrinol, Dichlobenil, Evital
Muhlenbergia uniflora Fern.	Smokegrass (Mass.)	Evital
Panicum agrostoides Spreng	Redtop panicgrass (Mass.)	Consult current Mass. recommendations
P. amarum Ell.	Beach grass (Mass., N.J.)	None known
P. clandestinum L.	Broad-leaved panicgrass (Mass.)	Mowing; late holding; Evital
P. dichotomiflorum Michx.	Corngrass (Mass.)	Maintain vigorous vines; Chloro-IPC, Devrinol, Evital, Fusilade
P. lanuginosum Ell.	Hairy panicgrass (Mass.)	Chloro-IPC, kerosene

(*continued*)

TABLE 8.7. (*Continued*)

SCIENTIFIC NAME	COMMON NAMES	CONTROL MEASURES
P. occidentale Scribn.	Western witchgrass (Oreg.)	Consult current Oreg. recommendations
P. spretum Schultes	Eaton's panicgrass (Mass.)	Spot spray with kerosene
P. verrucosum Muhl.	Warty panicgrass (Mass.)	Maintain vigorous vines; dichlobenil
P. virgatum L.	Switch grass (Mass., N.J.)	Pull out plants; Dalapon, Evital
Phalaris arundinaceas L.	Reed canarygrass (Mass., Oreg., Wis.)	None known
Poa annua L.	Annual bluegrass (Oreg.)	Consult current Oreg. recommendations
Setaria faberi	Foxtail (Wis.)	Consult current Wis. recommendations
Sieglingia decumbens (L.) Bernk.	Heathgrass	Consult current Oreg. recommendations
Sisyrinchium L. sp.	Blue-eyed grass (Mass.)	Dichlobenil
S. califonicum	Golden-eyed grass (Wash.)	Consult current Wash. recommendations
Sedges (Cyperaceae)		
Carex sp.	Fresh meadow grass (Mass.)	Dichlobenil + kerosene
C. bullata Schkuhr.	Cutgrass, Button sedge Marsh grass (N.J.)	Maintain good drainage
C. chorsoeehiza L.	Creeping sedge (Wis.)	Consult current Wis. recommendations
C. leporina L.	Hare sedge (Oreg.)	Consult current Oreg. recommendations
C. lyngbyei Hornem.	Lyngby's sedge (Oreg.)	Consult current Oreg. recommendations

TABLE 8.7. (*Continued*)

SCIENTIFIC NAME	COMMON NAMES	CONTROL MEASURES
C. obnupta L. H. Bailey	Slough sedge (Oreg.)	Consult current Oreg. recommendations
C. oligosperma Michx.	Wiregrass (Wis.)	Dichlobenil
C. rostrata Stokes	Wide leaf grass (Wis.)	Dalapon
C. scoparia Schkuhr.	Broom sedge (Mass.)	Spot treat with kerosene
C. vesicaria	Inflated sedge (Wash.)	Consult current Wash. recommendations
Cyperus dentatus Torr.	Toothed nutsedge (Mass.)	Devrinol, Dichlobenil, Evital
C. eragrostis Lam.	Tall umbrella plant Umbrella sedge (Oreg.)	Consult current Oreg. recommendations
C. esculentus L.	Yellow nutsedge (Wis.)	Consult current Wis. recommendations
Dulichium arundinaceum L.	Stargrass (Mass.)	Dichlobenil, kerosene
Eleocharis palustris (L.) R. & S.	Common or creeping spikerush (Oreg.)	Consult current Oreg. recommendations
E. tenuis (Willd.) Schultes	Needle grass (Mass.) Slender spike rush	Dichlobenil, Evital
Eriophorum chamissonis Mey	Russet cottongrass Cotton top (Wash.)	Consult current Wash. recommendations
E. virginicum L.	Tawny cottongrass (Mass.)	Dichlobenil
Scirpus americanus Pers.	Three-square grass (Mass.), American bulrush	Wipe with 2,4-D
S. cyperinus (L.) Kunt	Wool grass (Mass., Wis.) Sickle grass (N.J.)	Dichlobenil, kerosene

(*continued*)

TABLE 8.7. (*Continued*)

SCIENTIFIC NAME	COMMON NAMES	CONTROL MEASURES
S. validus Vahl.	Tussocks (Wash.), Soft-stem bulrush	Consult current Wash. recommendations
	Rushes (Juncaceae)	
Juncus acuminatus Michx.	Tapered rush (Oreg.)	Consult current Oreg. recommendations
J. bufonis L.	Toad rush (Mass., Oreg.) Louse grass (Wash.)	Maintain vigorous vines; kerosene
J. bolanderi Engelm.	Bolander's rush (Oreg.)	Consult current Oreg. recommendations
J. canadensis J. Gay	Canada rush (Mass.) Bog rush	Kerosene
J. effusus L.	Spike rush (Mass.) Soft rush (Wis.)	Dichlobenil, Evital, De-vrinol, kerosene,
var. *pacificus* Fern. & Wieg	Common rush (Oreg.)	Roundup
J. ensifolius Wikst.	Dagger-leaf rush (Oreg.)	Consult current Oreg. recommendations
J. pelocarpus Mey.	Mud rush (Mass.)	Dichlobenil
J. planifolius R. Br.	No common name (Oreg.)	Consult current Oreg. recommendations
J. tenuis Willd.	Slender rush (Oreg.)	Consult current Oreg. recommendations
	Ferns (Polyodiaceae)	
Dryopterus thelypteris Gray	Feather fern (Mass.) Marsh fern (Wis.)	Iron sulfate + salt
Onoclea sensibilis L.	Sensitive fern (Mass., Wis.)	Iron sulfate, Dichlobenil
Osmunda cinnamonea L.	Cinnamon fern (N.J.)	Iron sulfate
O. regalis L. var. *spec-tabilis* Willd.	Royal fern (Mass., N.J.) Flowering fern	Dichlobenil, Iron sulfate

TABLE 8.7. (*Continued*)

SCIENTIFIC NAME	COMMON NAMES	CONTROL MEASURES
Polystichum munitum (Kaulf.) Presl.	Sword fern (Oreg.)	Consult current Oreg. recommendations
Pteridium aquilinum Kuhn	Bracken fern (Wis.)	Iron sulfate
Woodwardia virginica (L.) Smith	Virginia chain fern (N.J.)	Dichlobenil

Compositae		
Ambrosia artemisiifolia L.	Common ragweed (Mass.), Bitter weed	Dichlobenil
Anaphalis margaritacea (L.) B. & H.	Pearly-everlasting (Oreg.)	Consult current Oreg. recommendations
Aster chilensis Nees	Chilean aster (Oreg.)	Consult current Oreg. recommendations
A. ericoides L.	White aster (Mass.) Small-leaved aster	Dichlobenil; wipe with Roundup
A. novi-belgii L.	New York aster (Mass.) Blue aster	Same as above
A. spectabilis Ait.	Showy aster (Mass.) Seaside purple aster	Wipe with Roundup
A. subspicatus Nees	Douglas' aster (Oreg., Wash.)	Consult current Oreg. and Wash. recommendations
Bidens frondosa L.	Devils beggarticks (Wis.) Pitchforks (Mass.) Spanish needle (Oreg.) a misnomer	Dichlobenil, Simazine
Chrysopsis falcata (Pursh) Ell.	Golden aster (Mass.)	Wipe with Roundup
Erechtites hieracifolia (L.) Raf.	Fireweed (Mass., Wash.) Cotton weed Pilewort	Dichlobenil, Simazine, Chloro-IPC

(*continued*)

TABLE 8.7. (*Continued*)

SCIENTIFIC NAME	COMMON NAMES	CONTROL MEASURES
E. minima (Poir.) DC.	Australian burnweed or fireweed (Oreg.)	Consult current Oreg. recommendations
Eupatorium dubium Willd.	Joe-Pye weed (Mass.)	Wipe with Roundup
Hypochaeris radicata L.	Spotted catsear (Mass., Oreg.)	None known
Leontodon mudicaulis (L.) Merat	Hairy hawkbit (Oreg.)	Consult current Oreg. recommendations
Senecio sylvaticus L.	Woodland groundsel (Oreg.)	Consult current Oreg. recommendations
Solidago altissima	Goldenrod (Wis.)	Consult current Wis. recommendations
S. canadensis L. var. *salebrosa* (Piper) Jones	Meadow goldenrod (Oreg.)	Consult current Oreg. recommendations
S. graminifolia (L.) Salisb.	Grassleaf goldenrod (Mass., Wis.)	Dichlobenil, Wipe with Roundup
S. rugosa Ait.	Rough goldenrod (Mass.)	Wipe with Roundup; Stoddard solvent
S. tenuifolia Pursh	Narrow-leaved goldenrod	Dichlobenil, Wipe with Roundup

Woody weeds		
Acer rubrum L.	Swamp maple (N.J.)	Hand pull
Andromeda glaucophylla	Bog rosemary (Wis.)	Consult current Wash. recommendations
Chamaecyparis thyoides (L.) BSP	White cedar (N.J.)	Hand pull
Chamaedaphne calyculata (L.) Moench	Leather leaf (N.J., Wis.) Brown brush (Mass.)	Wipe with 2,4-D
Clethra alnifolia L.	Sweetpepper bush (Mass., N.J.), White alder	Wipe with 2,4-D

TABLE 8.7. (*Continued*)

SCIENTIFIC NAME	COMMON NAMES	CONTROL MEASURES
Cornus canadensis L.	Dogwood (Wash.)	Consult current Wash. recommendations
Gaultheria shallon Pursh.	Salal (Oreg.)	Consult current Oreg. recommendations
Kalmia angustifolia L.	Sheep laurel (Mass., N.J.), Dwarf laurel, lambkill, Wicky	None known
Pyrus melanocarpa (Michx.) Willd.	Black chokeberry (Mass.) Chokeberry	Wipe with Roundup
Rhus radicans L.	Poison ivy (Mass., Wis.)	Wipe with Roundup
Rubus L. spp.	Bramble (Mass., Wis.) Blackberry	Dichlobenil + kerosene
R. discolor Weike & Nees	Himalaya blackberry (Oreg.)	Consult current Oreg. recommendations
R. hispidus L.	Swamp dewberry (Wis.) Swamp blackberry (N.J.)	Consult current Wis. and N.J. recommendations
R. laciniatus Willd.	Evergreen blackberry (Oreg.)	Consult current Oreg. recommendations
R. spectablis Pursh.	Salmonberry (Oreg.)	Consult current Oreg. recommendations
R. vitifolius Cham. & Schlecht	Western dewberry (Oreg.), Pacific blackberry	Consult current Oreg. recommendations
Salix sp.	Willows (Oreg., Wash.)	Consult current Oreg. and Wash. recommendations
Sanguisorba officinalis L.	Garden burnet (Oreg.)	Consult current Oreg. recommendations

(*continued*)

TABLE 8.7. (*Continued*)

SCIENTIFIC NAME	COMMON NAMES	CONTROL MEASURES
Smilex spp.	Green brier (N.J.) Bull brier	None known
S. glauca Walt.	Saw brier (Mass.) Silver leaf brier	None known
Spiraea alba Du Roi	Meadow sweet (Mass.)	Wipe with 2,4-D or Roundup
S. douglasii Hook	Buckbrush (Oreg., Wash.)	Consult current Oreg. and Wash. recommen- dations
S. tomentosa L.	Hardhack (Mass.) Steeple bush	Wipe with 2,4-D
Vaccinium angustifolium (Ait.)	Lowbush blueberry (Mass.)	Hand pull
V. corymbosum (Ait.)	Highbush blueberry (N.J.)	Hand pull

	Ditch and pond weeds	
Bidens frondosa L.	Begger-ticks (Oreg.), Spanish needle	Consult current Oreg. recommendations
Callitriche verna L.	Spring water-starwort (Oreg.)	Consult current Oreg. recommendations
Hypericum anagalloides C. & S.	Bog St. John's wart	Consult current Oreg. recommendations
Myriophyllum hyppuroides Nutt.	Wester water milfoil (Oreg.)	Consult current Oreg. recommendations
Nuphar advena Ait.	Yellow pond lily (Mass.) Spatter-dock Cow lily	Diquat outside of bog; Roundup in bog
N. variegatum Engelm.	Bullhead lily (Mass.)	Same as above
Nymphaea adorata Ait.	Pond lily (Mass., N.J.) Fragrant water lily	Remove manually if drainage is impeded

TABLE 8.7. (*Continued*)

SCIENTIFIC NAME	COMMON NAMES	CONTROL MEASURES
Pontederia cordata L.	Pickerelweed (Mass.)	Diquat or Roundup
Potamogeton natans L.	Broad or floating-leaved pondweed (Oreg.)	Consult current Oreg. recommendations
Sgittaria latifolia Willd.	Arrowhead (Mass.) Swamp-potato Duck-potato	Roundup, Diquat, Dichlobenil
Sparganium americanum Nutt.	Bur-reed (Mass.)	Dalapon in bog; Diquat outside bog

Root-spreading weeds		
Equisetum arvense L.	Field horsetail (Mass., Wash.), Marestail, meadow pine	Dichlobenil, Chloro-IPC
Lysimachia terrestris (L.) BSP	Yellow loosestrife (Mass.), Swamp candle (Wis.), Yellow weed (Oreg., Wash.), Mud weed	Dichlobenil; Wipe with 2,4-D; kerosene + Stoddard Solvent
Lythrum solicaria	Purple loosestrife (Wis.)	Consult current Wis. recommendations
Maianthemum canadense Desf.	Lily-of-the-valley (Wash.)	Consult current Wash. recommendations
M. dilatatum	False Lily-of-the-valley (Oreg.)	Consult current Oreg. recommendations
Rumex acetosella L.	Sheep sorrel (Mass., Wash.), Common sorrel, Little sorrel, Sour grass	Dichlobenil, Chloro-IPC
Triadenum virginicum L.	Marsh St. Johns-wort (Mass.)	Dichlobenil, Iron sulfate, Roundup

(*continued*)

TABLE 8.7. (*Continued*)

SCIENTIFIC NAME	COMMON NAMES	CONTROL MEASURES
	Runner-spreading weeds	
Fragaria chiloensis (L.) Duch.	Coast strawberry (Oreg.)	Consult current Oreg. recommendations
Lotus corniculatus L.	Lotus (Oreg., Wash.) Birdsfoot trefoil (B.C.)	Consult current Oreg. and Wash. recommendations
L. formosissimus Greene	Seaside lotus (Oreg.)	Consult current Oreg. recommendations
L. purshianus (Benth.) Clem. & Clem.	Spanish clover (Oreg.)	Consult current Oreg. recommendations
L. uliginosus Schkuhr	Birdsfoot trefoil (Oreg.)	Consult current Oreg. recommendations
Potentilla anserina L.	Silver leaf (Wash.) Cinquefoil, silverweed	Consult current Wash. recommendations
P. canadensis L.	Five-finger cinquefoil (Mass.)	Iron sulfate only treatment
P. pacifica Howell	Pacific silverweed (Oreg.)	Consult current Oreg. recommendations
Ranunculus repens L.	Creeping buttercup (Wash.)	Consult current Wash. recommendations
R. flammula L.	Small creeping buttercup (Oreg.)	Consult current Oreg. recommendations
Trifolium repens L.	White clover (Oreg.)	Consult current Oreg. recommendations
Vicia sativa L.	Common vetch (Oreg.)	Consult current Oreg. recommendations
	Tuberous weeds	
Achillea millefolium L.	Common yarrow (Mass.)	Wipe with Roundup
Apios americana Medic.	Wild bean (Mass.) Ground nut Potato bean	Only partial control with Dichlobenil and Devrinol

TABLE 8.7. (*Continued*)

SCIENTIFIC NAME	COMMON NAMES	CONTROL MEASURES
Rhexia virginica L.	Meadow beauty (Mass.) Deargrass	Easy to hand weed; Wipe with 2,4-D or Roundup

Seed-spreading perennial weeds		
Asclepias incarnata L.	Swamp milkweed (Wis.)	Consult current Wis. recommendations
A. syriaca L.	Common milkweed (Wis.)	Consult current Wis. recommendations
Lachnanthes tinctoria Walt.	Red root (N.J.)	Improve drainage; Increase vine vigor
Viola lanceolata L.	White violet (Mass., Oreg.), Lanced-leaved violet, Water violet	None known
V. palustris L.	Marsh violet	Consult current Oreg. recommendations

Seed-spreading annual weeds		
Cuscuta gronovii Willd.	Field dodder (Mass., Wis.) Goldthread, love-vine, Strangle-weed	Chloro-IPC, Dichlobenil, Nitrate of soda
Galium trifidum L.	Small bedstraw (Oreg.)	Consult current Oreg. recommendations
Ipomoea purpurea	Morning glory (Mass.)	Simazine
Polygonum hydropiper L.	Common smartweed (Mass.), Water pepper	Dichlobenil, Simazine
P. hydropiperoides Michx.	Mild smartweed (Oreg.)	Consult current Oreg. recommendations
P. pennsylvania L.	Pennsylvania smartweed (Wis.)	Consult current Wis. recommendations

(*continued*)

TABLE 8.7. (*Continued*)

SCIENTIFIC NAME	COMMON NAMES	CONTROL MEASURES
P. persicaria L.	Ladysthumb (Mass., Wash.)	Consult current Oreg. & Wash. recommendations
P. sagittatum	Saw grass (Mass.), Brier grass, Scratch grass	Chloro-IPC, Simazine
Solanum nigrum L.	Black nightshade (Wis.)	Consult current Wis. recommendations
	Mosses	
Polytrichum commune Hedw.	Hair cap moss (Mass., Oreg.), Green moss	Dichlobenil, Chloro-IPC
Sphagnum sp.	Sphagnum moss (N.J.)	Improve drainage

SOURCES: Cross 1952; Dana 1987; Demoranville 1984, 1986; Shawa et al. 1984.

the days of low oil prices, they were an economical as well as effective means of weed control. Today, they are no longer cheap, and they have been superceded for the most part by more effective herbicides. In addition to the petroleum products, the grower could use such salts as iron sulfate, copper sulfate, sodium nitrate, sodium chloride, and even sulfuric acid, which would be directed at the specific weed that needed to be controlled.

In the decades following World War II, a parade of organic herbicides became available for use on cranberry bogs. They included materials that could kill on contact, those that were absorbed by the weed plant and interfered with its metabolism and those that prevented germination of the weed seed. Because of the diversity of weed species that inhabited cranberry bogs and because the organic herbicides were only effective with specific weed species, it was necessary to develop an array of materials that would control as wide a spectrum of weeds as was needed to control. Hence, specific materials were developed to control the annual weeds, both narrowleaf and broadleaf, the perennial grasses and sedges, and the woody perennials. All of them needed to be carefully tested to make sure they were not harmful to cranberry plants or to man.

With the use of the petroleum derivative products, the cranberry grower was doing a fairly effective job of keeping many of the perennial grasses in check. The materials, however, were for the most part ineffective against the annual weeds. One of the first of the organic herbicides that filled this gap was the herbicide simazine (2-chloro-4,6-bis [ethylamino]-s-triazine). Dana (1960) found this preemergence herbicide to effectively control common ragweed, beggarticks, annual smartweed, and panic grass in Wisconsin cranberry bogs. Granular simazine at the rate of 1 to 2 pounds active ingredient per acre (1.15–2.3 kg/ha) applied early in the spring soon after the drawing of the winter flood gave good control and increased cranberry yields from very weedy bogs. In Massachusetts, simazine at the rate of 5 pounds per acre (5.75 kg/ha) of 80 percent wettable powder (80W) in 300 gallons (1.136 l) of water sprayed early in the spring before weed emergence controlled summer grass, cutgrass, morning glory, mannagrass, sand spurrey, cinquefoil, warty panicgrass, ragweed, pitchforks, fireweed, and some upland grasses (I. E. Demoranville and Cross 1962). Also developed at this time as a preemergent herbicide was Chloro-IPC (isopropyl N-[3-chlorophenyl] carbamate), which controls many of the same weeds controlled by simazine and is partially effective against dodder (I. E. Demoranville 1986).

Perennial grasses have always been the bane of a weedless cranberry bog. The petroleum derivatives helped keep them in check, but a more effective eradicant was needed. In the early 1950s, the herbicide amitrol (3-amino-1,2,4-triazole) was found to be effective against a broad spectrum of cranberry weeds which included the perennial grasses (I. E. Demoranville and Cross 1957b). The new herbicide was effective at rather low rates of application and did not seriously effect the cranberry plant (Dana 1959; Demoranville and Cross 1957a). Its effectiveness against a wide spectrum of weeds made it the favored herbicide of choice by cranberry growers on both coasts. When the compound became a suspected carcinogen and residues were found on cranberries (which led to the cranberry scare of 1959), amitrol disappeared from the cranberry grower's arsenal of herbicides.

Another effective herbicide used to combat these grasses was dalapon (2,2-dichloropropionic acid). On Massachusetts cranberry bogs, Cross and Demoranville (1962) were able to kill some of the most obstinate of these perennial grasses, including cutgrass, perennial summer grass, poverty grass, switch grass, warty panicgrass as well as sedge. Rates of 3 pounds per acre (3.5 kg/ha) of Dowpon (85% sodium dalapon) in 300 gallons (1,136 liters) of water applied to dormant plants in the spring controlled cutgrass. Applications rates of 5 and 10 pounds per acre (5.8 and 11.6 kg/ha) in October or November controlled the other grasses. In Wisconsin Dana (1956) found that dalapon controlled wide leaf grass, sickle grass, blue joint grass, bunch grass, and round rush.

Herbicides effective against a wider spectrum of weeds are desirable and have always been sought after. A material that would be effective against both narrow-leaved and broad-leaved annuals as well as perennial grasses and sedges would be the ideal herbicide. Approaching this ideal were the next group of herbicides that were released for use on cranberries. One of the most successful of these was dichlobenil (2,6-dichlorobenzonitrile), marketed under the product names Casoron and Norosac. Dana and his associates (1965) were able to control several annual and perennial sedges, grasses, and broadleaf weeds in Wisconsin cranberry bogs with the application of 4 to 6 pounds per acre (4.6–6.9 kg/ha) of a 4 percent granular dichlobenil formulation in either the spring or fall when applied to dormant cranberry plants. Only minor reduction in cranberry vine growth and berry size resulted. Devlin and Demoranville (1968) also found that dichlobenil treatment for two years in a row resulted in slight berry size and yield reduction. Sprinkling or shallow flooding after the application of the herbicide reduced its volatilization and therefore its phytotoxicity to the cranberry and increased its efficacy (Miller et al. 1967). With dichlobenil, Welker (1967) obtained good control of Virginia chain fern, a serious weed problem in New Jersey cranberry bogs. The wide spectrum of bog weeds controlled by dichlobenil makes it a valuable compound in cranberry weed control despite its potential for cranberry phytotoxicity.

Not quite as effective against the sedges and grasses were the broad-spectrum herbicides chlorpropham (isopropyl N-[3-chlorophenyl] carbamate) and naptalam (N-1-naphthyl phthalamic acid), although the combination of these two herbicides labelled for use under the product name Morcran was effective against germinating seedlings of annual grasses. At the rate of 100 pounds per acre (115 kg/ha) of granules, Morcran controlled sicklegrass, barnyard grass, tearthumb smartweed, and perennial smartweed. Growth of the difficult-to-control nutsedge and cutgrass was suppressed by Morcran but not eradicated (Devlin and Demoranville 1973). Morcran is no longer formulated and therefore not available for use on cranberries.

The most recent of these broad-spectrum herbicides to be released was norflurazon (4-chloro-5-[methylamino]-2-α, α, α-trifluoro-m-tolyl]-3[2H]-pyridazinone) marketed under the product name Evital and formulated as a 5 percent granular herbicide for cranberries. It is perhaps the best material available for control of most of the grasses (Dana 1975). A single application of up to 160 pounds per acre (184 kg/ha) of 5 percent granular Evital, applied in either early spring before weed growth starts or late fall after harvest, will control such grasses as poverty grass, wool grass, switch grass, cutgrass, needlegrass, barnyard grass, and smokegrass. Also controlled are nutsedges, spike rush, fall panicum, and red-root. It has given only marginal control of sedges and ferns. It is generally not effective against asters, loosestrife, or other broadleaf weeds found in cranberry bogs.

I. E. Demoranville and Devlin (1971) have reported a temporary chlorosis developing at the base of the cranberry leaf blade at an application of 16 pounds a.i. per acre (18.4 kg/ha) of norflurazon. No significant differences were detected, however, between control and treated berries when yield, berry size, berry dry weight, pectin content, and anthocyanin development were compared. Evital injury to cranberry is more likely to occur under conditions of marginal drainage and in sandy or hard-bottom bogs low in organic matter. Well-kept bogs with low-to-moderate weed populations and bogs with sprinkler irrigation are also more prone to vine injury by Evital application. Evital must not be applied during the most active growth stage of the cranberry in order to avoid injury to the cranberry plant. Because Evital must be absorbed through the roots of weed plants in order to produce the herbicidal action, it is generally less effective when applied to bogs with heavy vine growth or to bogs in which a heavy thatch exists. Evital must not be applied when another herbicide has been applied in the same year.

The herbicides discussed to this point have been highly successful in controlling many of the grasses and sedges that represent some of the most serious weed problems in cranberry culture. There remains, however, a host of weeds that can be significant problems in different areas and under specific growing conditions that are not controlled by any of these herbicides. Included in this group are many of the weeds in the Compositae family, such as the asters and the different species of goldenrod, most of the woody weeds, and the ditch weeds. One of the most effective herbicides recently introduced to fill this gap has been glyphosate (N-[phosphonomethyl] glycine) marketed under the product name Roundup. Shawa (1980) found glyphosate to give excellent control of *Aster* and *Spiraea,* two weeds that have been resistant to other herbicides available for use on cranberries in Washington. Since glyphosate is toxic to the cranberry plant, it can only be applied by spray when the cranberry plants are dormant. The powerful growth regulator effect of this compound was observed by Welker (1976). Glyphosate applied to actively growing cranberry plants greatly increased the number of new uprights that developed from buds along the runner, but it also resulted in vine injury and loss of current crop. During the growing season, glyphosate must be carefully swabbed or wiped on the problem weed with special applicators (Welker 1981). Using this method, such difficult-to-control weeds as *Spiraea,* goldenrod, poison ivy, and wild bean can be eradicated (I. E. Demoranville 1986).

Direct application by wiping with either glyphosate or the dimethylamine salt of 2,4-D (2,4 dichlorophenoxy acetic acid) is the method used to control many of the woody weeds such as the brambles, brown brush, and steeple brush. Ditch weeds can also be controlled by the wiping method using diquat

(6,7-dihydrodipyrido[1,2,-a:2',1'-C]tyrozinediium) in ditches located outside the bog and with Devrinol (2-[α-naphthoxy]-N-diethylpropionamide) in ditches located within the bog.

Three very-difficult-to-control weeds that are major weed problems on opposite coasts of the country are red-root in New Jersey, wild bean in Massachusetts, and inflated rush in Washington. Terbacil (3-tert-butyl-5-chloro-6-methyluracil) has been outstanding in controlling red-root and inflated rush. Terbacil sprayed at the rate of 2 kg/ha onto the emerging inflated rush plants while the cranberries were still dormant in the spring gave excellent control of this serious seed problem in Washington cranberry bogs (Shawa 1980). Welker (1979) found that terbacil at 2 kg/ha was the most effective herbicide tested to control red-root in New Jersey cranberry bogs. In Massachusetts Devlin and Demoranville (1978b) were able to control wild bean with the experimental growth regulator maleic hydrazide, but only at rates that were seriously detrimental to cranberry yield.

During this discussion of weed control measures, various methods of herbicide application have been alluded to. Since cranberry bogs (unless they are being prepared for a new planting) cannot be disked or harrowed, materials which are easily volatilized, such as the preemergent herbicides, must be applied in such a way as to reduce their loss to the atmosphere. One approach has been to apply the herbicide adsorbed to a sand or clay granule. This not only slows its volatilization but also aids in filtering the herbicide to the bog floor, where it is to carry out its function (Dana et al. 1965). The application of water at this point also greatly increases the efficacy of the herbicide by reducing its volatilization. Herbicides applied to bogs that are being prepared for planting can, of course, be worked into the soil mechanically or they can be thoroughly watered into the soil, where they will be most effective. In new bogs another approach may be to fumigate the unplanted bog with one of the available soil fumigants (Skroch and Dana 1965). In this case it is important that sufficient time elapses between the fumigation and the planting.

Herbicides that can be applied in solution without losing much of their efficacy can be sprayed on the bog with conventional spray equipment provided the herbicide is not toxic to the cranberry plant. Even where such phytotoxicity does exist, herbicides can be sprayed if the cranberry plants are dormant but the weeds have begun active growth. When both the weed and the cranberry plant are actively growing and the application of the herbicide is to be made to the growing weed, a special applicator is required. Various types of wiping equipment have been engineered for use on cranberry bogs, ranging from self-feeding, hand-held hockey sticks (Welker 1981) to elaborate self-propelled, herbicide-fed rollers.

Pollination Procedures

Pollinators

The need for insect pollination to insure good commercial yields has been well established (see chapter 6). Hutson (1925, 1926a) determined that the bumblebee *Bombus impatiens* was the most prevalent pollinating insect on cranberry bogs in New Jersey. At an average of 488 bumblebees per acre, Hutson calculated that there were enough bees to visit every flower every day during the entire blooming period. He determined that an average count of three bumblebees per square rod was sufficient for good pollination (Hutson 1926a). Hutson concluded that cranberry bogs in New Jersey had sufficient natural pollinators and, therefore, would not benefit from the addition of honeybees (Hutson 1926b). In Washington Johansen (1965) listed *Bombus mixtus, B. melanopygus,* and *B. vosnesenskii* as the most prevalent bumblebee pollinators of cranberries.

In 1940 Franklin was of the opinion that the populations of wild bees in Massachusetts bog areas were sufficient to promote adequate fruit set. In an effort to encourage the buildup of populations of wild bees, Chandler (1954a) suggested planting in the uplands surrounding cranberry bogs those species of plants that would provide nectar and pollen for native bees. Species that would not be competitive with cranberry—that is, would not bloom at the same time as cranberry, would not harbor cranberry insects, and would not become a cranberry weed problem—included wild lupine, white sweet clover, sweetpepper bush, forsythia, *Spiraea,* and buckwheat. Johansen and Hutt (1965) and Johansen (1967) also described methods, including the construction of nesting units, employed to encourage the most prevalent pollinator in Washington, *Bombus mixtus.*

By 1950, however, researchers were demonstrating that the use of domestic honeybees could markedly increase yields of cranberries (Stricker 1946; Farrar and Bain 1946; Filmer 1949). Intensive cultivation, the frequent burning of uplands, and the extensive use of insecticides appeared to work against the native pollinators, thus destroying their effectiveness as pollination agents. Another problem exists in that the pollen and nectar of flowers of competitive plants in the cranberry-growing area may provide better foraging for bees. Such plants as wild azalea (*Azalea viscosa*), privet Andromeda (*Kalmia liquistrina*), stagger bush (*Pieris mariana*), fetterbush (*Leucothoe racemosa*), blue huckleberry (*Gaylussacia frondosa*), black huckleberry (*Gaylussacia baccata*), and red-root (*Lachnanthes tinctoria*) are all significant competitors for bee visitations.

In Wisconsin, Farrar and Bain (1946) recommended one strong colony per two acres of cranberries under favorable pollinating conditions, and five to ten colonies under unfavorable conditions. In New Jersey the recommendation is for a minimum of one hive per two acres of cranberries and, possibly, one hive per acre to further insure against poor pollination in the event of poor pollinating conditions (Stewart and Marucci 1970). Oregon recommendations (Burgett and Poole 1987) call for two Oregon Grade A colonies (1,000 square inches of live brood and 24,000 adult workers) per acre. McGregor (1976) has recommended as many as ten colonies per acre under poor pollination conditions in order that bee saturation may occur, particularly when competitive plant species are in bloom.

Colony Requirement

The minimum requirements for a strong colony as suggested by the USDA (1968) specify that the colony consist of a two-story hive, contain 30,000 bees, and should have 6 to 12 standard frames of brood in all stages of development. On a warm day, bees should be in active flight with at least 50 to 75 workers leaving the nest each minute.

Recent evidence suggests that honeybee colonies may differentially collect cranberry pollen. Of six colonies of bees placed near a cranberry bog, one colony consistently collected more than 98 percent cranberry pollen. Other colonies collected between 0 and 86.8 percent cranberry pollen (Shimanuki et al. 1967). This interesting observation suggests the possibility of breeding bees specifically for cranberry pollination.

As a general rule, colonies should be located in the bogs when blossoms first appear and remain for the three-to-four-week bloom period. Marucci and Moulter (1978) observed that if bees were excluded from cranberry flowers for one or two weeks after full bloom, no reduction in fruit set occurred. However, if the bees were excluded for a single week at the beginning of flowering, fruit set was greatly reduced. Shimanuki et al. (1967) also found that maximum cranberry pollen collection occurred when colonies were placed near bogs before peak bloom. Moeller (1973) found the optimum time for hive placement was at full bloom. Hives that were in place two weeks before full bloom gathered significantly less cranberry pollen than hives placed in the bog at full bloom, suggesting that the bees from the early-placed hives were already working different plants. Burgett and Poole (1987), on the other hand, stress that the hives should be placed adjacent to the bogs no earlier than at 10 percent bloom and no later than at 25 to 30 percent bloom.

Honeybees usually pollinate flowers more thoroughly within 100 yards of their colonies, a factor that must be considered in colony distribution in the field. The placement of the hives along a windbreak and exposed to the early and full exposure of sunlight is the general consensus. The essentials of honey bee use in pollinating crops, including the scheduling of delivery of colonies and colony distribution in the field, are described in the USDA 1968 Leaflet No. 549, *Using Honey Bees to Pollinate Crops*. W. E. Tomlinson (1957) has emphasized the importance of protecting bees from insecticides. Similarly, USDA Leaflet No. 544, *Protecting Honey Bees from Pesticides* (1967), gives information on protecting bees from unnecessary decimation. Both USDA leaflets are available from the Superintendent of Documents, U.S. Government Printing Office, Washington, DC 20402.

Honeybee Requirements

Bees need water to cool off their hives. Without adequate moisture, bees would overheat in the hives and die very rapidly. In addition, bees require moisture to dilute stored honey before it is ingested, to produce royal jelly, to prevent dehydration of body tissues, and to aid in ingesting pollen grains before they are swallowed (*Cranberries* 1978).

Winter sites for hives must receive the maximum sunlight possible and have good water and air drainage. Bees must get out of the hive periodically during mild winter weather to rid themselves of wastes, or they may develop an intestinal disease known as Nosema. Bees may freeze to death in bitter cold weather; therefore, wrapping the hives in black paper will help warm the hives on the coldest days between January and March and thus insure some bee flight.

Recommendations for the Protection of Bees

The following procedures to be taken by the cranberry grower are strongly advocated for the preservation of the beekeeper's colonies (W. E. Tomlinson 1957; USDA 1967):

1. Do not spray while cranberries are in bloom. Apply insecticides when the cranberries are still in the bud stage or just after flowering.

2. Spray when bees are not flying. Bees are active on sunny days when the air temperature is above 50°F (10°C); they are most active between 8 a.m. and 5 p.m. Pesticide applications are preferably made in the early evening to allow decomposition time for the applied chemical and to allow unopened flowers to open overnight.

3. Do not contaminate the water with spray materials.

4. Use compounds that are least toxic to bees.

5. Use less toxic formulations:

   a. Dusts are more hazardous to bees than liquid formulations.

   b. Emulsifiable concentrates have shorter killing power than wettable powders.
   c. Ultra-low volume (ULV) formulations are often much more hazardous to bees than other liquid formulations.

   6. Eliminate attractive weeds. Before treating weed species with insecticides, mow the weed flowers so that bees are not subjected to the insecticide spray.

   7. Notify beekeepers. Some beekeepers will move bees from a spray area if given at least 48-hours notice, or they may want to cover their colonies.

   8. Protect colonies in the area. Locate hives to avoid direct insecticidal spraying of the hives. Sometimes beekeepers will cover the hives with coarse cloth to confine the bees; in these situations, frequent sprinkling with water will prevent bees from overheating.

   9. Never seal up colonies.

Other Pollinators

Contrary to what many growers might think, the honeybee is not the most efficient pollinator of fruit crops. Bees that do not make honey (non-*Apis* bees) are much more efficient. One such non-*Apis* bee is *Osmia lignaria,* which has been found to be an excellent orchard pollinator because it works longer hours and under more adverse weather conditions than do honeybees (*Cranberries* 1978). *Osmia* bees do not nest in hives but will readily accept synthetic nesting materials. If nesting materials are provided, a sufficient number of bees can be set up to handle any size orchard, and their emergence can be timed to coincide with the bloom period. They nest near the floral source and both males and females visit blossoms during their short flight period. Maximum pollination therefore occurs over a short period of time. These bees adapt to a wide range of environments and can be found from coast to coast. Although at present there is no commercial source of *Osmia lignaria,* they are easily captured and managed. Extensive research is being conducted by the federal government to investigate the feasibility of *Osmia* bees to serve as significant pollinators of crops.

   There are some 20,000 species of non-*Apis* bees compared to only four species of honeybee. A non-*Apis* wild bee that specializes in blueberries is *Colletes validus.* This bee is only active when blueberries are in bloom and spends the rest of the year underground. Perhaps someday such a non-*Apis* bee that will specialize in cranberries will be found.

Bog Maintenance

Sanding

One of the first cultural practices to be used in cranberry production was sanding. On Cape Cod in 1810, Henry Hall noted that sand blown in from the nearby beach improved the growth of the cranberries on his wild patch. This accidental discovery was recorded by the Hon. S. L. Deyo in his *History of Barnstable County* as follows (B. Tomlinson 1936, 4):

> Mr. Henry Hall of East Dennis owned a piece of low land on which wild cranberries grew, and adjoining this was a brush knoll, a low, round hill, partly covered with small trees. After these trees were cut the knoll was exposed to winds and erosion, and its sand was blown or washed down upon the wild cranberry vines at its base. Instead of injuring the cranberries, of which Mr. Hall had made some use, that layer of sand improved them, for the vines grew up through the sand and bore larger and better berries. Thus originated the fundamental idea of a layer of sand on a peat bog, which led to the successful cultivation of the cranberry industry.

Sanding has been an integral part of cranberry culture ever since. We have already seen the significance of its use in bog establishment and its use as a medium for vine propagation, but it has another significant application in line with Henry Hall's early observation of its invigorating effect. Sanding is used to rejuvenate old plantings and to curtail vine growth in excessively vegetative bogs. A layer of sand varying in depth from ¼ to 1 inch (0.64–2.54 cm) is broadcast evenly over the vines. If vine growth is particularly heavy, as much as 2 inches (5 cm) of sand may be beneficial. The amount of sand necessary to give the various depths is shown in table 8.2 (B. Tomlinson 1936).

The primary function of the sand is to cover the excessively long runners of mature plants and to stimulate the rooting of these runners (Cross and Demoranville 1969). These long vines, even though they may be in contact with the soil, do not root. Covering the stems encourages rooting and enables the vines to become more vigorous and productive. The kind of coverage needed to promote rooting generally requires that at least an inch (2.54 cm) of sand be broadcast evenly over the vines. In addition to the promotion of rooting, the sand serves to cover fallen leaves and other organic debris, thus encouraging their breakdown and incorporation into the bog soil. Bogs producing a moderate-to-heavy amount of vegetative growth are generally sanded every three to four years (Beckwith 1937).

Besides the primary purpose of promoting rooting, it was soon realized that there were other benefits to be gained by sanding. One of the first observations was that periodic sanding of a bog tended to reduce the tipworm population by covering the cocoons and thus preventing the emergence of the adult fly. Cranberry girdler infestations can also be reduced by covering the bog trash with a layer of sand, thereby creating an unfavorable environment for the tiny larvae (B. Tomlinson 1937).

Resanding has been observed to produce vigorous and healthy vine growth that successfully competes with vines weakened by false blossom disease. This was another benefit of sanding that was quickly recognized in the virus-infected bogs of the East. It is imperative, however, that these rejuvenated vines be protected with insecticide against the blunt-nosed leafhopper since these lush vines are particularly favored by the insect (Beckwith 1937).

Bogs that have been sanded will remain a few degrees warmer than unsanded bogs under identical frost-producing conditions. This is because the sand readily absorbs heat during the day and releases the heat rapidly during the night. Cross and Demoranville (1969) were also of the opinion that a layer of clean, white sand on the bog floor increases the amount of reflected light that impinges on the cranberry plant, thus contributing to increased photosynthetic activity. They postulated that this may be an important factor in bringing about the vigorous growth that usually follows sanding. Sanding also serves to reanchor plants that may have been torn loose by the harvest operation. This application would be particularly important where dry scooping is practiced as a harvest method.

With respect to benefiting weed control, sanding was originally thought to aid in weed control by covering existing weed seed. However, the conditions that favor cranberry rooting also favor new weed seed germination, particularly of annual weeds. This is especially true in the first growing season following sanding because an increased amount of the bog surface is opened to sunlight by the sanding operation. Also, certain perennials such as poison ivy are like the cranberry in that they respond with increased vigor to sanding. The beneficial weed control effects of sanding occur in later growing seasons when the increased cranberry vigor associated with sanding effectively crowds out the weed species.

For decades the general procedure for laying down the sand has been to wheelbarrow sand across broad planks on the bog and then spread the sand as evenly as possible by shovel. More recently, with the development of oversized pneumatic tires, motorized sand-spreading equipment has been developed that provides for a more efficient sanding operation with reduced vine injury (plate 8.7). When an adequate ice layer exists over the winter flood, the sanding operation can be greatly simplified by spreading the sand directly on the ice. The sand will melt down through the ice; this results in an even sand

PLATE 8.7. SANDING AN ESTABLISHED CRANBERRY BOG—A TECH-
NIQUE USED TO STIMULATE NEW CRANBERRY GROWTH
(Courtesy Massachusetts Cranberry Experiment Station)

application. One serious drawback to ice sanding, however, is the possibility of reducing the light intensity under the ice to the point that oxygen levels are depleted in the winter floodwater. Removing the water from under the ice will remedy this situation. Equipment has also been developed to enable sanding over flooded bogs from pontoon-supported vehicles (Kranick 1936; Norton 1972, 1982b).

Finally, there are specific precautions that should be taken when sanding is contemplated. It is recommended that the winter flood be withdrawn early in the spring on bogs that have been fall- or winter-sanded in order to insure an adequate crop. Bogs are not sanded within two to three weeks of either a fall or spring casoron treatment; if vines are weak, casoron-treated vines should not be sanded. Sanding may produce conditions favorable for fruit rot development, so precautions should be taken to maintain adequate rot control.

Pruning

Mature cranberry bogs, particularly those constructed on heavy muck, will tend to produce an excessive amount of vegetative growth. This excessive growth is manifested in long runners and old uprights that might reach lengths of more than 16 inches (40 cm) (Doehlert 1958). The effect of this excessive vegetative growth on cranberry production was recognized by Chambers

(1918) and led to his well-planned pruning experiments. Using a heavily vined Early Black planting that had declined steadily in production, he carried out a series of replicated treatments of different pruning severity and proceeded to record the effect on production. Although the pruning treatments resulted in about a 10-percent loss in production in the following year, the second year after the pruning revealed an average increase in production of 45 percent. The best yields were obtained with a moderate degree of pruning of these heavily vined cranberries (about three tons of prunings per acre). Two factors probably led to this delayed production response. The severance of most of the runners would have removed apical dominance in many of the vines, which would have encouraged more upright production from axial buds. These new uprights would have produced fruit in the second year after the pruning. Secondly, the removal of much of the top growth would have allowed more light to penetrate the vines and caused greater flower bud initiation.

Clearly, excessive vegetative growth is not compatible with maximizing yield. Heavy vine growth would certainly obstruct light, which appears to be critical for flower bud formation. In addition, heavy vine growth creates a microclimate that is conducive to fruit rot development, and it also presents a formidable problem to dry scooping at harvest. The question then is: How much pruning is optimum? Pruning runners will mean that some producing uprights are also removed. This was evident from the Chambers's (1918) production data in the first year after pruning. Doehlert (1955c) found that when he very carefully removed the new runner growth with hand shears, he still removed 7 percent of the uprights. More severe levels of pruning, which entailed the removal of more uprights with the runners, resulted in a 15-percent reduction in fruit buds. It would appear that a light annual hand pruning of vines, with rakes fitted with knives rather than tines, would be the best approach to controlling excessive vegetative growth. Most mowing machines would tend to remove too much upright growth along with the runners. The *Western Picker* has been designed to remove new runner growth without cutting into the bearing wood.

Renovation

Bogs that have been allowed to become overvegetative and have been in this state for some time may require more drastic remedial action to bring them back into productive bearing. In this instance, the bogs can be renovated by removing most of the top growth by either mowing the vines to the ground or burning off the tops (Darrow et al. 1924b). Burning is carried out during the winter when the vines are dormant. Care must be taken to keep water up in the ditches so that the burn does not extend into the root zone. Burning has the added advantage of destroying any insects that overwinter in the vines or in the surface trash. Mowing is generally easier and probably preferable to burning. Of course, no crop is realized in the year following the renovation, but by the second year a fair crop develops and by the third year the vines should again be in full production.

Although cranberry plants are perennial and cranberry plantings can therefore be considered as practically permanent, they do occasionally need to be replanted. Vines decimated by disease or insects may be best replanted. If an unproductive variety is to be replaced by a new cultivar, replanting is appropriate. Either of two procedures can be followed (B. Tomlinson and Franklin 1946). The vines can be destroyed by burning; in this case, a more severe burn is called for since the old cranberry roots are no longer desired. Alternatively, the vines can be killed with herbicide and then burned. After the vines are destroyed, the bog surface is plowed to a depth of 10 to 14 inches (25–36 cm). In lieu of plowing, some growers have merely spread a 3-inch layer of sand over the killed vines and replanted. An alternative procedures is to scalp the old turf, removing the vines and roots from the bog completely. There is another method of destroying the old vine, but it is not commonly used, and that is to flood the bog continuously for at least two years. This effectively destroys all vegetation, including weed species, as well as most insects. With the removal of the old vines, the bog is prepared for the new planting just as if a new bog were being established.

Cleaning Ditches and Upland

An important part of bog maintenance is keeping the bog ditches clean. Norton (1962a) estimated that a cranberry bog contains from 750 to 1200 linear feet of ditch per acre. In order to insure proper water movement, it is necessary to remove sand, mud, weeds, and vine growth from them every few years. Perimeter ditches that can be reached from the dams can be cleaned with power equipment such as backhoes or clamshells. However, the most common method of cleaning the lateral ditches still is by hand. The work is best done when the plants are dormant. The overhanging vines are severed with a grub axe, and the sediment and plant material is shoveled out and piled on the cranberry vines adjacent to the ditch and left to drain for a few days. The cleanings are then loaded onto wheelbarrows and carried ashore.

Norton (1962a) has attempted to mechanize the lateral ditch cleaning operation. His system consists of a mobile unit that straddles the ditch and is capable of chopping vegetative material while stirring up the sediments in the ditch. A water source supplying 600 to 1,000 gallons per minute takes the suspended material to a collection point, via a directed route, where it is

PLATE 8.8. *A,* THE WISCONSIN CRANBERRY BOOM; *B,* APPLYING CHEMICALS; *C,* MOWING GRASS (Courtesy University of Wisconsin Extension Service)

pumped into a disposal area, such as an abandoned sand pit, for settling. The ditch cleaning machine can be effectively operated by a two-person crew.

In Wisconsin, where many of the bogs have been laid out in a rectangular grid, bog maintenance is greatly facilitated by the *Wisconsin cranberry boom* (plate 8.8). This reinforced-steel boom is mounted on flatbed trucks on parallel sides of the bog and can thus be towed along. Various maintenance operations can then be carried out by workers suspended from the boom.

A final housekeeping chore the cranberry grower has to carry out is to mow the dams and the uplands surrounding the bogs. This accomplishes two important things. It destroys many weeds by preventing them from going to seed, and it serves to reduce the danger of forest fire. Removing the forest understory insures that any fire that does begin will not become too intense by feeding on dense undergrowth. Sometimes growers will control-burn the underbrush in the forest surrounding their bogs with the same results. Forest fires are always a significant danger to cranberry bogs as long as they are exposed.

NINE

Diseases

Introduction

In 1931 C. L. Shear, N. E. Stevens, and H. F. Bain produced USDA Technical Bulletin No. 258, which culminated three decades of research and observations on cranberry diseases. In *Fungous Diseases of the Cultivated Cranberry,* they reported on 69 species of fungi that occurred in the cranberry plant. Of these, they singled out 6 species that caused significant damage to the vines and 8 species that were associated with serious economic fruit loss. Another 24 species were designated as being of minor importance, and the remainder were considered to be of no economic significance to the cranberry. Since diseases are often classified on the basis of the plant part affected, that system of classification will be used in the following discussion of cranberry diseases. Accordingly, the diseases of the cranberry may be classified as those affecting the vines and those that affect the fruit. Furthermore, the diseases of the fruit may be divided into those that affect the fruit early in its development (in the field), and those that affect fruit in storage. Except for the mycoplasm that causes the serious false blossom disease, the major cranberry diseases are fungal diseases.

Diseases of the Vine

Leaf Diseases

Red Leaf Spot. Leaf diseases are generally not of economic importance in cranberry culture, although they may occasionally cause significant damage under certain environmental conditions in the various cranberry-growing regions. Red leaf spot caused by *Exobasidium vaccinii* (Fckl.) Wor. has been reported in all the cranberry-growing areas, but it is a particular problem in the Pacific Northwest where cloudy and misty weather favor the development and spread of the fungus which carries over on old diseased leaves and stems.

The most striking symptoms of the disease are the bright red circular spots that occur on the upper surface of the leaf. On the underside of the leaf, the spots appear paler and are covered with fine, spore-bearing hyphae that resemble a dense bloom or powder. Often two or more spots on a single leaf will coalesce. It appears that only young leaves and stems are susceptible to infection by this fungus. As striking as the leaf symptoms are, however, it is the infection and death of the growing shoot tip that causes the economic loss. The infection spreads from the leaf through the petiole to the growing stem, which becomes bright red and distorted in shape. Infected leaves will eventually turn brown and abscise prematurely and the growing shoots will become girdled. When conditions are particularly favorable for infection, the fungus will occasionally attack the fruit, causing elevated, circular, bright red spots on green berries.

Overly luxuriant vine growth, particularly in young beds, is especially susceptible to red leaf spot. The disease is more apt to be found in peat bogs rich in available nitrogen and on bogs that have been vegetatively overstimulated by excessive nitrogen fertilizer application. The heavy vine growth that often follows a bloom-killing frost is also prone to attack. Cultural practices that produce excessive vegetative growth should therefore be avoided. Captafol and maneb have inhibited the fungus under controlled conditions (Boone and Tontyaporn 1986), and in Washington spraying infected vines with Bordeaux mixture prevented the spread of the infection. The cultivars Ben Lear and Stevens appear to be particularly susceptible to red leaf spot.

Black Spot. Often associated with red leaf spot is the black spot fungus *Mycosphaerella nigro-maculans* Shear. The fungus often invades the red leaf spot lesions, turning them black. As in the case of red leaf spot, the fungus develops under conditions of excessive humidity, gaining entrance through the leaves and attacking the stems about the leaf base. Elongated black spots form and eventually coalesce and girdle the stem. The dead stems become thickly covered with black fungus fruiting bodies that produce spores for subsequent infection. If the infection is particularly severe, all the uprights in the infected area may be killed. When the fungus attacks the fruit, it causes conspicuous sunken black spots. Repeated applications of Bordeaux mixture have controlled the fungus on the West Coast.

Other Leaf Spots. Gibbera leaf spot (*Gibbera myrtilli* (Cooke) Petrak, and Cladosporium leaf spot (*Cladosporium oxycocci* Shear) are two leaf spot diseases that occasionally cause significant damage to cranberry plants in Wisconsin (Boone 1982b). Leaf spots caused by *Gibbera myrtilli* first appear in late September or early October as small, distinct red-to-purple spots on the upper surface of the current season's leaves. By the late spring of the following year, the spots have enlarged, become less distinctly outlined, and appear as large chlorotic spots with minute, black fungus fruiting bodies clustered in the centers. In Massachusetts and Nova Scotia, a similar leaf spot is caused by *Gibbera compacta* (Pk.) Shear (Carlson and Boone 1966; Lockhart 1970). Although more widespread than *G. myrtilli*, it is not considered very harmful.

Cladosporium leaf spots can be distinguished from Gibbera spots by the distinct gray-to-white center of the spot. By July the affected leaves become more chlorotic and the fungus appears as smudgy spots on the upper leaf surface. Premature leaf drop often occurs at this stage. The fungus may also cause small bright or deep red spots, sometimes with light-colored centers, to develop on the fruit, particularly before the fruit have developed their ripe red color. This berry speckle is superficial and, except for making the berries less attractive for fresh market, causes no appreciable harm. Berry speckle caused by *Gibbera* differs from the speckle disease of cranberry caused by the fungus *Botryosphaeria vaccinii*, in which the speckles appear light colored rather than red. The fungus overwinters in leaves and probably on unharvested fruit. The fruiting bodies ripen during July and infection occurs throughout July and August. Fungicides applied during this period generally control these two leaf spot diseases (Boone 1982b).

Rose Bloom. Another leaf disease attributed to an *Exobasidium* fungus is rose bloom, caused by the fungus *E. oxycocci* Rost. The fungus attacks the buds in the leaf axil, this stimulates the normally dormant buds to grow. The stimulated growth appears as abnormal lateral shoots bearing enlarged pink or light-rose-colored leaves that are crowded together, bearing a resemblance to a flower—hence the name rose bloom. Occasionally, the fungus attacks the terminal buds and blossoms, causing them to be deformed and unusually large. Berries that develop from infected blossoms will be deformed at the calyx end of the berry. Although the disease is considered of minor importance, it has been found to occur throughout the cranberry-growing regions and has been reported to reduce flower number and retard flower development (Bristow 1977). Rose bloom tends to be more prevalent in bogs having dense vine growth and impeded air and water drainage. The disease appears in early spring and can become widespread if cool rainy weather persists. Since the infected leaves lose much of their chlorophyll, a heavy infection can result in loss of vine vigor and crop yield. To control this fungus, a fungicide must be applied as soon as the symptoms are observed shortly after bud break in the spring.

More recently, Nickerson (1984) has described another disease believed to be caused by an *Exobasidium* fungus. A previously unreported disease of native cranberry plants in Nova Scotia and Newfoundland is believed to be caused by *E. perenne* sp. nov. The symptoms are an enlargement and reddening of the leaves and elongation of internodes caused by the perennial mycelium that invades the entire annual shoot. The new disease has been called red shoot disease in recognition of the characteristic symptoms expressed.

Stem Diseases

Twig Blight. Twig blight caused by *Lophodermium oxycocci* Karst may cause a serious loss of crop on West Coast cranberry bogs. Leaves, uprights, and even vines may be killed as the result of heavy infections by this fungus. Sporulation occurs from June to September with a peak period of infection occurring in July and August, at which time the new growth is inoculated. Symptoms of the infection are not evident until the winter after inoculation. By February, infected leaves turn from a normal dark red color to a bleached tan color, unlike a *Botryosphaeria* infection in which the leaves remain red. The uprights are killed by the fungus and the fungus fruiting bodies develop on the dead leaves which remain attached to the dead upright. The fruiting bodies appear as large, glossy black, football-shaped structures and occur only on the underside of the cranberry leaf. Sporulation occurs through a median slit on the fruiting body after it matures, and the cycle is completed with the inoculation of the new cranberry growth. There are no repeating secondary cycles. Only the new wood becomes infected. The organism appears to be excluded from two-year-old wood. Control is based upon maintaining an effective fungicide barrier between the fungus spores and the new cranberry growth. A series of maneb sprays beginning at the "popcorn" stage (first visible sign of flowers) of flower development and continuing on a prescribed schedule throughout the growing season is recommended by West Coast pathologists. The early spray application is particularly important because the fungicide must be in place before the infection begins. Bravo 500 and 720 are very effective in controlling twig blight and have been cleared for use on cranberries (Poole 1984).

Stem Blight. Another stem blight found on cranberries is that caused by the fungus *Guignardia vaccinii* Shear. The fungus *G. vaccinii* has been shifted to *Botryosphaeria vaccinii* (Shear) Barr, which has been shown to have *Phyllosticta elongata* Weidemann as the imperfect or conidial stage (Weidemann et al. 1982). More recently, Boone and Weidemann (1986a) have reported that the true causal agent for the diseases attributed to *Guignardia* is *P. vaccinii* Earle, a distinct species. This fungus is capable of infecting all the aerial parts of the cranberry plant, including the blossoms and fruit. The fungus overwinters as immature fruiting bodies on fallen twigs, leaves, and berries that were infected the previous season. The fruiting bodies appear as black, pinhead-sized, circular structures readily discernible from the large, glossy black, football-shaped structures of *Lophodermium oxycocci*, which causes a similar twig blight. The small black spots (perithecia) mature in the spring and produce ascospores that are forcibly ejected into the air, where they are carried throughout the bog by the wind. The cranberry plant becomes infected when the ascospore germinates after a prolonged period of

wetting. Within a few days of infection, additional small black bodies (pycnidia) appear on the surface of the infected plant part. After a prolonged wetting period, spores (conidia) produced in the pycnidia ooze out in a sticky
mass and carry out a secondary infection. When cool, moist weather conditions exist, this cycle of conidial infection can be repeated many times, resulting in a very rapid buildup of the disease. The organism is capable of infecting
the hooks and blossoms of the cranberry plant, causing them to turn brown
and die—a malady termed blossom blight. *Sporonema oxycocci* Shear is also
known to produce blossom blight as do many of the other organisms that produce fruit rot in cranberry.

Fruit can be infected by *Phyllosticta vaccinii* at any stage in its development. It is the cause of a major field rot known as early rot, and will be discussed later in the section on fruit rots. Control of this important disease is
accomplished in a number of ways. Dormant sprays of lime sulfur (applied to
the dormant plants) will kill the overwintering fungus on fallen leaves and debris. Sanding will also work against the fungus by covering the litter upon
which the fruiting bodies overwinter. Protective fungicide sprays will hold
down infection during the critical sporulation phases of the disease, and good
cultural practices that avoid rank vine growth and excessive weed growth will
prevent environments favorable for the spread of the disease. Late holding
the winter flood also helps combat this disease.

Tip Blight. Another organism that is capable of infecting both the cranberry shoot and its fruit is the fungus *Monilinia oxycocci* (Wor) Honey (*Sclerotinia
oxycocci* Wor) (Boone 1982c). The organism produces a tip blight on new uprights and a fruit rot referred to as hard rot or cotton ball. The tip blight stage
of the disease generally does not represent a significant economic loss to
growers, but fruit loss due to the disease can be serious on the West Coast
and in Wisconsin. In the case of the blight phase of the disease, there is generally no warning of the presence of the organism. Nearly full-grown uprights
that are infected suddenly wilt and collapse just behind their tips about the
beginning of bloom. The infected uprights become brown and shriveled and
soon are covered with grayish white powdery masses of conidia. A characteristic symptom of the tip blight phase of infection is the formation of an inverted "V" pattern of tan diseased tissue at the base of newly infected leaves.
Flowers, pedicels, and leafstalks can also become infected and covered with
the characteristic grayish masses of conidia. The diseased uprights are not
always easily discernible because they may be widely dispersed among the
erect and healthy uprights.

The berry symptom of Monilinia infection is easily recognized, as suggested by the descriptive terms of cotton ball and hard rot for this phase of the
disease. Infected berries fail to develop any red color. Instead, broad yellowish brown bands appear lengthwise on the berry and rapidly spread until the

whole berry is uniformly a yellowish brown color. The interior of the infected berry becomes filled with the cottony white mycelium of the fungus, which can be observed when the fruit is cut open. As harvest time approaches, the fungus becomes very active and hyphae invade all the tissues of the fruit, causing it to become hard and compact. The firm, leathery appearance of the fruit is in sharp contrast to the softened tissue produced by other fruit rots. The fruit becomes mummified, eventually turns black, and will either remain attached to the uprights or fall to the bog floor and become partly buried in the fallen leaves and trash. It is in this form that the fungus overwinters. In the spring, cup-shaped apothecia appear from the mummies (sclerotia) and produce the ascospores that infect the new growth and cause the tip blight. The conidia produced on the infected uprights infect the blossoms and developing berries in the second phase of the infection. Both phases of infection are favored by warm and prolonged wet periods during the spring and bloom period. New plantings and resanded bogs appear to be more susceptible to the disease than older established bogs.

Control sprays of fungicide must be made early in the growing season commencing with leaf bud break and repeated in 10 to 14 days. A third application is needed at early bloom and is repeated in two weeks. At present, triforine (Funginex) is registered for use in controlling the cotton ball disease in Wisconsin. The cultivars Bergman and Pilgrim are reported to be very susceptible to the disease, whereas McFarlin and Crowley appear quite resistant. The disease does not appear to be a problem in the eastern cranberry-growing regions.

Upright Dieback. Diaporthe vaccinii Shear (*Phomopsis vaccinii* Shear—imperfect stage) is capable of causing a serious vine disease as well as an economically important storage fruit rot known as viscid rot (Boone 1982d). Friend and Boone (1968a) have reported that the widely occurring upright dieback of cranberry observed in Wisconsin was associated with *D. vaccinii.* Both vines and uprights can be infected. The infection appears to start at the terminal end of the upright or vine and develops downward. The diseased tissue takes on a yellowish cast which may become orange or bronze and eventually brown as it dies. During the initial stage of infection, the leaves will often show a yellow mottling before turning completely yellow. Very often, diseased uprights will occur adjacent to healthy uprights along the same vine. The dieback disease has occasionally assumed economic significance in northern Wisconsin bogs that were particularly vegetative or following unusual hot spells (Friend and Boone 1968b). The dieback symptoms have been reported in Massachusetts and New Jersey as well. The fruit rot phase of infection can result in significant fruit loss in storage on both the West and East coasts.

Recently, a tip dieback of young cranberry shoots in Massachusetts cranberry bogs similar to the symptoms caused by an unidentified *Phomopsis*

species was observed by Uecker and Caruso (1988). They described the
dieback as occurring rapidly with the leaves on the blighted shoots turning
off-green, then yellowish, then brown and becoming dry. The researchers
isolated the fungus *Synchronoblastia crypta* from upright stems, fruits, and
runners, and successfully fruited the fungus on cornmeal agar media. Inoculation of young cranberry shoots with *S. crypta* produced the field symptoms
in as little as 18 days, thus adding a new fungus genus that is capable of causing economic loss in cranberry production.

Phytophthora. Another fungal vine dieback disease that has probably been
present in Massachusetts bogs for more than a decade is that caused by the
root pathogen, *Phytophthora cinnamomi* Rands, first isolated in October 1986
from the underground runners of plants showing dieback symptoms (Caruso
et al. 1987). The vines that appear to be the most susceptible to the disease
are those growing in the low areas of the bogs where water tends to accumulate after heavy precipitation or flooding because of poor soil drainage. Very
often the vines in these areas will die because of infection and the vines located peripheral to the area will be off-color and will produce fewer berries
than healthy vines. Infected plants will have poor root systems, and often
even apparent healthy roots will show an olive brown discoloration when the
epidermis is scraped away. Susceptible cultivars include Early Black, Howes,
Crowley, and Stevens. The disease is widespread through the entire
cranberry-growing area in Massachusetts, in some cases causing as much as
50 percent loss of vines in a given bog. The disease has also been found to
occur in New Jersey.

Control strategies include improving the drainage, sanding the areas to
raise the bog level, fertilizing the peripheral plants that have not yet died, and
treating with Ridomil. In Massachusetts and New Jersey, there is an emer-
gency registration for the use of Ridomil 2E and 5G applied in three applications (April, July, and postharvest). Dieback areas can be replanted after the
poor drainage is addressed, although there is no information on which
cultivars may be more resistant to the disease.

Red Gall. Red gall caused by *Synchytrium vaccinii* Thomas is recognized
by the small, shotlike, red galls on the young buds, leaves, and shoots. The
galls first appear just before bloom, and although the affected shoots produce
no fruit, it is not considered an economically important disease because of its
limited and erratic occurrence. The spread of the fungus is dependent on
water and is therefore more apt to occur in poorly drained bogs. The disease
appears to be relegated to the Eastern seaboard including Nova Scotia and is
particularly common in New Jersey. Early removal of the winter flood is an
effective prophylactic treatment for this disease.

Fairy Ring. This disease caused by the fungus *Psilocybe agrariella* Atk.
var. *vaccinii* Charles is especially apt to be found on old cranberry bogs. It can

be a frequent problem in Massachusetts and New Jersey bogs, where it was commonly referred to as ringworm. As descriptive as this term may be, it represents a misnomer inasmuch as the disease is entirely fungal in origin. When observed from high ground alongside the bog, the disease appears as distinct rings of dead or dying vines. The symptom first appears as a small area of dead or weak vines in the bog, often beginning close to a ditch. The dead area advances outward in all directions at the rate of one to two feet per year. After a few years, the center portion of the affected area will again begin supporting vine growth and thus a characteristic ring pattern is formed very similar to the "fairy rings" found in lawns and pastures. The vines die when the roots of the plants become smothered by the dense mat of fungal mycelium that develops. The actual death of the cranberry plant appears to be the result of having its water and nutrient supply cut off rather than to a direct parasitic effect of the fungus. It is no coincidence, therefore, that the disease is much more noticeable during dry seasons when moisture and nutrient stress are more apt to occur. The revining of the early infected portion of the bog occurs when the fungus dies in this area and can no longer produce its smothering mycelium.

In the past, control has consisted of ditching around the ring, complete removal of the infected area and replanting, or applying heavy doses of copper sulfate. More recently, the application of two tons of lime per acre to the infected area has given promising control (Zuckerman 1980). Ferbam also has been labelled for use against fairy ring disease and can be applied after the bog has been harvested.

False Blossom Disease. False blossom, perhaps the most serious of all the vine diseases, is not caused by a fungus but rather by a mycoplasma-like organism (Chen 1971) that is transmitted by the blunt-nosed leafhopper (Dobroscky 1929). The disease can be found in all of the major cranberry-growing regions of North America, except on the West Coast. By the second and third decade of this century, the disease had become extremely destructive, forcing many bogs out of production. False blossom was first observed in 1900 in Wisconsin, where it occurred in wild vines. The spread of the disease to the other major growing areas probably came about by the importation of infected vines from Wisconsin. The commercial production of cranberries in Wisconsin and on the East Coast is possible today because the insect responsible for its spread can be controlled with modern insecticides. There is no known cure once the mycoplasma has become established in the plant.

The extreme debilitating effect of this disease lies in its deformation of the cranberry flower, thereby preventing fruit development. As described by Beckwith and Hutton (1929), the cranberry flower, instead of drooping normally, stands erect like a daisy flower. The flower petals appear redder than normal and can be stunted in advanced stages of the disease. The calyx cup may be flattened and other flower parts may be malformed as well. In severe infestations, the floral parts may be green and small and hardly resemble a flower at all. A profusion of side stems may develop from a main stem, producing a witches'-broom effect. The leaves of plants infected with false blossom are smaller and redder than normal and grow more parallel to the stems.

The blunt-nosed leafhopper (*Euscelis striatulus* Fallen) is the most common leafhopper found in the cranberry bogs east of the Rocky Mountains. Its absence on the West Coast explains why false blossom disease in Oregon and Washington bogs failed to spread when infected vines from the East were imported. Cranberry selections from the wild appear to vary in susceptibility to the disease. The McFarlin cultivar appears to be the most resistant selection made from the wild, followed by Early Black, Jersey, Champion, Centennial, and Howes in increasing order of susceptibility to the disease (R. B. Wilcox and Beckwith 1933). Of the improved hybrids, Stevens is the most resistant cultivar, Franklin intermediate, and Beckwith the least resistant.

Control of false blossom disease consists primarily of controlling the blunt-nosed leafhopper with appropriate insecticides. Infected plants must be rogued out to prevent spread of the virus. There is evidence to indicate that late holding the winter flood may differentially destroy false-blossom-infected uprights and thereby aid in the roguing process (R. B. Wilcox and Beckwith 1935).

Ringspot. Boone (1966) has reported viruslike ringspot symptoms on cranberry fruits and leaves on the Searles and Howes cultivars in Wisconsin. The symptom was characterized by pale circular patches or whitish rings that developed on the surface of the berries and leaves. The ring symptoms on the berries were sometimes associated with blossom-end necrosis and malformation of the flowers in the Searles cultivar. Generally all the fruits of a given upright and all the uprights of an infected vine showed symptoms, which suggested that the disease was systemic. Virus particles very similar to those identified as the cause of red ringspot disease in the blueberry have been found in cranberry tissue showing ringspot symptoms (letter from K. S. Kim to A. W. Stretch 1981).

Stretch (1964) found a similar disorder on the Howes cultivar in New Jersey bogs, and recently there have been reports of its presence in Massachusetts bogs. Although the extent of the disease appears to be limited, the severity of its effect on the Searles cultivar may be of some concern to Wisconsin cranberry growers. Boone (1967) found that not only were diseased berries of the Searles cultivar apt to be misshapen but they also showed four to five times more spoilage after four months of storage at 47°F than berries from healthy vines.

Fruit Rots

Introduction

With the exception of false blossom disease and Phytophthora root rot, the fungal fruit rots are probably of most economic concern to cranberry growers. Although it is not always possible to distinguish visually between the different rots, one way they may be classified is on the basis of their time of occurrence. Early rots are generally observed to occur in the field and are sometimes referred to as field rots. Rots that develop after harvest are collectively referred to as storage rots. Fruit rots that are most apt to develop in the field are early rot, bitter rot, blotch rot, hard rot, and viscid rot. The latter appears late in the season in the field but more often develops after harvest in storage. In general, field rots are more of a problem on the East Coast than in Wisconsin or on the West Coast (Bergman and Wilcox 1936).

Early Rots

Scald. This early rot is caused by the fungus *Phyllosticta vaccinii* Earle. It was one of the first cranberry diseases found and described and was thought to be caused by *Guignardi vaccinii* Shear, by which it is referred to in the early literature (R. B. Wilcox 1940b). *G. vaccinii* has been reclassified as *Botryosphaeria vaccinii* (Shear) Barr, but according to Boone and Weidemann (1986b) many of the diseases formerly attributed to *B. vaccinii* are actually caused by *Phyllosticta vaccinii.* However, the asexual (imperfect) stage of *Botryosphaeria vaccinii* is *Phyllosticta elongata,* which appears to cause a latent infection that leads to rot in storage. Since many rots appear so very similar externally, the actual causal organism often must be identified from cultures of the diseased tissue. Early rot is more apt to be a problem in areas having long and hot growing seasons; therefore, it is chiefly a problem in New Jersey and Massachusetts. It does not appear to be of economic significance in either Wisconsin or on the West Coast.

The appearance of a small water spot on the cranberry fruit is the first indication of infection by *P. vaccinii.* The spot enlarges rapidly in a somewhat concentric manner until the whole berry becomes soft. A telltale symptom of the disease is the formation of dark concentric rings in the diseased area resembling a bull's-eye pattern. The infection occurs early in the fruit's development, and by the time the berry is half grown it has usually shriveled and become blackened. The blackening of the fruit is caused by the dark fungal pycnidia which become the source of inoculum for the following growing season. The organism is also capable of infecting the flower and young shoots, leading to blossom blast and twig blight. However, these forms of damage are usually minor compared to the fruit rot loss in the field. To control early rot, fungicides must be applied when the first scattered bloom becomes apparent. Another midbloom application and one or two sprays at ten-day intervals thereafter will normally control this disease (Boone and Weidemann 1986b).

Bitter and Blotch Rot. Bitter rot (*Glomerella cingulata vaccinii* Shear) and blotch rot (*Physalospora* [formerly *Acanthorhyncus*] *vaccinii* Shear) are two other early rots common to the East Coast cranberry regions (R. B. Wilcox 1940b). Infection normally occurs during bloom and the symptoms, characterized by softening of the fruit, occur during fruit development, although occasionally the rot may appear early in storage. Again, warm temperatures during the growing season favor the development of these rots. Refrigerating fruit immediately after harvest will greatly retard the development of the rot in storage.

Hard Rot. The development of hard rot (cotton ball) in the field has already been discussed in connection with tip blight caused by the same organism, *Monilinia oxycocci* (Boone 1982c). Berries infected with *M. oxycocci* grow normally throughout the growing season, reaching normal size by harvest time. The first indication of a problem is the failure of the berry to turn to its normal red color, rather they become a uniform yellowish brown. Instead of the fruit softening, as occurs with most of the fruit rots, the berry remains quite firm. The fungus can be easily seen by cutting open the suspect fruit and observing the cottony mycelium that has engulfed the seeds. The infected fruit are an important source of inoculum for infection the following spring. Fruit infected with hard rot when harvested must be removed by hand because they are capable of passing over the bounce boards used to separate soft rotten fruit.

Viscid Rot. Viscid rot is caused by *Diaporthe vaccinii,* the same organism that causes the upright dieback already discussed under vine diseases (Boone 1982d). Although the fruit rot phase of this disease normally occurs after harvest in storage, the rot can appear late in the season in the field. In Wisconsin it is the third most important fruit rot that must be dealt with. Again, it is difficult to distinguish visually between many fruit rots, but a very characteristic symptom of viscid rot is the stringing out of a viscous substance when a finger is touched to and then withdrawn from the cut surface of the rotted berry. The disease is difficult to control because *D. vaccinii* grows within the vascular tissues of the cranberry plant, necessitating the use of systemic fungicides that are as yet unavailable for use on cranberries.

Storage Rots

Rots that develop in storage have the potential for significant economic loss to the cranberry grower because not only do they require removal and, therefore, represent loss of marketable yield but they also can contribute to the loss of resales if the rot develops in fresh packs purchased by the consumer. Fruit that is processed immediately after harvest will not have sufficient time to develop rot, so in this case these rots are of little economic concern. Prolonged storage, however, runs the risk of breakdown, a risk that increases with increasing storage temperature. The principal storage rots are end rot, black rot, viscid rot, yellow rot, and Botrysphaeria fruit rot. Most of these storage rots can be found in all the major cranberry-growing areas.

End Rot. End rot caused by the fungus *Godronia cassandrae* Peck (*Fusicoccum putrefaciens* Shear—imperfect stage) is probably the most common storage rot. According to Boone (1982a), it is the most economically important fruit rot in Wisconsin. It has also been reported to cause stem blight in Oregon, and it can cause reddish brown leaf spots on the upper leaf surface of the plant. The fruit rot symptom only develops in storage. As its name suggests, the first signs of breakdown in the fruit occur at one end or the other. The rotted end becomes soft and watery and is clearly delineated from the sound portion of the berry. As the rot progresses, the whole berry becomes soft and elastic to the touch and becomes bloated because of the buildup of gas as the berry putrefies. The bloated berries are called "poppers" because of their tendency to burst and collapse when the internal pressure becomes too great. The shrunken fruit become yellowish or brownish. Although the fruit rot symptom does not develop until after harvest, the fungus has been isolated from berries soon after fruit set, usually at the blossom end where it may gain entrance through the senescent sepals. The suggestion is that the fungus can only become established through damaged or senescent tissue, which would include fruit that may have been bruised in the harvest operation.

The ubiquitous fungus is present year-round on the stems and leaves of the cranberry plant. To control end rot, fungicides must be applied from the late blossom period until mid-August in the warmer growing regions. Although refrigeration tends to delay the development of end rot in storage, it can develop at a slow rate even at temperatures as low as 40°F (4.5°C). In Wisconsin the cultivars Beckwith, Bergman, Early Black, Franklin, Howes, McFarlin, Pilgrim, Stevens, and Wilcox have been found to be relatively resistant to end rot, Searles relatively susceptible, and Ben Lear and Crowley very susceptible.

Black Rot. Black rot caused by the fungus *Ceuthospora lunata* Shear is another important storage rot of cranberry found in all the cranberry-growing regions. The fungus has recently been reclassified as *Apostrasseria lunata* (Shear) Nag Raj, which is the imperfect state of *Phacidium lunatum* (Nag Raj 1983). In New Jersey the same disease symptoms can be caused by the fungus *Strasseria oxycocci* Shear (Boone and Schwarz 1982). The jet black color of the rotted fruit is characteristic of the disease. The infected berry remains relatively firm and dry and will gradually wither and shrink, taking on the appearance of miniature prunes. Infection takes place comparatively late in the growing season, gaining entrance primarily through a wound. Because infection takes place so late in the season, fungicides are not always effective in reducing the incidence of the disease. Water raking increases the risk of infection because the spores of the organism are abundant in the floodwater and easily gain entrance through wounded tissue. Black rot tends to develop sooner in storage than end rot, but like end rot it is capable of developing even at low storage temperatures.

Yellow Rot. Yellow rot caused by a *Botrytis* species (*cinerea*-type) has at times caused heavy crop losses in Washington and Oregon, particularly in water-harvested bogs (Boone and Friend 1986). The disease has also been reported in Wisconsin and on the East Coast, although it is of minor significance compared to end rot and black rot. The identifying symptom of yellow rot is the bright yellowish orange color the fungus imparts to the infected fruit. Like black rot, the fungus gains entrance into the fruit through a wound, so it often exists in association with black rot. The water medium and the physical damage to the fruit caused by the water harvester are ideal for the development of this disease. The organism can grow on many different substrates, including dead or dying tissue; therefore, there is a constant supply of inoculum present. Severe infections have been reported following hail damage to cranberry bogs.

Botryosphaeria Fruit Rot. This fruit rot is characterized by the appearance of small, watery lesions on the surface of the fruit which give the berries a speckled appearance. Normally, the symptoms develop in storage, particularly if stored at relatively warm temperatures, although similar symptoms occasionally appear in the field late in the growing season. The disease is caused by the fungus *Botryosphaeria vaccinii* (Shear) Barr (=*Guignardia vaccinii* Shear), which previously had been thought to cause blossom blast and berry scald, now correctly attributable to *Phyllosticta vaccinii* (Boone and Weidemann 1986a). Infection by *Botryosphaeria vaccinii* usually occurs early in the growing season, but the infection remains latent until the infected tissues begin to senesce and the speckle symptoms appear. Fungicides must be applied early in the season prior to infection since the fungus seems to be able to withstand fungicide treatment during the latent period. The organism can be found in all the cranberry-growing regions.

Other Storage Rots. Other fungi that are capable of causing storage rots but are generally of minor importance are *Sporonema oxycocci* Shear, *Pestalozzia quepini vaccinii* Shear, *Synchronoblastia crypta*, *Penicillium* sp., and *Cytospora* sp. Most of these can be found in all the cranberry-growing districts. Storage rot caused by *Sporonema oxycocci* has become increasingly prevalent in Massachusetts and New Jersey in recent years (A. W. Stretch, verbal communication to author, 1988). *S. oxycocci* is now the most commonly isolated fungus from harvested berries in Massachusetts.

Physiological Breakdown. One of the major losses of fruit in storage cannot be attributed to fungi but rather to some form of physiological breakdown. This form of rot has also been termed *sterile breakdown* because tests failed to show the presence of fungi in the affected fruit. The severity of loss due to sterile breakdown appears to be directly related to the stage of maturity of the harvested fruit. Overripe fruit that have begun to soften are particularly vulnerable to storage breakdown of this type. Excessive nitrogen fertilization may also lead to soft fruit. During the harvest operation, such soft fruit is more susceptible to bruising, which appears to greatly hasten the senescence of the fruit. This suggests that the bruising may increase enzymatic activity in the cranberry. Since the disorder is not related to a fungus, fungicides are of no use in the amelioration of this problem. Harvesting at the proper stage of fruit maturity and storing fresh fruit at cold temperatures not lower than 38°F and with good ventilation appear to be the best methods of combating sterile breakdown.

TABLE 9.1. A COMPOSITE FUNGICIDE APPLICATION SCHEDULE FOR CRANBERRY DISEASES FOUND IN THE DIFFERENT GROWING AREAS

FUNGICIDE AND FORMULATION	RATE/A	APPLICATION TIMING	REMARKS
Rosebloom—Red Leaf Spot—Guignardia-Type Blights			
Bordeau mixture 8-8-10	24 lbs.	Dormant	Especially effective against rose-bloom and red leaf spot
Kocide 404 or	2 gals.	Apply when some new growth is present	Primarily for control of *Guignardia*-type blights but will also aid in control of stem and leaf blights caused by *Gibbera, Cladosporium,* and blossom blights
Kocide 101 or	8 lbs.		
Ferbam 76% WP or	4 lbs.		
Zineb 75% WP or	4 lbs.		
Maneb 89% WP or	4 lbs.		

(continued)

TABLE 9.1. (*Continued*)

FUNGICIDE AND FORMULATION	RATE/A	APPLICATION TIMING	REMARKS
Captan 50% WP	6 lbs.		caused by *Sporonema oxycocci* and *Phyllosticta vaccinii*
Zineb 75% WP or	4 lbs.	Apply at late hook stage just before bloom	For severe *Lophodermium* infections, apply two sprays of ferbam followed by two sprays of maneb at 14-day intervals
Ferbam 76% WP or	4 lbs.		
Maneb 80% WP or	4 lbs.		
Captan 50% WP or	6 lbs.		
Difolatan 4F or	4 qts.		
Phaltan 50% WP	9 lbs.		

| Cotton Ball or Hard Rot |||||

Triforine 1.6 EC	24 fl. oz.	Bud break, then at 7-to-10-day intervals	No more than four applications; do not apply through irrigation system
Captafol 80 sprills	3.75 to 6.25 lbs.	Early bloom, then 10–14 days later if needed	Three applications/yr maximum

| End Rot and Other Fruit Rots |||||

Captafol 80 sprills	3.75 to 6.25 lbs.	Early bloom, then at 10- to-14-day intervals	Three applications/yr maximum
Zineb 75% WP	7.5 lbs.	5% bloom, then 13 days later	Do not apply after midbloom; may cause some delay in fruit coloring

TABLE 9.1. (*Continued*)

FUNGICIDE AND FORMULATION	RATE/A	APPLICATION TIMING	REMARKS
Ferbam 76% WP	6 lbs.	Early bloom, then at 14-day intervals	Five applications/yr maximum; do not apply later than 28 days after midbloom
Folpet 59% WP	9 lbs.	Bloom, then 10–14 days later	18 lbs/a/yr maximum; may delay coloring of fruit
Anilazine 50% WP	6 lbs.	Bloom	
Mancozeb 80% WP or 37% F	3–6 lbs. or 2.5–5 qts.	Midbloom, then at 7-to-10-day intervals	Addition of a spreader-sticker may be necessary; may delay color
Chlorothalonil 40% F or 54% F	Bravo 500 6–10 pts. or Bravo 720 4–7 pts.	Scattered bloom, then at 7-to-10-day intervals	Three applications/yr maximum
Copper hydroxide 77% WP or 37.5% F	8 lbs. or 10.6 pts.	Late bloom, then at 10-to-14-day intervals	Continued use of copper sprays may cause plant injury

Sources: Dana and Klingbell 1966; Shawa et al. 1984.

Disease Control Recommendations

Fungicides are normally applied in spray applications either as dilute sprays of 100 to 300 gallons of water per acre, as concentrated sprays of 20 to 50 gallons of water per acre, or as ultrahigh concentrate sprays of 5 gallons of water per acre. Dilute sprays are generally applied with high-pressure sprayers but may also be delivered through the irrigation system or by helicopter. Concentrated sprays must be applied with special high-pressure spray equipment that produces a fine mist in order to obtain adequate vine coverage with the spray. Ultrahigh concentrates must be applied by aircraft. The addition of a commercial spreader-sticker to the spray material is good insurance for obtaining the spray coverage that is essential for good disease control, but they may cause phytotoxicity if added to fungicides, such as Bravo, which already have their own sticking agent. Spray materials are usually formulated as a liquid (F), wettable powder (WP), emulsifiable concentrate (EC), or occasionally as pelletized material (sprills).

A composite spray schedule for disease control in cranberries obtained from recommendations in the different cranberry growing areas is given in table 9.1. Since spray materials and recommendations continually change and differ from one growing area to another, this schedule can serve only as an example. Current spray recommendations should be obtained from appropriate agricultural specialists in the specific cranberry-growing regions.

TEN

Insects

The most definitive works on cranberry insects ever written are a series of bulletins prepared by H. J. Franklin (1948b, 1950, 1952). The publications were a thorough, clear, concisely written, and extensively illustrated compilation of the insects of economic importance to the cranberry industry in Massachusetts. Unfortunately, the publications are out of print and no longer easily accessed. In his bulletins Franklin grouped the injurious insects according to the type of damage inflicted upon the cranberry plant. First, there were the worms or wormlike forms attacking the foliage, buds, flowers, or fruits. Insects included in this group were the fireworms, spanworms, cutworms, hairy worms, fruitworms, and miscellaneous worms such as the bagworm, cranberry sawfly, and cranberry tipworm. Another group of insects were those that attacked foliage or fruit but were not wormlike. These included the weevils, leafhoppers, and mites. A third group of insects were those that attacked the stem. These included the cranberry girdler, scale insects, and spittle insect. Finally, there were the insects that attacked the roots, specifically the grubs (larval stages) of certain beetles. Included in this category were the cranberry white grub, grape anomala, cranberry root grub, striped colaspis, and cranberry rootworm.

The basic format used by Franklin to discuss the insects in his bulletins was to begin with a discussion of its distribution and economic importance, followed by a description of its injury and its life cycle, and finally a discussion of the treatments available to combat the insect. Although many of the chemical treatments that were available in the early 1950s are no longer used because of ecological and health reasons, many of the cultural and water management practices used to combat the insect are still applicable today. In this chapter the major cranberry insects of economic importance in the cranberry-growing regions will be discussed along a similar format, including current recommendations for their control. Throughout the discussion, the terms *larva, worm,* and *caterpillar* are used synonymously.

Worms That Attack Buds, Flowers, or Fruits

Fireworms

The fireworms include a number of species of relatively small worms that wriggle vigorously when disturbed. The worms attack mainly the terminal leaves of uprights, which they web together with silk, thus forming nests to protect themselves. The young caterpillar's feeding on the leaves causes them to become skeletonized and turns them brown. When large areas become infested with fireworms, they resemble vines that have been scorched by fire, hence the collective name of fireworm, although W. E. Tomlinson (1948) maintained that the spotted fireworm never browns a bog even in heavy infestations. Franklin (1948b, 5) lists five species of fireworms found on Massachusetts bogs, which he has keyed as follows:

Head black 1
Head not black 2
1. Body striped . . . . hill fireworm
    Body not striped . . . . black-headed fireworm
2. Body with conspicuous white spots
    along the back and sides . . . . spotted fireworm
    Body without such spots 3
3. Body with dull reddish lines along the
    back and sides . . . . red-striped fireworm
    Body pale yellowish, without reddish
    lines . . . . yellow-headed fireworm

Hill Fireworm (Tlascala finetella Wlk.). The hill fireworm is generally considered to be a minor pest. It is restricted to bogs that have been flooded for the winter and has on occasion caused serious damage to new bogs in Massachusetts. It may, however, also feed on heavily vined older bogs.

The small worms are capable of burrowing up through the stem toward the terminal leaves. In so doing, they produce a considerable amount of frass (chewing remains of insect) that combines with the silk of their tubes and the sand of the bog surface. The extraordinary amount of frass produced by this insect is an identifying characteristic of this species of fireworm. It normally feeds from late June to mid-August.

Moths emerge from overwintering pupae during late May and early June. Eggs are laid on the stems of the new cranberry growth during the first half of June, and the larvae hatch in five to six days. The mature worm is approximately ¾ inch long and has a black head and dark brown body with eight narrow, broken, yellow stripes running lengthwise on the back and sides. Most of the larvae mature and pupate by the beginning of August. Moths may emerge from some of the pupae during late August; the remaining pupae remain dormant throughout the winter.

Chemical treatment for the other major cranberry insects generally keeps this species in check. Bog reflows do not appear to be effective in controlling this pest.

Black-headed Fireworm (Rhopobota naevena naevana Hbn.). The black-headed fireworm is of major economic significance in all of the cranberry-growing regions including the Maritime Provinces of Canada. It is a particular problem in flooded bogs because the insect is quite capable of surviving the winter flood, whereas its natural predators are not. It is also quite capable of surviving without the benefit of the winter flood in the less vigorous climate of the Pacific Northwest. Another factor that contributes to its destructiveness is the ability to produce two broods a year. The first hatch can be found feeding by late April and early May when conditions are favorable. According to W. E. Tomlinson (1948), those species of fireworms that can be found feeding by mid-May are of greatest economic concern.

The newly hatched larvae of the first brood cause damage by mining (burrowing) the leaf upon which the eggs were laid. They then proceed to move onto the terminal buds, which they also mine. When new shoots appear, the caterpillars will web together the terminal leaves of the upright. It is at this stage of injury that the grower is first aware of the fireworms' damage: by this time, the larvae are feeding freely on the young leaves, flowers, and buds of the cranberry shoot. The vines may recover from the infestation of the first brood, although considerable loss of crop may have occurred. By early July a second brood begins to hatch that is often more damaging than the first. They feed extensively on the flowers and developing berries as well as the tips of new shoots, thus affecting the following year's crop as well as the current crop.

The black-headed fireworm overwinters in the egg stage laid in late summer and early fall by the adult moth of the second brood. The pale yellow, pinhead-sized eggs may hatch as early as April in early-drawn bogs or in bogs that were not flooded for the winter. The newly hatched larva penetrates the underside of the leaf on which the egg was laid and proceeds to feed on that leaf. When fully grown, the larva is about ⅓ inch long with a grayish yellow body and shiny black head. After about 30 days of feeding, it drops to the bog surface where it pupates as a naked pupa. In about two weeks, the adult moth emerges to begin the second brood. On heavy vines, hatching of the second brood may be greatly extended—giving the impression that more than two broods have occurred. The adult moth, or *miller* as it is sometimes referred to, is about ¼ inch long and has a grayish brown body with dark bands across the back, the rear band assuming the shape of the letter "V." The adult moths are usually active during calm, cloudy weather and during the late afternoon and evening. It flies with a characteristic jerky movement, rarely traveling more than a few feet at a time.

Control of the black-headed fireworm is best achieved with modern insecticides registered for control of the first brood, although a 10-hour flood at night or in cool weather when the first brood hatch has occurred and repeated once or twice as the worms appear can also be very effective in controlling this pest. Effective control of the first brood will prevent serious second brood infestations, but when second brood worms are present, they are usually controlled by sprays applied for cranberry fruitworm.

Spotted Fireworm (Archips parallela Rob.). The spotted fireworm is the largest of the fireworms, but it rarely causes enough damage to justify control measures for it alone. It has been reported to feed on cranberries in Massachusetts, New Jersey, and Wisconsin. It can often be found feeding on favorite weed species such as loosestrife and Saint-John's-wort in areas adjacent to cranberry bogs. Since it is larger than the other fireworms, it is capable of webbing a greater number of uprights into a nest, but it rarely browns a bog like the black-headed fireworm.

The spotted fireworm overwinters as a partially grown larva in the trash on the bog floor. The larva resumes feeding in early June. It attains a length of ¾ inch when fully grown and is similar in appearance to a *Sparganothis* fruitworm. The mature caterpillar has a light reddish brown head and an olive green body with conspicuous white spots along its entire length. The fully grown larva pupates within its nest in the webbed uprights by mid-July. The ¾-inch brown moths emerge in early August and very soon begin laying their eggs, which hatch in about 10 days. This species produces only a single brood in the year.

Infestations of this fireworm are rare in bogs that undergo periodic reflooding. It appears to be controlled by its natural enemies to a great extent. With the advent of the modern organophosphate insecticides that are used to control more serious economic pests of the cranberry, the spotted fireworm is seldom an economic threat to cranberry growers.

Red-striped Fireworm (Aroga trialbamacullella Chamb.). This fireworm is only a problem on dry bogs since the fully grown, overwintering larva is not able to withstand a winter flood. It has been reported on cranberry bogs in Massachusetts and New Jersey. It can be found feeding extensively on the wild blueberry, deerberry, and leatherleaf occupying the high ground surrounding cranberry bogs. This fireworm produces a tightly webbed nest of two or more uprights, forming a characteristic irregular, tubular case of silk that is covered with brown castings.

The mature caterpillar has a yellowish head and greenish yellow body with dull reddish lines running the length of the back and sides. It is about ⅓ inch in length when fully grown and pupates on the bog floor during May and June. The dark brown moth appears soon after to lay its eggs. Two broods are commonly produced during the growing season. The larvae of the first brood will pupate in their nest, and the larvae of the second brood will overwinter as full-grown worms.

The winter flood will prevent serious outbreaks of this pest. Infestations late in the growing season from second broods migrating from areas surrounding cranberry bogs are controlled by pesticides used to combat other insects. In addition, the larvae suffer extensive parasitization, which helps to keep their numbers in check.

Yellow-headed Fireworm (Acleris minuata Rob. = Peronea minuata Rob.). The yellow-headed fireworm can be a most destructive pest even though the overwintering adult moth is readily destroyed by the winter flood. As many as four broods can occur during the growing season, so infestations from surrounding upland hosts can readily migrate to cranberry bogs. If not checked during the growing season, they destroy vines much later in the season and leave bare uprights that are unable to survive the winter flood. The injury caused by this insect is similar to that produced by the black-headed fireworm, although it tends to gather more uprights into its web than does the black-headed fireworm.

The overwintering adult moth is slate grey in color, in contrast to the golden-orange-colored moths of earlier generations. The overwintering moths lay eggs in late April, and by early May the first brood is hatched. Subsequent broods are produced in July and August. The worms have a yellow head and pale yellow body and are about ½ inch long when mature. The larva pupates in its nest, producing a pupa that is easily distinguished from that of the other fireworms by a prominent knob at the head end.

The adult moth will not survive a winter flood. Infestations that develop from migrations of surrounding populations can be controlled by sprays against other spring insects. The insecticides used to control the black-headed fireworm will also control this insect.

Spanworms

The spanworms are the ubiquitous inchworms, or loopers, that are so named because of their peculiar means of locomotion. These caterpillars move by stretching out their bodies at full length, grasping the object they are traversing with their front legs, and pulling their hindquarters forward, bending the legless mid-portion of their body well up out of the way. The slender caterpillars are hairless and are open feeders, that is, they never web leaves together as do the fireworms. The larvae have the peculiar habit of stretching their bodies straight up from a rear-anchored position and remaining completely motionless whenever they are disturbed. Because the caterpillars are often of the same color as their surroundings, they appear as short twigs—a camouflage that serves to protect them from their enemies. The spanworms are a common problem in Massachusetts but apparently less of a nuisance in the other cranberry-growing areas. Franklin (1948b, 36) has keyed the common spanworms found in Massachusetts as follows:

Body mostly pale yellowish or pinkish
with reddish herringbone stripe along
the back . . . . *Eupithecia miserulata*
Body mostly yellow . . . . chain-spotted geometer
Body mostly green . . . . green cranberry spanworm
Body mostly brown or gray 1
1. With a row of conspicuous irregular
    reddish yellow spots along each side . . . . half-winged geometer
    Not thus marked 2
2. With a pair of noticeable tubercles a little
    way from the middle of the back 3
    Without such tubercles . . . . brown cranberry spanworm
3. The tubercles in front of the middle of
    the back . . . . cotton spanworm
    The tubercles behind the middle of the
    back . . . . big cranberry spanworm

Of this group of insects, *Eupithecia miserulata* and the half-winged geometer (*Phigalia titea* Cramer) are not of economic significance to cranberry growers. The green and brown cranberry spanworms are generally the most damaging to cranberry bogs.

Green Cranberry Spanworm (Itame sulphurea Pack.). This spanworm is the most common of the spanworms found on Massachusetts bogs. It has also been found in New Jersey and Wisconsin and appears to feed solely on cranberries. The insect causes damage to cranberries by eating the terminal buds and, later, by severing the stem at the juncture of the blossom. This resembles the injury caused by the cranberry blossom worm. The mature worms are green with inconspicuous white lines running the length of the back and are about an inch long.

The insect overwinters in the egg stage in the litter of the bog floor. The winter flood apparently does no harm to the eggs. The eggs begin to hatch about mid-May, and hatching can continue into July. The mature caterpillars pupate in the litter under the vines. Pupation lasts about 10 days. Moths can be found emerging from late June until early August, when the females lay their eggs. There is only one brood a year.

Because the larvae emerge fairly late in the growing season, reflows are not generally effective in controlling this insect. Insecticides applied in the spring to control other insects have kept the green cranberry spanworm in check. Since the insect overwinters in the egg stage, sanding has been an effective control measure because it buries the eggs.

Brown Cranberry Spanworm (Ematurga amitaria Gn.). The brown cranberry spanworm has become a serious economic pest on Massachusetts cranberry bogs in recent years where the species has occasionally become quite numerous. It has also been reported in Nova Scotia and Wisconsin. Unlike the green cranberry spanworm, it has many alternative hosts that are common to areas surrounding cranberry bogs. In addition to severing blossoms, the caterpillars chew on leaves, flower buds, and partly grown berries. Their attack on developing buds can effect crop production the following year as well. The mature worms are a little more than an inch long and are grayish brown in color.

The insects overwinter as pupae among the litter under the vines, quite able to withstand the winter flood during this dormant stage. The moths emerge during June and into July, depending on when the winter flood was drawn. The female moths lay their eggs among the litter on the bog floor.

Since the larvae are emerging about bloom time, control is somewhat difficult. Reflows are not possible because of the lateness of the season, and insecticide applications may need to be restricted because of the presence of pollinating insects. To effectively control the insect, insecticides must be applied thoroughly when the worms are ¼ to ½ inch long, but this application must not coincide with cranberry bloom. Often a second application of insecticide is needed to kill larvae originating from later-deposited eggs.

Chain-spotted Geometer (Cingilia catenaria Drury). This spanworm has caused serious economic damage to cranberry bogs in the Maritime Provinces and, on occasion, in Massachusetts. The chain-spotted geometer has many alternative hosts, among them the gray birch and the lowbush blueberry that is cultivated in Maine and the Maritime Provinces. The larvae are capable of stripping all the foliage off the plants in their path, causing the vines to turn brown.

The insect overwinters in the egg stage under the winter flood. The eggs hatch in late spring and the slow-developing larvae mature by early August. The mature larvae are nearly 1½ inches long and are yellow with round black spots on the head and neck shield. They have the peculiar habit of hanging very still—suspended downward—during the day and waiting until evening to resume active feeding. The larvae pupate by mid-August and remain in this stage for about a month. The moths emerge in September and lay their over-wintering eggs. There is only one brood produced. Maintaining clean peripheral ditches and keeping them partially filled with water help protect the bog from invading larvae.

Cotton Spanworm (Anavitrinella pampinarea Gn.). This spanworm is found over most of the country east of the Rocky Mountains. It is a more serious pest of other fruit and agronomic crops than it is on cranberry, although isolated cases of severe infestations have been reported. Damage is caused by the insect's voracious appetite for green tissue. Two broods are capable of browning an entire bog.

The first brood hatches from overwintering eggs in June. Within a month the larvae have matured into yellowish brown caterpillars about 1⅛ inches long. The worms crawl into the loose soil where they pupate, and the moths emerge in two weeks. Egg laying resumes and the caterpillars of the second brood mature in August. Again the larvae pupate, and the second generation of moths emerge in September to lay the overwintering eggs.

Because of the rarity of this insect, no specific recommendations for its control exist. In all probability, the insecticides used to control other cranberry insect pests will also control the cotton spanworm.

Big Cranberry Spanworm (Abbotana clemataria S. & A.). This spanworm has reportedly caused considerable damage on rare occasions in Massachusetts. It also feeds on apple and other tree species along the East Coast. It is by far the largest of the spanworms, reaching a length at maturity of 2½ inches. The caterpillars are black to chocolate brown and are for the most part very smooth surfaced.

The big cranberry spanworm overwinters as a coffee brown pupa that curiously never gets hard and firm (as most pupae do) but always yields to the touch. The moths emerge late in May and lay their eggs soon thereafter. The eggs hatch by mid-June, and by mid-July the worms have matured and pupated. There is only one brood produced in the year.

Again, this is a very minor economic pest and there are no specific pesticide recommendations made for its control. Insecticides used to control other cranberry insects probably keep this caterpillar in check.

Cutworms

Cutworms can be a serious pest to cranberries. They are the larvae of certain night-flying moths and are similar to the common garden cutworms, being of the same family of insects, the Noctuidae. The mature caterpillars range in length from 1½ to 2 inches, are without noticeable hair, and feed mostly at night. During the day they hide among the vines or in the litter on the bog floor. The damage they incur is out of proportion to the amount of vegetation they consume because they cut off leaves, flower buds, flowers, and small berries as the result of their stem chewing. Often the first signs of cutworm activity are green leaves floating in the ditches. Although the various species of cutworms are difficult to distinguish when the worms are small, the mature larvae do have distinctive colorations. Franklin (1948b, 23) has used these distinctions to identify the cutworm species that attack cranberry as follows:

With very conspicuous yellow stripes . . . . zebra caterpillar
Not so colored 1
1. Mostly dark, without definite side
   stripes . . . . black cutworm
   With a conspicuous strip along each side 2
2. With a row of two to four angular dark
   spots on each side of the hind part of the
   back . . . . spotted cutworm
   Without such spots 3
3. The back reddish brown and not marked
   with pale yellow dots . . . . cranberry blossom worm
   The back mostly dark, grayish, or
   green 4
4. Found on a bog not bared of a long flood
   after May 20 . . . . false armyworm
   Found on a bog bared of a long flood
   after May 20 5
5. With many small round or oval dark
   tubercles noticeable along the back . . . . fall armyworm
   The back without such tubercles 6
6. With a broken pale line along the middle
   of the back . . . . armyworm
   A narrow dark-brown stripe along the
   middle of the back . . . . Atlantic cutworm

The zebra caterpillar (*Ceramica picta* Harr.) and the Atlantic cutworm (*Polia atlantica* Grote) are rarely a problem in cranberry bogs.

Black Cutworm (Agrotis ypsilon Rott.). This cutworm can be a problem on late-held bogs. It can also be a problem on new plantings where it has a propensity for girdling the young vines. It is common to see the worms in association with the spotted cutworm and armyworm, often greedily devouring spotted cutworms as well as each other. Damage by the insect is manifested in the defoliation of the vines and, more seriously, in the severing of uprights. Although the larvae feed mostly at night, they have been observed traveling and feeding during the day as well, particularly on cloudy days.

The mature caterpillar has a dark brown and a grayish bottom half. A broad, light brown band traverses its back. The caterpillar's most distinguishing characteristic is its peculiar appearance, which can be best described as greasy. The black cutworm appears to overwinter as larvae in various stages of development or even as pupae. The gray moth with a reddish brown head is active from late May until late October. Two broods are normally produced; the first is most abundant in June and July, and the second in August and September. Eggs are laid throughout most of these months.

Infestations of the black cutworm are generally not a problem on early-drawn bogs; therefore, one prophylactic measure would be to draw the winter flood before 20 May. When cutworm counts in 50 sweeps of an insect net total eight or more, bogs should be reflooded for 10 hours at night. Carbaryl and Lorsban are two insecticides that are commonly used to control cutworms in bogs that can not be reflooded. The key to good control is to destroy the larvae when they are still small; therefore, timing of the reflood or spray is of utmost importance.

Spotted Cutworm (Amathes c-nigrum L.). Although the spotted cutworm is found from New England to the Pacific Northwest, it has only been reported to be a problem in Massachusetts cranberry bogs. It is a much more serious pest to vegetables and forage crops throughout its range. The insect generally only causes economic damage to bogs in which the winter flood was held to late May or early June. The caterpillar severs the stems of buds, flowers, and fruit as well as the petioles of leaves. It may also devour the internal tissue of young fruit.

The insect overwinters as a mature larva which pupates in May. The moths emerge in a few weeks to lay the eggs that produce the damaging larvae in late July and early August. The worms pupate in the soil and a second brood of moths emerge in three weeks to produce the eggs that hatch into the overwintering larvae. The color of the 1½-inch mature larva is dull gray or brown with greenish or olive brown tints. Its identifying characteristic is the whitish stripe along each side of the body and two to four rather conspicuous angular, blackish spots in a row on each side of the hind part of the back.

Since severe infestations of the spotted cutworm are seldom found on early-drawn bogs, one act of prevention prescribed in Massachusetts is to draw the winter flood before 23 May. On late-held bogs that can be reflooded, a 10-hour reflood may be effective against the newly hatched larvae. Early applications of insecticides may be effective—providing the applications are made before the larvae are half grown.

Cranberry Blossom Worm (Epiglaea apiata Gr.). This cutworm has caused serious economic losses to New Jersey cranberry growers on occasion (Beckwith 1929). A favorite alternative food for this insect is leatherleaf, which abounds in the cranberry-growing areas of New Jersey. Reinfestation of bogs from this alternative host contributes to the severity of this insect problem in New Jersey. The young larvae feed on the cranberry's terminal buds. As the larvae mature, they are capable of devouring entire leaves, severing blossom uprights, and even eating small berries. Severe infestations are capable of destroying the entire crop.

The insect overwinters as an egg which hatches in late May to early June. The newly hatched larva is yellowish green in color. As it matures it becomes chocolate brown in color, and a light, longitudinal stripe develops along each side and a dark stripe in the middle of the back. The larvae pupate in the trash on the bog floor, and adult moths begin to appear in early September. The overwintering eggs are deposited on cranberry foliage during October.

A 12-hour reflow in late May is an effective control measure for this pest. Since this cutworm feeds only at night, it is difficult to detect its presence until considerable economic damage is observed. Therefore, it is important to monitor for its presence by evening insect sweeps. Early insecticide applications also are effective deterrents. It is important, however, that the sprays be applied at an early stage of larval development before significant damage has occurred.

False Armyworm (Xylena nupera Lint.). This cutworm is a sporadic pest on Massachusetts cranberry bogs. It appears to limit its feeding to bogs in which the winter flood has been drawn before 15 May. It is capable of causing a great deal of economic damage because the young caterpillars eat out the center of the terminal buds. As the larvae develop, they devour new growth—often leaving little but a portion of the stem. Their feeding resembles that of the gypsy moth caterpillar. They can be found feeding freely in the daytime.

The insect overwinters as a moth that lays its eggs in late April and early May on early-drawn bogs. The eggs hatch in two-to-three weeks into whitish larvae marked with many black spots. A slender black spine emanates from each of these spots. As the caterpillar matures, it becomes green with whitish lines along the back and sides. The mature caterpillar is about two inches long and possesses a greenish yellow head. By late June the larvae are mature and penetrate the ground, where they remain dormant for two-to-six weeks before pupating. Moths emerge from mid-August until late September. There is only one brood produced per year. Late holding of the winter flood is one method of biological control that can be effective in preventing severe infestations of this insect. Reflooding early-drawn bogs for 10 hours on about 18 May or when 50 sweeps of an insect net pick up more than eight larvae is also an effective control measure. Carbaryl and chlorpyrifos insecticides give effective control of the false armyworm.

Fall Armyworm (Laphygma frugiperda S. & A.). Severe isolated infestations of this cutworm have been reported on late-held bogs in New Jersey and Massachusetts. Apparently the predators of this cutworm are eliminated by the prolonged flood, enabling the fall armyworm to reach epidemic proportions. The worm is seldom a problem on bogs drawn before July. The injury caused by this insect is similar to that caused by the armyworm. It can be found working during the daytime, and it cannibalizes its own species as well as other cutworms.

The moths invade the bog and lay their eggs on leaves during the night. The eggs hatch in a few weeks to produce caterpillars, each with a whitish body and black head. The mature larvae have markings that are similar to those of the armyworm, except that there is an inverted "Y" on the face of the head. The caterpillars pupate in the ground. There is only one brood produced in the cranberry-growing regions. The insect can be controlled by insecticide sprays used to control other cranberry insect pests.

Armyworm (Cirphis unipuncta Haw.). Although grasses rank as the favorite food of armyworms, these worms can seriously infest late-drained cranberry bogs. The moths appear to be carried on prevailing winds, which can result in sudden outbreaks of this notorious cutworm. They are a problem particularly after a cold and late spring. Like the black cutworm, they tend to nip off the leaves of the cranberry plant and to cut new uprights nearly off, leaving them to hang by a thread. As with most cutworms, they prefer to feed actively at night.

The armyworm appears to have two broods in the cranberry-growing regions, although it may have as many as six in warmer climates. It overwinters as partially grown larvae which mature in the spring and go on to pupate in the soil. After two weeks of pupation, the moths emerge and lay eggs in masses on the leaves. The moths are particularly attracted to light and may often be seen swarming around street lights. The plain brown moth has a white speck near the center of the upper surface of each forewing. The dark-colored caterpillar is about 1½ inches long. It has a yellowish brown head and a smooth, dark body with alternating dark and reddish yellow stripes on its side. Pale yellow lines separate the alternating stripes. Treatment procedures for combating the armyworm are similar to those outlined for the black cutworm.

Hairy Caterpillars

These caterpillars are similar to cutworms, but their bodies are covered with hair. There are four species of hairy caterpillars that have been known to attack cranberries. These may be distinguished as follows (Franklin 1948b, 46)

    Head red . . . . white-marked tussock moth
    Head not red 1
1. Working in late spring and early
    summer . . . . gypsy moth

Working in late July and early August ....*Datana drexelii*
Working in late August and in
September .... crinkled flannel moth

Of these four hairy caterpillars, only the gypsy moth is considered of economic importance by cranberry growers.

Gypsy Moth (Porthetria dispar L.). Economic outbreaks of this insect appear to occur about every 10 years in the northeastern United States. Oaks and other hardwoods that often surround cranberry bogs are favorite foods of this pest. The surrounding woodlands are, therefore, an abundant source of wind-disseminated immature larvae or migrating adult worms that can infest cranberry bogs. Young larvae feed on the terminal bud and the succulent new growth of the upright. Berry production is consequently severely affected.

The insect overwinters as an egg in buff-colored egg masses often attached to the trunks and branches of trees. The eggs are capable of withstanding temperatures as low as $-25°F$ ($-32°C$) and can survive the winter flood. The tiny slate-colored larvae emerge from mid-April to mid-July and are covered with aerostatic hairs that make it easy for them to be borne by the wind for up to 20 miles or more. The mature caterpillar possesses five pairs of blue spots at its front end and six pairs of red spots at its rear end. Pupation occurs amongst the litter or in the vines by mid-July and lasts two to three weeks. The white-colored female moths and buff-colored male moths emerge in late July and August. Unlike the slender-bodied male moth, the heavy-bodied female moth is incapable of flight; therefore, the female's egg masses are often found adjacent to their pupal case. There is only one brood produced during the year.

Late holding the winter flood until 25 May will eliminate the eggs laid in the bog the previous year and will drown many of the wind-disseminated young larvae. A late May reflood is also an effective treatment against wind-borne worms. It is critical to destroy the invading larvae as soon as possible; therefore, constant monitoring with insect sweeps is crucial. Fully developed larvae are more difficult to control with insecticides and their presence usually coincides with cranberry bloom, which limits the use of insecticides because of pollination considerations. The destruction of the insect egg masses in the surrounding woodlands is a significant prophylactic treatment.

Fruitworms

The fruitworms are perhaps the most economically serious of all the cranberry insects because of their debilitating effect on cranberry yield and because they are the most prevalent insect found in cranberry bogs. The two most important fruitworms that the cranberry grower must deal with are the cranberry fruitworm and *Sparganothis* fruitworm.

Cranberry Fruitworm (Acrobasis vaccinii Riley = Mineola vaccinii Riley). This fruitworm is considered to be the most serious cranberry pest that cranberry growers in the Maritime Provinces of Canada must deal with (Maxwell and Morgan 1966). It has caused severe crop losses in Massachusetts and can be a problem in the other major cranberry-producing regions as well. Injury is caused to the fruit by the newly hatched larva which bores through the stem end of the berry, closing the opening with a fine silken web. The larva proceeds to feed on the pulp of the berry. The invaded berry will prematurely turn red and eventually turn brown to black and resemble a raisin. When the berry pulp is consumed, the larva leaves the berry and enters a second berry, than a third, fourth, or fifth berry, usually boring through the side of the berry. The larva normally has completed its feeding cycle before harvest. The economic significance of this insect is thus quite apparent. Early-blooming cranberry varieties appear to be more prone to cranberry fruitworm attack than late-blooming varieties (Brodel 1980). No other part of the cranberry plant is affected by this pest.

The cranberry fruitworm overwinters as a full-grown larva in a cocoon made up debris from the bog floor. In the spring the larva enters the pupal stage, from which the moth emerges during late bloom. The dark brown moth has very noticeable white bands on its forewings. During the day the moths rest under the vines, but when disturbed they will fly 40 to 50 feet before coming back to rest on the vines. The female moth lays her eggs within the calyx cup of the berry. The pale green larva with a yellowish head migrates to the stem end, where it enters the berry by boring a tiny hole into the fruit. By early fall it has completed its feeding and leaves its last feeding place to construct the cocoon in which it hibernates.

Control is directed at the larval stage of this insect. Infestations are monitored by sampling 100 randomly picked berries from a bog and examining them for unparasitized eggs. The presence of two or more viable eggs in the sample is a signal to apply an insecticide. Berry samplings and egg counts are made every three to four days. Insecticides that are effective against cranberry fruitworm include parathion, azinphos-methyl, carbaryl, and diazinon.

Sparganothis Fruitworm (Sparganothis sulfureana Clem.). *Sparganothis* fruitworm also has been called the false yellow-headed fireworm because of its resemblance to that insect, but unlike the yellow-headed fireworm, this fruitworm infests fruits (Marucci 1953). It has become a significant pest in most of the cranberry-growing areas because of the general use of the organophosphate insecticides, which apparently reduced the number of parasites and predators that formerly kept the fruitworm in check naturally. Injury is caused by the feeding of the larva within the fruit. In its feeding process, it often scores many of the berries it comes in contact with, thus greatly increasing the amount of damage caused. Unlike the cranberry fruitworms, the larvae are not greenish, nor do they produce the castings characteristic of cranberry fruitworm feeding. The mature larva resembles the yellow-headed fireworm, although it is apt to be slightly larger.

The insect overwinters as a tiny caterpillar in flooded bogs. It comes out of hibernation when new cranberry tip growth appears in the spring. The larvae mature in June and July, during which time they may feed on developing blossoms. The most significant damage, however, is caused by a summer brood of larvae that mature in late summer and feed on the developing fruit. The entire life cycle from egg to moth requires 46 to 64 days in summer and 58 to 79 days in early fall.

The larvae are capable of withstanding prolonged flooding—often more than the cranberry plant can endure; therefore, water management is not a particularly effective means of control. The late larval stage of the insect is difficult to control with insecticides, and in addition one must deal with the problem of destroying the insect's predators. Parathion sprays are effective when directed at the young larval stage.

Miscellaneous Worms

Bagworm (Fumea casta Pallas). This hairless caterpillar was first reported feeding in cranberry bogs in Massachusetts in 1951. It feeds inside a bag that it constructs of small sticks glued lengthwise around its case of silk. It is reported to feed on a wide variety of plants. Since the bagworm is of such minor importance to cranberry culture, there is no special treatment for its control.

Cranberry Sawfly (Pristiphora idiota Norton). This species of sawfly occurs only on bogs that are not reflooded regularly. It feeds only on the cranberry and has been reported in the cranberry-growing areas of the East and in Wisconsin. The injury is caused by the larvae, which scallop the leaves irregularly. The insect produces as many as five generations in a year. This results in a long feeding season and the potential to do considerable harm.

The larvae overwinter in coffee brown silk cocoons in the trash on the bog floor. Pupation occurs in early May after the winter flood, and the adult sawflies emerge soon thereafter to lay their eggs in pockets between the upper and lower surfaces and at the edge of the leaf. By early June the first light yellowish green larvae appear, which have taken about a week to hatch. The cycle may be repeated as many as five times during the growing season, the last worms usually entering their winter cocoons in mid-October. A June reflow for 10 hours effectively controls this pest.

Cranberry Tipworm (Dasyneura vaccinii Smith). Tipworm injury has resulted in economic losses to cranberry producers in all of the growing areas. Marucci (1954) reported fruit losses in excess of 50 percent in severely infested New Jersey bogs, and the insect has been found in large numbers on many bogs in the Grayland district of Washington. Whenever there is new and succulent tip growth, there is the possibility for tipworm injury because this is the tissue favored by the female fly for egg laying. After being attacked by the tipworm, the shoot tips are cupped and resemble frost injury—in contrast to fireworm injury, in which an infected tip has an angular appearance. Instead of using its mouthparts, the maggot uses the rough underside of its body like a rasp for extracting the juices from the tender plant tips. Feeding results in the destruction of the shoot tip, which would have become the terminal bud and the following year's blossoms. There are normally two broods per year. Very often, vigorous plants that lose their shoot tips to the first brood can produce new tips that go on to mature and produce terminal buds. Injury by the second brood, however, results in new tip growth from which only leafy shoots rather than blossoms emanate the following year.

The larva of the second brood forms a cocoon on the underside of a leaf or in the trash on the bog floor, where it is capable of surviving the winter flood. In the spring after the winter flood has been drawn and temperatures are favorable, it pupates and emerges as a small, two-winged, gnatlike fly. The female fly lays her eggs at the base of the leaves of the new shoot. The newly hatched maggots feed on the developing leaflets, causing the characteristic cupping injury and eventual death of the growing tip. From one to five maggots may be found on an infested tip. The damage from this first brood occurs in late May and June. The yellow-to-orange legless maggot matures in about 10 days and constructs its cocoon in the injured tips. In a few days (often coinciding with full bloom) the adult flies emerge. It is this second brood that causes the most serious economic loss. Insecticides applied to control fireworm and fruitworm will also eliminate this pest.

Non-worms That Attack Foliage and Fruit

Weevils

Both the larvae and adult beetles of a number of weevil species are capable of injuring cranberry plants. The larvae can be found feeding on both the roots and aerial parts of the plant, and the beetles feed most often on the shoots and buds of the plant. The cranberry weevil is the most important weevil species attacking cranberries on the East Coast, and the black vine weevil is the dominant species of economic concern on the West Coast. To a lesser extent, the strawberry root weevils and other less prevalent weevils may be found occasionally on cranberry bogs.

Cranberry Weevil (Anthonomus musculus Say). Although not a major insect pest in Massachusetts cranberry bogs, this insect has the potential for becoming a serious economic problem because infestations can build to serious proportions over the years. Both the larvae and the adult beetles may injure the cranberry plant. The larvae tend to consume the flower parts within the flower, causing the unopened flower to change color from pink to orange. The adult beetles feed on the leaves, terminal buds, and blossom buds in the spring and on the fruit, foliage, and terminal buds in the summer and fall. The beetle's feeding is characterized by tiny holes drilled into the buds and by small crescent-shaped black spots on the underside of the leaves.

The cranberry weevil completes its life cycle in one year, carrying over the winter as an adult beetle under the winter flood. After the withdrawal of the winter flood, the adults hide in the trash under the vines and begin mating in early June. The female inserts its eggs between the petals of blossom buds. A legless white larva emerges from each egg to feed on the internal parts of the flower. The larva completes its feeding and pupates within the flower bud, from which the new generation adult beetle emerges in just six days. Thus, the entire period from egg to adult beetle takes only two months.

During the course of the growing season, the adults of two generations of beetles can be found in the sweeps of an insect net. Sweeps made from mid-May through mid-June will contain the adults of the previous generation, whereas sweeps after bloom will contain the adults of the new generation as well. Brodel (1980) maintains that whenever more than three beetles are recovered in 50 sweeps of the insect net, it would be economically advisable to apply an insecticide. Sprays of azinphos-methyl (when properly timed) have effectively controlled this insect. The cranberry weevil does appear to be parasitized by an unidentified wasp, but the extent of the wasp's effectiveness as an economic control has not been determined.

Black Vine Weevil (Otiorhynchus sulcatus Fabr.). In terms of economics, this root weevil is the most important weevil attacking cranberry bogs in the Pacific Northwest. The injury is caused by the larvae's feeding on the fine roots and on the bark of larger roots, often completely girdling the root. This feeding causes the plant to wilt and eventually die.

Upon hatching in early July, the half-moon-shaped white larva with a brownish head feeds on cranberry roots all summer, winter, and spring until it enters the pupal stage in April. Pupation lasts for two to three weeks, after which a black-snouted beetle about ⅓ inch long emerges. The adult beetles mate and lay their eggs in late June and early July at the soil surface beneath the vines, where they hatch in two to three weeks to repeat their life cycle. On occasion, the adults may live for a year on the bog surface and lay eggs for a second time the following season.

The overwintering larva cannot survive a winter flood, therefore it is mainly a problem on dry-harvested bogs and bogs which cannot be flooded. In the colder cranberry-growing areas where the winter flood is necessary, this insect is unable to survive. Flooding for three to four weeks during the dormant season will effectively control this insect. Bogs that cannot be flooded can be treated with repeat applications of Furadan in June and July in the Pacific Northwest only (Shanks 1979).

Other Weevils. The larvae of the strawberry root weevil (*Otiorhychus ovatus* Linn.) and the rough strawberry root weevil (*O. rugosostriatus* Geoze) feed on small roots and on the bark of larger roots in a manner similar to the larvae of the black vine weevil. The edges of cranberry bogs are particularly susceptible to injury by these two weevil species.

The adult stage of the obscure root weevil (*Sciopithes obscurus*) is a predominantly gray beetle about ¼ inch long with a wavy brown line across its wing covers. The adults feed on the foliage, causing a severe ragging of the leaves. The beetles may also become a source of fruit contamination at harvest. The woods weevil (*Nemocestes incomptus*) adult is a light or dark brown beetle about ¼ inch long with gray spots or patches on its posterior. Control of both the obscure root weevil and the woods weevil is directed at the beetle stage with sprays of azinophos-methyl at 21-day intervals whenever the adult weevils are present.

Blunt-nosed Cranberry Leafhopper (*Euscelis Striatulus* Fallen)

During the early decades of this century, this insect was the scourge of the cranberry industry because of its identification as the vector for the dreaded false blossom disease (Beckwith and Hutton 1929). With today's common usage of organophosphate insecticides, this insect is no longer such a serious threat. Franklin has counted as many as 400 to 500 leafhoppers in 50 sweeps of an insect net on badly infested bogs. At these concentrations, these sucking insects may also cause significant loss of vigor in the plants. The insect is not found on the Pacific Coast, which probably accounts for the failure of false blossom disease to spread when introduced on that coast with infected vines.

There are three stages in the life cycle of the blunt-nosed leafhopper: egg, nymph, and adult. There is but one brood per year. The insect overwinters as an egg thrust under the thin bark of the more tender cranberry stems, making it difficult to see them. Here they are able to survive the winter flood even when late held. The wingless nymphs begin hatching in June, with scattered hatchings continuing throughout July. The nymphs go through five molts before becoming winged adults in about a month. The adults generally do not feed much on the leaves.

The spray regimen used during the growing season on cranberry bogs, which includes the organophosphate insecticides, has effectively eliminated this insect from the bogs. However, the grower must be constantly vigilant because this leafhopper is abundant on the leatherleaf and dwarf huckleberry common to the cranberry-growing areas of the East Coast.

Southern Red Mite

Injury by this insect is caused by the mite's sucking of the contents of plant cells, which results in the removal of the chlorophyll from the cell and the consequent appearance of white spots or stipples at the feeding sites. The injury undoubtedly impairs the functioning of the cranberry plant, but to date it has not been determined whether mite feeding will lead to a reduction in crop.

The insects overwinter as eggs laid on both the upper and under surfaces of leaves, where they are capable of enduring the winter flood. In early spring the first of as many as eight broods of young mites are hatched. Each brood will undergo three instars, or moltings, before the young mites become adults. The mites readily migrate from heavily infested to less infested vines. Throughout the course of the growing season, the six to eight generations produced will overlap so that mites at various stages of development may be found on a single upright at one time.

Despite the uncertainty of whether mites reduce crop yield, growers are apt to apply a miticide whenever mite populations are observed. The efficacy of the treatment depends greatly upon the ability to wet both the upper and under surfaces of the leaves where the mites are to be found.

Insects That Attack the Stem

Cranberry Girdler (*Chrysoteuchia topiaria* Zeller)

This insect has been a spotty pest in all the cranberry-growing regions until recent years. It is becoming increasingly important as an economic pest as the prophylactic effects of the discontinued chlorinated hydrocarbons disappear from the soil. The buildup of cranberry girdler populations appears to be favored also by modern management practices, which include less frequent sanding, more liberal use of fertilizers, and greater accumulation of trash on the bog floor. The damage is done by the feeding of the larvae on the cranberry vegetation. In fact, the cranberry girdler is a member of a group of insects called sod webworms, which are known to cause considerable economic damage to certain grasses. The larvae conceal themselves in the leaf litter on the bog floor, where they feed on the outside layers of the cranberry vine covered with trash. Often the larvae feed on the underside of the vine, thus not completely girdling the vine. When this occurs, the vines are not completely killed but are sufficiently weakened so as to produce a great deal of unsound fruit. When the feeding results in the complete girdling of the vine or its severance, the vines are killed. Very seldom are bogs attacked with equal severity. More often than not the egg-laying moths will seek out those portions of the bogs that are dry, heavily vined, and well covered with trash. The injury first appears in the fall as patches of brown foliage indicating where vine death has occurred. The damaged areas become even more prominent in the spring after the removal of the winter flood when they appear as areas of defoliated vines.

The cranberry girdler survives the winter as a fully grown larva secure in its cocoon buried in the trash on the bog floor. After the withdrawal of the winter flood, the larva pupates within its cocoon, and moths begin to emerge in June. Moth emergence continues to early August with peak egg-laying activity occurring in early July. The adult moth is about ½ inch long with a snoutlike projection on its head. When it first emerges, it has a silvery color with light brown outer edges on the front wings. When at rest the moth appears long and narrow, which contrasts it from the fireworm or fruitworm. Beckwith (1934) maintained that when more than 25 moths are observed in a one-minute walk through the bog during their emergence period, there is apt to be considerable vine killing in the fall. The female moth scatters its eggs at random on the bog floor. The eggs, which are white at first, turn orange or red before hatching in 10 to 12 days. The small, dirty white larva with a brown head feeds sparingly at first, but by September it is feeding voraciously on the stems and runners, leaving fecal droppings that look like fresh sawdust. It will attain a length of ½ inch before it constructs its cocoon of silk intertwined with leaves and sand in preparation for overwintering, thus completing its life cycle. There is only one brood produced each year.

Traditional methods of control of the cranberry girdler have included flooding the bog after harvest but before the larvae have constructed their cocoons, and covering excessive vine growth and bog trash with a layer of sand (Beckwith 1925). The fall flooding must be maintained for at least five days and can therefore be injurious to a crop that has yet to be harvested. Application of the flood after the larvae are in their cocoons is of little value. Late holding the winter flood until 5 July followed by a 24-hour reflow in September is also an effective control measure if practiced before the vines show extensive dieback. This practice, of course, sacrifices one year's crop. Sanding with at least ½ inch of sand during the dormant season will cover the organic debris on the bog floor, thus eliminating the habitat most favorable for egg laying by the moth. Beckwith cautions against excessive drainage in the bog, which may also contribute to a habitat favorable for egg laying. In addition to spot sanding of infected areas, a regular sanding cycle of three to four years is advisable where the girdler is apt to be a problem. The larvae may also be killed with insecticide applications such as diazinon. The insecticide should be applied about three to four weeks after the peak flight of the adults to kill the young larvae before they are large enough to cause much damage (S. L. Roberts and Mahr 1982). Pheromone traps are particularly useful for monitoring the moth populations to ascertain peak flight. The moths may also be killed by fireworm and fruitworm sprays applied during the summer months.

Scale Insects

Heavy scale infestations can severely weaken cranberry plants. The insects, which can be recognized by their protective waxy coating, attach themselves to the stems, leaves, or fruits of the cranberry plant and suck its juices. This type of feeding eventually weakens the plant to the extent that premature plant senescence develops, as indicated by the early reddening of the vines. The insects are quite small, necessitating the careful inspection of vines to ascertain their presence. The woodlands surrounding cranberry bogs are a constant source of infestation of these insects.

Franklin has reported the existence of six different species of scale insects in Massachusetts bogs, which he has keyed for easy identification in the following key (Franklin 1952, 3):

     Mature female scales usually solitary 1
     Mature female scales not noticeably
     solitary 2
1. Female scales causing the cranberry
     stems to swell where they attach
     themselves .... Dearness scale
     Female scales attached mostly in
     crotches of cranberry stems, not
     causing the stems to swell; bodies of the
     insects themselves purplish .... Eriococcus scale
2. Mature female scales thin and delicate,
     mostly grayish; bodies of the insects
     themselves rather deep yellow .... Latania scale
     Mature scales mostly brown or
     brownish 3
3. Mature female scales mostly roundish or
     oval; bodies of insects themselves
     rather light yellow .... Cranberry scale
     Mature scales all elongate 4
4. Mature scales large and rather boat-
     shaped .... Lecanium scale

Mature scales resembling oyster shells
in shape .... Oystershell scale

In addition to these six species of scale insects, Scammell (1917) has reported injury to New Jersey cranberry bogs by the Putnam scale, and Crowley (1954) has reported San Jose scale infestations in cranberry bogs on the Pacific Coast.

Dearness Scale (Rhizaspidiotus dearnessi Ckll.). Although this insect may be found throughout the United States, it has only been found on cranberry bogs in Massachusetts. It does not appear to exist in numbers great enough to be very harmful. Seldom does more than one female scale occupy a single stem at a time; the stem becomes noticeably swollen where the female scale is attached. The female scales are pale gray, oval, convex, and 2 mm long—about twice the size of the white, elongated male. As many as 10 males may be found on a single upright. Infestations of this insect are generally not severe enough to warrant special control measures.

Eriococcus Scale (Eriococcus azaleae Comst.). Franklin (1952) noted that this species has caused economic damage on occasion to bogs that have had little or no winter flowage. It is the same scale that is a serious pest on greenhouse-grown azaleas as well as other *Rhododendron* species. Its most distinguishing characteristic is its propensity for lodging in the crotches of the cranberry stems, appearing as a small, white fluffy mass about 2 to 3 mm across. Each female will produce about 100 to 150 eggs in late June. By early July young crawlers emerge which show a strong tendency to cluster about the stem crotches. Eventually the crawlers migrate to the ground, where they overwinter; they move back onto the stems in the spring to mature. Although no chemicals are registered for control of this insect, azinphos-methyl or chlorpyrifos used to control fireworms and tipworms may control the crawler stage of *Eriococcus* scale.

Latania Scale (Hemiberlesia lataniae Signoret). This species of scale insect is commonly found in the subtropical regions of the world. It has occasionally been found on Cape Cod where it has caused economic damage on bogs fully flooded for the winter. No chemical control measures are available for this rather rare insect, although forsaking the winter flood would probably control this insect as would holding the winter flood until mid-July.

Cranberry Scale (Aspidaspis oxycoccus Woglum). The cranberry scale is by far the most harmful of all the scale insects. It has been found in cranberry bogs on both the East and West coasts. Unlike the previous scale insects described, this scale may become so numerous as to completely encrust the cranberry stem, killing whole areas of vines. It is commonly found on leaves and immature fruit as well; this results in the production of deformed and spotted fruit. The worst infestations often occur along the edges of the bog ditches.

The adult female scales are roundish oval, dark brown, and about the size of the head of a pin. The scales become loosely attached to the cranberry stem, and when they are brushed off they leave a characteristic white scar on the stem. Although there is but one brood per year, each female is capable of producing up to 100 eggs. The eggs are laid in June, and by the end of June the crawling young are evident. It is at this time that sprays used to control fireworm and tipworm may also control cranberry scale. The insect overwinters as the nearly mature adult under its scale, where it is capable of withstanding an ordinary winter flood. Late holding the winter flood until mid-July would probably destroy the insect.

Lecanium Scale (Lecanium corni Bouche). This scale insect is rather rare on the East Coast, having been reported in an isolated situation on a bog in Massachusetts that did not receive a winter flood. It appears to be a more serious problem on the West Coast, where bogs are less apt to receive a winter flood. It is the same scale known as brown apricot scale and European fruit Lecanium, and it can be found on many hosts in the woodlands surrounding cranberry bogs.

The adult scales are soft-shelled, brown insects about ⅛ inch in size, resembling a small brown split pea. The immature adult overwinters under its protective scale. In early spring the scale insects resume their feeding, and the females begin laying their eggs under their scale in June. As many as 1000 tiny white eggs may be deposited by a single female. The peak of the hatching is usually reached by mid-August. The newly hatched crawlers migrate to cranberry leaves, where they feed on the plant juices. As cold weather approaches, the crawlers move from the leaves to the stems, where they overwinter as immature scales. Sprays used to control fireworms and fruitworms will control Lecanium scale.

Oystershell Scale (Lepidosaphes ulmi Linn.). This is another scale insect that appears to be more of a problem in the milder growing regions of the Pacific Northwest. Crowley (1954) is of the opinion that it arrived in Washington State on vines imported from Massachusetts because no upland plants in the Washington area appear infected. In Massachusetts it has only been reported in isolated situations on bogs that did not receive a winter flood. The insect, however, is capable of causing severe vine damage, often turning the vines red in late July or August—making them appear as if they were suffering from drought.

The small brownish gray scales resemble miniature oyster shells, hence the name. The insect overwinters as a grayish white egg under the female scale. The female may lay as many as 250 of these tiny eggs under its scale before it dies. The overwintered eggs hatch in the spring about the time of early bloom. Small whitish nymphs roam the stems for a day or two before they attach themselves to the vines and begin feeding. Dormant oil sprays and lime-sulfur treatments have not been effective against this scale insect. The best control is achieved by eliminating the insect at the nymph stage with sprays used for the control of other cranberry insects.

San Jose Scale (Aspidiotus perniciosus Comstock). According to Crowley (1954), this scale insect causes serious injury to Washington cranberry bogs. Franklin (1952) questioned the accuracy of the reports of its existence in Washington because it had not been found in other cranberry-growing areas. Injury is to the fruit as well as to the vines.

The insect overwinters as a partially grown nymph under its scale, which is tightly fastened to bark of the stem. It can withstand submergence at this stage. In the spring the nymph completes its development by the time the cranberry blooms. The female remains under its scale, where it produces its live young soon after mating. The enormous number of young scales look like yellow mites and are soon crawling over leaves, stems, and berries. The prodigious numbers produced and the fact that the berries are permanently disfigured by their feeding contribute to the economic importance of this pest. Postbloom sprays of insecticide must be relied on for its control.

Cranberry Spittle Insect (*Clastoptera saint-cyri* Prov.)

When present in large numbers, this sucking insect can be very harmful. It can be found in most Massachusetts cranberry bogs, according to Franklin (1950). When heavy infestations exist, the masses of spittle are so great as to thoroughly wet the shoes of a person walking through the bog. It is also found in other cranberry-growing areas of the East Coast and is commonly found on much of the vegetation associated with cranberry bogs, thus providing a constant source of infestation. The injury is caused by the nymphs' sucking of the juice from the tender young cranberry shoots, which often results in the death of the upright.

The insect overwinters as an egg inserted into the bark of the cranberry vine, where it is capable of surviving the winter flood even on late-held bogs. The eggs hatch in early June, producing the nymphs that live singly in white masses of spittle which they form around themselves on the cranberry stem. By mid-July the nymphs are fully grown and crawl out of the protective spittle, dry off, and transform to the adult form within three days. The glossy adults are powerful jumpers and are easily disturbed by a person walking through the bog. The female inserts a single egg under the bark of the stem and the cycle is complete. There is only one generation produced in a year.

The nymphs, protected by their bubble of spittle, are remarkably free from attack by parasites and predators. They can be controlled very effectively, however, by a 24-hour June reflow just before bloom. This reflow treatment usually clears a bog of the insect for two to three years.

Insects That Attack the Roots

Grubs

Franklin lists grub infestation among the most serious of all the insect depredations. The grubs (larval stage) of five species of beetles are particularly debilitating to the fine root systems of cranberry plants. When infestations are severe, the damage to the root system may be so great as to enable one to roll up the vines as one would roll up a carpet. Only the adult beetles of the cranberry rootworm and the striped Colaspis are known to feed on the foliage of the cranberry plant. Franklin (1950, 40) has made the following key to aid in the identification of the grub stage of these beetles:

```
Tips of antennae nearly reaching tips of
jaws ...................................................... 1
Tips of antennae far short of tips of jaws ........................ 2
1. Hind part of abdomen appearing dark
   because of its contents ...................... cranberry white grub
   Hind part of abdomen not appearing
   dark .......................................... grape Anomala
2. Mature grubs much over a third of an
   inch long; front of head thickly pitted ............ cranberry root grub
   Grubs never much over a third of an inch
   long; front of head sparsely pitted ............................. 3
3. Tip of abdomen bifid (divided into two
   equal lobes) ..................................... striped Colaspis
   Tip of abdomen not bifid ..................... cranberry rootworm
```

Another helpful method of distinguishing amongst these insects is based upon the characteristics of their pupae, which are all formed in the soil. Franklin has constructed the following useful key based on these pupal characteristics:

```
Found in June ...................................................... 1
Found in August ........................... cranberry white grub
1. Never moving the abdomen ..................... cranberry root grub
   Waggling the abdomen freely ................................... 2
```

2. Over a quarter of inch long . . . . grape Anomala
   Not over a quarter of an inch long . . . . cranberry rootworm
   and striped Colaspis

Cranberry White Grub (Phyllophaga anxia Lec.). This grub may be found on young as well as old bogs; in fact, it can be a particular nuisance in new plantings of old cranberry bogs. Although it has an extensive range throughout Canada and the United States, it has only been reported to be a problem in Massachusetts. This rather large grub is capable of causing more individual damage than any of the other root grubs that attack cranberries.

The insect appears to have a three-year life cycle. The adult beetle as well as the immature larva is capable of overwintering under the winter flood. When mature, the grub pupates in late July and August in the soil. The beetles emerge in September and overwinter in the soil. The beetles emerge again in late May and June to lay their round, pearly white eggs, which hatch before mid-July. Grubs of different sizes can be found in the soil because the broods of different years overlap.

Control of cranberry white grub had been fairly complete with dieldrin applications. Summer flooding is the only effective control procedure that can be practiced today.

Grape Anomala (Anomala lucicola Fab.). The grub of this beetle has only been reported in Massachusetts, where it is seldom found in cranberry bogs less than 30 years old. The grubs may attack the roots of grasses and other plants as well as the cranberry. Although the beetles do not attack cranberry foliage, they are known to completely defoliate grape vines.

The grape *Anomala* has a one-year life cycle and is, therefore, capable of building up populations more rapidly after treatment than the cranberry root grub. The grubs overwinter in the soil under the winter flood. On early-drawn bogs they pupate by the end of May. The beetles emerge to lay their eggs in June, and the new larvae hatch in early July. The larva has the peculiar habit of straightening its abdomen and then bringing it up against the underside of its body rapidly and repeatedly. The pupa of this species also tends to waggle its abdomen freely.

Summer flooding is also an effective control measure for this pest. Since grape vines are a significant alternate feeding host for this insect, it would behove growers to eliminate wild grapes within the vicinity of their cranberry bogs.

Cranberry Root Grub (Lichnanthe vulpina Hentz). Next to the cranberry fruitworm, the cranberry root grub is probably the most important economic insect pest in the Northeast. Like the other beetle grubs, it is apparently only a problem on bogs that receive a winter flood, which would suggest that the insect is unable to survive the cold without the protection of the flood. It is rarely a problem until the bogs are 20 to 25 years old, and is a particular problem to Massachusetts cranberry bogs. When infestations are severe, as many as 20 grubs per square foot can be unearthed.

The grub overwinters in the soil under the winter flood. In fact, it is capable of surviving as a grub in the soil for years, so a given infestation may actually consist of grubs hatched in different years. The grubs move horizontally in the soil in response to the moisture in the soil. As the soil dries out, the grubs may migrate down into the profile—even out of the root zone. When fully grown, the grub will pupate in the soil. The beetles emerge in late June to lay their small white eggs singly throughout the soil at a depth of about 3 inches. The eggs hatch in July and early August. Grubs of all sizes from ¼ to 1 inch long can be found feeding on cranberry roots, reflecting the overlapping broods of different years.

During the years that chlorinated hydrocarbons such as dieldrin were applied to cranberry bogs, this pest (along with the other root-attacking grubs) was virtually eliminated. In 1975 the federal government banned the use of chlorinated hydrocarbons on all agricultural crops and, with it, the only known control for root grubs on cranberry bogs. Residues of dieldrin in the soil have undoubtedly kept infestations down, but in recent years new outbreaks have been reported in Massachusetts. Severe infestations can be curtailed by early drawing of the winter flood, followed by a reflooding of the thoroughly dried bog from the end of May until mid-July. This kills about 90 percent of the grubs but, of course, also sacrifices the crop for the year. The treatment would probably have to be repeated in 5 to 10 years.

Striped Colaspis (Colaspis costipennis Crotch). Beetles of this species have been found feeding on the foliage of azalea, wild aster, blueberry, cranberry, and grape from New England to Mississippi. Whereas the beetles feed on cranberry shoots, buds, and flowers, the grubs devour the fine roots of the plant.

The nearly mature grub overwinters under the winter flood and completes its development in early spring after the winter flood is drawn. The grub pupates in the soil by mid-June. The beetles emerge soon thereafter and feed on cranberry foliage for about a month. After mating, the beetles lay their eggs in the soil. There is only one generation per year. The adult beetles can be controlled with postbloom applications of insecticides when they are feeding on the cranberry foliage.

Cranberry Rootworm (Rhabdopterus picipes Oliv.). This insect can be found distributed along the coastal lowland from New England to Mississippi. It is a troublesome pest in New Jersey blueberry plantings and has also been reported to be a problem in New Jersey cranberry bogs. The beetle of this species is known to attack cranberry foliage, the damage can be severe at times. The grubs feed on the runners in contact with the soil as well as the fine roots of the plant and the bark of older roots.

The nearly mature grub overwinters deep in the bog soil under the winter flood. The grubs pupate near the surface of the soil in June, and the beetles emerge during July to lay their eggs. The eggs hatch in about a week, and the young larvae continue to feed until October. The grubs sometimes do not mature in one growing season, in which case they would spend two winters in the ground.

Since the beetles do feed on cranberry foliage, they are vulnerable to insecticide applications. Summer applications of diazinon or azinophos-methyl for fireworm control would probably control the beetle stage of this insect.

Nematodes

Occurrence

The earliest report of the association of nematodes with the cranberry was made by Cobb (1913) when he identified *Atylenchus decalineatus* in soil samples taken from a New Jersey bog. Later, Chitwood and Tarjan (1957) also reported the presence of this same stylet-bearing nematode in New Jersey cranberry soils. (So far as is known, all plant-parasitic nematodes possess stylets through which they feed, whereas most nonparasitic nematodes do not have stylets.) More recently, the widespread occurrence of parasitic nematodes in cranberry bogs has been reported in Massachusetts, New Jersey, and Wisconsin (Kisiel et al. 1971; Paracer et al. 1966; Reed and Jenkins 1963; Zuckerman, Reed, and Jenkins 1964.

In a Massachusetts survey (Zuckerman and Coughlin 1960), *Hemicycliophora* sp., the sheath nematodes, were the principal parasitic nematodes found in cranberry bogs (table 10.1). Most often, they were found in large numbers ranging from 19 to 83 percent of the nematodes obtained from 200-gram samples of soil. Although *Tylenchus* sp. were also found widespread throughout Massachusetts bogs, they were never the principal parasitic form. *Trichodorus* sp., the stubby-root nematodes, were found in large numbers and were found in 42 percent of the bogs sampled. *Tylenchorhynchus* sp., the stylet nematodes, were found in 16 percent of the bogs but made up the principal form only occasionally. Other stylet-bearing genera observed quite commonly were *Aphelenchoides, Dorylaimus, Helicotylenchus, Tetylenchus,* and *Tylencholaimus.* Of these, only *Tetylenchus* were found in large numbers. This Massachusetts survey demonstrated that these nematodes—proven plant pathogens in other crops—can be commonly found in cranberry bogs.

The most common parasitic nematodes found in New Jersey bogs were

TABLE 10.1. PERCENT OCCURRENCE OF PARASITIC NEMATODES IN CRANBERRY BOGS

NEMATODE	MASSACHUSETTS $N=160$ BOGS	NEW JERSEY $N=49$ BOGS	WISCONSIN $N=48$ BOGS
Aphelenchoides sp.	19	—	—
Atylenchus decalineatus	4	80	—
Criconemoides sp.	—	12	—
Criconemoides xenoplax	—	45	—
Dorylaimus sp.	63	—	—
Helicotylenchus sp.	18	82	19
Hemicycliophora sp.	73	45	19
Tetylenchus sp.	22	—	—
Tetylenchus joctus	—	4	—
Trichodorus sp.	42	—	4
Trichodorus christiei	3	24	—
Tylencholaimus sp.	22	—	—
Tylenchorhynchus sp.	16	—	—
Tylenchus sp.	73	37	81

SOURCES: Massachusetts data from Zuckerman and Coughlin 1960; New Jersey data from Bird 1963b; Wisconsin data from Boone and Barker 1966.

Helicotylenchus sp., the spiral nematodes (Bird 1963b). Also found in this New Jersey survey in order of their frequency of occurrence were *Atylenchus decalineatus*, *Hemicycliophora* sp., *Criconemoides* sp., and *Trichodorus* sp. Nematode populations in this survey ranged from 68 to 7222 nematodes per 250 cc of soil. These results indicate that stylet-bearing nematodes were found to be numerous and widespread in New Jersey cranberry bogs.

A Wisconsin survey by Boone and Barker (1966) indicated that the most common parasitic nematode genera found were *Tylenchus, Hemicycliophora, Helicotylenchus,* and *Trichodorus*. The concentration of these nematodes ranged from 1 to 200 per quart of soil, a relatively small number in terms of the concentration generally considered necessary to cause noticeable plant injury. Harmful nematodes in Wisconsin cranberry bogs, therefore, were much less prevalent than in Massachusetts and New Jersey. *Trichodorus christiei,* considered by Massachusetts and New Jersey researchers to be the most important parasitic nematode with respect to the cranberry, was not found in Wisconsin. Barker and Boone (1966), however, did recover *T. californicus* in low numbers from three bogs in which the plants showed viruslike ringspots on the leaves and fruit, but there was no evidence that this nematode was involved as a vector in the ringspot disease.

Distribution Patterns

In a young Massachusetts cranberry bog, the first six inches of soil were found to contain nearly 92 percent of the total nematode population in the bog (Zuckerman, Khera, and Pierce, 1964). The largest concentration of *Hemicycliophora similis,* the most prevalent nematode present, occurred in the four-to-six-inch zone. Apparently moisture and organic matter content were the two most important causal factors in the vertical distribution of the nematodes because as the soils dried out, the nematodes tended to migrate from dryer to wetter soil. In older bogs the largest concentration of *H. similis* was found at the two-inch depth, reflecting the higher organic matter content that developed at this depth as the result of the accumulation of organic debris throughout the years. Generally, when the organic matter content was less than 1 percent, the numbers of *H. similis* were smaller.

In addition to the vertical distribution patterns, there was a very noticeable horizontal fluctuation in nematode populations when soils were sampled at the two-inch depth at six-inch intervals across horizontal strata of uniformly low organic matter content. This horizontal variation in nematode population was characteristic of young and old bogs alike and was as great as 500 percent in some cases. Such variation in nematode populations is actually quite common in other crops as well.

Seasonal fluctuations in nematode density were observed by Zuckerman and his coworkers in 1962 (Zuckerman, Khera, and Pierce 1964). Nematode populations were low in the winter, built up throughout the spring, and peaked in early summer and again in November with an intervening decline presumably due to hot and dry weather conditions. The continuously changing cranberry bog environment apparently exacts its toll on these animals.

Parasitism

In order to determine whether the nematodes observed in cranberry bogs actually fed on cranberry roots, Bird and Jenkins (1964) inoculated cranberry roots with known concentrations of nematodes and determined whether the nematodes increased in quantity on the host tissue. The researchers concluded that 14 of the 16 different nematode species tested in their controlled inoculations must be parasitic to cranberry because after a given period of time they increased in population size.

The actual feeding of two species of nematodes, *Criconemoides curvatum* and *C. xenoplax*, was observed through special glass-sided boxes. The nematodes were observed feeding directly behind the root tip. Root tips that were being fed upon often turned brown and ceased growing. Wherever the nematodes fed, a brown frasslike material was observed.

Zuckerman (1960) observed that the feeding zone of nematodes often extended into the region of cell differentiation and occasionally as far back as 2 mm from the root tip. In studying the parasitism of *Tetylenchus joctus*, Zuckerman observed that feeding was generally confined to the epidermal cells. The nematodes fed on single cells for a period of 30 seconds to seven minutes by inserting their stylet about one-fourth its length into the cell and ingesting its cytoplasm, causing the cell to collapse. During the feeding the stylet did not move, but when feeding ceased, the nematode moved its stylet back and forth two or three times in a short probing motion prior to moving to another cell.

In subsequent studies Zuckerman (1961a) observed specimens of *Hemicycliophora similis* with their stylets imbedded to a depth of 55 microns reaching into the vascular cylinder of the plant root. This feeding was in contrast to the feeding habit of *Trichodorus christiei* and *Tylenchorhynchus clayatoni*, which were observed feeding on epidermal cells only. Zuckerman noted that as the result of the feeding of *Hemicycliophora similis*, the cells that were contiguous to the point of penetration of the stylet appeared to have stopped elongating. Normal growth continued on the side of the root opposite stylet penetration, causing a curvature of the root. Also characteristic of *H. similis* feeding was the formation of galls on the root of the cranberry plant. Some consequences of the feeding of *Trichodorus christiei* were the abortion of lateral roots, abnormal root proliferation, swollen tips, and a short-lived period of growth of lateral adventitious roots.

Pathogenicity

The pathogenicity of *Trichodorus christiei, Hemicycliophora similis, Pratylenchus penetrans,* and *Criconemoides curvatum* was established in cranberry cuttings by inoculating plants with these nematodes and observing the effects on plant growth (Bird 1963a). After 90 days cranberry plants showed a marked retardation in runner growth and fresh weight of both roots and runners. *Trichodorus christiei* was observed to cause the most severe symptoms on cranberry.

Independent work in Massachusetts (Zuckerman 1961a) showed that seedlings subjected to *Hemicycliophora similis* and *Trichodorus christiei* feedings were smaller than seedlings grown in a nematode-free environment. *T. christiei*-infected cuttings were also observed to produce smaller root systems than noninfected cuttings. The evidence, therefore, strongly supports the viewpoint that in cranberry bogs with high populations of such nematodes as *T. christiei* and *H. similis* some reduction in plant vigor and subsequent yield may be expected.

Control

Prophylaxis and chemical eradication are the two methods of nematode control generally employed. Some nematodes burrow within plant roots and will consequently be transmitted in transplant stock. The spread of nematodes to new bogs can be greatly curtailed by selecting only vigorous and healthy vines that are free from trash and soil, which might be harboring potentially damaging species.

Effective chemical control is obtained when the nematode population is materially depressed for a period of several months. Zuckerman (1964) was able to achieve this degree of control with the nematicide Zinophos (0,0-diethyl, 0-2 pyrazinyl phosphorothioate). Thirty-two pounds of granular Zinophos per acre reduced the nematode population for 176 days without adversely affecting crop yield. In New Jersey, Bird and Jenkins (1963) also achieved some degree of nematode control on established cranberry bogs with Zinophos, as well as with 1,2-dibromo-3-chloropropane (DBCP). A 67.2-percent-by-volume formulation of DBCP gave 70 to 88 percent control after 100 days when applied to bogs at the rate of three, four, and six gallons per acre (30–60 l per h). A 10 percent granular formulation of Zinophos gave 80 to 93 percent nematode control after 100 days when applied to bogs at the rate of 80, 160, and 320 pounds per acre (92–368 kg/ha). After 137 days all treated plots had a higher percentage of uprights and fruit buds than the nontreated controls. Flooding of the bog and a low concentration of oxygen in the floodwater would also tend to militate against nematodes and might explain much of the fluctuation in nematode population that is often observed in cranberry soils (Bird and Jenkins 1965).

Control Recommendations

General Considerations

Effective insect control is predicated on the correct identification of the insect and a knowledge of its life cycle, which will enable the most judicious timing of the treatment. The cranberry grower should have a thorough knowledge of the local insects economic importance and constantly monitor their presence.

Not only must the grower be able to recognize the different stages of development of each species but he or she must also be able to recognize the signs of their presence, such as webbing or accumulation of frass. Two indispensable tools for monitoring insect populations are the insect sweep net and the sex pheromone trap. It is important to begin monitoring insect populations early in the growing season. As the temperatures begin to increase, daily monitoring may become necessary to insure most efficient treatment. The indiscriminate use of insecticides is not only a waste of money but may also lead to more rapid development of resistance by the insect to the pesticide and unnecessary exposure of the applicator to these hazardous chemicals.

Another reason for early and frequent monitoring of the insect population is to be able to plan insecticide applications to avoid the cranberry bloom period. Most insecticides used in cranberry pest control are extremely toxic to bees. Only the relatively nontoxic methoxychlor may be used around bees

TABLE 10.2. A COMPOSITE SPRAY SCHEDULE FOR CRANBERRY INSECTS FOUND IN THE DIFFERENT GROWING REGIONS

INSECT	PESTICIDE FORMULATION	RATE a.i./a.*	DAYS TO HARVEST AND OTHER REMARKS
	Dormant Application		
Root Weevils	Flood Bog for 30 Days		Larvae Drown
	Delayed Dormant Application (Some new growth present)		
Cranberry weevil	Chlorpyrifos	1.5 lb	60 days
Fireworms	Carbaryl	3.0 lb	1 day
	(or) Parathion	0.75–1.0 lb	Check label
	(or) Diazinon	2.0 lb	7 days
	(or) Azinphos-methyl	1.0 lb	21 days
	(or) Malathion	2.5 lb	3 days
	(or) Chlorpyrifos	1.5 lb	60 days
	(or) Acephate	1.0 lb	90 days
Cranberry	Parathion	0.75–1.0 lb	Check label
tipworm	(or) Azinphos-methyl	1.0 lb	21 days
Spanworms	Chlorpyrifos	1.5 lb	60 days
	(or) Acephate	1.0 lb	90 days

(continued)

TABLE 10.2. (*Continued*)

INSECT	PESTICIDE FORMULATION	RATE a.i./a.*	DAYS TO HARVEST AND OTHER REMARKS
	Prebloom Application		
Cutworms	Diazinon	2.0 lb	7 days
	(or) Parathion	0.75–1.0 lb	Check label
	(or) Carbaryl	3.0 lb	1 day
	(or) Chlorpyrifos	1.5 lb	60 days
Cranberry weevil	Same as above		
Fireworms	Same as above		
Spanworms	Same as above		
Cranberry girdler	Diazinon (granular)	2.9 lb	Must irrigate 7 days
Root weevils	Carbofuran	2.0 lb	60 days Pacific Coast only
	Postbloom Application		
Second generation			
Fireworm and tipworm	Same as above		
Cranberry fruitworm	Parathion	1.0 lb	Check label†
	(or) Diazinon	3.0 lb	7 days
	(or) Carbaryl	3.0 lb	1 day
	(or) Chlorpyrifos	1.5 lb	60 days
	(or) Azinphos-methyl	0.5–1.0 lb	21 days
Cranberry girdler	Diazinon (granular)	2.9 lb	Must irrigate 7 days
	(or) Parathion	0.75 lb	Check label

SOURCES: Mahr et al. 1987; New Jersey Agr. Exp. Sta. 1987; Shawa et al. 1984.
*a.i/a = Active ingredient per acre.
†Higher rates of parathion and diazinon as well as multiple applications at 7-to-10-day intervals may be needed.

with a minimum amount of injury. In general, however, it is best to avoid all insecticide applications during the pollination period.

It is also imperative that all federal, state, and local laws be obeyed to insure the safe use of the pesticide. This means that all pesticides must be used strictly in accordance with label directions and only for those crops and pests specified in the labelling material.

A.

B.

PLATE 10.1. APPLYING PESTICIDES BY (*A*) POWER SPRAYER FROM THE DAM AND (*B*) BY HELICOPTER (Courtesy Massachusetts Cranberry Experiment Station)

Spray Schedules

Spray schedules evolve constantly in terms of chemicals available for use and their specific timing. As insects develop resistance to specific insecticides, the efficacy of that compound decreases. As research gives greater insight into the life cycle of a particular insect, the best timing of the treatment may change. Nonetheless, a review of the current spray schedules in use in the major cranberry-growing regions is presented to elucidate the treatments currently used to control the insects of economic importance to the cranberry grower (table 10.2).

Method of Application

Insecticides are generally applied in dilute formulations with power sprayers from the dam (plate 10.1). Both fixed-wing airplanes and helicopters are also frequently used when large areas need to be sprayed. Concentrated formulations are used when insecticides are applied by air, thus reducing the volume of spray material that needs to be applied. Recently, cranberry growers that have solid-set irrigation systems in place have been experimenting with the application of pesticides through the irrigation system.

ELEVEN

Harvesting and Handling

General Aspects

Importance

The ultimate determination of the profitability of a cranberry crop is often dependent on what happens in the final phases of cranberry growing–the harvesting and handling of the fruit. Assuming the crop has withstood the vicissitudes of weather, disease, and insect depredation, there are still a multitude of factors that can reduce the final marketable yield and, consequently, profit. The ultimate objective is to harvest 100 percent of a crop of highest quality fruit, which translated to maximum shelf life in the days when fresh fruit sales were paramount and today often means highly colored fruit for optimum processing quality. An excellent treatment of the subject can be found in the two *USDA Farmers' Bulletins* 1402 and 1882 (Franklin et al. 1924; Bain et al. 1942). The bulletins cover the period when cranberries were hand-picked or hand scooped—before the era of the mechanical harvester and water picking that dominates the cranberry harvest today—but they, nonetheless, include principles that are still valid.

Harvest losses are manifested as (1) unharvested fruit, either because of fruit dropped during picking or because of plantings that remained unpicked due to the unavailability of labor; (2) poorly colored fruit that results when berries are not allowed to fully ripen; (3) bruised fruit caused by the harvest or postharvest handling equipment or by freezing; (4) decayed fruit that develops either in the field or in storage; and finally (5) weight loss that occurs as the result of respiration and moisture loss during the postharvest period. These are the problems that the founders of the cranberry industry had to deal with during the harvest operation, and they are still the problems that the modern cranberry grower must address, albeit the relative significance of specific problems may have changed as today's modern methods of harvest evolved.

Harvest Season

Cranberry harvest begins in early September and is generally complete by November in all the growing regions. The exact timing of the harvest is dependent on the (1) maturity of the berry, which is in part cultivar dependent, yet also related to the size of the crop and the weather conditions experienced during the growing season, and (2) the prevailing weather conditions during the harvest season. The potential for freezing weather is a serious consideration in the determination of the length of the harvest season in the East and in Wisconsin. Not only is it necessary to protect the fruit from frost damage, but as the weather becomes progressively colder, the physical conditions that must be endured by the pickers, particularly those involved in water harvesting, become increasingly difficult. On average, the first frosts can be expected in Massachusetts and Wisconsin by mid-September but not until mid-October in New Jersey. On the Pacific Coast the first frost sometimes does not occur until mid-December, well after the cranberry harvest has been completed.

The predominant cultivar grown on the East Coast is the Early Black, which is an early-maturing cultivar that can usually be picked there early in September. Picking too early, however, can result in too many green fruit being harvested. This is particularly a problem when there is a heavy crop load and there are many berries buried in the vines (where they color slowly because of insufficient light) and when unusually warm growing conditions have prolonged the growing season. On the other hand, the Early Black cultivar will not keep well in storage if it is picked in an overripe condition. For maximum shelf life and quality, Early Black probably should be harvested by the end of September.

The other main cultivar in the East is the Howes, which is one of the latest cultivars to ripen. The Howes cultivar, however, must be harvested by the end of October to insure good shelf life for fresh market (Crooks 1988). It has the propensity for coloring while in storage, which means it can be picked slightly underripe. The McFarlin is a late-ripening cultivar important to the Wisconsin and Pacific Coast industries. Unlike the Howes cultivar, McFarlin must be fully colored before it is picked because it fails to color much in storage. An important midseason cultivar in Wisconsin is the Searles. This cultivar is also capable of coloring in storage, abut it keeps better if allowed to mature fully on the vine.

Color Development

The rapid gains made in the marketing of cranberry juice products in recent years have placed an even greater significance on the red color development of the cranberry as manifested in its anthocyanin content. More than ever, it is important to attempt to harvest the fruit at its optimum stage of color development. The minimum anthocyanin content for cranberry cocktail quality is set at 67 mg of anthocyanin per 100 grams of fresh fruit. The achievement of this level of red pigment content by its normal picking date can be difficult in an early cultivar such as Early Black because of the profound effects that sunlight and temperature have on anthocyanin development (Devlin et al. 1968). In most cases, the critical pigment level was only attained when harvest was delayed at least 10 days after the grower had deemed the crop mature and ready for picking. This placed the picking date for the required color level well into October in Massachusetts. In addition, the early-harvested fruit colored slowly in storage, often requiring at least 15 days of storage to reach cocktail quality. Delaying harvest by 10 days resulted in fruit that colored much more rapidly in storage and to a greater degree than the early-harvested fruit. Fruit that fails to meet the cocktail quality standard must be stored and eventually blended with more highly colored fruit to meet the required color content. Such undercolored fruit naturally brings a lower economic return to the grower.

The anthocyanin content of the cranberry has become so important that it has led to many attempts to enhance its level in the cranberry by chemical means, particularly in early-harvested fruit. One of the most effective chemicals to achieve such an acceleration and enhancement of anthocyanin in early-harvested cranberries was the insecticide malathion (Devlin et al. 1969; G. W. Eaton et al. 1969; Eck 1968, 1969, 1972a; Shawa and Ingalsbe 1968). Malathion 80% EC at the rate of 2½ pounds of active ingredient per acre applied in 200 to 300 gallons of water (3 kg/ha/2,000–3,000 l) two weeks before harvest was recommended. The large volume of spray was necessary in order to wet fruit located deep within the vines; apparently the material had to come in contact with the fruit in order to promote anthocyanin formation. It seemed to work on all the major cranberry cultivars being grown in the different cranberry-growing regions. Unfortunately, the use of malathion as a color enhancement treatment was never labelled and therefore may not be used for this purpose, although it is still registered for use as an insecticide for cranberries.

A chemical that has been labelled for color enhancement of cranberry is ethephon (2-chloroethyl phosphoric acid), a compound that breaks down in the cranberry plant to release ethylene (Bramlage et al. 1972; Devlin and Demoranville 1970, 1978a; Eck 1972b; Rigby et al. 1972; Shawa 1979a). Best results were obtained when the chemical was applied just as the berries began to turn red and when applied as a drench in 300 gallons of water to the acre (3,000 l/ha). (Consult current label for specific recommendation.) Other materials that have resulted in color enhancement have included the herbicide dichlobenil, applied either in the fall or spring (Devlin and Demoranville 1968) and the fungicide ferbam (Francis and Zuckerman 1962; Moore 1962). On the other hand, excessive nitrogen fertilizer may retard anthocyanin formation in the cranberry (Francis and Atwood 1961).

Harvest Methods

Hand Picking

For the first 100 years or more of the cranberry industry, cranberries were picked by hand (plate 11.1). Not until the end of World War I were hand scoops much in evidence. In 1922 J. D. Holman spoke of the lost art of handpicking cranberries in his address to the American Cranberry Growers' Association (Holman 1922). He recalled how, in his youth, the local population (or "natives" as they were called) would come as entire families to gather the cranberry crop, often earning enough money to clothe the whole family for the winter. With the development of the resort industry on the New Jersey coast toward the end of the nineteenth century, the natives forsook the cranberry bogs for more lucrative employment at the resorts. The growers eventually resorted to importing labor from surrounding cities. In New Jersey they came

PLATE 11.1. HANDPICKING ON CAPE COD CA. 1900 (Courtesy Massachusetts Cranberry Experiment Station)

from the Italian colonies in Philadelphia, and in Massachusetts the Portuguese from New Bedford were the dominant source of the new labor (Briggs 1967). Entire Italian families would migrate from the city to the bogs, where they would be housed right on the premises. Many of the old barracklike facilities may still be seen on New Jersey bogs—complete with the grape arbors that the Italians were fond of constructing (cranberry harvest coincided with grape harvest and wine making).

Hand harvesting required an almost inexhaustible supply of cheap labor. Two factors were to spell the end to handpicking cranberries, not to say that there were not other problems as well. Prior to the Great War, pickers averaged 25 cents per hour, but after the war these costs had more than doubled. Secondly, the ever-increasing amount of acreage in production made it increasingly difficult to find enough pickers. In this case, "necessity became the mother of invention," and soon cranberry growers were designing and building harvest aids, beginning with the cranberry scoop and continuing today with the development of sophisticated dry and wet mechanical pickers. By 1940 handpicking had all but disappeared in Massachusetts, and by the end of World War II, less than 25 percent of the crop in New Jersey and on the Pacific Coast was being picked by hand. Today, handpicking is virtually nonexistent. Even new bogs are water harvested when they are first picked three years after they are planted.

Scooping

The first mechanical harvest aids in the form of hand-held scoops began to appear on the scene at the turn of the century. The Rev. E. H. Durell exalted their coming as the salvation of the cranberry industry in his 1904 presidential address to the American Cranberry Growers' Association (Durell 1904). The failing labor supply was already making itself felt as the industrial revolution competed for able hands. The basic design of the scoop consisted of a series of wooden or metal tines that were set 1 cm apart in a wooden catch frame (plate 11.2). Three types were developed: (1) a small scoop called a *snap*, which had a hinged flap that aided in the removal of the berries from young, loosely rooted vines; (2) the *Eastern scoop*, which was used from the kneeling position, the teeth being pushed forward into the vines and berries stripped from them by rocking the scoop backward on its rounded bottom; and (3) the *Wisconsin scoop* or *rake*, which had two rigid bail handles attached to it that enabled it to be used from the standing position, being pulled from right to left in a long stroke with the teeth dipping into the vines at a slightly forward angle (plate 11.3). The Eastern scoop was used entirely in a dry bog situation, whereas the Wisconsin scoop was used on dry bogs or on the flood (so-called water raking). With both scoops, the vines were scooped in the same

PLATE 11.2. THE HAND SCOOP (Courtesy Massachusetts Cranberry Experiment Station)

direction year after year to help train the vines so as to minimize tangling. The typical scooping crew for 15 acres of cranberries consisted of a work supervisor, 15 scoopers, and 2 helpers who handled the picking boxes and transferred the berries to the roadway with modified wheelbarrows (plates 11.4 and 11.5).

The advantage of scooping cranberries over handpicking was immediate and obvious in the harvest cost savings realized. Handpickers, picking into six-quart containers, were able to pick 2 to 10 bushels of cranberries per day (depending on the crop) for which they received 20 cents per bushel. Scoopers were able to pick 10 times this amount in a day at a rate of 50 cents an hour, averaging $3 to $5 per day. By the beginning of World War II, harvesting costs were averaging 70 cents per barrel (100 quarts) for scooped berries compared to $2.50 for handpicked berries. Immediately after World War II, New Jersey scoopers were averaging $1.10 per bushel, or $3.30 per barrel (Boster 1946). Once given a scoop, pickers were not willing to go back to

PLATE 11.3. THE WISCONSIN SCOOP (Courtesy University of Wisconsin Extension Service)

PLATE 11.4. A SCOOPING GANG (Courtesy Massachusetts Cranberry Experiment Station)

PLATE 11.5. A MODIFIED WHEELBARROW USED TO CARRY QUAR-
TER-BARREL BOXES FROM THE BOG (Courtesy Massachusetts Cranberry Experiment Station)

handpicking because that work was more arduous and less rewarding (Durell
1914). Durell maintained that a major advantage of scooping was the reduction in the number of people, including children, who trampled over the bog
during hand harvesting, thus greatly lessening berry bruising. He stressed
the importance of properly pruning vines in order to reduce tangling and subsequent vine damage. Of great importance was the fact that the harvest could

begin later, insuring optimum maturity, and end sooner, which meant less loss to frost and a complete harvest.

Scooping, however, did not come without its problems. Paramount among them were the berry loss due to dropped fruit and the injury to the cranberry vine as the result of tearing plants up by their roots. In New Jersey, Doehlert (1936, 1937a, 1937b, 1939, 1941) carried out a long-term comparison of hand picking to scooping which addressed these problems. Doehlert found that handpickers dropped on average 10 percent of the crop, whereas scoopers missed up to twice as much fruit. Unfortunately, it was not small and rotted fruit that were missed by the scoopers but rather good-sized, sound berries. When excessive vine growth was present, fruit dropped by the scoopers increased to as high as 30 percent. In addition, Doehlert observed that over four years of the six-year experiment there was a 15 percent reduction in the average annual yield from the scooped plots compared to the handpicked plots, which may have resulted from loss in productivity because of vine injury. Scooping may also predispose the berry to greater rot in storage. In an experiment where scooped plots were compared to plots left undisturbed, Goheen (1953) found that after two months of storage a significant increase in fruit rot occurred in the scooped berries compared to fruit from plots left undisturbed the year before.

The problems of berry drop and vine injury associated with scooping were of major concern to cranberry growers. Procedures were developed that attempted to reduce these losses. Once the canning industry for cranberry products developed during the 1930s, it became profitable to retrieve the dropped berries by flooding the bogs and dislodging the trapped fruit by agitating the vines with flat-bottomed, air-powered boats. Doehlert (1950) maintained that these so-called floatboats could retrieve up to 33 percent of the dropped fruit. When properly dried and cleaned, the fruit was perfectly acceptable for processing.

This left the problem of vine injury. Most cranberry researchers and growers maintained that these losses could be contained by proper bog management and picker supervision. Franklin (1944) and Holman (1922) stressed the importance of good anchorage of the cranberry plant and the significance of sanding in obtaining this anchorage. Closer planting, according to Franklin, also encouraged deeper rooting and better anchorage. Beckwith (1944) advocated that bog soils should be kept moist during harvest so that vines and roots do not become brittle and break during the scooping operation. Holman expanded on Durell's (1914) observation on controlling vine growth by pruning to reduce scooping injury. He advocated pruning off as much as three to four feet of the new vine growth. He maintained that pruning forces uprights to develop 2 inches apart on the shortened vine rather than the normal 8 to 10 inches and that the number of producing uprights is, consequently, not reduced. The much shortened vines are easier to scoop and are less apt to smother existing vines and uprights.

Holman's analysis appears to be supported by the results of Doehlert's long-term harvest experiment. Each year Doehlert had lightly pruned the scooped plots, and by the final (sixth) year of the experiment the scooped plots had outyielded the handpicked plots by 17 percent. Varney (1955) included a new powered picking machine (*Darlington Picker*) in his comparison of picking methods and observed that mechanically picked plots yielded more fruit than carefully scooped plots because of less damage to the vines.

Powered Machines for Dry Harvest

The next logical step in the mechanization of the cranberry harvest was to replace the scooper with a machine. The first attempts were made in the early 1920s as growers put their ideas and engineering skills together to produce powered prototypes that simulated the scooping process. The first commercial cranberry picking machine was marketed by W. B. Mathewson of Quincy Adams, Massachusetts (Mathewson 1925, 1926). The *Mathewson picking machine,* (plate 11.6) as would all its successors, used a method of detach-

PLATE 11.6. THE MATHEWSON PICKING MACHINE (Courtesy New Jersey Agricultural Experiment Station)

ment that consisted of mechanically stripping the berries from the vines. It consisted of 14 rows of curved tines mounted on a hollow cylinder. Each row of tines represented a scoop that covered a width of 30 inches and combed 2 inches of vine surface, so that a single revolution of the cylinder harvested the fruit from 15 square feet of bog area. The scoops were operated by a cam arrangement that enabled them to open before they entered the vines and to close and turn over after going a short distance. The turning of the scoop kept the berries at the tip of the teeth rather than accumulating at the base of teeth as they did in the hand scoop. The adjustable, revolving cylinder pulled the scoops out of the vines, the berries being subsequently dropped from the scoop at the top of the cylinder onto a moving belt that carried them to a box at the left of the machine. The large cumbersome machine resembled a huge round revolving comb with curved teeth and was subject to frequent breakdowns. The Mathewson picking machine was quite expensive at $2,800 in 1925, but it was capable of harvesting three to four acres a day. The machine was used by the industry for the next two decades until smaller and more easily handled machines were developed (Norton and Cargill 1979).

One of these smaller, lightweight machines was developed by the Stankavich brothers of Coos Bay, Oregon, in the late 1940s (Hillstrom 1947). The *Western Picker* employed a passive system of predetachment and collection of berries. The picking head of the machine consisted of a set of 24 tapered tines turned up slightly at the tip. The tines were spaced 1¼ cm apart at the tips and converged until there was contact between adjacent tines. The 45-cm-long tines were mounted on the machine so that they made contact with the bog surface at a 30° angle. As the machine was propelled forward, the tines skimmed along the ground under the vines, collecting the berries on top (fig. 11.1). The berries were detached as the vines were stripped out between the rear of the tines. The detached berries were then elevated into the picking container by flat rubber flights sliding up the solid back of the machine. The Western Picker was also capable of severing long vines, which meant that it served the dual purpose of pruner.

Another lightweight mechanical picker was developed by T. B. Darlington of Whitesbog, New Jersey (Darlington 1958). In the *Darlington Picker* there were six rows of tines, resembling six large combs, emanating from a comb bar and controlled by a cam that positioned each comb to collect a small segment of berries lying in the path of the machine (plates 11.7 and 11.8). There was motion between the machine and the collection-detachment combs, which was the major difference between the Darlington Picker and the rigid passive detachment system of the Western Picker. At the apex of the revolution of the comb bar, the tines of the comb were in a vertical position (fig. 11.2). The angle of the tines changed slightly as the comb completed three-fourths of its course around the cam and the tines entered the vines. As the

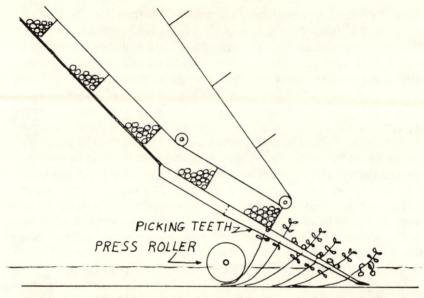

FIGURE 11.1. SCHEMATIC REPRESENTATION OF THE PICKING AC-
TION OF THE WESTERN PICKER. Teeth comb through
vines as machine moves to the right, stripping off berries,
which are then elevated to picking containers (Norton and Cargill 1979).

comb completed its revolution, the tines assumed a nearly horizontal position
pointing rearward toward a picking bar, at which point the berries were
stripped from the vines, which were held down firmly by the roller below the
picking bar.

Limitations of the Western and Darlington pickers included: (1) their relatively low harvesting capacity (one acre per day) due to the two-foot width of
their picking heads (wider widths resulted in decreased picking efficiency);
(2) the 20 to 30 percent field loss due to unharvested berries; and (3) the
bruising of the berries, which shortened their shelf life. University of Massachusetts agricultural engineer J. S. Norton addressed these limitations in
his design of an experimental harvester (Norton 1975). Norton's design was
based on the detachment method used in the Wisconsin wet rake (see section
on water picking), mainly that of retractable rows of curved teeth, because
this system seemed to be the least damaging to the berries. He replaced the
drum used in the Wisconsin rake with a belt mounted on two pulley systems.
The teeth were designed to retract through the belt as they passed over the
top pulley, much as they would into the drum of the Wisconsin water rake.
The retraction of the teeth served to release the berries to a transfer belt and
at the same time clear the teeth of all debris. By mounting a series of these

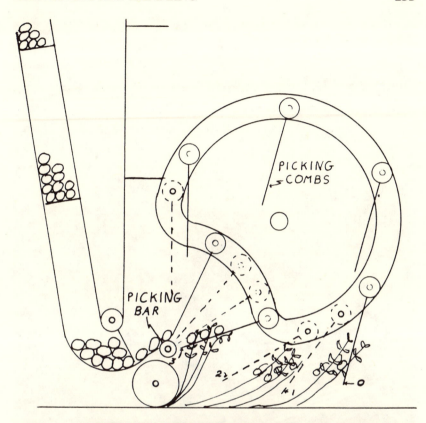

FIGURE 11.2. SCHEMATIC REPRESENTATION OF THE PICKING AC-
TION OF THE DARLINGTON PICKER. Picking combs enter
vines at position *0;* as machine moves to right, combs move to
left, smoothly assuming positions *1, 2,* and *3.* Upon assuming
position *3* the teeth pivot about the picking bar, stripping the
berries from the vines, which are held down firmly by the roller
below the picking bar (Norton and Cargill 1979).

12-inch belt-and-pulley systems in tandem, each with their own contour sensor, Norton hoped to increase the efficiency of the harvester. His initial prototypes did not appear to decrease the amount of bruising or the amount of
fruit left in the field when compared to the existing dry harvesters, although
the harvest capacity was increased fourfold. Norton was confident that modifications in design could greatly increase the efficiency of the picker and significantly improve the quality of the fruit. To date, the harvester remains an
experimental one.

Recent modifications of the fixed-head-type harvester have enabled an

PLATE 11.7. THE DARLINGTON PICKING MACHINE (Courtesy Massachusetts Cranberry Experiment Station)

increase in the width of the picking head without increasing fruit loss. This has made the *Furford Picker,* developed on the West Coast, more efficient than the shorter-width Western Picker. The Furford Picker also has pruning capabilities.

One other method of dry picking that must be mentioned because of its historical significance and because it was based on an entirely different principle was the *vacuum picker.* Initially developed on the West Coast, the suction force it generated was almost always insufficient to pull cranberries from their

PLATE 11.8. A BATTERY OF DARLINGTON PICKERS HARVESTING CRANBERRIES IN MASSACHUSETTS (Courtesy Massachusetts Cranberry Experiment Station)

pedicels. Only when the berries were mechanically detached were they sucked up (Harrison 1946). In addition, stones and debris vacuumed up with the berries were a serious drawback.

Throughout the 1940s and 1950s, the debate on the use of picking machines continued. Picking machines were faster and they were less damaging to the vines than scooping but more berries were left in the field. Trufant (1942) compared the costs and returns of different picking methods and showed that handpicking and hand scooping netted greater returns than machine picking when crops were heavy, but the reverse was true when crops were light. Another fact that might have tipped the debate in favor of hand scooping was the observation made by Zuckerman (1959) that machine-picked berries were twice as likely to break down in storage than were scooped berries. The ultimate factor to favor machine picking, however, was not so much economics as it was the unavailability of labor. By 1957 Cross estimated that 75 percent of the crop in Massachusetts was being harvested by the dry picking machines (Cross 1957). In the same article he spoke of the initial efforts in Massachusetts at water harvesting, drawing upon the successes of Wisconsin growers with this method decades earlier. Water harvesting was destined to become the single most important method of harvesting cranberries right up to the present.

Water Harvesting

This method of cranberry harvesting had its origins in Wisconsin (Franklin et al. 1924). Scooping or raking "on the flood" involved putting a shallow flood on the bog to lift the vines so that the berries could be easily raked as they floated near the surface. The Wisconsin scoop with its rigid bails was designed to be used from the standing position. The chief advantages of this method of harvest were the speed at which the berries were harvested, the elimination of harvest losses due to incomplete picking and dropped berries, and a reduction in vine injury.

The chief disadvantage of water raking became apparent almost immediately. Water-raked berries deteriorated much more rapidly in storage and had a shorter shelf life than dry-raked berries (Bergman 1919, 1922; Chaney 1940; Stevens and Bergman 1921). The deterioration appeared to have a pathological component manifested in increased fruit rot as well as a non-pathological component that appeared physiological in origins and was referred to as *smothering*. The submersion of the berries appeared to predispose the berry to fungal infection, and no amount of prophylactic treatment with fungicides appeared to protect against the fungal attack (Bain 1931, 1933b). Research was to reveal that key factors affecting both fungal infection and physiological breakdown were related to the environmental conditions and handling procedures used during the harvest operation. The conclusions arrived at were: (1) floodwaters should be cold, i.e., less than 55°F (13°C) (cold water contains more oxygen than warm water, and oxygen deficiency appears to be related to physiological breakdown); (2) berries should be removed from the water within three to four hours; (3) berries should be dried and cleaned as quickly as possible; and (4) only fully colored berries should be harvested because green berries appear to be more susceptible to injury. Bearing these limitations in mind, it becomes apparent why water harvesting had its origins in Wisconsin rather than on the East Coast. By September, the temperature of Wisconsin floodwater is often cold enough to use; Wisconsin bogs were originally constructed in small-acreage units (unlike the large bogs in the East, many of which exceed 20 acres); and the low humidity and drying winds of Wisconsin provided favorable conditions for the rapid drying of the fruit.

Despite the serious quality problem, Wisconsin growers were water harvesting more than half their acreage by the 1940s. Eastern growers were quick to adopt this new method of harvesting (C. F. Hall 1962). In the decades following World War II, the scoops gave way to picking machines. Both the passive fixed-head system of the dry picker and the nonpassive retracting-tine system of detachment (*Getsinger Retracto Tooth Picker*) were employed in the machines used to water harvest (plate 11.9). The Wisconsin drum rake with its retracting teeth (described earlier) was the model used by Norton in the design of his experimental dry harvester.

Another water harvester, developed in the early 1960s, beat the berries off the vines instead of stripping them off (plate 11.10). The new water harvester was referred to as a *water reel* or *beater*, which aptly describes its appearance and action (Norton and Cargill 1979). Still in use today, the lightweight machine consists of a small-horsepower engine that drives the large bicycle-like wheels and the berry detachment device, called a reel. The reel consists of several steel hoops, 60 to 75 cm in diameter, mounted about 50 cm apart on a common shaft with four or more steel rods, parallel to the shaft, attached at equal distances around the hoops. As the reel rotates with a peripheral speed of about 200 m per minute, the horizontal rods strike the berries or their stems, detaching the berries from the vines and permitting them to float to the surface. The reels have a width of 1 to 1½ m and can be mounted three abreast on larger, more heavily powered chassis.

The rapid increase in the use of the water reel to harvest cranberries coincided with the increased demand for berries for processing, particularly for the juice cocktail products being developed during this period. Since berry keeping quality was no longer paramount as it was for fresh fruit sales, this relatively harsh but efficient method of harvesting could be used. Growers were quick to design and build their own improved versions of the water reel for use on their own bogs (Carpenter 1982; *Cranberries* 1969). One particular problem that troubled Eastern growers was the large size and relative unevenness of their individual bogs. The amount of water required for an eight-inch (20-cm) flood on a level bog sometimes covered only half the large uneven Eastern bogs. This meant that the large individual bogs with their peripheral dams and crisscrossing ditches had to be redesigned. In New Jersey, bog sizes were reduced to four or five acres of perfectly level bogs with parallel dikes constructed at 200-feet (60-m) intervals (Mahn and O'Donnell 1966; O'Donnell 1968). These changes to small bogs with their intervening

A.

B.

PLATE 11.9. *A*, THE GETSINGER RETRACTO TOOTH PICKER; *B*, HARVESTING CRANBERRIES WITH THE GETSINGER PICKER (Courtesy University of Wisconsin Extension Service)

A.

B.

PLATE 11.10. *A*, THE WISCONSIN WATER REEL HARVESTER; *B*, HARVESTING WITH THE WATER REEL (Courtesy University of Wisconsin Extension Service)

dikes made it possible for a five-person crew to harvest, gather, clean, and dry the fruit from such a bog in a single day.

Handling

Dry-Harvested Fruit

Aprons and full skirts were perhaps amongst the first picking containers utilized by cranberry pickers. These eventually gave way to the six-quart measure and then to small measuring boxes of one-peck capacity into which the hand pickers picked directly. The picking containers were emptied into larger lug boxes of various dimensions equating to $\frac{1}{4}$-, $\frac{1}{3}$-, or $\frac{1}{2}$-barrel volumes. If the berries were to be stored in these same containers, the sides of these boxes would often be slotted so as to allow for ventilation. When berries were scooped or machine picked, they were often placed directly into these larger lug boxes. The filled boxes had to be carried from the bog directly over the vines to the nearest roadway. This was most often accomplished by open-sided wheelbarrows especially fitted with large pneumatic tires to minimize vine damage or by narrow-gauge track especially laid for the purpose (plate 11.11). From the bog they were transferred to the storage house by wagon or truck or, in some instances, by narrow-gauge track and car. Today the boxes are stacked on standard 40- by 48-inch pallets and moved by forklift truck and roller conveyor (Norton 1968a).

Careful handling was the byword during this early phase of berry handling as well as in the subsequent stages of milling, sorting, and packaging. It was recognized early (Shear et al. 1918) that bruising had a dramatic effect on the shelf life of the fruit even when injuries were not particularly noticeable. This was recently reemphasized by Massey and his coworkers (Massey et al. 1981) when they observed that visible defects often were not discernible in berries until several hours or even an entire day after berry impact. This means that berries that have passed inspection prior to packaging may break down within the consumer package. Most of this breakdown does not appear to be pathologically related but rather appears to involve a physiological breakdown of the fruit. Patterson and his coworkers (Patterson et al. 1967) have suggested that the berry bruising is related to an increase in polygalacturonase, an enzyme in the berry that contributes to its softening. More recently, Massey and others (1982) showed rough handling of berries resulted in a long-lasting stimulation of carbon dioxide evolution almost immediately after berry impact, a phenomenon that was not always associated with a visible bruise.

Although there are frequent opportunities to impact the berry during its handling in preparation for market, one of its most critical moments is the

PLATE 11.11. NARROW-GAUGE TRACK ESPECIALLY LAID IN THE BOG DURING THE HARVEST SEASON TO TRANSPORT PICKING BOXES (Courtesy Massachusetts Cranberry Experiment Station)

initial contact with the mechanical harvester. Modification of the picking machine to reduce berry bruising is one approach to reducing this loss. For example, Davis and Shawa (1983) were able to reduce berry bruising by the Furford Picker by modifying the elevator on the harvester. It was ascertained that the first paddle of the elevator was the major source of the injury, caused when the paddle pinched the berries between the paddle and the shaker bar. Moving the front elevator shaft forward and down resulted in a berry-paddle contact while the berries were moving, thus reducing the severity of berry impact and lessening the chance of pinching. Another approach toward reducing physiological breakdown in cranberries was suggested by Shawa's research (Shawa 1973). He reported that preharvest nutritional foliar sprays containing nitrogen, phosphorus, manganese, and zinc significantly reduced the amount of physiological breakdown of McFarlin berries in storage. He also observed that the growth regulator N[6]-benzyladenine significantly suppressed the respiratory rates of the harvested fruits.

Berries brought in from the field in their lug boxes are referred to as being "in chaff". If contained in slotted boxes and stored in well-ventilated areas, the berries may remain in this condition until ready for market preparation, although the separating, sorting, and packing operations usually begin simultaneously with the harvest (Shear et al. 1917). The first step in the preparation process is the separation of vines, leaves, and other field debris as well as rotted, small, and immature fruit. The sorting process was initially done by hand on wooden frames six to eight feet long and three to four feet wide (2 × 1 m) at one end and the width of a barrel top at the other end (plate 11.12). The screenlike bottom of the frames consisted of slats spaced about one-fourth inch apart. The process was known as *screening the berries,* a term that is still used in the East even though the wooden screens have long disappeared.

The cleaning process was first automated in the 1880s (Beckwith 1943). The principle of separation was based on an observation made by "Peg Leg" John Webb of Holmanville, New Jersey. Peg Leg John stored his cranberries on the second floor of his storehouse and screened them on the first floor.

PLATE 11.12. SCREENING BERRIES AT THE BOG ON CAPE COD CA. 1870 (Courtesy Massachusetts Cranberry Experiment Station)

One version of the legend has it that one day John's peg leg caught in a knot-hole on a step as he carried a box of cranberries from the loft, and the berries went cascading down the stairs. He must have been astounded when he found the sound berries had easily reached the bottom of the stairs, whereas the soft and rotted fruit collected on the treads as they failed to clear the descending steps.

In 1881 advertisements appeared for the first separating machine using the bounce principle. French & Company was the announced agent for the *Staniford cranberry cleaner and separator,* which was being offered at $40. D. T. Staniford of New Brunswick, New Jersey, who was aware of Webb's observations, applied the principle in the construction of the machine that bore his name. This original machine was similar to the separators in use today, except that it was much smaller and had only a single glass pane upon which the berries bounced. This was quickly followed by the *Buzby cranberry cleaner and separator* advertised at $60. The Buzby machine introduced a second pane of glass parallel to the first, giving the rejected berry a second opportunity to bounce clear, thereby improving the efficiency of the machine.

At about this same time a third machine was introduced, called the *Leland cranberry cleaner and separator.* The machine was based on an entirely different principle. Instead of bouncing berries off a glass pane, they were moved on a belt up an inclined plane. Sound berries rolled back against the belt's motion, whereas soft berries were carried off on the moving belt. Although it was very efficient against severely rotted berries, it probably allowed too many partially rotted berries to remain—because the principle was soon discarded. Instead, modifications to the early bounce machines were made. Blowers were introduced to remove the debris and immature berries, boards replaced the glass panes, and more of them were added in parallel. The width of the bounce boards was greatly increased and the feeding mechanism much improved in today's new *Hayden* and *Bailey mills* (plate 11.13). The principle, nevertheless, has remained the same. Sound berries bounce freely over a barrier, whereas soft berries drop without bouncing and are collected in boxes at the bottom of the machine. The separation is completed by passing the sound berries over a wire grader where the small pie berries are removed before the remaining berries move to the sorting tables.

The cleaned and separated berries are then carried on moving belts, from which decayed berries that have survived the bouncing are removed by hand along with green berries. At this point additional accessories may be added such as perforated belts, which allow dry air to be forced up around the berries to remove moisture, and soft brushes that remove the waxy bloom and any visible spray residue and leave the berries with a high polish. After this final sorting and inspection, the berries are ready to be packed into their market containers.

A.

PLATE 11.13. *A,* MODERN CRANBERRY SEPARATOR WITH AUXILIARY BLOWER AND BERRY ELEVATOR (NOTE THE VERTICAL ROW OF BOUNCE BOARDS); *B,* CLOSE-UP SHOWING THE BOUNCE ACTION; *C,* SOUND FRUIT EMERGING FROM SEPARATOR (Courtesy Massachusetts Cranberry Experiment Station)

Much of the trash collected by picking machines could be separated in the field, according to Norton (1968c). In his picking machine design, he incorporated an elevator belt as an integral part, over which the debris was separated and elevated away from the fruit and eventually brushed into its own container.

Water-Harvested Fruit

The unique problems of handling water-harvested fruit were first experienced by the Wisconsin growers who were using the water rake method of harvesting. Fruit had to be dried before it could be stored. To accomplish this,

B.

PLATE 11.13. (*continued*)

two systems of drying were used: (1) berries were spread thinly in drying crates measuring two feet square and four inches deep just as they came from the bog; and (2) vines and trash were removed by means of wire screens or revolving canvas belts before the berries were set out to dry. Removing the field debris greatly speeded up the drying process. The drying crate's sides and bottom were constructed of lath slightly set apart to allow for air circulation. The crates had cleats on the bottom edges which enabled them to be held apart when stacked for drying. The drying crates were stacked on the dikes in the open air so that the drying wind could blow through them. During inclement weather a canvas would be drawn over the crates to protect them from the rain.

So significant was the problem of lowered fruit quality of water-harvested cranberries because of increased rot that Wisconsin growers soon experimented with artificial methods of drying the berries (C. L. Lewis 1925). One of the first problems that had to be addressed before berries could be

C.

PLATE 11.13. (*continued*)

efficiently dried by artificial means was the tremendous amount of grass and trash that accompanied the berries to the dryer. Their solution was to construct an endless canvas belt 12 feet by 8 feet, which operated on an incline of about 45 degrees. The berries were dumped on the bottom of the belt as they arrived from the bog. Over 90 percent of the grass and chaff adhered to the belt as the berries were transported up the incline. The debris was carried away as the berries rolled back down to a belt that led to the drying machine. The actual dryer consisted of a hot-air furnace with a fan that forced heated air through pipes to the berries, which were being transported slowly over a slatted belt. This drying system had been in use in New Jersey to dry the "floaters" that had been gathered after dry harvest.

By the 1950s, 90 percent of Wisconsin's water-harvested fruit was being machine dried (Peltier 1957). The slatted wooden belt was replaced either by an endless mesh conveyor that moved fruit through the dryer (*Dana dryer*) or by a stationary mesh incline that enabled fruit to "flow" through the drier by gravity. Hot air from oil- or gas-fired furnaces was forced up through a layer of berries four to six inches deep (10–15 cm) at a rate of 28,000 cubic feet per minute (800 cu. m/min) as they berries descended the 26-foot (8-m) mesh belt. A second fan blasted cool air at the rate of 9,200 cubic feet per minute (260 cu. m/min) through the berries as they traversed the last six feet (1.8 m) of the belt. Key to the success of the dryer was the temperature used. The air needed to be heated only enough to evaporate the moisture from the berries. Too high a temperature ran the risk of heating the berries. The second, cold air blast insured that the berries were quickly returned to ambient temperature. This prevented moisture from condensing on the dried berries. The berries were then conveyed to the separators and graders to complete the screening process.

Although it was realized that this additional handling further exposed the fruit to bruising, it was so much more efficient than drying by the old method that its use became obligatory, especially with the universal movement to water harvesting. The strong demand for fruit for processing was a significant factor in this move to water harvesting. Interestingly, however, when Norton (1962b) compared the costs of dry harvesting with those of wet harvesting, he found no appreciable difference between the two methods. The chief economic advantage of water harvesting was the additional 20 percent of the crop harvested, which was normally left in the bog when dry harvesting.

The water reel has become the most popular method of water harvesting. It is not uncommon to see as many as a dozen of the small individually operated water reels being used in tandem on a bog. Its introduction has greatly increased the rate at which cranberries can be harvested and therefore has necessitated modifications in the handling of this increased volume of fruit. Berries harvested with the water reel float unimpeded on the surface of the water. In order to remove the berries from the bog, they must be concentrated in one section of bog in order to be conveyed out. This was not a problem with the water picking machines developed in Wisconsin because the harvested berries were directly conveyed into bins which were then lifted out of the bogs by various means, including helicopters. In the East the detached fruit was allowed to float on the floodwater and on windy days the floating fruit was often pushed to the lee side of the bog by the wind, which aided in its removal. A more reliable method, however, was to corral the fruit using a system of interlinked boards that literally formed the corral fence. As the berries were concentrated at the edge of the bog, sections of the corral fence were removed—further decreasing the area in which the berries were confined. In this way the berries could be efficiently conveyed by mesh-belt elevator into a convenient container. To assist in moving the collection boom, which may reach a length of 500 feet (152 m), Norton (1978) designed a motorized tug that was capable of corralling 1,000 barrels of cranberries in an hour. Later, Norton (1982a) developed an inflatable boom that consisted of a 2½-inch (6-cm) inflatable plastic tube with a narrow strip of weighted fishnet suspended below it. It was capable of corralling 2,200 barrels of cranberries in a single sweep, yet when deflated the 500-foot boom occupied only 10 cubic feet (0.3 cu. m) of space.

To handle the volume of fruit that could be harvested by the water reels, a bulk system for the transport of harvested berries became essential (Norton 1961, 1968b). The most expedient method was to convey the harvested fruit, trash and all, into bulk bins located on flatbed trucks parked on the dike adjacent to the harvested bog. Elevating the fruit into the transport bins was found to be less damaging to the fruit than pumping the fruit into them (Zuckerman and Cannon 1972). The transport bins were so constructed as to allow them to be moved by motorized forklift from truck to bin dumper, which emptied the fruit onto the detrashing conveyor.

The relatively violent impact of the water reel upon the berry and the immersion of the fruit in water for hours greatly affects the keeping quality of the fruit. This presents no problem if the fruit is to be processed soon after harvest but does preclude its use in the fresh market because of the rapid deterioration of the berry in storage. Much of this quality loss is due to the physiological breakdown of the berry manifested by the berry's soft and rubbery condition, its dull external appearance, and the diffusion of the red anthocyanin pigment throughout the berry mesocarp (Stretch and Ceponis 1978).

Water immersion has a dramatic effect in increasing the amount of physiological breakdown of both water-harvested and dry-scooped berries. In one study, dry-scooped berries that were immersed in bog water after harvest actually had more physiological breakdown in storage than water-harvested berries, suggesting that the bruising they received by scooping was equal to or more severe than that inflicted by water harvesting (Ceponis and Stretch 1981). Immersion for longer than four hours was particularly debilitating to the fruit, the breakdown being directly related to the length of time the fruit remained in the water. Most of the deterioration occurred within the first 2 weeks of storage, with little additional breakdown occurring after 10 weeks of storage. The authors also noted that, unlike earlier reports (Stevens and Bergman 1921), highly colored late-harvested berries were more susceptible to breakdown than were poorly colored early-harvested fruit. The cultivars Early Black and Wilcox were the most susceptible to physiological breakdown, and Ben Lear the most resistant, with Pilgrim, Stevens, and Franklin intermediate in susceptibility (Stretch and Ceponis 1986).

Bog water is an excellent medium for fungal spores. Schwartz and Boone (1981) found viable spores of *Ceuthosporo lunata,* the causal organism for black rot in cranberries, at concentrations of 50 spores/ml. Ceponis and Stretch (1983) found black rot to be the dominant fungal disease associated with water-harvested berries. Water-harvested fruit developed significantly more black rot in storage than did handpicked berries that were dumped into the bog water after they were picked. This tends to support Schwartz and Boone's observation that *C. lunata* is primarily a wound-invading organism. Early Black, Wilcox, and Ben Lear berries were significantly more susceptible to black rot infection when immersed than were Pilgrim, Stevens, and Franklin berries (Stretch and Ceponis 1986).

Anderson and Smith (1971) attempted to reduce postharvest spoilage in cranberries by hot-water treatments. Although temperatures above 125°F (52°C) resulted in berry damage, they observed that when the berries were immersed for only 2½ minutes at 125°F (52°C) and for longer periods at lower temperatures to 110°F (43°C), no damage occurred. The hot-water dips were effective in reducing the survival of pathogens contributing to storage rot—the longer the immersion time the more effective the treatment. Unfortunately, the hot-water dips were effective in reducing total spoilage only in early-harvested fruit. In fact, hot-water treatment of late-harvested fruit actually caused more spoilage to occur in storage because of increased physiological breakdown.

Storage

Chemical Changes in Fruit

As the cranberry ripens on the vine, its sugar content continually increases until it has become well colored (Morse 1927a). Morse and his coworkers (Morse et al. 1920) showed that the total sugar content in the mature cranberry ranges from a low of 3.75% in the McFarlin cultivar to 5.59% in Centennial berries. During storage there is a steady loss in the sugar content of the fruit (Morse 1919). The loss is accelerated at higher temperatures and when confined in airtight containers. On the other hand, the total acid content of the cranberry is relatively high at about 2.5% and varies little in storage. This relatively high acid-to-sugar ratio results in little flavor loss in the stored cranberry as often occurs in other fruits.

The harvested cranberry is a living entity which continues to undergo metabolic changes even though it is no longer attached to the cranberry plant. One such metabolic process is respiration, in which sugars are oxidized within the fruit to produce other metabolic products including CO_2. Morse and coworkers (Morse et al. 1920) were among the first to investigate this process in the cranberry by measuring carbon dioxide evolution from the fruit. They observed that the amount of carbon dioxide given off by the fruit doubled with each 10 C° rise in temperature above 1°C, thus confirming the sugar loss they observed in storage and its relationship to temperature.

Esselen and Fellers's (1937) measurements of cranberry respiration have shed light on the role of various environmental factors on the keeping quality of fruit. For example, they observed that cranberries that were left on the vines had a much higher rate of respiration than those which had been harvested about a month earlier and placed in storage. This would help explain why Crooks (1988) found that Howes picked early in the season had better shelf life than late-harvested fruit. Forsyth et al. (1973) later confirmed that cranberries that had begun to senesce in storage had higher respiration rates. This may explain in part the difficulty Anderson and his coworkers had in reducing total spoilage in late-harvested fruit with their hot water treatments. Esselen and Fellers also observed that fruit submerged in water had a much higher rate of respiration in storage than fruit that had not been subjected to submergence. This coincides with observations concerning the poorer keeping quality of water-submerged fruit (Wakabayashi 1925) and the poorer keeping quality of water-harvested fruit, as previously noted. Like Morse and his coworkers (1920), they also showed that temperature was directly related to fruit respiration and inversely related to keeping quality in storage. Within 20 days, cranberries stored at 24°C became soft, an indication of berry senescence. Levine et al. (1940) found that the CO_2/O_2 ratio of sound cranberries ranged from 0.3 to 1.0 and that such fruit possessed good keeping quality. These ratios were easily maintained when the berries were stored at 36°F (2°C), but after one week of storage at 70°F (21°C) they quickly exceeded this critical ratio.

Doughty et al. (1967) also observed that respiration rates and physiological breakdown of stored fruit were less in early-harvested than in late-harvested fruit, again alluding to the undesirability of allowing fruit to become overmature before harvesting. The Washington workers were able to reduce the amount of physiological breakdown in fruit stored for 24 weeks with experimental chemicals that inhibit senescence, including the retardants Alar and Phosfon-D.

The low pH (2.35–2.6) of sound cranberries and their relatively high benzoic acid content, which ranged from 0.029 to 0.098 percent among different cultivars, led Clague and Fellers (1934) to postulate that cranberries having high benzoic acid content would be more resistant to storage decay. Although the levels of benzoic acid found in cranberries were high enough to produce a preservative action in their in vitro studies, they found that cultivars with the highest benzoic acid content did not always have the best keeping qualities. This led them to conclude that factors other than benzoic acid content were paramount in determining the keeping quality of cranberries. They did note, however, that a large percentage of cultivars having poor keeping qualities had low total acid content, and conversely, good-keeping cultivars in the majority of cases had a high total acid content.

Another acid of importance in the cranberry is ascorbic acid (vitamin C). Fresh cranberries are an excellent source of vitamin C, containing on average 15 mg per 100 grams of fresh cranberries (Isham and Fellers 1933). Prolonged storage, however, can seriously erode the vitamin C content of stored cranberries. Licciardello et al. (1951) provided convincing evidence to this effect in their studies of a number of cranberry cultivars. Ascorbic acid content was nearly halved in the berries after three months of cool storage and halved once again after another three months of storage.

Cranberries are capable of increasing in color after they are harvested, although anthocyanin development proceeds much more rapidly in berries left on the vine than in berries held in common storage for the same period of time (Devlin et al. 1968). In cold storage, cranberries colored best at 45°F (7°C), but they tended to become too dark when stored at higher temperatures (Levine et al. 1940).

Common Storage

Until the advent of modern-day refrigeration equipment, cranberries were stored at the bogs in chaff in large ventilated rooms, or *screenhouses* as they were often referred to, and normally attained the ambient temperature of their surroundings. In this so-called common storage, berries might remain from a few weeks to several months before screening and shipment to market (Franklin et al. 1924). The traditional period for the fresh cranberry market usually extended from mid-September to the end of December.

The indirect relationship between temperature and keeping quality of the stored cranberry was recognized early by cranberry growers. One approach to enhance the storability of cranberry fruit was to pick the berries during the cooler part of the day, so that the berries went into storage at relatively low temperatures. The storage crates and storage building had to be so constructed as to allow for maximum ventilation, not only to insure that field heat was removed but also to minimize the condensation that might develop from daily temperature fluctuations. Fans were often used to enhance air movement, and insulated block buildings reduced daily temperature fluctuations.

Under such common storage conditions, Zuckerman (1956) determined that after 10 weeks of storage the Howes cultivar suffered approximately a 10 percent weight loss due to desiccation of the fruit. This loss was in addition to that incurred by fungal decay and physiological breakdown. In general, berries that tended to keep best in common storage came from mature fields, moderately sanded areas, dry areas, unfertilized fields, and bogs on which the winter flood was held until late in the spring. Both shrinkage due to desiccation and rot development were markedly reduced, however, by lowering the temperature at which the berries were stored.

Refrigerated Storage

Gunness (1942) compared the losses in storage of Early Black and Howes cranberries after two months of storage at different temperatures with the losses incurred in common storage. Cranberries stored at 30°F (−1.1°C) kept exceptionally well for two months, but when stored for an additional month at this temperature, they deteriorated very rapidly. Berries stored at 35°F (1.7°C) kept much better than those stored at 50°F (10°C), and all the refrigerated berries were superior to those stored at ambient temperatures. Storage losses were approximately halved when berries were kept at 35°F (1.7°C) when compared to berries kept in screenhouses. Wright et al. (1937) found that Early Black and Howes cranberries could be kept in marketable condition for as long as four months when stored at 36°F (2.2°C). Sixty-five percent of the Early Blacks and 73 percent of the Howes were still in excellent condition after this period. Lower storage temperatures resulted in extensive low-temperature injury after this prolonged storage period. Wright and coworkers determined that 70 to 75 percent relative humidity was best for storing cranberries at the recommended temperature.

Ringel and his associates (Ringel et al. 1959) also compared fruit losses between refrigerated and common storage. Not only were storage losses reduced as the result of refrigeration at 40°F (4.4°C) when compared to fruit stored at ambient temperatures, but the berries had better shelf life after storage as well. Cranberries that were kept in field lugs were found to cool more rapidly than prepackaged fruit in master cartons. In general, freshly harvested cranberries, when screened and prepackaged, could be kept in cold storage for 6 weeks without having to be rescreened. The limit for storing cranberries even under refrigeration appears to be somewhere between 12 and 19 weeks. Berries screened and prepackaged after 19 weeks of storage did not have very good shelf life, whereas fruit handled similarly after 12 weeks in cold storage held up well after storage.

Despite the fact that cranberries appear to store better when kept in bulk, the increasing consumer demand for prepackaged cranberries has led to considerable research on the keeping quality of stored prepackaged fruit (Hruschka and Kaufman 1949, 1951, 1952; Ringel et al. 1959). Hruschka and Kaufman determined that Early Black and Howes cranberries prepackaged in either perforated one-pound cellophane bags or unsealed one-pound cardboard window-boxes could be stored for 8 weeks between 33 and 38°F (0.6–3.3°C) and still have good shelf life. Ringel and his associates maintained that the storage length could be increased to 12 weeks if the berries were immediately cooled after harvest and packaged just before shipment. Losses after storage were held to less than 10 percent in the Howes cultivar using this approach. In general, it appears as though the Early Black cultivar lends itself best to prepackaged storage, followed by the Howes cultivar, with the McFarlin cultivar a poor third. Hruschka and Kaufman (1952) recommended that the prepackaged McFarlin cultivar be marketed as rapidly as possible and stored for only a short period if necessary.

Growers may either modify existing structures or construct entirely new cold-storage units to meet their storage needs. Cole (1951) in his discussion of cold-storage facilities for cranberry growers has given quite a detailed description of the requirements for a cold-storage structure, including costs. Based on an assumption that 6 cubic feet (0.2 cu. m) of space would be required to store a barrel of cranberries, he outlined the construction of a 6,000-cubic-foot (170-cu.-m) storage building to store 1,000 barrels of cranberries and arrived at a cost of approximately 80 cents per barrel to store them.

Controlled Atmosphere Storage

During the 1950s a great deal of interest was generated in the use of controlled atmosphere to improve stored fruit quality based on the successes with apples. The theory holds that fruit stored under reduced oxygen environment will keep longer than fruit stored in normal air because of the reduced respiration that would result. When Anderson and his coworkers (R. E. Anderson et al. 1963) stored cranberries at low temperatures (32° and 38°F [0 to 3.3°C]) at various reduced oxygen tensions, however, they were unable to detect any improvement in fruit quality over normal air storage after 18 weeks in storage. Stark and his colleagues (Stark et al. 1969) carried out similar studies in Nova Scotia but with fruit held in common storage rather than in refrigerated storage, and they came to the same conclusion. Fruit stored in 100-percent nitrogen actually developed a dull, watery appearance and acquired a slight aroma after only three weeks in storage.

In a separate experiment, however, the same workers (Lockhart et al. 1971; Stark et al. 1971) found that berries stored under refrigeration in an atmosphere of 100-percent nitrogen for three weeks had significantly less decay than berries stored at the same temperature in air. Unfortunately, there was greater physiological breakdown in the nitrogen-stored fruit, which precluded its use in the storage of fruit for the fresh market. The elimination of fungal decay by the nitrogen treatment, however, resulted in berries that had enhanced color and produced sauce that was superior in flavor to sauce from freshly harvested berries. Berries stored in nitrogen had significantly higher levels of titratable acidity in their juice. The complete exclusion of oxygen that 100 percent nitrogen storage would afford may, therefore, have some practical application in the processing of cranberries. However, when

Massachusetts workers (Norton et al. 1968) attempted to reduce the amount of fungal decay that develops in storage by injecting various concentrations of ozone into the storage room, they were unsuccessful.

Uniform color development of the berry has always been an important factor in the marketing of cranberries. With the introduction of new juice products, the total amount of anthocyanin produced by the berry has also become an important consideration. The postharvest treatment of stored fruit with ethylene was tried as early as the 1920s (Fudge 1930) in an attempt to improve the red color of harvested fruit. It was already known that stored fruit would increase in red color as the temperature increased, particularly if the berries were exposed to the light. By subjecting the stored fruit to various concentrations of ethylene gas, Fudge hoped to enhance color development of fruit in storage, thus increasing the market value of the crop. Although there was a slight increase in the appearance of red color in the berry, Fudge concluded that it was the result of ethylene's effect on chlorophyll degradation rather than on any increase in anthocyanin content of the fruit, although she did not actually measure the amount of anthocyanin present. When Craker (1971) studied the effect of ethylene on anthocyanin development in harvested cranberries under controlled laboratory conditions, he was able to show a marked increase in the anthocyanin pigment measured when berries were subjected to as little as 10 ppm ethylene. The ethylene treatment was greatly enhanced when supplied in the presence of light. He concluded that treatment of harvested cranberries with ethylene gas might be a practical method of increasing the anthocyanin content of cranberries, particularly those that may not meet the commercial grade.

Processing

Canning Sauce

The first cranberry sauce was commercially canned in 1888 by Burnham and Morrill of Portland, Maine. With the introduction of modern canning methods following World War I, more cranberries were beginning to be processed into sauce for canning. By 1922, 5,000 cases of cranberry sauce were being packed in South Hanson, Massachusetts, and by the late 1930s over a million and a half cases were being packed there. The new industry offered a profitable outlet for fruit that would not keep well and berries that were too small for the fresh fruit market. More importantly, it changed cranberries from a seasonal fruit to a year-round commodity and offered the growers a marketing outlet for crops during surplus production years. By the beginning of World War II, 25 percent of the cranberry crop was being canned. In 1957 the USDA published "U.S. Standards for Fresh Cranberries for Processing." Today more than 85 percent of the crop is processed either for sauce or juice products.

Cranberry sauce is produced by blending a mixture of cranberries, sugar, and water so that the mixture will form a gel. The gel-forming property of the sauce is dependent on the pectic substances, soluble solids, and acids of the fruit and upon the amount of sweetener added. In a study of jellies made from heat-extracted juice, Baker and Kneeland (1936) observed a strong correlation between jelly strength and the viscosity of the extracted juice. Maximum jelly strength was attained at a relatively low sugar concentration of 38 to 41 percent. Sugar concentration in commercially canned cranberry sauce generally ranges between 36 to 42 percent. Baker and Goodwin (1941) concluded that the major factor in loss of gel strength was the decomposition of the pectic substances that can occur when cooking temperatures are too high and the berries are cooked too long. They found that temperatures above 150°F (66°C) resulted in lowered gel strength, and they concluded that cooling the canned product rapidly (as practiced in the trade) was a good idea.

The gel-forming property of cranberries may vary not only with cultivar but also with maturity, season, horticultural practices, and conditions of storage (Zuckerman et al. 1967). The cultivars Franklin, Howes, and Wilcox were found to have relatively high gel strength, whereas Early Black and Pilgrim were consistently inferior in gel strength; their gel-forming properties varied more between bogs and seasons. The cultivars Stevens, Beckwith, and Bergman were intermediate in gel strength. The authors observed that within a cultivar the pigment content varied inversely with the viscosity of the juice. Both these factors appeared to be related to growing conditions and varied significantly between bogs. Esselen et al. (1948) have observed that sauces prepared with batches of berries containing approximately 15 percent spoiled berries had very weak gel characteristics.

To produce the desired gel characteristics of cranberry sauce, the amount of cranberries used to make the cranberry puree must be adjusted based on their ability to form a gel. If berries having low gel strength are used, it may be necessary to increase the concentration of cranberries or to increase the concentration of cranberry solids by the evaporation of water. If the cranberries have high gel strength, fewer cranberries can be used and less evaporation is necessary. Weckel and Swanson (1972) have developed the Gel Power Index, a simple and rapid test for measuring the gel strength of a given lot of cranberries. The index value is the minimum concentration of sugar necessary to form a satisfactory gel when a given quantity of cranberries is used in a mixture of cranberries, sugar, and water. When less sugar is required, the pectic substances present are capable of forming a gel in the presence of a greater concentration of water (less evaporation necessary). Using their simple test procedure and equations, the quantity of cranberries necessary to produce a satisfactory gel—or alternately, the concentration of sugar necessary to produce a satisfactory gel—can be calculated. The authors point out that with the increase of one unit gel power there is an increase in sauce production of 9 to 13 pounds for each 100 pounds of cranberries because of the higher water concentration that can be sustained at a lower cranberry concentration. The use of the Gel Power Index, the authors maintained, would not only enable better formulation for the processes used but also aid in the development of continuous rather than batch processes.

Cranberries can be processed either by the batch method or by a continuous operation process (Reich 1939). In the batch process, the washed and sorted berries are cooked with the proper amount of water in a steam-jacketed kettle. The cooking is finished when the skins pop, and the batch passes through a pulping machine to separate the seeds and skins from the juice. The hot juice (also referred to as the cranberry pulp or puree) is quickly pumped into steam-jacketed kettles where the steam is maintained at 85 pounds per square inch (psi). Here a determined amount of sugar is added to a measured amount of puree and mixed with a paddle to dissolve it as rapidly as possible to obtain the desired gel strength, which as previously indicated is at 40 percent sugar plus or minus 2 percent.

In the continuous process method, each required function is carried on without disturbing or unduly influencing any other function. The key to the operation is the elongated, narrow, jacketed copper kettle or evaporator into which a proportioning device feeds in exact amounts of sugar from a bin and cranberry puree from a constant-feed tank. The end of the evaporator that receives the sugar and puree is not jacketed, which enables the sugar to be mixed with the puree without caramelization. The required evaporation, carried out under 40 psi pressure, can be completed in two minutes because part of the water will combine with the added sugar to form invert sugar, which increases the density of the liquid without actual evaporation. To complete the sugar inversion process, the liquid flows into an inversion tank where it is kept below the boiling point of the liquid. The principal advantage of the continuous process over the batch process is that it greatly reduces the chance for overcooking the sauce.

Of great importance to the processing industry is the stability of the canned product, not only in terms of its culinary appearance but also from the standpoint of its shelf life and the preservation of the cranberries' natural vitamins. One of the first problems observed in the canning of cranberry sauce was the discoloration that sometimes developed after canning, transforming the sauce's natural red color to a dirty brown or even black. Morse (1927b) determined that the discoloration was due to the reaction of soluble iron formed from the inner surface of the can with the coloring matter (anthocyanin) and, to a lesser extent, with the tannin in the fruit. Improved methods of can preparation and welding have essentially eliminated this problem.

The color of cranberry sauce in the can after prolonged storage still remains, however, an important consideration. The color of the berries used to prepare the sauce greatly influences the color of the sauce (Servadio and Francis 1963). Over a two-year storage period, Servadio and Francis found that pigment degradation was dependent upon the length of storage and the storage temperature as well as the original pigment concentration. Sauce stored at 100°F (38°C) lost 75 percent of its pigment in three months, whereas sauce stored at 38°F (3°C) lost less than 50 percent of its pigment in two years. E. E. Anderson and Esselen (1950) found the use of pyrophosphates in the manufacture of cranberry sauce of little value in maintaining red color in the canned product.

Another important consideration in cranberry canning is its effect on the preservation of the cranberries' natural vitamins. Fresh cranberries are an excellent source of vitamin C and contain a small amount of vitamin A (2 units) but apparently contain no significant amounts of vitamins B complex, D, and G (Isham and Fellers 1933). Although fresh or boiled cold-pressed cranberry juice contained nearly as much vitamin C as the fresh berries, when the extracted juice was boiled and processed it lost most of its vitamin C. Licciardello and his associates (Licciardello et al. 1952) actually measured the vitamin C content after each unit of operation in the canning process and found that the loss in vitamin C was progressive with each operational step. They concluded that oxidation by atmospheric and dissolved oxygen, heat, and metal catalysts were all important factors in the destruction of the cranberries' natural vitamin C during the preparation of cranberry sauce.

An innovative approach to the preservation of cranberry sauce was that of freezing, as suggested by Boggs and Johnson (1947). Originally it was intended that the frozen sauce packaged in paper would be a replacement for the unavailable tin cans during World War II, but freezing had the added advantages of maintaining color, flavor, and vitamin C content during storage. The key to the operation was the addition of high-grade citrus pectin to a cranberry puree–sugar mix that was prepared without extensive heating. The added pectin was necessary to maintain the gel characteristic of the sauce during freezing. Freezing never became a viable commercial method of cranberry preservation, probably because of the added costs of the pectin and freezing.

Juice Products

During the 1960s the commercial production of cranberry juice products, marketed as cranberry cocktail or in combination with other fruit juices, became a significant new outlet for cranberries. Interestingly, however, the first cranberry beverage to be produced commercially was packed at Wareham, Massachusetts, in 1895 by B. P. Waters and R. C. Randall (Rice et al. 1939). The product was a cranberry syrup marketed under the name of "Ruby Phosphate" and was widely used as a base for soda-fountain-type beverages. The syrup was made from raw-pressed cranberry juice and sugar with a little wine added for flavor. In 1930 Cranberry Canners Inc., the predecessor to the Ocean Spray Cranberry Company, began packing and distributing cranberry cocktail, which was simply diluted cranberry juice with about 15 percent added sugar.

Juice is extracted from the cranberries by either heat extraction or by cold pressing. In the heat extraction method, water is added to the cranberries, which are heated until they soften, and the juice is expressed by pressing or by centrifugation. The press cake that remains after the juice is extracted contains much acid and color and most of the pectin; it is used in producing cranberry sauce. The expressed juice is then filtered, yielding about eight gallons per 100 pounds of fruit. The filtered juice is diluted with two parts of water and sufficient sugar to test 15 to 20 percent. The final cranberry cocktail consists of approximately 30 percent pure cranberry juice. When filled into sterile containers at 185°F (85°C), the juice requires no further pasteurization, but at lower temperatures a heat treatment of 20 minutes at 165°F (74°C) is needed.

Cold pressing is accomplished by grinding the raw berries and allowing them to set overnight before pressing out the juice. The juice yield by this method is slightly lower at seven gallons per 100 pounds of fruit. Another method of cold extraction would be to run frozen cranberries through a screw extractor. Sapers et al. (1983) were able to increase the juice yield by 50 percent and the pigment content by 15-fold using a freeze-thaw treatment before extraction. According to the authors, anthocyanin recovery could be further enhanced by tissue homogenization and by double pressing. Chiriboga and Francis (1970) went one step further and suggested that 90 percent of the anthocyanin content of the cranberry press cake could be extracted with multiple extractions using methanol containing 0.03% hydrochloric acid. The methanol would be distilled off and the anthocyanin purified by absorption on a Amberlite C G-50 resin. Juice from any of the methods of extraction must be clarified by means of Pectinol or other pectinase enzyme preparations, with subsequent settling and filtering with diatomaceous earth or some other filtering aid.

Since considerable dilution of the original cranberry juice is necessary, the product cannot be marketed as cranberry juice, but rather as cranberry cocktail. In addition to the unique flavor of the cranberry, cranberry cocktail offers very desirable marketing characteristics such as its brilliant red color, clarity, and ability to blend synergistically with other fruit juices. To date, successful combinations have been made with the juice of apples, raspberries, grapes, apricots, prunes, and, most recently, blueberries. One of the most successful of the combinations has been the cranberry-apple blend, which contains from 12 to 15 percent cranberry juice. Before blending, however, the apple juice must be flash pasteurized in order to inactivate the enzymes in the apple juice that would otherwise destroy the pigments in the cranberry juice (Esselen et al. 1948).

The success of the cranberry cocktail products has placed a tremendous demand on the anthocyanin (red pigment) production of the berry. Growers receive premium prices for highly colored berries that contain larger quantities of anthocyanin. This has necessitated the need for assessing the levels of the pigment in the harvested berries and monitoring the pigment content in the cocktail product. Fudge (1930) was probably the first person who tried to quantify the color in cranberries by extracting juice from frozen berries and comparing the color against a dye standard. Francis (1957) developed an extraction technique using an acid-ethanol extracting solution, which enabled him to remove all of the pigment and assay the total pigment content. Absorbance of the solution was read using a spectrophotometer, and the pigment concentration was expressed as milligrams of the dye Congo Red, which was used as a standard. Later, Fuleki and Francis (1968) established the extinction coefficients for the four major cranberry anthocyanins—from which point on anthocyanin content in the solvent system could be expressed in absolute quantities. Deubert (1978) introduced modifications in the original extraction procedures of Francis that enabled smaller samples to be used without affecting accuracy and, consequently, greatly speeded up the analysis process.

Another approach to assessing the pigment content in cranberries was the measurement of surface color of berries and the color of cranberry cocktail. Francis (1957) used the "a" reading of the Hunter Color and Color Difference Meter as an index of the surface color of a single layer of cranberries rotated below the exposure unit. The Hunter "a" was highly correlated (positively) with the total pigment content extracted from different cultivars of cranberries. Staples and Francis (1968) compared the pigment content of cranberry cocktail with color measurements obtained using various color-differentiating instruments. They found a high positive correlation of readings obtained with the Biospect and the G. E. spectrophotometers with readings obtained with the Lovibond Tintometer, indicating that the pigment content and color are very closely related. The authors concluded that it should be possible, therefore, to develop a system for continuous color measurement that could be utilized in a production line. Sapers et al. (1983) recently obtained high positive correlations between tristimulus reflectance measurements on whole or pureed cranberries and the juice color, determined by spectrophotometric or tristimulus transmission measurements.

The quality of the processed juice as manifested in the retention of its attractive red color upon storage and its nutritive value is of considerable importance. Francis and Servadio (1957) found that after 12 months of storage, juice stored at 38°F (3°C) retained its color much better than did juice held at 72°F (22°C). Juice prepared from highly colored fruit retained its color far better than juice prepared from light colored fruit. As discussed above, much of the natural vitamin C of the cranberry is lost in processing (Licciardello et al. 1951, 1952) and must therefore be replenished with ascorbic acid additives if the juice is to be heralded as a good source of vitamin C. According to Esselen and his coworkers (Esselen et al. 1946), this vitamin loss can be replaced with ascorbic acid at a rate that would give cranberry juice an amount of vitamin C equivalent to that in citrus juices. Not only did they find the added ascorbic acid to be quite stable but it also had a favorable effect on color retention in the juice during storage. Starr and Francis (1968), on the other hand, presented evidence which showed that adding ascorbic acid resulted in decreased pigment in the juice during storage. The pigment loss could be reduced somewhat by keeping the headspace oxygen content as low as possible.

Other Products

Cranberries had traditionally been thought of as a condiment to be served with the Thanksgiving turkey and the Christmas goose. This association was actually becoming a detriment to cranberry growers as their excess production was seen as a liability once the holiday season passed. It was little wonder, therefore, that imaginative entrepreneurs were constantly seeking new ways to market cranberries. Already mentioned was the successful cranberry syrup marketed as "Ruby Phosphate" in 1895. This highly concentrated juice prepared by cold pressing fresh cranberries and sweetened to 60 to 70 percent sugar solids can be used for blending and cooking and as a beverage base. When additionally treated with a pectin enzyme (such as Pectinol) to remove the pectin, a good quality beverage is obtained that can be further enhanced by light carbonation (Rice 1932). Until the recent introduction of a cranberry concentrate by Ocean Spray Inc., cranberry syrups have not been commercially exploited. Supposedly by preparing a range of such syrups, manufacturers give consumers the chance to satisfy their personal preferences for tartness and sweetness of the finished product.

In 1912 H. H. Harrison patented the machinery and the process whereby whole cranberries could be evaporated without loss of flavor and quality (Pascoe 1937). The new product was marketed under the label H & P Evaporated

Whole Cranberries. A one-pound tin of the condensed product was capable of making 22 pounds of whole fruit sauce and was sold to the hotel, restaurant, and institutional trade. Less successful, but no less innovative, was Dawson's attempt to produce "cranberry raisins" (Dawson 1925). Dawson realized that cranberries with their low sugar content could not be successfully dried. The resultant product would be a tough skin surrounding a group of sour seeds. Dawson patented a process whereby whole cranberries were impregnated with cold-pressed cranberry juice fortified with sugar and then dried. The resultant product was a berry with a soft, moist texture and a cavity filled with a 50 percent cranberry syrup. It is not known whatever came of Dawson's cranberry raisins, but the closest thing to it would probably be the *Craisin* recently patented by the Ocean Spray Cranberry Company. The sugar-infused cranberry is dried and marketed in cereal.

A somewhat similar product called *cransweets* was developed by K. G. Weckel at the University of Wisconsin (Woerpel 1956). Professor Weckel developed a process whereby cranberries could be pierced to provide a path for the sugar syrup. The berries are impregnated with the sugar syrup in a vacuum chamber, which prevents them from rupturing. Cranberry-filled chocolate cordials are very popular in Italy, so much so that the Italian government has sponsored research on growing the American cranberry in Italy just to fulfill this demand.

As already indicated, frozen cranberries are as suitable for processing (commercial or home use) as are fresh or stored cranberries. More pigment appears to be extracted from frozen berries, and after grinding, the pulp does not need to set before pressing. If the final product is to be the juice, however, it must be treated with a pectinase enzyme before it can be satisfactorily filtered because of its greater viscosity (Rice 1932). A distinct advantage that cranberries have over other fruits is that they can be frozen, thawed, and refrozen with no apparent ill effects (Knox 1952). During the 1950s a concerted effort was taken by the industry to promote frozen cranberries. A consumer opinion poll conducted by Hunter (Hunter 1957) indicated that this new product was readily accepted by homemakers with few complaints.

Recent bans by the FDA of certain synthetic red food dyes have led to considerable interest in the use of natural red pigments found in fruits and vegetables as substitutes. Because these natural pigments are very sensitive to processing conditions, their use as natural colorants are limited. Cranberry concentrate, however, has been successfully used as a color enhancement for cherry pie filling (Volpe 1976). It would appear that cranberry concentrate might be a suitable red coloring material whenever a food product with an acid pH is needed. The potential applications could include beverages, gelatins, canned fruits, and possibly maraschino cherries.

Cranberry-flavored yogurt has never been a popular product because the yogurt apparently lacks the impact flavor required for consumer acceptance. One approach to this problem suggested by Swanson and his associates (Swanson et al. 1972) was to intensify the cranberry flavor in yogurt with a synthetic cranberry flavoring. This became feasible with the identification of the flavor components of cranberries, thus enabling the synthesis of a more typical cranberry flavor. Taste panel tests showed that cranberry-flavored yogurt and sherbet fortified with the new synthetic cranberry flavoring were more acceptable than the unenhanced products.

Fermentation products utilizing cranberries are receiving increased attention. Cranberry cider—consisting of one part cranberry juice, two to three parts fresh apple juice, and 1.0 to 1.5 pounds of sugar to the gallon of the mixture—has been sold in cranberry-producing areas for many years. The addition of 0.25 ounce of sodium benzoate per gallon is needed if it is desired to keep the cider from going hard. Undiluted cranberry juice contains enough benzoic acid to prevent it from fermenting naturally. Cranberries have also produced an acceptable fruit wine. Lynard (1973) offers the following recipe to the amateur oenologist for the production of a gallon of cranberry wine:

> 3 lbs. fresh or frozen cranberries
> 1 lb. raisins
> 3 lbs. white granulated sugar
> 3½ quarts of warm water
> ½ of a small orange
> 1 package of wine yeast or ½ package dry, granulated baking yeast

The wine is a rosé in appearance and can be consumed soon after bottling.

There has always been a great deal of interest in utilizing the by-products of cranberry processing. The skins, seeds, and pulp, often mixed with rice hulls to improve extraction of juice, have been used to feed livestock, particularly goats. Besides its pigments, however, there are other chemical constituents found in cranberry scrap products that may have industrial value. Cranberries apparently contain a higher concentration of ursolic acid than anything else known (Nealy 1943). Ursolic acid produces a fine creamy emulsion when a small quantity is added to a mixture of mineral oil and water. It is used as an emulsifying agent in mayonnaise as well as in cosmetics and toothpaste. With the ursolic acid, cranberry wax and oil are also extracted. Cranberry oil has been used in cosmetics. A combination of ursolic acid, cranberry oil, cranberry wax, and distilled water has been made into a salve called Vaccinol used for skin lesions and burns.

TWELVE

Economics, Marketing, and Utilization

Economics

Costs of Bog Establishment

Perhaps one of the earliest records of the costs of developing a cranberry bog for commercial production can be found in the *Transactions* of the Middlesex County, Massachusetts, Agricultural Society for 1855. The report reprinted in Eastwood's manual, *Complete Manual for the Cultivation of the Cranberry* (1856), was entitled "Mr. Addison Flint's (of North Arlington, Mass.) Method of Cranberry Cultivation, with Statistics." In it Flint described how he converted a worthless bog meadow into two acres of profitable cranberry bog. In 1843 he built a dam to impound water on the meadow, which he kept flooded for three years. The water was drawn off and the swamp was burnt off (apparently there was no need to remove trees and stumps). Cranberry vines (probably taken from the wild) were cut up with a sharp hoe and set in hills in quart-sized bunches about 3½ feet apart. His first crop of 17 bushels was picked in 1850. He outlined his establishment costs as follows:

The cost of building my dam by contract . . . .$	20.00
Ox labor, furnished by myself, estimated.	5.00
Setting vines on about an acre	25.00
Total.	$50.00

Flint pointed out that his costs for preparing the land and setting the vines were well below the $1.50 to $1.87 per rod published in the first Annual Report of the Secretary of the Massachusetts Board of Agriculture. He went on to report his net gain as follows:

The cost of stopping and letting off water and, taking care of the same since
1846, yearly, at $10.00 ....$ 90.00
Reckoning the cranberries, for the past
six years, at six hundred bushels, and
the cost of picking and marketing the
same at 75 cents per bushel........................   405.00
Total $540.00

Gross returns for the years 1850–1855 .... 1,581.00
Net profit on $50.00, expended nine years 1,041.00
Yearly income on $50.00.............................   115.67

Flint's annual return of more than 130% on his original investment would be
the envy of all of today's cranberry growers.

Twenty years later Joseph White prepared detailed development costs for
publication in his monograph *Cranberry Culture* published in 1870. He
qualified his average expenditure estimates with the proviso that the costs
would vary with location, quality of the land, and the amount of damming required. Based on one acre, his calculated average costs for the following
were:

Original cost of land, say ....$ 30.00
Ditching and damming 10.00
Turfing, 25 cents per square rod........................   40.00
Removing turf (into fences, or other-
wise) 25 cents per square rod 40.00
Removing stumps, $2 per day,
say...   15.00
Leveling inequalities of surface 6.00
Plowing..   3.00
Harrowing and making drills for
vines 3.00
Ten barrels of vines, at $3.............................   30.00
Dropping and covering plants 8.00
                                                    $185.00

Expense of weeding
1st year ....$ 8.00
2nd year..   6.00

3rd year..	4.00
4th year...	2.00
Four years' interest on first cost, at 7	
per cent..	51.80
Total expense at the end of the 4th year	$256.80

Probable Receipts
(net profit at $4 per bushel)

1st year, 1 peck.....................................	$ 0.50
2nd year, 1 bu......................................	3.00
3rd year, 8 bu.	24.00
4th year, 80 bu.	240.00
Net receipts at the end of the 4th year	$267.50

White's figures, thus, show a positive cash flow by the end of the fourth year of establishment. These estimates were actually quite close to the establishment costs $1.50 to $1.87 per rod reported by the secretary of the Board of Agriculture (Mass.) to which Addison Flint alluded. White pointed out that if the planting was to occur on deep muck, sanding would be needed, which would raise the establishment costs another $275 per acre.

An indication of the escalating costs of establishing cranberry bogs was given in Andrew Searles's report to the Wisconsin Cranberry Growers' Association on the costs of rejuvenating an old cranberry bog (Searles 1925). These costs did not include original land or damming costs, but they do show the increasing costs of the new higher-yielding plant cultivars. Searles estimated the costs per acre for replanting an old bog as follows:

Plowing and leveling................................	$ 200.00
Putting on three inches of sand	150.00
Putting in new ditches	25.00
New flumes..	50.00
Searles Jumbo vines for planting	250.00
Planting...	100.00
Two season's weeding	225.00
Total costs for replanting one acre	$1,000.00

By the 1960s bog establishment costs had increased more than ten fold when compared to White's published figures of a century earlier. The director of the Minnesota State Agricultural Department's Division of Plant Industry estimated that it would take from $3,000 to $5,000 per acre to develop a cranberry bog in Minnesota (Schweitzer 1966). Today even these estimates would probably be quite conservative, considering the inflated land prices and interest rates of recent years. Another factor that would increase establishment costs considerably is the need for smaller bogs with precision leveling that modern water harvesting techniques require. The smaller the bog area, the more dike area is needed, which increases construction costs considerably. And finally, today's new high-yielding cultivars are in high demand and short supply and, therefore, command high prices when purchased from vine propagators.

Costs of Production

The first attempt in modern times to establish detailed costs of cranberry production was made by B. D. Crossman (Crossman 1951b). Crossman used a case approach wherein production costs for a range of bog operations were compared. The operations ranged from a part-time operation to a corporation employing ten full-time employees plus seasonal help. The acreage for the different production operations ranged from 8.5 acres in the part-time operation to 184 acres for the corporation. The detailed cost figures are taken from Crossman's article and are shown in table 12.1.

In arriving at his production cost estimates, Crossman did not attempt to include family labor. Neither did he include interest on owned investment or accrued depreciation, which he contended would be arbitrary and would tend to confuse costs with desired returns. His data indicated that over 60 percent of the cash expenses appear as labor costs. On small bogs labor costs were mainly for harvesting because this was usually the only time small growers needed to hire labor, whereas for the larger operations harvesting costs comprised about 25 percent of the total labor cost. Harvesting costs ranged from 87 cents to $2.46 per barrel, the highest costs being concurred at the lowest yield per acre. It is in this area, Crossman surmised, that the greatest economization could be obtained either by increasing production per acre and/or converting to mechanical harvesting (Crossman 1951a).

More recently, Ames and Christensen (1978) published a detailed evaluation of cranberry production costs in Massachusetts. The researchers obtained their data from 56 growers of operations that comprised seven different acreage classes. The data were further classified into four categories of productivity based on barrels per acre yield. In this way representative samples were obtained, which enabled the approximation of cost figures for the entire grower population in Massachusetts. The authors emphasized, however, that the costs reported were real costs for 16.6 percent of the cultivated cranberry acreage in Massachusetts—which represents a very large sample and can therefore be considered to be representative of the industry.

TABLE 12.1. CASH COSTS (IN DOLLARS) OF BOG PRODUCTION

	TYPE OF OPERATION					
	Part-Time Owner	Full-Time Owner	Owner + 2 Workers	Operator + 2 Workers	Operator + 4 Workers	Corporation + 10 Workers
Acreage	8.5	13	20	30	58	184
Expense items						
Regular labor*		1,404	4,200	6,754	8,378	17,820
Harvesting	355		1,620	2,216	4,734	21,360
Sanding	220			342	1,159	8,480
Other labor		49			483	
Insect control	74	79	370	220	1,215	
Weed control	4		155		2,732	2,780
Rot control	205	281	750	1,700	865	
Sanding	175	344				
Fertilizer	15	24			382	
Energy	74	93	578	314	637	5,180
Mach. repairs			325		680	4,230
Bldg. repairs	5	2	85		200	2,395
Taxes	113	140	568	1,147	3,604	4,510
Insurance					705	
Interest	480		36	440	335	3,490
Total cash items	1,720	2,416	8,687	13,133	26,109	70,245
Bog yields† (bbls.)	410	766	1,500	900	2,855	10,100
Cash cost per bbl.	4.20	3.15	5.79	14.60	9.15	7.00

SOURCE: Crossman 1951b.

*Owner's labor costs not included.

†Based on yield of previous year (1948).

The variable and fixed costs obtained by Ames and Christensen are shown in table 12.2.

The figures reported above are the weighted averages for each category of variable and fixed costs for the entire sample of 56 growers. Although Ames and Christensen did include depreciation under fixed costs, no cost provision was made for capital investment and/or land cost, factors that were also excluded from Crossman's cost estimates. The authors showed that the industry costs per barrel fall within the range of $9.75 to $10.25. They concluded that just under $10.00 was the best approximation for the industry as a

TABLE 12.2. VARIABLE AND FIXED COSTS OF PRODUCTION FROM SURVEY OF 56 MASSACHUSETTS CRANBERRY GROWERS, 1977

	ACRES REPORTING	AVERAGE COSTS PER ACRE	AVERAGE COSTS PER BARREL	PERCENT COSTS PER BARREL
Variable costs				
Hired labor	1,569	$277.56	$2.72	26.1%
Management salary	1,244	46.66	0.46	4.4
Supplies	1,374	29.04	0.28	2.7
Gasoline	1,671	25.49	0.25	2.4
Fertilizer	1,627	18.62	0.18	1.7
Professional serv.	1,643	19.90	0.20	1.9
Repairs	1,627	88.36	0.87	8.3
Outside hire	1,471	39.12	0.38	3.6
Pesticides	1,638	82.28	0.81	7.8
Sanding	1,195	19.14	0.19	1.8
Electricity	1,602	29.37	0.29	2.8
Telephone	1,240	7.29	0.07	0.7
Packaging sup.	1,527	5.00	0.05	0.5
Miscellaneous	1,499	36.27	0.36	3.4
Subtotal		724.10	7.11	68.1
Fixed costs				
Depreciation	1,759	80.82	0.79	7.6
Interest	1,532	83.57	0.82	7.8
Taxes	1,759	138.55	1.36	13.1
Insurance	1,676	35.86	0.35	3.4
Subtotal		338.80	3.32	31.9
Average total cost		1,062.90	10.43	100.0

SOURCE: Ames and Christensen 1978.

whole. These production cost figures were not too different from the figures Crossman reported for the commercial operations he sampled 30 years earlier.

Prices

In 1855 Addison Flint reported that he received $13.00 per barrel for his 50 barrel crop of cranberries that year (Eastwood 1856). In a letter to J. J. White for inclusion in his 1870 book *Cranberry Culture,* A. D. Makepeace of Hyannis, Massachusetts, indicated that he had received between $10.00 and $12.50 per barrel for his crop between 1867 and 1869. In the same book, White reported that his own 1869 crop brought him $25.00 per barrel in Philadelphia and that the U.S. government had recently adopted a plan of regularly issuing cranberries among its supplies to ships for the prevention of scurvy. With the rapid development of the whaling fleets, which would often put out to sea for years at a time, cranberries became an important staple for scurvy prevention. It was not uncommon for spot prices to reach $50 per barrel at the principal whaling ports. These early decades of the cranberry industry were truly the "golden years" of profitability, but by the end of the century the glitter was beginning to fade. It would be more than 100 years from the days of the great whaling fleets before cranberry growers could again dream of prices of $50 per barrel, let alone experience them (table 12.3).

Gilbert (1932) spoke of the problems of supply and demand and their influence on cranberry prices in his report to the Cranberry Producers Association of Wareham, Massachusetts, entitled "A Plan for the Stabilization of Cranberries." At the turn of the century, one of the biggest problems to face cranberry growers was the depressed prices that accompanied overproduction. Fresh fruit sales could no longer be relied upon to utilize all their production. An alternative use of the surplus had to be developed, and this need was unquestionably the impetus for the development of the canning industry. Gilbert had observed that by the 1920s the fresh market would absorb only about 500,000 barrels of cranberries before the surplus would begin to depress prices (table 12.3). He established $10 per barrel as the price at which cranberry production would be profitable; any price below this level would seriously erode profits. Production above one-half million barrels appeared to have this effect on prices. His plan to stabilize prices was simple and straightforward. He advocated a dual-price system whereby growers would receive on a proportioned basis $10 per barrel for the first 500,000 barrels produced and a base price of $4 per barrel for the excess production, which would be used in manufactured products. Thus, if production in a given year was at 550,000 barrels, a 10 percent surplus of 50,000 barrels would be declared, and the grower would correspondingly receive $10 per barrel for 90 percent

TABLE 12.3. TOTAL PRODUCTION, UTILIZATION, PRICE, AND
TOTAL VALUE OF CRANBERRIES FOR THE YEARS
1900–1987

Year	Production in Thousands of Barrels	UTILIZATION		Price	Value in Thousands of Dollars
		Fresh	Processed		
1900	318	100%	0%	$ 6.50	$ 2,067
1901	414	100	0	5.50	2,277
1902	317	100	0	6.20	1,965
1903	419	100	0	6.00	2,514
1904	385	100	0	5.00	1,925
1905	271	100	0	7.50	2,033
1906	412	100	0	6.30	2,596
1907	452	100	0	6.30	2,848
1908	344	100	0	7.50	2,580
1909	601	100	0	5.30	3,185
1910	569	100	0	5.60	3,186
1911	473	100	0	6.90	3,264
1912	512	100	0	6.50	3,328
1913	498	100	0	6.20	3,088
1914	664	100	0	4.00	2,656
1915	476	100	0	6.40	3,046
1916	571	100	0	6.50	3,712
1917	293	100	0	10.00	2,930
1918	375	100	0	8.70	3,263
1919	590	99	1	7.90	4,661
1920	472	99	1	10.30	4,862
1921	397	99	1	12.90	5,121
1922	597	99	1	10.50	6,269
1923	686	98	2	7.90	5,419

TABLE 12.3. (*Continued*)

Year	Production in Thousands of Barrels	UTILIZATION		Price	Value in Thousands of Dollars
		Fresh	Processed		
1924	610	95	5	10.00	6,100
1925	609	95	5	10.90	6,638
1926	762	94	6	7.20	5,486
1927	512	93	7	12.80	6,554
1928	559	87	13	14.40	8,050
1929	570	90	10	13.40	7,638
1930	584	94	6	10.90	6,366
1931	654	96	4	6.50	4,251
1932	580	94	6	7.70	4,466
1933	699	91	9	6.30	4,404
1934	445	92	8	11.30	5,029
1935	516	83	17	11.85	6,115
1936	504	82	18	13.20	6,653
1937	877	61	39	8.20	7,191
1938	474	92	8	10.90	5,167
1939	704	68	32	10.00	7,040
1940	571	63	37	12.70	7,252
1941	725	59	41	11.60	8,410
1942	812	49	51	12.10	9,825
1943	688	58	42	16.20	11,146
1944	376	55	45	24.60	9,250
1945	656	53	47	21.00	13,776
1946	856	34	66	31.40	26,878
1947	792	43	57	17.20	13,622

(*continued*)

TABLE 12.3. (*Continued*)

Year	Production in Thousands of Barrels	UTILIZATION		Price	Value in Thousands of Dollars
		Fresh	Processed		
1948	968	53	47	9.90	9,583
1949	841	68	32	5.80	4,878
1950	983	60	40	6.70	6,586
1951	910	49	51	12.30	11,193
1952	804	45	55	16.40	13,186
1953	1,203	36	64	12.50	15,038
1954	1,019	46	54	10.70	10,903
1955	1,026	47	53	8.60	8,824
1956	988	45	55	8.90	8,793
1957	1,050	43	57	11.00	11,550
1958	1,166	40	60	11.60	13,526
1959	1,252	44	56	9.20	11,518
1960	1,341	33	67	8.80	11,801
1961	1,236	49	51	8.61	10,642
1962	1,325	48	52	11.70	15,502
1963	1,255	37	63	12.10	15,186
1964	1,345	42	58	14.40	19,368
1965	1,437	35	65	15.60	22,417
1966	1,599	28	72	15.60	29,444
1967	1,424	29	71	15.50	22,072
1968	1,468	24	76	16.50	24,222
1969	1,823	22	78	16.30	29,715
1970	2,039	18	82	12.85	26,201
1971	2,265	18	82	10.35	23,443
1972	2,078	15	85	12.50	25,875

TABLE 12.3. (*Continued*)

Year	Production in Thousands of Barrels	UTILIZATION		Price	Value in Thousands of Dollars
		Fresh	Processed		
1973	2,100	19	81	12.40	26,040
1974	2,236	20	80	13.60	30,410
1975	2,075	15	85	11.10	23,033
1976	2,407	19	81	13.50	31,532
1977	2,102	22	78	18.10	38,046
1978	2,459	17	83	21.50	52,869
1979	2,476	13	87	26.70	66,109
1980	2,698	13	87	33.20	89,574
1981	2,593	11	89	41.50	107,610
1982	3,039	17	83	46.70	141,921
1983	2,986	11	89	52.00	155,272
1984	3,322	9	91	54.50	181,049
1985	3,485	9	91	54.50	189,932
1986	3,680	10	90	51.60	189,888
1987	3,675	10	90	51.60*	189,630*

*Estimated

SOURCE: USDA National Agricultural Statistics Service 1900–1987.

of his crop and $4 per barrel for the remaining 10 percent of his crop. The plan was to be administered by a marketing committee of cranberry growers representing the industry. Although never adopted by the industry at the time, Gilbert's plan did contain some of the rudiments for the National Marketing Order that cranberry producers operate under today.

As the nation emerged from the Great Depression, cranberry prices again began to increase in response to the increase in per capita consumer income (Wolf 1950). The war years were a period of sustained high prices, reflecting the increased demand for the military. In the decade following World War II, cranberry prices were for the most part at parity, as computed by the USDA

(Wolf 1956b). In 1955 the base price for cranberries was determined to be $15.80, whereas the parity price was calculated at $16.90 per barrel. Ominously, however, by the 1950s increases in per capita consumer income were no longer reflected in increased cranberry prices. Imbalances between production and consumption were again having a negative effect on cranberry prices. This period of depressed profitability reached its nadir with the "great cranberry scare" of 1959, which occurred when the Secretary of the U.S. Department of Health, Education, and Welfare, Arthur S. Fleming, nationally publicized that a certain amount of cranberries tainted with the weed killer aminotriazole, a suspected carcinogen, had entered the market chain. Even though only a minuscule amount of the cranberry crop was affected, the national revelation had a devastating effect on cranberry prices. For the next few years, prices were to remain depressed, and undoubtedly these years represented the most critical period for the cranberry industry since the turn of the century when the false blossom disease ravaged the industry. By this time the industry had to deal with yearly production levels of over a million barrels of cranberries. It was not until a strong new marketing thrust was in place, complete with new products and production restraints, that the industry was again to see profitable times.

The industry recovered slowly from the cranberry scare as production and prices increased steadily—thanks mainly to the increased demand for processed cranberries, which made cranberries a year-round fruit. The breakthrough in cranberry prices, however, came with the marketing of the highly successful new product, cranberry cocktail. By the end of the 1970s, prices began to skyrocket as production could not keep up with demand even though by now more than two million barrels of cranberries were being produced annually. In 1982 production amounted to more than three million barrels for the first time, and by 1983 cranberries were again bringing over $50 per barrel. Never in their wildest expectations could the cranberry growers of a generation ago ever believe that these price conditions, so reminiscent of the whaling era, could ever exist again.

Returns

In 1855 Addison Flint received $650 for the 50 barrels of cranberries produced from his recently developed two-acre cranberry meadow. The $325 per acre return realized by Flint was close to the $383 per acre that A. D. Makepeace averaged over a three-year period (1867–1869) from a young bog he had recently established. On his young bog, Makepeace had averaged a net profit of $273 for the three years indicated. More interesting, however, was the reference that Makepeace made in his letter to J. J. White of a bog he knew of which had returned its owner a net profit of $500 per acre per year for

TABLE 12.4. TEN-YEAR AVERAGE VALUES FOR CRANBERRY ACREAGE, YIELD PER ACRE, PRICE PER BARREL, TOTAL VALUE, AND RETURN PER ACRE FOR THE DECADES BETWEEN 1900 AND 1987

DECADE	ACREAGE IN HUNDREDS OF ACRES	YIELD PER ACRE IN BARRELS	PRICE PER BARREL	TOTAL VALUE IN MILLIONS	RETURN PER ACRE
1900–1909	252	16	$ 6.37	$ 2.462	$ 96
1910–1919	269	19	7.03	3.385	126
1920–1929	273	21	11.14	6.268	230
1930–1939	278	22	9.85	5.769	208
1940–1949	264	28	16.34	11.547	437
1950–1959	232	46	10.75	10.981	473
1960–1969	209	68	13.34	19.119	915
1970–1979	227	98	15.26	34.350	1,513
1980–1987	239	130	48.20	155.566	6,509

Source: Compiled from USDA National Agricultural Statistics Service 1900–1987.

the preceding ten years (White 1870). These kinds of returns led Makepeace to comment that the profits of cranberry culture were unusually large in comparison to other farm crops being raised in the area.

By the turn of the century, however, these extraordinary returns were a thing of the past. The first decade of the new century saw an average yearly return of only $96 per acre, more in keeping with other crops (table 12.4). Although returns per acre increased during the early decades of the new century (except for the depression decade of the 1930s), the so-called golden era of cranberry growing had apparently come to an end. It would not be until the war years of the 1940s that cranberry growers would again realize annual returns per acre comparable to those of the 1800s.

Throughout the 1950s gross returns continued to average more than $400 per acre, although profits were being squeezed by the poor prices being received. As pointed out by Wolf (1956a), the higher gross returns being realized by cranberry growers during this period was entirely due to the increasing population rather than to any increase in demand that might have been expected with increasing per capita income. Clearly what was needed was some stimulation in demand such as might be brought about by increased convenience in the use of the product. During this decade the use of new organic pesticides resulted in a marked increase in yield per acre. Yet growers were forced to retire marginal acres during this poor economic period in order to stay in business.

The 1960s saw a further retrenchment of the industry with the retirement of more acreage. Technology, however, was responsible for exponential gains in the average yields per acre being achieved. Included in these technological advances were the modern organophosphate insecticides, fungicides, and herbicides, the extensive use of sprinkler irrigation for frost control, and water harvesting—all of which boosted annual returns to over $900 per acre. During the latter part of this decade, prices were beginning to remain above the critical $10 per barrel break-even point, thus insuring profits. These prices reflected the ever-increasing utilization by the processing market. Increasing productivity and higher prices continued to insure increased returns and greater profitability throughout the 1970s and 1980s. By 1987 cranberry growers were realizing returns, and profits that were even greater than those their ancestors enjoyed in the mid-1800s.

Marketing

Packaging

The traditional shipping package for the cranberry has been the cranberry barrel, which held about 85 quarts and, when full, varied in weight from 90 to 105 pounds. It was in this container that cranberries went to sea with the early whaling ships and the U.S. Navy. Very often the cooperage plant would be set up where the grading and packing of the berries were to take place (Urann 1912). Hoops from the West, staves from Maine, and heads sawed from lumber on the property would be assembled at the cooperage, thus eliminating the necessity of transporting empty barrels. When filled, the barrels were conveyed to railcars located on a nearby siding for shipment to markets throughout the country. The standard barrel as a unit of measure was established by an act of Congress effective 1 July 1916, which fixed its dimensions so as to hold a content of 5,826 cubic inches. Today the barrel terminology is still used by the industry to express cranberry production, although the barrel has been standardized to equal exactly 100 pounds net weight (1 cwt.).

The barrel itself, as the favored method of transport, soon disappeared in the decades following World War I, being replaced by cranberry boxes of varying sizes (Salters 1936; J. L. Wilcox 1925). The boxes constructed of a good grade of pine were first made to hold a half barrel of cranberries; later, quarter-barrel and one-eighth-barrel boxes were built (plate 12.1). The boxes were constructed with slits on their tops, sides, and bottoms to allow for ventilation. The boxes—or crates, as they were often called—could therefore be used to store cranberries as well as to transport them. When the boxes were being filled, they would be vibrated to insure a tight pack (C. J. Hall 1939b). Not only were the boxes more attractive as a shipping container but the berries would arrive to market in better physical condition because they were subjected to less weight pressure in the smaller containers.

After World War II, a growing trend developed in the merchandising of fresh fruits and vegetables toward *prepackaging*. That term was used to denote the packaging of produce in individual consumer-size packages for retail sale. The rapid development of supermarkets and self-service stores increased the demand for prepackaged, ready-to-take-home food. The quarter-barrel shipping crate was rapidly becoming obsolete. Kraft paper bags were initially used as packaging material but were rapidly replaced by MST (moistureproof, heat-sealing, and transparent) cellophane film (Shank 1952b).

Early research by Hayes and his colleagues (Hayes et al. 1948) demonstrated that cranberries could be stored prepackaged in cellophane bags at 35° F for up to three months without serious spoilage loss. At room temperature, however, spoilage within the bags occurred rapidly. It did not appear to make any difference whether the bags were perforated or not. The cellophane film was an effective barrier against moisture loss, but it also impeded carbon dioxide exchange. A subsequent film developed by the DuPont Company called LST cellophane (less-moisture-protective film) allowed for carbon dioxide diffusion and alleviated this problem (Shank 1952a). Subsequent research showed that the new plastic films including polyethylene, Mylar, and Saran were superior to the cellophane films in terms of preventing

PLATE 12.1. PACKAGING CRANBERRIES IN QUARTER-BARREL BOXES—THE FAVORITE SHIPPING CONTAINER FOR COMMERCE JUST PRIOR TO THE INTRODUCTION OF MODERN PACKAGING MATERIALS (Courtesy Massachusetts Cranberry Experiment Station)

moisture loss by the berries and allowing for gas exchange (Ayres and Denisen 1958; Brown 1954). Today the plastic films have replaced cellophane as the favored packaging film for cranberries.

Two types of prepackaging containers appeared to meet the merchandizing need: the one-pound transparent bag and the one-pound window carton (Lebeau 1950). Lebeau determined that it cost only a few cents more per quarter-barrel unit to package cranberries in cellophane than in bulk (plate 12.2). Two types of filling machines were employed: one which filled readymade bags (plate 12.3) and the other which made and filled the pillow-shaped bags simultaneously (transwrap type). The latter type of filling machine appeared to be better adapted for heavy-volume operations, and the smaller

PLATE 12.2. HAND SCREENING CRANBERRIES BEFORE PACKAGING
(Courtesy Massachusetts Cranberry Experiment Station)

machines using ready-made bags seemed more appropriate for moderate-sized operations. The window carton, while slightly more expensive than the bag, did not require a significant investment in packaging equipment. The window of the carton was made of Celanese acetate, which was gas permeable, enabling the cranberries to breathe (Williams 1952). By the mid-1950s, virtually all of the crop that was marketed fresh was prepackaged. The new cranberry packages were not only a convenient unit of sale for the consumer but they also provided their own freezer container wherein the berries could be easily frozen. In addition, the transparent bags made for a handsome display of the fruit and also provided a surface for grower promotion.

Prepackaged cranberries were packed in corrugated paperboard cases (24 one-pound packages to a case) for shipment to retail outlets. When shipped via refrigerated transit, the berries maintained excellent quality if transit temperatures remained between 38° and 42°F (3°–5.5°C) (Kaufman et al. 1957). Precooling the prepackaged cranberries before transit was even better in

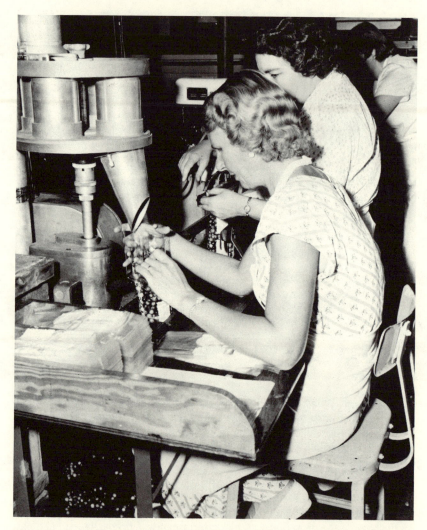

PLATE 12.3. AN EARLY CRANBERRY PACKAGING MACHINE PACKING
CRANBERRIES IN ONE-POUND CELLOPHANE BAGS
(Courtesy Massachusetts Cranberry Experiment Station)

terms of reducing decay in transit (Kaufman et al. 1958). Precooling the packages insured that the cases positioned in the center of the transit vehicle had
the desired reduced temperature.

Maintaining the quality of the packaged fruit on the grocer's shelf is a problem the cranberry shares with all perishable fruit crops. Attempts to control

fungal decay in packaged cranberries by including ammonia pellets in the package were only partially successful (Harding 1957). The desired reduction in fungal decay was attained but the ammonia also caused injury to the cranberry. Refrigeration still appears to be the preferred method of maintaining good cranberry shelf life. When Tolle (1959) compared retail display methods for cranberries, he concluded that the methods of display in decreasing order of desirable shelf life were (1) continuous display in mechanically refrigerated case; (2) continuous display on a false rack in a mechanically refrigerated case; (3) display on a nonrefrigerated counter in the daytime, followed by storage at 40° F at night; (4) continuous display on crushed ice; and (5) continuous display on a nonrefrigerated counter. After three weeks on a nonrefrigerated counter, cranberries suffered losses amounting to more than 80 percent.

Brands and Labels

Although cranberries were never marketed according to varietal names as apples are today, during the heyday of fresh fruit sales cranberries were sold by brand name (Franklin et al. 1924). The brands were established by individual growers or adopted by grower-selling organizations. The objective, of course, was to establish levels of quality that could be associated with a particular brand, whereupon premium prices could be obtained. For example, the New England Cranberry Sales Company had six brands for the Early Black cultivar and five for the Howes cultivar. The brands were distinguished on the basis of berry coloration, size, and shelf life. For the Early Black cultivar, the premium brand was Capitol, a uniform, red-colored berry, which was capable of withstanding a two-week transit without undue loss in shelf life. This was followed in decreasing order of quality by the brands Harvard, Minot's Light, Mayflower and Monarch, Chanticleer, and Skipper. The Howes cultivar was classified in decreasing order of quality by the following brand names: Santa Claus, Holiday, Honker and Mistletoe, Battleship, and Turkey. The brands (actually grades) were determined by an inspector appointed and paid by the producer or sales organization.

The Wisconsin Cranberry Sales Company developed grades for Wisconsin's major cranberry cultivars (Goldsworthy 1943). The principal cultivar, Searles Jumbo, was divided into the Fancy Antler brand and the Deer brand, the former representing the larger berry. The Howes cultivar was graded into the larger-fruited Roval brand and the smaller-fruited Star brand. The usual method of determining berry size was to count the number of berries in a standard half-pint cup; the fewer the number of berries needed to fill the cup, the larger the berries. McFarlin berries were designated as the Banner brand if their cup count did not exceed 90 berries or as the Fox brand if the cup count was higher. Vines taken from the wild marshes in Wisconsin were grouped under the Natives cultivar. Berries of the Natives cultivar were graded into the large-fruited Bouquet brand (<115 berries per cup) and the smaller-fruited Badger brand (115–140 berries per cup).

Color, size, and condition were also the criteria used by the Growers' Cranberry Company in New Jersey to establish brand names, or *labels* as they were called. The labels were established in 1911 by the Growers' Cranberry Company Label Committee consisting of H. L. Knight, C. E. Budd, and C. D. Makepeace. Labels of the Early Black cultivar, or Late Reds as they were sometimes called because of their cherry red color, were in order of lateness of harvest, namely, Heather, American Beauty, Silver Medal, Princeton, and Red Bell. The Early Red cultivar had only one label, Red Clover, which usually became available after 15 October. Later, the same label was also used for the Garwood Bell cultivar. The Jerseys, or Native Jerseys as they were sometimes referred to, were usually ready after 20 October and were labeled as Shamrock, Golden Rod Brand, Sunrise, Homestead, and Arbutus. The Jersey Long Keepers cultivar, or Jersey Blues as it were sometimes called, was marketed under the Plantation label and were also ready after 20 October. The Howes cultivar was marketed under the labels Excelsior, Rancocas, Laurel, Jersey Belle, Quail, and Monmouth. In addition, the Point Howes cultivar received the label of Atlantic. Liberty Bell, Fenwick, Hanover, and Swan were label names for the late-season Centennial cultivar. The Champion cultivar was marketed under the labels of Globe and Dixie, and the McFarlin cultivar under the labels of Mallard and Cottage. The Plum cultivar was marketed under its own name, and the Richards cultivar was sold under the Alpine label. The Howard Bell and Braddock Bell cultivars were marketed under the labels Olive and Ruby Brand, respectively.

In addition to these premium fruit labels, cranberries also received stock labels that denoted mixed cultivars or fruit of inferior quality. Two such stock labels were Arrow, which denoted berries that could survive 15 days of travel, and the Oak brand, consisting of berries that were unsuitable for shipping. When berries were shipped in the chaff, usually for long-term storage for the winter and spring trade, they did not receive labels but received marks on the ends of the crates or boxes in which they were stored. The mark "Ox" meant the berries were of medium color and average size, and "Rex" meant they were well cleaned and of average size.

Little is known about the origins of these colorful brand and label names. Clues as to why certain names were used and who gave the brands and labels their names are scarce. It is known that Jimmy Holman and H. L. Knight chose the Plum brand in 1911, and that Edith M. Haines chose the Silver

Medal label in 1901 when she sent cranberries from the Birches and Hog Wallow bogs to the Buffalo Exposition, where they won a Silver Medal. Individual growers would often establish their own brands, as did the Brick family when they designed their Pantry brand. Unfortunately, the stories behind most of the labels have been lost over time.

Sales Organizations

The fact that the cranberry was a perishable crop produced in widely disbursed geographic areas, the sales of which were restricted to a relatively short period, led producers to experiment with cooperative marketing organizations relatively early in the industry's development (Hobson 1923). One of the most successful of these early cooperative efforts was the Growers' Cranberry Company, established by a number of the larger growers of New Jersey and Massachusetts in 1895. The organization maintained efficient salespeople who, operating out of their Philadelphia office, kept in contact with market conditions and controlled the distribution of the crop. Berries were sold under the private brand labels of individual growers as described above. Each grower would receive the proceeds from the sales of his or her individual berries minus a 5 percent sales commission. Up until this time, growers had individually marketed their own crops to cash buyers or on consignment. Often the prices offered did not cover the costs of production because of unethical practices carried out by buyers and jobbers. Forming a united cooperative front proved to be a highly successful method of thwarting such cutthroat practices. In addition, a marketing strategy was absolutely essential to deal with the rapidly increasing production that was occurring by the turn of the century.

At about this same time, similar cooperative organizations were being established in Massachusetts and Wisconsin (Franklin et al. 1924). Massachusetts growers organized the Cape Cod Cranberry Sales Company in 1895 along the same lines as the Growers' Cranberry Company, although not as successful as the latter organization. In 1897 some of the leading cranberry growers of central Wisconsin formed the Cranberry Growers' Union, with headquarters in Wisconsin Rapids. This organization evolved into the Wisconsin Cranberry Sales Company by 1905 and established a sales manager in Des Moines, Iowa, and later one in Chicago. The Wisconsin Cranberry Sales Company developed the innovative approach of brand *pooling* whereby the price received for a particular brand was pooled over a season, and the returns distributed to the individual growers based on this pooled price and the amount of the particular brand submitted by the grower. In addition to simplifying the bookkeeping, this method had the advantage of smoothing out price fluctuations during the course of the marketing season. By 1906 the Wisconsin Cranberry Sales Company could boast that it was marketing the crops for over 90 percent of the growers in Wisconsin.

So successful was the Wisconsin organization that in 1907 similar marketing organizations patterned after the Wisconsin Cranberry Sales Company were organized in Massachusetts and New Jersey. The New England Cranberry Sales Company was formed in Massachusetts and the New Jersey Cranberry Sales Company in New Jersey (Benson 1938). Together, the three state sales organizations formed a separate central selling organization in 1907 known as the National Fruit Exchange, with headquarters in New York and a branch office in Chicago. At this point the Growers' Cranberry Company was in direct competition with the new marketing organization. The bumper crop of 1910 brought this competition to a head and led directly to the consolidation in 1911 of the Growers' Cranberry Company with the National Fruit Exchange, replacing the New Jersey Cranberry Sales Company on the Exchange. With this consolidation, the National Fruit Exchange became the American Cranberry Exchange, and by 1923 it was marketing 75 percent of the total crop in Wisconsin and about 65 percent in both New Jersey and Massachusetts. The remaining crop was being marketed by individual growers or through other marketing organizations such as the Cape Cod Cranberry Distributors in Massachusetts and the Pacific Cranberry Exchange, established in 1917 along the lines of the American Cranberry Exchange.

In 1919 each of the three state sales companies of the American Cranberry Exchange were reorganized into nonstock, nonprofit, cooperative organizations in order to comply with the Clayton Amendment of the Sherman Antitrust Law. The marketing operations and the grading and pooling systems, however, were retained. Basically, the state organization was to act as an intermediary between the grower and the central selling organization. An office was maintained in the local district where records of all shipments and sales were kept. Field agents were hired to oversee the picking, sorting, grading, and packing of the fruit. Central facilities for cleaning and packing the fruit were often provided. The state organization furnished the barrels and boxes needed for packing as well as any labels or other advertising that was to be placed on the containers. The state organization was also responsible for distributing the orders received from the central selling organization, making all transportation arrangements, overseeing the pooling system, and distributing the grower's money. It also had to take in any grower complaints and attempt to deal with them. For all of this, the local organization would receive 2 percent of the total sales for its expenses. Monies not used for expenses would be periodically refunded to the growers on a proportioned basis.

The American Cranberry Exchange functioned as the central selling agency for its member organizations, operating out of New York with A. U.

Chaney as its general manager for many years. The Exchange took charge of the carlots as they were made available from the local organizations and was responsible for all the selling and collections. The marketing success of the Exchange depended on the ability of their professional salespeople to coordinate demand with supply and to time shipments so that market gluts were avoided. The Exchange would arrange for cleaning and sorting of the fruit after transit (if needed) before the fruit was sent to the consumer. Another important function of the Exchange was to expend funds for advertising, which was absolutely essential if cranberries were to receive a greater portion of the consumer's discretionary food expenditures. Not only was it important to get more people to eat cranberries but it was also highly desirable to increase the per capita consumption of cranberries. To aid its marketing effort and to facilitate advertising, the Exchange developed the Eatmor trade name. By 1920, 1.5 percent of the gross return on a barrel of cranberries was being spent on advertising. To cover its expenses, the Exchange received 5 percent of the gross sales. Liaison between the Exchange and the member organizations was maintained via a board of directors that was comprised of grower members representing the individual state organizations. All growers marketing their fruit through the Exchange were members of the organization on a one-person-one-vote basis (Goldsworthy 1947). In 1953 the American Cranberry Exchange changed its name to Eatmor Cranberries, Inc., reflecting the domination in the public's eye of the Eatmor brand name over the marketing organization name.

The success of this marketing strategy could be seen in the percentage return to the grower of the consumer dollar. Based on a barrel containing 100 pounds of fruit and a retail price of 18 cents per pound, the cranberry grower was receiving 54 percent of the consumer dollar in 1920. This was far greater than returns normally realized on perishable food commodities. In addition to the 1.5 percent used for advertising, the remaining portion of the consumer dollar was allocated for the following costs: cooperative organizations (3.5%); transportation (7.4%); wholesale (11.2%); and retail (22.4%).

As successful as the American Cranberry Exchange was in marketing fresh cranberries, increasing production and decreasing demand for fresh fruit made it imperative to develop other marketing channels. Such an alternative marketing channel was provided by the cranberry canning industry, which had its origins with the United Cape Cod Cranberry Company (later to be called the Ocean Spray Preserving Company) founded by Marcus L. Urann of Hanson, Massachusetts (Peterson et al. 1968). Originally, canning was visualized merely as a method of utilizing fruit that was not suitable for fresh sales. By the 1930s the industry realized that canning was not only a way of using unsold fruit but was also a method of providing cranberries to the consumer all year round. Thus, in 1930 mass production canning techniques were introduced, and canning became a serious alternative to fresh sales. It was at this time that the Ocean Spray Preserving Company was reorganized into a growers' cooperative called Cranberry Canners, Inc.

No longer could the canning industry rely only on fruit unwanted by the fresh market; it needed its own sustained supply of good quality berries. This led to the active solicitation by the company's founder, M. L. Urann, of cranberry crops wherever he could find them. The competition for berries between the canning and fresh market was exacerbated by World War II, which created a great demand for the canned product for the military (C. L. Lewis 1944). By 1942, 44 percent of the national crop was being processed. Cranberry Canners, Inc. was receiving berries from independent growers in Massachusetts and New Jersey, from the New England Cranberry Sales Company, under special arrangements from the Makepeace and Urann cranberry properties, from the Wisconsin Cranberry Sales Company (which by now had become a large stockholder in Cranberry Canners, Inc.), and from the West Coast.

In 1946 Cranberry Canners, Inc. was renamed the National Cranberry Association. It marketed both fresh and processed cranberries under the Ocean Spray label. By 1949 the National Cranberry Association was marketing 55 percent of the nation's cranberry crop, compared to 28 percent for the rival American Cranberry Exchange cooperative, which was marketing fresh cranberries under the Eatmor brand (Pickett 1949). In 1957 the National Cranberry Association adopted the Ocean Spray name and became Ocean Spray Cranberries, Inc., which today has its headquarters in Middleboro, Massachusetts. By 1957 more than 50 percent of the national cranberry crop was being processed, and today this figure has increased to more than 80 percent.

Marketing Order

With the million-barrel-production years of the 1950s came the perplexing problem of crop *carry-over* (Wolf 1955). The carry-over in any given year represented the amount of fruit that remained unsold on the shelves and in the freezers of distributors at the end of the year. By the mid-1950s, carry-overs were amounting to the equivalent of hundreds of thousands of barrels of cranberries. Not even the burgeoning processing industry could deal with the problem. On 9 November 1959, just after the completion of the new harvest, the cranberry market was devastated by the aminotriazole residue revelations by the federal government. Not only was the 1959 crop practically unsalable (cranberry growers received over 8.5 million dollars in indemnification by the USDA that year) but in 1960 and 1961 crops could not be completely sold either. The industry was in desperate straits. It appealed to the USDA to help it sort out its marketing problem. So it was that the Cranberry Marketing Order was approved in a referendum vote of growers in July 1962. Administered by the USDA's Consumer and Marketing Service, the cranberry order permitted the industry to regulate the handling and marketing of cranberries in an orderly fashion.

The key to establishing an orderly market, thus stabilizing prices, was the *set-aside*. This amounted to restricting a certain amount of the new harvest from normal marketing channels. Cranberries withheld from the market could only be sold for export (excluding Canada), distributed to a charitable institution for consumption, or earmarked for any nonhuman food use (including research). To administer the program, a seven-person industrial committee, the Cranberry Marketing Committee, was established which was to meet with USDA representatives at the beginning of each harvest season to determine the set-aside for the year. Specifically, the committee was responsible for submitting to the Secretary of Agriculture a report setting the marketing policy for that crop year. The report was to contain (1) the estimated total production of cranberries; (2) the estimated general quality; (3) the estimated carryover of frozen fruit and other processed goods; (4) the expected demand conditions for cranberries; (5) figures on supplies of competing commodities; (6) trends and levels of consumer income; (7) the recommended quantity of marketable cranberries, including a recommended adequate carryover into the following crop year of frozen or other products; (8) the recommended allotment (set-aside) percentage for that year, if any; and (9) other factors having a bearing on the marketing of cranberries.

The new marketing order was needed the first year it was approved. It was deemed necessary to restrict the sale of 12 percent of the 1962 crop in order to stabilize the price. Most of this first set-aside was used in research to produce new cranberry products. Not all growers were happy with this turn of events (Goldsworthy 1963). Particularly grating was the fact that only berries receiving a USDA grade A rating could be used for the set-aside. This meant that the fruit to be set aside had to be graded and assured that it was fresh, clean, mature, fairly well colored, free of rot and decay, and free of bruises and scars. In addition, the fruit had to have a minimum diameter of $\frac{9}{32}$ inches. Marketers of fresh fruit apparently felt that the set-aside would discriminate against fresh fruit supplies since water-harvested fruit would not qualify as grade A berries. Fortunately, few set-asides ever had to be employed by the industry in the following years, although the marketing order is still in force. The development of new cranberry products, including the popular cranberry juice cocktail (which by 1966 accounted for half of the fruit processed), contributed to an increase in per capita consumption so that even two-million-barrel crops were being successfully marketed by the 1980s.

Utilization

Consumption

For the first 100 years of its commercial production, the American cranberry was sold primarily as fresh fruit. During much of this period, the fresh berries were distributed to the retailer in barrels and later in boxes from which he or she dispensed the berries to the consumer in paper bags. Subsequently, fresh berries were prepackaged and sold to the consumer in convenient one-pound plastic bags or boxes.

It was not until World War I that the first recorded amounts of the current season's crop were sold for processing (table 12.3). For the next nine years, however, processing did not represent a significant method of crop utilization, accounting for less than 10 percent of the crop. With the establishment of Cranberry Canners, Inc. in 1930, however, the percentage of the crop utilized for processing began to increase dramatically. By the end of the decade, more than 30 percent of the crop was being canned. World War II saw a dramatic increase in processed fruit utilization as supplies were mobilized for the war effort. For the next decade, fresh fruit utilization and processing used about equal amounts of each season's new crop.

With the 1950s came the first million-barrel crops, and with them the need to increase cranberry consumption. It was imperative that cranberries be made available the year round, so it was during these years that more cranberries were sold for canning than were sold fresh for the first time. From this period forward, fresh fruit sales would no longer be the dominant form of cranberry utilization. During the 1960s the importance of fresh fruit sales was further eroded as cranberry juice drinks were introduced to the market on a significant level. By the end of the 1960s, cranberry juice cocktail was utilizing half of the fruit made available for processing, which by now amounted to 70 percent of the crop. The increase in the percentage of crop utilized for processing, which amounted to 80 percent during the 1970s and 90 percent in the 1980s, was directly related to the phenomenal increase in consumption of cranberry fruit drinks that included a host of blended drinks using other fruit juices.

The rapid development and success of the processing technology were essential to the survival of the cranberry industry. An ominous development during the early decades of this century was the steady decline in the per capita consumption of cranberries (Kross 1950). In the decade from 1910 to 1919, the average per capita consumption of fresh cranberries in the United States was 0.54 pounds (245 g) (table 12.5). This value declined to 0.14 pounds (50 g) by 1987. Until the availability of processed cranberry products, this decline in fresh fruit consumption meant that per capita cranberry con-

TABLE 12.5. PER CAPITA CONSUMPTION OF CRANBERRIES (IN POUNDS) IN AMERICA FOR THE DECADES BETWEEN 1910 AND 1987

DECADE	FRESH	PROCESSED	TOTAL
1910–1919	0.54	0	0.54
1920–1929	0.47	0	0.47
1930–1939	0.38	0.06	0.44
1940–1949	0.27	0.18	0.45
1950–1959	0.23	0.28	0.51
1960–1969	0.23	0.42	0.65
1970–1979	0.17	0.80	0.97
1980–1987	0.14	1.11	1.25

SOURCE: Compiled from USDA National Agricultural Statistics Service Data 1900–1987.
NOTE: To convert pounds to grams multiply by 454

sumption on the whole was declining in this country, a problem that was being exacerbated by the increase in production that was occurring. When cranberries were made available the year round, intensive advertising programs could be initiated that emphasized the use of cranberries with all kinds of meals and not just Thanksgiving turkey. Even more significant was the effect the new cranberry products had on per capita consumption. By 1987 Americans were consuming more than one pound (454 g) of cranberries per man, woman, and child.

Uses

The uses that the Native Americans and the early colonists made of cranberries have already been addressed. The early seafarers must have eaten cranberries out of hand from the barrels stored on deck during their long voyages. Until the introduction of cranberry juice cocktail, however, the way of eating cranberries preferred by most consumers was as cranberry sauce. Until the modern canning industry developed, homemakers prepared their own sauce from the fresh cranberries that arrived on the market near the Thanksgiving and Christmas seasons. Cranberries therefore became associated with the holiday season—to be served with the Thanksgiving turkey and the Christmas goose. The delightful sauce was prepared by cooking the red berries with sugar and water until the skins popped. The pectin in the skins would cause the gelling of the sauce, which was then served as a condiment to the meal.

When canned cranberry sauce became available, an extensive effort was made by the industry to encourage consumers to use cranberry sauce as a condiment with all meat dishes throughout the year. Another approach the industry took to increase the consumption of cranberries was to develop and encourage other uses for cranberries such as in preserves, jellies, relish, barbeque sauce, candies, and of course cranberry juice cocktail. A significant effort was made to encourage the consumer to use the cranberry in baked products now that it was available the year round as a frozen berry. Food kitchens were established to test recipes that were then published and supplied with the cranberry packages. All these efforts contributed to the increase in per capita consumption that has occurred in recent years.

Nutritive and Therapeutic Value

From a chemical standpoint, the cranberry consists of water, plant fiber, sugar, acids, pectin, waxy materials, protein, and various ash constituents, namely, calcium, magnesium, potassium, and phosphorus (table 12.6). It is, in fact, 88.5 percent water, leaving the rest of the chemical constituents to make up the 11.5 percent of dry matter. The sugar content is relatively low and the acid content high. The fruit acids, mainly citric acid and malic acid, are metabolized by the body and used for energy much as the sugars are. According to Fellers (1936), this means that eating cranberries in normal amounts would not result in elevated blood acidity, or *acidosis*. The benzoic acid content is high enough to exert considerable preserving action on both the fresh fruit and manufactured products. Quinic acid is present at about ten times the concentration of benzoic acid. Both acids are converted to hippuric acid, which is eliminated by the body in the urine. Despite the relatively high acid content of the fruit, the ash is actually alkaline and consists largely of potassium, calcium, and phosphorus. The iodine content and manganese content of the ash are also relatively high. A four-ounce serving of cranberry sauce contains about 200 calories (kcal). The nutritive value of the cranberry as a food is given in table 12.6 for each constituent in an average serving of cranberry sauce (Fellers 1933).

Cranberries have very little protein, but they are high in vitamin C. Four ounces of fresh cranberries supply the minimum daily requirement of this vitamin for an average adult male (Fellers 1932). The fiber in the cranberry is concentrated in the skins and seeds and, when retained in processing, aids in elimination; cranberries can therefore be mildly laxative. Cranberries are also high in pectin, which enables cranberry jelly to set at a relatively low soluble-solids content of 42 percent compared to 65 to 70 percent for most fruits

TABLE 12.6. CHEMICAL COMPOSITION OF FRESH CRANBERRIES AND NUTRITIVE VALUE OF AN AVERAGE SERVING OF CRANBERRY SAUCE

CONSTITUENT	PERCENT*	MG PER 4-OZ. SERVING
Reducing sugars	4.2 %	48,590.0
Acids	2.4	916.0
Protein	0.4	172.0
Fat and wax	0.4	160.0
Fiber	3.2	3,600.0
Ash	0.25	107.0
Potassium oxide (K_2O)		33.0
Sodium oxide (Na_2O)		3.4
Calcium oxide (CaO)		10.7
Magnesium oxide (MgO)		4.7
Iron oxide (Fe_2O_3)		1.8
Manganese oxide (Mn_3O_4)		0.3
Copper oxide (CuO)		0.4
Phosphorus Pentoxide (P_2O_5)		9.8
Sulfur Trioxide (SO_3)		5.3
Chlorine (Cl)		1.7
Iodine (I)		0.002

SOURCE: Fellers (1933).
*Percentage of dry matter.

(Kohman 1938). Kohman has postulated that the digestion of pectin may contribute to the detoxification and elimination of toxic substances from the bowel. When pectin is digested it produces galacturonic acid, which can be converted to glycuronic acid. Both these acids are capable of conjugating with phenol-like substances and the higher alcohols, thus detoxifying those substances and aiding in their elimination.

It has long been observed that fresh fruit can greatly aid the digestive process and has often been used as a home remedy for the treatment of acute digestive disturbances accompanied by diarrhea (Esselen 1937). Cranberries may benefit the digestive process by virtue of their astringency and their acidity, which may discourage the growth of undesirable bacteria in the caecum and large intestine. Due to its high cellulose and pectin content, the cranberry absorbs moisture and swells to give voluminous soft stools, thereby scouring out the intestines and effectively removing bacteria that may be the cause of gastrointestinal difficulty. Cranberries have also been shown experimentally to increase body calcium retention in rats (Mindell et al. 1939). The researchers attributed this increased calcium retention to the increased acidity of the intestinal tract that occurred as the result of cranberry consumption. The cranberry treatment also resulted in a slight increase in the calcium content of the femur of the rat.

Researchers agree that the ingestion of the cranberry or its products leads to an increase in the acidity of the urine (Blatherwick and Long 1923; Fellers et al. 1933). Whereas fruit acids such as citric and malic are metabolized by the body and as such do not contribute to body acidity, the quinic and benzoic acids of the cranberry are converted to hippuric acid and eliminated in the urine. The amount of hippuric acid produced is directly proportional to the weight of cranberries eaten and is normally expelled within 24 hours. The hippuric acid can reduce the pH of the urine or, more likely, prevent it from becoming alkaline and may in itself have antibacterial properties, all of which may result in distinct therapeutic effects (Bodel et al. 1959). In a clinical trial, Papas and his co-investigators (Papas et al. 1966) found that over 70 percent of their patients suffering from acute urinary tract infections showed marked improvement as the result of consuming 16 ounces of cranberry juice daily for 21 days. The investigators concluded that the effect of cranberry juice in lowering urine pH and increasing its hippuric acid content gives it merit as an inexpensive, nontoxic, and palatable acidifying agent for the treatment of acute urinary infections.

Anecdotal evidence suggests that drinking cranberry juice can relieve the symptoms of dysuria (frequency and urgency of urination), a common complaint of older female patients (Moen 1962). Two 6-ounce glasses of cranberry juice taken daily have been known to relieve these urinary symptoms when other methods have failed. Other chronic urinary tract infections that have been treated successfully with a regimen of cranberry juice have included the chronic forms of urethritis, trigonitis, and pyelonephritis.

Clinical studies in nursing homes and in the incontinent wards of hospitals have indicated that the ingestion of cranberry juice by patients can alleviate the odor of fermenting urine (Dugan and Cardaciotto 1966; Kraemer 1964). Kraemer noted that the daily ingestion of 16 ounces of cranberry juice lowered the pH of test urines and reduced ammoniacal odor. When the juice treatment was discontinued, the odor returned. Acidification of the urine apparently was bacteriostatic enough to inhibit ammoniacal fermentation. Dugan and Cardaciotto also found a noticeable reduction in the ammoniacal odor in geriatric wards when patients were given as little as 3 to 6 ounces of cranberry juice daily. Although the reduction in odor was quite noticeable to the nursing staff, chemical measurements on the air sampled from the wards failed to reveal a significant change in ammonia content of the air after the patients received the cranberry juice. Nevertheless, the general consensus was that cranberry juice was a palatable and effective method of reducing ammoniacal urinary odors, thus improving the environmental status of nursing homes and hospitals.

Of much interest is the potential for cranberry juice to reduce recurrent kidney stones by its urinary acidification properties. One type of stone is formed as the result of the breakdown of urea by urease-positive organisms. This type of stone formation is often enhanced by infection. When urea is split by the enzyme urease, carbonic acid and ammonia are produced. This renders the urine alkaline, which favors the formation of calcium carbonate and struvite calculi. Zinsser and his associates (Zinsser et al. 1968) were of the opinion that urinary acidification, if carried out conscientiously, can stop stone growth and lead to diminution in stone size. The researchers successfully treated such calculi by administering urine-acidifying agents. They concluded that cranberry juice was one of the most effective acidifying agents because of greater patient acceptance or more consistent acidification—or as a result of some as yet unexplained effect of cranberry juice on stone formation. In this regard they later reported (Light et al. 1973) that in patients with renal stones, the urinary-ionized calcium was reduced by as much as 50 percent when cranberry juice was administered. The lower calcium concentration in the urine would mean less calcium precipitation and subsequent stone formation. It is interesting to note that at the U.S. Navy Hospital at St. Albans, New York, paraplegic patients with recumbent calculi are managed by an intensive medical regimen that includes the administering of cranberry juice (Kom 1968). Sternlieb (1963) has found that 8 ounces of cranberry juice fed four times daily for several days followed by 8 ounces twice daily thereafter was a valuable adjunctive therapy and prophylaxis in stone-forming patients whose renal stones were more soluble in an acid milieu.

The relatively high acidity of the cranberry has resulted in some concern over its effect on the blood alkali reserve and the potential for the development of excess acidosis of the blood. Large doses of fresh cranberries (100–254 g or 9–24 oz., of cranberry sauce) reduced the blood alkali reserve from 30 to 60 percent, which would be considered a mild-to-moderate degree of acidosis (Fellers et al. 1933). Smaller amounts of cranberry sauce (2–5 oz.) produced no demonstrable acidosis, suggesting that the blood's buffering system is capable of maintaining its blood alkali reserve and pH even in the presence of moderate amounts of free acids that are ingested in a normal serving of cranberry sauce.

Pharmaceutical uses of cranberries have included the syrup of cranberry as a vehicle for medicines and extracts of cranberry as a topical ointment for the treatment of some dermatoses. Lubitz and his coworkers (Lubitz et al. 1940) were of the opinion that its low cost, attractive color, and pleasant flavor made cranberry syrup an excellent candidate as a pharmaceutical vehicle. In palatability tests, cranberry syrup was second in preference only to raspberry syrup. It was very effective in masking the unpleasant flavor of a number of pharmaceutical compounds and was found to be compatible with most alcoholic preparations. An ointment known as Vaccinol, which had cranberry constituents as the active ingredient, was known to be effective in some dermatoses, including some alleged to be caused by fungi. Swartz and Medrek (1968) discovered that cranberry juice did indeed exert a significant in vitro antifungal effect on eight representative species of dermatophytes. They attributed the fungistatic action of cranberry juice to its benzoic acid content or to some other low molecular-weight component. The antifungal effect was particularly strong when the juice pH was kept at the natural value of 2.8; the juice lost some of its effect when the pH was raised to 5.6. Benzoic acid was also observed to lose some of its fungistatic property at the higher pH.

Recipes

Today there are literally hundreds of dishes that can be made using cranberries (*Better Homes and Gardens* 1971; Foley 1957). They include such exotic concoctions as cranberry borscht, cranberry soufflé crepes, and cranberry kugelhof (Ortiz 1971), but some of the more traditional favorites (Ocean Spray Cranberries, Inc.) are the following:

Whole Cranberry Sauce
4 cups (1 lb.) cranberries   2 cups sugar
2 cups water

Inspect the cranberries and wash the perfect fruit. Boil sugar and water together for 5 minutes. Add cranberries. Boil together without stirring until skins pop (about 5 minutes). Cool. If a thicker sauce is desired, cook 5 minutes longer.

Cranberry Jelly
4 cups cranberries   1½ cups water
2 cups sugar

Pick over berries, discarding the withered, soft, or damaged. Cook berries and water rapidly in a covered saucepan 15 minutes or until berries are soft. Strain through a fine sieve, add sugar, stir, and cook about 3 minutes or until the liquid gives the two-drop test from a spoon. Pour into jelly glasses. When cool and set, seal with paraffin.

The sauce and jelly have other uses besides being served as a condiment for meats. Either form can be added to frosting or hard sauce to give color and

PLATE 12.4. CRANBERRY CHEESE TARTS—ONE OF THE MANY DELI-CACIES MADE FROM CRANBERRIES (Courtesy United Fresh Fruit and Vegetable Association)

flavor or spread between layers of white cake. They are also excellent for use in a jelly roll.

Cranberry-Orange Relish
2 cups cranberries   1 whole orange
⅞ cup sugar

Pick over and wash cranberries and orange. Cut orange and remove seeds. Put cranberries and orange through food chopper. Add sugar. Mix thoroughly and let stand for several hours before using.

This simple but delightful relish is easy to prepare and requires no cooking. It also takes advantage of the synergistic effect that the orange has on cranberry flavor, as also suggested in the next recipe.

Cranberry Nut Bread

2 cups flour	1 cup cranberries, cut into halves
1½ tsp. baking powder	½ cup chopped nutmeats
½ tsp. baking soda	1 well-beaten egg
½ tsp. salt	Juice of 1 orange, plus warm
1 cup sugar	water to make 1 cup
	3 tbsp. melted shortening

Sift all dry ingredients together. Add cranberries and nut meats. Then add egg mixed with diluted orange juice and shortening. Stir slightly. Bake in greased and floured loaf pan for 1 hour at 350°F.

BIBLIOGRAPHY

Addoms, R. M., and Mounce, F. C.
1931 Notes on the Nutrient Requirements and the Histology of the Cranberry (*Vaccinium macrocarpon* Ait.) with Special Reference to Mycorrhiza. *Pl. Physio.* 6:653–668.

1932 Further Notes on the Nutrient Requirements and the Histology of the Cranberry (*Vaccinium macrocarpon* Ait.) with Special Reference to Mycorrhiza. *Pl. Physio.* 7:643–656.

Ahokas, H.
1971 Cytology of Hexaploid Cranberry with Special Reference to Chromosomal Fibres. *Hereditas* 68:123–136.

American Public Health Association
1965 Standard Methods for the Examination of Water and Waste Water. 12th ed. New York: APHA.

Ames, W. S., and Christensen, R. L.
1978 *A Preliminary evaluation of Cranberry Production Costs in Massachusetts.* Mass. Agr. Exp. Sta. Res. Bull. no. 656.

Anderson, E. E., and Esselen, W. B., Jr.
1950 *Influence of Pyrophosphates in the Manufacture of Cranberry Sauce.* Mass. Agr. Exp. Sta. Bull. no. 459:58.

Anderson, R. E.; Hardenburg, R. E.; and Vaught, H. C.
1963 Controlled-Atmosphere Storage Studies with Cranberries. *Proc. Amer. Soc. Hort. Sci.* 83:416–422.

Anderson, R. E., and Smith, W. L., Jr.
1971 *Effect of Postharvest Hot-Water Treatments on Spoilage of Cranberries in Storage.* U.S. Dept. Agr. Res. Rpt. no. 928.

Anjou, K., and von Sydow, E.
1968 The aroma of Cranberries. IV, *Vaccinium macrocarpon* Ait. *Arkiv for Kemi* 30:9–14.

Arnold, L. K., and Hsia, P. R.
1957 Solvent Extraction of Wax and Ursolic Acid from Cranberry Skins. *Ind. and Eng. Chem.* 49:360–363.

Atkins, T. E.
1940 Old Cape Cod Cranberry Notes, 1840–1890. *Cranberries—The Nat. Cranberry Mag.* 5 (8): 4, 6.

Atwood, W. M., and Zuckerman, B. M.
1961 The Effects of Fertilizer and Fungicide Combinations on the Quality of Cranberries. *Proc. Amer. Soc. Hort. Sci.* 77:359–366.

Ayres, J. C., and Denisen, E. L.
1958   Maintaining Freshness of Berries Using Selected Packaging Materials and Antifungal Agents. *Food Tech.* 12:562–567.

Bain, H. F.
1926   The Relation of Temperature during the Blossom Period to the Set of Cranberries. In *Proc. Wis. St. Cranberry Growers' Assoc. 40th Ann. Mtg.*, 23–26.

1931   Spraying and Water Raking Experiments. In *Proc. Wis. St. Cranberry Growers' Assoc. 45th Ann. Sum. Mtg.*, 14–17.

1933a   Cross Pollinating the Cranberry. In *Proc. Wis. St. Cranberry Growers' Assoc. 47th Ann. Sum. Mtg.*, 7–11.

1933b   Further Notes on Cranberry Spraying and Water Raking Experiments. In *Proc. Wis. St. Cranberry Growers' Assoc. 46th Ann. Mtg.*, 35–36.

1937   Production of Synthetic Mycorrhiza in the Cultivated Cranberry. *J. Agr. Res.* 55:811–836.

1940a   Experiments in Breeding Cranberries for False Blossom Control. *Cranberries—The Nat. Cranberry Mag.* 4 (11): 9–11.

1940b   Origin of Adventitious Shoots in Decapitated Cranberry Seedlings. *Bot. Gaz.* 101:872–880.

1943   Cranberry Tetraploids. In *Proc. 74th Ann. Conv. Amer. Cranberry Growers' Assoc.*, 12–13, 16.

1946   Blooming and Fruiting Habits of the Cranberry in Wisconsin. *Cranberries—The Nat. Cranberry Mag.* 10 (9): 11–14.

1948   Fruiting Characteristics of the Searles Cranberry. *Cranberries—The Nat. Cranberry Mag.* 13 (4): 6–8, 20–23.

Bain, H. F.; Bergman, H. F.; and Wilcox, R. B.
1942   *Harvesting and Handling Cultivated Cranberries.* U.S. Dept. Agr. Farmers' Bull. no. 1882.

Bain, H. F., and Dermen, H.
1944   Sectorial Polyploidy and Phyllotaxy in the Cranberry (*Vaccinium macrocarpon* Ait.) *Amer. J. Bot.* 31:581–587.

Baker, G. L., and Goodwin, W. M.
1941   Pectin Decomposition vs. Sugar Inversion in Jelly. *Food Ind.* 13:45–47.

Baker, G. L., and Kneeland, R. F.
1936   Cranberry Pectin Properties. *Ind. and Eng. Chem.* 28:372–375.

Barber, F. W.
1938   Wisconsin Grower Firmly Convinced of Merit of the McFarlin Berry. *Cranberries—The Nat. Cranberry Mag.* 3 (8): 2–8.

Barker, K. R., and Boone, D. M.
1966   Plant-Parasitic Nematodes on Cranberries in Wisconsin. *Pl. Dis. Rptr.* 50:957–959.

Barrowman, D. W.
1968   *Cranberry Objective Yield Analysis.* N.J. Crop Rep. Serv. Circ. no. 444.

Bates, E. M.
1971   Cranberry Bog Microclimate. *Cranberries—The Nat. Cranberry Mag.* 35 (9): 10–11, 13, 15, 20.

Baumann, T. E., and Eaton, G. W.
1986   Competition among Berries on the Cranberry Upright. *J. Amer. Soc. Hort. Sci.* 111:869–872.

Bear, F. E.
1949   What We Need to Know about Cranberry Soils. In *Proc. 79th Ann. Mtg. Amer. Cranberry Growers' Assoc.*, 26–30.

Beaton, G. T.
1959   The Cranberry Story. *Cranberries—The Nat. Cranberry Mag.* 23 (11): 16–17; 23 (12): 16–17; 24 (1): 10–11; 24 (2): 14–16.

Beaton, K. L.
1953   Advantages and Disadvantages of Late Held Water. *Cranberries—The Nat. Cranberry Mag.* 17 (11): 18–20.

Beckwith, C. S.
1919   The Effect of Certain Nitrogenous and Phosphatic Fertilizers on the Yield of Cranberries. *Soil Sci.* 8:483–490.

1921a   *A Complete Fertilizer for Savannah Cranberry Land.* N.J. Agr. Exp. Sta. Circ. no. 124.

1921b   The Effect of Fertilizer Treatments on Savannah Cranberry Land. *Soil Sci.* 12:183–196.

1922   *Cranberry Growing in New Jersey.* N.J. Agr. Exp. Sta. Circ. no. 144.

1925   *Control of the Cranberry by Submerging in Water.* N.J. Agr. Exp. Sta. Bull. no. 441.

1929   The Blossom Worm, a Cranberry Pest. *N.Y. Ent. Soc.* 37:409–416.

1930   *Effect of Fertilizer on Cranberry Land.* N.J. Agr. Exp. Sta. Bull. no. 501.

1931   *Cranberry Growing in New Jersey.* N.J. Agr. Exp. Sta. Circ. no. 246.

1934   *Cranberry Girdler.* N.J. Agr. Exp. Sta. Circ. no. 314.

1937   *Sanding Cranberry Bogs.* N.J. Agr. Exp. Sta. Circ. no. 371.

1940a   Flooding and Irrigation. In *Proc. 70th Ann. Mtg. Amer. Cranberry Growers' Assoc.*, 9–13.

1940b   Flooding and Irrigation—Water Table. *Cranberries—The Nat. Cranberry Mag.* 5 (3): 2, 11.

1940c   *Late Holding Water on Cranberry Bogs.* N.J. Agr. Exp. Sta. Circ. no. 402.

1943   Cranberry Separators. *Cranberries—The Nat. Cranberry Mag.* 7 (10): 5, 12.

1944   Suggestions on the Remaking of Old Bogs. In *Proc. 74th Ann. Mtg. Amer. Cranberry Growers' Assoc.*, 6–8.

Beckwith, C. S., and Fiske, J. G.
1925   *Weeds of Cranberry Bogs.* N.J. Agr. Exp. Sta. Circ. no. 171.

Beckwith, C. S., and Hutton, S. B.
1929   *Cranberry False Blossom and the Blunt-Nosed Leafhopper.* N.J. Agr. Exp. Sta. Bull. no. 491.

Bell, H. P., and Burchill, J.
1955   Winter Resting Stages of Certain Ericaceae. *Can. J. Bot.* 33:547–561.

Benson, A. D.
1938   Some Facts About the New England Cranberry Sales Company. *Cranberries—The Nat. Cranberry Mag.* 3 (1): 4–5.

Bergman, H. F.

1919   Comments on the Water Raking of Cranberries. In *Proc. Wis. St. Cranberry Growers' Assoc. 32nd Ann. Mtg.*, 13–16.

1920   Internal Stomata in Ericaceous and Other Unrelated Fruits. *Bull. Torrey Bot. Club.* 47:213–221.

1921   The Effect of Cloudiness on the Oxygen Content of Water and Its Significance in Cranberry Culture. *Amer. J. Bot.* 8:50–58.

1922   Observations on the Effect of Water-raking on the Keeping Quality of Cranberries. *Amer. J. Bot.* 9:245–252.

1925   The Respiratory Activity of Various Parts of the Cranberry Plant in Relation to Flooding Injury. *Amer. J. Bot.* 12:641–649.

1930a   The Oxygen Content of Water in Winter-Flooded Bogs under Ice. In *Proc. Wisc. Sta. Cranberry Growers' Assoc. 44th Ann. Mtg.*, 32–40.

1930b   Respiration of Cranberry Plants in Relation to Water Injury. In *Proc. 60th Ann. Mtg. Amer. Cranberry Growers' Assoc.*, 21–25.

1931   The Relation of Oxygen Content of Water to Flooding Injury in Cranberry Culture. In *Proc. 61st Ann. Mtg. Amer. Cranberry Growers' Assoc.*, 6–11.

1932   Directions for Taking and Titrating Water Samples for the Determination of Dissolved Oxygen. Mass. Agr. Exp. Sta. Mimeo. Sheet.

1940   Ice and Snow Cover on Winter-Flooded Cranberry Bogs in Relation to the Oxygen Content of the Water and to Vine Injury. *Amer. J. Bot.* 27:135.

1945   Oxygen Deficiency in the Winter Flood of Cranberry Bogs. In *Proc. 76th Ann. Conv. Amer. Cranberry Growers' Assoc.*, 7–13, 16.

1946   Oxygen Deficiency in the Winter Flood of Cranberry Bogs. *Cranberries—The Nat. Cranberry. Mag.* 10 (11): 21–27.

1947   Bud, Flower, and Fruit Production by Cranberry Vines in Relation to Depth of Winter Flooding. *Cranberries—The Nat. Cranberry Mag.* 12 (3): 9–10.

1948   Winter Conditions on Cranberry Bogs in Relation to Flower and Fruit Production. *Rev. Can. Biol.* 7:629–641.

1949   Winter Conditions on Cranberry Bogs in Relation to Flowers and Fruit Production. *Cranberries—The Nat. Cranberry Mag.* 14 (4): 6–10.

1950   Cranberry Flower and Fruit Production in Massachusetts. *Cranberries—The Nat. Cranberry Mag.* 15 (4): 6–10.

1953   Disorders of Cranberries. In *Plant Diseases—1953 U.S. Dept. Agr. Yearbook of Agric.*, 789–796.

1954   Flowering and Fruiting Characteristics of the Cranberry in New Jersey. In *Proc. 84th Ann. Mtg. Amer. Cranberry Growers' Assoc.*, 17–27.

Bergman, H. F., and Wilcox, M. S.

1936   The Distribution, Cause, and Relative Importance of Cranberry Fruit Rots in Massachusetts in 1932 and 1933, and Their Control by Spraying. *Phytopath.* 26:656–664.

Besse, S. A.

1966   Glimpse of the Past: Massachusetts Cranberry Growing. Part 1—An Early History of Massachusetts State Cranberry Bog. *Cranberries—The Nat. Cranberry Mag.* 31 (6): 7–9, 10.

Better Homes and Gardens
1971   *Better Homes and Gardens Five Seasons Cranberry Book.* Des Moines,
          Iowa: Meredith Publ. Serv.
Bird, G. W.
1963a   Effects of Plant-Parasitic Nematodes on Growth of Cranberry. *Phytopath.*
          53:871.
1963b   Host-Parasite Relationships and Nematode Control in Cranberries. In *Proc.
          93rd Ann. Mtg. Amer. Cranberry Growers' Assoc.,* 24–26.
Bird, G. W., and Jenkins, W. R.
1963   Nematode Control in Cranberry. *Phytopath.* 53:347.
1964   Occurrence, Parasitism, and Pathogenicity of Nematodes Associated with
          Cranberry. *Phytopath.* 54:677–680.
1965   Effect of Cranberry Bog Flooding and Low Dissolved Oxygen Concentra-
          tions on Nematode Populations. *Pl. Dis. Rptr.* 49:517–518.
Blatherwick, N. R., and Long, M. L.
1923   Studies on Urinary Acid. II. The Increased Acidity Produced by Eating
          Prunes and Cranberries. *J. Biol. Chem.* 57:815–818.
Bliss, G. S.
1922   Forecasting Minimum Temperatures for the Cranberry Bogs of New Jersey.
          Monthly Weather Rev. 50 (10): 529–533.
1924   Frost on the Cranberry Bogs. In *Proc. 54th Ann. Mtg. Amer. Cranberry
          Growers' Assoc.* 9:11, 14–16.
Bodel, P. T.; Cotran, R.; and Kass, E. H.
1959   Cranberry Juice and the Antibacterial Action of Hippuric Acid. *J. Lab. and
          Clinical Med.* 54:881–888.
Boggs, M. M., and Johnson, G.
1947   How Jellied Cranberry Sauce Is Preserved by Freezing. *Food Ind.* 19:1067–
          1069, 1174–1175.
Bonn, B.; Forsyth, F. R.; and Hall, I. V.
1969   A Comparison of the Rates of Apparent Photosynthesis of the Cranberry
          and the Common Lowbush Blueberry. *Natu. Can.* 96:799–804.
Boone, D. M.
1966   Ringspot Disease of Cranberry. *Pl. Dis. Rptr.* 50:543–545.
1967   A Cranberry Ringspot Disease Injuring Searles Variety. *Cranberries—The
          Nat. Cranberry Mag.* 31 (9): 14–15.
1982a   *End Rot of Cranberry.* Cranberry Pest Control Pub. no. A3196. Univ. Wis.
1982b   *Gibbera Leaf Spot and Berry Speckle of Cranberry.* Cranberry Pest Control
          Pub. no. A3193. Univ. Wis.
1982c   *Hard Rot and Tip Blight of Cranberry.* Cranberry Pest Control Pub. no.
          A3194. Univ. Wis.
1982d   *Viscid Rot and Upright Dieback of Cranberry.* Cranberry Pest Control Pub.,
          no. A3195. Univ. Wis.
Boone, D. M., and Barker, K. R.
1966   Plant Parasite Nematodes in Cranberry Marshes in Wisconsin.
          Cranberries—The Nat. Cranberry Mag. 31 (2): 24–25.

Boone, D. M., and Dana, M. N.
1971   Cranberry Cultivar Evaluation in Wisconsin. *Cranberries—The Nat. Cranberry Mag.* 35 (10): 13, 10–11.

Boone, D. M., and Friend, R. J.
1986   *Yellow Rot of Cranberry.* Cranberry Pest Control Pub. no. A3350. Univ. Wis.

Boone, D. M., and Schwarz, M. R.
1982   *Black Rot of Cranberry.* Cranberry Pest Control Pub. no. A3197. Univ. Wis.

Boone, D. M., and Tontyaporn, S.
1986   *Red Leaf Spot.* Cranberry Pest Control Pub. no. A3343. Univ. Wis.

Boone, D. M., and Weidemann, G. J.
1986a   *Botryosphaeria Fruit Rot and Leaf Drop.* Cranberry Pest Control Pub. no. A3351. Univ. Wis.

1986b   *Early Rot (Scald) of Cranberry and Blast of Blossoms and Young Fruit.* Cranberry Pest Control Pub. no. A3352. Univ. Wis.

Boster, D. O.
1946   Special Cranberry Acreage Survey. In *Proc. 76th Ann. Mtg. Amer. Cranberry Growers' Assoc.,* 10.

Bramlage, W. J.; Devlin, R. M.; and Smagula, J. M.
1972   Effects of Preharvest Application of Ethephon on Early Black Cranberries. *J. Amer. Soc. Hort. Sci.* 97:625–628.

Briggs, R. T.
1967   Life on a Cranberry Bog at the Turn of the Century. *Cranberries—The Nat. Cranberry Mag.* 32 (1): 7, 10–12.

Bristow, P. R.
1977   Diseases and Fungicides—Rose Bloom. *Cranberry Vine*—Pub. Coop. Ext. Serv., Coastal Wash.

Bristow, P. R., and Shawa, A. Y.
1981   The Influence of Fungicides on Pollen Germination and Yield of Cranberry. *J. Amer. Soc. Hort. Sci.* 106:290–292.

Brodel, C. F.
1980   Economic Thresholds and Cranberry Pest Management. *Cranberries—The Nat. Cranberry Mag.* 44 (10): 8–10, 12.

Brooks, R. M., and Olmo, H. P.
1950   Register of New Fruit and Nut Varieties. In *Proc. Amer. Soc. Hort. Sci.* 56:518–519.

1956   Register of New Fruit and Nut Varieties. In *Proc. Amer. Soc. Hort. Sci.* 68:618.

Brown, B. W.
1954   *A Study of the Storage and Packaging of Fresh Cranberries Made for the National Cranberry Association.* Nat. Cranberry Assoc. Mimeo. Rpt., Hanson, Mass.

Burgett, M., and Poole, A.
1987   An Evaluation of Pollinator Management As Applied in the Commercial Production of Cranberries—1987. *Dispatch from the Bog*—Pub. of Oreg. St. Univ. Coop. Ext. Serv., Nov., 1–5.

Camp, W. H.
1944   A Preliminary Consideration of the Biosystematy of *Oxycoccus. Bull. Torrey Bot. Club* 71:426–437.

Carlson, L. W., and Boone, D. M.
1966   A Berry Speckle Disease of Cranberry and Its Control. *Pl. Dis. Rptr.* 50 (8): 539–543.

Carpenter, E. G.
1982   N.J. Grower Perfects 3 Reel Water Harvester. *Cranberries—The Nat. Cranberry Mag.* 46 (2): 8–10.

Caruso, F. L.; Kusek, C. C.; and Wilcox, W. F.
1987   Phytophthora Root Rot/Dieback of Cranberry in Massachusetts. *Phytopath.* 77:1691 (Abstract).

Ceponis, M. J., and Stretch, A. W.
1981   The Influence of Water Immersion Times at Harvest on Physiological Breakdown of Early Black Cranberries in Storage. *HortSci.* 16:60–61.

1983   Berry Color, Water-Immersion Time, Rot, and Physiological Breakdown of Cold-Stored Cranberry Fruits. *HortSci.* 18:484–485.

Chambers, F. S.
1918   Cranberry Pruning Experiments. In *Proc. 48th Ann. Mtg. Amer. Cranberry Growers' Assoc.,* 3–7.

Chandler, F. B.
1944   Cranberry Breeding Investigations in 1944. In *Proc. 75th Ann. Conv. Amer. Cranberry Growers' Assoc.,* 16–17.

1951   Effect of Methods of Irrigating Cranberry Bogs on Water Table and Soil Moisture Tension. In *Proc. Amer. Soc. Hort. Sci.* 57:65–72.

1952a   Poor Draining Peat. *Cranberries—The Nat. Cranberry Mag.* 17 (3): 6–7.

1952b   Preliminary Report on the Development of Cranberry Fruit. *Cranberries—The Nat. Cranberry Mag.* 17 (4): 6–7.

1952c   The Use of Liquid Fertilizer on the Increase. *Cranberries—The Nat. Cranberry Mag.* 17 (8): 12–13.

1953a   Drainage. *Cranberries—The Nat. Cranberry Mag.* 18 (1): 17–18.

1953b   Relation of Different Methods of Expressing Size of Cranberries. *Cranberries—The Nat. Cranberry Mag.* 17 (9): 10, 12.

1954a   Bees and Food for Bees. *Cranberries—The Nat. Cranberry Mag.* 18 (12): 8–9.

1954b   Drainage Studies at Massachusetts State Bog. *Cranberries—The Nat. Cranberry Mag.* 19 (3): 12.

1954c   The Effect of Hailstones. *Cranberries—The Nat. Cranberry Mag.* 19 (7): 7–8.

1954d   Hurricane Injury to Cranberry Bogs. *Cranberries—The Nat. Cranberry Mag.* 19 (5/6): 7–9.

1955a   Dried Out or Brown Vines. *Cranberries—The Nat. Cranberry Mag.* 20 (4): 10.

1955b   Fertilizer Materials. *Cranberries—The Nat. Cranberry Mag.* 19 (11): 12–14.

1955c   Irrigation with Perforated Plastic Tubing. *Cranberries—The Nat. Cranberry Mag.* 20 (6): 14–15.

1955d   More Fertilizer in Use in Massachusetts. *Cranberries—The Nat. Cranberry Mag.* 20 (4): 12.

1956a   Cranberries: 1855 to 1955. *New Eng. Homestead* 129:6, 8, 28–29, 32.

1956b   Past, Present, Future Varieties of Cranberries. *Cranberries—The Nat. Cranberry Mag.* 21 (4): 7.

1956c   *Survey of the Cranberry Industry in Washington State.* Wash. St. Dept. Agr. Misc. Pub.

1956d   Timely Facts on Fertilization. *Cranberries—The Nat. Cranberry Mag.* 21 (1): 12–14.

1957   *A Survey of Oregon's Cranberry Industry.* Oreg. St. Col. Misc. Paper no. 38.

1961   *Fertilizer for Cranberries. Mass. Agr. Exp. Sta. Bull.* no. 499.

Chandler, F. B.; Bain, N. F.; and Bergman, H. F.

1950   The Beckwith, the Stevens, and the Wilcox Cranberry Varieties. *Cranberries—The Nat. Cranberry Mag.* 14 (12): 6–7.

Chandler, F. B., and Demoranville, I. E.

1958   *Cranberry Varieties of North America.* Mass. Agr. Exp. Sta. Bull. no. 513.

1959   *The Harmful Effect of Salt on Cranberry Bogs.* Mass. Agr. Exp. Sta. Misc. Pub. no. 1007.

1961a   Preliminary Report on Cranberry Soil Studies—1960. *Cranberries—The Nat. Cranberry Mag.* 26 (3): 9–10.

1961b   Some Recent Observations on Cranberry Breeding. *Cranberries—The Nat. Cranberry Mag.* 25 (12): 7–8.

1961c   Three New Cranberry Varieties. *Fruit Var. and Hort. Dig.* 15:65.

1964   Rest Period for Cranberries. In *Proc. Amer. Soc. Hort. Sci.* 85:307–311.

Chandler, F. B., and Hyland, F.

1941   Botanical and Economic Distribution of *Vaccinium* L. in Maine. In *Proc. Amer. Soc. Hort. Sci.* 38:430–433.

Chandler, F. B., and Murray, R.

1966   Cranberry Feasibility Study in Western Nova Scotia. Nova Scotia Dept. Agr. Mimeo. Rpt.

Chandler, F. B.; Wilcox, R. B.; Bain, H. F.; Bergman, H. F.; and Dermen, H.

1947   Cranberry Breeding Investigation of the U.S.D.A. *Cranberries—The Nat. Cranberry Mag.* 12 (1): 6–9; 12 (2): 6–10.

Chaney, A. U.

1940   Remarks on the Market and on the Practice of Water Raking. In *Proc. 71st Ann. Conv. Amer. Cranberry Growers' Assoc.*, 24–25.

Chaplin, M. H. S., and Martin, L. W.

1979   Seasonal Changes in Leaf Element Content of Cranberry, *Vaccinium macrocarpon* Ait. *Commun. in Soil Sci. and Pl. Anal.* 10 (9): 895–902.

Chen, T. A.

1971   Mycoplasmalike Organisms in Sieve Tube Elements of Plants Infected with Blueberry Stunt and Cranberry False Blossom. *Phytopath.* 61:233–239.

Chiriboga, C. D., and Francis, F. J.
1970   An Anthocyanin Recovery System from Cranberry Pomace. *J. Amer. Soc. Hort. Sci.* 95:233–236.
Chitwood, B. C., and Tarjan, A. C.
1957   A Redescription of *Atylenchus decalineatus* Cobb 1913. In *Proc. Helm. Soc. Wash.* 24:48–52.
Christ, E.
1977   Cross Breeding between Cranberries (*Vaccinium macrocarpon* Ait.) and Cowberries (*V. vitis idaea L.*). In *Proc. 2nd International Symposium on Vaccinium Culture.* Hannover, Germany 22–23 July, 1976.
Clague, J. A., and Fellers, C. R.
1934   Relation of Benzoic Acid Content and Other Constituents of Cranberries to Keeping Quality. *Pl. Physio.* 9:631–636.
Cobb, N. A.
1913   New Nematode Genera Found Inhabiting Fresh Water and Non-Brackish Soils. *J. Wash. Acad. Sci.* 3:434–437.
Colby, W. G.
1945   The Use of Commercial Fertilizer on Cranberries. *Cranberries—The Nat. Cranberry Mag.* 10 (6): 6–7.
1947   Cranberry Soils. *Cranberries—The Nat. Cranberry Mag.* 12 (2): 21–24.
Cole, W. R.
1951   Cold Storage for Cranberry Growers. *Cranberries—The Nat. Cranberry Mag.* 16 (1): 11–12.
Coppola, E. D.; Conrad, E. C.; and Cotter, R.
1978   High Pressure Liquid Chromatographic Determination of Major Organic Acids in Cranberry Juice. *J. Assoc. Off. Anal. Chem.* 61:1490–1492.
Cox, H. J.
1910   *Frost and Temperature Conditions in the Cranberry Marshes of Wisconsin.* U.S. Dept. Agr. Weather Bur. Bull. T.W.B. no. 443; 1–21.
Craker, L. E.
1971   Postharvest Color Promotion in Cranberry with Ethylene. *HortSci.* 6:137–139.
Craker, L. E., and Wetherbee, P. J.
1973   Ethylene, Carbon Dioxide, and Anthocyanin Synthesis. *Pl. Physio.* 52:177–179.
Cranberries
1969   New Jersey Cranberry Growers Develop an Improved Harvester. *Cranberries—The Nat. Cranberry Mag.* 33 (10): 6–7, 23.
1978   The Irreplaceable Bee. *Cranberries—The Nat. Cranberry Mag.* 45 (5): 6–8.
Crooks, J.
1988   Better Early Than Late for Fresh Fruit. *Harvest* 10 (3): 10–11.
Cross, C. E.
1937   Chemical Weed Control on Cranberry Bogs. In *Proc. 68th Ann. Mtg. Amer. Cranberry Growers' Assoc.,* 13–18.

1952   *Weeds of the Massachusetts Cranberry Bogs. Part I, The Grasses.* Mass. Agr. Exp. Sta. Bull. no. 463.

1953a   Cranberry Flowers and the Set of Fruit. *Cranberries—The Nat. Cranberry Mag.* 17 (12): 7–9.

1953b   Discussion on Cranberry Bog Irrigation. *Cranberries—The Nat. Cranberry Mag.* 17 (10): 7–8.

1954   A Study of the Size and Weight of Cranberries during the Harvest Season. *Cranberries—The Nat. Cranberry Mag.* 19 (8): 6–7.

1957   The Harvesting of Cranberries. *Cranberries—The Nat. Cranberry Mag.* 22 (8): 13.

1966   *Cranberry Flowers and Pollination.* Mass. Agr. Exp. Sta. Pub. no. 435.

1969a   Flood Management—Massachusetts Cranberry Bogs. In *Modern Cultural Practice in Cranberry Growing.* Mass. Agr. Exp. Sta. Pub. no. 39:5–8.

1969b   Relation of Weather Conditions to Production and Quality. In *Modern Cultural Practice in Cranberry Growing.* Mass. Agr. Exp. Sta. Pub. no. 39:38–40.

1983   Weather, As It Relates to Cranberry Production and Quality. In *Modern Cranberry Culture.* Univ. Mass. Coop. Ext. Serv. Bull. no. SP-126:52–58.

Cross, C. E., and Demoranville, I. E.

1962   Dalapon and Massachusetts Cranberries. *Down to Earth*—Summer 1962 Pub. Dow Chemical Co. 1–2.

1969   *Resanding of Massachusetts Cranberry Bogs.* Univ. Mass. Coop. Ext. Serv. Pub. no. 36.

Cross, C. E.; Demoranville, I.E.; and Rounsville, G. B.

1967   Frost Protection and Frost Warnings. *Cranberries—The Nat Cranberry Mag.* 31 (11): 1–2.

Crossman, B. D.

1951a   Harvesting Dollars or Deficits? *Cranberries–The Nat. Cranberry Mag.* 16 (6): 14–17.

1951b   Production Costs: the Area of Grower Choice. *Cranberries—The Nat. Cranberry Mag.* 15 (9): 7–8.

Croteau, R.

1977   Biosynthesis of Benzaldehyde, Benzyl Alcohol, and Benzyl Benzoate from Benzoic Acid in Cranberry (*Vaccinium macrocarpon*). *J. Food Biochem.* 1:317–326.

Croteau, R., and Fagerson, I. S.

1968   Major Volatile Components of the Juice of American Cranberry. *J. Food Sci.* 33:386–389.

1969   Seed Lipids of the American Cranberry (*Vaccinium macrocarpon*). *Phytochem.* 8:2219–2222.

1971a   The Chemical Composition of the Cuticular Wax of Cranberry. *Phytochem.* 10:3239–3245.

1971b   Volatile Substances Derived from the Cuticle Wax of Cranberry. *Phytochem.* 10:3247–3249.

1972   The Constituent Cutin Acids of Cranberry Cuticle. *Phytochem.* 11:353–363.

Crowley, D. J.
1940   Weed Control in the Cranberry Bogs of Western Washington. In *Proc. Amer. Soc. Hort. Sci.* 37:623–624.
1954   *Cranberry Growing in Washington.* Wash. Agr. Exp. Sta. Bull. no. 554.

Dana, M. N.
1956   Selective Herbicides for Cranberries. In *Proc. 13th N. Cent. Weed Cont. Conf.*, 63–64.
1959   Effect of Amitrol Sprays on the Growth and Development of the of the Cranberry. *Weeds* 7:277–283.
1960   Simazine for Annual Weed Control in Cranberries. *Weeds* 8:607–611.
1968a   Nitrogen Fertilization and Cranberries, Part I. *Cranberries—The Nat. Cranberry Mag.* 32 (12): 10–11.
1968b   Nitrogen Fertilization and Cranberries, Part II. *Cranberries—The Nat. Cranberry Mag.* 33 (1): 10–11, 15.
1975   A Review of Cranberry Weed Control. *Cranberries—The Nat. Cranberry Mag.* 40 (2): 9–11.
1981   Foliar Nutrient Concentration Studies. *Cranberries—The Nat. Cranberry Mag.* 45 (7): 9–10; (8): 4,6–7; (9): 8–10; (10): 10–11.
1983   Cranberry Cultivar List. *Fruit Var. J.*, 37:88–95.
1987   Cranberry Weed Lists. *Univ. Wis. Dept. Hort. Mimeo. Lists.*

Dana, M. N., and Klingbeil, G. C.
1966   *Cranberry Growing in Wisconsin.* Univ. Wis. Coop. Ext. Serv. Circ. no. 654.

Dana, M. N.; Skroch, W. A.; and Boone, D. M.
1965   Granular Herbicides for Cranberry Bogs. *Weeds* 13:5–7.

Darlington, T. B.
1958   The Cranberry Picker: Present Problems, Prospects for the Future. In *Proc. 88th Ann. Mtg. Amer. Cranberry Growers' Assoc.*, 18–19.

Darrow, G. M.
1951   Polyploidy in Fruit Improvement. *Cranberries—The Nat. Cranberry Mag.* 16 (3): 14–17.

Darrow, G. M.; Camp, W. H.; and Dermen, H.
1944   Chromosome Numbers in *Vaccinium* and Related Groups. *Bull. Torrey Bot. Club* 71:498–506.

Darrow, G. M.; Franklin, H. J.; and Malde, O. G.
1924a   *Establishing Cranberry Fields.* U.S. Dept. Agr. Farmers Bull. no. 1400.
1924b   *Managing Cranberry Fields.* U.S. Dept. Agr. Farmers Bull. no. 1401.

Davis, C. D., and Shawa, A. Y.
1983   Reducing Injury during Mechanical Harvesting of Cranberries. *J. Amer. Soc. Hort. Sci.* 108:444–447.

Dawson, B. M.
1925   Cranberry Raisins. Misc. Mimeo. Rpt. Boston, Mass.

Degaetano, A. T., and Shulman, M.
1987   A Statistical Evaluation of the Relationship between Cranberry Yield in New Jersey and Meteorological Factors. *J. Agr. and Forest Meteor.* 40:323–342.

Demoranville, C. J., and Deubert, K. H.

1987   Effect of Commercial Calcium-Boron and Manganese-Zinc Formulations on Fruit Set of Cranberries. *J. Amer. Soc. Hort. Sci.* 62:163–169.

Demoranville, I. E.

1960   Cranberries: Their Size in Relation to Weather. *Cranberries—The Nat. Cranberry Mag.* 24 (11): 10–11.

1974   The Effect of Temperature on Germination of Cranberry Seeds. *Cranberries—The Nat. Cranberry Mag.* 38 (11): 7.

1978   *Frost Forecasting and Frost Protection for Cranberries.* Univ. Mass. Coop. Ext. Serv. Misc. Pub.

1984   *Weeds of Massachusetts Cranberry Bogs, Part I.* Univ. Mass. Coop. Ext. Serv. Bull. no. SP-148.

1986   *Weeds of Massachusetts Cranberry Bogs, Part II.* Univ. Mass. Coop. Ext. Serv. Bull. no. SP-149.

Demoranville, I. E., and Chandler, F. B.

1957   Increased Yields with New Selections. *Cranberries—The Nat. Cranberry Mag.* 21 (12): 12.

1962   Rest Period. *Cranberries—The Nat. Cranberry Mag.* 27 (8): 12.

Demoranville, I. E., and Cross, C. E.

1957a   The Effects of Amino Triazole Sprays on Cranberry Vines and Their Fruit. *Cranberries—The Nat. Cranberry Mag.* 22 (1) 11–12.

1957b   Newest Cranberry Weed Killer. Amino Triazole. *Cranberries—The Nat. Cranberry Mag.* 21 (12): 16–17.

1962   Simazine, New Cranberry Weed-Killer. *New Eng. Homestead* 135:30.

Demoranville, I. E., and Devlin, R. M.

1971   Influence of Alachlor and Two Experimental Herbicides on Bud Break, Terminal Growth, and Root Development of Cranberry Cuttings. *Weed Res.* 11:310–313.

1976   The Effects of Two Growth Regulator Herbicides on Cranberry Plant Development. In *Proc. N. E. Weed Sci. Soc.* 30:152–155.

Dermen, H.

1945   The Mechanism of Colchicine Induced Cytohistological Changes in Cranberry. *Amer. J. Bot.* 32:387–394.

1947   Periclinal Cytochimeras and Histogenesis in Cranberry. *Amer. J. Bot.* 34 (1): 32–43.

Dermen, H., and Bain, H. F.

1941   Periclinal and Total Polyploidy in Cranberries Induced by Colchicine. In *Proc. Amer. Soc. Hort. Sci.* 38:400.

1944   A General Cytohistological Study of Colchicine Polyploidy in Cranberry. *Amer. J. Bot.* 31:451–463.

Deubert, K. H.

1969a   *Results of Studies on Massachusetts Cranberry Bog Soils.* Mass. Agr. Exp. Sta. Coop. Ext. Serv. Pub. no. 39.

1969b   Salt on Cranberry Bogs. *Cranberries—The Nat. Cranberry Mag.* 34 (1): 7.

1971   *Dieldrin on and around Cranberry Bogs.* Mass. Agr. Exp. Sta. Bull. no. 593.

1972	Cranberry Production and Water Quality. *Cranberries—The Nat. Cranberry Mag.* 37 (4): 13–14.

1978	A Rapid Method for the Extraction and Quantitation of Total Anthocyanin of Cranberry Fruit. *J. Agr. and Food Chem.* 26:1452–1453.

Deubert, K. H., and Demoranville, I. E.

1970	Pesticides in Water: Copper Sulfate in Flooded Cranberry Bogs. *Pest. Monitoring J.* 4:11–13.

Deubert, K. H., and Zuckerman, B. M.

1969	Distribution of Dieldrin and DDT in Cranberry Bog Soil. *Pest. Monitoring J.* 2:172–175.

Devlin, R. M.

1980a	Growth Inhibitor in Cranberry Leaves. *Cranberries—The Nat. Cranberry Mag.* 44 (3): 3,12.

1980b	Inhibition of Wheat Seed Germination and Growth by Cranberry Leaf Extract. *Pl. Growth Reg. Bull.* 8:7–8.

Devlin, R. M., and Demoranville, I. E.

1967	Influence of Gibberellic Acid and Gibrel on Fruit Set and Yield in *Vaccinium macrocarpon* cv. Early Black. *Physio. Planta.* 20:587–592.

1968	Influence of Dichlobenil on Yield, Size, and Pigmentation of Cranberries. *Weed Sci.* 16:38–39.

1970	Influence of 2-chloroethyl phosphoric Acid on Anthocyanin Formation, Size, and Yield in *Vaccinium macrocarpon* cv. Early Black. *Physio. Planta.* 23:1139–1143.

1973	Influence of the Herbicide R-7465 on Cranberry Fruit Development. *HortSci.* 8:400.

1978a	Influence of Two Ethylene-Releasing Compounds on Anthocyanin Formation, Size, and Yield in 'Early Black' Cranberries. In *Proc. N. E. Weed Sci. Soc.* 32:108–112.

1978b	Wild Bean Control on Cranberry Bogs with Maleic Hydrazide. In *Proc. N. E. Weed Sci. Soc.* 2:349–351.

Devlin, R. M., and Deubert, K. H.

1981	Presence of Natural Plant Growth Inhibitor in 'Early Black' Cranberry Leaves. In *Proc. N. E. Weed Sci. Soc.* 35:90–94.

Devlin, R. M.; Karczmarczyk, S. J.

1974	The Effect of Light on Cranberry Seed Germination. *Cranberries—The Nat. Cranberry Mag.* 38 (10): 3.

Devlin, R. M.; Karczmarczyk, S. J.; and Deubert, K. H.

1976	The Influence of Abscisic Acid in Cranberry Seed Dormancy. *HortSci.* 11:412–413.

Devlin, R. M.; Zuckerman, B. M.; and Demoranville, I. E.

1968	Effect of Delayed Harvest and Storage on the Pigment Development in Cranberries. In *Proc. Amer. Soc. Hort. Sci.* 92:793–796.

1969	Influence of Preharvest Applications of Malathion and Indole-3-Acetic Acid on Anthocyanin Development in *Vaccinium macrocarpon*, Var. Early Black. *J. Amer. Soc. Hort. Sci.* 94:52–55.

Dickey, G. L., and Baumer, O. W.
1985   Irrigation of Cranberries. In *Proc. and Tech. Ref. Man. for the Nat. Cranberry Conf.*, 30 April–2 May 1985, Hyannis, Mass., Mass. Coop. Ext. Serv. and Soil Cons. Serv., 46–62.

Dirr, M. A.
1974   Nitrogen Form and Growth and Nitrate Reductase Activity of the Cranberry. *HortSci.* 9:347–348.

Dobroscky, I. D.
1929   Cranberry False-Blossom Disease Spread by a Leaf Hopper. *Science* 70:635.

1931   Studies on Cranberry False Blossom Disease and its Insect Vector. *Contr. Boyce Thompson Inst.* 3 (1): 59–83.

Doehlert, C. A.
1936   A Comparison of Methods of Scooping and Handpicking the Cranberry Crop. In *Proc. 66th Ann. Mtg. Amer. Cranberry Growers' Assoc.*, 11–14.

1937a   Cranberry Harvesting and Some Notes on Dusting for the Bluntnosed Leaf Hopper. In *Proc. 68th Ann. Conv. Amer. Cranberry Growers' Assoc.* 22–24.

1937b   Cranberry Harvesting Methods. In *Proc. 67th Ann. Mtg. Amer. Cranberry Growers' Assoc.*, 10–18.

1939   Concluding Report on the Harvesting Investigation. In *Proc. 69th Ann. Mtg. Amer. Cranberry Growers' Assoc.*, 9–13.

1940   What Some New Jersey Growers Have Done to Improve Their Yields. In *Proc. 71st Ann. Conv. Amer. Cranberry Growers' Assoc.*, 17–24.

1941   Observations on Fertilizing and Harvesting Cranberries. In *Proc. 71st Ann. Mtg. Amer. Cranberry Growers' Assoc.*, 13–19.

1950   Cranberry Picking Methods and Costs per Barrel. In *Proc. 81st Ann. Conv. Amer. Cranberry Growers' Assoc.*, 6–10.

1951   Fertilizing Cranberries by Airplane. In *Proc. 81st Ann. Mtg. Amer. Cranberry Growers' Assoc.*, 8–11.

1953a   Fertilizing Cranberries. In *Proc. 83rd Ann. Mtg. Amer. Cranberry Growers' Assoc.*, 13–19.

1953b   Progress Report on What Makes a Cranberry Upright Produce Fruit. In *Proc. 84th Ann. Conv. Amer. Cranberry Growers' Assoc.*, 19–23.

1954   Composition and Timing of Cranberry Fertilizers. In *Proc. 84th Ann. Mtg. Amer. Cranberry Growers' Assoc.*, 9–17.

1955a   Cranberry Fertilizer Research in New Jersey. *Cranberries—The Nat. Cranberry Mag.* 19 (11): 10–12.

1955b   How Oxygen Deficiency Affected One Bog in New Jersey. In *Proc. 85th Ann. Mtg. Amer. Cranberry Growers' Assoc.*, 24, 26–28.

1955c   Pruning Cranberries. In *Proc. 85th Ann. Mtg. Amer. Cranberry Growers' Assoc.*, 15–19.

1956   Preliminary Notes on a Fruit Setting Hormone. In *Proc. 86th Ann. Mtg. Amer. Cranberry Growers' Assoc.*, 18–19.

1958   Pruning Cranberries. In *Proc. 88th Ann. Mtg. Amer. Cranberry Growers' Assoc.*, 14–18.

Doughty, C. C.
1961   *Protection from Frost.* Pacific County Ext. Serv. P.C. no. 4.
1962a   The Effects of Certain Growth Regulators on the Fruiting of Cranberries *Vaccinium macrocarpon* Ait. In *Proc. Amer. Soc. Hort. Sci.* 80:340–349.
1962b   Protection from Frost. *Cranberries—The Nat. Cranberry Mag.* 27 (1): 7–8.
1972   Fertility. In *Cranberry Vine*—Pub. Coop. Ext. Serv., Coastal Wash. 10 Aug. 1–2.
1984   Some Effects of Minor Elements on Cranberry (*Vaccinium macrocarpon* Ait.) Growth. *Can. J. Plant Sci.* 64 (2): 339–348.
Doughty, C. C., and Dodge, J. C.
1966   *Cranberry Production in Washington.* Wash. Agr. Exp. Sta. Pub. E.M. no. 2619.
Doughty, C. C., and Garren, R., Jr.
1970   Crowley, a New, Early Maturing Cranberry Variety for Washington and Oregon. *Fruit Var. and Hort. Dig.* 24:88–89.
Doughty, C. C.; Patterson, M. E.; and Shawa, A. Y.
1967   Storage Longevity of the McFarlin Cranberry as Influenced by Certain Growth Retardants and Stage of Maturity. In *Proc. Amer. Soc. Hort. Sci.* 91:192–204.
Doughty, C. C., and Scheer, W. P. A.
1969   Effect of Alar on Growth and Dormancy of Cranberry. *Cranberries—The Nat. Cranberry Mag.* 34 (6): 13–18.
Doughty, C. C., and Shawa, A. W.
1966   Cold Injury to Cranberries in 1965 in Washington. *Cranberries—The Nat. Cranberry Mag.* 30 (12): 20–24.
Driggers, B. F.
1924   *The Effect of the Height of the Water Table upon Cranberry Production.* N.J. Agr. Exp. Sta. Paper no. 229.
Dugan, C. R., and Cardaciotto, P. S.
1966   Reduction of Ammoniacal Urinary Odors by the Sustained Feeding of Cranberry Juice. *J. Psy. Nursing,* Sept.-Oct.
Durell, E. H.
1902   The Cranberry—A Unique Fruit. In *Proc. 32nd Ann. Mtg. Amer. Cranberry Growers' Assoc.,* 1–3.
1904   The Cranberry Scoop. In *Proc. 35th Amer. Ann. Conv. Amer. Cranberry Growers' Assoc.,* 1–3.
1914   Harvesting Cranberries: The Best Up-to-Date Method. In *Proc. 45th Ann. Conv. Amer. Cranberry Growers' Assoc.,* 4–6.
Eady, F., and Eaton, G. W.
1969   Reduced Chilling Requirement of McFarlin Cranberry Buds. *Can. J. Pl. Sci.* 49:637–638.
1972a   Effects of Chilling during Dormancy on Development of the Terminal Bud of the Cranberry. *Can. J. Pl. Sci.* 52:273–279.
1972b   The Role of Gibberellic Acid and Gibberellin-like Substances in the Dormancy of the Cranberry. *Can. J. Pl. Sci.* 52:263–271.

Eastwood, B.
1856   *Complete Manual for the Cultivation of the Cranberry.* New York: C. M. Saxton & Co.

Eaton, E. L.
1957   Cranberry Culture. In *The Cranberry.* Can. Dept. Agr. Pub. no. 810 (rev).

Eaton, G. W.
1966   The Effect of Frost upon Seed Number and Berry Size in the Cranberry. *Can. J. Pl. Sci.* 46:87–88.

1971a   Effect of N, P, and K Fertilizer Applications on Cranberry Leaf Nutrient Composition, Fruit Color, and Yield in a Mature Bog. *J. Amer. Soc. Hort. Sci.* 96:431–433.

1971b   Effect of N, P, and K Fertilizers on the Growth and Composition of Vines in a Young Cranberry Bog. *J. Amer. Soc. Hort. Sci.* 96:426–429.

1978   Floral Induction and Biennial Bearing in the Cranberry. *Fruit Var. J.* 32:58–60.

Eaton, G. W., and Kyte, T. R.
1978   Yield Component Analyses in the Cranberry. *J. Amer. Soc. Hort. Sci.* 103:(5):578–583.

Eaton, G. W., and MacPherson, E. A.
1978   Morphological Components of Yield in Cranberry. *Hort. Res.* 17 (2): 73–82.

Eaton, G. W., and Meehan, C. N.
1973   Effects of N, P, and K Fertilizer on Leaf Composition, Yield, and Fruit Quality of Bearing 'Ben Lear' Cranberries. *J. Amer. Soc. Hort. Sci.* 98:89–93.

1976   Effects on N and K Applications on the Leaf Composition, Yield, and Fruit Quality of Bearing 'McFarlin' Cranberries. *Can. J. Pl. Sci.* 56:107–110.

Eaton, G. W., and Ormrod, D. P.
1968   Photoperiod Effect on Plant Growth in Cranberry. *Can. J. Pl. Sci.* 48:447–450.

Eaton, G. W.; Zuckerman, B. M.; Shawa, A. Y.; Eck, P.; Dana, M. N.; Garren, R.; and Lockhart, C. L.
1969   The Effect of Preharvest Malathion Sprays upon Cranberry Fruit Color. *J. Amer. Soc. Hort. Sci.* 94:590–592.

Eck, P.
1964a   1962 Cranberry Fertilizer Studies. In *Proc. 92nd Ann. Mtg. Amer. Cranberry Growers' Assoc.,* 27–33.

1964b   Phosphorus Studies on Cranberries. In *Proc. 94th Ann. Mtg. Amer. Cranberry Growers' Assoc.,* 45–48.

1966   A Progress Report of Trace Element Studies on Cranberries. *Cranberries— The Nat. Cranberry Mag.* 31 (2): 13–14.

1968   Chemical Color Enhancement of Cranberry Fruit. *HortSci.* 3:70–72.

1969   Effect of Preharvest Sprays of Ethrel, Alar, Malathion on Anthocyanin Content of Early Black Cranberry (*Vaccinium macrocarpon* Ait.) *HortSci.* 4:224–226.

1971   Cranberry Growth and Composition as Influenced by Nitrogen Treatment. *HortSci.* 6 (1): 38–39.

1972a   Cranberry Yield and Anthocyanin Content As Influenced by Ethepon, SADH, and Malathion. *J. Amer. Soc. Hort. Sci.* 97:213–214.

1972b   Influence of 2-Chloroethyl Phosphoric Acid (Ethephon) on Color Development in Cranberry and Blueberry Fruit. *HortSci.* 7:322.

1976a   Cranberry Growth and Production in Relation to Water Table Depth. *J. Amer. Soc. Hort. Sci.* 101 (5): 544–546.

1976b   Relationship of Nitrogen Nutrition of 'Early Black' Cranberry to Vegetative Growth, Fruit Yield, and Quality. *J. Amer. Soc. Hort. Sci.* 101:375–377.

1985   Response of the American Cranberry to Phosphorus Fertilizer. *Acta Horticulturae* 165:299–301.

Eck, P., and Childers, N. F.

1966   *Blueberry Culture.* New Brunswick, N.J.: Rutgers University Press.

Esselen, W. B., Jr.

1937   Influence of Certain Fruits on Fecal Flora and Intestinal Reaction in Diets of Rats. *Food Res.* 2 (1): 65–72.

Esselen, W. B., Jr., and Fellers, C. R.

1937   Gas Content of Cranberries and Possible Relationship of Respiratory Activity to Keeping Quality. *Pl. Physio.* 12:527–536.

Esselen, W. B., Jr.; Fellers, C. R.; and Levine, A. S.

1948   Mold Counts on Strained Cranberry Sauce. *Fruit Prod. J. and Amer. Food Mfg.* 28:6–9.

Esselen, W. B., Jr.; Hayes, K. M.; and Fellers, C. R.

1948   *Apple-Cranberry Juice.* Mass. Agr. Exp. Sta. Bull. no. 449:51.

Esselen, W. B., Jr.; Powers, J. J.; and Fellers, C. R.

1946   The Fortification of Fruit Juices with Ascorbic Acid. *Fruit Prod. J. and Amer. Food Mfg.* 26:11–14, 29.

Farrar, C. L. and Bain, H. F.

1946   Honey Bees As Pollinators of the Cranberry. *Amer. Bee J.* 86:503–504.

Fellers, C. R.

1932   *Food Value of Cranberries and Cranberry Sauce.* Mass. Agr. Exp. Sta. Bull. no. C114.

1933   Nutritive Value of Cranberries. *Amer. J. Pub. Health* 23:13–18.

1936   Cranberries for Health. *Cranberry—The Nat. Cranberry Mag.* 1 (3): 12–13.

Fellers, C. R., and Esselen, W. B.

1955   *Cranberries and Cranberry Products.* Mass. Agr. Exp. Sta. Bull. no. 481.

Fellers, C. R.; Isham, P. D.; and Esselen, W. B.

1935   *Vitamins of Cranberries.* Amer. Cranberry Exchange Misc. Pub., New York.

Fellers, C. R.; Redmon, B. C.; and Parrott, E. M.

1933   Effect of Cranberries on Urinary Acidity and Blood Alkali Reserve. *J. Nutr.* 6:455–463.

Fernald, M. L.

1902   The Variations and Distribution of American Cranberries. *Rhodora* 4:231–237.

1950   *Gray's Manual of Botany.* 8th ed. New York: Amer. Book Co.

Ferris, I. G., and Lichtenstein, E. P.
1980   Interactions between Agricultural Chemicals and Soil Microflora and Their Effects on the Degradation of (^{14}C) Parathion in a Cranberry Soil. *J. Agr. and Food Chem.* 28:1011–1019.

Fiedler, H., and Christ, E.
1986   Experience with Cultivation of Cranberries (*Vaccinium macrocarpon*) on High Moorland in Southern Germany. *Erwerbsobstbau* 28 (4): 104–106.

Filmer, R. S.
1949   Cranberry Pollination Studies. In *Proc. 80th Ann. Conv. Amer. Cranberry Growers' Assoc.*, 14–22.

1953   Cranberry Pollination Studies. In *Proc. 84th Ann. Conv. Amer. Cranberry Growers' Assoc.*, 28–36.

1955   The Blooming and Fruiting Habits of Early Black Cranberries in New Jersey. In *Proc. 85th Ann. Mtg. Amer. Cranberry Growers' Assoc.*, 34–45.

Filmer, R. S., and Doehlert, C. A.
1959   *Use of Honeybees in Cranberry Bogs.* N.J. Agr. Exp. Sta. Circ. no. 588.

Filmer, R. S.; Marucci, P. E.; and Moulter, H. J.
1958   Seed Counts and Size of Cranberries. In *Proc. 88th Ann. Mtg. Amer. Cranberry Growers' Assoc.*, 22–30.

Fisher, R. A.
1951   Soil Data on Nutrition on Washington State Bogs. *Cranberries—The Nat. Cranberry Mag.*, 16 (2): 8–10.

Foley, M. E.
1957   *Ways with Cranberries.* Univ. Mass Coop. Ext. Serv. Spec. Circ. no. 218.

Forsyth, F. R., and Hall, I. V.
1967a   Oxygen Absorption and Ethylene Production by Developing Cranberry Fruit. *Can. J. Pl. Sci.* 47:153–156.

1967b   Rates of Photosynthesis and Respiration in Leaves of the Cranberry with Emphasis on Rates at Low Temperatures. *Can. J. Pl. Sci.* 47:19–23.

1969   Ethylene Production with Accompanying Respiration Rates from the Time of Blossoming to Fruit Maturity in Three *Vaccinium* Species. *Le Nat. Can.* 96:257–259.

Forsyth, F. R.; Hall, I. V.; and Lightfoot, H. J.
1973   Diffusion of CO_2, O_2, and Ethylene in Cranberry Fruit. *HortSci.* 8:45–46.

Francis, F. J.
1957   Color and Pigment Measurement in Fresh Cranberries. In *Proc. Amer. Soc. Hort. Sci.* 69:296–301.

1970   Color Measurement in Plant Breeding. *HortSci.* 5:102–106.

Francis, F. J., and Atwood, W. M.
1961   The Effect of Fertilizer Treatments on the Pigment Content of Cranberries. In *Proc. Amer. Soc. Hort. Sci.* 77:351–358.

Francis, F. J., and Servadio, G. J.
1963   Relation between Color of Cranberries and Stability of Juice. In *Proc. Amer. Soc. Hort. Sci.* 83:406–415.

Francis, F. J., and Zuckerman, B. M.
1962   Effects of Fungicide Treatment on Pigment Content and Decay of Cranber-
        ries. In *Proc. Amer. Soc. Hort. Sci* 81:288–294.
Franklin, H. J.
1920   *Monthly Weather Review.* Mass. Agr. Exp. Sta. Supple. no. 16:30.
1937   Glaciers of 20,000 Years Ago Part of Cape Cod Cranberry "Cradle." *Cran-
        berries—The Nat. Cranberry Mag.* 1 (11): 5–6, 12–16.
1940   *Cranberry Growing in Massachusetts.* Mass. Agr. Exp. Sta. Bull. no. 371.
1943   Miscellanea: Weather and Cranberry Size. Weather and Cranberry Ripen-
        ing. In *Weather in Cranberry Culture.* Mass. Agr. Exp. Sta. Bull. no.
        402:84–90.
1944   Discussion of New Jersey Bog Conditions. In *Proc. 75th Ann. Conv. Amer.
        Cranberry Growers' Assoc.,* 8–21.
1946   Weather and Cranberry Production. In *Weather and Water As Factors in
        Cranberry Production.* Mass. Agr. Exp. Sta. Bull. no. 443:3–36.
1948a   *Cranberry Growing in Massachusetts.* Mass. Agr. Exp. Sta. Bull. no. 447.
1948b   *Cranberry Insects in Massachusetts.* Mass. Agr. Exp. Sta. Bull. no. 445.
1950   *Cranberry Insects in Massachusetts.* Mass. Agr. Exp. Sta. Bull. no. 445.
1952   *Cranberry Insects in Massachusetts.* Mass. Agr. Exp. Sta. Supplement to
        Bull. no. 445.
Franklin, H. J.; Bergman, H. F.; and Stevens, N. E.
1943   *Weather in Cranberry Culture.* Mass. Agr. Exp. Sta. Bull. no. 402.
Franklin, H. J., and Cross, C. E.
1948   *Weather in Relation to Cranberry Production and Condition.* Mass. Agr.
        Exp. Sta. Bull. no. 450.
Franklin, H. J.; Darrow, G. M.; and Malde, O. G.
1924   Cranberry Harvesting and Handling. U.S. Dept. Agr. Farmers' Bull. no.
        1402.
Friend, R. J., and Boone, D. M.
1968a   *Diaporthe vaccinii* Associated with Dieback of Cranberry in Wisconsin. *Pl.
        Dis. Rptr.* 52:341–344.
1968b   Dieback of Cranberry in Wisconsin. *Cranberry—The Nat. Cranberry Mag.*
        32:9–10.
Fudge, B. R.
1930   *Increasing the Color of Cranberries after Removal from the Vines.* N.J. Agr.
        Exp. Sta. Bull. no. 504.
Fuleki, T., and Francis, F. J.
1967   The Co-occurrence of Monoglucosides and Monogalactosides of Cyanidin
        and Peonidin in the American Cranberry, *Vaccinium macrocarpon. Phy-
        tochem.* 6:1705–1708.
1968a   Quantitative Methods for Anthocyanins. 1, Extraction and Determination of
        Total Anthocyanin in Cranberries. *J. Food Sci.* 33:72–77.
1968b   Quantitative Methods for Anthocyanins. 2, Determination of Total Antho-
        cyanin and Degradation Index for Cranberry Juice. *J. Food Sci.* 33:78–
        83.

1968c   Quantitative Methods for Anthocyanins. 3, Purification of Cranberry Antho-
        cyanins. *J. Food Sci.* 33:266–274.
1968d   Quantitative Methods for Anthocyanins. 4, Determination of Individual An-
        thocyanins in Cranberry and Cranberry Products. *J. Food Sci.* 33:471–478.
Gilbert, A. W.
1932   *A Plan for the Stabilization of Cranberries.* Cranberry Prod. Assoc. Misc.
        Rpt. Wareham, Mass.
Goff, E. S.
1901   *Investigations of Flower Buds.* Wis. Agr. Exp. Sta. Ann. Rpt. no. 18:306–
        310.
Goheen, A. C.
1953   Effect of Dry-Scooping on Fruit Production and Keeping Quality of Twenty-
        One Cranberry Varieties and Selections in New Jersey. In *Proc. 83rd Ann.
        Mtg. Amer. Cranberry Growers' Assoc.*, 33–39.
Goldsworthy, V. C.
1933   A Preliminary Report on Cranberry False-Blossom in Wisconsin with Special
        References to Early Literature as Found in the Wisconsin Growers' Re-
        ports. In *Proc. Wis. St. Cranberry Growers' Assoc. 46th Ann. Mtg.*, 39–49.
1943   Unique Pooling of the Wisconsin Cranberry Sales Co. Proven 100% Efficient
        in Actual Operation. *Cranberries—The Nat. Cranberry Mag.* 8 (2): 11, 17.
1947   How the American Cranberry Exchange Has Met the Challenge of Forty
        Years. *Cranberry World* 1 (8): 3.
1963   What Has the Marketing Order Accomplished? *Cranberries—The Nat.
        Cranberry Mag.* 27 (11): 10.
Gray, R.
1972   Surface Water Quality in Drainage Areas of Cranberry Bogs. *Cranberries—
        The Nat. Cranberry Mag.* 37 (3): 8–9.
Greidanus, T., and Dana, M. M.
1972   Cranberry Growth Related to Tissue Concentration and Soil Test Phos-
        phorus. *J. Amer. Soc. Hort. Sci.* 97:326–328.
Greidanus, T.; Peterson, L. A.; Schrader, L. E.; and Dana, M. N.
1972   Essentiality of Ammonium for Cranberry Nutrition. *J. Amer. Soc. Hort. Sci.*
        97 (2): 272–277.
Greidanus, T.; Rigby, J. B. F.; and Dana, M. N.
1971   Seed Germination in Cranberry. *Cranberries—The Nat. Cranberry Mag.* 36
        (8): 13.
Gunness, C. I.
1942   Cranberry Storage Tests. *Cranberries—The Nat. Cranberry Mag.* 7 (5): 7–
        10.
Hall, C. J.
1939a   The Early Black Cranberry Was Developed at Pleasant Lake, Cape Cod,
        about 1860. *Cranberries—The Nat. Cranberry Mag.* 4 (3): 5.
1939b   Packing Machine Designed by Bruce & Hubbell Marks Step Forward for
        Growers. *Cranberries—The Nat. Cranberry Ma.* 4 (2): 6.
1941a   Cape Cod Winds Gave Idea of Cultivation of the Cranberry. *Cranberries—
        The Nat. Cranberry Mag.* 6 (1): 4.

1941b   An Old Indian Custom at Gay Head. *Cranberries–The Nat. Cranberry Mag.* 6 (7): 4–5, 11.

1941c   Pilgrims Heartened by Discovery of Wild Cranberries. *Cranberries—The Nat. Cranberry Mag.* 6 (4): 17–19.

1943   Developer of McFarlin Variety. *Cranberries—The Nat. Cranberry Mag.* 7 (12): 4–5.

1945   First Washington Bog Built When Region Was Still Little Known and Scarcely Settled. *Cranberries—The Nat. Cranberry Mag.* 9 (11): 6–9.

1947   Origin of Stankavich Berry. *Cranberries—The Nat. Cranberry Mag.* 11 (10): 10–11.

1948   Indians and English Use Them Much. *Cranberries—The Nat. Cranberry Mag.* 13 (8): 6–8.

1949a   The Chippewa Indians Had a Name for Cranberries. *Cranberries—The Nat. Cranberry Mag.* 13 (9): 6–8, 12.

1949b   "Cranberry Fever" Strikes Cape Cod and New Jersey in the 1850's. *Cranberries—The Nat. Cranberry Mag.* 14 (8): 6–7, 15–19.

1949c   Cultivation Began Early in Middlesex, Essex (Mass.) Counties. *Cranberries—The Nat. Cranberry Mag.* 14 (1): 10–12, 16–22.

1949d   Henry Hall, Pioneer Growers, a Vet of Revolutionary War. *Cranberries—The Nat. Cranberry Mag.* 13 (10): 6–8, 22–25.

1949e   Industry, with Mingled Wild and Cultivated Berries, Puts Out New Growth in 1830–40's. *Cranberries—The Nat. Cranberry Mag.* 14 (2): 18–21; 14 (3): 15–21.

1949f   More of the Start of Cranberry Cultivation at Dennis, Cape Cod. *Cranberries—The Nat. Cranberry Mag.* 13 (11): 12–16.

1949g   The Rising Sun of Cranberry Culture Touched Life to Industry in New Jersey Nearly as Soon as Cape Cod. *Cranberries—The Nat. Cranberry Mag.* 13 (12): 7, 12, 28.

1949h   With "Little Drops of Water and Tiny Grains of Sand" Cape Men Lay Up Industry Foundation in 40's. *Cranberries—The Nat. Cranberry Mag.* 14 (5): 14–16; 14 (6): 16–21.

1950a   "Cranberry Fever" Continues on Cape as Growers Produce "Red Gold." *Cranberries—The Nat. Cranberry Mag.* 14 (11): 8–9; 14 (12): 23–25.

1950b   1850's Find Growers Troubled with "The Rot" and Insects. *Cranberries—The Nat. Cranberry Mag.* 15 (7): 13–17.

1950c   Ending of 1850's Found Cranberry Cultivation Definitely Advanced. *Cranberries—The Nat. Cranberry Mag.* 15 (8): 11, 16–18.

1950d   Mid-years of 1850's Find Growers Troubled with Insects and "The Rot." *Cranberries—The Nat. Cranberry Mag.* 15 (6): 3–4.

1950e   Publishing of Eastwood Manual in Mid 50's Throws Fuel to Fire. *Cranberries—The Nat. Cranberry. Mag.* 15 (2): 15–17; 15 (3): 12–17.

1950f   A Reason for Wisconsin's Growing Production—Good Frost Forecasting. *Cranberries—The Nat. Cranberry Mag.* 15 (6): 7–9.

1952a   Cranberry Industry Is Booming As War of the Rebellion Rolls Up. *Cranberries—The Nat. Cranberry Mag.* 16 (11): 5, 18–20; 16 (12): 19–21.

1952b   I Put by My Chart and Glass, Took to Raising Cranberry Sass. *Cranberries—The Nat. Cranberry Mag.* 17 (7): 10–16.

1952c   War of the Rebellion Was No Obstacle to Cranberry Men. *Cranberries—The Nat. Cranberry Mag.* 17 (6): 7, 10, 13, 16–19.

1954   Where Did the "Early Black" Originate? *Cranberries—The Nat. Cranberry Mag.* 18 (10): 13–15.

1962   A Massachusetts Grower Tries Wisconsin Water Raking Harvest. *Cranberries—The Nat. Cranberry Mag.* 27 (7): 7–12.

1963   Long Beach Peninsula Was Site of Original Washington Bog. *Cranberries—The Nat. Cranberry Mag.* 28 (8): 10–12.

Hall, I. V.

1969   *Growing Cranberries—Culture.* Can. Dept. Agr. Pub. no. 1282.

1970   Cranberry Shoot Morphology as Influenced by Orientation of Vines. *Le Nat. Can.* 97:351–355.

1971   Cranberry Growth As Related to Water Levels in the Soil. *Can. J. Pl. Sci.* 51:237–238.

Hall, I. V., and Aalders, L. E.

1965   The Relation between Seed Number and Berry Weight in the Cranberry. *Can. J. Pl. Sci.* 45:292.

Hall, I. V., and Newberry, R. J.

1972   Floral Development in Normal and Frost Injured Cranberries. *HortSci.* 7:269–271.

Hall, I. V., and Nickerson, N. L.

1986   The Biological Flora of Canada. 7, *Oxycoccus macrocarpus* (Ait.) Pers., Large Cranberry. *Can. Field Natu.* 100 (1): 89–104.

Hall, I. V., and Stark, R.

1972   Anthocyanin Production in Cranberry Leaves and Fruit, Related to Cool Temperatures at a Low Light Intensity. *Hort. Res.* 12:183–186.

Hamilton, E. B.

1945   Wareham and the Cranberry Industry. *Cranberries—The Nat. Cranberry Mag.* 10 (7): 17–18.

Harding, P. R., Jr.

1957   Preliminary Tests of Ammonia Pellets for Control of Fungal Decay of Packaged Cranberries. *Pl. Dis. Rptr.* 41:564–566.

Harrison, I.

1946   Progress with the Vacuum Picker. In *Proc. 77th Ann. Conv. Amer. Cranberry Growers' Assoc.,* 24–25.

Hayes, K. M.; Fellers, C. R.; and Esselen, W. B., Jr.

1948   The Keeping Quality of "Pre-Packaged" Fresh Cranberries. In *Proc. Amer. Soc. Hort. Sci.* 52:257–262.

Hicks, J. L.; Hall, I. V.; and Forsyth, F. R.

1968   Growth of Cranberry Plants in Pure Stands and in Weedy Areas under Nova Scotian Conditions. *Hort. Res.* 8 (2): 104–112.

Hillstrom, R. J.

1947   The Western Cranberry Picker. In *Proc. 77th Ann. Mtg. Amer. Cranberry Growers' Assoc.,* 35–36.

Hintzman, A. J.; Estes, C. W.; and Morris, W. W.
1953   *Wisconsin Cranberries—Production, Varieties, Utilization, and Markets.*
        Wisc. St. Dept. Agr. Bull. no. 322.

Hobson, A.
1923   *Sales Methods and Policies of a Grower's National Marketing Agency.* U.S.
        Dept. Agr. Bull no. 1109.

Holman, J. D.
1922   Scooping of Cranberries. In *Proc. 52nd Ann. Mtg. Amer. Cranberry
        Growers' Assoc.,* 1–3.

Holmes, O. M.
1883   Address to the Members of the American Cranberry Growers' Assoc. In
        Proc. 11th Ann. Conv. Amer. Cranberry Growers' Assoc., 1–3.

Hovey, W. B., and Shulman, M. D.
1966   A Statistical and Synoptic Analysis of Factors Causing Frost in New Jersey
        Cranberry Bogs. *Bull. N.J. Acad. Sci.* 11:2–16.

Hruschka, H. W., and Kaufman, J.
1949   Storage of Prepackaged Cranberries. *Pre-Pack-Age* 3:18, 20, 22, 32.
1951   *Storage Tests with Prepackaged Cranberries.* U.S. Bur. Plant Indus. Off. Rpt.
        no. 235.
1952   Storage Tests with Prepackaged McFarlin and Late Howes Cranberries.
        Pre-Pack-Age 6:20–21.

Hunt, R.; Stribley, D. P.; and Read, D. J.
1975   Root/Shoot Equilibria in Cranberry (*Vaccinium macrocarpon* Ait.) *Ann. Bot.*
        39:807–810.

Hunger, J. S.
1957   *Purchaser's Opinions of Frozen Cranberries in Minneapolis–St. Paul.* U.S.
        Dept. Agr. Mktg. Res. Rpt. no. 183:27.

Hutson, R.
1925   The Honeybee as an Agent in the Pollination of Pears, Apples, and Cranber-
        ries. *J. Econ. Ent.* 18:387–391.
1926a   *Relation of the Honeybee to Fruit Pollination in New Jersey.* N.J. Agr. Exp.
        Sta. Bull. no. 434.
1926b   The Use of Honeybees as Pollinating Agents on Cranberry Bogs. In *Proc.
        57th Ann. Conv. Amer. Cranberry Growers' Assoc.,* 10–11.
1929   Cranberry Pollination. In *Proc. 59th Ann. Mtg. Amer. Cranberry Growers'
        Assoc.,* 19.

Isham, P. D., and Fellers, C. R.
1933   *Effect of Manufacturing and Preserving Processes on the Vitamins of Cranbe-
        rries.* Mass. Agr. Exp. Sta. Bull. no. 296:2–17.

Jankowski, K.
1973   Alkaloids of Cranberries, V. *Experientia* 29:1334–1335.

Johansen, C.
1965   *Cranberry Pollination Investigations,* 1962–1965. Wash. St. Univ. Coop.
        Ext. Serv. Mimeo. Rpt.
1967   *Encouraging the Bumble Bee Pollinator of Cranberries.* Wash. St. Univ. Col.
        Agr. Ext. Circ. E.M. no. 2262.

Johansen, C., and Hutt, R.
1965   Encouraging the Bumble Bee in Washington. *Cranberries—The Nat. Cranberry Mag.* 29 (12): 14, 16.

Kaufman, J.; Benfield, P. L.; and Harding, R. R., Jr.
1957   *Shipping Tests with Massachusetts Grown Cranberries in Conventual Refrigerator Cars with Standard Ventilation and in Mechanically Refrigerated Cars, 1955.* U.S. Dept. Agr. AMS no. 187.

Kaufman, J.; Ringel, S. M.; Hamer, A. A.; Atrops, E. P.; and Ramsey, G. B.
1958   *Effect of Precooling on Market Quality of Cranberries Shipped by Rail or Truck.* U.S. Dept. Agr. Marketing Res. Rpt. no. 287.

Kender, W. J., and Childers, N. F.
1959   Growth of Cranberry Plants (*Vaccinium macrocarpon*) with Various Sources of Nitrogen. In *Proc. Amer. Soc. Hort. Sci.* 74:407–413.

Kenny, H. S.
1949   Frost and Low Temperatures in the Wisconsin Cranberry Bogs. Unpublished Rpt. Chicago: U.S. Weather Bur.

Kisiel, M.; Castillo, J. M.; and Zuckerman, B. M.
1971   An Adhesive Plug Associated with The Feeding of *Hemicycliphora similis* on Cranberry. *J. Nematol.* 3:296–298.

Knight, R. J., Jr., and Scott, D. H.
1964   Effects of Temperatures on Self- and Cross-Pollination and Fruiting of Four Highbush Blueberry Varieties. In *Proc. Amer. Soc. Hort. Sci.* 85:302–306.

Knox, R.
1952   Freezing Fresh Cranberries. *Cranberry World* 6 (4): 5–6.

Kohman, E. F.
1938   Cranberries in the Diet. *J. Amer. Diet. Assoc.* 14 (8): 644–646.

Kom, C. J.
1968   Medical Management of Recumbent Calculi. St. Albens, N.Y.: U.S. Naval Hospital.

Konrad, J. G., and Bryans, M. A.
1975   Analysis of Cranberry Marsh Discharge. *Cranberries—The Nat. Cranberry Mag.* 39 (10): 7–11.

Kraemer, R. J.
1964   Cranberry Juice and the Reduction of Ammoniacal Odor of Urine. *Southwestern Med.* 45:211–212.

Kranick, E. M.
1936   A Homemade Sanding Scow for Cranberry Marshes. *Cranberries—The Nat. Cranberry Mag.* 1 (7): 4.

1937   The Stankavich Cranberry of Oregon, a Fine Variety with Good Possibilities. *Cranberries—The Nat. Cranberry Mag.* 2 (1): 6.

1940   Artificial Wind Machines Fight Frost in Oregon. *Cranberries—The Nat. Cranberry Mag.* 4 (10): 2,8.

Kross, J. I.
1950   Talk on Cranberry Marketing Problems. *Cranberries—The Nat. Cranberry Mag.* 15 (6): 16–21.

Lacroix, D. S.
1926   Cranberry Flower Bud Investigations. *J. Agr. Res.* 33:355–63
Lebeau, O. R.
1950   *Prepackaging Cranberries Cooperatively.* U.S. Farm Credit Admin. Coop.
        Serv. Div. Misc. Rpt. no. 138.
Lees, D. H., and Francis, F. J.
1971   Quantitative Methods for Anthocyanins. 6. Flavonols and Anthocyanins in
        Cranberries. *J. Food Sci.* 36:1056–1060.
1972   Standardization of Pigment Analyses in Cranberries. *HortSci.* 7 (1): 83–
        84.
Lenhardt, P. J., and Eaton, G. W.
1976   Cranberry Growth and Flowering in Response to Field Applications of
        Daminozide. *HortSci.* 11:599–600.
1977   Cranberry Flower Bud Initiation in British Columbia. *Fruit Var. J.* 31–44.
Lenhardt, P. J.; Eaton, G. W.; and Mahrt, B.
1976   Effect of Photoperiod and SADH on Cranberry Growth and Flowering in the
        Greenhouse. In *Report of the Res. Com. of Can. Hort. Coun.,* 252
        (Abstract).
Leschyson, M. A., and Eaton, G. W.
1971   Effects of Urea and Nitrate Nitrogen on Growth and Composition of Cranbe-
        rry Vines. *J. Amer. Soc. Hort. Sci.* 96:597–599.
Levine, A. S.; Fellers, C. R.; and Gunness, C. I.
1940   Carbon Dioxide–Oxygen and Storage Relationships in Cranberries. In *Proc.
        Amer. Soc. Hort. Sci.* 38:239–242.
Lewis, C. H.
1946   Study Oxygen Deficiency in Winter Flooding at Beaver Brook.
        Cranberries—The Nat. Cranberry Mag. 10 (10): 9–11.
Lewis, C. L., Jr.
1925   Artificial Drying of Water Raked Berries. In *Proc. Wis. St. Cranberry
        Growers' Assoc. 38th Ann. Mtg.,* 41–43.
1944   Orderly Marketing. *Cranberries—The Nat. Cranberry Mag.* 8 (9): 12–14.
Licciardello, J. J.; Esselen, W. B., Jr.; and Fellers, C. R.
1951   Stability of Ascorbic Acid in Fresh Cranberries during Storage. In *Proc.
        Amer. Soc. Hort. Sci.* 57:94.
1952   Stability of Ascorbic Acid during the Preparation of Cranberry Products.
        Food Res. 17:338–342.
Light, I.; Gursel, E.; and Zinsser, H. H.
1973   Urinary Ionized Calcium in Urolithiasis and the Effect of Cranberry Juice.
        Urology 1:1–10.
Lockhart, C. L.
1970   Isolation of *Gibbera compacta* from Cranberry and the Effect of Moisture and
        Temperature on Ascospore Development. *Can. Pl. Dis. Surv.* 50:108.
Lockhart, C. L.; Forsyth, F. R.; Stark, R.; and Hall, I. V.
1971   Nitrogen Gas Suppresses Microorganisms on Cranberries in Short Term
        Storage. *Phytopath.* 61:335–336.

Lubitz, J. A.; Fellers, C. R.; and Clague, J. A.
1940   Syrup of Cranberry, a New Pharmaceutical Vehicle. *J. Amer. Phar. Assoc. Sci. Ed.* 29:323–325.

Luke, N. C.; Chin, C. K.; and Eck, P.
1977   Dialysis Extraction of Gibberellin-like Substances from Cranberry Tissue. *HortSci.* 12 (3): 245–246.

Luke, N. C., and Eck, P.
1978   Endogenous Gibberellin-like Activity in Cranberry at Different Stages of Development as Influenced by Nitrogen and Daminozide. *J. Amer. Soc. Hort. Sci.* 103:250–252.

Lynard, D.
1973   A Wine for All Seasons. *Cranberries—The Nat. Cranberry Mag.* 38 (3): 8–9.

Mahn, F. A., and O'Donnell, W. H.
1966   New Jersey Growers Rearranging Bogs for Water Raking. *Cranberries—The Nat. Cranberry Mag.* 31 (1): 7–10.

Mahr, D. L.; Jeffers, S. N.; Stang, E. J.; and Dana, M. N.
1987   *Cranberry Pest Control in Wisconsin.* Wis. Coop. Ext. Serv. Pub. no. A3276.

Mainland, C. M., and Eck, P.
1968   Cranberry Fruit Set, Growth, and Yield as Influenced by Gibberellic Acid Alone and in Combination with Alar. In *Proc. Amer. Soc. Hort. Sci.* 92:296–300.

Makepeace, R.
1936   Cranberry "Most Villainous" of American Sauces. *Cranberries—The Nat. Cranberry Mag.* (5)5,7,15.

Markley, K. S., and Sando, C. E.
1934   Petroleum Ether and Ether Soluble Constituents of Cranberry Pomace. *J. Biol. Chem.* 105:643–653.

Marucci, P. E.
1953   The Sparganothis (*Sparganothis sulfureana*) Fruitworm in New Jersey. In *Proc. 83rd Ann. Mtg. Amer. Cranberry Growers' Assoc.*, 6–13.

1954   The Effect of Cranberry Tipworm Attack on the Fruit Bud Production of the Cranberry Plant. In *Proc. 84th Ann. Mtg. Amer. Cranberry Growers' Assoc.*, 1–10.

1967   Cranberry Pollination. *Amer. Bee J.* 107:212–213.

Marucci, P. E., and Filmer, R. S.
1957   Cranberry Blossom Blast in New Jersey. In *Proc. 87th Ann. Mtg. Amer. Cranberry Growers' Assoc.*, 32–41.

1964   Preliminary Cross Pollination Tests on Cranberries. In *Proc. 94th Ann. Mtg. Amer. Cranberry Growers' Assoc.*, 48–51.

Marucci, P. E., and Moulter, H. J.
1955   Oxygen Deficiency on New Jersey Cranberry Bogs during the Winter of 1954–1955. In *Proc. 86th Ann. Conv. Amer. Cranberry Growers' Assoc.* 17–24.

1957   The Suppression of Cranberry Runner Growth by Maleic Hydrazide. In *Proc. 87th Ann. Mtg. Amer. Cranberry Growers' Assoc.*, 18–20.

1958   The Effect of Maleic Hydrazide on the Cranberry Vine. In *Proc. 88th Ann. Mtg. Amer. Cranberry Growers' Assoc.*, 36–42.

1971   Oxygen Deficiency Kills Cranberry Insects. *Cranberries—The Nat. Cranberry Mag.* 35 (11): 13–15.

1978   Cranberry Pollination in New Jersey. *Cranberries—The Nat. Cranberry Mag.* 45 (4): 6–9.

Mason, G. F.

1905   The Occurrence of Benzoic Acid Naturally in Cranberries. *J. Amer. Chem. Soc.* 27:613–614.

Massey, L. M., Jr.; Chase, B. R.; and Starr, M. S.

1981   Impact-Induced Breakdown in Commercially Screened 'Howes' Cranberries. *J. Amer. Soc. Hort. Sci.* 106:200–203.

1982   Effect of Rough Handling on CO_2 Evolution from Howes Cranberries. *HortSci.* 17:57–58.

Mathewson, W. B.

1925   The Cranberry Picking Machine. In *Proc. 56th Ann. Conv. Amer. Cranberry Growers' Assoc.*, 9–10.

1926   Progress with the Picking Machine. In *Proc. 56th Ann. Mtg. Amer. Cranberry Growers' Assoc.*, 8–9.

Maxwell, C. W. B., and Morgan, G. T.

1966   Insects. In *Growing Cranberries*. Can. Dept. Agr. Pub. no. 1282:19–21.

McGregor, S. E.

1976   *Insect Pollination of Cultivated Crop Plants*. U.S. Dept. Agr. Handbk. no. 496.

Medappa, K. C., and Dana, M. N.

1968   Influence of pH, Calcium, Iron, and Aluminum on the Uptake of Radiophosphorus by Cranberry Plants. In *Soil Sci. Soc. Amer. Proc.* 32:381–383.

1970a   The Influence of pH, Ca, P, and Fe on the Growth and Composition of the Cranberry Plant. *Soil Sci.* 109:250–253.

1970b   Tolerance of Cranberry Plants to Manganese, Iron, and Aluminum. *J. Amer. Soc. Hort. Sci.* 95:107–110.

Miller, C. W.

1966   Dieldrin Persistence in Cranberry Bogs. *J. Econ. Ent.* 59:905–906.

Miller, C. W.; Demoranville, I. E.; and Charig, A. J.

1966a   Casoron Retention in Cranberry Soil. *Cranberries—The Nat. Cranberry Mag.* 30 (10): 10–12.

1966b   Persistence of Dichlobenil in Cranberry Bogs. *Weeds* 14:296–298.

1967   Effect of Water on the Persistence of Dichlobenil. *Weed Res.* 7:164–167.

Miller, C. W.; Tomlinson, W. E.; and Norgren, R. L.

1967   Persistence and Movement of Parathion in Irrigation Waters. *Pest. Monitoring J.* 1:47–48.

Miller, C. W.; Zuckerman, B. M.; and Charig, A. J.
1966   Water Translocation of Diazinon-C^{14} and Parathion-S^{35} off a Model Cranberry Bog and Subsequent Occurrence in Fish and Mussels. *Trans. Amer. Fisheries Soc.* 95:345–349.

Miller, C. W.; Zuckerman, B. M.; and Gunner, H. B.
1967   Pesticide Occurrence, Concentration, and Degradation in Free Water Systems. In *Proc. Water Res. Symp.*, 2 June 1967, 94–96.

Mindell, A.; Esselen, W. B., Jr.; and Fellers, C. R.
1939   The Effect of Apples and Cranberries on Calcium Retention. *Amer. J. Dig. Dis.* 6:116–119.

Moeller, F. E.
1973   Timing of Placement of Colonies of Honeybees for Pollination of Cranberries. *J. Econ. Ent.* 66:370–372.

Moen, D. V.
1962   Observations on the Effectiveness of Cranberry Juice in Urinary Infection. *Wis. Med. J.* 61:282–283.

Moore, D. H.
1962   New Formulation Restores Interest in Ferbam as a Means of Enhancing Berry Coloration while Combating Fruit Rots. *Cranberries—The Nat. Cranberry Mag.* 26 (11): 10–11.

Morse, F. W.
1919   Chemical Changes in Cranberry during Storage. *Science* 50:423.
1927a   *Chemical Changes in the Cranberry during Ripening and after Harvesting.* Mass. Agr. Exp. Sta. Bull. no. 247:328.
1927b   The Discoloration of Canned Cranberries. *J. Agr. Res.* 34:889–892.
1928   The Iodine Content of Cape Cod Cranberries. *J. Biol. Chem.* 79 (2): 409–411.
1929   The Mineral Constituents of Cranberries. *J. Biol. Chem.* 91:77–79.
1930   *A Chemical Study of Cranberries.* Mass. Agr. Exp. Sta. Bull. no. 265:88–102.

Morse, F. W.; Jones, C. P.; Rudolph, B. A.; and Franklin, H. J.
1920   *Studies of Cranberries during Storage.* Mass. Agr. Exp. Sta. Bull. no. 198.

Morzuch, B. J.
1982   Econometric Methods for Forecasting Cranberry Yields. Univ. Mass. Dept. Agr. and Resource Econ. Mimeo. Material.

Morzuch, B. J., and Dudek, D. J.
1984   Yield Predictions for Cranberries in Massachusetts Based upon Aggregate vs. Desegregate Data Series. Paper presented at Cranberry Workers Conference, Chatsworth, N.J., 17 Sept. 1984. Univ. Mass. Dept. Agr. and Resource Econ. Mimeo. Material.

Morzuch, B. J.; Kneip, J.; and Smith, D. C.
1983   *An Econometric Approach to Modeling the Effects of Weather and Technology on Cranberry Yields.* Mass. Agr. Exp. Sta. Res. Bull. no. 683.

Nag Raj, T. R.
1983   Genera *Coelomycetum.* XXI. *Strasseria* and Two New Anamorph Genera, *Apostrasseria* and *Nothostrasseria. Can. J. Bot.* 61:1–30.

Nash, G.
1938   History of the Wisconsin Cranberry Growers Association. *Cranberries—
        The Nat. Cranberry Mag.* 3 (4): 6, 11–12.
Nealy, W. A.
1943   Cranberry Dollars. *Business Week* 52,54.
Nelson, E. K.
1927   The Non-Volatile Acids of the Pear, Quince, Apple, Loganberry, Blueberry,
        Cranberry Lemon, and Pomegranate. *J. Amer. Chem. Soc.* 49:1300–
        1302.
New Jersey Agricultural Experiment Station.
1960   *New Jersey Fertilizer and Lime Recommendations.* N.J. Agr. Exp. Sta. Circ.
        no. 589.
1987   *Cranberry Pest Control.* N.J. Agr. Exp. Sta. Leaflet no. 346.
Nickerson, N. L.
1984   A Previously Unreported Disease of Cranberries Caused by *Exobasidium
        perenne* sp. nov. *Can. J. Pl. Path.* 6:218–220.
Norton, J. S.
1957   *Design of Minimum Gallonage Sprinkler Systems for Cranberry Bogs.* Mass.
        Col. Agr. Bull. no. 532.
1959   Frost Protection of Cranberries by Sprinkler Irrigation. Paper No. 1212,
        Ann. Mtg. North Atlantic Sect. Amer. Soc. Agr. Eng., 1–7.
1961   Water Raking and Bulk Handling of Cranberries. *Cranberries—The Nat.
        Cranberry Mag.* 25 (11): 11.
1962a   *Cleaning Cranberry Bog Ditches—A New Technique.* Mass. Agr. Exp. Sta.
        Bull. no. 527.
1962b   The Relative Cost of Harvesting Cranberries in Massachusetts. *Cranber-
        ries—The Nat. Cranberry Mag.* 27 (7): 13–14.
1963   *Application of Spray Materials and Fertilizers through Sprinkler Systems.*
        Mass. Agr. Eng. Series no. SW-6.
1967   A Telephone Frost Warning Device. *Agr. Eng.* 48:560.
1968a   *Equipment for Handling Pelletized Cranberries.* Univ. Mass. Coop. Ext.
        Serv. Pub. no. 21.
1968b   New Directions in Harvesting Techniques. *Cranberries—The Nat. Cranbe-
        rry Mag.* 33 (1): 6–7. 33 (2): 12.
1968c   *A Trash Separator for Cranberry Picking Machines.* Univ. Mass. Ext. Serv.
        Pub. No. 20.
1969   Low Gallonage Sprinkler Systems and Their Use. In *Modern Cultural Prac-
        tice in Cranberry Growing.* Mass. Agr. Exp. Sta. Pub. no. 39:9–18.
1972   Spreader Reel for Cranberry Bog Sanders. *Cranberries—The Nat. Cranbe-
        rry Mag.* 36 (12): 7–9.
1975   Development of a New Cranberry Harvester. *Trans. Amer. Soc. Agr. Eng.*
        18:20–26.
1978   A Tug for Towing Cranberry Collection Booms. *Cranberries—The Nat.
        Cranberry Mag.* 45 (8): 7–9.
1982a   Design of Inflatable Boom for Use in Water-Harvesting Cranberries.
        Cranberries—The Nat. Cranberry Mag. 46 (3): 3, 6–8, 11.

1982b   *Flood-Sander Barge for Cranberry Bogs.* Univ. Mass. Coop. Ext. Serv. Pub. no. J1341.

Norton, J. S., and Cargill, B. F.
1979   State of the Art of Harvesting Cranberries. Paper No. 79121A, presented before Amer. Soc. Agr. Eng.

Norton, J. S.; Charig, A. J.; and Demoranville, I. E.
1968   The Effect of Ozone on Storage of Cranberries. In *Proc. Amer. Soc. Hort. Sci.* 93:792–796.

Norwood, J. W.
1936   "Cranberry Eater"—an American King. *Cranberries—The Nat. Cranberry Mag.* 1 (3): 7.

Ocean Spray Cranberries, Inc.
n.d.   Twenty-Two best Fresh Cranberry Recipes from the Special Files of Ocean Spray's Cranberry Kitchen. Ocean Spray Cranberries, Inc. Hanson, Mass.

O'Donnell, W. H.
1968   Cranberry Growers Reshape Bogs for Water Picking. *Soil Conserv.* 33:185.

Ogle, D. W.
1983   Phytogeography of *Vaccinium macrocarpon* Aiton in the Southern United States. *Virginia J. Sci.* 35:31–47.

Ortiz, E. L.
1971   The All-American Cranberry. *Gourmet* 31:21, 58–66.

Papas, P. N.; Brush, C. A.; and Ceresia, G. C.
1966   Cranberry Juice for Treating Urinary Infections. *Southwestern Med.* 47:17.

Papke, A. M.; Eaton, G. W.; and Bowen, P. A.
1980   Airborne Pollen above a Cranberry Bog. *HortSci.* 15:756.

Paracer, S. M.; Brzeski, M. W.; and Zuckerman, B. M.
1966   Nematophagous Fungi and Predacious Nematodes Associated with Cranberry Soils in Massachusetts. *Pl. Dis. Rpt.* 50:584–586.

Pascoe, S. W.
1937   Whole Evaporated Cranberries Extend Use of Fruit to Many Parts of the World. *Cranberries—The Nat. Cranberry Mag.* 1 (10): 6–12.

Patterson, M. E.; Doughty, C. C.; Graham, S. O.; and Allan, B.
1967   Effect of Bruising on Post Harvest Softening, Color Changes, and Detection of Polygalacturonase Enzyme in Cranberries. In *Proc. Amer. Soc. Hort. Sci.* 90:498–505.

Peltier, G. L.
1954   Effect of Weather Conditions on Cranberries in Central Wisconsin. *Cranberries—The Nat. Cranberry Mag.* 19 (8): 8.

1955   Wisconsin Fertilizers. *Cranberries—The Nat. Cranberry Mag.* 19 (11): 14–16.

1957   Cranberry Machine Dryers. *Cranberries—The Nat. Cranberry Mag.* 22 (1): 13.

1959   Wisconsin's Unusual Hail Year of 1958—Facts About Hail. *Cranberries—The Nat. Cranberry Mag.* 24 (2): 10, 12.

1964   Soil Acidity of Wisconsin Marshes. *Cranberries—The Nat. Cranberry Mag.* 29 (8): 10–11.

1970   *A History of the Cranberry Industry in Wisconsin.* Detroit, Mich.: Harlo
         Press.
Peterson, T. S.; Cross, C. E.; and Tilden, N.
1968   *The Cranberry Industry in Massachusetts.* Common. of Mass. Dept. Agr.
         Div. Mktg. Bull. no. 201.
Pickett, C.
1949   Cranberry Growers Cooperative. *Nat. Agr.* 24 (8): 20–21.
Planer, T. D.
1986   *Cranberry Pest Control—Weed Identification Series.* Univ. Wis. Coop. Ext.
         Serv. Spec. Pub.
Poole, A.
1984   Lophodermium Control Guidelines Given. *Dispatch from the Bog*—Pub. of
         Oreg. St. Univ. Coop. Ext. Serv. June, 1–7.
1986   Climatological Aspects of Oregon Cranberry Production. Paper presented
         at the Cranberry Research and Extension Workers Conf., Kentville, Nova
         Scotia, 15 Sept. 1986.
Porsild, A. E.
1938   The Cranberry in Canada. *Can. Field Natu.* 52:116–117.
Puski, G., and Francis, F. J.
1967   Flavonol Glycosides in Cranberries. *J. Food Sci.* 32 (5): 527–530.
Rayner, M. C., and Levisohn, I.
1940   Production of Synthetic Mycorrhiza in the Cultivated Cranberry. *Nature*
         45:461.
Reed, D. J.
1987   In Support of Frank's Organic Nitrogen Theory. *Angewandte Botanic* 61:25–
         37j.
Reed, J. P., and Jenkins, W. R.
1963   *Hemicycliophora vaccinium* n. sp. (Nematoda: criconematidae) from Cran-
         berry. In *Proc. Helm. Soc. Wash.* 30:211–212.
Reich, G. T.
1939   New Sauce Machine Developed for Minot Food Packers, Inc. is Regarded of
         Great Importance. *Cranberries—The Nat. Cranberry Mag.* 4 (1): 7.
Rice, C. C.
1932   Preservation, Utilization, and Properties of Cranberry Juice. M.S. thesis.
         Mass. St. Col., Amherst.
Rice, C. C.; Fellers, C. R.; and Clague, J. A.
1939   Cranberry Juice—Properties and Manufacture. *Fruit Prod. J. and Amer.
         Food Mfg.* 18:197–200.
Rider, A. J.
1909   Early History of the American Cranberry Grower's Association and a Brief
         Review of Its Work. In *Proc. 40th Ann. Conv. Amer. Cranberry Growers' As-
         soc.,* 4–7.
Rigby, B., and Dana, M. N.
1971   Seed Number and Berry Volume in Cranberry. *HortSci.* 6:495.496.
1972a   Flower Opening, Pollen Shedding, Stigma Receptivity, and Pollen Tube
         Growth in the Cranberry. *HortSci.* 7:84–85.

1972b   Rest Period and Flower Development in Cranberry. *J. Amer. Soc. Hort. Soc.* 97:145–148.

Rigby, B.; Dana, M. N.; ad Binning, L. K.
1972   Ethephon Sprays and Cranberry Fruit Color. *HortSci.* 7:82–83.

Ringel, S. M.; Kaufman, J.; and Jaffe, M. J.
1959   *Refrigerated Storage of Cranberries.* U.S. Dept. Agr. Mktg. Res. Rpt. no. 312.

Ripa, A. K.
1984   Cultivation of *Vaccinium* in the Latvian SSR. *Sadovodstvo* 11:31.
1985   Introduction of Varieties of American Cranberry into the Latvian SSR. *Latvijas PSR Zinatny Akademijas Vestis* 3:126–132.

Robbins, W. W.
1931   *The Botany of Crop Plants.* Philadelphia: Blakiston's Son. 517–522.

Roberts, R. H., and Struckmeyer, B. E.
1942   Growth and Fruiting of the Cranberry. In *Proc. Amer. Soc. Hort. Sci.* 40:373–379.
1943   Blossom Induction of the Cranberry. *Pl. Physio.* 18:534–536.

Roberts, S. L. and Mahr, D. L.
1982   *The Cranberry Girdler* Univ. Wis. Ext. Cranberry Pest Control Pub. no. A3188.

Rupasova, Z. A.
1984   Characteristics of Nutrient Absorption of *Oxycoccus macrocarpus* Pers. during the First Year of Life. *Botanika:Issledovanie* 26:159–160.

St. Pierre, J. C.
1966   Objective Measures to Determine Cranberry Yields. *Cranberries—The Nat. Cranberry Mag.* 31 (3): 14.

Sakamura, S., and Francis, F. J.
1961   The Anthocyanins of the American Cranberry. *J. Food Sci.* 26 (3): 318–321.

Salters, R. E.
1936   Your Cranberry Package. *Cranberries—The Nat. Cranberry Mag.* 1 (5): 11–15.

Sapers, G. M.; Graff, G. R.; Phillips, J. G.; and Deubert, K. H.
1986   Factors Affecting the Anthocyanin Content of Cranberry. *J. Amer. Soc. Hort. Sci.* 111 (4): 612–617.

Sapers, G. M., and Hargrave, D. L.
1987   Proportions of Individual Anthocyanins in Fruits of Cranberry Cultivars. *J. Amer. Soc. Hort. Sci.* 112 (1): 100–104.

Sapers, G. M.; Jones, S. B.; Kelly, M. J.; Phillips, J. G.; and Stone, E. C.
1986   Breeding Strategies for Increasing the Anthocyanin Content of Cranberries. *J. Amer. Soc. Hort. Sci.* 111 (4): 618–622.

Sapers, G. M.; Jones, S. B.; and Maher, G. T.
1983   Factors Affecting the Recovery of Juice and Anthocyanin from Cranberries. *J. Amer. Soc. Hort. Sci.* 108 (2): 246–249.

Sapers, G. M.; Phillips, J. G.; Rudolph, H. M.; and Divito, A. M.
1983   Cranberry Quality: Selection Procedures for Breeding Programs. *J. Amer. Soc. Hort. Sci.* 108 (2): 241–246.

Sargent, E. H., & Co.
1966   The Galvanic Cell Oxygen Analyzer. Bull. 638A. Springfield, N.J.

Sawyer, W. H., Jr.
1931   Stomatal Apparatus of the Cultivated Cranberry, *Vaccinium macrocarpon.*
         Amer. J. Bot. 19:508–513.

Scammell, H. B.
1917   *Cranberry Insect Problems and Suggestions for Solving Them.* U.S. Dept.
         Agr. Farmers' Bull. no. 86.

Schlatter, F. P.
1916   *Report of Cranberry Investigations. I. Experiments with Fertilizer on Cran-
         berries.* N.J. Agr. Exp. Sta. Ann. Rpt., 329–366.

Schultz, J. H.
1944   Some Cytotaxonomic and Germination Studies in the Genus *Vaccinium.*
         Ph.D. thesis. Wash. St. Univ., Pullman.

Schwartz, M. R., and Boone, D. M.
1981   The Effect of Wounding and Wet Raking on the Incidence of Black Rot of
         Cranberries in Wisconsin. *Phytopath.* 71:253–254 (Abstract).

Schweitzer, J. W.
1966   Wasteland Transformed into Multi-Million Dollar Industry with Time, Mon-
         ey, and Water. *Cranberries—The Nat. Cranberry Mag.* 31 (4): 916.

Scoggan, H. J.
1979   *The Flora of Canada.* Nat. Museum of Natu. Sci. Pub. in Botany, no.
         7:1213.

Scorza, R.; Welker, W. V.; and Dunn, L. J.
1984   The Effect of Glyphosate, Auxin, and Cytokinin Combinations on *in Vitro*
         Development of Cranberry Node Explants. *HortSci.* 19:66–68.

Servadio, G. J., and Francis, F. J.
1963   Relation between Color of Cranberries and Color and Stability of Sauce.
         Food Tech. 17:124–128.

Searles, A.
1925   Cost of Building a Cranberry Bog. In *Proc. Wis. St. Cranberry Growers' As-
         soc. 38th Ann. Mtg.,* 37–39.

Shank, M. E.
1952a   Cellophane Bagged Cranberries. *Cranberry World* 5 (10): 10–11.
1952b   Cranberries in Cellophane. *Cranberry World* 5 (9): 10–12.

Shanks, C. H., Jr.
1979   Granular Carbofuran for Black Vine Weevil Control in Nonflooded Cranberry
         Bogs. *J. Econ. Ent.* 72:55–56.

Sharstsyanikina, A. V., and Zaranchuk, L. G.
1986   Effect of Lime on the Growth and Utilization of Basic Mineral Elements by
         Large-Fruited Cranberry Plants. *Vestsi Akademii Navuk BSSR Biyalagich-
         Nykh Navuk* 5:60–65.

Shaw, F. R.; Shaw, W. M.; and Weidhaas, J.
1956   Observations on Sugar Concentrations of Cranberry Nectar. *Gleanings in
         Bee Culture,* March, 1–2.

Shawa, A. Y.
1972a   Fertilizer. In *Cranberry Vine*. Pub. Coop. Ext. Serv. Coastal Wash. May, 2–3.
1972b   Response of Cranberry Bogs to Sulfur-Coated UREA: A Slow Releasing Nitrogen. *HortSci.* 7 (3): 333 (Abstract).
1973   Prolonging the Life of Harvested McFarlin Cranberries. *J. Amer. Soc. Hort. Sci.* 98:212–214.
1979a   Effect of Ethephon on Color, Abscission, and Keeping Quality of McFarlin Cranberry. *HortSci.* 14:168–169.
1979b   Effect of Lime on Yield and Keeping Quality of 'McFarlin' Cranberries. *HortSci.* 14 (1): 50–51.
1979c   *Effect of Slow-Release Nitrogen on Cranberries: Sulfur-Coated Urea and Isobutylidene Urea*. Wash. St. Univ. Bull. no. 0880.
1980   Control of Weeds in Cranberries (*Vaccinium macrocarpon*) with Glyphosate and Terbacil. *Weed Sci.* 28 (5): 565–568.
1981   Response of McFarlin Cranberries to Minor Elements. *HortSci.* 15:699 (Abstract).
1982   Response of McFarlin Cranberry to Nitrogen Sprays. *HortSci.* 17:949–950.
1984   *The Cranberry Vine*. Pub. Coop. Ext. Serv., Coastal Wash.
Shawa, A. Y.; Doughty, C. C.; and Johnson, F.
1966   Effect of Fungicides on McFarlin Cranberry Pollen Germination and Fruit Set. In *Proc. Amer. Soc. Hort. Sci.* 89:255–258.
Shawa, A. Y.; Eaton, G. W.; and Bowen, P. A.
1981   Cranberry Yield Components in Washington and British Columbia. *J. Amer. Soc. Hort. Sci.* 106 (4): 474–477.
Shawa, A. Y., and Ingalsbe, D. W.
1968   Anthocyanin Enhancement in McFarlin Cranberries at Optimum Maturity. In *Proc. Amer. Soc. Hort. Sci.* 93:289–292.
Shawa, A. Y., and Kresge, C. P.
1976   Response of Cranberry Bogs to Sulphur-Coated Urea. *Sulphur Institute J.* 12, nos. 3–4.
Shawa, A. Y.; Shanks, C. H., Jr.; Bristow, P. R.; Shearer, M. N.; and Poole, A. P.
1984   *Cranberry Production in the Pacific Northwest*. Pacific Northwest Ext. Pub., no. PNW 247.
Shear, C. L.
1915.   Utilization of Peat Land for Cranberry Culture. *J. Can. Peat Soc.* 4:15–18.
Shear, C. L.; Stevens, N. E.; and Bain, H. F.
1931   *Fungous Diseases of the Cultivated Cranberry.* U.S. Dept. Agr. Tech. Bull. no. 258.
Shear, C. L.; Stevens, N. E.; and Rudolph, B. A.
1917   *Observations on the Spoilage of Cranberries Due to Lack of Proper Ventilation.* Mass. Agr. Exp. Sta. Bull. no. 180:235–239.
Shear, C. L.; Stevens, N. E.; Wilcox, R. B.; and Rudolph, B. A.
1918   *Spoilage of Cranberries after Harvest*. U.S. Dept. Agr. Bull. no. 714.
Shimanuki, H.; Lehnert, T., and Stricker, M.

1967 Differential Collection of Cranberry Pollen by Honey Bees. *J. Econ. Ent.* 60:1031–1033.

Sidorovich, E. A.; Rupasova, Z. A.; Rusalenka, V. R.; and Ignatsenka, V. A.
1986 Seasonal Dynamics of Phosphorus Accumulation in Plants of Large-Fruited Cranberry. *Akademii Navuk BSSR, Biyalagichnykh Navuk* 4:25–31.

Sidorovich, E. A.; Rupasova, Z. A.; Zubkova, G. P.; Ignatsenka, V. A.; and Rudakovskaya, R. N.
1987 Characteristics of Seasonal Zinc Accumulation in Large-Fruited Cranberry Plants in Commercial Cultivation. *Sel'skokhozyaistvennaya Biologiya* 4:28–33.

Sieckmann, S., and Boe, A. A.
1978 Low Temperature Increases Reducing and Total Sugar Concentrations in Leaves of Boxwood (*Buxus sempervirens* L.) and Cranberry (*Vaccinium macrocarpon* Ait.) *HortSci.* 13 (4): 439–440.

Sleumer, H.
1941 Vaccinioden Studien. *Bot. Jahrb. Sonder.—Abdr.* 71:375–510.

Skroch, W. A., and Dana, M. N.
1965 Sources of Weed Infestation in Cranberry Fields. *Weeds* 13:263–267.

Smith, G. N.
1870 *Cranberry Growing in Wisconsin.* Wis. St. Agr. Soc. for 1870.

Smith, J. B.
1903 *Insects Injurious in Cranberry Culture.* U.S. Dept. Agr. Farmers' Bull. no. 178.

Somogyi, L. P.; Childers, N. F.; and Eck, P.
1964 Influence of Nitrogen Source and Soil Organic Matter on the Cranberry (*Vaccinium macrocarpon* Ait.) In *Proc. Amer. Soc. Hort. Sci.* 84:280–288.

Sorensen, L. A.
1955 Fertilizers on Wisconsin Marshes. *Cranberries—The Nat. Cranberry Mag.* 19 (11): 7–8.

Stang, E. J., and Dana, M. N.
1984 Wisconsin Cranberry Production. *HortSci.* 19 (4): 606–607.

Stang, E. J.; Ferree, D. C.; and Struckmeyer, B. E.
1982 Effect of Four Light Levels on Net Photosynthesis and Leaf Anatomy in Cranberry (*Vaccinium macrocarpon* Ait.). Paper presented at 21st Int. Hort. Cong., Hamburg, Germany, 29 Aug. to 4 Sept. 1982 (Abstract).

Staples, L. C., and Francis, F. J.
1968 Colorimetry of Cranberry Cocktail by Wide Range Spectrophotometry. *Food Tech.* 22:77–80.

Stark, R.; Forsyth, F. R.; Hall, I. V.; and Lockhart, C. L.
1971 Improvement of Processing Quality of Cranberries by Storage in Nitrogen. *Can. Inst. Food Tech. J.* 4:104–106.

Stark, R.; Hall, I. V.; and Dean, P. R.
1969 Cranberries Evaluated for Fresh Fruit and Processing Quality after Reduced Oxygen Storage. *Cranberries—The Nat. Cranberry Mag.* 34 (6): 14, 18; 34 (7): 14, 16.

Starr, M. S., and Francis, F. J.
1968   Oxygen and Ascorbic Acid Effect on the Relative Stability of Four Antho-
          cyanin Pigments in Cranberry Juice. *Food Tech.* 22:1293–1295.
Sternlieb, P.
1963   Cranberry Juice in Renal Disease. *The New England J. Med.* 268:57.
Stevens, C. D.; Cross, C. E.; and Piper, W. E.
1957   *The Cranberry Industry in Massachusetts.* Mass. Dept. Agr. Bull. no. 157.
Stevens, N. E.
1927   Cranberries Used in Trial Forecasts As to Keeping Quality. In *1927 U.S.
          Dept. Agr. Yearbook of Agric.,* 238–240.
1931   *The Spread of Cranberry False-Blossom in the United States.* U.S. Dept. Agr.
          Circ. no. 47.
1932   Thickness of Cuticle in Cranberry Fruits. *Amer. J. Bot.* 19:432–435.
1944   An Outstanding Cranberry—Fifty Years of the Searles Variety. *Wis. Hort.*
          34:83–84.
Stevens, N. E., and Bergman, H. F.
1921   *The Relation of Water-raking to the Keeping Quality of Cranberries.* U.S.
          Dept. Agr. Bull. no. 960.
Stevens, N. E.; Rogers, L. M.; and Bain, H. F.
1940   Alkaline Flooding Water in Cranberry Growing. *Trans. Wis. Acad. Sci.*
          32:351–360.
Stevens, N. E., and Sawyer, W. H., Jr.
1926   The Distribution of Cranberry False Blossom. *Phytopath.* 16:223–227.
Stevens, N. E., and Thompson, N. F.
1943   Factors Influencing Injury to Cranberry Plants during Flooding. *Trans. Wis.
          Acad. Sci.* 34:73–81.
Stevens, P. F.
1971   Taxonomic Studies in the *Ericaceae. Bot. J. Linn. Soc.* 64:1–53.
Stewart, J. D., and Marucci, P. E.
1970   *Honeybees for Cranberry Pollination.* N.J. Agr. Exp. Sta. Circ. no. 588-A.
Stieber, T., and Peterson, L. A.
1987   Contribution of Endogenous Nitrogen toward Continuing Growth in a
          Cranberry Vine. *HortSci.* 22 (3): 463–464.
Stone, E. G.
1982   Germination of Stored Cranberry Seed on Three Media. *HortSci.* 17:58–59.
Stretch, A. W.
1964   Cranberry Diseases Investigations—1962. In *Proc. 93rd Ann. Mtg. Amer.
          Cranberry Growers' Assoc.,* 32–33.
Stretch, A. W., and Ceponis, M. J.
1978   Relative Importance of Black Rot in Postharvest Disease of Water-harvested
          Cranberries. *Phytopath. News* 12:173 (Abstract).
1986   Fungal and Physiological Breakdown in Six Cranberry Cultures Following
          Water Harvesting and Cold Storage. *HortSci.* 21 (2): 265–267.
Stribley, D. P., and Reed, D. J.
1974   The Biology of Mycorrhiza in the Ericaceae. IV, The Effect of Mycorrhizal

Infection on Uptake of [15]N From Labelled Soil by *Vaccinium macrocarpon*. *New Phytologist* 73 (6): 1149–1155.

1976   The Biology of Mycorrhiza in the Ericaceae. V, The Effects of Mycorrhizal Infection and Concentration of Ammonium Nitrogen on Growth of Cranberry (*Vaccinium macrocarpon* Ait.) in Sand Culture. *New Phytologist* 77 (1): 63–72.

1980   The Biology of Mycorrhiza in the Ericaceae. VI, The Relationship between Mycorrhizal Infection and the Capacity to Utilize Simple and Complex Organic Nitrogen Sources. *New Phytologist.* 86:365–371.

Stricker, M. H.
1946   Bees and Pollinating Cranberries. In *Proc. 76th Ann. Mtg. Amer. Cranberry Growers' Assoc.*, 16–19.

Swanson, B. G.; Weckel, K. G.; and Lindsay, R. C.
1972   Intensifying Cranberry Flavor in Yogurt and Sherbert with Synthetic Flavoring. *Cranberries—The Nat. Cranberry Mag.* 37 (5): 13–16.

Swartz, J. H., and Medrek, T. F.
1968   Antifungal Properties of Cranberry Juice. *J. App. Micro.* 16:1524–1527.

Szpunar, J. W.
1985   Acidification of Soil and Water for Cranberry *Vaccinium macrocarpon* Ait. Growing. *Acta Horticulturae* 165:333–336.

Tallman, K. S., and Eaton, G. W.
1976   A Comparison of Growth Habit of "Bergman" and "McFarlin" Cranberry Cultivar on Commercial Bogs in British Columbia. *Fruit Var. J.* 30:55–59.

Thienes, J. R.
1955   Fertilizing in Oregon. *Cranberries—The Nat. Cranberry Mag.* 19 (11): 8.

Tolle, W. E.
1958   *Maintenance of Quality of Prepackaged Cranberries during Retail Display.* U.S. Dept. Mktg. Res. Rpt. no. 320.

Tomlinson, B.
1936   *Resanding Cranberry Bogs.* Univ. Mass. Coop. Ext. Serv. Spec. Circ. no. 36.

1937   Proper Sanding of Great Importance in Good Bog Management. *Cranberries—The Nat. Cranberry Mag.* 1 (9): 4, 8–11.

Tomlinson, B., and Franklin, H. J.
1936   *Weed Control in Cranberry Bogs.* Univ. Mass. Coop. Ext. Serv. Spec. Circ. no. 29.

1946   *Renovation of Cranberry Bogs.* Univ. Mass. Coop. Ext. Serv. Spec. Circ. no. 55.

Tomlinson, W. E., Jr.
1945   Influence of Cranberry Variety on the Rate of Development and Survival of the Blunt-Nosed Leafhopper, *Ophiola striatula.* In *Proc. 76th Ann. Conv. Amer. Cranberry Growers' Assoc.*, 25–26.

1948   Cranberry Fireworms and Blossom Worm. In *Proc. 78th Ann. Mtg. Amer. Cranberry Growers' Assoc.*, 8–12.

1957   Don't Forget the Bees. *Cranberries—The Nat. Cranberry Mag.* 21 (12): 12–13.

Torio, J. C., and Eck, P.
1969   Nitrogen, Phosphorus, Potassium, and Sulfur Nutrition of the Cranberry in Sand Culture. *J. Amer. Soc. Hort. Sci.* 94:622–625.

Torio, J. C.; Stretch, A. W.; and Eck, P.
1966   Influence of Glomerella Infection on Cranberry Vegetative and Fruiting Characteristics and Nutritional Effects on Fruit Rot Symptom Expression. *Pl. Dis. Rptr.* 50:346–348.

Townsend, L. R., and Hall, I. V.
1971   Nutrient Levels in Leaf and Soil Samples from Three Cranberry Bogs in the Anapolis Valley of Nova Scotia. *Cranberries—The Nat. Cranberry Mag.* 36 (3): 11–12.

Trufant, R. A.
1942   The Economics of the Cranberry Picking Machine. *Cranberries—The Nat. Cranberry Mag.* 4 (10): 10–11.

Uecker, F. A., and Caruso, F. L.
1988   *Synchronoblastia crypta,* a New Coelomycetous Pathogen of Upright Stems and Fruits in Cranberry. *Mycologia* 80:344–347.

U.S. Department of Agriculture.
1900–87 *Cranberries.* Agr. Stat. Board Publ., Washington, D.C. 20250.
1950   *New Cranberry Varieties Announced by Experiment Stations and U.S.D.A.* USDA Variety Release, 1.
1957   *United States Standards for Fresh Cranberries for Processing.* 22 F.R. 5853.
1961   *Notice to Fruit Growers and Nurserymen Relative to the Introduction of Three New Cranberry Varieties—The Bergman, Franklin, and Pilgrim.* U.S. Dept. Agr., ARS Crops Res. Div., Variety Release Notice.
1967   *Protecting Honey Bees from Pesticides.* U.S. Dept. Agr. Leaflet no. 544.
1968   *Using Honey Bees to Pollinate Crops.* U.S. Dept. Agr. Leaflet no. 549.

Urann, M. L.
1912   *Cranberry Harvesting and Packing under Modern Methods.* United Cape Cod Cranberry Co. Bull. no. 101.

Vander Kloet, S. P.
1983   The Taxonomy of *Vaccinium* and *Oxycoccus. Rhodora* 85:1–44.

Varney, E. H.
1955   Effect of Various Harvest Methods in One Year on Production and Rots of Early Black Cranberries the Following Year. In *Proc. 85th Ann. Mtg. Amer. Cranberry Growers' Assoc.,* 32–33.

Volpe, T.
1976   Cranberry Juice Concentrate as a Red Food Coloring. *Food Product Development,* Nov.

Voorhees, J. H.
1914   *Experiments with Fertilizers on Cranberries.* N.J. Agr. Exp. Sta. Ann. Rpt., 247–251.

Vorsa, N., and Welker, W. V., Jr.
1985   Relationship between Fruit Size and Extractable Anthocyanin Content in
         Cranberry. *HortSci.* 20 (3): 402–403.

Wakabayashi, S.
1925   *The Injurious Effect of Submergence on the Cranberry Plant.* N.J. Agr. Exp.
         Sta. Bull. no. 420.

Waksman, S. A.
1918   The Occurrence of Azotobacter in Cranberry Soils. *Science* 48:653–654.
1919   Microbiological Studies on the Cranberry Bog Soil. I, The Effect of Liming
         upon the Microbial Population of the Cranberry Soil. *Bot. Abstr.* 5:298–299.

Wallis, W. R.
1964   The Effectiveness of Wind Machines for Cold Protection in a Wisconsin
         Cranberry Marsh. *Cranberries—The Nat. Cranberry Mag.* 28 (10): 13–15.

Wang, P. L.; Du, C. T.; and Francis, F. J.
1978   Isolation and Characterization of Polyphenolic Compounds in Cranberries. *J.
         Food Sci.* 43:1402–1404.

Warrington, P., and Eaton, G. W.
1968   A Novel Inflorescence in *Vaccinium macrocarpon* cv. Beaver. *Can. J. Bot.*
         46:1162–1663.

Washington State College.
1963   *Cranberry Fertilizer.* Wash. St. Col. Agr. and Home Economics Res. Prog.
         Rpt. no. 9.

Weckel, K. G., and Swanson, B.
1972   Gel Power Index of Cranberries. *Cranberries—The Nat. Cranberry Mag.*
         34 (6): 6–8, 14.

Weidemann, G. J.; Boone, D. M.; and Burdall, H. H., Jr.
1982   Taxonomy of *Phyllosticta vaccinii* (Coelomycetes) and a New Name for the
         True Anamorph of *Botryosphaeria vaccinii* (Dothideales, Dothioraceae).
         Mycologia 74 (1): 59–65.

Welker, W. V., Jr.
1967   Virginia Chain Fern Control in Cranberry Bogs. *Weeds* 15:179.
1976   Effect of Glyphosate on Cranberries. In *Proc. N.E. Weed Sci. Soc.*, 30:157
         (Abstract).
1979   The Control of Red-root (*Lachnanthes tinctoria*). In *Proc. N.E. Weed Sci.
         Soc.* 33:142 (Abstract).
1981   A Self-Feeding, Hand-Held Herbicide Wiper. In *Proc. N.E. Weed Soc.*
         35:345–346 (Abstract).

Welker, W. V., Jr. and Vass, G. D.
1983   Influence of Size and Orientation of Cranberry Cuttings upon Plant Develop-
         ment. *HortSci.* 18 (5): 722–723.

White, J. J.
1870   *Cranberry Culture.* New York: Orange Judd Co.

Whittlesey, S. N.
1937   The Picking of $100,000 Worth of Wild Cranberries, A Real Start of Wiscon-
         sin Cranberry Industry. *Cranberries—The Nat. Cranberry Mag.* 2 (3): 4, 9.

Wilcox, J. L.
1925   Cranberry Boxes. In *Proc. Wis. St. Cranberry Growers' Assoc. 38th Ann. Mtg.*, 34–37.

Wilcox, R. B.
1940a   Blossom Blast of Cranberries. In *Proc. 70th Ann. Mtg. Amer. Cranberry Growers' Assoc.*, 14–22.
1940b   *Cranberry Fruit Rots in New Jersey,* N.J. Agr. Exp. Sta. Circ. no. 403.
1951   Tests of Cranberry Varieties and Seedlings for Resistance to the Leafhopper Vector of False-Blossom Disease. *Phytopath.* 41:722–735.

Wilcox, R. B., and Beckwith, C. S.
1933   A Factor in the Varietal Resistance of Cranberries to the False-Blossom Disease. *J. Agr. Res.* 47:583–590.
1935   *The False-Blossom Disease of Cranberries.* N.J. Agr. Exp. Sta. Circ. no. 348.

Wilcox, R. B., and Delap, J. M.
1946   Tests of Cranberry Hybrids in 1945 for Probable Resistance to the False Blossom Disease. In *Proc. 77th Ann. Conv. Amer. Cranberry Growers Assoc.*, 12–16.

Williams, L. R.
1952   Prepackaging Fresh Cranberries. *Pre-Pack-Age* 5 (11): 26–27, 30.

Woerpel, M.
1956   New Confectionery Ingredient. Special Process Permits Use of Cranberries in Candies. *Cranberries—The Nat. Cranberry Mag.* 20 (12): 15–16.

Wolf, A. F.
1950   *Effect of Consumer Income on Cranberry Prices.* Rpt. to Cranberry Inst.
1955   *The Cranberry Carry-Over.* Cranberry Inst. Surv. Rpt.
1956a   Maximization of Returns to Cranberry Growers. *Cranberries—The Nat. Cranberry Mag.* 21 (8): 7–8.
1956b   The Parity Price of Cranberries. *Cranberries—The Nat. Cranberry Mag.* 20 (11): 8–9.

Wood, J. H.; Warner, L.; and Powers, W. L.
1950   Water and Nutrient Relations for Cranberries. Oreg. Agr. Exp. Sta. Mimeo., 10.

Wright, R. C.; Demaree, J. B.; and Wilcox, M. S.
1937   Some Effects of Different Storage Temperatures on the Keeping Quality of Cranberries. In *Proc. Amer. Soc. Hort. Sci.* 34:397–401.

Zapsalis, C., and Francis, F. J.
1965   Cranberry Anthocyanins. *J. Food Sci.* 30:396–399.

Zinsser, H. H.; Seneca, H.; Light, I.; Mayer, G.; Karp, F.; McGeoy, G.; and Tarrasoli, H.
1968   Management of Infected Stones with Acidifying Agents. *N.Y. St. J. Medicine* 68:3001–3010.

Zuckerman, B. M.
1956   Shrinkage of Cranberries Held in Common Storage. *Cranberries—The Nat. Cranberry Mag.* 20 (10): 10–13.
1959   Harvesting Methods, Fungicides, and Keeping Quality. *Cranberries—The Nat. Cranberry Mag.*, 23 (9): 7–8.

1960   Parasitism of Cranberry Roots of *Tetylenchus joctus* Thorne. *Nematological*
            5:253–254.

1961a   Parasitism and Pathogenesis of the Cultivated Cranberry by Some Nema-
            todes. *Nematological* 6:135–143.

1961b   Reduction of Frost Injury in Cranberries by Fungicide Treatments. *Pl. Dis.
            Rptr.* 45:253–254.

1964   The Effects of Zinophos on Nematode Populations and Cranberry Yields. *Pl.
            Dis. Rptr.* 48:172–175.

1980   Cranberry Disease Control Experiments in Massachusetts, 1980. In
            Modern Cranberry Culture: Univ. Mass. Coop. Ext. Serv. Bull. no.
            SP-126:90–92.

Zuckerman, B. M., and Cannon, W. C.
1972   Water Harvest Procedures and Quality of Early Black Cranberries in Mas-
            sachusetts. *Cranberries—The Nat. Cranberry Mag.* 36 (9): 6–7, 10.

Zuckerman, B. M., and Coughlin, J. W.
1960   *Nematodes Associated with Some Crop Plants in Massachusetts.* Mass. Agr.
            Exp. Sta. Bull. no. 521.

Zuckerman, B. M.; Demoranville, I. E.; Francis, F. J.; Hayes, K.; Norgren, R. L.;
Regling, S.; Miller, C. W.; and Paracer, S. M.
1967   Pigment and Viscosity of Juice and Sauce of Several Cranberry Varieties. In
            Proc. Amer. Soc. Hort. Sci. 89:248–254.

Zuckerman, B. M.; Khera, S.; and Pierce, A. R.
1964   Population Dynamics of Nematodes in Cranberry Soils. *Phytopath.* 54:654–
            659.

Zuckerman, B. M., and Mackiewicz, M.
1969   The Rate of Disappearance of Parathion from Water Associated with Two
            Massachusetts Cranberry Bogs. *Cranberries—The Nat. Cranberry Mag.*
            34 (8): 6–8.

Zuckerman, B. M.; Reed, J. P.; and Jenkins, W. R.
1964   Notes on *Hemicycliophora vaccinium* Reed and Jenkins. *Nematological*
            9:648.

INDEX

Boldface page numbers indicate illustrations (figures and plates).

Abbotana clemataria S. & A. (big cranberry spanworm), 254

abscisic acid (ABA), in seeds, 128

abscission zone(s), effect of winter injury on, 82

acephate (insecticide), 279 table

Acer rubrum L. (swamp maple), 166 table

acid(s), 130–131, 352; content, 130 table, 131 table

acidity: breeding for in fruit, 61; caecum bacteria, 353; calcium retention in rats, 354; effect on blood (acidosis), 352; kidney stones, 355; urine, 354

acidosis, 352–355

acid-sugar ratio (berry), effect of storage on, 311

Acleris minuata Rob. = *Peronea minuata* Rob. (yellow-headed fireworm), 251

acreage: Canada, 28; Massachusetts, 23–25, **24**; New Jersey, 25–26, **25**; Oregon, **28**; U.S., 19, 20 table, **24**; Washington, **27**; West Coast, 26; Wisconsin, 26, **27**

Acrobasis vaccinii Riley = *Mineola vaccinii* Riley (cranberry fruitworm), 260

Actinomyces, in soil, 102

advertising, 347

Agrotis ypsilon Rott. (black cutworm), 255

air drainage, importance of, 169

Alar: effect on vegetative growth, 115–116; as an inhibitor of berry senescence, 312

alder (*Alnus rugosa*), 166 table

algae: control with copper sulfate, 163; effect of winter flood on, 185

aliphatic alcohols, in fruit, 133

aliphatic aldehydes, in fruit, 133

alkaloids, in leaves, 135

Alnus oregona Nutt. (alder), 166

Alnus rugosa Koch (alder), 166 table

alpha-terpineol, in fruit, 133–134

aluminum, 161

Amathes c-nigrum L. (spotted cutworm), 256

Ambrosia artemisiifolia L. (common ragweed), 207 table

American Cranberry Exchange, 12; formation of, 346; name change in 1953, 347

American Cranberry Growers Association, origin of, 11

American Indian, use of cranberries by, 3–4

aminotriazole, and cranberry scare of 1959, 336

amitrol (herbicide), 215. *See also* aminotriazole

ammonia pellets, for control of decay, 343

ammonium (fertilizer): effect on fruit quality, 154–155; response to, 149–150

ammonium nitrate (fertilizer), 181

ammonium sulfate (fertilizer), 194

anatomy, 52, 54

Anavitrinella pampinarea Gn. (cotton spanworm), 254

Andrews, W. A., 76

anilazine, fungicide recommendation, 245 table

annual smartweed (*Polygonum hydropiper*), 213 table; control with simazine, 215

Anomala lucicola Fab. (grape *Anomala*), 272

anther(s), frost injury to, 83

anthocyanin(s): analysis of, 132; breeding for, 61, 133; climate effect on, 105; effect of ethylene in fruit, 129; effect of ethylene gas in storage, 316; in fruit, 128–129, 132–133; malathion, 285; minimum content for juice cocktail, 285; nitrogen fertilizer, 155; storage, 285, 313; temperature and formation of, 88. *See also* color; pigment

Anthonomus musculus Say (cranberry weevil), 262

Anthony cultivar, 63

antifungal effect, of cranberry juice, 356

Aphelenchoides sp., nematode occurrence of, 274–276, 275 table apical dominance, 112–113; in relation to propagation, 178

Apostrasseria lunata (Shear) Nag Raj: reclassification of *Ceuthospora lunata*, 241; imperfect stage of *Phacidium lunatum*, 241

Applegate cultivar, 63

aquatic life, effect of pesticides on, 103–104

Archips parallela Rob. (spotted fireworm), 250

armyworm, 258

Aroga trialbamacullella Chamb. (red-striped fireworm), 250

aromatic compounds, in fruit, 133

ascorbic acid: added to processed products, 322; breeding for, 61; content in fruit, 132, 313; effect of storage on, 313. *See also* vitamin C

ash, content of, 130 table, 131–132, 352

Aspidaspis oxycoccus Woglum (cranberry scale), 268

Aspidiotus perniciousus Comstock (San Jose scale), 270

Atlantic cutworm, 255

Atwood, Stephen, 63

Atwood cultivar, 63

Atylenchus decalineatus, nematode occurrence of, 274–276, 275 table

auxins, for fruit set, 125

Aviator cultivar, 63

azinphos-methyl: for control of cranberry fruitworm, 260; for control of cranberry and other weevils, 263–264; insecticide recommendations, 279–280 table; and scale insects, 268

Azotobacter, in soil, 102

bagworm, 261

Bain, H. F., 15, 57, 78

barrel usage, in shipping cranberries, 338–339

Bartlett, Bradford, 8

Bass River cultivar, 63

Batchelder, George, 7, 68, 73

batch process, of sauce production, 317

Bates, Norman, 5

Beach Berry cultivar, 63

Beaver cultivar: description of, 63, 64 table; origin of, 57

Beckwith, C. S., 13, 16, 57

Beckwith cultivar: description of, 63, 64 table, 66; original hybrid from USDA breeding program, 58–59; relative gel strength of, 317

Beese, Samuel, 8

beggarticks (Devil) (*Bidens frondosa*), 207 table; control with simazine, 215

Bell and Bugle cultivar, 66

Bell and Cherry cultivar, 66

Bell of the Cape cultivar (Centerville), 66

Belvedere cultivar, 66

Benjamin cultivar, 66

Ben Lear cultivar: calcium content in plant, 145 table; description of, 64 table, 66; iron content of, 146 table; luxury nitrogen level in, 148; magnesium content of, 145 table; manganese content of, 147 table; nitrogen content of, 141–142 table; phosphorus content of, 143 table, 157; photosynthesis in, 114; potassium content of, 144 table; resistance to physiological breakdown, 310; response to nitrogen fertilizer, 148, 149 table, 192 table; susceptibility to black rot disease, 311; susceptibility to red leaf spot disease, 231; yield components in, 120

Benn, Edward, 6

Bennett, A. C., 66

Bennett cultivar (Bennett Jumbo): description of, 66; resistance to false blossom disease, 60; use in USDA breeding program, 58

benzaldehyde, in fruit, 134

benzoic acid: content in fruit, 130 table, 134, 352; effect on storage decay, 312

N^6-benzyladenine, effect on berry respiration, 304

benzyl alcohol, in fruit, 134

benzyl benzoate, in fruit, 134

Bergman, H. F., **15,** 57

Bergman cultivar: description of, 64 table, 66; flower bud induction in, 117; hybrid from USDA breeding program, 59; relative gel strength of, 317; susceptibility to tip blight disease, 235; uprights in, 118; yield components in, 119 table, 120

Berlin cultivar: description of, 67; susceptibility to false blossom disease, 60

Berry, Albert, 67

berry, 50–51, **53;** effect of Alar and Phosfon-D on senescence, 312; effect of storage on acid-sugar ratio, 311; effect of weather on size, 106; frost injury to, 84; hail damage to, 106; oxygen deficiency injury to, 91, 93 table. *See also* fruit

Berry Berry cultivar, 58, 67

Berryland sand: fertilizer response in, 190–191; nitrogen response in, 153; optimum water table depth in, 188

berry screening, 304

berry size: in relation to seed number, 121; weather and, 106; as a yield component, 118–120, 119 table
berry speckle disease, 232
Bidens frondosa L. *See* beggarticks
biennial bearing, 116–117; effect of nitrogen on, 154
big cranberry spanworm, 254
biological oxidation demand (BOD), in flood-water, 95–96
biotin, content in fruit, 130 table
bitter rot disease, 240
black cutworm, 255–256
Black Diamond (Bugle) cultivar, 67
black-headed fireworm, 249–250; controlled by late holding of the winter flood, 184–186; reflow as method of protection against, 186–187
blacklock soils, 167
black rot disease, 241–242; cultivar suscepti-bility to, 311; effect of berry immersion on incidence of, 310
black spot disease, 231
Black Veil cultivar: description of, 67; use in breeding for low fruit acid content, 61
black vine weevil, 263–264; control of by re-flows, 187
blast, 87
Bliss formula(e), 86
blood alkali reserve, effect of cranberry con-sumption on, 352, 355
blossom blast, 124
blossom blight disease, 234
blossom induction, 116
blotch rot disease, 240
blunt-nosed cranberry leafhopper, 264–265; controlled by reflows, 187; cultivar re-sistance to, 58; feeding trials, 60; vector of false blossom disease, 60, 237
bog establishment, 170–181, **172, 173, 174, 175,** 177 table, **179, 180;** costs of, 325–328
bog maintenance, 223–229, **225, 228**
bog rejuvenation, 186
bog renovation, 226–227
Bombus impatiens, 219
Bombus melanopygus, 219
Bombus mixtus, 219
Bombus vosnesenskii, 219
booms, for collecting water-harvested fruit, 309–310
Boone, D. M., 15
Bordeaux mixture, 243 table; for control of black spot disease, 231; for control of red leaf spot disease, 231

boron (B), 163–164; content in plant, 147 table; deficiency level in shoot, 139 table; effect on fruit set, 194; interaction with manganese, 162; interaction with molyb-denum, 163; seasonal distribution in plant, 137 table; standard value in shoot, 139 table
Botryosphaeria fruit rot disease, 242
Botryosphaeria vaccinii (Shear) Barr (formally *Guignardia vaccinii*), 233; causal agent of *Botrysophaeria* fruit rot disease, 242
Botrytis sp., causal agent of yellow rot dis-ease, 242
boxes (crates), **290,** 302; construction of, 339; sizes, **340**
Bozarthtown Pointer cultivar, 67
Braddock, W. R., 5, 67
Braddock Bell cultivar: brands (labels) of, 344; description of, 67
brands and labels, 343–345
Bravo fungicide: for twig blight control, 233; recommendation, 245 table
breeding: for anthocyanin, 61, 133; methods, 61–62; objectives of, 59–61
British Columbia: flower bud induction in, 117; flowering in, 111; yield components in, 119 table, 120
brown cranberry spanworm, 253
Buckalew cultivar, 67
buckbrush (*Spirea douglasii*), 166
bud(s), 45–46, **48;** chilling requirement of, 110–112; gibberellic acid activity in, 113; types of, 112–113
Budd, Theodore H., 8, 67
Budds Blues cultivar, 67
Bugle (Black Diamond) cultivar, 67–68
bulk bins, for handling water-harvested fruit, 310
bumblebees, as pollinators of cranberries, 219–220
Bumpus cultivar, 68
Burgess, Prince, 8
burning: controlled burning of uplands, 229; for bog rejuvenation, 186; for bog renova-tion, 226–227
Burr, D. R., 66
button bush (*Cephalanthus calyculata*), 166 table
Buzby cranberry cleaner and separator, 305

Cahoon, Cyrus A., 7, 56, 63
Calamovilfa brevepilis Hack (saucer grass, reed grass), 185, 202 table
calcium (Ca), 159; content in fruit, 130 table, 145 table; content in plant, 145 table; defi-

calcium (Ca) (*continued*)
  ciency level in shoot, 139 table; seasonal
    distribution in plant, 137 table; standard
    value in shoot, 139 table
caloric value, 130 table, 352
Canada: acreage, 28; production, 33
Canada Department of Agriculture, release of
    Beaver cultivar, 63
Canadian Maritimes, winter flood in, 184
canning sauce, 316–319
Cape Cod: birthplace of cranberry industry,
    4–5; industry during the 1800s, 6–8
Cape Cod Beauty cultivar, 68
Cape Cod Cranberry Distributors, 346
Cape Cod Cranberry Growers' Association,
    origin of, 12
Cape Cod Cranberry Sales Company, organi-
    zation of, 345
captafol, fungicide recommendation, 244
    table
Captan: effect on pollen germination, 124;
    fungicide recommendations, 244 table
carbaryl: for control of cranberry fruitworm,
    260; for control of false armyworm, 257;
    insecticide recommendations, 279–280
    table
carbofuran, insecticide recommendations,
    280 table
carbon dioxide: evolution from fruit, 311; in
    floodwater, 95; oxygen ratio, 312; stimula-
    tion of in bruised berries, 302
Carex bullata Schkuhr. (cut grass), 185
Carver Bell cultivar, 68
Carver Red cultivar, 68
Casoron, persistence in soil, 102. *See also*
    dichlobenil
Castalia odorata (white water lily), 165
catfaced berry: as a result of copper deficien-
    cy, 163; as a result of frost injury, 83
cation-exchange capacity: in soil, 101; in
    Massachusetts soils, 167
cellophane, in prepackaging, 339–340
Centennial cultivar: brands (labels) of, 344;
    description of, 68; sugar content in, 131
    table; susceptibility to false blossom dis-
    ease, 60; use in breeding for high fruit
    sugar content, 61; use in USDA breeding
    program, 58
Centerville cultivar: description of, 68; sugar
    content in, 131 table; use in breeding for
    high fruit sugar content, 61
cephalanthus occidentales L. (button bush),
    166 table
Ceramica picta Harr. (zebra caterpillar), 255
Ceuthospora lunata Shear: bog water as a

medium for, 310; causal agent of black rot
    disease, 241; dominant fungus associated
    with water-harvested berries, 311
Chabot, Anthony, 6
chain-spotted geometer, 253–254
Chamaecyparis thyoides B.S.P. (white cedar),
    166 table
Chamaedaphne calyculata Moench (leather-
    leaf), 166 table
Champion cultivar: brands (labels) of, 344;
    description of, 68; seed number in, 128
Chaney, A. U., 12, 347
Chapman, Abner, 5
Chapman, H. W., 74
Cherry Bell cultivar, 68
Cherry Red cultivar, 68
chilling requirement (hours), 110–112
Chipman cultivar, 68
chloride(s), 103
chlorine (Cl), in fruit, 130 table
2-chloroethyl phosphoric acid (CEPA): effect
    on fruit size, 127; ethephon effect on berry
    color enhancement, 285
Chloro-IPC (herbicide), 215
p-chlorophenoxyacetic acid (CPA), for fruit
    set, 125
chlorophyll, in fruit, 128
chlorosis (leaf): caused by norflurazon, 217;
    correction with iron, 161; correction with
    manganese, 162; correction with zinc, 162;
    due to copper toxicity, 163
chlorothalonil. *See* Bravo fungicide
chlorpropham (herbicide), 216
chlorpyrifos: for control of false armyworm,
    257; insecticide recommendations, 279–
    280 table
chromosome number, 54–55
Chrysoteuchia topiaria Zeller (cranberry
    girdler), 265
Cingilia catenaria Drury (chain-spotted ge-
    ometer), 253
cinnamon fern (*Osmunda cinnamomea*), 165
Cirphis unipuncta Haw. (armyworm), 257
citric acid, in fruit, 130 table, 352
Cladosporium leaf spot disease, 231–232
Cladosporium oxycocci Shear, causal agent of
    Cladosporium leaf spot disease, 231
Clastoptera saint-cyri Prov. (cranberry spittle
    insect), 270
Clethra alnifolia L. (sweet pepperbush), 166
    table
climacteric, in fruit, 129
climate, of the major growing regions, 104–
    105, 105 table
Coastal Washington Experiment Station, 14

Colaspis costipennis Crotch (striped *Colaspis*), 273
colchicine: use in cranberry to study phyllotaxy, 54–55; use in production of tetraploids, 61–62
cold storage units, 315
color: development of, 284–286; in fruit, 128–129
Columbia cultivar, 68
common ragweed (*Ambrosia artemisiifolia*), 207 table; control with simazine, 215
common storage, 131
Compositae, 207–208 table
composition: of fruit, 129–135, 130 table, 131 table, 353 table; of plant, 137 table, 139 table, 141–147 table
consumption, 350–351, 351 table
continuous process, for sauce production, 317
controlled atmosphere storage, 315–316
convection current, in flood water, 96
copper (Cu), 163; content in fruit, 130 table; content in plant, 147 table; deficiency level in shoot, 139 table; effect on fruit quality, 194; interaction with manganese, 162; seasonal distribution in shoots, 137 table; standard value in shoot, 139 table
copper hydroxide (fungicide), 245 table
copper sulfate, in floodwater, 104, 163
copper toxicity, 163
costs: of bog establishment, 325–328; of production, 328–331, 329 table, 330 table
cotton ball, 240
cotton spanworm, 254
Craisin, 323
cranberry barrel, 338–339
cranberry blossom worm (*Epiglaea apiata*), 256–257; controlled by reflows, 187
Cranberry Canners, Inc., 348, 350
cranberry cider, 324
cranberry concentrate, as a natural coloring material, 323
cranberry-flavored yogurt, 323–324
cranberry fruit wine, 324
cranberry fruitworm, 260; insecticide recommendations for, 280 table
cranberry girdler, 265–267; control by late holding of the winter flood, 185; insecticide recommendations for, 280 table
Cranberry Growers' Union, 345
cranberry jelly, recipe for, 356
cranberry juice (cocktail), 284, 319–322, 349; and ammonical odors, 354–355; antifungal effect of, 356; and calcium content of urine, 355; and cranberry prices, 336; for dys-

uria, 354; for kidney stones, 355; percentage of crop used for, 350; preparation of, 319–321; urinary pH, 354; for urinary tract infections, 354
Cranberry Marketing Committee, 349
Cranberry Marketing Order, 349
cranberry nut bread, recipe for, 358
cranberry-orange relish, recipe for, 357–358
cranberry root grub, 272–273
cranberry rootworm, 273–274
cranberry sauce: pectin in, 134; preparation of, 316–318; vitamin C content of, 132; recipe for, 356
cranberry sawfly, 261
cranberry scale, 268–269
cranberry scare of 1959, 336
cranberry sherbet, 324
cranberry spittle insect, 270–271
cranberry syrup, 322; pharmaceutical use of, 355–356. *See also* ruby phosphate.
cranberry tipworm, 261–262; insecticide recommendations for, 279 table
cranberry weevil, 262–263; insecticide recommendations for, 279–280 table
cranberry white grub, 272
crates. *See* boxes
Crinconemoides sp., nematode occurrence, 274–276, 275 table
Crinconemoides curvatum: pathogenicity of, 277–278; parasitism by, 277
Crinconemoides xenoplax: occurrence of, 275 table; parasitism by, 277
crinkled flannel moth, 259
Crocker cultivar, 68
crop: production, 332 table; returns, 336–338, 337 table; utilization, 332 table; value, 40–43, **41**, 332 table
Cropper cultivar, 69
Cross, C. E., 13
Crowell, Calvin, 8
Crowley, D. J., 14, 18, 79
Crowley cultivar: description of, 64 table, 69; hybrid released by Washington State University, 59; photosynthesis in, 114; resistance to tip blight disease, 235; susceptibility to phytopthora disease, 236
cultivar(s): descriptions of, 62–77, 64 table; trials, 77–80
Cumberland cultivar, 69
cut grass (*Carex bullata*), control of, 185
cuticle, composition of, 135
cuttings, used for propagation, 178
cutworms, 254–258; insecticide recommendations for, 280 table
cyanidin-3-glucoside, content in fruit, 132

cyanidin-3-monoarabinoside, content in fruit, 132
cyanidin-3-monogalactoside, in fruit, 132
cytology, 54–55
cytospora sp., causal agent for storage rots, 242

dalapon (Dowpon), 215
daminozide [succinic acid-2,2-di-methylhydrazide], 115. *See also* alar
dams, 171–176, **172, 173;** maintenance of, 229
Dana, M. N., horticulturist, 17–18
Dana dryer, 308
Darlington Picker, 293–295, **295, 296;** effect on vine damage, 292
Dasyneura vaccinii Smith (cranberry tipworm), 261–262, 279 table
Datana drexelii, 259
DBCP, for control of nematodes, 278
DDT, persistence in soil, 102
dearness scale, 268
Demoranville, I. E., 13
Devrinol (herbicide), 218
Diaporthe vaccinii Shear: and upright dieback disease, 235; and viscid rot disease, 240
diazinon: insecticide recommendations for, 279–280 table; for control of cranberry fruitworm, 260; for control of cranberry girdler, 267; in floodwater, 103
dibble, used in planting, 178, **180**
1,2-dibromo-3-chloropropane (DBCP), for nematode control, 278
dichlobenil (Casoron and Norosac): effect on berry color enhancement, 285; as herbicide, 216
2,4 dichlorophenoxy acetic acid (2,4-D), to control woody weeds, 217
dieldrin: in floodwater, 103; persistence in soil, 102
0,0-diethyl, 0-2 pyrazinyl phosphorothioate (Zinophos), for nematode control, 278
Difolatan, fungicide recommendation, 244 table
Dill Eagle cultivar, 69
Dillingham, F., 67–68
diquat (herbicide), 217–218
disease control recommendations, 243 table, 245–246
diseases of the vine, 230–238
distribution, 43–45
ditch and pond weeds, 210–211 table
ditches, 171–176, **174;** cleaning, 227–229; depth of, 169; used for irrigation, 189–190
diurnal influences, on oxygen content of floodwater, 97

Doehlert, C. A., 13, 17
dormancy: of seeds, 128; photoperiod requirement for, 113
Dorylaimus sp., nematode occurrence, 274–276, 275 table
Doughty, C. C., 14, 18
Dowpon, 215
drainage, 169–170, **182;** for controlling phytophthora disease, 236
dried blood (fertilizer), 194
drought, effect on yield, 109
dry harvesting, 286–298
dry matter, content of fruit, 131 table
dysuria, treatment of with cranberry juice, 354

Early Black cultivar: anthocyanin response to nitrogen fertilizer, 155; brands (labels) of, 343, 344; description of, 64 table, 69; effect of low temperature on fruit, 84; first planting, 7; flower bud induction in, 117; fruit development of, 125–127, **126;** harvest season of, 284; nitrogen content in, 140, 141–142 table; nitrogen deficiency level in, 140; optimum water table depth for, 188; origin of, 56; phosphorus content of, 143–144 table, 156; pollination of, 123; potassium content of, 144–145 table; preference of the blunt-nosed leafhopper for, 58; relative gel strength of, 317; resistance to false blossom disease, 60; respiration in, 115; rest requirement for, 110; response to boron, 164; response to molybdenum, 163; response to nitrogen, 148, 149 table; response to phosphorus, 156; response to potassium, 157–158; seed number in, 128; storability of prepackaged fruit, 315; sugar content in, 131 table; sulfur content of, 147 table; susceptibility to black rot disease, 311; susceptibility to oxygen deficiency injury, 93–94, 93 table; susceptibility to physiological breakdown, 310; susceptibility to phytophthora disease, 236; temperature influence on storability of, 314; yield components in, 119 table, 120
early drawing. *See* winter flood
Early Ohio cultivar, 69
Early Red cultivar, 69
Early Richard cultivar, 70
early rots (field), 239–240
East Coast: cranberry spittle insect on, 270; harvest season on, 284; importance of cranberry weevil on, 262; occurrence of bitter and blotch rot diseases, 240; water harvesting on, 299, 309
Eastern scoop, 287, **288**

Eastwood, B.: *Complete Manual for the Cultivation of the Cranberry*, 7; on bog establishment costs, 325–326; prices, 331
Eatmor Cranberries, Inc., 347
Eaton, E. L., 18, 57
Eaton, G. W., 18
economics, 325–338, 329 table, 330 table, 332 table, 337 table
elements: seasonal distribution in plants, 136–137, 137 table, 148, 157, 159, 160, 161, 162–163; standard values in plants, 137–138, 139 table. *See also specific elements, i.e.*, boron, copper, iron, *etc.*
Ematurga amitaria Gn. (brown cranberry spanworm), 253
end rot disease, 241
energy value, of fruit, 130 table, 352
Epiglaea apiata Gr. (cranberry blossom worm), 187, 256
Ericaceae family, 43, 136
Eriococcus azaleae Comsto (*Eriococcus* scale), 268
ethephon, for berry color enhancement, 285
ethylene: effect on anthocyanin, 129; production in fruit, 129; to promote berry anthocyanin formation in storage, 316
Eupithecia miserulata, 252
Europe, cultivar trials in, 80
Euscelis striatulus Fallen (blunt-nosed leafhopper), 187, 264; vector of false blossom disease, 238
evaporative cooling, for control of berry scald, 87
Evital, 216
Excelsior cultivar, 70
Exobasidium oxycocci Rost, causal agent of rose bloom disease, 232
Exobasidium perenne sp. nov., causal agent of red shoot disease, 232
Exobasidium vaccinii (Fckl.) Wor., causal agent of red leaf spot disease, 230

fairy ring disease, 236–237
fall armyworm, 256–257
false armyworm, 257
false blossom disease, 237–238; "cafeteria" test for leafhopper resistance, 58; cultivar resistance to, 58, 238
fat, content in fruit, 130 table
Fenwick, J. A., 8, 11
Ferbam: for control of fairy ring disease, 237; effect on berry color enhancement, 286; effect on pollen germination, 124; recommendations of, 243, 244 tables
ferns (*Polyodiaceae*), 206–207 table

fertilization (flower): indication of, 123; time after pollination, 118, 123
fertilization (nutrient): of new plantings, 179, 181; response to calcium, 159; response to nitrogen, 148, 149 table, 151–155; response to phosphorus, 155–157; response to potassium, 158; response to sulfur, 160
fertilizer(s): materials, 194–195; methods of application, 197–198; rates and ratios, 195–197, 196 table; requirements, 190, 191 table; response to, 190–194, 192 table, 193 table; time of application, 197
fiber, content in fruit, 130 table, 352, 353 table
Filmer, R. S., 16
fireworms, 248–251; insecticide recommendations for, 279–280 table
flash flooding, for irrigation, 190
flavonol(s), 128, 132
flavor components, for use in yogurt, 324. *See also* volatiles
Fleming, A. S. (Secretary of U.S. DHEW), 336
floatboats, 291
flooding: for black vine weevil control, 263–264; for cranberry girdler control, 266; for frost control, 84–85; for grub control, 272–274; measures to minimize oxygen deficiency during, 98–100; for nematode control, 278; for winter protection, 82
floodwater: biological oxidation in, 94–96; color of, 90; copper sulfate in, 104; dieldrin in, 103; factors affecting oxygen level in, 94–97; increasing the oxygen content of, 98–100; nitrogen in, 104; optimum temperature for water harvest, 298; oxygen level in, 89–90, 92; parathion in, 103–104; phosphorus in, 104; pH of, 103
flower(s), 49–52, **50–51, 52**; effect of false blossom disease on, 237–238; frost injury to, 83–84; oxygen deficiency on number of, 90–91, 93 table; potential number of, 123; production response to nitrogen, 154; respiration rate of, 92; ringspot disease, 238; rose bloom disease, 232; winter injury on, 82
flower bud: effect of low temperature on, 84; oxygen deficiency injury to, 90–91, 93 table
flowering, 116–118; chilling requirement for, 110–112; relationship to winter flood, 184; response to sulfur, 160; in the Stevens cultivar, 117; as a yield component, 118–120, 119 table, 139
foliage, non-worms that attack, 262–265

foliar fertilizer: effect on McFarlin cranberry, 193–194; liquid urea sprays, 195

Foxboro Howes cultivar, 70

Franklin, H. J.: director of Massachusetts Cranberry Experiment Station, 12–13, **17;** entomologist, 16

Franklin cultivar: description of, 64 table, 70; hybrid released from USDA breeding program, 59; relative gel strength of, 3₁7; rest requirement for, 110; susceptibility to black rot disease, 311; susceptibility to physiological breakdown, 310

freezing (frozen fruit): for preservation of vitamin C, 319; marketing of, 323

frost: injury, 83–87; critical temperatures, 83; on fruit, 84; influence of sanding on, 224; protection against, 84–87; types of, 84

frost forecasting: alarm systems for monitoring, 86–87; formulae for, 86

fruit. *See also* berry
—chemical changes of in storage, 311–313
—composition, 129–135, 130 table, 131 table, 141 table; calcium, 130 table, 145 table; chlorine, 130 table; copper, 130 table; iodine, 130 table, 132; iron, 130 table; magnesium, 130 table, 145 table; manganese, 130 table; nitrogen, 142 table; phosphorus, 130 table, 143 table; potassium, 130 table, 144–145 table; sodium, 130 table; sulfur, 130 table, 147 table
—development of, 125–129, **126**
—drying, 306–309
—effect of low temperature on, 84, 186
—maturity of, 129
—non-worms that attack, 262–265
—oxygen deficiency injury to, 91, 93 table
—quality: effect of copper on, 194; effect of machine harvesting on, 298; effect of nitrogen on, 154–155; and late holding winter flood, 185; and manganese and zinc, 193; and ringspot disease, 238; and water harvesting, 298, 310; and weather, 107
—respiration rate of, 92
—ripening (maturity): effect of temperature on, 107; in relation to respiration, 312
—rot(s), 239–243; effect of scooping on, 291; effect of sulfur on, 160; influence of sanding on, 225
—set, 123–125; and boron, 164, 194; factors affecting, 124; and gibberellic acid, 125; importance of, 123; and nitrogen, 154; and oxygen deficiency, 93 table; and sulfur, 160; and temperature, 87–88; and winter flood, 185; as a yield component, 118–120, 119 table, 139

—size, 125–127, **126;** and nitrogen, 154; and potassium, 158; and sulfur, 160; and zinc, 162

fruiting habit, 116–121; effect of nitrogen on, 154

fruitworms, 259–261

fuel oil, use in weed control, 201, 214–215

Fuller, P. A., 68

Fumea casta Pallas (bagworm), 261

fungicide(s): applications of, 243; effect on frost tolerance of fruit, 84; effect on fruit set, 124

Funginex. *See* triforine-EC

Furadan, for control of black vine weevil, 264

Furford Picker, 296; modification of, 303

Fusicoccum putrefaciens Shear, imperfect stage of *Godronia cassandrae,* 241

Garwood, I., 70

Garwood Bell cultivar, 70

Gaultheria procumbens L. (wintergreen plant), 165

Gaynor, Judge, 12

Gebhardt, H. H., 70

Gebhardt Beauty cultivar, 70

Gel Power Index, 317–318

gel strength, 317

genus, 43

germination: of pollen, 117–118, 123, 124; of seeds, 128

Getsinger Retractor Tooth Picker, 299, **300**

Gibbera compacta (Pk.) Shear, causal agent of Gibbera leaf spot disease, 232

Gibbera leaf spot disease, 231–232

Gibbera myrtilli (Cooke) Petrak, causal agent of Gibbera leaf spot disease, 231

gibberellic acid: effect on fruit set, 125; effect on rest requirement, 112; effect on vegetative growth, 113–114

gibberellin activity: effect of nitrogen on, 153; in the plant, 113–114

Gibrel, 125

Gifford cultivar, 70

Glomerella cingulata vaccinii Shear, causal agent of bitter rot disease, 240

glyphosate (herbicide), 217–218

Godfrey cultivar, 70

Godronia cassandrae Peck, causal agent of end rot disease, 241

golden club (*Orontium aequaticum*), 165

grape *Anomala,* 272

grasses (*Gramineae*): key to, 200, 202–204 table

green cranberry spanworm, 252–253

grower organizations, 11–12

Growers' Cranberry Company (New Jersey): brand names (labels) of fruit, 344–345; consolidation with the National Fruit Exchange, 346; organization of, 345

growing season: of the major growing regions, 105 table; requirements of, 104

growth habit, 110–116

growth inhibitors (retardants): exogenous, 115–116; natural, 116

growth regulators: effect on apical dominance in tissue culture, 113; effect on fruit size, 127; effect on vegetative growth, 113–114

grubs, 271–274

Guignardia vaccinii Shear: causal agent of stem blight disease, 233; originally thought to be causal agent for scald disease, 239; reclassified as *Botryosphaeria vaccinii*, 239

gypsy moth, 259

hail, crop losses caused by, 106

hairy caterpillars, 258–259

half-winged geometer, 252

Hall, Henry, 4

Hall, I. V., 18

Hall, Thomas, 4

Hall cultivar, 70

Hamilton, T. F., 71, 72

handling: dry-harvested fruit, 302–306, **303, 304, 306–308**; water-harvested fruit, 306–311

hand picking, 286–287, **286**

hand weeding, 200

Handy, L., 70

hardiness, effect of temperature on, 81

hardpan, in soils, 167

hard rot (cotton ball) disease, 240

Hardy Howes cultivar, 70

Harlow cultivar, 70

Harrison, Isaac, 8

harvest
—machines: for dry harvest, 292–298, **292, 294, 295, 296, 297;** for water harvest, 298–302, **301–302**
—methods, 286–302, **286, 288–290, 292, 294, 295, 296–297, 300–301**
—season, 284

Harwich cultivar, 70

Haskins, L. P., 69

Hawthorne cultivar, 70

Hayden and Bailey mill, for berry sorting, 305, **306–308**

heat, injury by, 87

Helicotylenchus sp., nematode occurrence, 274–276, 275 table

Hemiberlesia lataniae Signoret (latania scale), 268

Hemicycliophora similis: distribution patterns of, 276; pathogenicity of, 277–278; parasitism by, 277

Hemicycliophora sp., nematode occurrence, 274–276, 275 table

Henry Griffith cultivar, 70

herbicides, 214–218. *See also* specific materials

Hewitt Berry cultivar, 70

hill fireworm, 248–249

hippuric acid: content in urine in relation to fruit consumption, 354; conversion of benzoic acid and quinic acid to, 352

Hockanum cultivar, 70

Holliston cultivar (Mammoth), 58, 71

honeybees: application recommendations, 219–220; colony requirements, 220–221; protection of, 221–222; requirements of, 221

Horseneck cultivar, 71

Howard, M., 71

Howard Bell cultivar, 71, 344

Howes, Elias, 56

Howes, J. W., 72

Howes cultivar: brands (labels) of, 343, 344; calcium content of, 145 table; description of, 65 table, 71; effect of low temperature on fruit, 84; flower bud induction in, 117; fruit development of, 125–127, **126;** harvest season for, 284; iron content of, 146 table; magnesium content of, 146 table; manganese content of, 147 table; nitrogen content of, 142 table; optimum water table depth for, 188; origin of, 56; phosphorus content of, 143 table; photosynthesis in, 114–115; potassium content of, 144 table; resistance to blunt-nosed leafhopper, 58; respiration in, 115; relative gel strength of, 317; response to boron, 164; rest requirement for, 110; ringspot disease symptoms in, 238; seed number in, 127–128; storability of prepackaged fruit, 315; sugar content in, 131 table; susceptibility to false blossom disease, 60; susceptibility to oxygen deficiency injury, 93–94, 93 table; susceptibility to phytophthora disease, 236; susceptibility to storage losses, 313; temperature effect on storability of, 314; yield components in, 119 table

Howland cultivar, 71

H & P Evaporated Whole Cranberries, 323

hurricanes, effect of on water quality, 103

ice: on floodwater, 95; formation in cells, 83–84; sanding on, 224–225

Improved Howes cultivar, 71
Indian Head cultivar, 71
indicator plants, 165–167, 166 table
industry: origins of, 1–6; early development of, 6–11
inflorescence, 49–52, **50–51, 52.** *See also* flower
insect(s): control recommendations, 278–282, 279–280 table; effect of late holding of winter flood, 184–185; effect of reflows on, 186; spray schedule for, 281
insecticides, method of application, **281,** 282
interspecific hybridization, 62
iodine, content in fruit, 130 table, 132, 352
iron (Fe), 161; content in fruit, 130 table; content in plant, 146 table; deficiency level in shoot, 139 table; seasonal distribution in plant, 137 table; standard value in shoot, 139 table
iron chelate (FeEDTA), 161
iron chlorosis, 161
irrigation, 187–190
isobutylidene diurea (fertilizer), 195
Itame sulphurea Pack. (green cranberry spanworm), 252

Jerseys cultivar (Natives): brand names (labels) for, 344; description of, 71; origin of, 57; seed number in, 128
Jones, Albert, 69
juice products, 319–322
Juneau cultivar, 71

Kalmia polifolia Wang, 166
kerosene, use in weed control, 201, 214–215
ketones, in fruit, 133
Keystone cultivar, 71–72
kidney stones, effect of cranberry juice on, 355
Klondike cultivar, 72
Kocide fungicide, 243 table

Lachnanthes tinctoria (red root), 185
Laphygma frugiperda S. & A. (fall armyworm), 257
latania scale, 268
Late Cape cultivar, 72
late holding. *See* winter flood
Late Jersey cultivar, 72
late-water flood, use in Massachusetts, 185
Leach, C. D., 74
leaf: calcium content of, 145 table; diseases of, 230–232; gibberellic acid activity in, 114; iron content of, 146 table; magnesium content of, 145–146 table; manganese con-

tent of, 147 table; nitrogen content of, 141–143 table; oxygen deficiency injury to, 92; phosphorus content of, 143–144 table; potassium content of, 144 table; respiration rate of, 92; sulfur content of, 147 table
leatherleaf: as host for the blunt-nosed cranberry leafhopper, 265; as host for the cranberry blossom worm, 256–257; as an indicator plant for site selection, 166 table
Lecanium corni Bouche (*Lecanium* scale), 269
Lecanium scale, 268
Ledum columbianum Piper, 166
Leland, Augustus, 4–5
Leland cranberry cleaner and separator, 305
LeMunyon (Norman?), 72
Leonard Robbins cultivar, 72
Lepidosaphes ulmi Linn. (oystershell scale), 269
Lichnanthe vulpina Hentz (cranberry root grub), 272
light: effect on vegetative growth, 113; limitation in floodwater, 94–95. *See also* photoperiod
limestone (lime): effect on pH of soil, 100–101; for control of fairy ring disease, 237; response to, 159
lime sulfur, for control of stem blight, 234
lingonberry, 2-methylbutyric acid content in, 134
Lophodermium oxycocci Karst, causal agent of twig blight disease, 233
Low, Winthrop, 5
low-life pumps, 176

McFarlin, Charles D., 6
McFarlin, Joseph T., 67, 68
McFarlin, Thomas H., 56
McFarlin cultivar: anthocyanin response to nitrogen in, 155; boron content of, 147 table; brands of, 343; bud types in, 112–113; calcium content of, 145 table; copper content of, 147 table; description of, 65 table, 72; effect of Alar on, 115–116; fertilizer response in, 192–194; first planting in Oregon, 6; fruit development in, 125–127, **126;** harvest season for, 284; iron content of, 146 table; magnesium content of, 145–146 table; manganese content of, 146–147 table; nitrogen content of, 141–142 table; origin of, 56; phosphorus content of, 143 table, 157; pollination of, 123; potassium content of, 144 table; preference of the blunt-nosed leafhopper for, 58; resistance to false blossom disease, 60; resistance to

oxygen deficiency injury, 93–94, 93 table; resistance to tip blight disease, 235; response to copper, 163, 194; response to iron, 161; response to lime, 159, 192; response to manganese, 193; response to potassium, 158; response to zinc, 162, 194; rest requirement for, 110–111; storability of prepackaged fruit, 315; sugar content in, 131 table; uprights in, 118; yield components in, 120

magnesium (Mg), 159–160; content in fruit, 130 table, 145 table; content in plant, 145 table; deficiency level in shoot, 139 table; seasonal distribution in shoot, 137 table; standard value in shoot, 139 table

Magnolia virginiana L. (swamp magnolia), 166 table

Makepeace, A. D., 71

malathion, effect on berry anthocyanin content, 285

Malde, O. G., 66

maleic hydrazide: control of vegetative growth, 116; for wild bean control, 218

malic acid, content in fruit, 130 table, 352

Mammoth cultivar (Holliston), 72

mancozeb, fungicide recommendation, 245 table

Maneb fungicide: effect on pollen germination, 124; effect on twig blight disease, 233; recommendations, 244 table

manganese (Mn): content in fruit, 130 table, 352; content in plant, 146–147 table; deficiency level in shoot, 139 table; effect on fruit quality, 193; foliar use of, 193; seasonal distribution in shoot, 137 table; standard value in shoot, 139 table

Maritime Provinces: black-headed fireworm in, 249; chain-spotted geometer in, 253; cranberry fruitworm in, 260

marketing, 338–349, **340, 341, 342;** of fresh fruit, 313

marketing order, 348–349

Marucci, P. E., 16

Massachusetts: acreage, 20 table, 23, **24, 25;** bog establishment in, 171; climate of, 105 table; copper toxicity in, 163; cultivar trials in, 78–79; drainage of bogs in, 169; fruit development in, 125–127, **126;** growing season in, 105 table; indicator plants for site selection in, 165; infestations of fall armyworm in, 257; occurrence of fairy ring disease, 237; oxygen deficiency in, 88; phytophthora disease in, 236; production, 29, 20 table; productivity, 33–40, **34, 35,** 36 table; scald disease in, 239;

soils in, 167; winter flood in, 99, 183–186; yield components in, 119–120, 119 table

Massachusetts Cranberry Experiment Station, 12–13; cultivar trials at, 78–79

Mathewson picking machine, 292–293, **292**

Matthews, Isaiah, 72

Matthews cultivar, 72

Maxim Randall cultivar (Randall), 72

mechanical harvesting, 292–302; breeding for, 61

Metallic Bell cultivar, 60, 72

2-methylbutyric acid, in fruit, 134

microclimate, effect on bog temperature, 85–86

Middleboro cultivar, 72–73

Middlesex cultivar, 73

mineral(s), content of fruit, 130 table, 131–132

moisture, content in fruit, 130 table

molybdenum, 163–164

Monilinia oxycocci (Wor) Honey (formally *Sclerotinia oxycocci* Wor), 234; causal agent of hard rot disease, 240

Monmouth cultivar, 73

Morcran (herbicide), 216

morphology, 45–51, **46, 47, 48, 50–51**

Mosquito Damn cultivar, 73

moss, control with copper sulfate, 163; varieties of, 214 table

mowing: as a method of weed control, 200; dams, 229; machines for, 226, **228;** for pruning, 226

muck (mud bottom): in New Jersey and Massachusetts, 167–168; optimum water table for, 188; in soil, 101

Murdock cultivar, 73

mycorrhiza: in cranberry plant, 47–49; effect on nutrient uptake, 138; role in nitrogen metabolism, 150–151

Mycosphaerella nigro-maculans Shear, causal agent of black spot disease, 231

Myrica gale (sweet gale), 166

myricetin-3-arabinoside, content in fruit, 132

myricetin-3-digalactoside, content in fruit, 132

Nancy LeMunyon cultivar, 73

1-naphthaleneacetic acid (NAA), to produce fruit set, 125

β-naphthoxyacetic acid (NOA), to produce fruit set, 125

naptalam (herbicide), 216

National Cranberry Association, 348

National Cranberry Sales Company, 12

National Fruit Exchange, 346

National Marketing Order, 335

Natives cultivar: calcium content of, 145 table; description of, 73; iron content of, 146 table; labels of, 344; magnesium content of, 146 table; manganese content of, 147 table; nitrogen content of, 142 table; phosphorus content of, 143 table; potassium content of, 144 table

natural blast, 124

nectar: effect of oxygen deficiency on production, 91; sugar content of, 122

nectaries: frost injury to, 83; oxygen deficiency injury to, 91

nematodes: control of, 278; distribution patterns of, 276; occurrence of, 274–276, 275 table; parasitism by, 276–277; pathogenicity of, 277–278

Nemocestes incomptus (woods weevil), 264

New England Cranberry Sales Company: brands (labels) for, 343; organization of, 346

Newfoundland, red shoot disease in, 232

New Jersey: acreage in, 20 table, 25–26, **25**; Berryland sand in, 101; climate of, 105 table; cultivar trials in, 79–80; damage to cranberry blossom worm, 256; damage to cranberry tipworm, 261–262; drainage of bogs in, 169; fertilizer materials in, 194; fertilizer rates and ratios in, 195; fertilizer response in, 190–192; first cultivation in, 5; growing season for, 105 table; honeybee recommendations for, 220; indicator plants for site selection in, 165, 166 table; industry during the 1800s, 8–10; infestation of fall armyworm in, 257; occurrence of oxygen deficiency, 88; occurrence of fairy ring disease, 237; occurrence of phytopthtora disease, 236; occurrence of red gall disease, 236; occurrence of scale disease in, 139; production, 29, 30 table; productivity, 33–40, **35**, 36 table; sanding in, 177; savanna soils in, 101; settler's use of cranberry, 3–4; upright types in, 118; winter flood in, 99, 183–186; yield components in, 118–120, 119 table

New Jersey Cranberry and Blueberry Research Laboratory: cultivar trials at, 79–80; origin of, 13

New Jersey Cranberry Sales Company, organization of, 346

New Jersey Crop Reporting Service, 121

Newton cultivar, 73

nicotinic acid, content in fruit, 130 table

nitrate(s) (fertilizer), plant response to, 149–150

nitrate reductase: activity in plant, 150; role of mycorrhiza in nitrate reduction, 151

nitrogen (N), 140–155, 141–143 table, 149 table; deficiency level in Early Black cultivar, 140; deficiency in shoots, 139 table; deficiency symptoms, 140, 148, 151–152; effect on berry coloring, 286; effect on phosphorus, 157; effect on red leaf spot disease, 231; effect on tissue manganese, 162; form of, 149–150; interaction with sulfur, 160; response to, 148, 149 table, 151–155; seasonal distribution in shoot, 137 table, 148; standard value in shoot, 139 table

nitrogen gas, as a storage atmosphere, 315

non-*Apis* bees, as pollinators of cranberries, 222

nonflurazon (Evital) (herbicide), 216

Norosac. *See* dichlobinil

North Cape Howes cultivar, 73

Northeast, cranberry root grub in, 272

Nova Scotia: flower bud induction in, 117; red gall disease in, 236; red shoot disease in, 232

Nova Scotia Bell cultivar, 73

nutrient(s): calcium, 159; deficiency levels in shoot, 139 table; influence of mycorrhiza on uptake, 138; nitrogen, 140; phosphorus, 155; potassium, 157–158; requirement for, 136; standard values in shoot, 139 table. *See also* elements

nutritive and therapeutic value, 352–356, 353 table

Nye, G. N., 68

Nyssa sylvatica Marsh (sour gum), 166 table

obscure root weevil, 264

Ocean Spray Cranberries, Inc., 348

ointment, 355–356. *See also* Vaccinol

Old Homestead cultivar, 73

Ophiola striatula Fall. (*Euscelis striatulus*), vector of false blossom disease, 60

Oregon: acreage in, 20 table, 26, **28**; honeybee recommendations for production, 29, 30 table; seasonal distribution of elements in plants, 137 table; sprinkler irrigation in, 176; yellow rot disease in, 242

organic acids, in fruit, 130–131, 130 table

organic matter: depth of, 167; in floodwater, 95–96, 100; in soil, 101

organic nitrogen, utilization of, 151

Orontium aequaticum L. (golden club plant), 165

Osmia lignaria (non-*Apis* bee), 222

Osmocote (fertilizer), 195

Osmunda cinnamomea L. (cinnamon fern), 165
Osmunda regalia L. (royal fern), 165
Otiorhynchus ovatus Linn. (strawberry root weevil), 264
Otiorhynchus rugosostriatus Geoze (rough strawberry root weevil), 264
Otiorhynchus sulcatus Fabr. (black vine weevil), 187, 263–264
Oxhart cultivar, 73
Oxycoccus macrocarpus [Ait.] Pers. (*Vaccinium macrocarpon* Ait.), 43–44
O. microcarpus Turcz. (*Vaccinium oxycoccus* L.), 43–44; chromosome number of, 54
O. ovalifolius Por., 43–44
O. quadripetalus Gilib. (*Vaccinium quadripetalus*), 43–44; chromosome number of, 54; use in breeding, 62
oxygen
—content in floodwater, 92–93
—deficiency, 88–100, 93 table; correction of, 97–100; effect on fruit set, 124; factors affecting oxygen level in floodwater, 94–97; forms of injury, 90–91; occurrence of, 88–90; oxygen level for, 91–94; relation to winter flood, 184
—measurement of in floodwater, 97–98
—methods of increasing in floodwater, 97–100
—requirement for, 91–94
oystershell scale, 269–270
ozone, as a storage atmosphere, 316

Pacific Beauty cultivar, 73
Pacific Coast: climate of, 105; growing season for, 105 table; harvest season on, 284; scale insects of the, 268; use of windbreaks on, 170. *See also* Pacific Northwest
Pacific Cranberry Exchange, 346
Pacific Northwest: adaptability of Crowley cultivar to, 59; black-headed fireworm in, 249; black vine weevil in, 263; flowering in, 111; origins of cranberry industry in, 6; red leaf spot disease in, 230; species found in, 44; sulfur-coated urea in, 195; use of evaporative cooling, 87. *See also* Pacific Coast *and* West Coast
packaging, 338–343, **340, 341, 342**
Palmeter, D. C., 73
Palmeter cultivar, 60, 73
panicgrass (hairy) (*Panicum lanuginosum*), 203 table; control with simazine, 215
Panicum lanuginosum Ell. (hairy panicgrass), 203 table
pantothenic acid, content in fruit, 130 table

Paradise Meadow cultivar, 58, 73
parathion: for control of cranberry fruitworm, 260; for control of *Sparganothis* fruitworm, 261; degradation of by soil microflora, 102; effect on aquatic life, 103–104; in floodwater, 103–104; insecticide recommendations for, 279–280 table
parthenocarpy, 125
Paul cultivar, 73
peat: in soil, 101; problems in using, 168
pectin: content in fruit, 130 table, 134, 352–353; effect on elimination of body wastes, 353–354; and gelling property of sauce, 317–318, 352
Peffer, G. A., 6
Pembroke, Thomas, 7
pemmican, Indian use of cranberries in, 2
Penicillium sp., causal agents of storage rots, 242
peonidin-3-glucoside, content in fruit, 132
peonidin-3-monoarabinoside, content in fruit, 132
peonidin-3-monogalactoside, content in fruit, 132
Perkins cultivar, 73
Perry, J., 73
Perry Red cultivar, 73
Pestalozzia quepini vaccinii Shear, causal agent of storage rot, 242
pesticide(s): contamination of water, 103–104; effect on aquatic life, 103–104; residue in soils, 102
pH: effect on aluminum availability, 161; effect of limestone on soil, 100–101; effect on manganese availability, 162; effect on nitrogen response, 149; effect on soil microflora, 102; effect on weeds, 165; of floodwater, 102–103; of fruit, 312; of soil, 100–101; of urine in relation to hippuric acid content, 354; sulfur effect on, 100–101, 160
Phacidium lunatum, 241
Phaltan: effect on pollen germination, 124; fungicide recommendation, 244 table
pheromone trap, 279
Phigalia titea Cramer (half-winged geometer), 252
Phoma radicis, 49, 138, 151
Phomopsis vaccinii Shear, imperfect stage of *Diaporthe vaccinii*, 235
Phosfon-D, as an inhibitor of fruit senescence, 312
phosphorus (P), 155–157; content in fruit, 130 table, 143 table; content in plant, 143–144 table; deficiency level in shoot, 139

phosphorus (P) (*continued*)
table; deficiency symptoms in plant, 156;
seasonal distribution in shoots, 137 table;
standard value in shoot, 139 table
photoperiod: effect on flower bud induction, 116; effect on vegetative growth,
113
photosynthesis: occurrence under floodwater, 94–95; in the plant, 114–115
Phyllophaga anxia Lec. (cranberry white
grub), 272
Phyllosticta elongata Weidemann: imperfect
or conidial stage of *Botryosphaeria vaccinii*,
233, 239
Phyllosticta vaccinii Earle: believed to be true
causal agent of stem blight disease, 233;
causal agent of scald disease, 239
phyllotaxy, 45–46
Physalospora (formerly *Acanthorhyncus*)
vaccinii Shear, causal agent of blotch rot
disease, 240
physiological blast, 124
physiological breakdown (fruit): effect of
bruising, 302; effect of water immersion
on, 310; sterile breakdown of, 243
Phytophthora cinnamomi Rands, causal agent
for phytopthora disease, 236
phytophthora disease, 236
Picea sitchensis (spruce), 166
pigment(s): breeding for, 60–61; content in
fruit, 132–133; degradation in cans, 319;
quantitative determination of, 132, 321–
322; in relation to surface area of berry,
133; response to phosphorus fertilizer,
155; temperature effect on stabilization in
stored juice, 322
Pilgrim cultivar: description of, 65 table, 74;
hybrid from USDA breeding program, 59;
relative gel strength of, 317; susceptibility
to black rot disease, 311; susceptibility to
physiological breakdown, 310; susceptibility to tip blight disease, 235
Pilgrims, use of cranberries, 1–2
Pinus rigida Mill (pitch pine), 166 table
Pihus toxiocodendron L. (poison sumac), 166
table
pistil: frost injury to, 83; respiration rate of,
92
pitcher plant (*Sarracenia purpurea*), 165
pitch pine (*Pinus rigida*), 166 table
Pittsberg cultivar, 74
plastic, used in prepackaging, 339–340
plastic pipe (PVC): for irrigation and
drainage, 190; use in sprinkler irrigation,
176
Plum cultivar, 74

poison sumac (*Pihus toxicodendron*), 166
table
Polia atlantica Grote (Atlantic cutworm), 255
pollen (grains): effect of fungicides on, 124;
frost injury to, 83; germination of, 117–
118, 123; transfer of, 121–122
pollination, 121–124; mechanism of, 117–
118; method of, 121–122; procedures,
219–222; requirement for, 121; respiration
rate during, 92; self- vs. cross-, 122–123
pollinators, 219–220, 222
polygalacturonase enzyme, influence of berry
bruising on, 302
Porthetria dispar L. (gypsy moth), 259
potassium (K), 157–159; content in fruit,
130 table, 132; content in plant, 144–145
table; deficiency level in shoot, 139 table;
effect of nitrogen fertilizer on tissue level,
148; effect of magnesium fertilizer on
tissue level, 160; seasonal distribution in
shoots, 137 table; standard value in shoot,
139 table
Potter, M. O., 74
Potter cultivar (Potter's Favorite), 58, 74
polyvinylchloride (PVC) pipe, use in sprinkler
irrigation, 176
Pratylenchus penetrans, pathogenicity of,
277–278
prepackaging (fruit), 339–343, **342;**
storability of, 314
pressure, effect on oxygen level in floodwater, 94
price(s), 40–42, 41 table; 331–336, 332 table
Pride cultivar (Vose's Pride), 60, 74
Pristiphora idiota Norton (cranberry sawfly),
261
processing, 316–324; canning sauce, 316–
319; juice products, 319–322; other products, 322–324
production, 29–33, 30 table; costs of, 328–
331, 329 table, 330 table; during the
1800s, 9 table; effect of technology on,
338; response to nitrogen, 153–154
productivity, 33–40, **35,** 36 table; effect of
technology on, 338; potential, 123
products (other): 322–324; other methods of
utilization, 352
Prolific cultivar: description of, 74; susceptibility to false blossom disease, 60; use in
USDA breeding program, 58
propagation and planting, 176–181, 177 table,
179, 180; importance of sanding to, 223–
225
protein, content in fruit, 130 table
pruning(s), 225–226; effect on apical dominance, 113; to reduce scooping injury,

291–292; used for propagation, 178–179
Psilocybe agrariella Atk. var. *vaccinii* Charles, causal agent of fairy ring disease, 236
Putman scale, 268
pyridoxine (B_6), content in fruit, 130 table

quercetin, content in fruit, 132
quercetin-3-arabinoside, content in fruit, 132
quercetin-3-galactoside, content in fruit, 132
quinic acid, content in fruit, 130 table, 352

rainfall: effect on yield, 109; in relation to berry size, 106
Randall, George, 77
Randall, L., 72
recipes, 356–358, **357**
Reckless cultivar, 74
red gall disease, 236
red leaf spot disease, 230–231
red root (*Lachnanthes tinctoria*), control by late holding winter flood, 185
Reds cultivar, 74
red shoot disease, 232
red-striped fireworm, 250–251
reducing sugars, content in fruit, 130 table
Reeves, Sylvester, 5
reflow(s), 186–187; for control of black-headed fireworm, 250; for control of cranberry sawfly, 261; for control of cranberry spittle insect, 271; for control of false armyworm, 257; for control of gypsy moth, 259; for control of spotted cutworm, 256; oxygen levels in, 89; precautions in the use of, 98. *See also* flooding
refrigeration: for fruit display, 343; retarding bitter and blotch rot development, 240; to prevent physiological breakdown, 243; and shipping, 341–342; and storage, 314–315
relative humidity, for storing berries, 314
reservoirs, 168, **182**
respiration: of N^6-benzyladenine on harvested fruit, 304; in different plant tissues, 92, 115; effect of temperature on rate of, 91–92; of fruit maturity on, 312; under floodwater, 94–95; of water immersion on berry, 312
rest requirement, 110–112
Rhabdopterus picipes Oliv. (cranberry rootworm), 273
Rhizaspidiotus dearnessi Ckll. (dearness scale), 268
Rhode Island cultivar, 74
Rhopobata vacciniane (formerly *R. naevena naevana* Hbn.) (blackheaded fireworm), 187, 249
riboflavin (B_2), content in fruit, 130 table

Richard, A., 70
Ridomil, for control of phytophthora disease, 236
ringspot disease, 238
Robbins, N., 69
rock phosphate (fertilizer material), 194
Rogers, L. S., 63
root(s): insects that attack the, 271–274; morphology of, 47–49, **47**; nematode pathogenicity of, 277–278
rooting, 178; effect of water table depth on, 188. *See also* propagation and planting
root-spreading weeds, 211 table
root weevils, insecticide recommendations for, 280 table
rose bloom disease, 232
rough strawberry root weevil, 264
Round Howes cultivar, 74
Round Red cultivar, 75
Roundup glyphosate, 217
royal fern (*Osmunda regalia*), 165
Ruby Phosphate, 320, 322
runner(s), 45–46, **47**; nematode pathogenicity of, 277–278; nitrogen content of, 141 table; response to nitrogen, 152; response to phosphorus, 156. *See also* vines
runner-spreading weeds, 212 table
rushes (*Juncaceae*), 206 table; key to, 199
Russell Bell cultivar, 75
Rutherford cultivar, 75

Sackett, Edward, 10
St. Clair cultivar, 75
sales organizations, 345–348
Salix sp. (willow), 166
saltwater, intrusion by hurricanes, 103
Samuel Small's Bugles cultivar, 75
sanding, 223–225, **225**; for control of cranberry girdler, 224; effect on apical dominance, 113; effect on green cranberry spanworm, 253; effect on stem blight disease, 234; over peat for propagation, 176–178, 177 table; relationship to water movement, 189; relationship to water table depth, 188; sand supply for, 170
San Jose scale, 270
Sarracenia purpurea L. (pitcher plant), 165
saucer grass (*Calamovilfa brevepiles*), control of, 185
savanna(s) (gray sands): effect of pH on soil microflora in, 102; of New Jersey, 101, 167; nitrogen response in, 153; potassium response in, 158; sanding on, 178
scald (temperature): definition of, 87; effect of weather on, 108–109
scald disease, 239–240

scale insects, 267–270

scalping (turfing), 171; used in bog renovation, 227

Scammell, H. B., 16

Sciopithes obscurus (obscure root weevil), 264

Sclerotinia oxycocci Wor, 234

scooping, 287–292, **288–289**

screenhouses, for berry storage, 313

scurvy: use of cranberries for prevention of, 2, 7; use by the U.S. Navy, 331. *See also* vitamin C

Searles, Andrew, 56

Searles cultivar (Searles Jumbo): brands of, 343; description of, 65 table, 75; harvest season for, 284; optimum upright density for, 113, 152; origin of, 56; photosynthesis in, 114; ringspot disease symptoms on, 238; sugar content in, 131 table; susceptibility to false blossom disease, 60; susceptibility to red leaf spot disease, 238; yield components in, 118–119, 119 table

Sears, Elkanah, 4

sedges (*Cyperaceae*), 204–205 table; key to, 200

seeds, 127–128; effect of frost on seed count, 83; relationship to berry size, 121

seed-spreading weeds: annual, 213–214 table; perennial, 213 table

selections, from the wild, 56–57

senescence (fruit), in storage, 312

Settler cultivar, 75

Shaw, A. M., 75

Shaw, E. W., 68

Shaw, J. W., 76

Shaw's Success cultivar, 58, 75

Shawa, A. Y., 14

Shear, C. L., 15

shelf life (fruit): effect of bruising on, 302; effect of temperature on, 314; display methods for maximum, 343

Sherman Antitrust Act, industry compliance with, 346

shipping: containers, 339, **340**, 341; refrigerated, 341

shoot(s), 45–47, **47, 48**; nitrogen content in McFarlin, 141 table; nutrient deficiency levels in, 139 table; phosphorus content of, 156; respiration rate of, 92; sampling for tissue analysis, 138; standard nutrient values for, 139 table

Shreve, D. H., 8

Shurtleff cultivar, 75

Silver Lake cultivar, 75

simazine (herbicide), 215

site selection: drainage, 169–170; indicator plants for, 165–167, 166 table; sand supply, 170; soils, 167–168; water supply, 168–169

Smalley, James A., 63, 75

Smalley Howes cultivar, 75

Smith, Captain John, discovery of cranberries by, 1

Smith, J. B., 16

Smith R., 75

Smith cultivar, 75–76

Smith No. 1 cultivar, 76

Smith No. 2 cultivar, 76

smothering, of water harvested fruit, 298

snap, 287

Snipatuit cultivar, 76

sodium nitrate (fertilizer), 194

soil(s), 100–102; aluminum levels in, 161; drainage of, 214; iron levels in, 161; microflora, 101–102; miroorganisms in, 101–102; pH of, 100–102, 136; phosphorus levels in, 156; potassium levels in, 158; types of, 167–168

sour gum (*Nyssa sylvatica*), as an indicator plant for site selection, 166 table

southern red mite, 265

spanworms, 251–254; insecticide recommendations for, 279–280 table

Sparganothis fruitworm, 260–261

Sparganothis sulfureana Clem. (*Sparganothis* fruitworm), 260

species, 43–45

sphagnum moss, 165

Spirea douglasii Hook (buckbrush), 166

Sporonema oxycocci Shear: causal agent of blossom blight disease, 234; storage rot, 242

spotted cutworm, 256

spotted fireworm, 250

sprinkler irrigation: after herbicide application, 216; for evaporative cooling, 81; for fertilizer application, 198; for frost control, 85; for irrigation, 187; installation of, 176; water need for, 168

spruce (*Picea sitchensis*), 166

Staniford cranberry cleaner and separator, 305

Stankavich cultivar, 57, 64–65 table, 76

Stankiewicz, Joseph (Stankavich), 57

Stanley cultivar, 58, 61, 76

Staten, E., 74

stem(s): insects that attack, 265–271; oxygen deficiency injury to, 90–91. *See also* uprights

stem blight disease, 233–234

stem diseases, 233–238

Stevens, N. E., 15.
Stevens cultivar: calcium content of, 145 table; description of, 64–65 table, 76; flower induction in, 117; flowering in, 117; iron content of, 146 table; magnesium content of, 146 table; manganese content of, 147 table; nitrogen content of, 141 table; nitrogen deficiency level in, 140, 148; phosphorus content of, 143 table, 156; deficiency symptoms in, 156; origin of, 58–59; potassium content of, 144 table; relative gel strength of, 317; rest requirement for, 111–112; stigma receptivity in, 123; susceptibility to black rot disease, 311; physiological breakdown, 310; phytophthora disease, 236
stigma, receptivity of, 123
Stoddard Solvent, use in weed control, 214–215
stolon, 45–46, **47**
stomata, 52, 54
storage, 311–316; chemical changes of fruit in, 311–313; common storage, 313; controlled atmosphere storage, 315–316; refrigerated storage, 314–315; rots, 240–243
storage life: effect of benzoic acid content, 312; effect of berry bruising on, 310; hot-water treatment and, 311; water immersion on, 310
Strasseria oxycocci Shear, 241
strawberry root weevil, 264
striped *Colaspis*, 273
style, frost injury to, 83
sugar(s): breeding for in fruit, 61; concentration in sauce, 317; content of nectar, 122; effect of ripening, 311; effect of storage on, 311; in fruit, 129–130, 130 table, 131 table
sulfate of potash (fertilizer), 194
sulfur, 160–161; content in fruit, 130 table; content in plant, 147 table; effect on tissue phosphorus, 157; for adjusting soil pH, 101–102
sulfur-coated urea, 160; as a fertilizer material in the Pacific Northwest, 195
sulfur dioxide, 160
sunshine: effect on yield, 108; percent in different growing regions, 105 table; relationship to berry size, 106
swamp magnolia (*Magnolia virginiana*), 166 table
swamp maple (*Acer rubrum*), 166 table
sweet pepperbush (*Clethra alnifolia*), 166 table
Swift, H., 69

Synchronoblastia crypta: causal agent for tip dieback disease, 236; causal agent for storage rots, 242
Synchytrium vaccinii Thomas, causal agent of red gall disease, 236

tamarack (*Larix laricina*), 166
taxonomy, 43–45
Taylor, G., 76
Taylor cultivar, 76
technology, effect on production, 338
temperature(s), 81–88; critical temperatures, 81, 186; for drying water-harvested fruit, 309; effect on carbon dioxide evolution from stored fruit, 311; effect on fruit ripening, 107; effect on fruit set, 124; effect on oxygen level in floodwater, 94; effect on photosynthesis, 94, 115; effect on storability of canned sauce, 319; effect on yield, 108; and frost injury, 82–87; for fruit storage, 312; and heat injury, 87; for hot-water treatment of water-harvested fruit, 311; of refrigerated storages, 314; relationship to berry size, 106; and winter injury, 82
terminal bud(s), oxygen deficiency injury to, 90–91. *See also* bud
terpene derivatives, in fruit, 133
tetraploid(s): hybrids produced by colchicine treatment, 61–62; natural, 44
Tetylenchus sp., nematode occurrence, 274–276, 275 table
Tetylenchus joctus: occurrence of, 275 table; parasitism by, 277
Thanksgiving, role of cranberries at first feast, 4
thiamine (B$_1$), content in fruit, 130 table
Thomas, Benjamin, 5
tip blight disease, 234–235
tip dieback disease, 235–236
tissue culture, effect of growth regulators on apical dominance, 113
Tlascala finetella Wlk. (hill fireworm), 248
Tomlinson, W. E., Jr., 16
trace elements, 161–164
2,4,5-trichloroacetic acid (2,4,5-T), to produce fruit set, 125
2,4,5-trichlorophenoxypropionic acid (2,4,5 TP), to produce fruit set, 125
Trichodorus sp., nematode occurrence, 274–276, 275 table
Trichodorus californicus, occurrence of, 276
Trichodorus christiei: occurrence of, 275 table, 276; pathogenicity of, 277–278; parasitism by, 277

triforine-EC: effect on pollen germination, 124; for control of tip blight disease, 235
trunk gates, 174–175, **175**
tuberous weeds, 212 table
turfing, 171, 227
Turner, W. P., 73
twig blight disease, 233
Tylencholaimus sp., nematode occurrence, 274–276, 275 table
Tylenchorhynchus sp., nematode occurrence, 274–276, 275 table
Tylenchorhynchus clayatonia, parasitism by, 277
Tylenchus sp., nematode occurrence, 274–276, 275 table

umbrella bloom, 110–111
United Cape Cod Cranberry Company, 347
United States: acreage, 19, 20 table, **24;** production, 29, 30 table; productivity, 33–40, **35,** 36 table
United States Department of Agriculture (USDA), breeding program, 57–59
University of Wisconsin Cooperative Extension Service, criteria for site selection, 166–167
upland soils, production on, 167
upright(s), 45–47, **46, 47;** boron content, 147 table; calcium content, 145 table; copper content, 147 table; effect of fertilizer on flowering in, 190; effect of pruning, 291; iron content, 146 table; length in relation to fertilizer requirement, 193 table; magnesium content, 145 table; manganese content, 147 table; nitrogen content, 141 table, 152, 154; optimum density for Searles cultivar, 113; phosphorus content, 143 table; potassium content, 144 table, 158; and tip blight disease, 234; and tip dieback disease, 236; and twig blight disease, 233; types of, 118; and upright dieback disease, 235; and water table depth, 188; as a yield component, 118–120, 119 table, 139
Urann, Marcus L., 347
urea (fertilizer), 195
urea formaldehyde (fertilizer), 195
urine: effect of fruit consumption on acidity of, 354; calcium content of, 355; elimination of ammoniacal odor in, 354–355
urinary tract infections, treatment of with cranberry juice, 354
ursolic acid, a processing byproduct, 324
utilization, **42,** 350–358, 351 table, 353 table; in geriatric wards, 354–355

Vaccinium hagerupii, chromosome number of, 54
Vaccinium macrocarpon Ait. (*Oxycoccus macrocarpus* [Ait.] pers.), 43–44; chromosome number of, 54
Vaccinium oxycoccus L. (*O. microcarpus* Turcz.), 44
Vaccinium quadripetalum (*O. quadripetalum*), (wild cranberry), 166
Vaccinium vitis-idaea L. 45; use in breeding, 62. *See also* lingonberry
Vaccinol, 324, 356
vacuum picker, 296–297
vegetative growth, 112–114; effect of growth inhibitors on, 115–116; effect on respiration, 115; response to nitrogen, 151–153
ventilation, for fruit storage, 313
vine(s), 45–47; cranberry girdler damage to, 265–266; effect of excessive growth on harvest, 291; freezing temperature on, 186; growth response to potassium in McFarlin cultivar, 158. *See also* runner and stolon
viscid rot disease, 240
vitamin(s), content in fruit, 130 table, 132
vitamin A, content in fruit, 130 table, 132, 319
vitamin C: breeding for, 61; content in fruit, 130 table, 132, 352; effect of canning on, 319. *See also* ascorbic acid
volatiles, components of cranberry juice, 133–134
Vose, B. F., 74
Vose's Pride cultivar (Pride), 58, 74

Wales Henry cultivar, 60, 76
Walker, Saunders, 7
Washington (state): acreage, 20 table, 26, **27;** copper toxicity in, 163; cranberry tip worm damage in, 262; cultivar trials in, 79; fertilizer responses in, 192–195; indicator plants for site selection in, 166; production, 29, 30 table; productivity, 33–40, **35,** 36 table; sanding recommendations for, 177; yellow rot disease in, 242; yield components in, 120
Washington Cranberry and Blueberry Station, 14, 79
water: movement in bog, 189; pH of, 102–103; quality of, 102–104
water harvesting, 298–302, **300–301;** and black rot disease, 242; and yellow rot disease, 242
water management, 181–190, **182;** for control of black cutworm, 256; for control of

cranberry girdler, 266; for control of false armyworm, 257; for control of grubs, 273–274; for control of gypsy moth, 259; for control of spotted cutworm, 256; importance in weed control, 201

water raking, 287, **289**

water reel (beater), 299, **301**

water supply, 168–169; amount needed for winter flood, 183; control gates, 174–176, **175**

water table, for irrigation, 187–190

weather, 106–109; and fruit set, 124; and fruit quality, 107; and fruit ripening, 107; and oxygen deficiency, 94–97; and production, 107–109; and stem blight disease, 234; use in predictive yield models, 107–109

Webb, J. J. ("Peg Leg John"), 5, 304–305

weeds: available publications on, 198–199; control measures, 200–201, 214–218, 202 table; effect of late holding of winter flood on, 185; major problems, 199–200; influence of sanding upon, 223–224

weed wipers, 218

weevils, 262–264

Wellman Cherry cultivar, 77

West Coast: black spot disease on, 231; tip blight disease on, 234; twig blight disease on, 233; scale insects on, 269

Western Picker, 293, **294;** pruning ability of, 226

wetland soils, production on, 167

White, Barclay, 8

White, Elizabeth, 25–26

White, J. J.: New Jersey cranberry pioneer, 8; author of *Cranberry Culture*, 10; on costs of bog establishment and production, 326–327; on drainage, 169; on prices, 331; on sanding, 176–177; secretary of American Cranberry Growers Association, 11

white cedar (*Chamaecyparis thyoides*), 166 table

white-marked tussock moth, 258

Whitesbog, cultivar trials at, 80

white water lily (*Castalia odorata*), 165

Whiting Randall cultivar, 77

Whitman Park cultivar, 77

Whittlesey cultivar, 58, 77

Wilcox, R. B., 14–15, **15**

Wilcox cultivar: description of, 65 table, 77; hybrid released from USDA breeding program, 58–59; relative gel strength of, 317; susceptibility to black rot disease, 311; susceptibility to physiological breakdown, 310

wild cranberry (*Vaccinium quadripetalum*), 166

willow (*Salix* sp.), 166

wind, effect on oxygen content of floodwater, 96–97

windbreaks, use of, 170

wind machines, for frost control, 85

Winslow cultivar, 77

winter flood, 183; effect on false blossom disease, 238; effect on red gall disease, 236; effect on stem blight disease, 234; late holding for cranberry girdler control, 266; late holding vs. early drawing of, 183–186; for preventing winter injury, 82; quantity of water needed for, 168, 183; relationship to sanding, 224–225

wintergreen (*Gaultheria procumbens*), 165

winter injury, 82

Winter Queen cultivar, 77

Wisconsin: acreage, 20 table, 26, **27;** alkaline water in, 102–103; climate of, 105 table; cultivar trials in, 77–78; drainage of bogs in, 169; end rot disease in, 241; false blossom disease in, 237; fertilizer practices in, 196–197; growing season for, 105 table; harvest season in, 284; honeybee recommendations for, 219–220; indicator plants for site selection in, 166; industry beginnings, 5–6; industry during the 1800s, 10; oxygen deficiency in, 88; production, 29, 30 table; productivity, 33–40, **35**, 36 table; standard tissue element values for, 139 table; tip blight disease in, 234; upright dieback disease in, 235; upright types in, 118; viscid rot disease in, 240; water harvesting in, 298–299, 309; winter flood in, 99, 183; yield components in, 118–120, 119 table

Wisconsin cranberry boom, 228 table, 229

Wisconsin Cranberry Sales Company: brands (labels) for, 343; organization of, 345

Wisconsin Cranberry Sales Growers' Cooperative, 12

Wisconsin Cranberry Station: cultivar trials at, 77–78; origin of, 14

Wisconsin cultivar, 77

Wisconsin scoop (rake), 287, **289, 298**

Wisconsin State Cranberry Growers' Association: cultivar trials at, 77–78; origin of, 11–12

witches'-broom symptom, caused by false blossom disease, 238

woods weevil, 264

woody weeds, 208–210 table

Woolman, A. W., 77

Woolman cultivar, 77
worms, that attack buds, flowers, or fruits, 248–262

Xylena nupera Lint. (false armyworm), 257

yellow-headed fireworm, 251; control by late holding, 184
yellow rot disease, 242
yield: and iron, 161; and nitrogen, 149 table, 153–154; and oxygen deficiency, 93 table; and phosphorus, 155–156; and potassium, 158; and pruning, 225–226; and rainfall, 109; and rose bloom disease, 232; and sulfur, 160; and sunshine, 108; and technological advances, 109; use of weather in predictive modeling of, 107–109. *See also* production

yield analysis, 120–121
yield components, 118–120, 119 table; in relation to nutrition, 138–139

zebra caterpillar, 255
zinc (Zn), 162–163; content in plant, 147 table; deficiency level in shoot, 139 table; effect of nitrogen fertilizer on level in plant, 148; effect on fruit quality, 193; foliar use of, 193; phosphorus induced deficiency, 156; seasonal distribution in shoots, 137 table; standard value in shoot, 139 table
zinc chelate, 162
zineb, fungicide recommendations, 243–244 table
Zinophos, for control of nematodes, 278